A HISTORY OF EARLY MODERN
WOMEN'S WRITING

A History of Early Modern Women's Writing is essential reading for students and scholars working in the field of early modern British literature and history. This collaborative book of twenty-two chapters offers an expansive, multifaceted narrative of British women's literary and textual production in the period stretching from the English Reformation to the Restoration. Chapters work together to trace the contours of a diverse body of early modern women's writing, aligning women's texts with the major literary, political, and cultural currents with which they engage. Contributors examine and take account of developments in critical theory, feminism, and gender studies that have influenced the reception, reading, and interpretation of early modern women's writing. This book explicates and interrogates significant methodological and critical developments in the past four decades, guiding and testing scholarship in this period of intense activity in the recovery, dissemination, and interpretation of women's writing.

PATRICIA PHILLIPPY is Professor of English Literature at Kingston University London. She has published widely in early modern literature and culture, with a special focus on women's writing. Her books include *Women, Death and Literature in Post-Reformation England* (Cambridge, 2002), *Painting Women: Cosmetics, Canvases, and Early Modern Culture* (2006), and *Shaping Remembrance from Shakespeare to Milton* (Cambridge, 2018). She has edited the writings of Elizabeth Cooke Hoby Russell for *The Other Voice in Early Modern Europe* (Toronto Series).

A HISTORY OF EARLY MODERN WOMEN'S WRITING

EDITED BY
PATRICIA PHILLIPPY
Kingston University London

CAMBRIDGE
UNIVERSITY PRESS

CAMBRIDGE
UNIVERSITY PRESS

University Printing House, Cambridge CB2 8BS, United Kingdom

One Liberty Plaza, 20th Floor, New York, NY 10006, USA

477 Williamstown Road, Port Melbourne, VIC 3207, Australia

314-321, 3rd Floor, Plot 3, Splendor Forum, Jasola District Centre, New Delhi - 110025, India

79 Anson Road, #06-04/06, Singapore 079906

Cambridge University Press is part of the University of Cambridge.

It furthers the University's mission by disseminating knowledge in the pursuit of education, learning and research at the highest international levels of excellence.

www.cambridge.org
Information on this title: www.cambridge.org/9781107137066
DOI: 10.1017/9781316480267

© Cambridge University Press 2018

First published 2018

A catalogue record for this publication is available from the British Library

Library of Congress Cataloging in Publication data
Names: Phillippy, Patricia Berrahou, 1960- editor.
Title: A history of early modern women's writing/edited by Patricia Phillippy.
Description: First edition. | New York : Cambridge University Press, 2018. | Includes bibliographical references and index.
Identifiers: LCCN 2017042281 | ISBN 9781107137066 (hardback)
Subjects: LCSH: English literature—Early modern, 1500-1700—History and criticism. | English literature—Women authors—History and criticism. | Women and literature—Great Britain—History—16th century. | Women and literature—Great Britain—History—17th century. | Literature and society—Great Britain—History—16th century. | Literature and society—Great Britain—History—17th century. | BISAC: LITERARY CRITICISM / European / English, Irish, Scottish, Welsh.
Classification: LCC PR113 .H57 2018 | DDC 820.9/928709031—dc23
LC record available at https://lccn.loc.gov/2017042281

ISBN 978-1-107-13706-6 Hardback
ISBN 978-1-316-50205-1 Paperback

Contents

Figures

Contributors

ELAINE V. BEILIN is Professor of English and Director of the Center for Excellence in Learning, Teaching, Scholarship, and Service at Framingham State University, Massachusetts. Her recent work includes an essay on the Countess of Pembroke's *Discourse of Life and Death* for the *Ashgate Research Companion to the Sidneys 1500–1700* and entries on Anne Askew in the *Encyclopedia of Renaissance Philosophy* and the *Handbook of Women Biblical Interpreters*. She is currently completing a book on representations of Askew and *The Examinations* from the 1540s to the present.

PAMELA J. BENSON, Emerita Professor of English at Rhode Island College, is currently writing a book on Aemilia Lanyer in her cultural contexts. She is author of *The Invention of the Renaissance Woman: The Challenge of Female Independence in the Literature and Thought of Italy and England* (1992) and editor of *Italian Tales from the Age of Shakespeare* (1996) and of *Texts from the Querelle, 1521–1640* (2008). She co-organized (with Victoria Kirkham) the conference *Strong Voices/ Weak History: Early Women Writers and Canons in England, France, and Italy* and coedited the volume of essays drawn from it (2004). She completed most of the research for her chapter at the Folger Shakespeare Library, Washington, DC, thanks to a short-term fellowship.

JULIE D. CAMPBELL is Professor of English at Eastern Illinois University, Charleston. She is the author of *Literary Circles and Gender in Early Modern Europe* (2006) and the editor and translator of Isabella Andreini's pastoral tragicomedy, *La Mirtilla* (2002). With Anne R. Larsen, she has edited and contributed to *Early Modern Women and Transnational Communities of Letters* (2009). With Maria Galli Stampino, she has edited and contributed to *In Dialogue with the Other Voice in Sixteenth-Century Italy: Literary and Social Contexts for Women's Writing* (2011).

MARIE-LOUISE COOLAHAN is Professor of English at the National University of Ireland, Galway. She is the author of *Women, Writing, and Language in Early Modern Ireland* (2010), as well as articles and essays about Renaissance manuscript culture, women's writing, early modern identity, and textual transmission. She is currently Principal Investigator of the ERC-funded project, RECIRC: The Reception and Circulation of Early Modern Women's Writing, 1550–1700 (www.recirc.nuigalway.ie). She has recently coedited two special issues of the journal *Women's Writing* ("Katherine Philips and Other Writers," 2016; "Katherine Philips: Form and Reception," 2017) with Gillian Wright.

PETER DAVIDSON is Senior Research Fellow and Archivist at Campion Hall, Oxford. Scotland. His research, often conducted in collaboration with Jane B. Stevenson, interrogates the interrelations of the arts in the early modern period. He is the author of *The Universal Baroque* (2007) and the editor of *Poetry and Revolution: An Anthology of British and Irish Verse 1625–1660* (1998). As Honorary Curator of Aberdeen University's Manuscript, Rare Book and Museum Collections from the Renaissance and Baroque periods, he has produced a history of the collections. His publications have been at the forefront of material cultural studies of early modern women's writings and artworks.

MARGARET J. M. EZELL is Distinguished Professor of English and the John and Sara Lindsey Chair of Liberal Arts at Texas A&M University, College Station. She is the author of *The Patriarch's Wife: Literary Evidence and the History of the Family, Writing Women's Literary History, Social Authorship and the Advent of Print*, and *The New Oxford Literary History, 1645–1714*. She has edited the works of Mary Chudleigh, Anne Killigrew, and Mary More.

SUSAN M. FELCH is Professor of English at Calvin College, Grand Rapids, Michigan, and Director of the Calvin Center for Christian Scholarship, also in Grand Rapids. Her publications include *The Collected Works of Anne Vaughan Lock* (1999), *Bakhtin and Religion: A Feeling for Faith*, with Paul J. Contino (2001), *Elizabeth Tyrwhit's Morning and Evening Prayers* (2008), *Elizabeth I and Her Age*, with Donald Stump (2009), *Selected Readings of Bible Stories*/圣经故事选读, with Xing Ling (2011), *Teaching and Christian Imagination*, with David I. Smith (2016) and *The Cambridge Companion to Literature and Religion* (2016).

JAIME GOODRICH is an Associate Professor of English at Wayne State University, Detroit, Michigan. In addition to writing numerous articles and book chapters on early modern Englishwomen's texts, she has published a monograph on the social and political functions of early modern Englishwomen's devotional translations called *Faithful Translators: Authorship, Gender, and Religion in Early Modern England* (2014). She is currently editing the writings of early modern English nuns and researching a book on textual production and communal identity in English Benedictine convents on the Continent.

W. SCOTT HOWARD received his PhD in English and Critical Theory from the University of Washington, Seattle, Washington. He is the founding editor of *Appositions: Studies in Renaissance/Early Modern Literature & Culture*, coeditor, with Sara van den Berg, of *The Divorce Tracts of John Milton: Texts and Contexts* (2010), and editor of *An Collins and the Historical Imagination* (2014). His work has received support from the Modern Language Association, the Pew Charitable Trusts, the National Endowment for the Humanities, and the Beinecke Library, Yale University, New Haven, Connecticut.

CLARE R. KINNEY is Associate Professor of English Literature at the University of Virginia, Charlottesville. She is the author of *Strategies of Poetic Narrative: Chaucer, Spenser, Milton, Eliot* (1992) and editor of *Ashgate Critical Essays on Women Writers in England, 1550–1700, Volume 4: Mary Wroth* (2009). Her recent research on the Sidney circle appears in the articles, "Continuations and Imitations of the *Arcadia*," *Ashgate Research Companion to the Sidneys*, ed. M. Brennan, M. Hannay and M. E. Lamb (2015) and "Turn and Counter-Turn: Reappraising Mary Wroth's Poetic Labyrinths," in *Rereading Mary Wroth*, ed. K. Larson, N. Miller and A. Strycharski (2015).

DANA E. LAWRENCE is Assistant Professor of English at the University of South Carolina Lancaster. She received her PhD from Texas A&M University, College Station, where her work focused on the poetry of Aemilia Lanyer, Isabella Whitney, Veronica Franco, and Marie de Romieu. Her research interests include early modern women poets, literary tourism, Shakespeare adaptations, and children's Shakespeare. She is currently working on an article examining the role of Romeo and Juliet tourism in Verona.

JESSICA L. MALAY is Professor of English Renaissance Literature at the University of Huddersfield, England. She has published widely on early modern women's writing and culture. She actively researches early modern textual production and had edited the works of Anne Clifford and the autobiography of Mary Hampson. She has published on Sibylline prophesy in the medieval and early modern periods. Her work also engages with early modern materiality and concepts of space.

MEGAN MATCHINSKE is Professor of English Literature and Comparative Literature at the University of North Carolina, Chapel Hill. With two monographs, *Writing, Gender and State in Early Modern England: Identity Formation and the Female Subject* (1998), *Women Writing History in Early Modern England* (2009) and an edition in "The Other Voice" series, *Mary Carleton and Others: The Carleton Bigamy Trial* (2018), as well as numerous essays, Matchinske offers theoretical and practical approaches to reading early modern writing through the lens of postmodernism.

PAULA MCQUADE is an Associate Professor at DePaul University, Chicago, Illinois, and is the author of multiple articles on gender and religion in early modern England. Her article on the female catechist Dorothy Burch was selected by the Society for the Study of Early Modern Women Writers as the best article of 2010. Her book, *Catechisms and Women's Writing in Seventeenth-Century England*, was published by Cambridge University Press in 2017.

PATRICIA PENDER is Senior Lecturer in English and Writing at the University of Newcastle, New South Wales, Australia. She is the author of *Early Modern Women's Writing and the Rhetoric of Modesty* (2012) and coeditor, with Rosalind Smith, of *Material Cultures of Early Modern Women's Writing* (2014). She is currently working on an Australian Research Council Discovery Project on Early Modern Women and the Institutions of Authorship (2014–2017), from which an edited collection, *Gender, Authorship, and Early Modern Women's Collaboration*, appeared in 2017.

SARAH C. E. ROSS is Associate Professor of English at Victoria University of Wellington, New Zealand. Her publications include *Women, Poetry, and Politics in Seventeenth-Century Britain* (2015), *Editing Early Modern Women*, with Paul Salzman (2016) and *Katherine Austen's 'Book M': British Library, Additional Manuscript 4454* (2011). She is currently working on women and complaint in early modern England, on a

Royal Society of New Zealand Marsden-funded project with Michelle O'Callaghan and Rosalind Smith.

PETER SHERLOCK is Vice-Chancellor of the University of Divinity, Melbourne, Australia. His research interests include the commemoration of the dead in early modern Europe, especially sepulchral monuments, and representations of gender. He is author of *Monuments and Memory in Early Modern England* (2008) and is presently working on a history of the monuments of Westminster Abbey.

EDITH SNOOK is Professor of English Literature at the University of New Brunswick, Fredericton. She is the author of the award-winning *Women, Beauty and Power in Early Modern England: A Feminist History* (2011) and *Women, Reading, and the Cultural Politics of Early Modern England* (2005). Her current research focuses on recipes. A book in progress examines the literary impact of seventeenth-century Englishwomen's medical practices, while another project, funded by the Social Sciences and Humanities Research Council of Canada, is investigating early modern recipes archived in what are now the Maritime provinces of Canada.

JANE B. STEVENSON is Senior Research Fellow at Campion Hall, Oxford. She is the author of *Women Latin Poets: Language, Gender and Authority from Antiquity to the Eighteenth Century* (2005) and coeditor, with Peter Davidson, of *Early Modern Women Poets: An Anthology* (2001). She has published extensively on early modern women's education, translation, and Latin and neo-Latin poetry. With her frequent collaborator, Peter Davidson, she has produced numerous significant studies of early modern women's writing in print, manuscript and material texts.

MIHOKO SUZUKI is Professor of English and Director of the Center for the Humanities at the University of Miami, Florida. She is the author of *Subordinate Subjects: Gender, the Political Nation, and Literary Form in England, 1588–1688* (2003) and coeditor, with Mary Lindemann and Anne J. Cruz, of *Early Modern Women: An Interdisciplinary Journal*. She edited *The History of British Women Writers, Volume 3: 1610–1690* (2012) and coedited, with Hilda L. Smith and Susan Wiseman, a four-volume collection of manuscript and printed texts, *Women's Political Writings, 1610–1725* (2007). She is completing a book, *Antigone's Example*, on early modern women's political writings in times of civil war.

MICHELINE WHITE is Associate Professor in the College of the Humanities, Carleton University, Ottawa, Canada. She is editor of *English Women, Religion, and Textual Production, 1500–1625* (2011) and *Secondary Work on Early Modern Women Writers: Whitney, Lanyer, and Lock* (2009). She has published on women and religion in publications such as the *Times Literary Supplement, Renaissance Studies, ELR, Modern Philology*, and *Sixteenth-Century Journal*. Her work on Katherine Parr has been featured in radio interviews with CBC's *Tapestry* and Radio Canada's *Les Voies du Retour*.

RAMONA WRAY is Reader in English Literature at Queen's University, Belfast, Northern Ireland. She is Coprincipal Investigator on a network project, "Memory and Community in Early Modern Britain," supported by the Arts and Humanities Research Council. She has edited Elizabeth Cary's *Tragedy of Mariam* (2012) and written extensively on early modern women's writing and Shakespeare on film. She is coeditor of *Reconceiving the Renaissance: A Critical Reader* (2005) and author of "Cary, Community and Audience" in *Community-Making in Early Stuart Theatres: Stage and Audience* (2015). She is currently at work on a literary biography of Elizabeth Cary.

Acknowledgments

I owe a great debt to Ray Ryan at Cambridge University Press, whose inspiration it was to embark upon this project, and whose careful and prompt guidance has shaped this work from the start.

It has been a great pleasure to work with my contributors during the preparation of this volume. Their enthusiasm, profound expertise, and meticulous scholarship have excited and inspired me. I have learned a great deal from each of these colleagues. Special thanks go to Margaret Ezell, who has been to me a source of wisdom for many years and whose counsel has enriched this volume in many ways. Jaime Goodrich and Sarah C. E. Ross offered sound advice and cheerful support throughout.

Fouad Berrahou's patient companionship made this project much easier. Finally, I must thank my daughter, Iman K. Berrahou, whose strength and generosity keep me awake, alert, and alive.

Abbreviations

BCP   Book of Common Prayer
BL   British Library
Bod   Bodleian Library, Oxford
CUL   Cambridge University Library
Folger   Folger Shakespeare Library
GB   Geneva Bible, Geneva: Roland Hall, 1560
Hunt   Huntington Library
KJV   The Bible (King James Version, London: Robert Barker, 1611)
ODNB   *The Oxford Dictionary of National Biography: From the Earliest Times to the Year 2000*, edited by Matthew H. C. G. Harrison and Brian Howard (Oxford University Press, 2004; online edition, 2008)
OED   *Oxford English Dictionary* (2nd edition, Oxford University Press, 1989; online edition, 2009)
NRO   Northampton Record Office, Northampton
STC   *A Short-Title Catalogue of Books Printed in England, Scotland and Ireland, and of English Books Printed Abroad 1475–1640*, edited by A. W. Pollard and G. R. Redgrave (2nd edition, revised and enlarged, begun by W. A. Jackson and F. S. Ferguson, completed by K. F. Pantzer, 3 vols., London: The Bibliographical Society, 1976–91)
TNA   The National Archives, Kew

Introduction
Sparkling Multiplicity

Patricia Phillippy

Concluding the chapter that opens this volume, Margaret Ezell predicts that the continued relevance and value of early modern women's writings lie neither in "their anomalous nature nor their female uniformity, but their sparkling multiplicity." The chapters in *A History of Early Modern Women's Writing* mirror this feature of their subject. This collaborative volume of twenty-two chapters offers an expansive, multifaceted narrative of British women's literary and textual production in the period stretching roughly from the Reformation to the Restoration. These chapters work together to trace the contours of a diverse body of early modern women's writing, aligning women's texts with the major literary, political, and cultural currents informing them and which they, in turn, influenced. At the same time, this volume explicates and interrogates significant methodological and critical developments guiding and testing scholarship in the past four decades, a period of intense activity in the recovery, dissemination, and interpretation of women's writing.

This project responds to two challenges posed by early modern women's writing to the genre of literary history as it has traditionally been conceived. First, the vast diversity of genres and media in which early modern women's writing survives demands that our notion of "literature" be expanded to accommodate writing beyond the standard generic categories of poetry, fiction, drama, and essays.[1] While chapters in this volume explore women's works in these forms, they also position women's contributions among the various discursive strands constituting the fabric of literate activity in early modern Britain. Secondly, a lack of critical agreement concerning the status of a female tradition or canon – stemming from the desire to avoid facile essentialism in its defining term, on the one hand, and the contested relationship of women's writing to the

---

[1] See Loewenstein and Mueller, "Introduction," in *Cambridge History of Early Modern English Literature*, 6–7, for a useful discussion of that volume's similarly expansive treatment of literature.

literary mainstream, on the other – has fostered "separate but equal" areas
of study and their attending literary histories. When women's writing has
been inserted into comprehensive literary histories, its inclusion has been
both partial and strategic: a small number of "anomalous" works disrupt
the monolithic narrative of the masculine canon.[2] More often, women's
writing has been treated as if enacted remotely, distinct from masculine
practice and canonicity and incommensurate with conventional standards of merit or value. "On the one hand," as Mary Ellen Lamb sums up
the dilemma, "it is important not to ghettoize women writers. To take
their rightful place in the mainstream of the literary canon, their works
must be understood in terms of their male contemporaries. On the other
hand, to discount the formative role of gender is to ignore the condition
under which women wrote and lived."[3]

This volume offers an innovatively conceived literary history, responsive to the unique features of early modern women's writing and conveying essential information and exposition of this body of work. Individual
contributions employ fresh approaches to the subject and to the task
of writing literary history, seeking points of contact between women's
local histories and the broader literary histories of the period. Employing
approaches from historicism to new formalism, from intertextual analysis
to material cultural and manuscript studies, these chapters speak to the
robust fortunes of women's texts not only in the past and present, but
also in a future attuned to "the dazzling ways in which they disrupt [tra-
ditional models] and challenge us to see our own assumptions, aesthetic
as well as historical."[4]

From Pre-History to Post-History

The literary history of early modern women writers in Britain begins in
what might be termed a pre-history composed in these authors' lifetimes

---

[2] See Clarke, "Nostalgia," who calls for editions of women's writing that "are attentive to specific features of women's writing" rather than conforming to canonical conventions (191). This concern
also attends the inclusion of women's writing in standard literary anthologies. See Wray,
"Anthologizing," who calls for "a new politics of selection" (57). See also Ross and Scott-Baumann,
"Anthologizing Early Modern Women's Poetry," in their edition of *Women Poets of the English Civil
War*, a self-described "populist text which nonetheless attends to textualist and historicist concerns"
(217). For recent anthologies that approach in different ways the rival demands of diversity and
conformity in women's writing, see Ostovich and Sauer (eds.), *Reading Early Modern Women*, and
Millman and Wright (eds.), *Early Modern Women's Manuscript Poetry*.
[3] Lamb, "Out of the Archives," 204.
[4] Margaret J. M. Ezell (Chapter 1) in this volume.

in works celebrating the accomplishments of "illustrious" women. Rooted in the long literature of the *querelle des femmes*, where defenses of women routinely included catalogues of classical women deemed remarkable for their erudition, early modern catalogues worked to contain women's writing within orthodox social and familial structures. William Barker's *Nobility of Women* (written in Henry VIII's reign and revised in Elizabeth I's) characteristically praises women's literary achievements as testimonies to the humanist pedagogy of male governors: his list of luminaries includes "the two systers of the moste noble Prince Edward the Sixt," "the daughters of the Duke of Somersett," "the two daughters of the Earl of Arondell," and "dyvers other lords and gentlemen ... whose daughters prove very well learned, in especiallye the daughters of Syr Anthony Cooke, a knight, which, for greke and lattyn, be not inferior to any we have namyd."[5] More than a century later, in her *Essay to Revive the Antient Education of Gentlewomen* (1673), Bathsua Makin bolsters her argument for the education of women by recalling examples of learned women living and dead, among them Lady Jane Grey, Margaret Cavendish, and "the four Daughters of Sir Anthony Cook."[6] Brief lives of early modern women writers, often copied from earlier accounts, were transmitted in antiquarian works, most prominently George Ballard's *Memoirs of Several Ladies of Great Britain* (1752), through the eighteenth century.[7]

In part following the clues contained in compilations such as Ballard's, scholars in the 1980s began the full-scale project of recovering early modern women's writing.[8] Initial forays into the field carried the essentialist trace of the antiquarian sources from which they emerged. In her foundational study, *Writing Women's Literary History* (1993), Ezell called attention to the gendered assumptions tacitly conveyed from catalogues into the critical tendency to read women's works as transparent biographical records rather than as crafted textual performances.[9] Feminist scholars

---

[5] Barker, *Nobility of Women (1559)*, 154–5.
[6] Makin, *Essay*, 10 and 20. In this volume: Julie Campbell's chapter on the Seymour sisters and the Cooke sisters (Chapter 8); Jaime Goodrich on Anne Cooke Bacon (Chapter 2); Elaine Beilin on Elizabeth Tudor and Jane Grey (Chapter 7); Mihoko Suzuki on Cavendish (Chapter 20).
[7] Ballard, *Memoirs*.
[8] See, among many other studies: Greer et al. (eds.), *Kissing the Rod*; Ezell, *Patriarch's Wife*; Beilin, *Redeeming Eve*; Hannay (ed.), *Silent but for the Word*; Ferguson, Quilligan, and Vickers (eds.), *Rewriting the Renaissance*; Graham et al. (eds.), *Her Own Life*.
[9] Ezell, *Writing Women's Literary History*, 66–103. See also: Grundy and Wisemen (eds.), *Women, Writing, History, 1640–1740*; Brant and Purkiss (eds.), *Women, Texts and Histories, 1575–1760*; Ezell (Chapter 1) and Jane Stevenson (Chapter 19) in this volume.

in the period scoured the archives, rediscovering a wealth of women's writings in a wide range of genres, on every imaginable topic, sacred and secular. The first biographical and topical guide to women writers appeared in 1990, while a growing body of critical studies sought to read this diverse corpus in its historical dimensions and in relation to contemporary feminist debates.[10] The body of women's writings available for recovery was greatly enlarged by the recognition that, for early modern women, manuscript circulation was an established method of publication, one often preferred to print.[11]

While the project of reclaiming women's writing in the 1980s and 1990s resurrected the woman writer and her history, this exhumation took place in the shadow of "the death of the author."[12] As women's literary history approached the new millennium, critics struggled with the unviability of "life and works" approaches that linked writing to biography; of the "essentialist and positivist" assumptions underpinning their textual recoveries and analyses; and of authorial intention as the mainstay of interpretation.[13] Sharing with cultural materialism an understanding of literature as both a product of and an agent in culture, late twentieth-century criticism stressed the changing historical and material contexts of writing and, responding to the non-traditional forms often employed by women, embraced the view of literary texts as cultural documents.[14] Contemporary scholarship, influenced by new textualism, has taken up this method, examining sites of textual production, circulation, and reception, describing patterns of "social authorship," and retrieving "a sociology of writing" within which women's works were situated.[15] Recognizing "the paradigm shift from study of learned women as isolated anomalies to study of them as numerous, vital participants in learned

[10] See: Blain, Grundy, and Clements (eds.), *Feminist Companion*; Hobby, *Virtue of Necessity*; Cora Kaplan, *Sea Changes: Essays on Culture and Feminism* (London: Verso, 1986).

[11] See: Ezell, *Social Authorship*; Burke and Gibson (eds.), *Early Modern Women's Manuscript Writing*.

[12] See: Roland Barthes's 1967 essay, "The Death of the Author," in *Image, Music, Text*, trans. Stephen Heath (London: HarperCollins, 1977), 142–7; Michel Foucault, "What Is an Author?" in Donald Bouchard (ed.), *Language, Counter-Memory, Practice: Selected Essays and Interviews* (Ithaca, NY: Cornell University Press, 1980), 113–38.

[13] Clarke, "Nostalgia," 192.

[14] This approach, until the recent resurgence in formalism, discouraged engagement with the aesthetic features and value of women's writing. On new formalism, see: Roberts, "Feminist Criticism and the New Formalism"; Scott-Baumann, *Forms of Engagement*; Burton and Scott-Baumann (eds.), *Work of Form*; Ross, *Women, Poetry and Politics*; Millman and Wright (eds.), *Early Modern Women's Manuscript Poetry*; Ross and Scott-Baumann (eds.), *Women Poets of the English Civil War*.

[15] See: Ezell, *Social Authorship*; Bicks and Summit, "Introduction," in *History*, 2; Hurley and Goodblatt (eds.), *Women Editing*, xi.

networks," Julie Campbell's contribution to this volume, for instance, unfolds the transnational literary circles in which women humanists took part. Sarah C. E. Ross's exploration of "the complexity of literary culture" in elite circles of the mid-seventeenth century deftly affirms that networks and coteries were "'essential material conditions' for literary production," including the social production of the female author. This dominant methodology has brought forth a growing body of scholarship that displays the diversity of women's textual productions and the multiplicity of literate practices at play in discrete cultural moments and locations.

This critical approach, clearly, challenges the attempt to script a unified, inclusive literary history – a challenge akin to that posed by post-structuralist scholars in the late 1990s approaching the "grand narratives" of traditional literary history from marginalized or excluded positions.[16] In response to the move toward cultural studies dominant in early modern scholarship at the turn of the century, *The Cambridge History of Early Modern English Literature* (2002) adopted the "situational" model as its overarching structural principle, reading canonical works and authors alongside less familiar male and female writers, all set in relation to various institutional sites of writing in the period. Recent literary histories of early modern women's writing have followed suit. The situational model provides the linchpin for *The Cambridge Companion to Early Modern Women's Writing* (2009), which surveys sites of production in a central section framed by chapters on the material aspects of early modern writing and key genres and modes. Most recently, both of the two early modern volumes in Palgrave's multi-volume *History of British Women's Writing* place at their core sections on "Writing Places" and "Sites and Modes," accompanied by sections on material practices, networks, genres, and developing methodological approaches to "contexts" and "histories."[17] This emphasis on the sites of writing accords with a view of literature as embracing multiple voices and subject positions, a literature whose histories are necessarily plural and whose aesthetic aspects are inseparable from the historical locations and social functions of writing.[18]

---

[16] See, for example: David Perkins, *Is Literary History Possible?* (Baltimore and London: Johns Hopkins University Press, 1992); Mario J. Valdes and Linda Hutcheon (eds.), *Rethinking Literary History: A Dialogue on Theory* (Oxford: Oxford University Press, 2002).

[17] See: Loewenstein and Mueller (eds.), *Cambridge History of Early Modern Literature*; Knoppers (ed.), *Cambridge Companion to Early Modern Women's Writing*; Bicks and Summit (eds.), *History*; Suzuki (ed.), *History*.

[18] See Clarke and Coolahan, "Gender, Reception, and Form," for an argument of an expanded notion of form that shifts focus from authorial production to reception, allowing for one to take account of both aesthetics and utility.

The absence to date of an *integrated* literary history of woman's writing, viewed in this light, may not come as a surprise. Shaped by the widely accepted principles governing scholarship in the field, literary histories of women's writing, understandably, have generally refused an integrative structure, opting instead for an arrangement of accretion and compilation, collections much like the miscellanies assembled by early modern women themselves.[19] The intention of this volume, by contrast, is to present a history that respects and acknowledges the multiplicity of women's writing while at the same time seeking grounds in the subject to support a unified narrative and to work against the unfeatured accretion of names and titles that can easily result in a disjointed account of unrelated textual events.

Six Themes

The organization of this literary history differs from previous examples in the field, adopting a design that enables a unified but multifaceted view of early modern women's writing as it has taken shape as a scholarly discipline, and as it developed chronologically in the cultural, political, religious, and social landscapes of early modern Britain. The period covered here corresponds roughly to the beginning of the Reformation under Henry VIII to the Restoration of the monarchy with the return of Charles II. The initial and terminal dates are fixed with reference to two milestone early modern women's texts: Margaret More Roper's translation of Erasmus's *Precatio Dominica*, published in 1526 as *A Deuoute Treatise upon the Pater Noster*, and the Lady Anne Clifford's *Great Books of Record*, a massive manuscript project that ended with her death in 1676.[20] The volume is divided into four parts (see Table I.1). Part I, as I discuss below, functions non-chronologically to interrogate key debates in the field. Parts II–IV move chronologically across the period to provide a historical account of developments in early modern women's writing. At the same time, these chapters are arranged to encourage synchronic comparisons of the state of women's writing in relation to six themes or subject areas that traverse the period and change over time. These themes provide a template for highlighting points of contact and

---

[19] See Burke, "Manuscript Miscellanies."

[20] Richard Hyrde's dedicatory epistle to Roper's volume is dated October 1, 1524 (see Erasmus, *A Deuoute Treatise*, trans. Roper, sig. B3ᵛ). In this volume, Felch (Chapter 5) notes that the text may have been printed as early as 1524, and Campbell (Chapter 8) dates the treatise to that year. Since the earliest edition extant is 1526, I accept this date, not least for the utilitarian motive of establishing a timeframe for this history of exactly 150 years. On Clifford, see Malay (Chapter 22) in this volume.

Table I.1. *Organization of the volume*

Part I – Critical Approaches and Methodologies			
Ch. 1 – Invisibility Optics: Aphra Behn, Esther Inglis and the Fortunes of Women's Works	Ch. 2 – Reconsidering the Woman Writer: The Identity Politics of Anne Cooke Bacon	Ch. 3 – The Critical Fortunes of the Tenth Muse: Canonicity and Its Discontents	Ch. 4 – When We Swear to Tell the Truth: The Carleton Debates and Archival Methodology
Margaret J. M. Ezell	Jaime Goodrich	Patricia Pender	Megan Matchinske
Themes	**Part II – The Tudor Era**	**Part III – The Early Stuart Period**	**Part IV – Civil War, Interregnum, and Restoration**
Reformations	Ch. 5 – Common and Competing Faiths	Ch. 11 – Aemilia Lanyer's Radical Art: "The Passion of Christ"	Ch. 17 – Prophecy, Power, and Religious Dissent
	Susan M. Felch	Pamela J. Benson	W. Scott Howard
Collaborations and Coteries	Ch. 6 – Isabella Whitney's "Slips": Poetry, Collaboration, and Coterie	Ch. 12 – Memory, Materiality and Maternity in the Tanfield/Cary Archive	Ch. 18 – Coteries, Circles, Networks: The Cavendish Circle and Civil War Women's Writing
	Dana E. Lawrence	Ramona Wray	Sarah C. E. Ross
Transmissions	Ch. 7 – Transmitting Faith: Elizabeth Tudor, Anne Askew, and Jane Grey	Ch. 13 – Mary Wroth Romances Ovid: Refiguring Metamorphosis and Complaint in *The Countess of Montgomery's Urania*	Ch. 19 – Inventing Fame
	Elaine V. Beilin	Clare R. Kinney	Jane B. Stevenson
Transnationalities	Ch. 8 – Humanism, Religion, and Early Modern Englishwomen in Their Transnational Contexts	Ch. 14 – Nuns' Writing: Translation, Textual Mobility and Transnational Networks	Ch. 20 – Political Writing across Borders
	Julie D. Campbell	Marie-Louise Coolahan	Mihoko Suzuki
Form and Genre	Ch. 9 – Women in Worship: Continuity and Change in the Prayers of Elizabeth Tyrwhit and Frances Aburgavenny	Ch. 15 – Motherhood and Women's Writing in Early Seventeenth-Century England: Legacies, Catechisms, and Popular Polemic	Ch. 21 – English Women's Writing and Indigenous Medical Knowledge in the Early Modern Atlantic World
	Micheline White	Paula McQuade	Edith Snook
Material Textualities	Ch. 10 – Spatial Texts: Women as Devisers of Environments and Iconographies	Ch. 16 – Monuments and Memory	Ch. 22 – Lady Anne Clifford's *Great Books of Record*: Remembrances of a Dynasty
	Peter Davidson	Peter Sherlock	Jessica L. Malay

continuity between texts and traditions. Each historical section consists of six chapters, located not in relation to usual categories of genre, situation, or medium but based on their participation in a specific discursive field at a specific cultural moment. The six themes governing these chapters, as mapped across three historical periods, are as follows.

Reformations

Like other areas of early modern literary and cultural studies, scholarship on women's writing has been influenced by "the return of religion."[21] This subject has been framed by two watershed scholarly collections. Contributors to Margaret P. Hannay's *Silent but for the Word* (1985) establish that religion was an approved, productive discursive site for early modern women. Chapters in Micheline White's *English Women, Religion, and Textual Production, 1500–1700* (2011) address anew the challenges to feminist literary criticism (centrally, the contested claims of subversion and orthodoxy, as discussed below) posed by early modern women's religious writing.[22] Three chapters in the present volume move scholarship forward by attending to the nuances of religious debate at key moments within the period. Susan Felch explores how early-Reformation co-religionist circles, both Catholic and reformed, enabled rather than subsumed women as devotional speakers. Pamela Benson's intertextual reading of Aemilia Lanyer's "radical reformulation" of the Passion sees gender at the core of Lanyer's innovations, revealing heretofore unrecognized Catholic sources with which Lanyer engages only to refute. W. Scott Howard locates Civil War sectarian writings "within networks of devotion and dissent, prophecy and protest," where authorial identity takes shape as "interventions into converging and diverging fields of [religious] reform."

Collaborations and Coteries

Chapters by Sarah C. E. Ross, Ramona Wray, and Dana Lawrence focus on the material textuality of women's writing, viewing these works as collaborative, "culturally mediated," and "choral."[23] Ross follows performative traces in manuscript and print from the Cavendish sisters

---

[21] See Ken Jackson and Arthur Marotti, "The Turn to Religion in Early Modern English Studies," *Criticism*, 46(1) (Winter 2004), 167–90.
[22] Hannay (ed.), *Silent but for the Word*, 4–14; White (ed.), *English Women*, 1–16.
[23] Pender and Smith, *Material Cultures*, 2 and 4.

to Alice Egerton – partially unmasking the Lady of Milton's *Comus*. Wray restores "occluded networks and praxes" enfolding Elizabeth Cary to argue that attending to "disparate materialisations" (print, manuscript, portraiture, and effigial sculpture) can revise views of women's authorship as inextricably bound to biography. Dana Lawrence's reading of Isabella Whitney locates collaboration *within* the single-authored work, *A Sweet Nosgay*, as an intertextual strategy that scripts Whitney's authorship as a shared coterie practice. The fiction of Whitney's *Nosgay*, in Lawrence's reading, is an allegory of contemporary critical engagements with woman writers, which cast them less as solitary authors and more as agents within networks of textual exchange.

Transmissions

Women's writings were often transmitted to posterity through interventions by male editors and scribes, figures who, to some extent, must be read as co-authors. In a recent discussion of Katherine Philips's print and manuscript transmissions, Marie-Louise Coolahan evocatively describes these mediations – and thus the "woman writer" they produce – as creating "refracted versions of authorship that concatenate around a single historical figure."[24] In this volume, Elaine Beilin traces the transmissions (by John Bale, Thomas Bentley, and others) of women's devotional writings in the Reformation, illustrating Danielle Clarke's perceptive sense of "editing as a form of authorship and authorship as a kind of editing."[25] Clare Kinney focuses not on the transmission of Mary Wroth's publications, but on Wroth's revisionary transmission of the Petrarchan and Ovidian "canon[s] of myth." Jane Stevenson surveys the often treacherous routes leading to women's literary fame in their lifetimes, focusing on the fortunes of Katherine Philips, Lucy Hutchinson, and Elizabeth Melville – as Stevenson notes, "the most successful published woman poet of the English-speaking world in the early modern period."[26]

Transnationalities

The "paradigm shift" from single authorship to collaborative textual production has encouraged comparative readings of the transnational

---

[24] Coolahan, "Single-Authored Manuscripts," 193.
[25] Clarke, "Producing Gender," 42.
[26] Stevenson (Chapter 19) in this volume.

networks in which women took part. While Julie Campbell explores
women's participation in the humanist republic of letters spanning
England and Europe, Marie-Louise Coolahan attends to the transnational avenues of textual exchange among English nuns in houses on
the Continent, a body of writings, she notes, that challenges traditional
ideas of authorship in their promotion of collective identity and elision
of "markers of female authorship." Mihoko Suzuki draws on the model of
the French *frondeuses* to enrich a reading of Margaret Cavendish's textual
self-fashioning and, more broadly, to demonstrate that civil wars in both
England and France opened up possibilities for women to intervene in
politics and public affairs.

Form and Genre

Recent attention to the formal aspects of women's writing has worked to
bridge the divide between aesthetic and historicist interpretations. Three
chapters in this volume respond to Elizabeth Scott-Baumann's call for "a
feminist formalism or a formalist feminism," engaging in close reading
and exploring the cultural encoding of gender within genres and forms.[27]
Micheline White's meticulous textual analysis of prayers by Elizabeth
Tyrwhit and Frances Aburgavenny demonstrates how each woman nego-
tiates formal constraints by adapting the available devotional lexicon in
novel ways. Paula McQuade shows how women appropriate traditional
forms by exploiting "the cultural prestige of maternity": mastering the
restrictive form of the catechism, for instance, women mobilize the genre
within doctrinal and political debates. Edith Snook studies women's
recipes – "a socially significant form of writing at an historical moment in
which domestic medical practice was integral to the provision of care in
England" – in relation to Indigenous American "practices and technologies," retained in the form while their "history of sources" is left behind.

Material Textualities

Evolving from manuscript studies, criticism of women's authorship has
increasingly turned toward the recovery of the material cultures of writing. Recent studies of "women's textualities" have moved beyond the
printed book and manuscript, reading women's literate engagements

---

[27] Scott-Baumann, *Forms of Engagement*, 9.

with material forms such as sewing and embroidery, monumental texts and sculpture, visual arts, and commissions and acts of patronage.[28] Peter Davidson surveys women's activities as collaborative "devisers" of spatial textualities, from painted domestic interiors, to sacred and secular embroidery, to gardens, noting women's creative management of the environments in which they lived. Peter Sherlock traces women's self-representations in the places where they were laid to rest, arguing that funerary sculptures and texts constitute a surprisingly rich archive of early modern women's writing. Finally, Jessica Malay reads Anne Clifford's magisterial project, the *Great Books of Record*, as a composite work laboriously crafted to produce a book "of national identity" in the shadow of the Civil War and an autobiography of Clifford herself.

Four Debates

In preface to the chronological history presented in this volume, Part I, "Critical Approaches and Methodologies," contains four chapters that interrogate debates at the heart of the study of early modern women's writing. These chapters give a general grounding in the field but also provide sophisticated engagements with key issues by critics who have led scholarly dialogue and practice. The four contested topics are: (1) Recoveries and Transmissions; (2) Authorial Agency and Identity Politics; (3) Subversion, Orthodoxy, and the Canon; and (4) Tradition and Truth in the Archives. The significance of each of these debates within the field is discussed briefly here.

Recoveries and Transmissions

The past four decades have witnessed an ever-increasing number of critical reclamations of early modern women's texts that had been veiled in obscurity for centuries. The sheer quantity of texts now available has profoundly changed critical views of the period, and these views continue to evolve as scholarship takes account of diverse genres, media, and modes of women's textual production. Printed and manuscript texts by early modern women are now widely accessible in digital archives (*Women Writers Online; Perdita Manuscripts Online, 1500–1700; Who Were the*

---

[28] Frye, *Pens and Needles*.

Nuns?; digital editions of single authors).[29] Published editions, such as Caroline Bowden's six-volume *English Convents in Exile, 1600–1800*, and series such as Oxford University Press's *Women Writers in English, 1350–1850* and Ashgate's facsimile series of essential works by early modern Englishwomen, have made women's writing available to students and scholars. The Other Voice in Early Modern Europe series recently supplemented its list of English translations of Continental women's writing with a series dedicated to editions of women's writing in English.[30]

While the available body of writing by early modern women has grown rapidly, this recovery is a work in progress, one that labors in the wake of new textualism's challenge to authorship. Authorial agency, as Hurley and Goodblatt put it, is now "diffused."[31] Registering the vast body of women's writings returned to circulation and the unfinished, revisionary scholarship attending it, *Orlando: Women's Writing in the British Isles from the Beginnings to the Present* provides "a feminist literary history centered in women's production." This expansive and inclusive database "emphasizes the intellectual, material, political and social conditions (including writing by men) that have, over time, helped to shape writing by women."[32] Treating all writing and authors as equal, this digital catalogue presents detailed biographical and critical accounts of the lives and works of its subjects. Individual texts and writers are displayed as actively engaged in multiple cultural and literary networks and traditions.

---

[29] See: *Women Writers Online*, www.wwp.northeastern.edu/wwo; *Perdita Manuscripts*, www. Perditamanuscripts.amdigital.co.uk/default.aspx; "Who Were the Nuns?", http://wwtn.history. qmul.ac.uk/database/index.html; *Bess of Hardwick's Letters: A Complete Correspondence, c.* 1550–1608, www.bessofhardwick.org; Salzman (ed.), *Mary Wroth's Poetry: An Electronic Edition*, http:// wroth.latrobe.edu.au/all-poems.html; "RECIRC: The Reception and Circulation of Early Modern Women's Writing, 1550–1700," ww.nuigalway.ie/English/marie_louise_coolahan.html. For discussions of the contingent nature of women's writing as particularly amenable to digital editions, see: Ezell, "Editing Early Modern Women's Manuscripts"; Pender and Smith, "Editing Early Modern Women."

[30] See: Bowden (ed.), *English Convents*; *Women Writers in English, 1350–1850*, Woods (ed.), https:// global.oup.com/academic/content/series/w/women-writers-in-english-1350-1850-wwe/?cc=gb&la ng=en&; Betty S. Travitsky, Anne Lake Prescott, and Patrick Cullen, *The Early Modern Englishwoman: A Facsimile Library of Essential Works* (Ashgate Press, www.ashgate.com/default. aspx?page=1797); Margaret King, Albert Rabil, Jr., and Elizabeth H. Hageman, "The Other Voice in Early Modern Europe" (ACMRS/ITER, https://acmrs.org/publications/other/ other-voice-early-modern-europe-toronto-series).

[31] Hurley and Goodblatt (eds.), *Women Editing*, xii.

[32] Susan Brown, Patricia Clements, and Isobel Grundy, *Orlando: Writing by Women in the British Isles from the Beginnings to the Present* (Cambridge University Press), http://orlando.cambridge.org.

In many ways, the Orlando Project completes a circle begun by the antiquarian catalogues that conveyed the memories of early modern women writers to contemporary criticism alongside those of many other women who would not have considered themselves "writers" in a traditional sense. Although the "invisibility optics" produced by male-authored catalogues and histories of women's writing have long been evident, the field's lingering indebtedness to this body of writing has been less apparent. When the Orlando Project's editors name writing by men as one of the "social conditions" giving shape to women's writing, they imagine this engagement in specific historical terms: early modern men's literary practice creates a condition (among others) for early modern women's literary practice to take place. Yet the influence of writing by men on the transmission of women's writing is often more definitive than this contextualization suggests. "Studies in intertextuality, history of the book, material culture, and manuscript circulation," Elaine Beilin affirms in this volume, "have repeatedly demonstrated that women writers functioned actively in a nexus of literary, political, social and economic relationships on both sides of the confessional divide and sometimes in between." Yet her study of male editors' interventions in writings by Anne Askew, Elizabeth Tudor, and Jane Grey shows how, in the service of religious belief, these women and their works were plucked from this nexus to create singular female authors and exemplars.

While contemporary scholarship in the field has deployed new textual, material, and situational strategies to move beyond the essentialist and biographical focus which was the legacy of antiquarian catalogues, critics have generally embraced rather than refused the taxonomy also emergent from the catalogue tradition which presupposes and dictates the separate history and trajectory of women's writing from men's. Studies and histories of early modern women's writing, as a result, frequently remain insular and inward-turning, aimed primarily at a community of scholars and students already familiar with this material. The specter of catalogue transmission is eerily resurrected in critical studies of women's writing that compile lists of women writers, some more familiar than others, working in a specific mode or genre in the given period. These latter-day catalogues attend to their subject, but tend neither to address the development of genres over time, nor to seek connections among women's works or between women's writing and relevant texts in the masculine canon.

Certainly one of the institutional sites informing early modern women's writing – perhaps the most pressing location – is the web of expectations, choices, limitations, and opportunities constructed by the masculine canon and men's literary practice. Recent efforts to revise or refuse the relevance of traditional categories of textual production to women's writing raise valid concerns about the unique characteristics – the difference – of women's texts.[33] In this volume, Margaret Ezell's study of the challenges posed by Esther Inglis's corpus to "traditional ways of classifying authorship" underscores the need for "alternative narratives embracing multiple literary traditions rather than tidy inclusions into a single, dominant, pre-existing one." Yet if we are to remedy the pattern of "loss-recovery-loss" suffered by early modern women's works,[34] the literary history of women's writing must position these works in an accessible narrative addressed to as wide an audience of scholars and students as possible. If the literary history of early modern women's writing is to move beyond the separate sphere in which the catalogue tradition placed it, disengaged from the broader histories of the literature and culture in which it participates, it must find means to enter into conversation with other narratives of literary production. In this volume, intertextual studies by Benson, Lawrence, and Kinney address men's and women' shared literary cultures. Chapters engaging the "sociology of writing" – by Felch, Campbell, Howard, Wray, Ross, Stevenson, Coolahan, Suzuki, Davidson, and Sherlock – stress the participation of men as well as women in coteries and circles. Formalist studies by White, McQuade, and Snook attend to adaptions and revisions of conventional forms and genres by women. By acknowledging the collaborative transmission of much of early modern women's writing and its imbrication with writing by men, a history of women's writing need not be an exclusive history, nor need it address an exclusive audience.

Authorial Agency and Identity Politics

In their emphasis on cultural sites informing literate practices, recent literary histories of women's writing destabilize not only the category of "literature" but also the idea of "the author." Organizing their literary history around the literate practices of "ordinary women from across the social spectrum and their encounters with the written word," for example, Caroline Bicks and Jennifer Summit suggest a breakdown of the dichotomy between author and reader: "the multiplicity of women's literate practices," they assert, "challenges us to rethink the boundary between

---

[33] See, especially, Wray, "Anthologizing". See also Clarke, "Nostalgia."
[34] Janet Todd, as quoted by Ezell (Chapter 1) in this volume.

reading and writing ... that has artificially limited our understanding of early literary culture."[35] Troubling the binary of reading and writing, recent histories of reading attest to the need to align early modern textual production with reception. The contention that reading is continuous with, and may effectively constitute, writing helps to make sense of early modern women's literate practices. Traditionally passive acts of reception – reading, but also, for example, translation, transcription, and editing – qualify the image of an autonomous author as the sole creator of her work. "Intentionality, then," Marie-Louise Coolahan concludes, "is as much a question to be asked of the reader-compiler-editor as of the author."[36]

Views of authorial agency as occurring within collaborative networks of readers and writers are better attuned to the conditions of textual production informing early modern writing, and enable a more accurate and inclusive view of literate practice in early modern Britain. Yet the qualification of authorial agency that they involve poses significant problems to narrating the development of early modern women's writing over time. The poststructuralist denunciation of authorial intention and the proclaimed "death of the author" have led feminist histories of women's writing toward constructionist views of gender and performance. As Laura Lunger Knoppers puts it, "with a focus on gender in history, we can move away from both essentializing and deconstruction of identity, grounding our work in historical particulars that include – among other factors – biography and women's life-writing."[37] Yet calling upon biography and autobiography to explicate writing as the product of *feminine gender* rather than *female sex* nonetheless seems to posit a figure of authorial presence, a subject through whose activity a piece of writing has come into being. The waning desire to describe a female tradition, where women writers engage implicitly or explicitly with female peers or precursors, underscores the critical preference for treating the contingent circumstances of textual production, a situational contingency that threatens to mark women's writing as "occasional" in a pejorative sense.

[35] Bicks and Summit, "Introduction," 4. See also: Hackel, *Reading Material*; Hackel and Kelly (eds.), *Reading Women*; Ferguson, *Dido's Daughters*.
[36] Coolahan, "Single-Authored Manuscripts," 193.
[37] Knoppers, "Introduction: Critical Framework and Issues," in Knoppers (ed.), *Cambridge Companion to Early Modern Women's Writing*, 9. Knoppers registers the continuing influence of Judith Butler's formulation of performativity on the field: see *Gender Trouble: Feminism and the Subversion of Identity* (New York and London: Routledge, 1999).

If the literary history of women's writing is to be imagined as more than a series of tenuously related (or perhaps unrelated) occasions of composition, it seems fruitful to embrace a version of authorship that corresponds with, without acquiescing to, a conservative view of writing as a medium within which a recognizable subject or identity comes into being. Claims for authorial agency must take into account the central dilemma of identity politics as Joshua Gamson describes it: clear identity categories are both necessary to affirm membership in a group with common political aims and social values, and they are "dangerous distortions," stigmatizing the communities they unite. Thus, Gamson reasons, "it is as liberating and sensible to demolish a collective identity as it is to establish one." Viewed in this light, this dilemma may foster rather than unravel a proactive view of identity undergirding creative practice.[38] One suggestive way to negotiate this conflict is available in Linda Alcoff's idea of positionality and its recent iterations in corporeal feminist and post-humanist theory. Identity, in Alcoff's view, is relative to, but not determined by, a constantly changing context, engaged in and responsive to shifting networks of cultural conditions and institutions. Female identity is "a construction yet also a necessary point of departure," Alcoff writes. "Being a 'woman' is to take up a position within a moving historical context and to be able to choose what we make of this position and how we alter this context."[39] Rosi Braidotti, adapting and refashioning Adrienne Rich's notion of the "politics of location," sees "subjectivity [as] a process of auto-poiesis or self-styling which involves complex and continuous negotiations with dominant norms and values and with multiple forms of accountability."[40] Positional agency works against the "occasional" aspects of early modern women's writing, enabling "gestures of collective self-styling," as Braidotti puts it, where self-reflexive subjects are constituted through a shared repertoire of styles, "an interactive process which relies on a social network of exchanges."[41] This politics of location

---

[38] Joshua Gamson, "Must Identity Movements Self-Destruct? A Queer Dilemma," *Social Problems* 42(3) (August 1995), 401 and 403.

[39] Linda Alcoff, "Cultural Feminism versus Post-Structuralism: The Identity Crisis in Feminist Theory," *Signs*, 13 (1988), 443.

[40] Braidotti, *Posthuman*, 30. See also Adrienne Rich, "Notes Towards a Politics of Location," in *Women, Feminist Identity and Society in the 1980s: Selected Papers*, Myriam Díaz-Diocaretz and Iris Zavala (eds.) (Amsterdam: John Benjamins, 1985), 7–22.

[41] Braidotti, *Posthuman*, 74; and Rosi Braidotti, *Metamorphoses: Towards a Materlialist Theory of Becoming* (Cambridge: Polity, 2002), 13.

embodies and embeds the subject not within a circle but at a point of departure.[42]

Taking into account these refinements of identity politics, we are able to move beyond explicating situational conditions and institutions informing women's writing toward defining a shared repertoire of creative and self-creative choices available to women to respond to and alter these conditions. Recognizing the degree to which women's writing is intertwined with processes of historical and literary change, these chapters interrogate the place of gender among other defining features of identity. Jaime Goodrich's reading of Anne Bacon's identity politics in this volume agrees that an author's "identifiable voice ... is dependent upon complex material histories of production that shift over time."[43] Goodrich locates Bacon's writing within spheres of literate practice, employing a flexible idea of authorship as a product of "overlapping identities." "What if the female author was viewed as just a writer, not as a woman writer?" Goodrich wonders, and she deploys the insights of intersectional studies to decenter essentialist and intentionalist readings of Bacon's authorial agency. While Bacon sought to construct authorship at the intersection of overlapping identities, Goodrich recounts how male readers (in this case, Bacon's unruly son Anthony) could undercut the woman writer's plural identities by focusing exclusively on gender. This challenge to the woman writer's intersectional identity at the hands of a dissenting reader is a tale repeated and reversed in Jane Stevenson's account of the fortunes of Elizabeth Melville's *Ane Godlie Dreame*: when Melville's son published a parody of his mother's widely read work, he censured "the impoverished poetics of his mother's [Calvinist] circle." "Melville was received," Stevenson concludes, "whether by admirers or detractors, as a Calvinist poet, not a woman poet."

Goodrich's model of intersectional identity is shared by chapters in this volume that focus on religious writing. Felch sees women's writing in co-religionist circles as marked but not confined by their authors' gender: they are "gender-inflected but not gender-exclusive."[44] Micheline White's assessment of Aburgavenny's prayers illustrates quiet revisions of "masculine or gender-neutral nouns to describe the Christian community"

---

[42] Braidotti, *Metamorphoses*, 2.
[43] Pender and Smith, *Material Cultures*, 4. They further note that an emphasis on the material histories of textual production "uncouple[s] a static model of historical woman writer and text and replac[es] it with one that views this relationship as temporally, spatially, and textually contingent."
[44] Felch, "The Backward Gaze," 24.

toward the feminine options, "widow" and "sister." W. Scott Howard notes the "complex, cross-gender identit[ies]" and "hybrid subjectivities ... [common] among Baptists, Quakers, and Fifth Monarchists," calling attention to An Collins's "autobiographical, devotional, and prophetic personae" in her *Divine Songs and Meditations*. Yet intersectionality proves useful beyond studies of religious writing as well. Peter Sherlock argues that plural identities are revealed in women's "serial use of monuments." Ramona Wray explores Cary's multiple versions of the woman writer to disrupt "life and works" readings, while the plural identities of Isabella Whitney's poetic persona emerge in Dana Lawrence's mapping of her migration from impoverished solitude to panoptic control of the city she owns.

Subversion, Orthodoxy, and the Canon

If early modern catalogues, such as William Barker's *Nobility of Women*, strove to contain women's writing within orthodox, patriarchal power structures, twentieth-century criticism tended to value subversion and heterodoxy in women's writing. Nascent scholarship in early modern women's writing often adopted a formulaic pattern: details of an unknown author's biography were presented, based in large part on evidence gleaned from her recovered text; a survey of the work's contents, genre, and mentalities followed; and an argument for the author's protofeminism demonstrated how she challenges or subverts masculine cultural and political hegemony. As Sarah Ross and Paul Salzman put it, "'protofeminism' could be seen to constitute a new kind of female exemplarity."[45]

Twenty-first-century approaches to women's writing have refined these reductive readings on a number of fronts. New attention has been paid to women's works and genres overlooked because they appear to maintain rather than subvert religious, political, and gender hierarchies. Paula McQuade's chapter in this volume on mother's legacies and catechisms, for instance, shows how writers in these genres exploit maternity as "a culturally sanctioned space for female authorship" while documenting women's interventions into mainstream political and spiritual discourses.[46] The relevance of traditional ideas of canonicity to women's works is pressingly interrogated in recent work on editing women's

---

[45] Ross and Salzman, *Editing Early Modern Women*, 4.
[46] See, for example, McQuade, "A Knowing People."

writing. Danielle Clarke suggests that "the canon has been something of a *canard*" for women's writings insofar as the textual features of women's works defy the "fields of regularity" governing canonicity.[47] As a "female canon" of early modern women's writing – one attentive to the material culture, formalism, and "sociologies" of texts – coalesces, the place of women's writing in relation to the traditional, masculine canon remains a contested subject of critical and pragmatic concern.[48]

If uncertainties attend the status of a canon of early modern women's writing, the persistent critical preference for subversion over orthodoxy stands at the heart of this debate. As scholarship has embraced a wide and diverse field of early modern women's writing, the value of establishing a female canon at all has been as unclear as the criteria on which individual works would acquire canonical status. The field has been centrifugal, moving toward diversity and multiplicity that scuttle the notion of a centralized group of major texts or authors representative of early modern women's writing. Although certain women writers have emerged as canonical – perhaps most obviously "the triumvirate," in Mihoko Suzuki's phrase, of Mary Sidney Herbert, Mary Wroth, and Aemilia Lanyer – a female canon has seemed as superfluous and outmoded as appeals to maintain and protect the traditional male canon of great works from the encroachment of arguably less artful works by minor writers, female as well as male.[49]

In this volume, Patricia Pender's intervention into this debate traces developments in contemporary editorial practice that can work to deconstruct the binaries – stable/diffuse, single-authored/collaborative, and, most significantly, subversive/orthodox – that have attended women's canonicity. If Adrienne Rich sought to confer canonical status on Anne Bradstreet in order to rescue her from "the Woman's Archive,"[50] Pender's comparison of two recent editions of Bradstreet's poems explores a "variety of new canon formations" that might enfold her works. One, a modernized anthology, adopts the orthodox format of mainstream collections yet aims to subvert the "politics of selection" governing them; the other,

---

[47] Clarke, "Nostalgia," 188.

[48] See Marcus, "Editing Queen Elizabeth I," and Ross and Scott-Baumann, "Anthologizing Early Modern Women's Poetry," for discussions of the advantages of modernized editions of women's texts, with which students are more capable of engaging.

[49] Suzuki (ed.), *History*, 7. The canonical status of these writers is largely based upon standard editions by prestigious presses and editors. See: Herbert, *Collected Works*; Lanyer, *Poems*; Wroth, *Poems;* Wroth, *Urania* (first and second parts).

[50] Rich, "Foreword," in Henley (ed.), Bradstreet, *Works*, xvii. See Pender's discussion (Chapter 3) in this volume.

a digital edition, subverts the desire for a stable text by attending to the material transmissions of Bradstreet's poems, an approach, as Pender points out, "increasingly being painted as a new orthodoxy."[51] Calling for "a collective, multidisciplinary approach to early modern women's writing," Pender argues that the capacious field exceeds the limitations of inherited critical methodologies and the restrictive binaries on which they rely.

Yet a *history* of early modern women's writing may not be best conceived as a disjointed record of textual dispersal. Balancing the centrifugal and centripetal forces that have influenced scholarship in the field, chapters in this history account for the scope and plurality of women's writing while investigating how and why some texts and authors move beyond the conditions of textual production and reception to achieve continued or renewed relevance for readers, scholars, and students. In some, if not all, cases, this is as much an achievement of the industry of scholars, archivists, and editors as it is of the women writers to whom they attend. Thus there is as much a place in this canon for Lucy Knatchbull and Dorothy Burch as for Anne Bradstreet and Aphra Behn. The female canon advanced by this project does not uproot texts from the social locations of their composition or describe their achievements as extraordinary, prodigious, or transcendent. Rather, this volume views those works as "major" which carry the traces of the conditions of social authorship and display creative, innovative responses to these cultural and literary fields. A description of these benchmark works can begin to establish a recognizable, if flexible and fluid, canon of early modern women's writing, a collaboratively authored, "choral" canon that moves not toward protection and separatism, but toward inclusion, commonality, and likeness.

Tradition and Truth in the Archives

Historically, attempts to identify a tradition of women's writing – one within which established links between authors and works might ideally be retrieved or, failing such evidence, accurately theorized – have struggled to find terms flexible enough to accommodate the multifarious nature of this work. If feminist scholars in the 1980s took an essentialist view of their female subjects, a third-wave "strategic essentialism" has

---

[51] The editions are: Ross and Scott-Baumann, *Women Poets of the English Civil War*; and Pender, "Anne Bradstreet," EMWRN Digital Archive.

more recently been called forth to support a unified, common tradition among women writers. Following the implications of strategic essentialism for coalescing collective identity, some critics have adapted standpoint theory – most often articulated in the situational model of women's literary history – to describe early modern women's shared social location and experience as grounds for constructing a uniquely feminine perspective. Relying on an identity politics based on subject position, Mihoko Suzuki claims that the potentially male authors known pseudonymously as Constantia Munda and Esther Sowernam "wrote from the subject position of women and had the effect of galvanizing women's identity as a subordinate group with common interests."[52] Yet in the field of literary history, as in feminist theory, poststructuralism has troubled the notion of stable identities grounded in normative categories of experience or viewpoint. Paul Salzman usefully opts for and describes "identifications" among women writers rather than shared "identities" by relying upon strategies of affiliation (with male authors, with other powerful women, with feminine genres, through collective activism) to enact "self-conscious authorship." His effort to move from localized performances of authorship to a tradition of similar acts, however, falters as it confronts the challenge posed by difference: "these women were, if not always consciously, at least through print and manuscript circulation of their work, establishing something like a tradition of women's writing, even if that tradition was discontinuous."[53]

Very infrequently, early modern women writers demonstrate or express their knowledge of and indebtedness to earlier examples of women's writing. In Aemilia Lanyer's poem on the passion of Christ, the female speaker presents herself as a literary heir to Mary Sidney Herbert in a dream vision of a "golden Chaine" joining the poets, Reason, the Graces, and the Muses in a timeless, if nebulous, coterie.[54] Sarah C. E. Ross's *Women, Poetry and Politics in Seventeenth-Century Britain* (2015) makes a valuable contribution to the twenty-first-century project of mapping a pattern of literary inheritance like that imagined by Lanyer. Although Ross acknowledges that the women she studies were most likely not directly influenced by each other's works, she excavates "a female political

---

[52] Mihoko Suzuki, "Introduction," in Suzuki (ed.), *History*, 2. See Nancy C. M. Harstock, "The Feminist Standpoint: Toward a Specifically Feminine Historical Materialism," in Sandra Harding (ed.), *The Feminist Standpoint Reader: Intellectual and Political Controversies* (New York and London: Routledge, 2004), 35–54.
[53] Paul Salzman, "Identifying as (Women) Writers," in Suzuki (ed.), *History*, 41.
[54] Lanyer, *Poems*, 21.

poetic" at work in their creative productions. This tradition, for Ross, demands more subtle critical engagement than did the search for subversive or protofeminist inflections pursued by second-wave feminist scholars. Here we are attentive to multilayered representations, recurring tropes, shared sources – the "echoes [and] prefigurations" – that rise to the surface in formalist treatments of women's works.[55]

Although critics may not agree on what we are searching for when we enter the archives – who or what is "the woman writer" we seek – there is agreement, I believe, that whatever shape the tradition or history of early modern women's writing takes is largely determined by the scholarly, aesthetic, and ethical values we adopt as we approach women's works. Megan Matchinske's chapter in this volume explores the possibility of unearthing historical "truth" in the written records the archives intractably hold. Calling on the legal case of a notorious liar, Mary Carleton, Matchinske considers the irony in Carleton's evocation of the classical philosopher Epimenides – Cretan and Sophist, famous for speaking the self-referential paradox that "all Cretans are liars" – to support the truth of her testimony. We might wonder about the credibility of the textual account of Carleton's court appearance in light of this erudite allusion, but this is the least of the challenges posed by Epimenides's paradoxical presence. As Matchinske points out, the philosopher's "double call to truth asks ... for a greater field of vision, to hold on to more than one meaning at a time, to accept as possible the likelihood that something could be right as well as wrong, good as well as bad, and true as well as false." Mapping Carleton's double truths onto archival methodology, Matchinske reminds us of the "'storied' nature of our tellings": we must labor – patiently, responsibly – to piece together a story of the past from slips and fragments. And she turns us back to the world outside the archives as well, to the current "post-truth" world, where the "pluralizing" images of Mary Carleton and her sophistic instructors – with their "alternative facts" and multiple truths – seem unnervingly at home.[56]

---

[55] Ross, *Women, Poetry, and Politics*, 3 and 214. A similar impulse informs Ross and Scott-Baumann's *Women Poets of the English Civil War*, which brings together five mid-century poets, a decision which itself gestures toward a shared tradition among these writers.

[56] In November 2016, Oxford Dictionaries declared "post-truth" the word of the year (see https://en.oxforddictionaries.com/word-of-the-year/word-of-the-year-2016, accessed February 27, 2017). See also Jon Swaine, "Trump Team Defends 'Alternative Facts' after Widespread Protest," *The Guardian*, January 23, 2017, www.theguardian.com/us-news/2017/jan/22/donald-trump-kelly-anne-conway-inauguration-alternative-facts, accessed February 27, 2017.

Certainly the tellings contained in this volume are "storied." When Ramona Wray observes that Elizabeth Cary's "competing attempts at memorialisation ... attest to the fraught processes of writing women's literary history in the seventeenth century," her equivocation suggests that those processes are fraught not only for twenty-first-century critics but also for their seventeenth-century counterparts. Several contributors share an interest in the methods employed by early modern women themselves to craft histories. Peter Sherlock, Jane Stevenson, and Marie-Louise Coolahan explore strategies pursued by women in multiple forms and media for "reputation management," as Coolahan puts it. Yet if our tales are storied – if our truths are multiple – they are fraught but not failed. If our patron saint is the fallen Epimenides, he need not consign us to the closed circuit of both/and, neither/nor – an endless wavering between two equally impossible truths. Epimenides's statement is only paradoxical if we assume that the inevitable opposite of "all Cretans are liars" is "all Cretans are truthful." Viewed from another angle, though, other possibilities – pluralities of truths – come into view. If we understand the alternative truth to be "not all Cretans are liars," the paradox is solved; the closed circuit is opened. We learn to suspect binaries and their seemingly inevitable oppositions, to remain open to surprising alternatives. Our choices are still plural, our answers multiple – but they *are* choices, answers, solutions.

This volume concludes with two storied tellings crafted by early modern women. Edith Snook's reading of early modern women's recipes displays the processes by which Indigenous knowledge is appropriated from sources that are quickly forgotten and erased from historical record. "'The truth about stories,'" she writes, quoting the Cherokee American/Canadian writer Thomas King, "'is that that is all that we are.'" Snook censures women's implication in the invisibility optics that elide Indigenous actors, a view that, in other circumstances, might apply to the situation of women's writing in the literary history of Britain: "The story that we tell," she writes, "should include all participants." Jessica Malay's study of Anne Clifford's *Great Books of Record* is a tale of seventeenth-century women in the archives: of Clifford and her mother, Margaret Russell, industriously rifling through records, retrieving primary sources to support Clifford's claim to her inheritance, and pulling them together to craft a narrative – Clifford's own literary history, intended to manage her reputation in the historical afterlife. *The Great Books of Record* are composite texts in form and content, compiling a plurality of truths and identities, pieced together and arranged to tell the story of Lady Anne Clifford that Malay would compile, arrange, and retell four centuries later.

Together, the chapters in this volume describe a kinetic female tradition, a literary history that views women's writing as carrying traces of lost networks of creative options and opportunities, embodying choices made in response to and influencing the literary, political, social, and cultural traditions available to their authors. Lanyer's "golden Chaine" aptly figures the shared desire of the contributors to this volume and its editor to join – and join with – early modern women's diverse, expansive, multiple writings in a processual, collective history. Each brilliant chapter is a sparkling link in that chain.

PART I

Critical Approaches and Methodologies

Invisibility Optics
Aphra Behn, Esther Inglis and the Fortunes of Women's Works

Margaret J. M. Ezell

The Bee draweth naught (Most Noble and Vertuous Ladie) hway from the fragrant herbs of the garding for hir self: no more haue I payned my self many yearis to burie the talent God hes geuen me in oblivion.

> Esther Inglis, dedication to Susanna, Lady Herbert (1605)[1]

The following Collection of Plays needs no other Recommendation than that they were writ by the incomparable Mrs. A. Behn; a Person whose Character is so universally known, and whose Performances have met with such a general Applause, that 'tis needless to bespeak the Reader's Favour on her behalf.

> "Preface", *Plays Written by the Late Ingenius Mrs. BEHN in Four Volumes* (1724)[2]

Late in the last century, a great and collaborative work of recovery was undertaken by literary scholars to exhume women poets, story tellers, and playwrights whose works of genius were lurking, dusty and undiscovered, in the archives of major research libraries ... But their stories have not yet been adopted for the classroom, or for the book club, or for bedside reading. There are many reasons for that, none of them good ones.

> Donald W. Foster, *Welcome to Women's Work*[3]

In the twenty-first century, reading about early modern women writers and the fortunes of their works, one typically encounters two different but interlocking narratives. The first celebrates the recovery of a host of women writing in multiple genres between 1450 and 1700. The second

---

[1] Harvard University, Houghton Library MS 428, Esther Inglis, *Argumenta singulorum capitum Geneseos per Tetrasticha*, 1605, fol. 1ʳ.
[2] Aphra Behn, *Plays Written by the Late Ingenious Mrs. Behn in Four Volumes*, 3rd ed., 4 vols. (London: Mary Paulson, 1724), vol. I, fol. A2ʳ.
[3] Donald W. Foster, *Women's Works*, 4 vols. (Salem, MA: Wicked Good Books, 2013), vol. I, xxiii.

laments the lack of a significant, lasting impact of newly discovered women on the long-existing canon, and points to the resistance of change in the typical English literature curriculum, scholarship, and the public perception of women in the past by readers in the present.

The energy of scholars in the 1980s and 1990s devoted to the rediscovery of early modern women writers was extraordinary and the claims made for early modern women's texts were large. One of the early leading figures in the scholarly editing of early modern women's texts, Josephine Roberts, declared that in the last decades of the twentieth century "the recovery of works by early modern women has become one of the most important developments in the field of bibliographical and textual studies."[4] Betty S. Travitsky and Patrick Cullen began the ambitious and still ongoing series *The Early Modern Englishwoman – A Facsimile Library of Essential Works* in 1996, declaring in each volume that the recovery of texts by and for women has "become one of the most important – indeed perhaps the most important – means for the rewriting of early modern history."[5] A later anthology stated that its goal was to represent "the sheer energy and diversity of women's cultural activity in the British islands," noting that "the study of early modern women's poetry is an academic industry of twenty years' growth, which has seen an extraordinary amount of activity."[6]

As the general editors of another 1990s pioneering print series devoted to scholarly editions of early modern women's works observed, "most of the writers represented in the series were well known and highly regarded until the professionalization of English studies in the later nineteenth century coincided with their excision from canonical status and from the majority of literary history."[7] One highly influential early anthology of the period, *Kissing the Rod*, however, remained cautious about this recovery process. "In seventeenth-century England literary activity was exclusively oriented to the concerns of the classically educated males" and "if poetry is 'making' then all women were poets, but they did not make primarily with words, and certainly not with characters inscribed upon a page."[8] Some ten years later, Germaine Greer, one of the anthology's

[4] Roberts, "Editing the Women Writers," 63.

[5] Betty S. Travitsky and Patrick Cullen (general eds.), "Preface," *The Early Modern Englishwoman: A Facsimile Library of Essential Works. Part 1: Printed Writings, 1500–1640 Vol. 1, Anne Askew*, introduction by John N. King (London: Routledge, 1996), vii. The series continues to the present day.

[6] Stevenson and Davidson (eds.), *Early Modern Women Poets*, xxviii and lii.

[7] Susanne Woods and Elizabeth H. Hageman, "Foreword," in Anna Weamys, *A Continuation of Sir Philip Sidney's Arcadia*, Patrick Colborn Cullen (ed.) (Oxford: Oxford University Press, 1994), ix.

[8] Greer et al. (eds.), *Kissing the Rod*, 1.

editors, concluded in her study of women poets that "the dilemma of the student of poetry who is also passionately interested in women is that she has to find value in a mass of work that she knows to be inferior."[9]

The seeming lack of enthusiasm for reading the newly recovered works by women was remarked upon nearly twenty years after those ground-breaking anthologies and editions, when Nigel Smith pointed to the gap between "academic readers ... with specific agendas of interest and enquiry that make us look at – and teach – material that no one out there in high-street land would bother to read."[10] What makes a writer highly visible and celebrated at some moments in time and invisible in others? Susanne Woods posed early on a pertinent question, still to be answered: "how can we recover early women's writing in English once and for all?"[11] Elizabeth Clarke was equally troubled two decades after Woods that "what I find almost entirely lacking in the field of early modern women's writing at present is a narrative, however tentative, of how an excluded class of potential authors – women – might become recognized as literary successes, in the twenty-first century if not in their own time."[12] As Clarke notes, the lack of a narrative concerned with emergence of women authors "leaves us at the mercy of the kind of thinking that drives canon formation: an ahistorical, mystical assertion of the literary genius at work, which is constructed by largely unspoken aesthetic and political judgements," detrimental to our being able to perceive and appreciate any group outside of the dominant literary culture of a period.[13]

What have been the persistent narratives about early modern women writers affecting their subsequent fame and fortune, and what might be possible alternatives? Taking as case studies Esther Inglis and Aphra Behn, who wrote for profit, as well as women writing for noncommercial audiences, and the fortunes of their works, we can reconsider the mechanisms driving what Janet Todd has described as the cycle of loss-recovery-loss of women's texts and shaping our perceptions of early modern women's participation in literary culture. How might we understand "author" as applied to women's works?[14]

[9] Germaine Greer, *Slip-Shod Sibyls: Recognition, Rejection and the Woman Poet* (New York: Viking Press, 1995), xi.

[10] Smith, "The Rod and the Canon," 232.

[11] Susanne Woods, "Recovering the Past, Discovering the Future: The Brown Women Writers Project," *South Central Review*, 11.2 (1994), 19.

[12] Clarke and Robson, "Why Are We 'Still Kissing the Rod'?," 184–5.

[13] Ibid., 185.

[14] For Behn, see Janet Todd, *The Critical Fortunes of Aphra Behn* (Martlesham: Camden House, 1998). See also Jane Spencer *Aphra Behn's Afterlife* (Oxford: Clarendon Press, 2001).

Invisibility: Presence, Absence, or Erasure?

[The] marginalization of women's writing arises from the ways in which early modern women's poetry was received, redacted and valued.[15]

The starting premise of many late twentieth-century studies of early modern women writers was their absence; therefore, each individual found was a "discovery" of an assumed previously unknown type, a surprising anomaly.[16] Virginia Woolf famously speculated in 1929 about the Elizabethan period that "it is a perennial puzzle why no woman wrote a word of that extraordinary literature when every other man, it seemed, was capable of song or sonnet."[17] Speaking of early women writers, the feminist poet and early anthologist Louise Bernikow observed, "poets did generally congregate at court, in men's clubs, at Cambridge, in living rooms, in bars, where they shared whatever was to be shared and spread a certain infectious energy among themselves." "Male poets that is," she concludes, "women had almost nothing to do with such congregating except perhaps to serve tea or sit in a back room copying over manuscripts so the work of the men would make marks for posterity."[18] Furthermore, given the 1980s configuration of early modern literacy (based on the absence of their signatures on various legal documents, mostly ecclesiastical court records) that 90 percent of women of all social classes were presumed to be illiterate until around 1700, to envision a sixteenth-century woman writing seriously, much less a group of women writing in association, would have been a formidable leap of the imagination.[19]

The assumption of absence or a merely silent presence in the background not surprisingly permeated the apparatus of the emerging anthologies of early modern women's writings in the 1980s and 1990s. The original edition of the *Norton Anthology of Literature by Women: The Tradition in English* (1985) gave 172 pages to women's writing prior to 1800 out of 2,390; the editors declared that it was not until the eighteenth century and Aphra Behn that the emergence of "productive,

---

[15] Patricia Pender and Rosalind Smith, "Afterword," 244–52 at 247.
[16] Ezell, "The Laughing Tortoise."
[17] Woolf, *A Room of One's Own*, 32.
[18] Louise Bernikow (ed.), "Introduction," in *The Women Split Open: Women Poets 1552–1950* (London: The Women's Press, 1979), 16.
[19] The most influential study on early modern literacy was David Cressy, *Literacy and the Social Order: Reading and Writing in Tudor and Stuart England* (Oxford: Cambridge University Press, 1980), 72–3 and 191–201; also Table 6.1 and Graph 7.2, which has been strongly challenged in the following decades.

publishing women ... began to form a tradition of their own." The earlier women who did manage to write, the editors assured their readers, were scattered and isolated individuals, not part of larger "literary communities comparable to the loosely organized groups of male writers who supported and encouraged the works of artists like Marlowe."[20] Given the prevalence of the assumption that there were no women writing, little wonder early modern women who wrote were invisible.

As Jennifer Summit has argued, "despite their cultural prevalence, representations of women writers as lost are by no means reliable descriptors of women writers' actual absence from literary history" and the "lost woman writer ... has a complex history that participates in the broader histories of authorship and English literature."[21] What scholarly practices lead to invisibility? The assumption that women writers are rare and anomalous requires that the identity of a writer as being a female be confirmed. Virginia Woolf may have believed that "Anon, who wrote so many poems without signing them, was often a woman," but this has not been the view of most literary historians, in part based on the assumption of women's illiteracy and the potency of prevalent cultural prescriptions against female speech.[22] Ballads, for example, the vast majority of which are anonymous publications, often feature a woman speaker, appealed to women buyers, and were hawked by female ballad singers. This female environment in which ballads were circulated and enjoyed has suggested, as critics have noted, that "gender distinctions tended to blur at every stage of production," but nevertheless it is currently believed that "most ballad writers were probably men and there is no concrete evidence that women at this time wrote ballads."[23] This statement sits uneasily alongside Germaine Greer's pragmatic observation that "for hundreds of years women put their children to sleep with lullabies that nobody thought to write down ... each mother would have invented her own verses ... the pattern of such female creative activity is that everybody does it."[24]

Even when a woman's name is attached to a work, that is no guarantee that the text will be read as female authored. In one early feminist polemic, *How to Suppress Women's Writing*, Joanna Russ targeted the

[20] Gilbert and Gubar (eds.), *Norton Anthology of Literature by Women*, 1 and 3.
[21] Summit, *Lost Property*, 209.
[22] Woolf, *A Room of One's Own*, 38.
[23] Kris McAbee and Jessica C. Murphy, http://ebba.english.ucsb.edu/ballad/31176/player; on women as the audience for ballads, see Sandra Clark, "The Broadside Ballad and the Woman's Voice," in Malcolmson and Suzuki (eds.), *Debating Gender*, 103–20.
[24] Greer, *Slipshod Sibyls*, xiv.

"denial of agency" as creating a literary landscape in which women as writers are invisible. "What to do when a woman has written something? The first line of defense is to deny that she wrote it. Since women cannot write, someone else (a man) must have written it," Russ suggests, possibly her father, brother or husband.[25] A related form of literary invisibility occurs when the optic lens focuses narrowly on the woman's relationships. Lady Margaret Douglas (1515–78) was a famous figure in her time: she was the niece of Henry VIII, one of Anne Boleyn's and Katherine Parr's ladies in waiting, the scandalous love interest of Lord Thomas Howard and later his nephew Sir Charles Howard, and the mother-in-law of Mary Queen of Scots. What this focus overlooks is her importance as a contributor in several ways to the poetry manuscript miscellany created in the 1530s and 1540s, "The Devonshire Manuscript."[26] Until the twenty-first century the volume was primarily valued as a source for establishing the poetic *oeuvre* of Sir Thomas Wyatt.[27]

Historically, several other mechanisms preserved notable women's names, if not the works of their hands. The catalogues of learned, noble women formed a genre in itself: the celebration of "Female Worthies" made use of such biographical, historical lists of women to praise and to contextualize their respective queens.[28] The tutor of Charles I's daughter, Bathsua Makin, in her *Essay to Revive the Antient Education of Gentlewomen* (1673) urged her readers educate their daughters in the pattern established by literate, literary ladies of the past; the London merchant's wife and artist Mary More, likewise included a catalogue of admirable learned women as a means of establishing precedent for her challenges to seventeenth-century English property law and the status of wives.[29] The antiquarian George Ballard provided an invaluable resource for the study of early modern women writers in his encyclopedic 1752 *Memoirs of several ladies of Great Britain, who have been celebrated for their writings, or skill in the learned languages, arts and sciences*, still the starting point for the recovery of many literary women in the past, including Esther Inglis. As Philip Hicks has argued, this genre of history-writing

---

[25] Joanna Russ, *How to Suppress Women's Writing* (Austin: University of Texas Press, 1983), 20–1.
[26] Lady Margaret Douglas and Others, "The Devonshire Manuscript: A Woman's Book of Courtly Poetry," Elizabeth Heale (ed.) (Toronto: CRRS/ITER, 2012).
[27] Ibid., 30–3.
[28] Celeste Turner Wright, "Elizabethan Female Worthies," *Studies in Philology*, 43.4 (1946), 628–43. See also Philip Hicks, "Female Worthies and the Genres of Women's History," in Ben Dew and Fiona Price (eds.), *Historical Writing in Britain, 1688–1830* (New York: Palgrave Macmillan, 2014), 18–33.
[29] See Teague and Ezell (eds.) and Walker (assoc. ed.), *Educating English Daughters*.

grounded upon lists of notable women was central in eighteenth-century women writers – for example, Mary Astell's assessment of the place of women in contemporary society.[30]

Paradoxically, the same strategy that preserved early modern women's names could also be a first step in rendering their works invisible. The eighteenth-century theater historian John Doran listed the names of many late seventeenth-century women writing for the theater, but his catalogue surely begins the process of erasing them: of the group of women "more or less distinguished as writers for the stage," he lists, "the virtuous Mrs. Philips, the audacious Aphra Behn, the not less notorious Mrs. Manley, the gentle and learned Mrs. Cockburn, the rather aristocratic Mrs. Boothby," concluding with the "fat Mrs. Pix."[31] Visibility, yes, but of the imagined personal characteristics of the writers – virtuous, audacious, notorious, gentle, aristocratic, fat – not of the nature of the works. The list effectively implies the texts they wrote need not be read.

Is there such a thing as too much visibility for an early modern woman writer? In the nineteenth century, Aphra Behn's name is typically a tiny note in larger literary histories, but not because of her works. Repeatedly paired with the chaste matron Katherine Philips as representing the polar ends of the range of female writers, Behn's reputation for profligate living as well as risqué writing caused one critic to declare "it is a pity that even such plots and such dialogue should suffice to preserve on any shelves the writings of so impure a pen."[32] Virginia Woolf may have wished flowers for the grave of Aphra Behn to celebrate her as the originator of a tradition of women's commercial writing, but Woolf and her contemporaries also forged an image of Behn which established a pattern of directing critical attention away from her works and her audience.

Another of the long-standing twentieth-century narratives about early modern women writers impeding our perception of them was that, unlike Behn, they shunned public display and were veiled by layers of modesty tropes when they appeared at all. This mode of reading early modern women's protestations of inferiority as sincere autobiographical utterances, an expression of internalized patriarchal repression, has created "certain problematic legacies for feminist scholarship, most crucially

---

[30] On Ballard's impact on eighteenth- and nineteenth-century biographers of women writers, see Ezell, *Writing Women's Literary History*, chapter 3; Philip Hicks, "Women Worthies and Feminist Argument in Eighteenth-Century Britain," *Women's History Review* 24.2 (2015), 174–90.

[31] John Doran, *"Their Majesties' Servants": Annals of the English Stage from Thomas Betterton to Edmund Keen*, 2 vols. (New York: Armstrong, 1880), vol. I, 163.

[32] Quoted in Ezell, *Writing Women's Literary History*, 92–3.

in the priority it places on 'original' composition and 'self-expression.'"[33]
As Patricia Pender has pointed out, while the expanding body of criticism
about early modern women and self-representation views the rhetoric of
modesty as more complex and acting in multiple ways, "the broad pedagogical story – the anthologized and anthologizing narrative ... continues
to present, perhaps even to promote, women's literary expressions of
modesty as evidence of their historical oppression."[34]

Genre definitions have also rendered invisible the works of women
writers, whether works of multiple genres or writings that fall outside
literary tradition, no matter how widely read they were. "The Mother's
Legacy" enjoyed sustained popularity for both women writers and readers, with some twenty of them being composed between 1575 and 1675;
among the best known was *The Mother's Blessing* (1616) by Dorothy
Leigh (d. 1616), which had twenty-eight editions by 1729, yet it has not
been until recently that these women's texts have been considered part of
a female literary tradition.[35]

Likewise, as critics have noted, books of religious devotion far outsold
even those of the most popular poets and dramatists, but until recently
there has been little consideration of them as meriting literary study.[36]
Although visible to social literary historians as a phenomenon because
of their prolific publications and personalities, the works of Quaker
women have most often been viewed through a historical rather than
a literary lens.[37] Speaking in 1996 of the radical sectarian women writing in the seventeenth century, Hilary Hinds asserted that none of these
texts, according to traditional criteria, "would be likely to qualify as literary works worthy of sustained critical attention," even though "many of
them deal with issues of enduring and ... 'universal' significance, such
as liberty, justice and godliness."[38] They fall outside the literary canon as
being too topical, too ephemeral, and too female, all the while challenging "the boundaries which have been erected around the canonical literary genres."[39]

---

[33] Pender, *Early Modern Women's Writing*, 6–7. See also Beilin, *Redeeming Eve*.
[34] Ibid., 8–9.
[35] Heller, *The Mother's Legacy*, 2. See also Paula McQuade (Chapter 15) in this volume.
[36] Green, *Print and Protestantism*, 637; Matthew Brown, *The Pilgrim and the Bee: Reading Rituals and Book Culture in Early New England* (Philadelphia: University of Pennsylvania Press, 2007), 7; Longfellow, *Women and Religious Writing*.
[37] Ezell, *Writing Women's Literary History*, chapter 5; Catie Gill, *Women in the Seventeenth-Century Quaker Community: A Literary Study of Political Identities, 1650–1700* (Aldershot: Ashgate, 2005), 1.
[38] Hinds, *God's Englishwomen*, 4–5.
[39] Ibid., 5.

Additionally, these women's works, although visible as textual objects, have baffled bibliographers because of practices of collaborative authorship, being texts created by a community as opposed to a named individual.[40] The notion of early modern authorship as residing in a singular inspired individual in elite culture has been strongly challenged by recent scholarship on early modern dramatic texts, which increasingly has depicted the world of Shakespeare's stage and Jonson's masques as being fluid and highly collaborative; the works themselves are comfortably intertextual rather than discrete objects created by solitary genius. Recent work on the women of the courts of Queen Anna of Denmark and Queen Henrietta Maria highlight the ways in which the women were active participants in the commissioning and interpretation of the masques and entertainments in which they appeared, even if their names do not appear as authors.[41]

Looking away from authorship as an isolated individual act to view the cultural context in which texts are created and consumed helps to reveal women active as literary agents. Julie Crawford has drawn attention to the importance of women such as Mary Sidney Herbert, Lucy Russell, Countess of Bedford, and Mary Wroth as members of "'coteries' and 'alliances'" in the production of early modern texts, noting that "like the communities that produced them, literary texts were often … dialogic, contentious, even confrontational."[42] Likewise, Helen Smith draws attention to women's involvement in various aspects of textual creation: "texts, rather than being the product of a solitary author, transmitted direct from fertile mind to well-stocked bookshelf, are the products of numerous processes populated by diverse persons."[43] When one changes the lens through which one sees a literary text, from evaluating it as the product of a single inspired vision to how it involves multiple creative minds and actions, a different conceptualization of literary "work" comes more clearly into focus, involving labor beyond that of a single genius whose name is inscribed on a printed page.

---

[40] Gill, *Women in the Seventeenth-Century Quaker Community*, 5. See also the pioneering study by Hobby, *Virtue of Necessity*, 206.

[41] See: Susan Cerasano and Marion Wynne-Davies (eds.), *Renaissance Drama by Women: Texts and Documents* (New York and London: Routledge, 1996); Clare McManus, *Women on the Renaissance Stage: Anna of Denmark and Female Masquing in the Stuart Court (1590–1619)* (Manchester University Press, 2002); Karen Britland, *Drama at the Courts of Queen Henrietta Maria* (Cambridge University Press, 2006).

[42] Crawford, *Mediatrix*, 7 and 8. See also the early study by Margaret P. Hannay, *Philip's Phoenix: Mary Sidney, Countess of Pembroke* (Oxford: Oxford University Press, 1990).

[43] Smith, *"Grossly Material Things,"* 2.

Esther Inglis (1570/1–1624) and the fortunes of her texts offer challenges to the traditional ways of classifying authorship as well as insights
into conditions creating both visibility and vanishing. In her most recent
ODNB entry she is listed simply as being a "calligrapher."[44] Her twentieth-
century biographer Dorothy Judd Jackson, while clearly writing with
respect for Inglis's manuscript books, noted that her works were "much
admired in her time and, today, we may enjoy them for their undeni-
able charm," although she concludes Inglis is "limited" in her abilities.[45]
Inglis's subsequent cataloguers, while preserving the bibliographical
record of her work, nevertheless note that while she was an "extraordinary calligrapher," she "was not an inventive draughtswoman and preferred to copy existing models."[46]

Her eighteenth-century biographer George Ballard, in contrast, enthusiastically declared that "all that see her writing are astonished at it
upon the account of its exactness, fineness and variety, and many are
of opinion that nothing can be more exquisite."[47] Her reputation for
highly skilled workmanship and collectability is announced throughout
eighteenth- and nineteenth-century biographical notices, in no small
part because works such as Mary Hays's multi-volume *Female Biography*
(1803) often drew verbatim from Ballard's enthusiastic account. Inglis's
books were continually valued by antiquarian enthusiasts and book col-
lectors throughout the century.[48]

Included in Ballard's encyclopedia, although not in Woolf's narrative of women writers, Inglis continued in the twentieth century to
appear in collections of biographies of notable women. Dorothy Judd
Jackson published a brief life and preliminary bibliography in *Esther
Inglis Calligrapher, 1571–1624* in a remarkable limited edition volume,
Bookmaking on the Distaff Side (1937), a collection of essays individually
printed and designed by women involved in the print trades.[49] Inglis also

---

[44] See *ODNB*.

[45] Dorothy J. Jackson, *Esther Inglis, Calligrapher* (New York: privately printed at the Spiral Club, 1937), fol. 1ʳ.

[46] A. H. Scott-Elliot and Elspeth Yeo, "Calligraphic Manuscripts of Esther Inglis (1571–1624): A Catalogue," *The Papers of the Bibliographical Society of America*, 84.1 (1990), 10–86 at 17 and 19.

[47] Ballard, *Memoirs of Several Ladies of Great Britain*, 254; Mary Hays, *Female Biography: Or, Memoirs of Illustrious and Celebrated Women, of All Ages and Countries. Alphabetically Arranged*. 6 vols. (London: R. Phillips, 1803), vol. II, 451–2.

[48] Worcester & Worcester Antiquities, *Descriptive catalog of the museum formed at Worcester ... July 22 to 29, 1862* (1862), 61–2. See also David Laing, "Notes relating to Mrs. Esther (Langlois or) Inglis," *Proceedings of the Society of Antiquaries of Scotland*, 6 (1864–6), 284–309.

[49] Bruce Rogers, et al. (eds.), *Bookmaking on the Distaff Side* (New York: Distaff Side, 1937), n.p.

was featured in some early anthologies devoted to women writers, including *The Paradise of Women*, which noted that "unlike most of the other women discussed in this chapter and almost all the women in the period, [Inglis] wrote professionally, i.e., for profit."[50]

During her lifetime, Inglis had the support of her family, the admiration a group of prominent Scottish men of letters, and the patronage of the royal family. Of the fifty-nine currently known manuscript volumes she created, Esther Inglis's first seems to have been *Livret contenant diverses sortes de letters* (BL Sloane MS, 987, 1586) which contained commendatory verses by her father in Latin. Its primary contents were translations into French of Psalms 2 and 94 done by Clément Marot and Théodore de Bèze and in Latin by Helius Eobanus Hessus, but the point of the book is to showcase the fifteen-year-old Inglis's ability to use five different calligraphic alphabets.[51]

Ballard and subsequent biographers reliant on him make specific mention of several of Inglis's books preserved in the Bodleian Library, one presented to Queen Elizabeth and another dedicated to the Earl of Essex. The 1599 volume *Les Proverbes de Salomon* dedicated to Robert Devereux, 2nd Earl of Essex (1566–1601) includes a Latin poem by Andrew Melville, Principal of Glasgow: "Much we the work, much more the hand admire;/Her fancy guiding this, our wonder raises higher." This volume also has a self-portrait of the author in the act of writing; the dedication praises Essex for his virtues and begs him to accept "mien petit labeur."[52] As Scott-Elliot and Yeo note, it bears a strong resemblance to two other volumes done around the same time, *Le Livre des Pseaumes* (1599) (Christ Church, Oxford, MS 189) dedicated to Queen Elizabeth and *Le Livre de l'Eccleiaste, ensemble le Cantique de Salomon*, dedicated to the diplomat Anthony Bacon (1558–1601) who was in the household of Essex at the time (BL Add. MS 27927).[53] Each of these volumes had similar ornamentation – a "balls-and-bead" border on the pages, a self-portrait, ornamental figures based on those found in the Geneva Bible (1588), and commendatory verses by Inglis's male supporters.[54]

---

[50] Travitsky (ed.), *Paradise of Women*, 24.
[51] Scott-Elliot and Yeo, "Calligraphic Manuscripts of Esther Inglis (1571–1624): A Catalogue," 25–6.
[52] Bodleian Library MS 990, Esther Inghlis, "Les Proverbes de Salomon escrites en diverses sortes de lettres par Esther Anglois Françoise." *A Lislebourg en Ecosse* (1599), xi.
[53] Scott-Elliot and Yeo, "Calligraphic Manuscripts of Esther Inglis," 33–5 and 39–41.
[54] Georgianna Ziegler, "'More Than Feminine Boldness': The Gift Books of Esther Inglis," in Mary E. Burke et al. (eds.), *Women, Writing and the Reproduction of Culture in Tudor-Stuart Britain* (Syracuse University Press, 2000), 19–37 at 34; Jackson, *Esther Inglis*, 2ʳ; Sarah Gwyneth Ross,

Each volume, however, is unique and personalized for the intended reader. Essex's includes his coat of arms; Elizabeth's has her coat of arms within a frame depicting two women, one holding a book and the other a pair of scales; Bacon's arms have been slightly modified and the title page shows Apollo and Mercury on either side of an archway, on which is depicted a reclining figure holding a pen and another with a branch of leaves. Her volumes often featured the motif of a pair of golden pens crossing through a wreath of laurel, with the motto "Vive la Plume" or *Nil Penna Sed Usus*, drawing attention to her skills, claiming the book as "feminine territory."[55]

Recently it has been decided that Inglis did include some of her own poetry in these volumes as well as customizing the dedications. Given that the greatest proportion of text inside her books was "recycled" from printed texts and often incorporated design elements from them as well, is she an author or merely a copyist? Her works were never "printed" and each copy is unique; as Georgianna Ziegler notes, the career of Esther Inglis thus complicates our understanding of patronage systems, scribal publication, and even the notion of authorship itself.[56] Susan Frye argues that "the most significant aspect of her books lies in the relation between their existence as handmade objects and the ways that she uses them to represent herself as a woman author."[57] As Ziegler also stresses, we can clearly see in Inglis's manuscript books her "melding design, purpose, and text into a creative object that ties together time," and in the same manner as modern "book artists," deliberately playing with the "(dis)-placement of familiar book structures and formats to create highly individualized objects that invite readers and viewers to find the unexpected in the anticipated."[58]

With seven known self-portraits in her works, Inglis self-consciously presents herself as a professional woman writer, with pen in hand and books open before her, several with the motto *De L'Eternal le bien, de Moi le mal ou rien*, suggesting to Frye that "she is eager to place in circulation a complex representation of her identity as writer, artist, and woman."[59] In fact, Frye argues, Inglis's use of printed texts and ornaments is a form of appropriation of "male-controlled forms of textual production," and

"Esther Inglis: Calligrapher, Miniaturist, and Christian Humanist," in Campbell and Larsen (eds.), *Early Modern Women and Transnational Communities*, 159–82 at 173.

[55] Frye, *Pens and Needles*, 111.
[56] Ziegler, "More Than Feminine Boldness," 19–37.
[57] Frye, *Pens and Needles*, 103.
[58] Ziegler, "Hand-Ma[i]de Books," 84.
[59] Frye, *Pens and Needles*, 108.

she "returns to print as her copy source not only to craft a book more valued because more preciously jeweled and miniature than a printed one, but also to make print culture yet another aspect of the textual world with which she collaborates."[60]

What do the fortunes of Inglis and her works show us? Although applauded during her lifetime, until very recently she has not been perceived as being part of a woman's literary tradition, in part because of the type of writing she did and in part because of the ways in which her writings have been contextualized. Inglis's name and her exquisite works have remained visible through the subsequent generations largely because of their original audience: she created embroidered, jeweled textual gifts valued by royalty and important courtiers, to be carefully preserved in libraries as beautiful, valuable artifacts. Her works survived their original function to secure patronage because they were collectible, unique literary curiosities as well as art books. The narratives about her works, however, shifted from the celebration of her genius by contemporaries to praise of her as an industrious craft worker, praise which reminds us of her failings as much as her strengths. "Compared to the finest French, Italian, and Spanish manuscripts, her abilities were limited," Jackson states bluntly on the first page, "yet there is no other woman of the period, either in England or on the Continent, whose signed manuscript books survive in such numbers."[61] Because of their survival as beautiful artifacts, Inglis's works still challenge traditional models of authorship, editing, and literary canons.

Visibility and Viability: Distant Fame, Future Fortunes

We have reached something of a tipping point in the study of early modern women's writings.[62]

[Katherine Philips] was a vital figure in British literary history, a history that we now understand as more complicated and interesting than we knew before Philips and a host of other early modern women writers – Mary Sidney, Isabella Whitney, Anna Trapnell, Anne Bradstreet, and Margaret Cavendish, for example – were "rediscovered" in the 1970s and 1980s.[63]

---

[60] Ibid., 110.
[61] Jackson, *Esther Inglis*, 1r.
[62] Paul Salzman (ed.), "Introduction," in *Expanding the Canon of Early Modern Women's Writing* (Newcastle: Cambridge Scholars Press, 2010), 1.
[63] Hageman, "Afterword," 311–12.

Through the publication of early modern women's works, visibility is established, but for how long and to what purpose? The drive in the 1980s and 1990s to anthologize women's works in volumes aimed at classroom use ensured that at least the woman's name and a brief glimpse of her accomplishments were preserved.[64] While the increasing presence of women's works, whether in mixed anthologies or ones devoted only to women, was clearly desirable, the format itself subsequently has emerged as problematic. Critics charge that feminist criticism has largely failed to confront the editorial issues involved in the selection of writers included.[65] Danielle Clarke observed that "the editing of early modern women's texts is often marked by unacknowledged impulses," which include "a nostalgic desire for stable texts ... and the related anachronistic desire for a body of texts from the Renaissance with which modern readers can identify."[66] One concern was that the anthologies' selections give the impression that gender trumps class, religion, and region, and that there exists an identifiable "early modern woman's voice."

The terms in which texts by women should be evaluated are related concerns. In a way similar to Jackson's treatment of Inglis as both worthy of attention yet of comparatively limited abilities, Woolf and her contemporaries in the first decades of the twentieth century contextualized Aphra Behn's works with a mixture of defiant praise for her life and apologetic dismissal of her works. Montagu Summers's six-volume edition of Behn's works in 1915 foregrounded Behn's detractors in his introduction. He quotes a 1738 article in the *Gentleman's Magazine*, "The Apotheosis of Milton," which has Aphra Behn crashing the assembly of laureate poets, demanding her seat among them: "Observe that Lady dressed in the loose *Robe de Chambre* with her Neck and Breasts bare; how much Fire in her Eye! ... Observe what an Indignant Look she bestows on the President [Chaucer], who is telling her, that none of her Sex has any Right to a Seat there."[67] Such views, Summer observes tartly, show "how early condemnatory tradition had begun to incrustate around Astrea," but excuses Behn's flaws as due to her need to write quickly.[68]

---

[64] See Wiesner, *Women and Gender*, chapter 5; Salzman, "Introduction," for excellent summary overviews of critical editions and anthologies of early modern women's writings in the 1980s through the early twenty-first century.

[65] Wray, "Anthologizing the Early Modern Female Voice," 58.

[66] Clarke, "Nostalgia," 188.

[67] Behn, *Works of Aphra Behn*, ed. Summers, vol. I, lix.

[68] Ibid.

Vita Sackville-West's *Aphra Behn: The Incomparable Astrea* (1927) mocks Doran's earlier representation of Behn as "a mere harlot who danced through uncleanness," but bluntly states, "let us say straight away that Aphra Behn is no Shakespeare."[69] It is a pity, she concludes, that Behn did not cultivate her abilities and rival Defoe as a novelist; she confesses that "in the course of these three months spent in her company, it is Aphra the woman of whom I have grown fond, to the extent of forgiving Aphra the writer for the tedious hours she has compelled me to spend over her volumes."[70] A similar sigh of regret was voiced by Earnest A. Baker in his 1905 edition of a selection of Behn's fiction, which did not include *Oroonoko*: "it must be confessed that, apart from *Oroonoko*, Mrs. Behn's fiction is of very little importance in the history of our literature."[71] Behn achieved visibility again in Woolf's generation, but the critical apparatus applied to her works – the attempt to fit her within an existing model of critical evaluation and her failure in comparison to male canonical writers – established the vocabulary to lessen her significance and even paradoxically to support her erasure.

In the recovery period of the 1980s, the goal became to document the material existence of women's texts, and arguing the technical or aesthetic merits of women's writing seemed of lesser urgency. "I am much more interested in what women's writings show us about female struggles within and against the demand made of them, than I am in their use of rhyme or complexity of characterization (to take some extreme examples of the narrowness of conventional literary-critical concerns)," observed Elaine Hobby in 1988.[72] That same year Janet Todd advocated "a kind of historically specific, archival, ideologically aware but still empirically based enterprise."[73] Given the previous scarcity of early modern women's texts, the necessity of documenting early modern women's voices foregrounded the significance of women's texts as historical artifacts rather than literary ones.

Twentieth-century anthologists who began including women in compilations featuring both men and women poets typically highlighted the historical, political interest of the women's verses, one editor declaring, "I have included several items mainly for their historical or

---

[69] Vita Sackville-West, *Aphra Behn: The Incomparable Astrea* (London: Gerald Howe Ltd., 1927), 11.
[70] Ibid., 77 and 84.
[71] Behn, *Novels*, xxvii.
[72] Hobby, *Virtue of Necessity*, 25.
[73] Janet Todd, *Feminist Literary History: A Defence* (Cambridge: Polity Press, 1988), 7.

human interest."[74] However, twenty-first century critics now resist what Stephanie Hodgson-Wright terms the "either/or" historical/aesthetic reading of women's texts in favor of the "both/and."[75] Writing in 2007, Alice Eardley believed that "at present, research into women's writing continues to emphasize historical context" but "embedded in this approach is the possibility that it may now be possible to start considering the literary nature of women's poetry."[76]

Sasha Roberts argued for a dialogue to be established between literary formalism and feminist criticism: "it is not just a matter of understanding that access to forms and formal play has a gendered history … if we neglect early modern women's interest in questions of literary form, we fail to do justice to their work as readers and writers."[77] This turn is emphasized in the essay collection *Early Modern Women and the Poem* (2013), which points to what it sees as "a critical shift in the field itself surrounding early modern women's engagements with genre."[78] Elizabeth Scott-Baumann urges a "feminist formalism or a formalist feminism" when reading women's texts, believing that their reworking of poetic forms was a declaration of the woman writer's engagement with the pressing issues of the cultures in which they wrote. Similarly, Sarah C. E. Ross draws attention to early modern women's "political poeticization" as forming its own literary tradition.[79]

In a related move, critics have begun to argue that many early modern women practiced "reading as resistance" rather than passive indoctrination, seeing women's works in the context of "re-creation, challenge, and appropriation."[80] Gillian Wright has argued for "reading women's poetry for genre," allowing us to "recognize her willingness and competence to engage in literary forms … and ideas central to [her] culture."[81] By changing the frame through which early modern women's texts are read to include the material cultures of manuscript and print practices as well as appreciating how they challenge traditional definitions of genre, recent criticism seeks alternative narratives embracing multiple literary traditions rather than tidy inclusion into a single, dominant pre-existing one.

---

[74] Eardley, "Recreating the Canon," quoting Alistar Fowler (ed.), *The New Oxford Book of Seventeenth-Century Verse* (Oxford: Oxford University Press, 1991), xliv.
[75] Hodgson-Wright (ed.), *Women's Writing*, viii.
[76] Eardley, "Recreating the Canon," 277.
[77] Roberts, "Feminist Criticism and the New Formalism," 69.
[78] Pender and Smith, "Afterword," 246.
[79] Scott-Baumann, *Forms of Engagement*, 9; Ross, *Women, Poetry, and Politics*, 213.
[80] Scott-Baumann, *Forms of Engagement*, 7 and 8.
[81] Wright, *Producing Women's Poetry*, 20.

To sustain such critical discussions, scholars and students require access to stable texts and critical editions, while acknowledging the inherent instability of early modern texts. In this, too, women's writing has necessitated a revision of editorial assumptions about what is suitable for editing and how the text is presented. Since the 1990s, notable stand-alone editions of early modern women's texts have been produced by major university presses and organizations including the Medieval and Renaissance Text Society and the Renaissance English Text Society, as well as "The Other Voice" series begun at the University of Chicago, which partners with ITER to create both print and electronic editions, and Broadview Press, which produces affordable modernized classroom editions.[82] Nevertheless, there is still a noticeable dearth of standard scholarly editions to be found in the lists of either Oxford or Cambridge University presses, traditionally considered the gold standard. In 2014, one editor of the Oxford Scholarly Editions Online considered how "the most celebrated women writers from the period 1500–1700 are represented in this new digital format," and concluded, "in short, early modern English women writers have fared, perhaps predictably, badly."[83] One can, for example, access the print editions electronically of *The Farming and Memorandum Books of Henry Best* and the complete poems of Patrick Cary, but there are no comparable editions of his mother, Elizabeth Cary, or of any of the "Mother's Legacy volumes," or the works of Margaret Cavendish.[84]

In addition, however, to the numerical imbalance of editions by women writers in comparison with male authors, Danielle Clarke argues that "editorial procedures need to be appropriate to the texts that they attempt to describe, represent, and pass on."[85] As critics have increasingly pointed out, editing an early modern woman for a scholarly edition poses issues that are infrequently a feature when editing male writers from the period.[86] Unlike most canonical male authors, many early modern

---

[82] Elizabeth I, *Elizabeth I: Collected Works*; Wroth, *The Poems of Lady Mary Wroth*; Wroth, *The First Part of The Countess of Montgomery's Urania*; Wroth, *The Second Part of the Countess of Montgomery's Urania*.

[83] Andrew Zurcher, "Entitling Early Modern Women Writers." http://blog.oup.com/2014/03/entitling-early-modern-women-writers.

[84] www.oxfordscholarlyeditions.com. The first volume of four of the complete works of Lucy Hutchinson, gen. ed. David Norbrook, appeared from Oxford University Press in 2011; a three-volume complete works of Katherine Philips, ed. Elizabeth H. Hageman and Andrea Sununu, is under contract to Oxford University Press, and the multi-volume Cambridge University Press edition of the complete works of Aphra Behn, gen. ed. Elaine Hobby, has received major funding, with the first volume to appear in 2018.

[85] Clarke, "Nostalgia," 208.

[86] Flanders, "The Body Encoded."

women's texts exist in a manuscript copy or a single print edition; documents about their lives are often lacking, making the typical "life and works" format for editing problematic. In response, proponents of "new textualism" in editing women's writings urge an editorial approach that highlights the material properties of the manuscript text or printed book, and the sociology of the texts, i.e. the cultures in which they were created and read, thus shifting the critical gaze from the solitary author to the text itself, its functions, and its multiple audiences.[87]

One solution to the problems posed by selection and space in anthologies and the critical apparatus necessary for a scholarly edition is clearly offered by the advances in digital archiving and editions. In contrast to expensive university press print editions, anything can become part of the digital world, freely available on demand. Surely this will ensure both visibility and viability? Sadly, no. Of the sites listed in a 2001 annotated bibliography of web resources on women writers, fewer than half of those links are still alive and accessible.[88] Likewise, the sites included in Robert C. Evans's 2002 list of digital resources for teaching women writers have mostly vanished or not been updated for many years.[89] As Laura Mandell has observed, so many digital projects devoted to women's writings have become dead links that it feeds into the perception that "women's writings must come, in the end, not to count after publication, only ever recovered and re-recovered."[90] Again, the dead links do preserve the woman's name, but the works themselves are inaccessible. "The loss of a digital presence of an often-reproduced canonical author may not hurt the awareness and study of the canonical author," observes Amy Earhart, "but the loss of the single digital instance of a recovered text by a little-known author will, in effect, send the author back into the hidden archives that scholars worked to expose."[91]

[87] Ann Hollinshead Hurley and Chanita Goodblatt, "Preface" in Hurley and Goodblatt (eds.), *Women Editing/Editing Women*, xi.
[88] Ziegler, "Women Writers Online."
[89] See Laura Estill, "Digital Futures: Long-Term Planning for Your Project," keynote address, The Digital Humanities Summer Institute, University of Victoria, BC, June 2016. This trend has been confirmed when looking at links relating to digital humanities projects in general; Robin Camille Davis found that 45% of the digital projects presented at the 2005 Digital Humanities Conference at the University of Victoria were no longer accessible in 2015. "Taking Care of Digital Efforts: A Multiplanar View of Project Afterlives," www.robincamille.com/presentations/mla2015.
[90] Laura Mandell, "Gendering Digital Literary History: What Counts for Digital Humanities," 511–23.
[91] Amy Earhart, *Traces of the Old, Uses of the New: The Emergence of Digital Literary Studies* (Ann Arbor: University of Michigan Press, 2012), 80.

As with the recent calls to reconceptualize critical and editorial approaches using a feminist lens, so, too, do women's texts challenge developing digital archives. *Orlando: Women's Writing in the British Isles from the Beginning to the Present* and the *Women Writers Project* have survived and flourished, in part by reconceiving the infrastructure of women's writing in opposition to traditional editorial models. The emerging challenge to the editing and archiving of women's texts electronically, however, may be the shift in the field toward funding projects offering "big data" for computer analysis. As Mandell has warned, given that women tended to publish in small print runs or via manuscript, "the digital adds a new threat to render women writers invisible: its valuation of countlessness. Big data threatens to eradicate the history of women writers altogether."[92]

What will best ensure the future fortunes of early modern women's works? Given the trajectory of recovery and interest in these works over the last decades of the twentieth century and the opening ones of the twenty-first, the attempt to insert women and their works cleanly into the existing canon of male authors and the model of authorship as an act of solitary creative genius runs the danger of preserving them only as curious historical artifacts, always secondary to the main players. Similarly, counting solely on a new publication technology to rescue women writers from disappearing is equally problematic without the safety nets of traditional print publications, given the current fragility of new media. If women's works, from Esther Inglis's unique books for courtiers to Aphra Behn's risqué representations of changing manners for the popular stage and page, are to be kept viable in scholarly conversations and visible in the classroom, it must be because of what we see and value in them: neither their anomalous nature nor their female uniformity, but their sparkling multiplicity; not the way they bulk up traditional lists and gracefully yield to traditional models, but the dazzling ways in which they disrupt both and challenge us to see our own assumptions, aesthetic as well as historical.

[92] Mandell, "Gendering Digital Literary History," 521; Ezell, "Editing Early Modern Women's Manuscripts."

2

Reconsidering the Woman Writer
The Identity Politics of Anne Cooke Bacon

Jaime Goodrich

In 1589, Thomas Wilcox dedicated his commentary on Solomon's proverbs to his longtime patron, Anne Cooke Bacon (c. 1528–1610). One of the many "hotter" Protestant ministers supported by Bacon during her long widowhood, Wilcox carefully catalogs the signs of God's favor that testified to Bacon's place among the elect predestined for salvation:

> For though to be borne not onlie of worshipful parents, but of a sanctified stock, be some thing both before God and man: and though learned and holie education bee a good helpe towards the reformation of our corruption ... and though to be richlie joyned in holy matrimonie be a token doubtles of Gods great favour and love: and though to have in the undefiled mariage bed, a blessed seed and lawfull issue, be a special blessing & mercie from God: & though to leade and live a vertuous and unreproveable life in the sight of men ... bee a happie thing: (with all which favours you have by the divine providence, been even laden as it were in your birth, bringing up, youth, old age, virginitie, mariage, widowhood and posteritie) ... me thinketh you have wherein to rejoyce.[1]

Wilcox evokes the entire arc of Bacon's life from "birth" to "widowhood," positioning her in a familial context as a daughter ("borne ... of worshipful parents"), a wife ("joyned in holy matrimonie"), and a mother ("blessed seed and lawfull issue"). As this curriculum vitae indicates, Bacon's life offers an excellent case study for understanding the various identities available to early modern women. Daughter to Sir Anthony Cooke, she received an outstanding and unusual education in Latin, Greek, and Italian. As a staunch Protestant, Anne Bacon used this training to produce three English translations that advanced religious reform: nineteen Italian sermons by Bernardino Ochino (*Sermons of Barnardine Ochine*, 1548; *Fourtene Sermons of Barnardine Ochyne*, 1551) and a Latin

---

[1] T. W. [Thomas Wilcox], *A Short Yet Sound Commentarie Written on ... The Proverbes of Salomon* (London: Thomas Orwin for Thomas Man, 1589), sig. A3ʳ. See *ODNB* on Wilcox.

defense of the Church of England by John Jewel (*An Apologie or Answere in Defence of the Churche of Englande*, 1564). In 1553, she married Sir Nicholas Bacon, who was already enjoying a distinguished legal career and served as lord keeper of the great seal under Elizabeth I. Besides becoming stepmother to six children from her husband's first marriage, Bacon gave birth to two daughters, who died young, and two sons, who would become well known in their own right: Anthony Bacon (1558–1601), a spy and associate of the Earl of Essex, and Francis Bacon (1561–1626), attorney general and essayist. After her husband died in 1579, Bacon devoted her widowhood to maintaining the familial estate at Gorhambury, looking after her sons' interests, and advancing Puritanism.

Taking Bacon's life and writings as its subject, this chapter offers a starting point for exploring the multifaceted identities that shaped early modern women's textual production. A survey of critical responses to Anne Bacon over the past century reveals that her long, rich life has become a prism of sorts for scholarly treatments of women writers. As new critical lenses such as feminism, historicism, and deconstruction reshaped the field of literary studies, they also opened up new ways of viewing the identity politics of femininity in early modern England. Once viewed primarily as a mother, Bacon is now understood to have had multiple identities. Despite this decentering of gender, the female author's identity is nonetheless still defined by womanhood, as suggested by the very term "woman writer." The chapter proposes two new ways of reconsidering the identity politics of women writers: first, by viewing women writers simply as writers, not as women; and second, by considering how female authority emerged from a variety of overlapping identities. By providing new paradigms for understanding the identities constructed by and for female authors, this chapter reconsiders the very nature of the woman writer.

From Matriarch to Cultural Construct: Anne Bacon and Critical Models of Female Identity

In the first half of the twentieth century, scholarly models of early modern women's identities were essentialist in nature, assuming a fundamental continuity in women's experiences across all eras. Many of these first scholars of gender history surveyed prescriptive conduct literature in order to explore early modern women's performance of apparently timeless female roles. In her pioneering study *Doctrine for the Lady of the Renaissance* (1956), Ruth Kelso observed, "The lady, shall we venture to say, turns out to be merely a wife."[2] As Kelso's phrasing ("merely a wife") indicates, the domestic role of the "wife" is self-evident and thus requires no further definition. The first scholars to recover Bacon's writings likewise viewed her in terms of essentialist female identities. An early essay by Mary Bradford Whiting opens by describing Bacon in strictly familial terms as "the wife of the Lord Keeper and the mother of two brilliant sons – Anthony and Francis Bacon."[3] Whiting finds Bacon remarkable due to her refusal to disappear completely into a domestic role:

> her keen interest in the religious questions of the day kept her from sinking into a mere household drudge, and when Bishop Jewell's *Apologia Ecclesiae Anglicanae* ... was published, she not only read it eagerly in the Latin, but resolved upon translating it. It was in the year 1563, when her younger son was only three years old, that it appeared, but once set upon her self-imposed task she carried it through in spite of all the other claims upon her.[4]

Although Whiting celebrates Bacon for refusing the life of a "drudge," she nonetheless frames Bacon's translation in familial terms by mentioning her three-year-old son. Muriel St. Clare Byrne employed a similar approach in her 1934 article "The Mother of Francis Bacon," which also begins by foregrounding Bacon's domestic identity: "Anne, wife of Sir Nicholas Bacon, Lord Chancellor and Keeper of the Great Seal to Queen Elizabeth, is usually described as 'the second learned daughter of Sir Anthony Cooke,' or alternatively as 'the mother of Francis Bacon.'"[5] Rather than deviating from these precedents, Byrne offers an essentialist reading of maternity in Bacon's letters. Identifying Bacon as the "eternal matriarch," Byrne appeals to archetypal roles of mother and child in order to present matriarchy as a form of domestic tyranny: "it takes two to make a matriarchy – mother and child. Neither Anthony nor Francis ever took the necessary steps to free himself from her tyrannous affection."[6] Thus Bacon's reclamation as a subject of legitimate scholarly inquiry was premised on an essentialist view of her maternal identity.

In the 1980s, a new generation of feminist scholars drew on radical feminism and New Historicism in order to offer a fresh perspective on female identity in early modern England. Influenced by radical feminist

[2] Kelso, *Doctrine for the Lady of the Renaissance*, 1.
[3] Mary Bradford Whiting, "The Learned and Virtuous Lady Bacon," *The Hibbert Journal*, 29 (1930–1), 270–83 at 270.
[4] Whiting, "Lady Bacon," 272.
[5] Muriel St. Clare Byrne, "The Mother of Francis Bacon," *Blackwood's Magazine*, 234 (1934), 758.
[6] Byrne, "Mother," 758 and 764.

critiques of patriarchy, these critics viewed women's relegation to the domestic sphere as part of a patriarchal agenda to subordinate female agency. In the 1989 preface to her important anthology *The Paradise of Women*, Betty Travitsky depicts women as largely passive victims of patri- archal power: "Fixed within respectable familial and Christian orienta- tions and tending not to question the orthodoxies of those orientations, [early modern women writers] nevertheless often poignantly express the position of the marginalized."[7] Travitsky's analysis of how domestic and religious "orthodoxies" justified the "marginalized" position of women efficiently illustrates how ideological pressures and structural circum- stances reinforced the subordinate identity of women in early modern England. The rise of New Historicism, and an attendant critical interest in the trope of subversion and containment, made this feminist explo- ration of patriarchal power timely. Reexamined in this light, Bacon's translations provided ample material for analyzing female identity in relation to patriarchy. In an influential essay on the Cooke sisters, Mary Ellen Lamb approaches Bacon's translations not only as household works but also as the product of her relationships with men. After wondering if Anthony Cooke encouraged Bacon to translate Ochino, Lamb asks similar questions about Bacon's translation of Jewel: "Was Anne Cooke Bacon at all influenced by her brother-in-law [William Cecil] to trans- late this work? How important was her husband's approval to her? Did it motivate her?"[8] Although Lamb recognizes the political status of the Jewel translation, she situates the translation as a product of patriarchal power by referring to William Cecil and Nicholas Bacon in terms of their familial roles rather than their governmental positions. Meanwhile, Elaine Beilin's groundbreaking monograph *Redeeming Eve* (1987) argues that Matthew Parker's dedicatory preface to Bacon's translation of Jewel uses female stereotypes to make Bacon's learned work acceptable to con- temporary readers:

> He praises her modesty three times: for submitting the book to his judg- ment, for disliking flattery, and for her putative disinclination to have the work published. Each instance represents her possession of a feminine virtue: obedience to men, humility, and privacy ... Indeed, only under these conventional terms would Parker and his readers also admit to the brilliance and public usefulness of Bacon's achievement.[9]

---

[7] Travisky (ed.), *Paradise of Women*, xix.
[8] Lamb, "The Cooke Sisters," 111.
[9] Beilin, *Redeeming Eve*, 59.

As Beilin's analysis indicates, Parker inscribes Bacon's text within a patri-archal framework predicated on "obedience to men" by associating its translator with "conventional" expectations of femininity. While Beilin and Lamb continue to focus on Bacon's domesticity, their analysis of the way that patriarchy informed Bacon's writings added fresh complexity to the essentialist interpretations of previous scholars.

In the 1990s, a more nuanced view of femininity as a cultural con-struction arose as deconstructionist critiques of essentialism problema-tized any monolithic understanding of female identity. In his seminal book *Desiring Women Writing* (1997), Jonathan Goldberg responds to Denise Riley's deconstruction of the category of woman by observing, "For a woman to write as a woman must involve the revelation that woman is not a self-evident or tautological category, indeed, that it may have no ontological ground."[10] Although his repetition of the term "woman" might seem to create a tautology, the third appearance of this word decenters the category of woman by suggesting that femininity may have "no ontological ground," or basis in reality. This conceptual-ization of womanhood as a cultural construction led critics to analyze how Bacon's texts participate in the social production of female identity. A 1994 monograph on women writers by Louise Schleiner broke fresh ground by demonstrating that Bacon's writings emerged from more than one identity position. After arguing that Bacon's translations of Ochino asked readers to view themselves as part of an elite Calvinist community of the elect, Schleiner contends that for the Cooke sisters, Calvinism was "an aristocratic identity that in some measure counteracted the silenc-ing import of their identity as women."[11] By presenting Bacon's writings as the product of competing identities based in gender and religion, Schleiner implicitly counters essentialism. Another classic example of this deconstructionist approach occurs in Alan Stewart's elucidation of how Bacon's various personae resist any fixed idea of womanhood: "Far from recognizing a 'women's literature' or even a 'woman's voice,' [Bacon's con-temporaries] heard a number of different women's voices – the maiden, the wife, the mother, the widow – and it was to these differentiated voices that they responded. These were voices that were at once tacitly doubled by the man who defined that woman's social role (the father, the husband, the son), and yet clearly heard as the voices of women."[12]

[10] Goldberg, *Desiring Women Writing*, 137.
[11] Schleiner, *Tudor and Stuart Women Writers*, 39.
[12] Stewart, "Voices of Anne Cooke," 88.

Stewart's interpretation decenters both essentialism and patriarchy, suggesting that we cannot view Bacon as an archetypal female because her works contain "voices" that are "confused and contradictory," both male and female at the same time.[13] Thus deconstructionist criticism allows for a new sense of the multiplicity of female identity, which is seen less as biological fact than as the construction of particular cultural frameworks.

By 2000, then, two competing ideas of female identity had come to dominate scholarship on early modern women writers. While the process of canon formation still relied on an essentialist understanding of womanhood, the instability of this category undermined any synthetic view of the female author. In his 2006 book, Paul Salzman neatly expresses the dilemma that scholars now faced, asking "how we can steer between the Scylla of homogenizing transparently identifiable early modern women writers, and the Charybdis of deconstructed texts which call any identity into question."[14] Like many scholars of this era, Salzman overcame this critical conundrum by using historical context to develop a more nuanced understanding of early modern women's agency. This methodological shift toward historicism resulted in a veritable Renaissance of scholarship on Bacon, including new editions of her letters and translation of Jewel.[15] Several scholars have focused squarely on Bacon's participation in the dynamic social process of constructing female identity. In an important article from 2001 on female authority in Bacon's letters, Lynne Magnusson compellingly argues that maternity was a culturally contested site of power: "Motherhood as a self-identical and unchanging construct can be a potent ideological blinder to critical analysis ... My point is not to suggest that Lady Bacon is without motherly affection but rather to be more specific about the local contexts and structural relationships inflecting her dialogue and emotional engagement with her sons."[16] Explicitly responding to the essentialist paradigm of previous scholarship on Bacon, Magnusson uses microhistory to sketch "local conflicts" that permit a reconstruction of the complexities of Bacon's particular maternal role. Increasingly, critics have paid attention to the way that religious context informs Bacon's authorial identity. In a 2010 piece on Bacon's translation of Jewel, Magnusson contends that translation allowed Bacon

---

[13] Ibid., 99.
[14] Salzman, *Reading Early Modern Women's Writing*, 8.
[15] Bacon, *Letters*, ed. Allen; Bacon, *Apology*, ed. Demers. Subsequent quotations of Bacon's letters are to Allen's edition and appear parenthetically.
[16] Magnusson, "Widowhood and Linguistic Capital," 14.

to fulfill a public vocation that was informed by her dual identity as a Calvinist and humanist: "Women's writing is often associated with marginal or *anonymous* voices, but here Bacon's work was celebrated for producing the *unanimous* voice for a church countering charges from Rome of heresy and schism and confidently pronouncing, as a unified spiritual community, what 'wee beleeue,' what 'we make no doubt' of."[17] Magnusson's focus on the collective voice of "spiritual community" subordinates gender to religious identity, subverting our expectations of what "[w]omen's writing" should look like. Gemma Allen's recent treatment of the Jewel translation likewise offers a complex assessment of the text's evocation of gender. While Allen argues that Bacon's insertion of the first-person plural "we" transforms the text into a creed suited to national needs, she also notes that Bacon reminds the reader of the female translator's presence by adding a first-person singular voice ("I") that creates a subtle "authorial presence."[18] Over the past hundred years, critical representations of Anne Bacon have foregrounded different representations of her identity, from essentialist matriarch to patriarchal pawn, from a deconstructed maiden/wife/mother/widow to a savvy participant in her own cultural construction. Yet even though gender has been decentered, it nonetheless remains at the heart of the critical enterprise to understand female identity in Bacon's writings and, by extension, works by other women writers.

A "Venerable Theologian": Religious Identity in Bacon's 1548 Ochino

Magnusson's comment about the anonymity of the female voice gestures toward a completely different way of approaching the woman writer's identity. What if the female author was viewed as just a writer, not as a woman writer? This methodology counters the critical tendency toward what Danielle Clarke has termed "gynocritical feminism": a focus on women writers primarily *as* women.[19] By emphasizing historical context rather than gender, scholars have already begun to develop a more nuanced understanding of the way that Bacon's translations participated in broader cultural shifts. In a recent discussion of Bacon's translation of Jewel, Patricia Demers foregrounds "the specific context of Lady Bacon's

---

[17] Magnusson, "Imagining a National Church," 44, her emphasis.
[18] Allen, "'a briefe and plaine declaration,'" 75. See also Allen, *The Cooke Sisters*, 61–71.
[19] Clarke, *Politics of Early Modern Women's Writing*, 2.

work," offering a detailed comparison of Bacon's translation with an anonymous version of the text printed in 1562.[20] Moving beyond earlier analyses of Bacon's subordination within a patriarchal framework, Demers draws attention to the stylistic success of her translation: "the achievements of Bacon's language – its rhetorical vigor and steely determination along with its lucid and intuitive grasp of the resonances of English syntax – account for the strength of this translation."[21] This sort of comparative, historicist approach is particularly useful for understanding Bacon's 1548 translation of Ochino. Published anonymously, Bacon's first translation eschewed gender identity altogether and therefore resists being read as women's writing. As Whiting observed, "its quaint phrases read all the more strangely when it is remembered that they were penned, not by a venerable theologian, but by a girl scarcely out of her teens."[22] This slippage between the "venerable theologian" and the young "girl" seems intentional, allowing Bacon to participate in the Edwardian Reformation on the same terms as her male contemporaries. Feminist scholars have labored valiantly to recover anonymous works by women, but attempting to read these texts in a gendered framework may obscure the virtues of anonymity.[23] In the case of Bacon's first translation of Ochino, anonymity allowed her authorial identity to be viewed in terms of Protestantism, not gender.

As scholars have argued, Bacon's translation should be read in relation to both religious politics and the print market.[24] Henry VIII had sought to censor reformist publications as soon as the Lutheran threat emerged in the 1520s, but Edward VI's government saw the press as a vital aid in religious reform. Bacon was one of many translators who took advantage of the loosened restrictions on print that accompanied Edward's accession. In 1548 alone, texts by key Continental theologians such as Heinrich Bullinger, John Calvin, Martin Luther, Philipp Melanchthon, and Ulrich Zwingli became available to English readers. Indeed, Anne Bacon was not the only translator to realize that Ochino's sermons could help popularize Protestant beliefs. In 1548, Richard Argentine

---

[20] Demers, "'Nether bitterly nor brablingly,'" 209.
[21] Ibid., 216.
[22] Whiting, "Lady Bacon," 271.
[23] On anonymity, see Marcy North, *The Anonymous Renaissance: Cultures of Discretion in Tudor-Stuart England* (Chicago: University of Chicago Press, 2003).
[24] Jaime Goodrich, "Early Modern Englishwomen as Translators of Religious and Political Literature, 1500–1641," unpublished PhD thesis, Boston College (2008), 150–7; Hosington, "Tudor Englishwomen's Translations," 126–7.

published three English translations: six sermons by Ochino, a sermon by Luther, and a treatise by Zwingli. A comparison of Bacon's Ochino with Argentine's output shows that she was very much in touch with the *zeitgeist*. Argentine viewed translation as a means of spreading Protestant devotion, rendering Zwingli into English in order to instill reformed faith in children: "suche maye be trayned unto Christe/that as yet have not the parfect use of reason/whereby fayth maye the most surely be graffed in them/withoute the whych it is impossyble to please God."[25] Argentine represents his other translations as contributions to the political aims of the Edwardian Reformation. The preface to his translation of Luther praises Edward for purifying the church: "It hath pleased almightie god of his great mercy/to send unto us a Josias/and a Kynge of moost worthye fame/clene to weede oute the same/commaundyng god and his holye woorde frelie to be geven unto all his lovinge subjectes."[26] Dedicating his translation of Ochino to Edward Seymour, Duke of Somerset, Argentine likewise suggests that God has favored the reformers' cause through Somerset's regency: "the mig[h]tye LORD hath appointed your grace unto the same office for the comfort of all the faithful/as the necessary hande of a Kynge gyven unto us by God. And to that purpose these syx Sermons of the famous clerke Bernardinus Ochinus are translated out of the Italyan tongue."[27] Bacon also views translation as a political activity that can propagate reformist devotion and doctrine:

> I shalbe redye and wyllynge hereafter when god geveth better knowlege (accordyng as my talent wyll extende) to turne mo godly sermons of the sayd mayster Barnardine into Englishe for the enformacion of all that desyre to know the truth. For they truely conteyne moch to the defacyng of al papistrie, and hipocrysie, and to the advancement of the glorye of god, and of the benefytes of Christ Jesus.[28]

This charged anti-Catholic language ("papistrie," "hipocrysie") positions Bacon's publication within an ecclesiastical project to refashion English religion by rejecting Catholicism. Much like Argentine, Bacon's identity as a translator is constituted through politicized religious beliefs, and

---

[25] Ulrich Zwingli, *Certeyne Preceptes Gathered by Hulrichus Zuinglius*, trans. Richard Argentine (London: Anthony Scoloker, 1548), sig. A2ʳ.

[26] Martin Luther, *A Ryght Notable Sermon Made by Doctor Martyn Luther*, trans. Richard Argentine (London: Anthony Scoloker, 1548), sig, A2v.

[27] Bernardino Ochino, *Sermons of the Ryght Famous and Excellent Clerke Master Bernardine Ochine*, trans. Richard Argentine (London: Anthony Scoloker, 1548), sig. A4ʳ.

[28] Ochino, *Sermons of Barnardine Ochine*, trans. Bacon, sig. A4ʳ. This work will be referred to hereafter parenthetically.

contemporaries would thus have viewed both Bacon and Argentine as supporters of the Edwardian Reformation.

At the same time, Bacon's reference to the "benefytes of Christ" signals that her translation contributes to a very specific political agenda: defending the Protestant tenet of justification by faith, which holds that faith in Christ alone is sufficient to guarantee salvation. The Edwardian government had endorsed this doctrine with the publication of Thomas Cranmer's *Homelies* on July 31, 1547. Intended to be read in all churches as sermons, the *Homelies* provided a summation of Edwardian theology, and its support for justification by faith addressed a doctrinal problem created by Henry VIII's inconsistent attitude toward reform. While Henry denied the existence of purgatory, he nonetheless supported justification by a combination of faith and works: "although suche workes of penance be required in us, towardes the atteinyng of remission of sinnes and justificacion: yet the same justificacion and remission of sinnes is the free gyft of God."[29] Henry's views were inherently contradictory because both purgatory and good works suggested that man could achieve salvation in part by his own actions. "An Homelie of the Salvation of Mankynd" resolved this issue by establishing and affirming mainstream Protestant doctrine: "we be justified by faithe onely, freely, and without woorkes."[30] In 1548, several publications explicitly defended justification by faith and thus offered support for the government's theological position. Dedicating his translation of Philipp Melanchthon's *The Justification of Man by Faith Only* to Somerset, Nicholas Lesse noted that this work could popularize justification by faith among readers of all kings as this tenet is "so playnly: so openly set forthe" by Melanchthon that "everye plowman, which can fynde in hys herte to learne to knowe to whome he shal cleave for his salvation: may with no great payns ... in passing of his tyme come to the knowledge."[31] Meanwhile, an anonymous translation of Luther's *Chiefe and Pryncypall Articles of the Christen Faythe* foregrounded justification by faith in its very first article: "S. Paull sayth. We suppose that a man is justifyed by faith, withoute the dedes of the lawe. Item, That he onely be counted juste, and a justifyer of hym that beleveth on

---

[29] Henry VIII, King of England, *A Necessary Doctrine and Erudicion for Any Chrysten Man* (London: Thomas Berthelet, 1543), sig. T4ʳ.
[30] Thomas Cranmer, *Certayne Sermons or Homelies Appoynted by the Kynges Majestie* (London: Rychard Grafton, 1547), sig. E1ʳ–E1ᵛ.
[31] Philipp Melanchthon, *The Justification of Man by Faith Only Made ... by Phylyp Melanchton*, trans. Nicholas Lesse (London: William Powell, 1548), fol. 6ʳ.

Jesus."[32] Thus by 1548, English reformers were consciously attempting to make justification by faith an essential component of English theology.

Bacon would have been well aware of the theological and political importance of this doctrine, thanks to her personal and familial connections at the Edwardian court, and her translation of Ochino aided royal efforts to combat any lingering adherence to justification by works. The table of contents suggests that the sermons' content is primarily devotional and thus noncontroversial: "How a Christyan oughte to make hys last wyll and testament," "How we shuld answere the deveil, when he tempteth us and namely in the ende of our lyfe," "How answere is to be made at the judgement seate of god," "By what meane to come to heaven," and "How god hath satisfyed for our synnes and hath purchasyd Paradice for us" (*Sermons*, A1ᵛ). While Hosington has argued that Bacon's translation only "indirectly" advances justification by faith, Bacon's preface situates the final two sermons in relation to this tenet by describing them as a means to learn "the true workes that god requireth of us, and the way to go to heaven" (A3ᵛ).[33] Despite their apparently divergent topics, the five sermons themselves are linked by their endorsement of justification by faith, thereby rejecting Catholic doctrine and Henrician equivocation about the efficacy of works. According to the first sermon, Christ has already redeemed the elect, or those chosen by God for salvation: "I am well assured that in purgatorye I shal not come, both bicause ther is found no other purgatory but christ in whom at the full be purged and punished al the synnes of the elected, and also bycause … Chryste not by my merytes, but by hys mere goodnes dothe satisfie for al my synnes trespasses, & paynes" (sig. B2ᵛ–B3ʳ). Since Christ has already "purged and punished" the elect through his sacrifice, the Catholic doctrine of purgatory is redundant and the elect have no need for works: "not by my merytes, but by hys mere goodnes." This passage links the loss of purgatory with justification by faith, inviting readers to see the relationship between previous English doctrine and this new tenet. In the fifth sermon, Christ himself again contends that his death has fully justified the souls of the elect: "I have taken on me al the sinnes, love hath layde them on my shulders, therfore … let my disciples and my elected passe as innocentes" (sig. E3ᵛ–E4ʳ). This parallel between Christ's "disciples" and the "elected" associates justification of faith with the primitive church, implicitly

---

[32] Martin Luther, *The Chiefe and Pryncypall Articles of the Christen Faythe* (London: [by S. Mierdman] for Gwalter Lynne, 1548), sig. A7ᵛ.
[33] Hosington, "Tudor Englishwomen's Translations," 127.

asserting its spiritual authority and rebutting potential objections to its novelty. The sermons also characterize justification by works as a diabolical invention. In the second sermon, Ochino portrays justification by works as a satanic stratagem for tempting the elect: "he wyll thus labour to bryng the[e] under the law, to thinke that thou must be justified not by christ, but by perfourmynge and fulfyllynge of the lawe, to the ende that thou shulde despayre" (sig. B7ʳ–B7ᵛ). Ochino urges readers to respond to such temptation by reaffirming their belief in Protestant doctrine: "I trust not to be saved by my workes ... I hope onelye to be saved by Christ, and hys workes" (sig. B8ʳ). This contrast between "my workes" and Christ's "workes" reinforces the idea that the soul relies on divine grace, not merit, for salvation. On a personal level, acceptance of justification by faith takes on greater importance as a means of combating the devil. In political terms, Bacon's translation of Ochino's sermons provides yet another opportunity for English readers to encounter Continental theology aligned with official agendas. By staying alert to the way that Bacon's authorial persona is mediated by religious identity rather than gender, we can better perceive the cultural resonance of her translation. Anonymity allowed Bacon to become just one of many Protestant translators who hoped to influence popular acceptance of religious reforms then afoot.

A "Christian and Naturall Mother": Intersectionality and Female Identity

While anonymity allowed Anne Bacon to construct an authorial identity based on religious affiliation, her remaining translations foregrounded her gender by providing Bacon's initials and by identifying her as a woman. It seems as though the political aims of these texts were better served by attribution rather than anonymity. For example, Bacon's role as the wife of a leading statesman underscored the official nature of Jewel's treatise. Richard Verstegan, a Catholic controversialist, certainly understood the political connotations of Bacon's authorship, representing her as part of a female cabal that abetted the Church of England: "The apologie of this Church was written in Latin, & translated into English by A. B. with the comendation of M. C., which twaine were sisters, & wives unto Cecill and Bacon, and gave their assistance and helping hands, in the plot and fortification of this newe erected synagog."[34] The preface to the

---

[34] Richard Verstegan, *A Declaration of the True Causes of the Great Troubles* ([Antwerp: Printed by J. Trognesius?] 1592), 12.

Jewel translation was signed by "M. C." (Matthew Parker, Archbishop of Canterbury), and Verstegan's misattribution of this dedication to Mildred Cooke Cecil, Bacon's sister, reveals the importance of Bacon's triple identities as reformist, translator, and wife. At the same time, his implicit dismissal of these "sisters, & wives" indicates that public acknowledgment of Bacon's identity also risked potential backlash due to negative female stereotypes that associated women with lustiness, talkativeness, and unruliness. Bacon's later translations mitigated this possibility by juxtaposing gender with other identities that conferred social prestige. Schleiner and Magnusson have already noted that Bacon's authority emerged from the interplay of her humanism, Protestantism, and rank.[35] However, to date there has been no sustained examination of how these identities related to one another or how they were viewed by Bacon and her contemporaries.

Kimberlé Crenshaw's groundbreaking work on the intersectional identity of black women offers a valuable method for theorizing the interrelationship of these various identities. Arguing that scholars need to move from a "single-axis framework" based solely on gender to a multidimensional view that involves multiple vectors of identity, Crenshaw proposes a model that resembles a traffic intersection where accidents, or discrimination, can occur in multiple directions: "If an accident happens in an intersection, it can be caused by cars traveling from any number of directions and, sometimes, from all of them. Similarly, if a Black woman is harmed because she is in the intersection, her injury could result from sex discrimination or race discrimination."[36] Intersectionality studies has since provided a useful tool for analyzing the relationship between power and identity: "intersectionality helps reveal how power works in diffuse and differentiated ways through the creation and deployment of overlapping identity categories."[37] Although Anne Bacon and other early modern Englishwomen were white, "overlapping identity categories" nonetheless provided an essential means of negotiating stereotypical female weaknesses. Critics have already explored how Elizabeth I exploited the distinction between her female body personal and her masculine body politic in order to legitimize her rule.[38] Women of lower classes carried out similar manipulations of identity, although these

[35] Schleiner, *Tudor and Stuart Women Writers*, 36 and 39; Magnusson, "Widowhood and Linguistic Capital," 13.
[36] Crenshaw, "Demarginalizing the Intersection of Race and Sex," 139 and 149.
[37] Cho, Crenshaw, and McCall, "Toward a Field of Intersectionality Studies," 797.
[38] See, for example, Carole Levin, *The Heart and Stomach of a King: Elizabeth I and the Politics of Sex and Power* (Philadelphia: University of Pennsylvania Press, 1994), 121–48.

maneuvers have received less scholarly attention. Taking a cue from intersectionality studies, the following discussion will analyze how Bacon constructed female authority through her overlapping identities as a woman, an aristocrat, a Protestant, and a humanist.

As contemporary portrayals of Bacon reveal, her femininity was often inflected by other factors. A neo-Latin poem addressed to Bacon by Andrew Willet provides a particularly rich example of these various identities. Entitled "Materfamilias" (mother of the family), the poem is dedicated to Bacon as "Doctissimae faeminae & prudentissimae Matronae Dominae Baconae" (the most learned woman and most prudent wife, Lady Bacon).[39] Even before the poem begins, Willet locates Bacon in terms of gender (mater, "mother"; matronae, "wife"), humanism (doctissimae; "most learned"), and rank (Dominae; "Lady"). Yet while the poem's title might seem to suggest that Willet will emphasize gender, he contrasts Bacon with an idealized housewife:

> At tua laus maior Domina est, quae tempora libris,
>   rebus in augendis conterit illa suis.
> Altera pauperibus doctis tu munera praebes,
>   hanc famuli laudant, te pia turba beat.
> Sic omnes utinam caperet sacra pagina mentes
>   omnium ita votis cresceret ordo sacer.

> (But your praise is greater, Lady, you who spend time with books,
>   she in increasing her goods.
> You offer gifts to the learned, this other to the poor,
>   the servants praise this one, a pious crowd blesses you.
> Would that the sacred page would seize all minds so,
>   that thus the sacred company would grow by the vows of all.)[40]

Bacon's domestic roles of mother and wife are complicated and enriched by her learning and Protestantism, both of which distinguish her from being a "merely a wife," to borrow Kelso's phrase. Her aristocratic rank adds yet another dimension to the poem, positioning her as a role model for the entire community of the godly (*pia turba*; "pious crowd"). Bacon thus gains authority as a mater familias from the intersection of multiple identities.

Bacon's gender roles were based on her relationships with men, and her other forms of identity were often viewed in relational terms as a result.

---

[39] Andrew Willet, *Sacrorum Emblematum Centuria Una* (Cambridge: John Legate, 1592), sig. F1ʳ.
[40] Willet, *Centuria*, sig. F1ᵛ, my translation. All subsequent translations are my own.

In the dedicatory preface to *Christian Meditations upon Eight Psalmes of the Prophet David* (1582), Theodore Beza consistently represents Bacon's various personae through her familial ties to men:

> I perswaded my selfe that it should not be displeasing to you, if this small volume carying your name upon the browe, were offered to you … hoping withall that this estate of widowehode whereunto it hath pleased God to call you by decease of that right vertuous and of right renowmed Lord, my Lord Nicolas Bacon your husband, & most worthy Keeper of the seale of England, you might perhaps therein finde some consolation, after the reading of those great and holy doctors Greeke and Latine so familiar to you, for your better confirming in the meditation of spiritual things, and in this constancie and Christian patience wherewith God hath so beautified you, that in you is verily acknowledged that Christianly high minded courage which I sawe in these partes shining in the deceased, of very happy memorie, Syr Anthony Cooke Knight, during those great calamities publique to the realme, and particular to him & his whole familie.[41]

Beza gestures at Bacon's aristocracy by referencing her marriage to a man with political power and social status. Her Protestantism is firmly established through Bacon's role as the daughter of Anthony Cooke, who entered exile during the "great calamities" of Mary I's reign. Although Beza mentions Bacon's delight in classical texts and notes that Bacon has sent him "latin letters" that show "the great and singular, yea extraordinarie graces" of God, he also describes her son Anthony Bacon as "a very paterne" of these same "graces."[42] Thus while Bacon enterprisingly used her humanist training to participate in the international Protestant community, Beza subsumes even that learning within a maternal identity. As this portrayal indicates, Bacon's status as a virtuous woman – whether daughter, mother, wife, or widow – was, in the eyes of her contemporaries, informed by her relationships with men. As a result, other forms of identity – such as education, rank, and religion – could be understood in relational terms.

When Bacon's translations were publicly attributed to her, these forms of identity played an important role in legitimizing her appearance in print. Her second translation of Ochino declares on its title page that "A. C." was the translator, and a preface to the reader by "G. B." (possibly William Baldwin) describes the translator as "a wel occupied Jentelwoman, and verteouse meyden," thereby evoking gender and

---

[41] Theodore Beza, *Christian Meditations upon Eight Psalmes of the Prophet David* (London: Christopher Barker, 1582), sig. A5ᵛ–A6ᵛ.
[42] Beza, *Meditations*, sig. A5ᵛ.

class.[43] G. B. underplays Bacon's learning by noting that any defects in the translation result from her domesticity: "it is a womans, yea, a Jentylwomans, who commenly are wonted to lyve Idelly, a maidens that never gaddid farder then her fathers house to learne the language" (sig. A2ᵛ). Mentioning her gender identity three times in this sentence ("a womans, yea, a Jentylwomans," "a maidens"), G. B. qualifies Bacon's femininity in terms of class, domesticity, and familial relationships. These accepted female roles neutralize Bacon's erudition by circumscribing it within her twin identities as a gentlewoman and daughter. Matthew Parker performs a similar maneuver while dedicating Bacon's translation of Jewel to the translator herself, "the right honorable learned and vertuous Ladie A. B."[44] This phrasing evokes Bacon's intersectional identity by referencing gender, class, and education. Elaborating in particular on her gender, Parker praises Bacon for showing proper deference to male authority by sending her translation to him for approval: "You have used your accustomed modestie in submittinge it to judgement, but therin is your prayse doubled, sith it hath passed judgement without reproche." If Bacon's gender necessitated such caution, her religious and humanist identities legitimized the inherently political task of translating Jewel's defense of the English church: "you have expressed an acceptable dutye to the glorye of GOD, deserved well of this Churche of Christ, honourablie defended the good fame and estimation of your owne native tongue ... [and] done pleasure to the Author of the Latine boke, in ... makinge his good woorke more publikely beneficiall." Both G. B. and Parker justify the publication of Bacon's translations by positioning these works as the product of an author who was not just a woman, but also a scholar, an aristocrat, and a Protestant.

In her own writings, Bacon also sought to construct an authority that drew on the intersections among her various identities. Dedicating her second translation of Ochino to her mother, Bacon identifies herself as a "humble Daughter" to "the right worshypful and worthyly beloved Mother, the Lady F.," or Anne Fitzwilliam Cooke (*Fourtene Sermons*, sig. A3ʳ). Bacon's juxtaposition of familial and class identities is further complicated by her mother's pious concerns about the frivolity of Italian: "it hath pleased you, often, to reprove my vaine studye in the Italyan tonge, accompting the sede thereof, to have bene sowen in barayne, unfruitful

---

[43] Ochino, *Fourtene Sermons of Barnardine Ochyne*, trans. Cooke, sig. A2ʳ. This text will hereafter be cited parenthetically.
[44] Jewel, *An Apologie*, trans. Bacon, n.p.

grounde" (sig. A3ʳ–A3ᵛ). This allusion to the parable of the sowers uses implicitly maternal language while also suggesting the superiority of biblical study over vernacular languages. Bacon extends this metaphor to justify her study by describing the sermons as yielding the "excelent fruit" of Protestant doctrine and by categorizing her translation as "some parte of the fruite of your Motherly admonicions" (sig. A4ʳ and A4ᵛ). Bacon thus constructs a relational identity for herself as an obedient daughter, which in turn informs her religious affiliation. Bacon's letters to her son Anthony reveal a similar propensity to use other identities as a means of augmenting her maternal role. When warning her son Anthony about the spiritual dangers of his intimacy with Thomas Lawson, a Catholic, she observes, "This one cheffest cownsell your christian and naturall mother doth geve yow, even before the Lorde, that above all worldely respects yow carie yourself even at your first coming as one that doth unfeinedly profess the tru religion of Christ" (*Letters*, 99). Much as in her dedicatory preface to the 1551 Ochino, Bacon constructs maternal authority in a twofold sense, through both reproductive and spiritual roles ("christian and naturall mother"). Using her Protestantism in order to enhance her authority as a "naturall" mother, Bacon urges Anthony to show his own fidelity to "the tru religion of Christ." In another letter, Bacon took a similar approach in order to warn Anthony of political dangers at court: "*matris monita nihil estimantur* [a mother's warnings are not valued]. I think for my long attending in coorte and a cheeff cownsellour's wyffe few *preclarae feminae meae sortis* [noblewomen of my lot] are able or be alyve to speak and judg of such proceadings and worldly doings of men" (*Letters*, 217). Well aware that "a mother's warnings are not valued," Bacon proceeds to heighten her maternal authority by pointing to other aspects of her identity. Bacon's very use of Latin here and elsewhere in the letter gestures at her humanism, subtly contending that her knowledge exceeds that of a mere mother. Bacon also establishes her political credentials by citing her status as a courtier ("long attending in coorte") as well as "a cheeff cownsellour's wyffe." Bacon thus evokes multiple forms of identity in an attempt to forestall any dismissal of her advice as simply a mother's warning.

Revealingly, Anthony Bacon undercut his mother's authority by focusing solely on her maternal identity. For example, he rejects Bacon's counsel about Lawson by emphasizing her femininity: "howsoever your Ladyship dothe pretende and alledge for reason your motherlie affection towards us in that which concernethe Lawson, yet anie man of judgme[nt] and indifferentcy must needes take it for a meere passion"

(*Letters*, 186). Characterizing her "motherlie affection" as "meere passion" and stating that "anie man" would concur with this opinion, Anthony pointedly rejects his mother's self-construction as a *godly* mother. In another letter, Anthony again diminishes his mother's authority by emphasizing her gender:

> As from a mother sicklie and in yeares, I am content to take in good parte anie misconceite, misimputatione or causeles humorous threates whatsoever, onlie this I maie withe reason and must for mine upon the warrant of a good conscience remonstrate unto your Ladyship, that your sonne's poore credite dependethe uppon judgement and not uppon humour; and that your Ladyship cannot utter anie thinge in your passion to your sonne's lacke, so longe as God gives him the grace to be more carefull in dutie to please and reverence your Ladyship as his mother, then your Ladyship seemeth manie times to be towardes me as your sonn. (*Letters*, 241)

In addition to representing her as "a mother" who is subject to excessive emotions ("passion"), Anthony further undermines Bacon's authority by referencing her age and ill-health ("sicklie and in yeares"). Stripped of the identities of class, humanism, and piety, Anne Bacon only retains her gender and its association with frailty. This phenomenon may help to explain Godfrey Goodman's infamous comment, "for Bacon's mother, she was but little better than frantic in her age."[45] Stewart has argued that this statement reflects the contemporary dismissal of Bacon's independent voice as insane.[46] Viewed from an intersectional angle, this observation may suggest that without a relational identity to buttress her "naturall" maternity, Bacon's expectation of authority might well seem "frantic." These gendered constructions of Bacon's identity demonstrate just how important intersectionality was for crafting female authority in the period. Shakespeare's *King Lear*, moreover, suggests that intersectionality was important for men. After Lear has given away his kingdom, the Fool calls him a fool, explaining, "All thy other titles thou hast given away; that thou wast born with."[47] Like Anne Bacon's "frantic" disposition, Lear's madness could be understood as a response to loss of identities that complemented his masculinity: king and father. Indeed, Lear seems to

---

[45] Godfrey Goodman, *The Court of King James the First*, ed. John S. Brewer, 2 vols. (London: Richard Bentley, 1839), vol. I, 285. See also Lisa Jardine and Alan Stewart, *Hostage to Fortune: The Troubled Life of Francis Bacon* (New York: Hill and Wang, 1999), 225–6 and 321.

[46] Stewart, "Voices of Anne Cooke," 88–102.

[47] William Shakespeare, *King Lear (Conflated Text)* in *The Norton Shakespeare*, Stephen Greenblatt et al. (eds.), 2nd edition (New York: W. W. Norton, 2008), 1.4.130–1.

recognize that he is left with only a maternal role: "O, how this mother swells up toward my heart!"[48]

Conclusion

The title page of a 1617 pamphlet from the *querelle des femmes* identifies its author as "*Ester Sowernam*, neither Maide, Wife nor Widdowe, yet really all, and therefore experienced to defend all."[49] Sowernam's claim to be both "all" kinds of women and none may hint that this female persona was merely a pseudonym for a male writer. Yet Sowernam's self-identification also indicates the instability of these essentialist categories, much like Lucio's assertion in *Measure for Measure* that Mariana may be "a punk, for many of them are neither maid, widow, nor wife."[50] Sowernam was responding to an infamous treatise by Joseph Swetnam, who also problematized stereotypical female identities: "There are six kinds of women which thou shouldest take heed that thou match not thy selfe to any one of them: that is to say, good nor bad, faire nor foule, rich nor poore."[51] In a pioneering monograph, Linda Woodbridge contended that this controversy over women reflects an early modern inclination to view women only through gender:

> the Renaissance rejoiced in systems of classification. As human beings might be divided into sub-classes along social lines (royalty, aristocracy, commonalty), religious lines (clergy, laity), spiritual lines (the saved, the damned), or into dichotomies like military/civilian, so women had their own sub-classes – usually maid/wife/widow, plus whore. These categorizations defined women solely on grounds of their relationships with men.[52]

Yet Woodbridge's reference to "human beings" implicitly admits that these social, religious, and spiritual "systems of classification" applied generally across the gender binary. As this chapter has shown, Anne Cooke Bacon was identified within many different frameworks: gender (maid/wife/widow), family (daughter/mother), education (humanist), religion (Protestant/Puritan), and rank (aristocrat). Contemporaries may have viewed her largely through the lens of gender, but Bacon's first translation

[48] Shakespeare, *King Lear*, 2.4.54.
[49] Esther Sowernam, *Ester Hath Hang'd Haman* (London: [Thomas Snodham] for Nicholas Bourne, 1617).
[50] William Shakespeare, *Measure for Measure* in *Norton Shakespeare*, 5.1.177–8.
[51] Swetnam, *Arraignment*, 36.
[52] Linda Woodbridge, *Women and the English Renaissance: Literature and the Nature of Womankind, 1540–1620* (Urbana: University of Illinois Press, 1984), 84.

of Ochino reveals the benefits of using religion as a primary identity. Meanwhile, an intersectional analysis of her various identities shows that Bacon and her contemporaries used other affiliations to complement gender. By questioning the notion of womanhood itself, we can gain a better understanding of how early modern women and their writings gained cultural authority from a variety of intersecting identities that include, but are not limited to, gender.

3

The Critical Fortunes of the Tenth Muse
Canonicity and Its Discontents

Patricia Pender

Anne Bradstreet's poetic career has signaled a profound investment in the idea of a female canon, from the title of her first volume of poetry, *The Tenth Muse, Lately Sprung Up in America*, to the 1970s feminist reclamation of her "personal" poetry, and the current century's revivification of her "political" interests. Each major movement in Bradstreet's critical reception has paid deliberate attention to the ways in which her poetry subverts or re-inscribes different orthodoxies in literary history – both historical and current. This confluence of concerns, and the dramatically divergent results they have produced, makes Bradstreet an ideal subject for examining the notion of a female canon in early modern women's writing. Against what did the notion of a female canon oppose itself in the seventeenth century, and against which critical traditions has this same notion been harnessed in subsequent literary criticism? A transhistorical examination of Bradstreet's critical reception (even one as abbreviated as this chapter can provide) offers insights into canon building (and dismantling) from a unique perspective: Bradstreet is at once an obvious anomaly, a clear contender for canonicity, and a test case from which arguments about subversion and orthodoxy in early modern women's writing continue to flourish.

For a writer who might now be considered a relatively canonical figure in early modern women's studies, and who occupies such a seminal position in early American literary history, the full story of Anne Bradstreet's critical reception has received surprisingly scant attention. The "pirated" London publication of her first volume of poetry, *The Tenth Muse Lately Sprung Up in America* in 1650, her expressed shock and dismay at seeing her poems in print, and her written response to this "theft" in her second edition, *Several Poems*, published posthumously in Boston in 1678, have become the stuff of literary legend. But while the broad brushstrokes of Bradstreet's seventeenth-century reception are generally well known, less is understood about the ways her work has traveled from the seventeenth century to our own period, and the concomitant ways in which her relationships with various canons – of literature and scholarship – have evolved.

Bradstreet exemplifies the utility of studying the transmission of women's writing across time because her critical reception is demonstrably and deeply tied, at crucial historical junctures, to the particular manuscript and print editions that constitute her evolving *oeuvre*. In a sense, of course, this is true of every author's corpus, but in Bradstreet's case, the critical apparatus tied to her editions might be seen as especially significant, not least to those concerned with women's literary history, because the epistles and commendatory verse (and later introductions and forewords) that have framed Bradstreet's poetry have so fundamentally influenced the critical reception of her work. Importantly, this is not necessarily the result of editorial hostility or the unintended consequence of disdain or disinterest – in fact, quite the reverse. Indeed, Bradstreet's early modern and late modern editors, and the literary-critical credentials they bring to their editions, are authoritative and have accrued corresponding longevity.

Famously, for instance, when Bradstreet's brother-in-law John Woodbridge took her manuscripts to London in 1650 and published them, purportedly without her permission, he described the author in his epistle to the "Kind Reader" in terms that have been repeated almost verbatim through centuries of subsequent criticism. When Woodbridge described Bradstreet as "a woman, honoured, and esteemed where she lives, for her ... exact diligence in her place, and her discrete managing of her family occasions" and her poems as "the fruit but of some few hours, curtailed from her sleep and other refreshments," he presented a presumably unintentionally patronizing picture of a woman poet which might have been expected to appeal to the restrictive gender norms of her contemporary seventeenth-century audience.[1] But this sense of Bradstreet as a decorous dilettante whose potentially transgressive foray into print requires biographical amelioration on the part of her male editors has persisted to the extent that even as late as 1981, Joseph R. McElrath and Allan P. Robb, in the introduction to their *Complete Works*, felt the need to assure the reader that despite Bradstreet being a poet, "No scandal attached itself to her life."[2]

---

[1] John Woodbridge, "Kind Reader," in Bradstreet, *Tenth Muse*, n.p. See also Kathryn Zabelle Derounian-Stodola, "'The Excellency of the Inferior Sex': The Commendatory Writings on Anne Bradstreet," *Studies in Puritan American Spirituality*, 1 (1990), 129–47.
[2] Bradstreet, *Complete Works*, xi.

Similarly, but from a very different political position, in the "Foreword" and "Postscript" to Jeannine Hensley's 1967 *Works of Anne Bradstreet*, Adrienne Rich offered a newly inspirational Bradstreet to an emerging second-wave feminist audience. For Rich, Bradstreet "was one of the few women writers I knew anything about who had also been a mother."[3] Valuing Bradstreet's depiction of the "simple events in a woman's life," Rich's endorsement gave birth to a strong tradition of gender-focused Bradstreet scholarship that continues to flourish today.[4] More problematically, Rich expressed a decided preference for the second edition of Bradstreet's poems – particularly those that deal with mother-hood and the family – over the first edition, which she deems amateur-ish and derivative, the result of a "nostalgia for English culture," written in a detached, impersonal style which would not have stood the test of time.[5] As a consequence, and until only recently, Bradstreet's early politi-cal poetry has been dismissed, perhaps especially by feminist scholars, as rote-like imitations of male models.

In prefacing editions of her poetry designed to introduce Bradstreet to new audiences – one in the mid-seventeenth and one in the late twentieth century – John Woodbridge and Adrienne Rich offered assess-ments of the poet and her work that have each been enormously influ-ential. On the face of it, these assessments are inimical. The patronizing paternalism that Woodbridge extended to a contemporary female poet was an attitude that Rich challenged repeatedly and vigorously through-out her own long and justly celebrated poetic career. Rich's affirmation of the minutiae of women's daily lives as it appears in Bradstreet's poetry would have seemed anathema to Woodbridge, for whom such concerns would have been deemed incidental or irrelevant; and yet these introduc-tions, separated by two centuries, share similarities of structure, rhetoric, and even ideology that belie their obvious differences.

Structurally, Woodbridge's dedicatory epistle and Rich's foreword func-tion as vindications – however compromised – of the work that follows. As such, they engage, implicitly and sometimes quite explicitly, with the contemporary notions of literary merit and value against which Bradstreet's poetry could assume to be measured. Rhetorically, both introductions are encomia, and employ tropes of praise and censure to represent how the author in question sees Bradstreet fitting, and perhaps more importantly

---

[3] Rich, Foreword: "Anne Bradstreet and Her Poetry," xx–xxi.
[4] Ibid., xvii.
[5] Ibid., xiii–xv.

challenging, current notions of merit and value, categories that are clearly freighted with gendered expectations. Thus Woodbridge defends Bradstreet against potential animadversions against her neglect of feminine responsibility by employing the trope of nocturnal studies: she wrote her poems in the few hours left to her after the performance of family duties.[6] Rich upholds Bradstreet's poetry against potential slurs of ineptitude, not by validating her corpus as a whole, but by siphoning off a subsection that escapes the general censure with which she evidently agrees: Bradstreet's later, personal, "genuinely feminine" poetry is deemed accomplished; her earlier, public, derivatively masculine verse is judged as substandard.[7] Both Woodbridge and Rich defend Bradstreet's poetry against canonical expectations by recourse to alternate gendered expectations. Ironically, however, her normative femininity is the key to both defenses.

The equivocal vindications of Bradstreet offered by Woodbridge and Rich have each received sustained scholarly scrutiny, to the extent, perhaps, that one might wonder whether anything new might be said about them. My aim in placing them together in this way is to shed light on submerged similarities that are illuminated by viewing them as vehicles for charged representations of the poet and her works. Each evinces an intimate investment in ideas of orthodoxy and subversion that issues of canonicity invoke almost by fiat. Woodbridge is concerned to preempt charges of transgression by an appeal to gender orthodoxy, which paradoxically makes Bradstreet exceptional in the conventional literary canon of his day. Rich is keen to repudiate charges of rote-like literary orthodoxy by an appeal to gender transgression, which paradoxically makes Bradstreet exemplary in a female literary tradition that Rich would come to figurehead herself.[8] In a further twist, Rich simultaneously wishes to "rescue" Anne Bradstreet from what she calls the "Women's Archives" – clearly for Rich a place of historical ignominy – in order to argue for both her acute relevance to twentieth-century women and the timeless quality of her personal poetry.[9]

---

[6] The nocturnal studies trope is analyzed in Patricia Pender, "Rethinking Authorial Reluctance in the Paratexts to Anne Bradstreet's Poetry," in Wiseman (ed.), *Early Modern Women and the Poem*, 165–80.

[7] The phrase "genuinely feminine" comes from my analysis of Rich and Bradstreet in Pender, *Early Modern Women's Writing*.

[8] See, for example: Wendy Martin, *An American Triptych: Anne Bradstreet, Emily Dickinson, Adrienne Rich* (Chapel Hill: University of North Carolina Press, 1984); Marion Rust, "Making Emends: Adrienne Rich, Audre Lorde, Anne Bradstreet," *American Literature: A Journal of Literary History, Criticism, and Bibliography*, 88.1 (2016), 93–125; Showalter, *A Jury of Her Peers*.

[9] Rich, Foreword, xvii.

The canons toward which Woodbridge and Rich endeavor to usher Bradstreet's poetry and the methods they employ to facilitate this process thus bear similarities and differences in an uncomfortable mixture that resists any easy political polarization. We might start to untangle these strains by recognizing that each presents Bradstreet as worthy of entering a conventional canon of some sort: Woodbridge by presenting her as a precociously gifted practitioner of English Renaissance verse, and Rich by presenting her as having evolved from that practice to produce poems of feminine authenticity. But both also draw attention to an alternative gendered tradition – Woodbridge in his allusions to the Nine Muses of classical antiquity, and Rich in her rejection of the "Women's Archives." For both Woodbridge and Rich, it is inclusion in the conventional canon that matters, regardless of the way Rich might seek to open, and ultimately succeed in opening, that canon to other gendered concerns.

In what follows I outline some of the conflicting positions in the canon debate as it has developed in early modern women's studies before turning to assess our current critical moment, where we can see many of these issues still actively in play. In the early twenty-first century, as, indeed, at any other point in time, there is not "one" Anne Bradstreet, and neither is there one definitive canon.

To Canonize or Not to Canonize: That Is One Question

As Patricia Phillippy outlines in her introduction to this volume, the different desires to uncover the influence of earlier women's writing on later practitioners, and to "avoid facile essentialism" in its definition, have led to "a lack of critical agreement concerning the status of a *female tradition*," resulting in "a pattern of 'separate but equal' fields of study and their attending literary histories." When women's writing has been inserted into comprehensive literary histories, she writes, "its inclusion has been both partial and strategic: a small number of anomalous works disrupt the monolithic narrative of the masculine canon." More often, however, "women's writing has been treated as if enacted remotely, distinct from masculine practice and canonicity and incommensurate with conventional standards of merit or value." According to the overarching rationale for the present volume, and the brief for this chapter in particular, a "persistent critical preference for subversion over orthodoxy stands at the heart of this debate," and ongoing uncertainties about the status of a canon of early modern women's writing are a direct consequence.[10]

---

[10] Phillippy, Introduction: "Sparkling Multiplicity" in this volume.

Questions about the relevance of the conventional literary canon (and what this canon might entail), the efficacy of producing a counter-canon of women's writing (and what this canon might entail) and the associated possibilities and pitfalls of incorporation, expansion, occlusion, and ghettoization might be said to have reached their zenith in the 1980s, following the academy's uptake of and ensuing struggle over the identity politics of race, class, gender, and sexuality, among other important markers of difference.[11] Almost forty years later, questions of canonicity might be (mistakenly) thought to have reached their nadir: scholars are understandably exhausted and frustrated by the lack of clear pathways through what can often seem a critical minefield, even if a largely abandoned one.[12] For some, the question has been settled pragmatically: if the institutional or economic viability of a discipline rests with canonization, alternatives are clearly not worth pursuing. For others, the question itself is wrongheaded or irrevocably reductive ("the master's tools will never dismantle the master's house")[13]; for still others, it is simply counterproductive, capable only of rehashing past battles between diametrically opposed ideological and practical positions. The problem here is that fields such as early modern women's writing – which evolved from a primary focus on one demarcation of difference, even when they involved the consideration of other differences – cannot help but beg the question of canonicity, even, ironically, in the very refusal of that question.

In their 2010 introduction to Palgrave's *History of British Women's Writing, 1500–1610*, for instance, Caroline Bicks and Jennifer Summit write that: "[r]ather than inserting women into a pre-existing literary canon or defining an autonomous female tradition," they propose "a new approach" to women's literary history, one which focuses on "the diverse practices of women's writing in order to discern a broad but obscure landscape of female literacy and literary practice in the early modern period."[14] This is an approach which has gained considerable traction (and with which I personally feel much critical sympathy), but it is clear that even in such a concerted circumvention of its conflicts, it is impossible to fully escape the question of canonicity. Bicks and Summit reject previously polarized attempts to deal with the problem, but in doing so

---

[11] Now-classic texts in this field include: Robinson, "Treason Our Text"; Showalter, *A Literature of Their Own*; Gilbert and Gubar, *Madwoman in the Attic*.
[12] The minefield analogy is explored adroitly in Annette Kolodny, "Dancing through the Minefield: Some Observations on the Theory, Practice and Politics of a Feminist Literary Criticism," *Feminist Studies*, 6 (1980), 1–25.
[13] Audre Lorde, "The Master's Tools Will Never Dismantle the Master's House," in *Sister Outsider: Essays and Speeches* (Berkeley: Crossing Press, 1984), 110–13.
[14] Catherine Bicks and Jennifer Summit, "Introduction," in *History*, 1.

they have to propose an alternative in its place, thereby contributing, even if reluctantly, a "new approach" to the idea of a women's canon. This is less a criticism than an acknowledgment of the inevitability – and inescapability – of the conundrum of canonicity. Like proverbial conversations about politics itself, it cannot be sidestepped or evaded by a pronouncement that one is "not talking about politics."

From one perspective, the concept of the canon is unavoidably coercive; it relies on politics and practices of inclusion and exclusion that are fundamentally anathema to many working from the position of marginalized literatures. Phillippy notes that, as the field of early modern women's writing has expanded, "the value of establishing a female canon at all has been as unclear as the criteria on which individual works would acquire canonical status." An established female canon, she suggests, "has seemed as superfluous and outmoded as appeals to maintain and protect the traditional male canon of great works."[15] At the same time the concept of the canon is a "real world" force: despite or perhaps indeed because of differing and fluctuating definitions, it influences what kinds of teaching, textbooks, editions, and even scholarship remain economically viable. In the neoliberal academy, invocations of canon, and through them, appeals to relevance, have the capacity to "make or break" the following, for example: university courses and, in consequence, administrative units such as disciplines, schools and faculties; publishing enterprises such as teaching texts, critical editions, and scholarly monographs; and, increasingly, applications for funding and international research collaboration. All of these things have the potential to impact individual careers as well as whole fields.

My portrayal of this institutional environment might seem unnecessarily bleak and skeptical (and I hope this proves the case), but even this grim picture fails to make any one path through the canon debate indisputably preferable or more promising. In 2005, Nigel Smith claimed (to an audience of scholars who had devoted or were about to devote their careers to early modern women writers) that the only way forward for the field was to court the "High Street" audience – members of the general public for whom the conventional male canon presumably still held firm sway.[16] But scholars of early modern women's writing have been nothing if not tenacious in their commitment to disrupting prevailing narratives

[15] Phillippy, Introduction: "Sparkling Multiplicity 15," in this volume.
[16] Smith, "The Rod and the Canon." For a framing of and partial response to Smith's call, see Clarke and Robson, "Why Are We 'Still Kissing the Rod'?"

of literary history and the concepts of canon that underwrite these narratives. Smith's suggestion conforms and calls out to a certain postfeminist discourse in academia, a rhetoric of "commonsense" that past feminist principles might now be judiciously jettisoned in light of small but significant gains and the very real presence of economic pressures. I disagree with this proposal, and the gender politics that give rise to it, but that does not mean that clear solutions to the conundrums of the canon are any easier to articulate or advocate for.

Twenty-First Century Bradstreets: Modern Editions and Their Audiences

Today's publishing industry creates what might seem to scholars some surprising alternative "Anne Bradstreets" for different reading publics. Some popular and niche presses, for instance, package Bradstreet to presumably generalist audiences as a spiritual exemplar, combining the poems with evangelical biography and a basic historical overview ("King James I of England was angry"),[17] sometimes with an overtly didactic cast: "In contrast to the common delusion that we control our lives in today's society, we can gain in Bradstreet the perspective of one who recognized God's sovereign hand in every aspect of her life."[18] Others promote her poems and their geographical contexts as pilgrimage destinations: the assumed locations of Bradstreet's households, her authorship of specific poems, and her death are advertised to readers seeking access to an earlier form of Puritan devotion or to the later New England literary scene with which she was subsequently linked.[19] Nigel Smith's call for "High Street" recognition of early modern women writers seems to be met by these publications, but without producing any discernable promotion of Bradstreet as a canonical poet. The idea that canonicity is in fact conferred by the High Street, or in the American context, Main Street, can be seen as something of an obfuscation of the institutional power of the academy in this case.[20]

---

[17] Faith Cook, *Anne Bradstreet: Pilgrim and Poet* (Carlisle, PA: EP Books, 2010), 11.

[18] Heidi L. Nichols, *Anne Bradstreet: A Guided Tour of the Life and Thought of a Puritan Poet* (Phillipsburg, NJ: P&R Publishing, 2006), 14.

[19] Kristin Bierfelt, *The North Shore Literary Trail: From Bradstreet's Andover to Hawthorne's Salem* (Charlestown: The History Press, 2009).

[20] On institutional understandings of canon-formation see Gayatri Chakravorty Spivak, "The Making of Americans, the Teaching of English, and the Future of Cultural Studies," *New Literary History*, 21 (1990), 781–98; and Alan Golding, *From Outlaw to Classic: Canons in American Poetry* (Madison: University of Wisconsin Press, 2009).

Beyond popular or trade press editions such as these, publications that present Bradstreet to different reading publics include the teaching anthologies that introduce students to the poet in various canonical incarnations. While more comprehensive assessments of such collections have been ably conducted by others, it is useful to flag here the different "Bradstreets" that emerge from the pages of the widely used Norton anthologies of American literature and (Anglophone) women's literature, both counter-canon building enterprises in their own right.[21] *The Norton Anthology of American Literature* presents Bradstreet's *Tenth Muse* as the "first published volume of poems written by a resident in the New World," noting that it was widely read and that fellow New England Puritan poet Edward Taylor had a copy of the second edition in his library, thus conferring canonicity on Bradstreet through priority ("the first"), popularity, and through association with a contemporary male poet. The editors state that "[a]lthough she herself probably took greatest pride in her long meditative poems on the ages of man and on the seasons, the poems which have attracted present-day readers are the more intimate ones which reflect her concern for her family and home and the pleasures she took in everyday life rather than in the life to come," a view clearly indebted to Adrienne Rich's revisionist analysis of Bradstreet's output discussed above.[22]

The Norton Anthology of Literature by Women also focuses on Bradstreet's position within "New World" Puritan culture but with additional attention to her status as a woman writer. Editors Sandra Gilbert and Susan Gubar write that, given contemporary cultural strictures against female ambition, "it is no wonder" that the poems collected in the *Tenth Muse* "betray little overt rebellion against such a lot."[23] A tenacious gynocritical predilection for detecting patriarchal subversion is evident in the editors' subsequent affirmation: "Even in the 1650 edition of *The Tenth Muse*, though, we can discern, if not a rebellion against woman's domestic 'place,' a rising of the heart against female intellectual subordination." Like the editors of the *Norton Anthology of American Literature*, Gilbert and Gubar note that Bradstreet's later poetry "depended heavily on images and metaphors drawn from her life as a

[21] See: Ezell, "Myth of Judith Shakespeare"; Ezell, *Writing Women's Literary History*; Wray, "Anthologizing"; Eardley, "Recreating the Canon."

[22] Nina Baym et al. (eds.), *The Norton Anthology of American Literature*, 3rd ed. 2 vols. (New York: W. W. Norton, 1989), vol. I, 92.

[23] Gilbert and Gubar (eds.), *Norton Anthology of Literature by Women*, 81–2.

woman," but they omit what is by-now customary aesthetic praise of these poems, noting instead that they demonstrate the way Bradstreet "confronted her role as a domestic helpmate with a sharp wit."[24] For an anthology explicitly designed to champion the work of women writers, the editors' overall assessment strikes a somewhat discordant note: Bradstreet's popularity waned in the centuries following her death, and despite acknowledgment from various individuals, her poetry is viewed primarily as an achievement in the context of the hardships and limitations she experienced.[25] Despite the overt premise of the collection, then, this seems a fairly clear-cut case of what Linda Woodbridge describes as the critical double standard where "men inhabit literature-land; women inhabit history-land."[26]

Two quite recent editions of Bradstreet's poetry provide different, more specialized access to selections of her work. Sarah C. E. Ross and Elizabeth Scott-Baumann's anthology *Women Poets of the English Civil War* aims to present the work of five poets, including Bradstreet, "in clear, modernised texts for use by students at undergraduate level and above," according to "the broad editorial principles behind anthologies such as *The Norton Anthology of English Literature*."[27] In their "Textual Introduction," Ross and Scott-Baumann make the claim that "[m]odernised editions are not only easier for students and beginning scholars to use, encouraging close reading and comparisons with other well-known examples of early modern poetry; they also undoubtedly carry with them the whiff of canonicity, of 'great literary authorship,' and engender more serious approaches to the work."[28] As Leah Marcus has argued in the context of editing Elizabeth I's works, "[w]hether appropriately or not, the modern-spelling Shakespeares have set a standard for other authors of the period ... [m]odern spelling, or at least the availability of modern spelling editions, makes an author appear more like Shakespeare, which is to say more canonical."[29] In a reflective essay on their own editorial practice, Ross and Scott-Baumann pose the challenge their volume faces in the following way: "To invite students to read women's poems in

[24] Ibid., 82.

[25] Ibid., 82–3.

[26] Linda Woodbridge, "Dark Ladies: Women, Social History, and English Renaissance Literature," in Viviana Comensoli and Paul Stevens (eds.), *Discontinuities: New Essays on Renaissance Literature and Criticism* (Toronto: University of Toronto Press, 1998), 52–71 at 62.

[27] Sarah C. E. Ross and Elizabeth Scott-Baumann, "Textual Introduction," in Ross and Scott-Baumann (eds.), *Women Poets of the English Civil War*, 317–19 at 317.

[28] Ibid., 317.

[29] Marcus, "Editing Queen Elizabeth I," 143.

genuine conversation and comparison with those of canonical men, we
need to meet like with like: to present them with texts that have been
afforded mainstream editorial parity, whatever the limitations of mainstream editorial protocol may be."[30] A poignant musical analogy brings
this message home: "students and scholars need to be able to encounter
women's poems in full symphony orchestra renditions, not just on period
instruments, because whatever its distortions and anachronisms, a full
symphony orchestra sound is what our ear is attuned to."[31]

    Women Poets of the English Civil War, as its editors readily acknowl-
edge, is "frankly populist," an "avowedly mainstream" anthology which
aims to present poems that are, in Nigel Smith's formulation, "a good
read," to students who are "exploring the literary canon for the first time,
whose sense of 'the literary' is under construction, and whose attention to
women writers will inevitably be constructed by the 'great works' focus
that continues to dominate twelve-week undergraduate courses at ter-
tiary level."[32] The editors' investment in canonicity is explicit: "We chose
poems that would speak to the most-taught works of Donne, Herbert,
Marvell and Milton, and also those that would speak among themselves;
those that articulate themselves most clearly in relation to canonical
poetic traditions, and also those that do not."[33] Encouraging formal
analysis of the selected poets is a key aim of the anthology: pushing back
against a perceived critical trajectory that favors historical over aesthetic
inquiry, Ross and Scott-Baumann assert that "there remains a concur-
rent need to make women's poetry available in ways that make it easy
to explore the verbal, imagistic and formal qualities of a poem, and its
participation in the cultural aesthetics of its day."[34] The editorial rationale
informing this anthology thus aims to redress what Danielle Clarke and
Marie-Louise Coolahan describe as the "evasion of discussion of form"
seen as symptomatic of previous biographical, historical and material
accounts of early modern women's writing.[35]

    My own representation of Bradstreet's poetry in the digital archive,
Material Cultures of Early Modern Women's Writing, was produced at the
same time and often in conversation with the editors of *Women Poets
of the English Civil War*. As the title of the overarching archive suggests,

---

[30] Ross and Scott-Baumann, "Anthologizing Early Modern Women's Poetry," 223.
[31] Ibid., 224.
[32] Ibid., 217 and 229, quoting Smith, "The Rod and the Canon," 233.
[33] Ross and Scott-Baumann, "Anthologizing Early Modern Women's Poetry," 219–20.
[34] Ibid., 224.
[35] Clarke and Coolahan, "Gender, Reception, and Form," 151.

its approach is decidedly material, and my Bradstreet selection focuses exclusively on its textual apparatus – the title pages, dedicatory epistles, addresses to the reader, and commendatory poems – that accompanied her two seventeenth-century editions of poetry into print. While several print and online resources currently offer access to the poems themselves, the print editions have almost uniformly misrepresented their paratexts, through grouping together the individual texts that prefaced each volume, while the online resources are generally "unedited." As I argue in my "Textual Introduction," such conflation and omission has the probably unintended result of collapsing together, and thus diluting, the specific ways that Bradstreet's poetry was presented to different reading publics in 1650 and 1678.[36]

The rationale behind my approach to presenting Bradstreet's poetry in this way stems from a conviction that each edition of Anne Bradstreet makes a different claim to represent the poet – claims that inevitably reflect their own cultural and literary moment. Editorial choices, introductions, tone, and format play important roles in shaping and staging Bradstreet's poetry; they also work to construct, modify, champion and reject existing representations of Anne Bradstreet herself. The "selection" I present of Bradstreet's poetry is in fact very limited, and reproduces little in the way of her authorial "voice," but this is a deliberate choice, designed to encourage further studies of the transmission of Anne Bradstreet's works that might tell us more about the ways in which her texts were produced in their specific literary-historical milieu and the ways in which they subsequently circulated as material objects.[37]

These two recent representations of Bradstreet's poetry clearly pursue different agendas, and it would be easy, if simplistic, to see them as projects distinctly at odds. The model of scholarship that views disciplinary developments through the binary viewfinder of orthodoxy versus subversion would no doubt construe them thus, with previous turf wars between aesthetics and history reconfigured here as conflicts between new formalism and materialism. But which project stands for orthodoxy and which for subversion has become happily complicated in our current critical climate. *Women Poets of the English Civil War* makes an explicit appeal to canonical orthodoxy but also makes an embedded bid to subvert what it sees as the trend for historically focused studies of early modern women writers in favor of promoting aesthetic inquiry. The *Material*

---

[36] See *Anne Bradstreet*, ed. Pender.
[37] Gillian Wright has done just this in her chapter on Bradstreet in *Producing Women's Poetry*.

Cultures of Early Modern Women's Writing digital archive eschews questions of canonicity, and takes a History of the Book approach, endeavor-
ing to foreground the historical and material specificity of selected early
modern women's texts, an enterprise that has previously been seen as subverting traditional literary methodologies but which is increasingly being
painted as a new orthodoxy.

   As might be expected of concrete examples as opposed to theoretical
arguments, however, the representations of Bradstreet's poetry in these
very different editions are not entirely dissimilar. Both are products of the
present moment in early modern women's studies that address limitations
in the way that her poetry is currently available.[38] Each relies on previous
editions of Bradstreet, even as they branch out in new directions. Thus
Women Poets of the English Civil War is predicated on the fact that the previous editions of the poets exist, a scenario that allows its producers to *edit
for* specific goals in the anthology.[39] The Bradstreet section of the *Material
Cultures of Early Modern Women's Writing* digital archive similarly relies
on the complete seventeenth-century editions being available online, and
instead provides a scholarly apparatus for the paratexts that are not normally accorded such editorial attention. Even methodologically – where
the differences between these editions might seem most acute – it would
be premature, and possibly misguided, to see these different editions of
Bradstreet as inimical. Ross and Scott-Baumann state clearly that "we
have not abandoned an interest in the poems' conditions of production,
and in the contexts in which they originally occurred."[40] And, despite ani-
madversion to the contrary, nowhere, to my knowledge, have studies of
the material production of early modern women's texts claimed that the
writing itself is irrelevant to further investigation.

   A collective, multidisciplinary approach to early modern women's
writing strikes me as a win-win situation. Canonical literary history

---

[38] The need for a new critical edition of Bradstreet today rests partly with the problems of McElrath
and Robb's *Complete Works* of 1981 and partly with its inaccessibility: it went out of print shortly
after publication, severely restricting its circulation. McElrath and Robb also remove the paratexts
to both the 1650 *Tenth Muse* and the 1678 *Several Poems* and place them in an appendix of
Commendatory Writings. Jeannine Hensley's teaching edition for Harvard places the dedicatory
and commendatory texts written by Bradstreet and others at the beginning of her collection but
combines paratexts from the *Tenth Muse* and *Several Poems*, thus conflating accolades to the poet
from two separate periods – the pre- and post-publication periods – of her writing life. Both editorial decisions disturb the integrity of the early modern book as material artifact, and homogenize
the history of Bradstreet's works in transmission.

[39] Ross and Scott-Baumann, "Anthologizing Early Modern Women's Poetry," 230.

[40] Ross and Scott-Baumann, "Textual Introduction," 318.

might be based, *pace* Harold Bloom, on the assumption that precocious sons devour their authoritative father figures, agonistically and *ad nauseam* (and some of those father figures might be very hard on digestion indeed). This is clearly not the case with whatever canon we can construct for early modern women writers, and it need not dictate the forms our scholarship takes either. Our inherited models of literary criticism might proffer the bald binary of subversion and orthodoxy with a certain siren-like simplicity, but the growing field of early modern women's studies deserves better models. These can really only be achieved by talking across purported methodological and critical divides. In the following, final section of this chapter I look very briefly at some of the emerging critical trajectories that are currently reproducing Anne Bradstreet for twenty-first century readers.

Scholarly Interventions: Bradstreet's New Canonical Contexts

We have seen above how Adrienne Rich's championing of Bradstreet's personal poetry has had a profound impact on how her work has been received since the late 1960s. This has taken two forms: scholarship which extends and adumbrates Rich's literary preference and gender focus, and more recently, scholarship that has sought to contest Rich's dismissal of the early public poems as unworthy of sustained scholarly inquiry. In the capable hands of scholars such as Susan Wiseman and Catharine Gray among others, a "political turn" in Bradstreet scholarship has brought the historical, religious, national, transatlantic, and generational resonances of Bradstreet's early poems into much sharper focus.[41] Thus poems previously dismissed as dull and derivative, such as "The Four Monarchies," "The Four Elements," and "The Four Seasons" have been revealed as rich repositories of political theory, cultural and

---

[41] See: Wiseman, *Conspiracy and Virtue*; Susan Wiseman, "Anne Bradstreet's Poetry and Providence: Earth, Wind and Fire," in Johanna Harris and Elizabeth Scott-Baumann (eds.), *Intellectual Culture of Puritan Women*, 135–49; Gray, *Women Writers and Public Debate*. See also: Andrew Hiscock, "'Dialogue Between Old England and New': Anne Bradstreet and Her Negotiations with the Old World," in Andrew Hiscock (ed.), *Mighty Europe, 1400–1700: Writing an Early Modern Continent* (Bern, Switzerland: Peter Lang, 2007), 195–220; Patricia Pender, "Disciplining the Imperial Mother: Anne Bradstreet's 'A Dialogue Between Old England and New,'" in Jo Wallwork and Paul Salzman (eds.), *Women Writing 1550–1750* (Bundoora: Meridian, 2011), 115–31; Gillespie, "'This Briny Ocean Will O'erflow Your Shore.'" For earlier work in this area, see Jane D. Eberwein, "Civil War and Bradstreet's 'Monarchies'," *Early American Literature*, 26.2 (1991), 119–44; Helena Maragou, "The Portrait of Alexander the Great in Anne Bradstreet's 'The Third Monarchy,'" *Early American Literature*, 23.1 (1988), 70–81.

religious contestation, and lively negotiation with literary precedent. As its inclusion in Ross and Scott-Baumann's anthology attests, Bradstreet's poetry has become a fertile site of scholarly investigation into Civil War politics, conflicting and evolving attitudes toward the monarchy and the Commonwealth, and relationships between both "Old" World and "New" and Puritan and Catholic faiths. In one sense this reorientation subverts what by the 1990s had become a new orthodoxy of rejecting Bradstreet's political poetry in favor of her personal poetry. But this intervention should not be seen as wrenching Bradstreet from "literature-land" to relocate her in "history-land." Reassessing Bradstreet's ambitious, scholarly narrative poems requires a critical reevaluation of their formal qualities, and of the particular genres she chose to work in, some of which are undoubtedly less familiar (and less immediately palatable) to us than they were to her contemporary audience.

A particular extension of the renewed focus on Bradstreet's political poetry has been the drive to understand her as a transatlantic poet, one who was connected in complex ways to both "Old" England and "New" but is not considered fully a "native" of either. The compelling postcolonial analysis that Stephanie Jed provided of Bradstreet in 1994 has been supplemented by Kate Chedgzoy's positioning her in the "British Atlantic world," Tamara Harvey's reading of her "across the Americas," and Katharine Gillespie's analysis of her "'Second World' Atlanticism."[42] Recent studies pursuing this critical trajectory include Jim Egan's consideration of "creole" Bradstreet, Gabriele Rippl's analysis of transatlantic colonial melancholia, and a special edition of *Symbiosis* exploring "transatlantic continuities" from Bradstreet to Plath.[43] While the political analyses of Bradstreet's poetry offered by Wiseman, Gray, and others collectively mount a sustained challenge to the view of the poet put forward by Rich and the *Norton Anthology of Women's Literature*,

---

[42] Jed, "The Tenth Muse"; Chedgzoy, *Women's Writing in the British Atlantic World*; Tamara Harvey, *Figuring Modesty in Feminist Discourse Across the Americas, 1633–1700* (Aldershot: Ashgate, 2008); Gillespie, "'This Briny Ocean Will O'erflow Your Shore.'"

[43] Jim Egan, "Creole Bradstreet: Philip Sidney, Alexander The Great, And English Identities," in Ralph Bauer and José Antonio Mazzotti (eds.), *Creole Subjects in the Colonial Americas: Empires, Texts, Identities* (Chapel Hill: University of North Carolina Press, for Omohundro Institute of Early American History and Culture, 2009), 219–40; Gabriele Rippl, "Mourning and Melancholia in England and its Transatlantic Colonies: Examples of Seventeenth-Century Female Appropriation," in M. Middeke and Christina Wald (eds.), *The Literature of Melancholia: Early Modern to Postmodern* (Basingstoke: Palgrave Macmillan, 2011), 50–66; Richard Gravil (ed.), "The Republic of Poetry: Transatlantic Continuities from Bradstreet to Plath," Special issue of *Symbiosis*, 7, 1 (2003).

these transatlantic studies mount a concerted critique of the "national literatures" premise that underwrites the *Norton Anthology of American Literature* and others of its ilk. For some scholars, the fact that Bradstreet has never seemed either "English" enough or "American" enough has been a source of concern. Transatlantic scholarship refuses the conventional boundaries of nation-state-based counter-canon building and embraces the ambivalent position Bradstreet occupies between ostensibly discrete national literatures as the source of interest and inquiry.

One final recent scholarly intervention worth noting here is Bradstreet's emergence as part of the eco-critical canon: in a transhistorical study structurally reminiscent of Wendy Martin's *An American Triptych*, Robert Boschman considers "ecology and Westward expansion" in the poetry of Anne Bradstreet, Elizabeth Bishop and Amy Clampitt; Michael Ziser compares Bradstreet with Edward Taylor as others have done before him but through an intriguingly specific lens in his essay "The Pomology of Eden: Apple Culture and Early New England Poetry"; and Irish poet Eavan Boland provides a meditative account of her encounters with Bradstreet's poetry, similar to Adrienne Rich's, in *Green Thoughts, Green Shades: Essays by Contemporary Poets on the Early Modern Lyric.*[44]

Recent political, transatlantic, and eco-critical approaches attest to the way that Bradstreet is appearing today in a variety of new canon formations. At the same time, scholarship on her work continues to flourish in the now established academic orientations of gender and religious studies. Recent scholarship on Bradstreet's poetry pursuing such topics is by no means limited to the original articulations and demarcations of these fields and it would be a mistake to perceive them as conservative (or transgressive) simply on the basis that their general approach has been adopted by parts (but by no means all) of the academy.[45] If we can determine

---

[44] Robert Boschman, *In The Way of Nature: Ecology and Westward Expansion in the Poetry of Anne Bradstreet, Elizabeth Bishop and Amy Clampitt* (Jefferson, NC: McFarland, 2009); Michael Ziser, "The Pomology of Eden: Apple Culture and Early New England Poetry," in Thomas Hallock, Ivo Kamps, and Karen L. Raber (eds.), *Early Modern Ecostudies: From the Florentine Codex to Shakespeare* (New York: Palgrave Macmillan, 2008), 193–215; Eavan Boland, "Finding Anne Bradstreet," in Jonathan F. S. Post (ed.), *Green Thoughts, Green Shades: Essays by Contemporary Poets on the Early Modern Lyric* (Berkeley: University of California Press, 2002), 176–90.

[45] Recent gender studies include: Abram Van Engen, "Advertising the Domestic: Anne Bradstreet's Sentimental Poetics," *Legacy: A Journal of American Women Writers*, 28.1 (2011), 47–68; Laura Major, "Anne Bradstreet: The Religious Poet as Mother," *Journal of the Association for Research on Mothering*, 7.1 (2005), 110–20; Alice Henton, "'Once Masculinities ... Now Feminines Awhile': Gendered Imagery and the Significance of Anne Bradstreet's *The Tenth Muse*," *New England Quarterly: A Historical Review of New England Life and Letters*, 85.2 (2012), 302–25. Recent religious studies include: Constance Furey, "Relational Virtue: Anne Bradstreet, Edward Taylor, and

anything from such a brief analysis of Anne Bradstreet's relationship to canonicity, it is that concepts such as orthodoxy and subversion inevitably create a domino effect: subversion follows orthodoxy follows subversion. And, to mangle the metaphor horribly, it does not always matter, ultimately, which domino is the chicken and which is the egg. It is the pattern and the process that determines what results can be produced.

Early modern women's studies have inherited a subversion versus orthodoxy model of canon formation, for both literary and critical canons, that, given the conditions governing the institutional emergence of the field, has been both understandable and unavoidable. But I would like to question a continued reliance on such a Bloom-based, clearly cannibalistic, model. I have no desire to overcome or consume my grandmothers, mothers, sisters and potential daughters in the field of early modern women's studies. Frankly, I think we could do better. Agonism is, after all, only one way that such relationships can be pursued. In suggesting alternatives, I do not discount the sometimes severe institutional pressures that exhort us to present our work as exceptional – as the chapter or book or grant project that will rip the veil away from our past misunderstandings and shine a bright new light on early modern women writers. A formalist analysis might be useful here: antagonistic techniques work well with conventional genres of disputation; rhetorically, they aim to shore up one end of a black and white argument that, despite forays into a grey area, will only be resolved by a binary conclusion of yes or no. My call for a deconstruction of these binaries might strike some as a retreat to what they see as a new critical orthodoxy – a theoretical indeterminacy of "neither and both" that satisfies no one. I would like to suggest that early modern women's studies has to a large extent been produced in that critical context and that we cannot expect conventional ideas of canonicity to adequately account for it.

Puritan Marriage," *Journal of Medieval and Early Modern Studies*, 42.1 (2012), 201–24; Richard J. DuRocher, "'Cropt by Th' Almighties Hand': Allegory as Theodicy in Anne Bradstreet's Poems on Her Grandchildren" in Ken Hiltner (ed.), *Renaissance Ecology: Imagining Eden in Milton's England* (Pittsburgh: Duquesne University Press, 2008), 217–28; Ludwig Deringer, "Religious Poetry and New England Verse: Anne Bradstreet's 'Here Followes Some Verses Upon the Burning of Our House' and Edward Taylors 'Huswifery,'" in René Dietrich, Oliver Scheiding, and Clemens Spahr (eds.), *A History of American Poetry: Contexts – Developments – Readings* (Trier, Germany: Wissenschaftlicher Verlag Trier [WVT], 2015), 7–22; Roxanne Harde, "'Then Soul and Body Shall Unite': Anne Bradstreet's Theology of Embodiment," in Michael Joseph Schuldiner and Roxanne Harde (eds.), *From Anne Bradstreet to Abraham Lincoln: Puritanism in America* (Lewiston, NY: Mellen Press, 2004), 1–50.

4

When We Swear to Tell the Truth
The Carleton Debates and Archival Methodology

Megan Matchinske

Eighty-five mentions of the word "truth" or "untruth" are on display in the Mary Carleton bigamy debates. "True" or "untrue" account for another fifty-six separate references.[1] Oftentimes several iterations of each can be found in a single passage. This should come as no surprise. These are, after all, a collection of pamphlets and broadsheets focusing on a trial – a trial that depends on legal truths to make its case. As the Clerk of the Peace warns jurors in *The Arraignment*: "*The evidence that you shall swear between our sovereign lord the king and the prisoner at the Bar, shall be the truth, the whole truth, and nothing but the truth.* So help you God."[2] Truth, then, is *the capstone issue* worrying speakers on both sides of the Carleton debate question, worrying but also motivating. Writers entering into the bigamy debate saw the questions of what is right and what is true as opportunities to think about how the world was changing. Adaptation and innovation were bringing new and more capacious understandings to bear on rigid and narrow categories of what constituted truth, categories that rejected those who did not share in sexual makeup, cultural antecedents, or social privileges. This debate is not just a matter of who is married to whom and how many times. The stakes, and we can feel them in the raucous approval that this woman generates from her supporters, are considerably higher, having more to do with

---

[1] There are another 128 adverbial mentions of truth ("truly," "forsooth," "verily"). The numbers would jump exponentially were I to begin enumerating general qualities that imply truthfulness such as "honesty, sincerity, and veracity." These tallies include only eleven of the sixteen pamphlets dating from 1663. The four that remain unchecked, as yet unavailable on EEBO and so not easily searchable, are: *The articles and charge of impeachment against the German lady* (London: G. Winnam, 1663); *The Westminster Wedding, or, Carlton's Epithalamium* (London: S.B., 1663); *The Tryall of Mis Mary Carleton (formerly the German Lady, Henereta Maria de Woolva)* (London: Printed for N. Brook, 1663); *The Female Hector, or, the Germane Lady turn'd Monsieur* (London: N. Dorrington, 1663).
[2] Mary Carleton, *The Arraignment, Tryal and Examination of Mary Moders, otherwise Stedman, Now Carleton* (London: N. Brook, 1663), 5.

what people make of themselves and what comes to define the verity of one's life. When we look at the Mary Carleton bigamy tracts, we see not simply one definition of truth or even two, but rather myriad, sometimes radically different, notions of what counts as real vying for our attention.

The writers of these tracts cannot agree precisely on what happened, how it happened, to whom it happened, or which member of the Carleton couple – husband or wife – has suffered the most as a result of its uncertain consequences. And so for each of them, what is true and what is false carries separate meanings. Yet taken together, in community, their jarring and discordant voices do on occasion extend the notion of truth in its entirety. Like magnets that both attract and repel, the two main participants possess mirror traits, often antagonistic and ineffectual but on occasion useful and productive. I want to think about the sites they hold in common and alone, the conversations they generate together and apart as a foray into the question of critical methodology. Engaging the problem of their wide-ranging and often disparate "truths," I consider what it means to be part of a cacophonous, debating community of truth speakers who, despite their disagreements, share the same goals.

Of course, we are not they. Early modern feminist scholars DO NOT engage in brawling. And, in any case, accusations of bigamy seem unlikely to inspire confidence in lasting truths, much less the very concept of what it means to keep faith. Or do they? Again and again, this trial illustrates, both in its performance and in its debates, some of the methodological quandaries that continue to beset modern-day truth seekers who disagree as to the nature of what constitutes the past, what qualifies as evidence, and how one goes about proving things that happened long ago.

And as for the trial itself … Let me offer a few facts for those less familiar with the litigants. After a hasty romance that may or may not have been designed by one or both parties with the aim of bilking the other, Mary and John are wed. Additional funds not forthcoming, it is quickly discovered that Mary (née Moders or Wallway) may be already married to another. She is thrown in prison, defends herself at trial, and is acquitted. Within two weeks of the trial's conclusion there appears a rash of publications on both sides of the debate.

Two Truths

Two passages, one from John and a second from Mary reveal their different perspectives on what truth means. I want to begin our discussion by looking at both, taking into account their use of one particular formal evidentiary site – the letter – first to tease out their separate standards and then to pull them forward into an interrogation of contemporary method. Our first encounter, drawn from *The Replication*, nostalgically pines for a truth undressed, a truth without disguise. It also seeks for a sense of shared value – common ground. John explains:

> I am not ignorant of the various rumours, reports, stories, fancies, daily increasing fables, and Proteus shapes wherein the different humours and dispositions of the world bring forth the late acted project and cheat. And though I might be justly angry with some, yet I scorn to take notice of any. For should I begin to undress all these prodigious shapes and set them out singly in the naked truth, into what a confused chaos should I bring myself? How endless should I make my sufferings? How many years might I lead my life in discontent before I could hear, answer, and satisfy the many niceties, questions, curiosities, and objections of the giddy-headed vulgar? Qui non ad veritatem rei, sed ad opinionem prospiciunt. I am satisfied, that as a little time will make a distinction between the report and the reality, so it will put a conclusion to both, by burying them in oblivion.[3]

For John, an undressed truth is truth in its purest form. And the sooner it is exposed, the faster its detractors' "curiosities" will be buried in "oblivion." John knows truth when he sees it. Using clothing metaphors to describe both the gaudy overreaching of an obscene costume and the hidden horrors of a misshapen lie, John attempts to winnow out all social, cultural, and material factors that may affect a single searcher for a communal truth. He begins by describing the protean shapes that populate Mary's truth-claims, insisting that their formal changes have radically deformed them, altering their ability to speak honestly; now they are little more than *rumours, reports, stories, fancies,* [and] *daily increasing fables.*

When we strip John's metaphoric truth of its clothes, what remains is an essential purity – a truth that is stable, universal, and timeless. In order to achieve this elemental thing, John must rid himself of externals: things that, ostensibly, don't count; ephemera, jewels, and costume, of course, but also time of day, situation, and context. Should it matter if it was raining, or if it happened on a Thursday? Ostensibly not. Think for a moment of truth as a platonic ideal – an absolute certainty on which all can agree, or perhaps the Aristotelian belief that what renders us human

[3] John Carleton, *The Replication* ([S.I] Printed by the author's appointment, 1663), 2.

is our shared view on matters of good and evil. Material manifestations fall away before a timeless, placeless, and perhaps even prelingual truth.

Before we leave John's metaphoric truth, let's try to be aware of what is torn asunder as we seek out essence. What else shouldn't count? Status, nationality, and gender? Are all of our truth quests invariably without motive or provocation? Are they always or inherently absent of interested parties? Might there be certain bodies that suffer that exposure more often than others? Women's bodies perhaps? Foreign bodies? Poorer bodies? Not all truth motivations are unbiased. John's family wanted Mary as a daughter when they believed her to be a German princess and were willing to do anything to secure that connection no matter how duplicitous. They spent well beyond their means to convince her that their son was a gentleman of some worth, when clearly he was not.

John may be well intentioned in his efforts to tease apart truth from rumor, but his awkward avowal of his own participation in its defrocking clearly unsettles him. *For should I begin to undress all these prodigious shapes and set them out singly in the naked truth, into what a confused chaos should I bring myself*? He wonders, and the memory uncomfortably recalls for readers another brutal unveiling, one that occurs as he and his family rip Mary's clothing from her body in their attempt to elicit truth, presumably through forced confession. In that scene of torture, Mary describes how John's "father cometh to my lodging … [with] my husband and … [they] called me [a] cheat and [a] harlot, [and] violently stripped me of all my apparel and jewels, pulled off my silk stockings from my legs, cut the lace of my bodice, and scarce left me anything to cover my nakedness with."[4]

Now let's turn to Mary's handling of truth. It is longer and more capacious. It is also more capricious. Mary cites sources – classical sources – as if she is about to offer a disputation on truth.[5] Ventriloquized through noted philosophers, Epimenides and Anaxarchus, her discussion, is filled with qualifiers that define truth metaphorically. While some of Mary's points seem coincident with those of her husband, others are more

---

[4] Mary Carleton, *An Historical Narrative* (London: Charles Moulton, 1663), 6.
[5] Mary also quotes Chilon of Sparta, one of the seven sages. All three of the philosophers that Mary cites may derive from the same source: a nineteenth-century American self-help book contains almost identical references, suggesting that the citations come from one source. See Henry Davenport Northrup, "The Cardinal Virtues," in *Character Building: Or Principles, Precepts and Practices Which Make Life a Success* (Philadelphia, PA: International Publishing Co., 1896), 226–8. Northrup discerns no irony in the text whatsoever.

enigmatic, withholding information and leaving readers to fill in the blanks. Here are the "truths" that she gives us:

> *Epimenides,*[6] the philosopher being asked by the *Rhodians* what that virtue called *truth* was, answered [that] *truth* is that thing whereof ... the gods do make profession and the virtue that illuminateth the heaven and the earth, maintaineth justice, governeth, preserveth, and protecteth a state or kingdom, and ... maketh all doubtful and ambiguous matters clear and apparent.
>
> The *Lacedemonians*, inquisitive after this rare virtue, importuned *Anaxarchus*[7] to delineate *truth* to them. He drew its portraiture in these faire lines, *viz. Truth* is a perpetual *health* and *welfare*, a life without ending, an unguent that healeth all misfortunes, a sun always shining that never suffereth by eclipse, a gate never shut, [and] a journey in which none can wax weary: it's a virtue, without which all strength is feebleness and infirmness itself; wisdom, [both] folly and madness.

Like John, Mary seems to be seeking a truth that's already been discovered. She purportedly finds it in the classical past, among reputable authorities. The answers she offers seem banal enough, at least at first glance: truth is a virtue and a light – it illuminates all things. Truth heals, it journeys, it is tireless, strong, and wise. But are those really the answers she wants us to take away? And are these philosophers likely to impart such advice sincerely? Epimenides, like Chilo, whom Mary also cites, are sophists. In some early modern circles, both were reviled, often simplistically so, for their failure to articulate what might be understood as a foundational truth. By the mid-seventeenth century, however, such early Greek thinkers, once celebrated for their wisdom (*sophia*) had largely been reappropriated, brought back into the fold. No longer dismissed as empty rhetoricians, "sophistical" in their use of deceptive or confusing argumentation, they now served a variety of political, religious, social, and ethical functions within seventeenth-century thought. For those who had lived through the wars, both thinkers offered ideas about knowledge transmission that seemed presciently aware of the complexities of a rapidly changing environment. Speculative and human-centered, amenable to disagreements between and across perceptive categories, they were used to open up new and different ways to interpret religion, law, and

---

[6] A Cretan philosopher who lived in the sixth century BC. Diogenes Laertius mentions three men named Epimenides: see *Lives of Eminent Philosophers, Volume I,* trans. R. D. Hicks, Loeb Classical Library 184 (Cambridge, MA: Harvard University Press, 1925), 121.

[7] A fourth-century BC Greek philosopher and companion to Alexander the Great.

political will that played an important role in coping with the vagaries of a shifting landscape.[8]

So when Mary tells us that Epimenides answered that "*truth* is that thing whereof ... the gods do make profession" what exactly does she mean? Is she hailing perhaps the *one True God* with whom this philosopher is most closely associated: Zeus? We know him today for the "Epimenides Paradox": "All Cretans are liars," he swears, attacking his people for building a tomb to house a god who is not dead but immortal. A Cretan himself, Epimenides seems either to have forgotten his own implication in his rush to judgment or to be toying with his audience, fully aware that he has caught himself and his listeners in a catch-22.[9] If he says all Cretans are liars, and he's a lying Cretan, then ... not only is the passage not true, but it cannot be false either. While *our* Epimenides is most familiar for his paradox, it is clear that Renaissance writers already recognized the philosopher's compromised stance as a lying Cretan.[10]

It seems to me that Mary isn't simply playfully admitting the fraud that ballasts her case, though I suppose we could argue as much. Rather Epimenides's double call to truth asks readers for a greater field of vision, to hold on to more than one meaning at a time, to accept as possible the likelihood that something could be right as well as wrong, good as well as bad, and true as well as false, making "all doubtful and ambiguous matters clear and apparent." When we credit the content of the lines

---

[8] See: Brendan Dooley, *The Social History of Skepticism: Experience and Doubt in Early Modern Culture* (Baltimore and London: The Johns Hopkins University Press, 1999); Luciano Floridi, *Sextus Empiricus: The Transmission and Recovery of Pyrrhonism* (Oxford: Oxford University Press, 2002); Melissa Caldwell, *Skepticism and Belief in Early Modern England: The Reformation of Moral Value* (New York: Routledge, 2017), 224–8.

[9] In his *Cretica*, Epimenides vows that Zeus "livest and abidest forever" while attacking his own people for building a tomb to house his dead body. Our evidence for reading the Epimenides paradox through the *Cretica* comes from a biblical scholar writing at the turn of the twentieth century: see a series of articles by J. Rendel Harris in *The Expositor*: 7.2.4 (1906), 305–17, 7.3.4 (1907), 332–7, and 8.4.4 (1912), 348–53. In Titus 1.12, Paul appropriates *Cretica's* verse, and Aratus further revises its last line (see his *Phaenomena*, in *Callimachus, Hymns and Epigrams: Lycophron: Aratus*, trans. A. W. Mair and G. R. Mair, Loeb Classical Library 129 (Cambridge: Harvard University Press, 1921), lines 1–5).

[10] "[Y]et notwithstanding the people of that countrey [Crete] were noted to be vicious, and shamefull lyers, as Epimendides wrote in a verse, recited by Saint Paule, in his Epistle to Titus, saying: Cretes always bene lyers, ungracious beastes, and slouthfull panches," in Thomas Cooper's *Thesaurus linguae Romanae & Britannicae tam accurate congestus* ([London: Henry Denham, 1578], s.v. "creta, æ, fœ, g. and e, es"). While Paul cites no sources in Titus, Clement of Alexandria makes the connection explicit: see *The Fathers of the Church: Stromateis, Books 1–3*, vol. 85, trans. John Ferguson (Washington, DC: Catholic University of America, 1991), book 1, Chapter 14, 66ff. Speculating that Epimenides might be the last of the seven sages, Clement acknowledges the philosopher's link to lying, his connection to the Pauline reference, and the irony of his status as a Cretan accusing Cretans.

themselves, Epimenides's reprimand against his own people isn't only the collapse of an impossible truth, it also carries a religious charge that depends on just such illogical, faith-based thinking; in their ignorance, the philosopher's lying countrymen have failed to acknowledge the divinity of the one true God, and for that they have damned themselves and all of Crete. Understood from this perspective, Epimenides's willingness to take a stand against his people based on *true* faith may underscore the risk that Mary is willing to undertake in order to defend her own position, come what may.

Moving to the second of Mary's sources, we can see how far she is willing to go to reinforce in her audience this sense of wider vision. Anaxarchus, slightly later than Epimenides, offers us an even more pluralizing image. Mary begins by telling us about his depiction of truth as if in portraiture, and the connection is apt. A student of Metrodorus of Chios, Anaxarchus can be defined, like Epimenides, as a skeptic, closely attracted to both Democritean atomism and the Pyrrhonism of Sextus Empiricus.[11] Where his mentor was ostensibly supposed to have claimed that he knew nothing, not even the fact that he knew nothing, Anaxarchus was himself attacked for sabotaging the validity of truth claims by likening real-life objects to scene paintings and arguing that both were equivalent to the experiences of madmen and dreamers.[12] Here the idea of perception is literally called into question as it is shifted onto the landscape that orders its interactions. Mary hints at the representationally mirroring truths alive in her commentary, mentioning both the "delineat[ion of] *truth* [as] … portraiture" and the "folly and madness" that belie wisdom. In drawing our attention to sophists and skeptics, with their more challenging notions of truth and its perceptually fractious qualities, Mary seems intent on introducing potentially satirical elements into her discussion, not again, I think, simply to call attention to the fact of her own fraud but rather to ask us to linger over the idea of truth as that which cannot be fully or finally defined or confined.

John talks of an essential truth, and Mary recognizes the degree to which truth adapts to both its moment and speaker. John understands truth as a means to correct something that has gone awry; Mary sees it

---

[11] Laertius tells us that Anaxarchus was key to the development of Pyrrho's philosophical disposition, including his own focus on the suspension of judgment in cases where to judge will do no good: see Diogenes Laertius, *Lives of Eminent Philosophers, Volume 2*, trans. R. D. Hicks, Loeb Classical Library 185 (Cambridge: Harvard University Press, 1925), book 9, chapter 10, lines 271–3.

[12] Sextus Empiricus, *Sextus Empiricus: Against the Logicians*, trans. R. G. Bury, Loeb Classical Library 291 (Cambridge: Harvard University Press, 1935), book 1, line 88.

as untapped potential. So what do we make of their different definitions? Of their shared goals? Can truth restore a past that never was by readjusting already perfect categories with a new set of as yet untried players? John believes he belongs in that "truth" scenario as one of its natural winners. In contrast, truth, Mary promises, is whatever you make of it; it will serve you in good stead; it will allow you to recreate your life, fitting it to your dreams and aspirations. All it takes are the voices of men known for their wisdom and valor, willing or able to speak on your behalf, a ready wit, quick to take advantage of whatever circumstances come your way, and the belief in oneself and the faith in one's convictions: the certainty that your own personal truths will remain rock solid in the face of adversity and public denial. Because she has yet to find what she is looking for, her truth is somewhere up ahead, undefined, negotiable, and still open for debate. In contrast, her husband seems to understand a world where certainties have already been established and order simply needs to be restored. How do two such simple claims give rise to the vexed business of writing history, of reading the archives, and thinking about early modern gender?

Modern Methodologies and the Trouble with Truth

In the following discussion, I want to talk about problems of method in light of these separate understandings and how they affect our choice and framing of our arguments. I want to suggest as well that these problems persist *regardless of content* (the things that we choose to study). We are trained to be attentive to the archive. We have been taught best practices and appropriate investigative methods, we can ably recognize protocols, we understand the importance of working within communities to ensure that our work is carefully vetted and know when to get the help we need on the issues with which we are less familiar or inadequately skilled. We also realize, because we are dealing with the past, that there are invariably things still out there that we cannot understand, materials as yet not discovered that may shed further light on our subject and change what we think about it. We understand as well that much has been lost. Large swaths of information are simply unrecoverable. We have no access to them, nor will we, however diligently we seek. Further complicating this scenario, we recognize that the kinds of material that we are able to locate – texts, monuments, structures, artifacts – limit what we can know. Were we able somehow to embrace other forms of experience or knowledge, if we could, for instance, slip back in time to feel the chaotic terror of the Bailey court when the gallows beckon, or catch the horrible scent of midden in London streets, we would "know" in a very different way.

Because we are reaching back to times, places, and figures that left only a few traces behind them (for me, a late seventeenth-century bigamy trial in London and a woman named Mary Carleton),[13] we are often left with gaps, holes that we cannot fill but must instead simply attempt to imagine.[14] These aporia can be frightening to new scholars. There is a sense too that we would get it more right if only we had more information. And that makes sense. Obviously, our accuracy should improve when we are better informed, when we have more materials upon which to ground our studies. This idea of more is better has been around for some time. In the preface to his *Britannia*, William Camden adheres to an accretive model, suggesting that later historians will take up the banner and carry on in his footsteps. Writers can ultimately create a more *perfect* truth, he believes, provided that they continue to take their archival work seriously.[15] While writers like John Milton are more skeptical about the likelihood of ever reaching that perfection in this world, he is perhaps more savvy as well about the degree to which different "truths" may bear the same foundational integrity and yet be remarkably different in voice,

[13] Unknown aside from her scandalous trial, Mary left no life documentation. Not a holder of public office, not qualified to put her name to assembly vote or a tax assessment, she lacked one essential quality – she was not male. While other reasons might keep people from the historical record, we as feminist scholars recognize the often restrictive limitations imposed on our historical endeavors. Unless we are writing about someone like Elizabeth I or Marguerite de Navarre, traditional resources can be scarce. The traces that we seek are often more *ephemeral* than other archival matter, perhaps because they were printed without proper imprimatur or formal licensing, perhaps because the paper that marks their record was cheaply made or printed in limited supplies, perhaps because they only circulated in manuscript copies among an elite coterie, or perhaps because of one of the many and varied restrictions that have so ably been identified by feminist scholars dealing with the textual afterlives of women writers in our period. See, for instance, Natalie Zemon Davis, "Gender and Genre: Women as Historical Writers, 1400–1820," *University of Ottawa Quarterly*, 50, 1 (1980), 123–44.

[14] For accounts that attempt to theorize the imaginative aspect of our scholarship, see Jed, "The Tenth Muse"; Matchinske, *Writing, Gender and State in Early Modern England*, chapter 2.

[15] See William Camden, *Britannia* (London: Georgii Bishop & Ioannis Norton, 1610), fol. 5ᵛ. See also: Thomas Blundeville, *The True Order and Methode of Writing and Reading Hystories* (London: Willyam Seres, 1574; reprint Frankfurt: Verlag Peter Lang, 1986); Walter Ralegh, *The History of the World* (London: William Stansby, 1614), fols. Aʳ–C3ʳ. The idea of "more is better" has hurt early modern feminist studies and other underrepresented arenas of thought in that it is often difficult to access *as much* archival material on women as it is on men. The same can be said for attempts to access information about other low-status commoners of either sex; those who left little to no record behind of their doings are at a disadvantage when truth scales only value the quantity of evidence that scholars are able to bring forth in proving their case.

intent, and meaning.[16] We often find ourselves struggling with what may seem to be a rather limited set of options: too little evidence; tired and worn patterns of study; gender mindsets that are distinctly anti-feminist.

We've got a job to do, and we want to do it responsibly. We also want our work to be recognized by our peers. Ideally we may wish too that it could receive a wider audience, that somehow our students were listening, that the words we exchange in our courses matter and that they might go beyond the walls of our classrooms. We strive to ensure that our articles find that broader community of readers and listeners. And, like any writer worth her salt, we do ourselves great harm if we forget the "storied" nature of our tellings. It behooves us then to provide folks with a throughway – a means of deciphering what we have found. Negotiating across disparate materials, uncertain as to how to navigate the blanks where time and memory have simply dropped away, we must tread carefully, speak openly as to what we see and what we cannot see. We must not forget that we are writing to the present and to an audience who will only care if we make them care. Mary's tale of her trial worked, and it worked better and longer because she told it so well. Responding to the back and forth bickering of the pamphlets that preceded her account, picking up on their abusive rhetoric and making it her own, Mary recreated herself not only as London's *cause célèbre* but also as one of its preeminent storytellers: "Let the world now judge, whither being prompted by such plain and public signs of a design upon me, to coun- terplot them, I have done any more then what the rule and a received principle of justice directs: *to deceive the deceiver, is no deceit.*"[17] Whatever other truths, then, are on the table – getting the facts right, securing leave time to visit the archive, making sure we've obliged our dissertation com- mittee, completing our tenure requirements – making sure we've got a story worth telling is the one truth we ought not to forget.

Have I scared you already, with that word "storied"? Gotten your hackles up? What is she talking about? Scholars don't make things up. We try our best to tell the truth, paying special heed to ideas of due dili- gence. Yet in a case like this, we must continually decide between *differ- ent versions* of what is right and what is true. Marked by fabrications and

---

[16] While Milton is referring here to the central metaphysical Truth rather than a purely historical truth, he applies the same term – truth – to both categories: see John Milton, *Areopagitica*, in Merritt Y. Hughes (ed.), *Complete Poems and Major Prose* (Indianapolis: Hackett Publishing Company, 1957), 742.

[17] Mary Carleton, *The Case of Madam Mary Carleton* (London: Sam: Speed and Hen: Marsh, 1663), 38.

mis-sayings bearing the imprimatur of truth, the Carleton tracts make that task difficult. Mary claims that she is the daughter of a German barrister of considerable wealth and prestige, that she was orphaned young and brought up in a convent. John, on the other hand, avers that she is the daughter of a Canterbury fiddler. Both of them use different kinds of proof to state their claims. While I cannot know definitely that Mary is likely to have lived in England longer than she claims she has, that her background is lower than she led her husband to believe, and that she has pulled a few cons before, I suspect that this is so. Should I let that "assumption" inform the way that I talk about this material? I am also passionately committed to working on women and gender in early modern England, to thinking about whatever I work on through that lens. How do I allow that predisposition to *responsibly* inform my handling of this material without *doing jeopardy* to the archival and historical matter that I discover?

Is it our job as historians and literary critics of the past to simply describe what we see or are we doing more than that every time we reach out to engage with these writers? As careful as we necessarily must be in attending to the materials, to heeding the archive, and looking deeply at the evidence, we actively shape what we encounter according to dispositions that matter to us.[18] Unlike John, I believe that time changes perception and that language, meaning, emotion – all of these human concepts – are constantly evolving as a result of the ways in which they are deployed. Looking back offers us an opportunity to gauge how and when those shifts are likely to occur. Looking back at women's words allows me an opportunity to test those boundaries in an area that is directly relevant and meaningful to me in my life. I want to see that women can effect change – for better and for worse.

So ... back to the question I just posed: what *is* our responsibility when we engage these subjects? The Carleton trials are messy. The woman they describe may be *very very* guilty: a con artist, already wed to two or three or four husbands by the time we hear about her; she may also be a thief. Should her criminal background change how we approach her as the subject of our study? Do we simply gather our evidence and let it build or are we being disingenuous in making such claims? Can evidence

---

[18] Felski, "Context Stinks," 582, reminds us of the bait and switch techniques we often employ to mask our self-interest: "We explicate the puzzle of our attachments by invoking veiled determinations and covert social interests, while paying scant attention to the ways in which texts may solicit our affections, court our emotions, and feed our obsessions."

really speak for itself or does it always need a little bit of intellectual prodding (even if that prodding only happens at a subconscious level)?

The questions I'm asking here, posed philosophically in one mode or
another of historical writing since Herodotus (or his scribe) first put ink
to papyrus, apply across the board to the studies that currently occupy
gender scholars in our field.[19] Take for example our recent interests in
new formalism. Focusing on the disposition of texts within a discursive field, new formalism asks us to pay attention to the forms that we
examine as we engage the past – to consider their aesthetic power and
the myriad social, representational, and historical effects to which they
can be put (history operating in the service of form). Once upon a time,
new historicism wanted us to position these same texts within time, to
think about all types of writings, no matter their form, within a shared
network of institutions, practices, and politics, trying to gauge their
relationships accordingly (form succumbing to history, place, and position). Presumably, if we are serious about what we do, it is likely that we
come out somewhere within the bailiwick of these two theoretical frames,
attentive to both formal and temporal questions as we approach our
materials.

For the purposes of my discussion here, I am going to assume as
much, returning for a moment to the preeminent truth-site in the
debate – to the letters that demand both their attention and ours. Again
and again we find Mary and John turning to epistles to justify and con-
solidate their proof claims. Letters evince a material reality above and
beyond the other matter that makes up these tracts. Both speakers seem
intent to possess, post, intercept, debunk, destroy, and display epistolary
content. Letters in the debate *appear to embody* three types of unfiltered
truth. In matters of love, exchanged between two people, they ostensibly
reveal authentic feelings not easily expressed. In matters of personal communication, they suggest proof of status and income. And in matters
accusatory, they offer material evidence of a particular disposition that
can be entered into court record. Within the litigious world of the trial,
letters serve as legal ballast. "A true copy of the letter I will here insert,"[20]
John tells us in one instance. "[My husband] sent me this letter," Mary

---

[19] See, for instance: Johann Gottfried von Herder, *Outlines of a Philosophy of the History of Man*,
trans. T. Churchill (London: J. Johnson, 1800); Friedrich Nietzsche, "On the Use and Abuse of
History for Life (1874)," in *Untimely Meditations*, Daniel Breazeale (ed.), trans. R. J. Hollingdale
(Cambridge: Cambridge University Press, 1997); Wilhelm Dilthey, *Pattern and Meaning in
History: Thoughts on History & Society*, H. P. Rickman (ed.) (New York: Harper, 1962).
[20] John Carleton, *The Ultimate Vale of John Carleton* (London: J. Jones, 1663), 27.

avers in another, "the copy of which I here insert *verbatim*, the which I have now by me and shall keep it as a relict." While letters hold documentary power above and beyond other words spoken in the Carleton debate, it is clear that the fascination continues and commodifies, becoming for a time an integral component of budding novelistic practices and giving rise to several epistolary fictions outside and beyond the world of this trial.[21] Printers producing these tracts recognize the residual aesthetic power that letters evoke – the thing that makes them seem *more real* – and so distinguish them by the use of unusual typographic markers (i.e., italics, indents, changes in font, etc.).

Ironically, though, as we well know, at least since Derrida's mock send-up of *la carte postale*,[22] claims to authenticity are about the only thing you *cannot count on* in letter writing. John calls Mary's efforts *chimera-letters*[23] and, given Mary's more ample understanding of what constitutes truth, this insult may not be that far off. She certainly admits to encoding her letters, hoping either to withhold information that could harm her reputation or to suggest more to avid listeners than meets the eye: "I knew very well the uncertainty of my condition here, and therefore … [my] letters were merely ciphers."[24]

Aware that letters begin and end in an already finished moment, creating odd and interesting time stutters when they are placed within other temporalities that continue around them unabated, we traverse the narrative of the debate letters through their formal and their historical registers. We can talk about the post, but only prior to its formal beginnings; we can speculate about the qualities of parchment, but only in the abstract; and the same goes for the hands found in the letters, as again, everything we read in these debates is merely representational. No letters exist for them to reference.

And so we are back to the same problem. In a study devoted to form and its aesthetic power, what do we do when the materiality that authorizes these letters is absent? How do we account for what's missing? As new historical formalists we find we are just as vulnerable to

---

[21] M. Carleton, *An Historical Narrative*, 12. See Edmé Boursault, *Lettres de respect, d'obligation et d'amour* (Paris: Theodore Girard, 1669), and Gabriel-Joseph de la Vergne, comte de Guilleragues, *Lettres portugaises* (Paris: Claude Barbin, 1669). Aphra Behn's *Love-Letters between a Nobleman and His Sister* was published in three parts in 1684, 1685, and 1687.

[22] Jacques Derrida, *The Post Card: From Socrates to Freud and Beyond*, trans. Alan Bass (Chicago: University of Chicago Press, 1980).

[23] J. Carleton, *Ultimate Vale*, 24.

[24] M. Carleton, *Case*, 136.

improvisation as new historicists; we just improvise around different artifacts. Our truths veer as we command them; sometimes the frames they fit are shaped with purpose; at other times they bend of their own accord. But bend they do, and stretch they often will.

In a world where we expect our broadcasters to spin our news rather than relay it, the problem of ungrounded truth is particularly vexed. While many of us recognize the fluidity of truth claims at one and the same instant that we aspire to accuracy, heed facts as they appear, and respect established protocols of right and wrong, growing currents in contemporary culture seem intent on shattering the pact of civil discourse, on breaking apart those relational agreements that support how we as humans interpret and evaluate not just what happens around us but also the way we ought to conduct our lives. This leads me to my last and most important point. Methodology can be a murky business. Sometimes deciding which path to take can make us uncomfortable. Sometimes it can even push us past our ethical limits. What constitutes a sound history? And how can we be sure we've written one?

Historical Community

Much like modern witnesses to the past, Mary and John participate in an extended debate about the nature of evidence and worry about what counts as true. They also spend a portion of their time in a trial setting where the early vestiges of court protocols are being set in place – the selection of jurors, beginnings of *voir dire* process, the calling of witnesses, the presentation of material evidence, and the recording and documenting of trial proceedings. I want to introduce one last element into this discussion of methodological principles.

Something significant and something communal happens every time we as scholars engage with the past; something that speaks to the essence of historical awareness and occurs over time and in a shared space. This experience is further developed during the writing process as we piece our ideas together and gather our research into a coherent whole. As we research the past, time slows, creating a productive and oddly communal space, a space where we may quietly interact with our peers, engage with our evidence, disagree with ourselves, and mull over what it is that we are doing.[25] Writing reinforces "exchange by prolonging its debates and

---

[25] Megan Matchinske, "Women's Kinship Networks: A Meditation on Creative Genealogies and Historical Labor," with Michelle Dowd, Julie Eckerle, and Jennifer Kopalcoff, in Merry

inscribing them in print. History writing keeps participant positions synchronically present by committing them to memory and to narrative."[26]

As I've mentioned elsewhere,

> [T]he process of history writing is complicated and arduous. We rely on multiple sources to make sense of prior events – we visit the archive, we converse with others who share our historical interests, we contact specialists who carry expertise in less familiar fields, we worry over niggling details, over pieces that do not fit, we debate with our colleagues over method and matter, and finally we share our precious insights with our students – all of this "work" makes up the laborious business of remembering (and labor is key term here).[27]

Our labors, the business of method, take space and time. And that is when our work, inextricably linked to the communities we value, is examined, judged, and juried.

The Carleton debate tracts are dissonant, raucous, and anarchic. No one agrees about anything. Every new point of contention must be painstakingly fought over and talked about. For us, encounters with already familiar sites of study are more generously shared, more openly valued. We read the work of those who came before us and take to heart the lessons that we will not have to learn entirely alone. I remember early on in my graduate career worrying over the possibility of having my work "scooped," of writing too slowly on a subject that was gaining momentum in another university. Little did I know how absurd that concern would be, not because I would in the end write fast enough, but because such concerns rarely matter. Each of us *truly* sees a different facet of history's rich tapestry, following one of many wandering paths through to its various representations of "truth". We build on one another's work, and, yes, we bicker over what seems right and how to make it so, but we are the stronger for our collective and communal truths.

So far scholars have located sixteen separate pamphlets and broadsheets written about the Carleton bigamy trial in 1663, a total of twenty-six published by 1673, the year Mary was finally executed. Several of the pamphlets repeat verbatim elements of earlier tracts, phrases, letters ostensibly exchanged by the married couple, folios borrowed whole cloth from one text to another. It is clear as well that the writers, several of them perhaps authoring several tracts at once, read each other, borrowing words and

---

Weisner-Hanks et al. (ed.), *Attending to Early Modern Women: Remapping Routes and Spaces* (Delaware: Associated University Presses, 2015), 247.

[26] Matchinske, *Women Writing History*, 130 and 150.

[27] Matchinske, "Women's Kinship Networks," 247.

ideas. Commentaries take sides, actively countering opponents who may disagree. In addition to the pamphlets, we also find evidence of the trial available through the Old Bailey Online, the National Archives (London Sessions Records and the Middlesex Sessions Records), the London Metropolitan Archives (St Mary Woolchurch Parish Register Records), and, of course, the State Papers.[28] More helpful even than those archival documents, at least for those of us who were not formally trained as historians, are the numerous references that we rely on to educate us in all of the matters both arcane and esoteric in which we are ill-informed. And so, again and again I find myself turning to friends and colleagues: to Eileen Spring and Amy Louise Erickson for discussion of women and property; to Cynthia Herrup for information on the criminal courts; to Fran Dolan and Laura Gowing for work on gender and domestic space; and to so many others. The debts, my obligations to my peers, are endless and ongoing.[29]

In the cacophony of voices, my argument takes shape, borrowing from one strand of text and then another. Sometimes the material I use is more synthesized, sometimes less. In all cases at least some degree of prior meddling has occurred, even before I begin to fiddle. But, I want to return for a moment to the trial and to the initial debaters. They are talking to one another. Their voices do not exist in a vacuum. Indeed, the richness of this site comes from that density, from the myriad voices that make it happen. The same is true for the matter we study and the means by which we acquire our knowledge. The tools we use are multiform, and with each encounter we are further educated. As we learn more, our truths change; they are not rendered incoherent. All of a sudden an image of the Washington mall is not read to contain three times as many

---

[28] We sometimes track down "non-evidence" as well. When, for instance, Mary's detractors tell us about her former marriage to Thomas Steadman, a cobbler, in St Mildred's Parish, Canterbury, Kent, we look for clues in places where we expect to find none. We have been told that the Parish Register recording the marriage was not kept: *"the former clerk did seldom or never register any marriage"* (J. Carleton, *Ultimate Vale*, 34). The same is true in regard to Mary's first bigamy trial (a rather more likely site to find concrete data). We go to the Dover quarter sessions to find the indictment and the trial. And again, neither exists.

[29] On property, see Amy Louise Erickson, *Women and Property in Early Modern England* (London: Routledge, 1993), and Eileen Spring, *Law, Land, and Family: Aristocratic Inheritance in England, 1300 to 1800* (Chapel Hill: University of North Carolina Press, 1997). See also Ng, *Literature and the Politics of Family* and Lawrence Stone, *Family, Sex, and Marriage in England, 1500–1800* (London: Weidenfeld & Nicholson, 1977). On law, see: Cynthia Herrup, *The Common Peace: Participation and the Criminal Law in Seventeenth-Century England* (Cambridge: Cambridge University Press, 1987); J. M. Beattie, *Crime and the Courts of England, 1660–1800* (Ann Arbor: University of Michigan Press, 1986); Thomas A. Green, *Verdicts According to Conscience: Perspectives on the English Criminal Trial Jury, 1200–1800* (Chicago: University of Chicago Press, 1987). On domesticity, see Dolan, *Dangerous Familiars* and Gowing, *Domestic Dangers*.

people as we actually see in attendance.[30] Instead, what we know shifts as a result of evidentiary claims that we as group have recognized as valid, claims that speak to our shared sense of what constitutes legitimate historical protocol. As we correspond with each other, ask questions, read articles, attend conferences, listen to papers, teach classes, engage with our students, do our administrative work, all of those activities impinge on our truths in like fashion. And in like fashion, they make rich the work we create. They also make it "honest."

Like Mary, we exist in a skeptical world, where foundational truths and historical certainties are hard to come by. What is less difficult is the realization that language is the only medium we have through which to evaluate truth and that our strength as scholars comes in our willingness to labor hard together in order to understand how different formal, social, and historical categories operate, to use our expertise and the expertise of those around us to navigate across a terrain increasingly marked by truth wars. That is our strength. "Collaborative" peer investigation and evaluation – multifaced scholarly input – these are the elements that ensure our continued attention to source material, that secure the validity of our work, and that will, in the future, better expand our audiences, are we to more frequently involve our colleagues in joint research projects.

When Mary hears John talking about her "excellent parts," she makes sure to include those passages verbatim in her accounts.[31] His words become the foundational frame for the way that she styles the ensuing recreations of herself, turning his "parts" into hers. Part of an ongoing conversation, our works accrete as well. So, I ask again, what "truths" are tapped when history is considered and compiled? What phenomena mark its duration? What do we acquire in the willing act of remembering above and beyond the facts, events, and circumstances that we unearth? There is something that is essential to what history does for us and to us that occurs not simply in direct and easy recall but rather in the struggle to retrieve and refigure, to read through and debate. Our efforts make "true" what is past by bringing it into the present and by giving it a relational value that locates and secures its content in time – our time. More than simply a sum of "excellent parts," those truths become "truly" meaning-full in that past-future totality.

---

[30] Tim Wallace, Karen Yourish, and Tory Griggs, "Trump's Inauguration vs. Obama's: Comparing the Crowds," *New York Times*, January 20, 2017, www.nytimes.com/interactive/2017/01/20/us/politics/trump-inauguration-crowd.html?_r=0.

[31] J. Carleton, *Ultimate Vale*, 10.

PART II

The Tudor Era (1526–1603)

Common and Competing Faiths

Susan M. Felch

During the Christmas season of 1525–6, John Langland, Bishop of Lincoln, traveled to London, bearing a gift from Cardinal Wolsey to King Henry VIII. The king, Langland reported back in a letter to Wolsey, was pleased both with the present and with reports about the newly founded Cardinal's College at Oxford, under construction on the grounds of the recently suppressed Augustinian Priory of St. Frideswide.[1] The celebratory mood, however, was overshadowed by uneasy currents at court and the threat of contamination from abroad. Langland had brought Henry more than a gift and a progress report on Wolsey's college. He also presented a proposal to the king: Lutheran books were flooding into England from the Continent, and Wolsey sought Henry's approval for a sermon at Paul's Cross. Wolsey wanted a public denunciation of Luther and the English merchants who smuggled in Lutheran books, and he asked that the owners of such books bring them to be burned, under pain of excommunication and possible death. In addition, Wolsey suggested fines for merchants and stationers who continued to import the books. Henry, Langland reported, agreed enthusiastically with the plan, suggesting the Bishop of Rochester, John Fisher, as the preacher and noting that the fines would likely cause more consternation among the merchants than the threat of excommunication. Later that day, Langland also reported to Wolsey that later that day he and the king visited Queen Catherine in her chambers, and Henry encouraged him to tell her about the plans for Cardinal's College. According to the letter, the plans they discussed were not building blueprints, but rather the curriculum, the "literature" of the college, including an emphasis on the

---

[1] The letter, no. 995, is calendared in "Henry VIII: January 1525, 1–14," in J. S. Brewer (ed.), *Letters and Papers, Foreign and Domestic, Henry VIII, vol. 4, 1524–1530* (London: Her Majesty's Stationery Office, 1875), 431–3. British History Online, www.british-history.ac.uk/letters-papers-hen8/vol4/pp431-443.

exposition of the Bible, that promised to make this new English college
a desired destination for students "from all parts of Christendom." The
queen, Langland reported, "gave Wolsey great thanks, and was marvel-
lously glad."

This episode at the Tudor court draws in broad strokes the English
landscape on the cusp of the Reformation and provides a framework for
understanding the religious literary history of the sixteenth century, with
its common and competing faiths. First, the incident underscores the significance of female patrons, a strategic role that women had held and would
continue to play throughout the century. The Bishop of Lincoln did not
visit Catherine for idle chitchat. While it was fitting that he pay his respects,
more importantly both Henry and Langland knew that the queen would
be particularly interested in Wolsey's curricular plans for the new Cardinal's
College, in the "literature" that attract scholars from "all Christendom."

England had, in its distant and near past, a history of royal female
religious patrons. The Tudor reign itself was marked by Lady Margaret
Beaufort's establishment of Christ's College (1505) and, posthumously,
St Johns (1511–16) at Cambridge, her patronage of monastic orders, and
the publication of her translations of the fourth book of *The Imitation of
Christ* (1503) and *The Mirror of Gold for the Sinful Soul* (1506).[2] Three
of Henry's queens and both his daughters maintained and developed
this tradition of supporting religious scholars and writers; in addition,
Katherine Parr, Mary, and Elizabeth wrote religious texts themselves.
Catherine of Aragon maintained chaplains, purchased religious books
for her household, possibly commissioned *The Instruction of a Christian
Woman* from Juan Luis Vives, and gave up to two hundred pounds
annually to the poor.[3] John Foxe summarized the life of Anne Boleyn
by noting that she "wythoute all controuersye was the priuye and open
comforter and aider of al the professors of Christes gospel, as well of the
learned as the vnlearned."[4] Katherine Parr educated Henry's children at

---

[2] Hosington, "Lady Margaret Beaufort's Translations."

[3] Cotton App. B. M. no. 6121 in "Henry VIII: December 1529, 16–29," in Brewer (ed.), *Letters and Papers*, 2720–37. British History Online, www.british-history.ac.uk/letters-papers-hen8/vol4/pp2720-2737.

[4] John Foxe, *The Unabridged Acts and Monuments Online* or *TAMO* (1563 edition) (Sheffield: HRI Online Publications, 2011), 564–5. Available from: www.johnfoxe.org. Although some scholars question the significance of Anne Boleyn's religious activities, this skepticism is countered by: Maria Dowling, "Anne Boleyn and Reform," *Journal of Ecclesiastical History*, 35 (1984), 30–46; Eric Ives, *Anne Boleyn* (Oxford: Blackwell, 1986); Thomas S. Freeman, "Research, Rumour and Propaganda: Anne Boleyn in Foxe's 'Book of Martyrs,'" *The Historical Journal*, 38 (1995), 797–819; James P. Carley, *The Books of King Henry VIII and His Wives* (London: British Library, 2004), 124–33, who

court, published her own theological writings, and oversaw the translation of Erasmus's paraphrases into English, a work to which Mary Tudor contributed. As supreme governor of the Church of England, Elizabeth dispensed religious patronage throughout her life, but she also wrote her own prayers and made a Christianized translation of Boethius's *Consolation of Philosophy*. Royal English women, in other words, were integral to the cultural production of religious writing; they were engaged in protecting and encouraging writers, reading and transmitting texts, and writing such texts themselves.

Second, Henry and Wolsey's concern over the stationers who were printing and the merchants who were importing Lutheran books into the English market points toward the increasing importance of laypeople in the religious life of sixteenth-century England. Although royal female patrons and writers remained active throughout the century in both Roman Catholic and Protestant contexts, gentlewomen and merchant-class women – particularly those from well-connected London households – became ever more visible within the circles of co-religionists that incorporated both women and men.[5] At the same time, Henry's worry in the 1520s over the evangelical merchants and his growing rift with the Roman Catholic Church, already foreshadowed in the ongoing suppression of monasteries, was mirrored in his children's reigns by continued struggles among circles of reformed, Catholic, and prayer book Christians for ecclesiastical power.[6]

The significance of these lay circles is strikingly illustrated in a 1576 dedicatory preface to Sir Christopher Hatton, written by James Sanford. In the course of a sustained panegyric to Queen Elizabeth, in which Sanford compares her to Plato's philosopher king, the biblical King Solomon, the Virgin Mary, and Christ himself, Sanford suggests that the queen would do well to look closer to home for models of godly learning: "Englande hath had and hath at this day noble Gentlewomen famous for their learning, as the right honorable my Lady Burleigh, my Lady Russel, my Lady Bacon, Mistresse Dering, with others."[7] "My Lady Burleigh" is

---

notes that Boleyn's surviving manuscripts reveal a deep commitment to the reformist texts she encountered at the court of Marguerite de Navarre.

[5] See, for instance, White, "Women Writers and Literary-Religious Circles."

[6] Appropriate terms for religious groups in the sixteenth century are notoriously difficult: "evangelical" here stands for early Lutheran-inflected reformers; "reformed" for those who tilted toward Geneva and Presbyterianism; "Catholic" for those loyal to papal authority; "prayer book" for those who accepted the Book of Common Prayer and the authority of the English bishops.

[7] James Sanford, *Houres of Recreation, or Afterdinners, Which May Aptly be Called the Garden of Pleasure* (London: Henry Binnemin, 1576; *STC* 12465), sig. A4ʳ.

Mildred Cooke Cecil (1526–89), eldest daughter of Sir Anthony Cooke and Ann Fitzwilliam; Elizabeth Cooke Hoby Russell (1540–1609) was her third sister; Anne Cooke Bacon (1527/8–1610) was her second sister; Mistress Dering is Anne Lock (1534–c. 1590).

Although the Cooke sisters were well connected at court and Anne Lock's parents had both served Henry VIII and his queens, none of the "noble Gentlewomen" were intimates of Queen Elizabeth. They were, however, politically and literarily active, using their learning to advance the cause of reformed religion. They supported the Scottish reformation at court, wrote and circulated letters among co-religionists, translated and published works from continental reformers, and in 1572 collaboratively produced a presentation manuscript, along with Lock's second husband, Edward Dering, intended to regain the queen's favor after Dering lost his preaching privileges when he warned Elizabeth not to become like "an untamed and unruly Heiffer."[8] That this particular circle of co-religionists was sufficiently well known such that Sanford could allude to them along with famous classical, biblical, and continental exemplars, suggests not so much their exceptionality as the recognition of their circle within the contemporary religious and political landscape.

Third, to return to the 1525–26 Christmas episode at the Henrician court, the conversations among Langford, Henry, and Catherine limn the continued entangling of the old and new faiths, their status as quarreling cousins rather than distant enemies. The English Church's break with Rome, the virulent rhetoric from all sides, the incompatible interpretations of Christ's statement, "This is my body," and the subsequent religious wars on the Continent conspire to lure modern scholars into drawing sharp lines of demarcation between Catholic and Protestant literary culture. Political divisiveness, often justified by religious language, highlighted the differences between what would become the Roman Catholic and Protestant Churches. In fact, even in theological debate and more so in devotional and poetic writings, as well as in the fictional prose and drama that were inflected by religion, the common fund of Christian images, rhetoric, and thought bound religious culture together more than it distinguished between its various forms. Both Roman Catholic and

---

[8] For details on letter writing and other patronage activities, see Phillippy, "Living Stones"; Susan M. Felch, "'Deir Sister': The Letters of John Knox to Anne Vaughan Lok," *Renaissance and Reformation/Renaissance et Réforme*, 19.4 (1995), 47–68. For the 1572 manuscript, see Schleiner, *Tudor and Stuart Women Writers*, 39–45, and Brenda M. Hosington, "'Minerva and the Muses': Women Writers of Latin in Renaissance England," *Humanistica Lovaniensia*, 58 (2009), 9–43.

Protestant authors relied on the common primary text of the scriptures – even when they disagreed on precisely what books could be considered sacred. Both produced new texts that nevertheless drew from traditional commentaries, sermons, histories, mystical visions, catechetical and other reading aids, and numerous lay prayer books. Both laid claim to the history of the Church – even though they spun its narrative thread in distinctive ways. Not only was Christianity central to sixteenth-century life – nearly half the books printed in this period were religious – but religious discourse also provided, as Debora Shuger has pointed out, one of the most potent forms of analytics in the Tudor era.[9]

Tellingly, in the episode at hand, Wolsey simultaneously plans to thwart Lutheran influence in England and suppress an Augustinian priory, whose property he covets. Henry, as befits his title *Fidei Defensor*, conferred by Pope Leo X in 1521, puts forward John Fisher, the probable co-author of his published attack on Luther, as the preacher for the Paul's Cross sermon and concurrently reduces Rome's presence in England by approving Wolsey's land grab. The fate of Cardinal's College itself – suppressed in 1531 after the fall of Wolsey, refounded the following year as King Henry VIII's College, and refounded yet again within the Church of England as Christ Church in 1546 – mirrors both the turbulence and continuity of the early Reformation, its unstable landscape of common and competing faiths.

What these faiths had in common – the role of female patrons, the rise of laywomen within co-religionist circles, and the intertwining of Catholic and Protestant literary culture – was complicated, however, by a seismic shift in the way words, particularly the words of scripture, were understood to take effect in the hearts and lives of those who heard them. On the one hand, the mere repetition or even physical possession of a written psalm, gospel text, or prayer could be regarded as spiritually efficacious; on the other hand, there was increasing momentum to reposition religious language from magical talisman to intelligible word. Erasmus himself, early in the century, advocated for both the talismanic and intelligible properties of sacred words in his *Enchiridion militis christiani*. While the serious lay Christian ought to pursue knowledge through a "fervent study of the sacred scriptures," Erasmus allowed that those with lesser mental capacity could still benefit from merely reciting words they did

9 Debora K. Shuger, *The Renaissance Bible: Scholarship, Sacrifice, and Subjectivity* (Berkeley and Los Angeles: University of California Press, 1994).

not understand "as in magical formulas."[10] But the shift from formal recitation to reading with understanding was unmistakable, as we see in the
work of two women associated with Erasmus' friend, Sir Thomas More.

Margaret More Roper and Joan Fish

Margaret More Roper (1505–44), the daughter of Sir Thomas More,
was the most prominent literary figure in his circle, after More himself.
Educated as a humanist, conversant with and admired by her father's
friends, Roper translated Erasmus's commentary on the *Pater Noster* as
a young matron of nineteen; it was published prior to Wolsey's fall in
1529, possibly as early as 1524.[11] Her accessible but elegant text extended
Erasmus's desire for intelligible words to an English-speaking public, and
did so by using familiar rhythms from earlier English devotional texts,
particularly the doubling of verbs as in "desyre and long" to translate
anhelantium or "knowe and vnderstande" to translate *intelligunt* in the
very first sentence.[12] Regrettably, Roper's work has received less attention
than it should, partly because translation traditionally has not been considered as creative as other forms of prose, but largely because she appears
to have been subsumed within the circle of her famous father.

Participation in a family or co-religionist circle, however, does not
negate female authorial agency – quite the reverse. Sixteenth-century
men and women rarely, if ever, acted as autonomous individuals but
rather functioned within larger and smaller networks. The household, in
particular, was the locus of economic, social, and religious activities. The
word "private," for instance, used to designate the numerous primers and
prayer books printed during the century, meant family, as distinct from
the secret or closet prayers of an individual or the common public prayers
in the church.[13] For the More family, as Stephen Greenblatt has argued,

---

[10] Desiderius Erasmus, *The Handbook of the Christian Soldier*, translated and annotated by Charles
Fantazzi, in John W. O'Malley (ed.), *Collected Works of Erasmus, Volume 66: Spiritualia* (Toronto:
University of Toronto Press, 1989), 32 and 36.

[11] Erasmus, *Precatio dominica* (1523); Erasmus, *A Deuoute Treatise* (1526; *STC* 10477).

[12] Erasmus, *A Deuoute Treatise*, sig. B4ʳ. See also Elizabeth McCutcheon, "Margaret More Roper's
Translation of Erasmus's *Precatio Dominica*," in Stella P. Revard, Fidel Rädle, and Mario A. Di
Cesare (eds.), *Acta Conventus Neo-Latini Guelpherbytani: Proceedings of the Sixth International
Congress of Neo-Latin Studies* (Binghamton, NY: Medieval & Renaissance Texts and Studies, 1988),
664.

[13] The tripartite distinction is formalized in the 1646 Westminster Confession: "God is to be
Worshipped every where in Spirit and Truth; as in private Families daily, and in secret, each one by
himself; so, more solemnly, in the publique Assemblies" (Anon., *The Humble Advice of the Assembly*

establishing the reputation of their family circle as a center of virtue and learning was crucial for maintaining Sir Thomas More's role as wise advisor to the king, as were continued efforts to portray him as a reluctant scholar-turned-politician.[14]

The dedicatory preface of *A Deuoute Treatise* participates in this portrayal of the More circle.[15] Although Roper's name does not appear, the preface is written from Chelsea, the More's residence, by Richard Hyrde, tutor to the More family; it is addressed to Roper's cousin Frances Stafferton, and identifies the writer as young Frances's "forenamed kynswoman," who is "as lothe to haue prayse gyuyn her, as she is worthy to haue it."[16] The reference to Roper could hardly be missed.[17] In the context of praising women for their steadfast character, virtue, and learning, Hyrde locates Roper as an exemplary female figure, occupied at home with "good or necessary busynesse," who functions as a lodestar for men who, in living "amonge company dayly," are tempted "to vtter suche crafte as [they] hath gotten by [their] lernynge."[18] Private and public intersect in the development of virtuous behavior, which is cultivated by the Classical and Christian learning that is fostered in the home. Hyrde, in fact, links male and female education together, holding out for commendation Roper and her husband who "hath by the occasyon of her lernynge/and his delyte therin/suche especiall conforte/pleasure/ and pastyme/as were nat well possyble for one vnlerned couple/eyther to take togyder or to conceyue in their myndes/what pleasure is therin."[19] As Jaime Goodrich has argued, the publication of *A Deuoute Treatise* was part of a program that positioned Roper, from the unassailable site of a learned household, as a public representative and promoter of her family and particularly her father, a position she retained throughout his subsequent arrest, death, and establishment as a Roman Catholic martyr.[20] That outward gaze from the household study is replicated in the initial

---

[footnotes]

of Divines (London: Printed for the Company of Stationers, 1646); Wing 1427, chapter 21, para.6, fol. E2ʳ).

[14] Stephen Greenblatt, *Renaissance Self-Fashioning from More to Shakespeare* (Chicago: University of Chicago Press, 1980), 11–73.

[15] Mary Ellen Lamb, "Margaret Roper, the Humanist Political Project, and the Problem of Agency," in Peter Herman (ed.), *Opening the Borders: Inclusivity in Early Modern Studies: Essays in Honor of James V. Mirollo* (Newark, DE: University of Delaware Press, 1999), 83–108.

[16] Erasmus, *A Deuoute Treatise*, sig. A7ʳ⁻ᵛ.

[17] See Goodrich, "Thomas More and Margaret More Roper," 1031.

[18] Erasmus, *A Deuoute Treatise*, sig. A3ᵛ.

[19] Ibid., sig. B1ʳ.

[20] Goodrich, "Thomas More and Margaret More Roper," 1023, deploys Jürgen Habermas's concept of "representative publicity" to understand Roper's role.

woodcut: rather than imitating the posture of the Virgin Mary, looking attentively downward at a Book of Hours whilst the angel announces her imminent pregnancy, Roper is portrayed as a scribe amongst her many books, looking upward and outward as she offers her learning to the attentive reader. Although the visual parallels between the annunciation scene and Roper's study are undoubtedly meant to accentuate Roper's piety, the difference in posture underscores her agency. She does not merely receive the word of God. Rather, through her translation of the *Pater Noster*, she mediates that word to her compatriots; she makes it intelligible to those who do not understand Latin. If Mary bears the enfleshed word and births it into the world, Roper now carries the written word into the vernacular public sphere.[21]

Indeed, this particular translation and publication of the *Pater Noster* may have been predicated on the perceived need to shore up Erasmus's reputation in England following his reluctance to forthrightly repudiate Luther.[22] In this way, Roper functioned as a patron for the eminent humanist, providing access to his work for English-speaking readers whilst also offering the imprimatur of England's foremost humanist family. Goodrich has argued that Erasmus's explication of the *Pater Noster* reaffirms distinctive Roman Catholic doctrines against the barrage of Protestant theological critique, but the work is not polemical. Instead, it draws both on the tradition of vernacular catechetical materials, which had been steadily increasing in the previous century, and on the close reading of the scriptural text that was a hallmark of humanist education.[23]

Erasmus's exposition of the fourth petition, "Give us this day our daily bread," for instance, focuses as did Luther and other reformers on Christ as the bread of life, mediated both in scripture and in the Eucharist. Hence Erasmus, while acknowledging that it is God who gives us food for our physical bodies, for which we should be properly thankful,

---

[21] Although Goodrich emphasizes Roper's public stance, she reads the woodcut as re-enclosing her domestically within a private study. Rather than noting that Roper's eye contact with the reader reinforces public agency, Goodrich sees her as "gazing out into space" ("Thomas More and Margaret More Roper," 1031).

[22] Goodrich, "Thomas More and Margaret More Roper," 1028–30.

[23] For late medieval vernacular catechetical materials, see Henry Littlehales, *The Prymer or Prayer-Book of the Lay People in the Middle Ages* (London: Longmans, Green, and Co, 1891). On close reading, see Erasmus's rule against the evil of ignorance where he enjoins readers "to understand fully what the Scriptures tell us about Christ and his Spirit ... [for] there is not one tiniest detail contained therein that does not pertain to your salvation" (Erasmus, *The Handbook of the Christian Soldier*, 55).

commends his readers, in Roper's translation, to "desyre and craue" the spiritual bread, which is "thy worde full of all power." This bread-word, Erasmus explains is both "the blessed body of thy dere sonne" and the "teachyng of the gospell" and he further commends those that teach "the lernyng of the gospell" as ones who "gyueth vs forthe this breed."[24] Similarly, Luther's exposition of this petition reminds readers not to be anxious for physical bread, which God will provide, but rather to desire the heavenly bread, the word of God, by which "the whole church, and the soul of every Christian, is ... nourished and supported and defended." This bread is Christ himself, given to us outwardly through preaching and the sacrament and inwardly "by the teaching of God himself."[25] Although Luther excoriates clerical abuses – "it is a grievous matter that men celebrate so many masses ... while alas! the chief thing for which the mass was instituted, that is, the preaching of the word of God, is left out" – Erasmus contents himself with noting that the sacramental bread "indifferently belongeth to vs all" but must be mingled with "heuenly grace" in order to be efficacious.[26] William Taverner's later translation of Wolfgang Capito's psalm paraphrases, well known in England, explicates the twenty-third psalm in words compatible with both Erasmus's and Luther's expositions of the *Pater Noster*: the green pasture to which the sheep are led are "the fedynge groundes of thy plenteous worde"; the shepherd's staff is glossed as "the staffe of thy worde"; and the table laid in the presence of enemies is "the bourde of thy worde [spread] before me."[27]

Roper's text forms part of the ongoing work of Bible translation and vernacular catechetical instruction.[28] As Frans van Liere has documented, medieval vernacular Bible translations were commonly accepted, as long

---

[24] Erasmus, *A Deuoute Treatise*, sig. E2r–E4r at E3r, E3v, and E4r. For discussions of Roper's translation choices, see: McCutcheon, "Margaret More Roper's Translation," 659–66; Rita M. Verbrugge, "Margaret More Roper's Personal Expression in the *Devout Treatise Upon the Pater Noster*" in Hannay (ed.), *Silent but for the Word*, 30–42.

[25] Luther, *Exposition*, 59, 62, and 64–6.

[26] Ibid., 65; Erasmus, *A Deuoute Treatise*, sig. E3ʳ⁻ᵛ.

[27] Richard Taverner, *An Epitome of the Psalmes, or Briefe Meditacions upon the Same, with Diuerse other Moste Christian Prayers* (London: (By R. Bankes? for A. Clerke?), 1539; *STC* 2748), sig. C4ʳ. This is a translation of Wolfgang Capito, *Precationes Christinae ad imitationem psalmorum copositae* (Strasbourg: Rihel, 1536).

[28] See, for example, the mid-fifteenth-century CUL MS Ff. 2.38, Frances McSparran and P. R. Robinson (eds.), *Cambridge University Library MS Ff 2.38* (Leicester: Scolar Press, 1979), which includes standard catechetical materials such as the Ten Commandments, the penitential psalms, the various "sevens" (works of mercy, deadly sins, bodily senses, seven sacraments), and didactic prose works; For a survey of late medieval vernacular teaching materials, see Duffy, *Stripping of the Altars*, 53–87.

as they were not associated with heretical or politically subversive views.[29] Such translations, however, were usually piecemeal, interlined in gospel books and prayer books or included in sermons along with the authorized Latin version. The growing pressure in the sixteenth century from both humanists and reformers was for a translation of the compete Bible into English. In fact, the 1530 censorship act that banned Tyndale's New Testament as well as other evangelical works also promised an English Bible translated "by great, learned, and Catholic persons," when it should seem "convenient" for the king to authorize it.[30] Yet in the charged atmosphere of the 1520s, calls for an English Bible translation were politically and religiously fraught. Consequently, it is not particularly surprising that a young London laywoman, Joan Fish, ran afoul of Sir Thomas More in 1529 for insisting that the scriptures be read in English rather than in Latin in her house.

We do not know a great deal about this incident. John Foxe notes that Joan Fish, whose first husband had published the anticlerical *A Supplicacyon for the Beggers* "had by chaunce displeased the friers for not suffering them to saye their gospelles in Latine in her house, (as they did in others) on lesse they would say it in Englishe."[31] As a result, she was summoned to appear before the Lord Chancellor, and only the illness of her young daughter, sick with the plague, kept her from "muche trouble." This brief narrative probably refers to Joan's repudiation of the custom of friars begging for alms in exchange for reciting the prologue to the Gospel of John (John 1:1–14), also known from its opening words as the *In principio*.[32] The value of the *In principio* in England may have been enhanced by the belief that Clement V had dispensed an indulgence of one year and forty days for anyone who heard or recited it.[33]

---

[29] Frans van Liere, *An Introduction to the Medieval Bible* (Cambridge: Cambridge University Press, 2014), 177–207.

[30] Paul L. Hughes and James F. Larkin (eds.), *Tudor Royal Proclamations, Volume I: The Early Tudors, 1485–1553* (New Haven: Yale University Press, 1964), 196.

[31] Foxe, *TAMO* (1563), 500–1. Foxe probably heard this anecdote from Joan Fish herself, when he interviewed her about her second husband, James Bainham. See also Simon Fish, *A Supplicacyon for the Beggers* ((Antwerp?: J. Grapheus?, 1529?); *STC* 10883).

[32] William Tyndale, for instance, criticizes "the limeteriers sayenge of in principio erat verbum from housse to housse": see Anne M. O'Donnell and Jared Wicks (eds.), *An Answere Vnto Sir Thomas Mores Dialoge* (Washington, DC: The Catholic University of America Press, 2000), 60.

[33] See Christopher Wordsworth (ed.), *The Tracts of Clement Maydeston with the Remains of Caxton's Ordinale* (London: Harrison and Sons, 1894), 173, as referenced by E. G. Cuthbert Atchley, "Some Notes on the Beginning and Growth of the Usage of a Second Gospel at Mass," *Transactions of the St. Paul's Ecclesiological Society*, 4 (1900), 161–76.

Mistress Fish's refusal to let the friars say the Latin gospel in her house was both a statement about her commitment to the vernacular scriptures and a defiant stand against the popular piety that More defended in *A Dialogue Concerning Heresies* and in *The Supplication of Souls*, his response to her husband's *Supplicacyon*.[34] It aligned her publicly, as a merchant-class laywoman, with the "new religion."[35] By insisting that the friars recite John 1 in English, Joan repositioned the scriptures from magical talisman to intelligible word, and she pressured the friars to demonstrate their theological competency either by providing their own translation or by quoting the Lollard Bible or Tyndale's New Testament, both of which were banned books.[36] That More took the time to prosecute a young London woman and to write a ninety-page response to Simon Fish's sixteen-page pamphlet confirms that he felt these London households, and their commitment to evangelical literature, posed a serious threat to England.[37]

This is somewhat surprising, given that the condemnation of clerical abuses in Fish's *Supplicacyon* (wealthy monastic foundations, burdensome mortuaries and other ecclesiastical payments, lustful priests) was hardly new or confined to emerging Protestants and that Fish's theological justification for reform, the denial of Purgatory, was stated but not developed. With only a few changes, the pamphlet could have been written – or preached – by any number of reform-minded traditional clerics. The threat, however, as More saw it, may have been exacerbated

[34] Thomas More, *The supplycacyon of soulys Supplycacyon of Soulys* (*STC* 18092). See "Supplication of Souls" in Thomas More, *The Complete Works of St. Thomas More*. Frank Manley, Germain Marc'hadour, Richard Marius, and Clarence H. Miller (eds.), 15 vols. (New Haven and London: Yale University Press, 1990), vol. VII, 107–228.

[35] For a less public stand by a London woman, see the memoir of Anne Lock's sister-in-law, Rose Lock Hickman Throckmorton, who recalled that her mother read evangelical English books to her daughters, although "very privately for feare of troble bicause those good books were then accompted hereticall." See BL Add. MS 43827, "Certaine old stories recorded by an aged gentlewoman a time before her death, to be perused by her children and posterity," fols. 3ʳ–4ʳ; transcribed by Maria Dowling and Joy Shakespeare, "Religion and Politics in mid Tudor England through the eyes of an English Protestant Woman: the Recollections of Rose Hickman," *Bulletin of the Institute of Historical Research*, 55 (1982), 94–102 at 97.

[36] The Wycliffe or Lollard Bible had been proscribed by Archbishop Arundel's Constitutions (1408). The preface to Henry VIII's published 1527 reply to Martin Luther notes that copies of Tyndale's New Testament are to be burned on the advice of More, and readers of such are to be sharply corrected: see Henry VIII, *A Copy of the Letters* (London: Richarde Pynson, 1527; *STC* 13086), sig. A6ʳ.

[37] Richard Marius, *Thomas More: A Biography* (New York: Alfred A. Knopf, 1984), 351, suggests that More would have known Simon Fish as part of the close-knit networks of London lawyers. It is possible that Simon and Joan Fish's second husband, James Bainham, were associated with William Roper during the years that More's son-in-law professed the evangelical faith. See Susan Brigden, *London and the Reformation* (Oxford: Clarendon, 1989), 116 and 120.

by Anne Boleyn's role in transmitting Fish's *Supplicacyon* to the Henrician court. Although there are complications in the chronology, it appears that Anne Boleyn received a copy of *A Supplicacyon* and gave it to Henry, possibly via his footman, Edmund Moody, and two evangelical merchants, George Elyot and George Robinson. At some later point, servants who noted the king's interest in the book told Joan Fish that it might be safe for Simon, who was in exile on the Continent, to return home.[38] "Wherupon," John Foxe notes, Joan "therby being incoraged came first & made suet to the king for the safe returne of her housband. who vnderstanding whose wife she was, shewed a maruelous gentle chearfull countenaunce towardes her asking where her husband was, she answered if it like your grace not farre of." Indeed, Simon had already returned to England and was living in London. Joan brought him to court, where he received safe conduct from the king. Simon himself died shortly thereafter from the plague; Joan then married James Bainham from Gloucestershire, who was burned as a heretic on April 30, 1532, and she was herself arrested, imprisoned, and had her household goods confiscated during her second marriage.[39]

Although these stories of Margaret Roper, intimate of the More household, and Joan Fish, antagonist to Sir Thomas More himself, are divergent in many respects, together they represent the role of women and outline the characteristic features of the English religious landscape on the cusp of the Reformation in England. Both Roper and Fish, as laywomen, were active participants in their respective co-religionist circles; they sought to promote the reading and understanding of religious texts; and they shared a common fund of orthodox Christian beliefs, images, and scripture.

---

[38] Foxe notes two introductions of *A Supplycacyon* to the Henrician court: one by Anne Boleyn, first recorded in Foxe, *TAMO* (1563), fol. 500; the other by Moody and the merchants, first recorded in Foxe, *TAMO* (1570), fol. 1192. Both incidents are included in subsequent editions, and Foxe makes no attempt to harmonize the accounts. The most likely explanation is that Henry first encountered *A Supplicacyon* early in 1529, when he received a copy from Anne Boleyn and was asked by Wolsey to surrender it. After Wolsey's fall in October of that year and the seating of the "Reformation Parliament," the *Supplicacyon* was sufficiently uncontroversial for Joan to sue for the return of her husband. The positive encounters of Joan and Simon Fish at court presumably occurred prior to the banning of *A Supplicacyon* by the bishops on May 24, 1530: see BL Cotton Cleop. E. v, fol. 321ʳ, "A proclamation against erroneous books and heresies, and against translating the Bible in English, French, or Dutch," anno reg. Henr. VIII.xxii, in David Wilkins (ed.), *Concilia Magnae Britanniae et Hiberniae*, 4 vols. (London: Gosling, 1737), vol. III, 740–2.

[39] See Thomas S. Freeman, "The Importance of Dying Earnestly: The Metamorphosis of the Account of James Bainham in 'Foxe's Book of Martyrs'" in R. N. Swanson (ed.), *The Church Retrospective, Studies in Church History*, 33 (Woodbridge: Ecclesiastical History Society, 1997), 267–88 at 274.

Anne Lock and Anne Dacre Howard

This same amalgam of traditional and reformist stances can be seen in the work of two women who were active in the second half of the sixteenth century: Anne Lock and Anne Dacre Howard.

Anne Lock's two published books were dedicated to female patrons at court, Katherine Brandon Bertie, Dowager Duchess of Suffolk, and Anne Russell Dudley, Countess of Warwick, both of whom she recognized as co-religionists and urged to further service in reforming the English Church.[40] The Duchess of Suffolk is asked in 1560 to mediate John Calvin's sermons, through Lock's translation, to Queen Elizabeth – a daring move, as Micheline White has pointed out, given the new queen's antipathy toward all things Genevan.[41] Thirty years later, the Countess of Warwick is reminded to use her position at court "to give light unto manie" and particularly to promote the cause of the Puritans, many of whose leaders were in exile, in prison, or dead in the wake of Archbishop Whitgift's ascendancy and the Martin Marprelate controversy.[42]

In both prefaces, Lock not only appeals to patrons at court, but also includes them within her own co-religionist circle. The Duchess of Suffolk is counted among the "we" who know how to seize the medicine of God's word "bycause we knowe it wyll heale us."[43] The Countess of Warwick is counted among the "we" who in experiencing persecution know they are "under the crosse."[44] Furthermore, Lock stitches the continental male authors John Calvin and Jean Taffin into the same circle. If the Duchess of Suffolk is to receive good medicine from the hand of God, it is medicine that is mediated through the combined efforts of Calvin and Lock herself: "This receipte God the heavenly Physitian hath taught, his most excellent Apothecarie master John Calvine hath compounded, and I your graces most bounden and humble have put into an Englishe box."[45] If the Countess of Warwick is to let her light shine in the late Elizabethan court, she must accept the instruction on

---

[40] Anne Lock, *Sermons of John Calvin, Upon the Songe that Ezechias Made After He Had Bene Sicke, and Afflicted by the Hand of God, Conteyned in the 38. Chapiter of Esay* (London: John Day, 1560; STC 4450); Anne Lock, *Of the Markes of the Children of God, and of Their Comforts in Afflictions* (London: Thomas Orwin, for Thomas Man, 1590; STC 23652). Both texts are included in Felch (ed.), *Collected Works of Anne Vaughan Lock.*
[41] White, "Perils and Possibilities of the Book Dedication."
[42] Lock, *Collected Works*, 77.
[43] Ibid., 8.
[44] Ibid., 76.
[45] Ibid., 5.

suffering that Lock has selected from Taffin. Male theologians and lay women are equally bound by virtue of their spiritual calling to build up the Church; in Lock's words, "to doo somewhat to the furtherance of the holie building."[46]

In addition, it is worth noting that despite the growing divisiveness among religious factions in England, Lock continues to draw not just on the common fund of scripture, but also on traditional Christian images and tropes. In the preface to her 1560 book, she takes as a central image the ancient comparison of a vibrant spiritual life to good physical health. She then threads the biblical stories of the Good Samaritan's healing oil (Luke 10:25–37), the parable of the wise and foolish virgins and their oil or lack thereof (Matthew 25:1–13), and the wilderness story of the brass serpent, which later becomes an idolatrous snare to Israel (Numbers 21:4–9; 2 Kings 18:4), into a coherent narrative that draws on the common funds of scripture and tradition whilst also positioning good medicine with Protestant teachings, bad medicine with that of the "papists." In the poem that concludes her 1590 volume, Lock crafts a classic meditation on the cross and the contemplation of heaven as aids to the suffering Christian that would not have been out of place in a medieval prayer book or in the mouth of a Roman Catholic believer or prayer book Protestant. It ends with these words: "Then for religion love the crosse/ though it doo bring some paine:/The joy is great, small is the losse,/but infinite the gaine."[47]

Indeed, these sentiments, if not the very words, could have been uttered by Lock's younger contemporary, Anne Dacre Howard, Countess of Arundel (1557–1630), a convert to and supporter of Catholicism in England.[48] Placed under house arrest in the early 1580s, interrogated, and later separated from her husband who was confined to the Tower of London from 1585 until his death in 1595, Howard, like Lock, experienced the late Elizabethan reign as a time of increasing persecution. Although no writings can be securely attributed to her, her support of co-religionists included patronage of the Jesuit priest and poet Robert Southwell, who lived in her household and whose first printed book, *Epistle of Comfort*, was published with her support.[49]

---

[46] Ibid., 77.

[47] Ibid., 189.

[48] For the life and works of Howard, see Susannah Brietz Monta, "Anne Dacre Howard, Countess of Arundel, and Catholic Patronage," in White (ed.), *English Women*, 59–81.

[49] Robert Southwell, *An Epistle of Comfort to the Reuerend Priestes* (London: John Charlewood? 1587?; *STC* 22946).

Southwell's *Epistle* argues for endurance in the face of suffering in much the same terms that Lock and Taffin do in *Of the markes of the children of God* and, highlighting the same scriptural text – "For whom the Lord loueth, he chasteneth, and scourgeth euery sonne that he receaueth" (Hebrews 12:6, *Bishops' Bible*) – presses home the point that persecution is a sign not of God's displeasure but rather of his tender, disciplinary care.[50] Both books are replete with biblical examples that, as in Lock's dedicatory preface to the Duchess of Suffolk, weave a continuous narrative of human suffering and divine grace; and both draw on selected theologians of the past, chief among them Augustine and Bernard of Clairvaux, as well as on familiar images of pilgrimage, physical illness and health, military campaigns, storms, and buildings. Lock's famous picture of the Church as the tumbled-down walls of Jerusalem to which all are called to bring their stones "to the strengthening" of those same walls, is prefigured by Southwall's metaphor of true Catholics as spiritual pillars in the Church who stand "more firm and vnmoueable" as persecution presses upon them such that they are not "broaken of from the members of Christes misticall bodye."[51]

Lock's translation of Taffin found a wide readership in England: it was reprinted seven times before 1615. Similarly, Southwell's works were disseminated widely and read by Catholics and Protestants of various persuasions. As Susannah Brietz Monta has noted, Southwell's *Short Rule for a Good Life*, written originally for Howard, found a Protestant readership in both manuscript and print versions, often in forms in which overt Catholic references were silently removed.[52]

Conclusion

From the distance of some 400 years, the religious landscape of the sixteenth century can appear factious and sectarian. Certainly the fault lines between and among Protestants and Catholics – to use that too simple dichotomy – can be seen in conflicting beliefs and practices and in the shift from an efficacious recitation of sacred words to an insistence upon intelligible reading. These fault lines often did erupt into physical, political, and economic persecution. Although Lock and Southwell both published books of comfort centered around the hope of the cross

---

[50] Lock, *Collected Works*, 76; Southwell, *An Epistle*, sig. B4ᵛ.
[51] Lock, *Collected Works*, 77; Southwell, *An Epistle*, sig. Z4ʳ⁻ᵛ.
[52] Monta, "Anne Dacre Howard," 69.

and heaven, they singled out their own beliefs as the true religion, and they urged practices that laid hold of that hope in different ways. For Southwell and his patron Anne Howard, continued good works of confession, mercy, and daily pious exercises "necessarye to saluation" were enjoined to steer a safe course through life "by the example of former Saintes."[53] For Taffin and Lock, the faithful Christian was one who participated actively in a Church where "the word of God is trulie preached, the Sacraments are purelie ministred, and one onelie God is called upon in the name of his onelie sonne Jesus Christ."[54]

Although by the end of the century such differences in belief and practice, exacerbated by political fiat, had severed religious communities from one another, the vocabulary and imagery of Catholic and Protestant literary culture still remained intertwined, supported by the ongoing roles of female patrons and the active work of laywomen within their own co-religionist circles.

[53] Southwell, *An Epistle*, sig. M4ʳ and N1ᵛ.
[54] Lock, *Collected Works*, 90.

6

Isabella Whitney's "Slips"
Poetry, Collaboration, and Coterie

Dana E. Lawrence

Frequently identified as the first Englishwoman to publish a collection of secular poetry, Isabella Whitney has secured her place within the current canon of early modern women writers.[1] In general, very little is known about her life, though attempts have been made to reconstruct her biography based on her two published volumes, *The Copy of a Letter* (1567) and *A Sweet Nosgay* (1573).[2] Both of these texts demonstrate Whitney's familiarity with a variety of literary genres, which she utilizes to create space for her original work. In this chapter, I argue that Whitney's engagement with past and present literary traditions and trends through imitation, adaptation, and appropriation functions as a mode of collaborative writing. Though she does not actually write *with* these other authors, Whitney's *A Sweet Nosgay* layers texts, genres, and conventions to create a palimpsest, an example of what Gérard Genette terms *transtextuality*: "the textual transcendence of the text, [defined as] all that sets the text in a relationship whether obvious or concealed, with other texts."[3] Within this category of transtextuality, Genette identifies five types, two of which – intertextuality and hypertextuality – are most relevant to this discussion.

Genette describes intertexuality as "a relationship of copresence between two texts or among several texts," whereas a hypertext is, more specifically, "any text derived from a previous text either through simple transformation ... or through indirect transformation, which I shall label

---

[1] See Whitney, *The Copy of a Letter*.
[2] For more on Whitney's biography, see: R. J. Fehrenbach, "Isabella Whitney (fl. 1565–75) and the Popular Miscellanies of Richard Jones," *Cahiers Elisabethians: Late Medieval and Renaissance Studies*, 19 (1981), 85–7; Jessica L. Malay, "Isabella Whitney, 'Sister Eldershae,' and Cheshire Recusancy," *English Language Notes*, 43 (2005), 18–22; Averill Lukic, "Geffrey and Isabella Whitney," *Emblematica*, 14 (2005), 395–408.
[3] Genette, *Palimpsests*, 1.

imitation."[4] Employing elements of intertextuality and hypertextuality, Whitney participates in multiple masculine and feminine traditions, constructing imagined literary and social collaborations that she uses to authorize her own voice. Whitney's use of popular literary forms is well established, and Linda Hutcheon argues that adaptation (a form of hypertextuality) "has an obvious financial appeal" because the reworking of already successful texts is a "safe bet."[5] It is possible that Whitney's choice of genres in both her volumes was influenced by her printer, as Lynette McGrath has suggested: "[Richard] Jones's publishing goal was clearly to whet contemporary appetites, and certainly his poetic collections appealed to current literary fashion."[6] However, from the outset of *A Sweet Nosgay*, Whitney establishes her intent to publish and her desire for patronage, and she presents herself and her volume as collaborators in a broad literary circle that includes source texts, genre conventions, social and cultural discourses, and readers.

Whitney presents *A Sweet Nosgay* as an act of appropriation, acknowledging her theft from Hugh Plat's *Floures of Philosophie* (1573) even as she calls attention to her labor in gathering the poems: "The which to get some payne I tooke,/and travayled many houres."[7] By citing Plat as her source, Whitney subordinates her text to his,[8] but through her imitation and adaptation of Plat's "floures" she demonstrates her mastery of the text and makes it her own – even granting her readers permission to gather their own posies from his garden.[9] Moving from a textual collaboration with a potentially unwilling author to a fictional coterie that confirms the speaker's narrative of abandonment, Whitney continues to appropriate popular literary forms and traditions. In her epistolary exchanges with friends and family, Whitney recasts the role of the Heroidean beloved as that of a disillusioned maidservant-turned-writer. The *Nosgay*'s final poem, the "Wyll and Testament," blends legacy (legal

---

[4] Ibid., 1 and 7.
[5] Hutcheon, *A Theory of Adaptation*, 5. On Whitney's formal choices, see Betty Travitsky, "The 'Wyll and Testament' of Isabella Whitney," *English Literary Renaissance*, 10 (1980), 76–95; Jones, "Apostrophes to Cities"; Beilin, "Writing Public Poetry"; Laurie Ellinghausen, "Literary Property and the Single Woman in Isabella Whitney's *A Sweet Nosgay*," *Studies in English Literature 1500–1900*, 45 (2005), 1–22; Hutson, *Usurer's Daughter*, 116–28; Paul A. Marquis, "Oppositional Ideologies of Gender in Isabella Whitney's Copy of a Letter," *Modern Language Review*, 90 (1995): 314–24; and Wall, *Imprint of Gender*, 296–310.
[6] McGrath, *Subjectivity and Women's Poetry*, 125.
[7] Whitney, *Sweet Nosgay*, sig. C5ʳ. Subsequent citations are to this edition and appear parenthetically.
[8] Julie Sanders, *Adaptation and Appropriation* (London: Routledge, 2010), 9.
[9] Jean I. Marsden, *The Appropriation of Shakespeare: Post-Renaissance Reconstructions of the Works and the Myth* (New York: St. Martin's Press, 1991), 1.

and literary) and chorography as the speaker/writer enacts a literary appropriation of London.

Throughout this palimpsestic volume, traces of Christine de Pizan's *Book of the City of Ladies* emerge. While Whitney may not have known the medieval writer by name, she easily could have read the text, which had been available to non-courtly readers since Bryan Anslay's 1521 edition. Christine the author did not receive credit on Anslay's title page, but "Christine" the speaker narrates the text, and the influence of *City of Ladies* on early modern English women writers and the *querelle des femmes* is evident.[10] This influence is particularly visible in Whitney's opening scene, in which her speaker, like "Christine," finds herself surrounded by volumes of misogynist discourse, which she rejects. When the City of Ladies is echoed in Whitney's thematic map of London in the "Wyll," "Christine" becomes a collaborator in Whitney's literary project, participating in what Catharine Gray terms a "coterie of ghosts."[11] This spectral female author not only associates the poet with past literary traditions but also allows her to assume the role of heir to the literary present. Although this present, for Whitney, is one of shame and misery, she combines the conventional union of gardens and poetry with the specter of plague to appropriate and re-direct the shaming gaze.

Shame and Plague

Isabella Whitney employs a rhetoric of shame in *A Sweet Nosgay*, presenting her volume as a textual Panopticon which renders visible the wrongs committed by those who have abandoned London and its most oppressed citizens. Assuming the guise of an unemployed maidservant, Whitney evokes the association of plague with sin and shame in the minds of early modern readers to emphasize her maidservant's subjection.[12] In cities like London, households suspected of harboring plague

---

[10] See: Malcolmson, "Christine de Pizan's *City of Ladies*"; Susan Groag Bell, *The Lost Tapestries of the City of Ladies: Christine de Pizan's Renaissance Legacy* (Berkeley: University of California Press, 2004); Barbara K. Altman and Deborah L. McGrady (eds.), *Christine de Pizan: A Casebook* (New York: Routledge, 2003).

[11] Gray, *Women Writers and Public Debate*, 145–81.

[12] For discussions of the experiences of early modern maidservants, see: Sara Mendelson and Patricia Crawford, *Women in Early Modern England, 1550–1720* (Oxford: Clarendon, 1998), 92–108; Bernard Capp, *When Gossips Meet: Women, Family, and Neighbourhood in Early Modern England* (Oxford: Oxford University Press, 2003), 127–72; Jones, "Maidservants of London"; Patricia Fumerton, *Unsettled: The Culture of Mobility and the Working Poor in Early Modern England* (Chicago: University of Chicago Press, 2006); Phillippy, "The Maid's Lawful Liberty";

victims were quarantined for weeks, and families would conceal the sick
and the dead to avoid this fate.[13] Servants were particularly vulnerable
because of their "uncontrolled contact with the world outside," and those
who fell ill were likely to be hidden and given little to no care.[14] In addition to being "shut in," plague-stricken people and households were made
to display public markers of their illness: hanging bundles of straw from
the windows, crosses on the door, or carrying a white pole in the streets.[15]
These responses, designed to protect the population from the disease,
also served as shaming devices, as the infected were publicly marked
and exposed for their sins. In *Discipline and Punish*, Michel Foucault
likens this environment of strict and constant surveillance to Bentham's
Panopticon, the power of which lies in its ability "to induce in the inmate
a state of conscious and permanent visibility that assures the automatic
functioning of power"; in other words, someone is always watching.[16]
When victims were seen as innocent, Ernest B. Gilman attests, the only
other explanation was that "the nation itself must be guilty."[17] While
individuals might escape sickness by fleeing the city or simply by luck,
they could not avoid the fear of possible infection or God's judgment.

In her literary construction of collaborative relationships, Whitney
uses her text to enlist readers as co-conspirators in her efforts to shame
the very authorities who would shame her. Whitney's invocation of the
all-seeing eye of God repeats a warning already ingrained in early modern culture. To enforce adherence to social and moral codes of conduct,
Elizabeth A. Clark argues, "Church Fathers ... attempted to construct
a gendered disciplinary apparatus through the rhetoric of shame."[18] The
"constant repetition" of this rhetoric implies that not even the watch-
ful eye of God was "entirely effective as a disciplinary device."[19] While
Whitney's state of abandonment and her tour of London's moral failings
serve as evidence of its ineffectiveness, the power to shame is not exclusively within the purview of the clergy. Shame, as a social construct, is

---

Paul Griffiths, *Youth and Authority: Formative Experience in England 1560–1640* (Oxford: Clarendon Press, 1996).

[13] Joseph P. Byrne, *Daily Life during the Black Death* (Westport, CT: Greenwood Press, 2006), 194.

[14] Ibid., 69.

[15] Paul Slack, *Impact of Plague in Tudor and Stuart England* (Oxford: Clarendon, 1985), 201.

[16] Michel Foucault, *Discipline and Punish: The Birth of the Prison*, trans. Alan Sheridan (1975; repr., New York: Vintage Books, 1979), 201.

[17] Ernest B. Gilman, *Plague Writing in Early Modern England* (Chicago: University of Chicago Press, 2009), 45.

[18] Clark, "Sex, Shame, and Rhetoric," 221.

[19] Ibid., 222.

also collaboratively produced by and within communities as a regulatory system – one fundamental to the Panopticon. Stephanie Chamberlain argues that this community surveillance "ultimately functions as a moral corrective to force the offending individual to conform to accepted community standards."[20] Ewan Fernie dismisses the role of the public in shaming, stressing the individual's private pain, "because the shamed self is *literally not fit to be seen*."[21] As an unemployed maidservant, Whitney's speaker is inherently shameful: an unsupervised young single woman whose unemployment leaves her economically vulnerable and marks her as a criminal.[22] The speaker passively accepts her shame at first, but through her fictional collaborations she illustrates her virtues, thus allowing her to turn her detractors' accusations against them. Insisting on the accountability of others, Whitney asserts her own innocence. Exonerating herself of guilt for their crimes, she represents the weak, who, like the *Nosgay*'s speaker, have been abandoned.

From the volume's opening words, Whitney presents her gathering of Plat's "floures" as an act of appropriation. She begins the dedicatory epistle to George Mainwaring with an assertion of her authorship: "When I … had made this simple Nosegaye." However, she quickly assumes a veil of modesty, claiming, "although the Flowers bound in the same were good: yet so little of my labour was in them" (sig. A4ʳ). Though she briefly downplays her authorial role here, Whitney goes on to emphasize her labor in the dedication, asserting that the poems "be of my owne gathering and makeing," and she asks Mainwaring to "respect my labour and regard my good wil" (sig. A4ᵛ). She claims ownership of her work, taking possession of the bouquet that is of her own arrangement: her repetition of the possessive "my" anticipates the privileging of her voice, her labor, and her "wyll" in the volume's final poem. Minimizing the social distance between writer and patron, Whitney imbues her poetry with the very protective powers that she seeks from her dedicatee, assuring Mainwaring that "when you come into a pestilent aire that might infect your sound minde: yet favour to these SLIPS in which I trust you shall finde safety" (sig. A5ʳ). Here, Whitney foreshadows the plague that looms over the *Nosgay* and alludes to her curative authorial role.

---

[20] Stephanie Chamberlain, "Rotten Oranges and Other Spoiled Commodities: The Economics of Shame in *Much Ado About Nothing*," *Journal of the Wooden O Symposium*, 9 (2010), 1–10 at 5.

[21] Ewan Fernie, *Shame in Shakespeare* (London: Routledge, 2002), 16.

[22] Queen Elizabeth's 1563 Statute of Artificers made it a crime for single women between the ages of twelve and forty to *not* be in service. See also Jones, "Maidservants of London," 22.

By referring to her poems as "slips," Whitney connects the paper on which she writes with the "flowers" plucked from Plat's garden. However, the term also highlights Whitney's collaboration with Plat, because, within the context of gardening, a *slip* is "a twig, sprig, or small shoot taken from a plant ... for the purposes of grafting or planting."[23] Whitney Trettien convincingly ties the *Nosgay*'s "slips" with contemporary rhetoric surrounding writing and embroidery. Though Trettien acknowledges the term's meaning within the context of gardening, her analysis focuses on embroidered and illustrated flowers rather than actual gardening practices.[24] Exploring an analogy between gathering and reading these slips, Trettien argues that Whitney both fashions her role as writer and "transforms the role of the reader into one that allows her to be an active participant in the sharing and circulation of texts."[25] The act of reading inspires the act of writing, and Whitney highlights her authorship as appropriation: "& not havyng of mine owne to discharg that I go about," she claims, "[I] did step into an others garden for these Flowers" (sig. A4ᵛ). Plat's maxims serve as grafts for Whitney's poetry, "so as to allow the sap of the latter to circulate through the former."[26] Whitney uses the garden as a site of self-authorization which is also an act of theft, and embeds her voice in the work of her predecessors, cultivating her poetic persona until the dispossessed maidservant grows into London's sole benefactress.

In the same way that she asserts her authorial voice in the dedication to George Mainwaring, Whitney uses her address to the reader to introduce the themes of plague, abandonment, and shame that bind the volume together. "The Auctor to the Reader" begins with Whitney's speaker sitting in a study surrounded by books that provoke her resistant readership. She picks up and sets aside several canonical texts, including the Bible, various "Histories," and the works of Virgil, Ovid, and Mantuan. Like "Christine" in the *City of Ladies*, Whitney finds herself disheartened by the misogynistic texts. In her critique of the discarded texts, Whitney's speaker complains that, "wantying a Devine" (sig. A5ᵛ), she cannot understand scripture well enough to find comfort.[27] Instead,

---

[23] *OED*, s.v. "slip."

[24] Trettien, "Isabella Whitney's Slips."

[25] Ibid., 515.

[26] *OED*, s.v. "graft."

[27] A thorough examination of Whitney's religious beliefs is not within the purview of this chapter, but it is worth noting that, while she frequently invokes God throughout *Nosgay*, the material symbols of God on earth are given only cursory attention. For discussions of Isabella Whitney's

Whitney focuses on the ways in which people fail to do God's work in taking care of each other. Her speaker's rejection of history is likewise critical of human behavior: "Wherein I found that follyes earst,/in people did exceede./The which I see doth not decrease,/in this our present time/ More pittie it is we folow them,/in every wicked crime" (sig. A5ᵛ). Again like "Christine," Whitney's study of authoritative texts leads her to question their value and weight.

Whitney emphasizes her speaker's powerlessness even as she locates agency within her shameful state. The speaker's "leasure" to read is the result of unfortunate circumstances: "This Harvest tyme, I Harvestlesse,/ and servicelesse also:/And subject unto sicknesse, that/abrode I could not go" (sig. A5ᵛ). By describing herself as "Harvestlesse," the speaker hearkens back to the fact that her flowers are picked out of someone else's garden, underscoring both her economic and intellectual poverty. Even if she was not punished for her unemployment, Ann Rosalind Jones notes, "a woman's failure to find work risked landing her in debtors' prison."[28] Whitney's speaker demonstrates her awareness of this threat, both in her desperate requests for money from family members in the "Familier Epistles" and in the lingering attention she pays London's prisons in her "Wyll and Testament." However, despite the many challenges faced by maidservants in their attempts to preserve their livelihoods and reputations, they also enjoyed a freedom denied married or very wealthy women.

In *A Sweet Nosgay*, the speaker's mobility and unmastered state provide an opportunity to engage in intellectual pursuits like reading and writing. Becoming "wery of those Bookes" that brought her no comfort, the speaker seeks to "refresh my … muse,/and cheare my brused brayne" by taking a walk outside (sig. A5ᵛ). She immediately encounters a passing male friend, who warns her of "the noysome smell and savours yll," advising her to leave the city "if you regard your health" (sig. A6ʳ). Whitney's use of the plague as both setting and metaphor reflects the ever-present threat of disease and death in early modern England. Just ten years before the publication of *A Sweet Nosgay*, bubonic plague swept through the country. Citing John Stowe's figures, J. F. D. Shrewsbury estimates that 85 percent of deaths in London were caused by plague in 1563: "bubonic

---

connections to Protestantism, see: Patricia Crawford, "Women's Published Writings 1600–1700," in Mary Prior (ed.), *Women in English Society 1500–1800* (London and New York: Methuen, 1985), 211–82; Averill Lukic, "Geffrey and Isabella Whitney," *Emblematica*, 14 (2005), 395–408; Malay, "Isabella Whitney."

[28] Ann Rosalind Jones, "Maidservants of London," 22.

plague must have destroyed at least one-quarter of [the population], and when the panic exodus of a considerable part of the population is taken into account, it seems probable that the disease exterminated one-third of the available human material."[29] This "panic exodus" is seen in the *Nosgay* when the speaker's friend urges her to leave London; it may also explain the absence of her friends and family in the "Familier Epistles." Meredith Skura suggests a more immediate threat of plague, citing first-hand descriptions of illness in London records for 1573.[30] Whether the plague in Whitney's text is literal or figurative, it provides a mandate for placing her *Nosgay* in readers' hands.

Slips and Plots

Before she can unleash her damning critique of London, Whitney must first develop a persona whose credibility and authoritative voice can rival the prevailing discourse of shame. Against the backdrop of a plague epidemic, the speaker guides her readers through the "maze" of Plat's text, presenting her adaptations as an improvement upon the original (sig. A8^{v}). The pestilence in the air sends the speaker of "The Auctor to the Reader" back home, where, in another moment reminiscent of the *Book of the City of Ladies*, Lady Fortune serves as her "guyde" and "she to Plat his Plot mee brought" (sig. A6^{r-v}). Her physical presence in the garden may allude to a late-Elizabethan trend that Christine Coch describes as "putting beautiful women in their gardens." This practice, she explains, not only reflected "the period's moral ambivalence about art's sensual appeal," but also "allowed a poet further to enrich his work with resonances from earlier well-known texts that featured it."[31] Whitney again appropriates literary conventions, focusing on woman's labor rather than her dangerous beauty. Instead of the shameful object, Whitney's speaker becomes a writing subject. She explores Plat's garden for just an hour because "leasure lackt,/and businesse bad mee hye" (sig. A6^{v}). The remainder of Whitney's "The Auctor to the Reader" makes it clear that her writing is what called her away. Before she leaves Plat's book behind, "A slip I tooke to smell unto,/which might be my defence./In stynking

[29] J. F. D. Shrewsbury, *The History of Bubonic Plague in the British Isles* (Cambridge: Cambridge University Press, 1970), 192.

[30] Meredith Anne Skura, *Tudor Autobiography: Listening for Inwardness* (Chicago: University of Chicago Press, 2010), 156.

[31] Christine Coch, "Woman in the Garden: (En)gendering Pleasure in Late Elizabethan Poetry," *English Literary Renaissance*, 39 (2009), 102.

streetes, or lothsome Lanes/which els might mee infect" (sig. A6ᵛ). In these lines, Plat's poems are the "slips" onto which Whitney grafts her own poetic voice, and she goes on to claim unlimited access to Plat's work: "to come when as I wyll:/Yea, and to chuse of all his Flowers,/ which may my fancy fill" (sig. A7ʳ). She grants herself the right to rifle Plat's poems, which she then presents as both a source of pleasure and a preventative.

In her grafting of Plat's "floures," Whitney adapts and appropriates the poems she "picks" from his textual garden, embracing her role as trespasser and introducing the arguments made in the "Familier Epistles" and her "Wyll." For the most part, Whitney follows the order of Plat's *Floures of Philosophie*, with her numbered poems corresponding to the same in the source text. However, when Plat's adage number 101 brings up the subject of lawyers, Whitney seems driven to expand upon his critique, skipping around to "pluck" other statements about lawyers, wealth, gossip, and "the wicked." Her last ten poetic adaptations vilify the law, arguing that it favors the wealthy, as in number 102 (Plat's 391):

> A little gould in law wyll make,
> Thy matter better speede:
> Then yf thou broughtest of love as much
> As might in kindreds breed. (Sig. C4ʳ)

Lacking both love and money, Whitney's abandoned maidservant illustrates through her own experiences and through her observations of London's forgotten citizens the threat of death or imprisonment faced by those without means or support. In the world as she knows it, Whitney asserts, wealth trumps virtue (poem 103), lawyers exploit the poor (poem 104), loose tongues are dangerous (poems 105–7), and when wicked men prosper, everyone suffers (poem 110). In her minor (but meaningful) revisions to and deliberate selections from Plat, Whitney "plants" her voice and enables its originality to flourish even in an adaptation borrowed from another's authorial stock.

Whitney not only rewrites Plat's aphorisms in charming rhyming couplets, but also selects and revises the advice contained within. The brief hour that she claims to have spent with Plat's text could explain the fact that Whitney adapts just over 100 of Plat's nearly 900 tenets. However, the subjects of the flowers chosen for her *Nosgay* have strong thematic ties to the volume's other sections. Whitney's "Phylosophicall Flowers" provide guidance on the topics of (in the most general terms) friendship, virtue, generosity, and death. Perhaps these sayings inspired her to

leave Plat's book behind to tend to the "businesse" of writing her original
poetry. For example, Whitney's seventh quatrain takes Plat's "Out of
sight, out of minde"[32] and binds it to the question of friendship:

> A saying olde, once out of sight,
>   And also out of minde:
> These contraries, that absent frends
>   Much joy at meeting finde. (Sig. B2ᵛ)

The problem of absent friends is at the center of the "Familier Epistles,"
and Whitney forces the reader to see those who have been out of sight
and out of mind in her "Wyll." Similarly, in Whitney's number 60 (Plat's
59), Whitney take's Plat's maxim, "The poore man hath no friende to
participate his sorrow withal," and she shifts focus from the individual to
emphasize a more common plight:

> The poore, they have no friends at al
>   For to participate,
> The sorrow and the griefe they finde
>   In their most wretched state. (Sig. B8ʳ)

This sense of abandonment is felt by Whitney's speaker in particular
and the marginalized people of London in general throughout *A Sweet
Nosgay*. In fact, the failure of "friends" to provide financial assistance to
those in need becomes Whitney's primary complaint.

Whitney, Ovid, and a New Coterie

In her "Familier Epistles," a coterie enters the *Nosgay*, allowing the poet
to move from the role of solitary writer engaged with other texts to an
actual literary exchange with individual men and women. The correspondence presents a more direct confrontation with the social and economic forces that threaten Whitney's speaker and others in her position.
In another collaboration through appropriation, the epistles refigure the
abandoned Heroidean woman who, after receiving unsatisfying responses
(or none at all), carries out her threats of suicide in the form of her fictional death. Echoing the letters of Ovid's *Heroides*, Whitney's epistolary
verses attempt to rewrite the story of a shamed maidservant who has been
dismissed from her post and seeks to clear her name. At the same time,
Whitney appropriates the tradition of humanist dialogues and epistles,

---

[32] Plat, *Floures of Philosophie*, 1.

which Judith Deitch contends allows women writers to "imagine for themselves not only the intimate relation with a friend but also, explicitly, the wider circle of readers, male and female, who will carry on its discussions."[33] Whitney collaborates with her fictional coterie to graft her speaker's identity with that of the writer, narrating the countless ways she has been forsaken.

The first epistle, "To her Brother G. W.," imagines the addressee's absence from London as a response to plague, immediately tying the communications in the second section to the occasion of the first. Isabella Whitney ("the Auctor") is identified as the letter writer, blurring the line between poet and speaker in a way that is again similar to Christine de Pizan's *Book of the City of Ladies*. Whitney writes, "Good Brother when a vacant time/doth cause you hence to ryde" (sig. C5^v). The "vacant time" that prompted G. W.'s departure points to the fact that, as Ian Munro states, "[t]he city under plague is a depopulated city."[34] Londoners who could afford to do so often fled the city in times of plague, with "servants, apprentices, and hangers-on ... left to shift for themselves."[35] It appears that G. W. has also abandoned his sister, and she indicates that he is (or was) her primary source of support: "You are, and must be chiefest staffe/that I shal stay on heare" (sig. C6^v). The imagery of the garden is also echoed here, as a staff is used to support the stalk of a new or weak plant.[36] Whitney's male addressees continue to prove unhelpful, and Whitney goes on to describe her great suffering in "A carefull complaint by the unfortunate Auctor," in which she laments the cruelty of Fortune, who has turned the speaker's health "to heapes of payne" (sig. D3^r). In response, her friend, T. B., chides her for wallowing, while another correspondent, C. B., offers sympathy and well wishes – but no material support. In her exchanges with men, Whitney apologizes for her writing, as in her letter to B. W.: "Then wyll I wryt, or yet resyte,/ within this Paper weake" (sig. C7^r). Her tone is less familiar than in the letters to her sisters, and she seems resigned to her suffering with little hope of relief. While all of Whitney's letters to male correspondents clearly seek support, she uses her letters to other women to serve a different purpose.

---

[33] Judith Deitch, "'Dialoguewise': Discovering Alterity in Elizabethan Dialogues," in Helen Ostovich, Mary V. Silcox, and Graham Roebuck (eds.), *Other Voices, Other Views: Expanding the Canon in English Renaissance Studies* (Newark: University of Delaware Press, 1999), 249.

[34] Munro, "The City and Its Double," 250.

[35] Byrne, *Daily Life*, 69.

[36] *OED*, s.v. "staff."

The epistles addressed to Whitney's sisters illustrate the ways in which women's lives were constrained by domestic responsibilities, whether in service or in marriage. Rather than inquiring about their health or location, the letters participate in a tradition of female legacies, which Wendy Wall defines as "a form not crucial for its feminine difference, or for its marking of a female consciousness, but for its provision of a stance from which women could publicly challenge cultural demands for their silence."[37] Mother's legacies developed as a means for pregnant women facing the risks of childbirth to provide posthumous guidance to their children.[38] Whitney appropriates this tradition to offer advice to her sisters, and she uses her misfortune as a source of authority in the same way that pregnancy "presented … a demarcated and culturally acknowledged moment of peril that made it natural for women to be both the authors of and the audience for articulations of wisdom and counsel."[39] This legacy of advice allows Whitney to prove her virtue through the admission of past errors and evidence of her newfound wisdom. Anticipating her own absence in "Modest Meane for Maids," Whitney prepares readers for her final testament:

> Good Sisters mine, when I
>   shal further from you dwell:
> Peruse these lines, observe the rules
>   which in the same I tell. (Sig. C7ᵛ)

This time Whitney is the one leaving loved ones behind – a reversal of her correspondence with male friends and relatives. However, Whitney attempts to offer more than mere platitudes as support. She goes on to detail the ways in which young women in service can ensure their place in the household. Her advice reiterates that of the "Phylosophicall Flowers," urging her sisters to avoid gossip, be modest, please their employers, and, above all, trust in God. Whitney reminds the young women,

> Refer you all to hym,
>   that sits above the skyes:
> Vengeance is his, he wil reveng,
>   you need it not devise. (Sig. C8ᵛ)

This description of an all-seeing, vengeful God foreshadows the panoptic view of London that Whitney provides in the volume's final poem, her

[37] Wendy Wall, "Isabella Whitney and the Female Legacy," *English Literary History*, 58 (1991), 46.
[38] See Paula McQuade's discussion of the Mother's Legacy (Chapter 15) in this volume.
[39] Wall, "Isabella Whitney," 38.

"Wyll and Testament." In her advice to leave vengeance to God, Whitney may be reminding herself as well. Whitney will model this counsel in the generosity of her "Wyll." Whitney's legacy of advice for her sisters privileges the speaker's experience and adds weight to her words.

In addition to her use of the legacy tradition to authorize her writing in general, Whitney uses the epistles to her sisters to proclaim her status as a professional writer. To her younger sisters in service, she insists:

> I some things must write,
>   take paynes to read the same:
> Hencefoorth my lyfe as wel as Pen
>   shall your examples frame. (Sig. D1ʳ)

Connecting her lived experience with her writing, Whitney merges the two and claims writing not as a diversion but as something she "must" do (and as something of value to readers). Her use of "Hencefoorth" may suggest that, until this point, her life has not been as exemplary as her writing. This may be Whitney's way of telling her sisters, "Do as I say, not as I do," accepting her past indiscretions as shameful. However, in shamelessly asserting writing as essential, she merges her "lyfe" and her pen to declare her poetry honorable. Her married sister, "Misteris A. B.," appears to have provided financial support in the past, and Whitney does not want her to think she "vainely had bestowed expence" (sig. D2ᵛ). She praises her sister and her family, wishing them long, happy lives, then closes the epistle with a rather pointed comparison:

> I know you huswyfery intend,
> though I to writing fall:
> Wherefore no lenger shall you stay,
> From businesse, that profit may.
>
> Had I a Husband or a house,
> and all that longes therto
> My selfe could frame about to rouse,
> as other women doo:
> But til some houshold cares mee tye,
> My bookes and Pen I wyll apply. (Sig. D2ʳ)

Marriage and authorship, according to Whitney, are not compatible. In fact, it is the speaker's current freedom from the "household cares" of a maidservant that allows her to write at all. She suggests that her sister's "businesse" of being a wife barely leaves her time to read the letter. The second stanza compares the poet to "other women" and emphasizes her identity as a single "servicelesse" woman who is free from all "tye[s]." Whitney concludes that, while she remains unbound, she will devote herself to her writing. However, in the final epistle, declaring herself "wery of writyng," Whitney decides, "For now I wyll my writting cleane forsake/ till of my griefes, my stomack I discharg" (sig. E2ʳ). Here the stomach could stand in for the heart or breast "to designate the inward seat of passion, emotion, secret thoughts, affections, or feelings."[40] Alternatively, Whitney may be blaming her physical illness on the grief caused by her abandonment. In either case, Whitney's need to "discharg" her grief leads the reader to her "Wyll and Testament." She again draws on the female legacy tradition, using the occasion of her fictional death to privilege her voice as she shifts from epistolary dialogue to a monologic critique of London's abandonment of the poor.

Poetry, Palimpsest, Panopticon

Within *A Sweet Nosgay*'s final poem, the continued influence of Christine de Pizan's *Book of the City of Ladies* is apparent, most prominently in Whitney's acknowledgment that power can be located on the periphery of society through a collaborative effort to rewrite the dominant discourse. Upon being visited by the Ladies Reason, Rectitude, and Justice, Susan Schibanoff asserts, Christine "come[s] to realize that her own feelings and thoughts about women ... are more authoritative than the opinions of all the poets and philosophers she has studied."[41] The women serve as the material from which the city is constructed, built on a foundation cleared of the evils of misogyny by means of female labor. Because the city is literally made of women, the space and the women who occupy it cannot be separated. Jill E. Wagner observes that Christine's history of women is organized thematically rather than chronologically, which allows readers to "mentally picture a part of the city and focus on the virtues of the women within it."[42] Whitney adopts this strategy in her literary construction of London in the "Wyll," imposing her own order by grouping sites thematically to show the interconnectedness of commerce and human suffering.

---

[40] *OED*, s.v., "stomach."

[41] Susan Schibanoff, "Comment on Kelly's 'Early Feminist Theory and the *Querelles des Femmes*, 1400–1789,'" *Signs*, 9 (1983), 324.

[42] Jill E. Wagner, "Christine de Pizan's City of Ladies: A Monumental (Re)construction of, by, and for Women of All Time," *Medieval Feminist Forum (MFF)*, 44 (2008), 76.

Like Christine de Pizan, Whitney locates her legitimacy among the people on whose backs London is built. This connection of bodies and space was particularly meaningful to early modern readers, because of the parallel development of cartographic and anatomical representations during the period. In her examination of these parallels, Caterina Albano argues, "the body is itself a site for the recognition of spatial organization in the distinction between surface and internal parts, and ... bodily positions and movements organize the space in which they exist."[43] Drawing attention to her poor health throughout the *Nosgay*, Whitney emphasizes the ways in which her embodiment both liberates and hinders. In the "Wyll and Testament" the speaker's impending (fictional) death frees her body to move about the streets of London as she enacts her own survey of the city. In doing so, she participates in an activity reserved for men, one that was of particular interest to the landowning gentry, John M. Adrian notes, "not only because [surveys] describe familiar topography ... but because they enact the very order that was the chief political function of the gentry."[44] In her appropriation of this genre, Whitney instead reveals the *dis*order threatening London and its inhabitants, through both her nonlinear reordering of familiar sites and her paradoxical positioning of London's consumer culture alongside the suffering of its impoverished citizens. As chorographical texts, surveys engage in what Howard Marchitello describes as "the typically narrative and only occasionally graphic practice of delineating topography not exclusively as it exists in the present moment but as it has existed historically as well."[45] In Whitney's narrative tour of London, she engages past and present, reimagining the city not as a fixed place but as a palimpsestic space on which she can write herself into the story of her beloved "famous Citie" (sig. E2ʳ).[46]

The city itself is constructed as an unfaithful male lover, appropriating and reversing traditional comparisons of the city to a woman's

---

[43] Albano, "Visible Bodies," 90.

[44] John M. Adrian, "Tudor Centralization and Gentry Visions of Local Order in Lambarde's *Perambulation of Kent*," *English Literary Renaissance*, 36 (2006), 307–34 at 310.

[45] Howard Marchitello, "Political Maps: The Production of Cartography and Chorography in Early Modern England," in Margaret J. M. Ezell and Katherine O'Brien O'Keefe (eds.), *Cultural Artifacts and the Production of Meaning: The Page, the Image, and the Body* (Ann Arbor: University of Michigan Press, 1994), 13–40 at 22.

[46] See Jonathan Gil Harris, *Untimely Matter in the Time of Shakespeare* (Philadelphia: University of Pennsylvania Press, 2009), 95–118, for a palimpsestic reading of John Stow's *Survey of London*. My argument, unlike Harris's, stresses gender as a central feature of the chorographic palimpsest.

body.[47] In her blazon of the city, Whitney usurps the male poetic gaze and turns it away from the female body toward the bustling and dirty streets of London. Readers see the city through Whitney's eyes, meeting vendors, tradesmen, criminals, and other members of London's "common" population, for whom the city's wealth is out of reach. Rather than directly criticizing those in power, Whitney reveals the experiences of the poor and powerless, ultimately undermining the authorities of London and usurping that authority for herself as the voice of the oppressed. Whitney's bequeathals to the city begin with "Brave buildings rare, of Churches store,/and Pauls to the head" (sig. E3ᵛ). From the top of St Paul's Cathedral, the most prominent structure in London, Whitney establishes a vantage point high above the city. Citing Michel de Certeau, Andrew Gordon argues that such a position "construct[s] an image of the city which remains oblivious to the activities of those on the ground."[48] Whitney, however, quickly reminds her readers that "Betweene the same: fayre streats there bee,/and people goodly store" (sig. E3ᵛ). This abrupt shift highlights the distance between the two, even as it recognizes their proximity. Helen Wilcox contends that Whitney "does not think of [St Paul's] in terms of its spiritual influence but as a physical presence."[49] However, the view from St Paul's reiterates Whitney's repeated reminders that God is watching, and the cathedral acts as a Panopticon from which the poet becomes the all-seeing eye.

Like the City of Ladies, Whitney's London is constructed thematically. Appropriating the perambulation, a literary mode concerned with boundaries and order, Whitney reads the city through the lens of one who has been relegated to its margins. In her comparison of Whitney's description with Queen Elizabeth's 1559 progress through the city, Rhonda Lemke Sanford states, "Whitney uncovers what is covered up and hidden in the coronation pageant as we move from the seen to the unseen, from the *scene* of the pageants to the *obscene* of the back streets."[50] In her first move, Whitney connects the specter of St Paul's with commerce and government, providing butchers, bakers, and brewers

---

[47] See: Phillippy, "The Maid's Lawful Liberty"; Wall, *Imprint of Gender*, 296–310; Paul Gleed, "'I lov'de thee best': London as Male Beloved in Isabella Whitney's 'The Manner of her Wyll,'" *The London Journal*, 37 (2012) 1–12.

[48] Andrew Gordon, "Performing London: The Map and the City in Ceremony," in Andrew Gordon and Bernhard Klein (eds.), *Literature, Mapping, and the Politics of Space in Early Modern Britain* (Cambridge: Cambridge University Press, 2001), 69.

[49] Wilcox, "'ah famous citie,'" 24.

[50] Rhonda Lemke Sanford, *Maps and Memory in Early Modern England: A Sense of Place* (New York: Palgrave, 2002), 115.

to feed London's residents, as well as fish markets for those "such as orders doo observe,/and eat fish thrice a weeke" (sig. E3ᵛ). Along with these provisions, Whitney later recognizes St Paul's as a site of intellectual sustenance, praising the bookbinders, printers, and booksellers "because I lyke their Arte" (sig. E6ᵛ). For her own printer, she "wyll[s] my Friends these Bookes to bye" (sig. E6ᵛ), using this opportunity for self-promotion. Whitney groups together these spaces for spiritual, edible, and textual nourishment, demarcating their transactions as both different and more valuable than the sites of commerce, wealth, and punishment that follow.

The bulk of Whitney's "Wyll" juxtaposes the excesses of consumption with the cruel and indifferent treatment of those who, like her, do not have access to London's material wealth. She details the various goods one might purchase and where they are found, like linen on Friday Street, jewelry and other luxury items on Cheapside, footwear in St Martins, and tailors scattered throughout the "Streetes or Lanes" (sig. E4ᵛ). Whitney's inventory abruptly shifts to the armories and other sites that use fear of violence to assert power, like posting the heads of traitors and conspirators on iron spikes at Temple Bar or the permanent scaffold and gallows built on Tower Hill (sig. E4ᵛ). This brutality is linked back to London's wealth as Whitney directs her readers to the Mint, housed in the Tower of London – another site that inspires fear of punishment. Moving away from symbols of wealth and power, Whitney turns her attention to the poor, to whom she leaves prisons, sites of execution, ill-reputed hospitals, and a workhouse.[51] Throughout this ironic bequeathal, Whitney situates herself among those who face these consequences as a result of their poverty. Whitney concludes her "Wyll" by leaving lawyers to assist the wealthy as they "strive for House or Land" (sig. E7ʳ), repeating the critique of lawyers levied in her "Phylosophicall Flowers." In the end, those who are in a position to help the poor abandon them, and Whitney prepares for death.

Whitney's *Nosgay* is bound by a rhetoric of shame, though the speaker's shame will become that of the city by the end of the "Wyll." In her request for burial, Whitney admits she cannot contribute to the cost, but she asks a personified London to "consider that above the ground,/ annoyance bee I shall" (sig. E7ᵛ). With this reminder, Whitney again

---

[51] See Whitney, *Sweet Nosgay*, E5ᵛ–E6ʳ: Counter Prison, Newgate Prison, Holborn Hill (site of hangings), Ludgate Prison, Smithfield (site of commerce and executions), Bartholomew Hospital, Bethlehem Hospital, and Bridewell (a royal palace converted into a workhouse for the poor).

evokes the presence of plague, which created so many corpses that bodies were wrapped in sheets and thrown into plague pits.[52] As a final gesture to her omniscience and London's shameful state, Whitney makes a request: "let me have a shrowding Sheete/to cover mee from shame" (sig. E7^v). In this fatal image, the *Nosgay* alludes to Christ's crucifixion, a "spectacle of shame" that, unlike Whitney's body, cannot be buried "in oblivyon" (sig. E7^v).[53]

---

[52] Gilman, *Plague Writing*, 58.
[53] Virginia Burrus, *Saving Shame: Martyrs, Saints, and Other Abject Subjects* (Philadelphia: University of Pennsylvania Press, 2008), 44.

7

Transmitting Faith
Elizabeth Tudor, Anne Askew, and Jane Grey

Elaine V. Beilin

Princess Elizabeth's *The Glasse of the Synnefull Soule* still exists written in her own hand in a presentation copy given to her stepmother, Queen Katherine Parr. While we might wish that Anne Askew's *Examinations* and Jane Grey's letter to her sister still survived in holograph, we have yet to find them. As many scholars realize, however, the missed opportunity to pore over Askew's handwritten account of her interrogations is countered somewhat by the advantages of possessing editors' responses and commentaries in the early printed versions of her text.

Bringing these three writers together creates an opportunity to review a historical moment when these and other women writers participated in vigorous religious communities and possessed some authority as voices of faith. Although fiery persecution certainly marks the life-and-death debates over doctrines such as transubstantiation in the mid-1540s, the decade from 1544 to 1554 may also be generally characterized by its overlapping religious doctrines, when Catholics and Reformers shared traditional texts and piety. Janel Mueller describes Queen Katherine Parr's 1545 *Prayers or Meditations*, a recasting of Richard Whitford's English translation of Thomas à Kempis's *De Imitatione Christi*, as an attempt "to foster Reformed devotion among the literate laity of the late Henrician Church of England by performing a generic reorientation on the masterpiece of late medieval Catholic spirituality." Similarly, Lucy Busfield finds "fluidity" and "confessional interplay" in examples of Passion meditations drawing on late medieval sources adapted to the doctrines of the new dispensation, and Elizabeth Malson-Huddle shows how Askew's texts reveal "both her radical defiance of church doctrine and her continued attachment to aspects of the late medieval Catholic liturgy."[1] Each writer considered

---

[1] Parr, *Katherine Parr*, 373; Lucy Busfield, "Women, Men, and Christ Crucified: Protestant Passion Piety in Sixteenth-Century England," *Reformation and Renaissance Review*, 15 (2013), 217–36 at 219; Elizabeth Malson-Huddle, "Anne Askew and the Controversy over the Real Presence," *Studies in English Literature 1500–1900*, 50 (2010), 1–16 at 1.

here contributes to the ongoing shaping of belief, and whether translating, bearing witness, or exhorting, she teaches her chosen audience about faith.

Tracing the complicated history of textual transmission raises similar questions about each writer: why were Elizabeth's, Askew's, and Grey's works continually reproduced and why and how were they repeatedly revised and adapted? Just as interesting an inquiry centers on how these three authors figure in both written and visual texts, continually adapted to play new roles. While all their writings deserve study to answer these questions fully, this chapter will focus on three texts written at a moment when religious devotion centered on reading the English Bible, an unmediated relationship with God, and habits of intense spiritual self-examination: the young Princess Elizabeth's *The Glasse of the Synnefull Soule* (1544), her translation of Marguerite de Navarre's poem, *Le miroir de l'âme pécheresse;* passages in Askew's *Examinations* related to her faith community (1546); and Jane Grey's letter to her sister written in her Greek New Testament (1554). As an intense expression of Christ's saving grace for the sinner guided by Scripture, Elizabeth's translation looks back to late medieval devotion and forward to the full validation of English Bible reading. Similarly grounded in Scripture, Askew's texts attest to the dangerous confrontations during Henry VIII's last years between the evangelical community and their conservative opponents.[2] Grey fiercely preaches the doctrines of the Edwardian Reformation, writing when they were threatened by a Catholic resurgence. At the heart of their work is the conviction that Scripture provides the key to living and dying. Each text is memorably first person, giving the powerful sense of an individual expression of faith, and each writer creates a voice that directly encourages readers' self-examination and spiritual participation. This rhetorically clear voice seems to be a key element male editors seize upon when they introduce, praise, and adapt each text. As the texts are reedited and republished, however, the dominant persona of the Christian soul exhorting her readers to search their own souls, once separated from her original audience and networks, reappears as a self-contained female figure exemplifying certain designated virtues, such as piety, constancy, or nobility. Elizabeth, Askew, and Grey emerge as solitary female figures, repositioned as icons of faith, rather than as participants in rich intellectual and religious networks.[3]

---

[2] See Alex Ryrie, "The Strange Death of Lutheran England," *The Journal of Ecclesiastical History,* 53 (2002), 64–92.

[3] In "Representations of Women in Tudor Historiography: John Bale and the Rhetoric of Exemplarity," *Renaissance and Reformation/Renaissance et Réforme,* 22 (1998), 41–61, Krista Kesselring shows how Bale configures Elizabeth and Askew as exemplary historical and political agents.

This chapter will focus on the religious-political environments in which these women wrote in the 1540s and 1550s, drawing on scholarship that has amassed evidence of women writers' active participation in the English Reformation, positioning them ever more precisely in multiple historical, theological, and cultural contexts. An essential strand of this investigation has focused on the many networks and collaborations in which women writers participated, whether within families, instructional relationships, reading circles, religious settings, or book editing, publishing, and selling networks. Studies in intertextuality, the history of the book, material culture, and manuscript circulation, all assisted by the continuing archival recovery of letters and papers, have repeatedly demonstrated that women writers functioned actively in a nexus of literary, political, social, and economic relationships on both sides of the confessional divide and sometimes in between.[4] Even if the community of believers who formed their initial audience was small, circumscribed by rank or access – as in Elizabeth's case – eventually, these texts and their authors reach far beyond their first readers, fulfilling the interests of their later editors and publishers.

Elizabeth Tudor, *The Glasse of the Synnefull Soule* (1544)

Particularly through Queen Katherine Parr's tutelage and example, young Elizabeth found an intensely self-reflective form of devotional thought and feeling, first expressed in her translation, *The Glasse of the Synnefull Soule*, and its dedication. Elizabeth presented her translation to Parr at an eventful moment in her stepmother's life, and the evidence suggests that Elizabeth's work relates closely to Parr's activities. In 1544, Parr was regent during Henry VIII's absence in France, and in 1544–1545 she was also working on *Psalms or Prayers*, a translation of John Fisher's Latin Psalm collage with added original prayers, and on *Prayers and Meditations* – both texts that demonstrate the continuities and differences between late medieval Catholic and early Reformation devotion. On July 31, 1544, Elizabeth sent an Italian letter to Parr from Saint James, marking her months of close association with her stepmother, who brought the absent Henry's three children to Hampton Court and then out into the countryside with her during a plague outbreak.[5] When Henry returned in the autumn, Elizabeth went back to Ashridge in Hertfordshire, from where she dates her translation of Marguerite's poem. In the next year,

---

[4] See Summit, *Lost Property*, chapter 3, and all the essays in White (ed.), *English Women*.
[5] Letter 1, translated in Marcus, Mueller, and Rose (eds.), *Elizabeth I: Collected Works*; and Susan Doran, *Queen Elizabeth I* (New York: New York University Press, 2003), 22.

she completed her translation into Latin, French, and Italian of Parr's *Prayers and Meditations*, presenting her work to her father in December 1545 as "the most excellent tribute that my capacity and diligence could discover."[6] At the same time, she presented her English translation of chapter 1 of Calvin's *Institution de la Religion Chrestienne* to Parr "as testimony that not for anything in this world would I want to fall into any arrears in my duty towards your grace." Significantly, Elizabeth adds the wish that "the organ of your royal voice may be the true instrument of His Word, in order to serve as a mirror and lamp to all true Christian men and women."[7] From Parr's example – and likely with her active guidance – Elizabeth appears to recognize the role a politically prominent translator might play in establishing reformed devotion, and she adds her texts to that enterprise. As Jonathan Gibson argues, Elizabeth's texts "were produced at a key moment of transition and accommodation between medieval 'Catholicism' and early modern 'Protestantism.' Texts produced at this liminal point by Elizabeth and others – women active in the shaping of the English Reformation – helped set the parameters for a good deal of pious writing in prose and poetry in early modern England."[8]

As every reader of *The Glasse of the Synnefull Soule* confirms, Marguerite's poem and Elizabeth's translation articulate a direct relationship between the sinner and God, faith in the saving grace of Christ, and a profound reliance on the Bible as the source of knowledge, faith, and wisdom. These elements place the translation squarely in the religious milieu fostered by Parr, recalling medieval devotion, even as it contributed to the future of Protestant piety – although readers must still navigate the shoals of Marguerite's particular choice of metaphor and Elizabeth's renderings. The central trope rings the changes on family relationships, as the sinner represents Christ treating his soul like a "father, brother, childe, and spowse" to whom the sinner is daughter, sister, mother, and wife.[9] As Anne Prescott finds, *Le miroir* "explores a set of analogies through which mortals can indicate otherwise incommunicable religious feelings, expressing them in terms of familial and erotic relationships."[10]

---

[6] Letter 3, translated from Latin, in *Elizabeth I: Collected Works*.

[7] Letter 4, translated from French, in *Elizabeth I: Collected Works*.

[8] Jonathan Gibson, "Katherine Parr, Princess Elizabeth, and the Crucified Christ," in Burke and Gibson (eds.), *Early Modern Women's Manuscript Writing*, 33.

[9] Princess Elizabeth's Translation of Marguerite de Navarre's *Le miroir de l'âme pécheresse*, 1544 (original-spelling version) in Scodel and Mueller (eds.), *Elizabeth I: Translations*, 66.

[10] Anne Lake Prescott, "The Pearl of the Valois and Elizabeth I: Marguerite de Navarre's *Miroir* and Tudor England," in Hannay (ed.), *Silent but for the Word*, 61–76 at 68.

Perhaps, as Prescott and others have argued, Elizabeth saw the knot of family relationships in the French poem as a way to write about her own painful relationships and her anger; or by dedicating a work by Marguerite de Navarre to Katherine, she was trying to attract Henry's attention. Seeing it as a fully reformist text, Maureen Quilligan argues that as the memorial nature of the Eucharist replaces the priestly mediator with an intensely direct relationship between the sinner and God, Elizabeth's incest trope "layers the fullness of filial affection onto the potency of sexual desire, making a newer and more powerfully intimate contact out of the mix."[11] Roger Ellis sees Elizabeth's "juvenile translations" as aiming "to make her position at court more secure," although he also identifies *The Glasse* with Marguerite's work as a "mystical text of (Erasmian) Catholic persuasion" resembling its medieval forerunners.[12] In his edition of the text, Marc Shell finds that the translation may be a predictor of "how a preadolescent young woman of 1544 formed her spirit but also how that spirit informed the political identity of the English nation."[13] That its metaphors inform such varied psychological, political, sociological, and religious interpretations suggests that *The Glasse of the Synnefull Soule* cannot be read merely as a juvenile first attempt.

In John Bale's 1548 edition, *A Godly Medytacyon of the Christen Sowle, Concerninge a Love Towardes God and Hys Christe*, almost every sentence is edited, many rhetorically or grammatically improved. Whether Katherine Parr or Bale or both are the improvers and editors is difficult to say, but Jaime Goodrich shows that this version "definitively established Elizabeth's reformist credentials."[14] In view of Parr's active writing life and patronage from 1544 to 1548, we may imagine her attending to Elizabeth's text as the young princess had requested. In her dedicatory letter, Elizabeth writes:

> yet do i truste also that oubeit it is like a worke wich is but newe begonne, and shapen: that the fyle of youre excellent witte, and godly lerninge, in the reding of it (if so it vouchsafe youre highnes to do) shall rubbe out, polishe; and mende (or els cause to mende) the wordes (or rather the order of my writting), the wich i knowe in many places to be rude, and nothinge done as it shuld be.[15]

[11] Quilligan, *Incest and Agency*, 50.
[12] Roger Ellis, "The Juvenile Translations of Elizabeth Tudor," *Translation and Literature*, 18:2 (2009), 157–80 at 158 and 160.
[13] Shell, *Elizabeth's Glass*, 7.
[14] Goodrich, *Faithful Translators*, 90. Goodrich suggests changes Parr and Bale might separately make.
[15] Elizabeth I, *Elizabeth I: Translations*, 42.

Elizabeth's perfect metaphor of the file shows her writerly gifts, as she imagines Parr's editing skills as the metal instrument that smooths the roughness. This humble wish for help seems somewhat at odds with the text that follows, for Elizabeth quite ably translates the mature voice of Marguerite's sinner lamenting a lifetime of original and volitional sin and yet seeking salvation. Prescott describes Marguerite's poem as having "a definite direction: from self-loathing to joyful anticipation, from death in life to life in death, from dismay at her betrayal of God to faith in his steadfast love, and therefore to her acceptance of her own role as the beloved."[16] The narrative arc of Elizabeth's translation surefootedly traces the journey from abject horror at sinfulness, to gratitude for God's merciful and salvific grace. At base are the sinner's "personal" experience and instructional voice, melded in sentence after sentence where "I" becomes "our": "Than i se to haue no other accuser, but iesuschrist wich is my redeemer, whose death hath restored vs, oure inheritaunce for he made hymselfe oure man a lawe, shewynge hys so worthy merites afore god, wherewith my g great dette is so surmounted, that in iudgemente she is accompted for nothinge."[17]

If Elizabeth had Marguerite's immediate guidance through the tangles of the human-divine relationship, more speculatively, we may also place her as heir to her great-grandmother, Lady Margaret Beaufort, who herself set a precedent for publishing translations of devotional texts by translating *Le mirouer dor de lame pecheresse tres utile et profitable*, a French version of *Speculum aureum animae peccatricis*, a fifteenth-century Carthusian work, as *The mirroure of golde for the synfull soule* (printed 1522, 1526).[18] Possibly, Elizabeth's mother, Anne Boleyn, may have been another influence, since she may have owned a copy of Marguerite's *Le miroir*, and she corresponded with Marguerite during 1534 and 1535.[19] Significantly, the voice of the young scholar in the dedicatory letter and the voice of the adult sinner meet in the persona of the godly woman, who derives her learning from Scripture, which glosses every page of the original and the translation.

Indicative of the continuing religious significance of both the writer and the work, the translation appeared in five sixteenth-century editions.

[16] Prescott, "Pearl of the Valois," 64.
[17] Elizabeth I, *Elizabeth I: Translations*, 106–8.
[18] Hosington analyzes Lady Margaret's translations in "Lady Margaret Beaufort's Translations."
[19] Mueller and Scodel (eds.), in *Elizabeth I: Translations*, 25, acknowledge scholars' speculation about Boleyn's copy of *Le miroir*, but "no such manuscript or printed volume has yet been found."

After Bale adapted it for his militantly Protestant agenda, the translation reappeared edited by James Cancellar in 1568 and 1580 before its publication in 1582 in Thomas Bentley's anthology, *The Monument of Matrons*. The final sixteenth-century printing was Roger Ward's 1590 reprint of Bale's edition, with some adjustments.[20] When Mueller and Scodel note that Elizabeth's early translations establish her "learned, pious persona – her first public identity, and an enduring one – " they describe well Elizabeth's early representation as a daughter and sister of kings who is also a figure of faith. They also assert that both Bale and Cancellar make extensive changes to "regularize" Elizabeth's text "to validate its religious authority and utility for a sixteenth-century readership."[21] Princess Elizabeth's figuration as the godly woman appears inseparable from her political presence, as the woodcut used at the beginning and end of Bale's edition demonstrates. The long title to Bale's volume ends by identifying *Elyzabeth/doughter to our late soverayne Kynge Henri the viii*. Directly below these words is the woodcut featuring a crowned Elizabeth, kneeling before the immense figure of a risen Christ, who points heavenward. As Princess Elizabeth offers her book to Christ, his gesture may imply salvation for the princess or a declaration that the book teaches its readers how to achieve salvation. Goodrich analyzes the woodcut closely, proposing that Christ displaying his pierced foot makes Elizabeth another Mary Magdalene witnessing the resurrection, and through this direct relationship, establishing "Elizabeth as a royal scion whose learned devotion both embodies and authorizes reform."[22]

Bale's edition is an important step towards making Elizabeth into a Reformation icon. As the epitome of "nobility," which Bale defines as believing and seeking "to do the wyll of the eternall father," Elizabeth is a royal figure of learning and piety, as "the translacyon of thys worke, were evydence strenge ynough."[23] Elizabeth's worldly nobility may derive from her parentage, but she achieves true nobility by her learning and active faith. As in his earlier editions of Askew's *Examinations*, published in 1546 and 1547, Bale attacks the faith, doctrine, and Church hierarchy of England's Catholic past in favor of establishing a Reformed Church,

---

[20] See Quilligan, *Incest and Agency*, 76–101, for key distinctions among the editions. Quilligan relates the incest trope to female agency and Reformation theology.

[21] Elizabeth I, *Elizabeth I: Translations*, 26. Mueller and Scodel show every change Bale and Cancellar made, demonstrating the printed versions' "muting" of Elizabeth's translations of Marguerite's "passionate religious feelings" and their insuring the text's religious orthodoxy (37–8).

[22] Goodrich, *Faithful Translators*, 97.

[23] John Bale, *A Godly Medytacyon of the Christen Sowle* (Wesel: (Marburg), 1548), sig. 6ᵛ and 41ʳ.

representing these two young women as valuable assets in the religious-political conflict, particularly given Elizabeth's political position.

Anne Askew, *The Firste Examinacyon* (1546) and *The Lattre Examinacyon* (1547)

Two years before his publication of Elizabeth's *Godly Medytacyon*, Bale, in exile in the Protestant Duchy of Cleves during the last years of Henry VIII, communicated with Dutch merchants who apparently brought him Anne Askew's manuscripts, which Bale's collaborator, Dirik van der Straten, printed as *The Firste Examinacyon* (1546) and *The Lattre Examinacyon* (1547), each including Bale's introductions and extensive "elucidations." Four further editions appeared from different presses by 1560, as well as an edition of *The Firste Examination* around 1585. John Foxe included *The Examinations* in every edition of *Actes and Monuments*, so that they were always in print, and had a wide readership.[24] The texts first circulated to serve Bale's writing of Protestant history, where he identified Askew as a martyr comparable to the earliest Christian martyrs in her "infatygable" and "myghtye" spirit and her resistance to "the enemyes of truthe."[25] Extrapolating the more specific community to which Askew belonged is largely a matter of circumstantial evidence. Whereas Elizabeth's biography is relatively full, Askew's is disappointingly sparse and her own writing provides no information about her domestic life and very little about her fellow reformers. She alludes to her earlier years in Lincolnshire only to illustrate her narrative of persecution and triumph, as when she confronts the priests in Lincoln minster, although her "fryndes" advised her not to go. Her silence appears to have motivated Bale to supply his own account of her marriage, motherhood, and violent expulsion from her home, although he does not identify his sources other than to write, "as I am infourmed … I heare saye … I thynke."[26] He may be alluding to an evangelical network that provided information, but he may also be constructing a biographical context for a figure he was shaping as a Protestant martyr.[27]

While many later sources connect Askew and Katherine Parr, only circumstantial evidence from the 1540s links them. Askew declares that

---

[24] See Beilin, "Textual Introduction," in Askew, *The Examinations*, xlv–liv.
[25] Askew, *The Examinations*, 12.
[26] Ibid., 56 and 92.
[27] See Beilin, "A Woman for All Seasons."

Richard Rich and "one of the counsell" questioned "if I knewe man or woman of my secte," and she says that they asked about "my ladye of Sothfolke, my ladye of Sussex, my ladye of Hertforde, my ladye Dennye, and my ladye Fizwyllyams. I sayd, if I shuld pronounce anye thynge against them, that I were not hable to prove it."[28] Countering Susan James's claim that all the women about whom Askew was questioned were in Parr's "inner circle," Thomas Freeman finds that "This claim might be made for the countess of Hertford and the duchess of Suffolk ... but it can hardly be made for the countess of Sussex or Lady Denny and there are no discernible ties at all between the queen and Lady Fitzwilliam."[29] As Freeman clarifies, Askew does not say that she was questioned about the queen or about the three women who were closest to Parr and under earlier suspicion for heretical reading (her sister, Anne Herbert; her cousin, Maud Lane; and Elizabeth Tyrwhit, who was most likely Foxe's main source of information about Parr). Whether Askew actually met Katherine Parr is unknown. The first text to make that claim appears to be Robert Persons' *The Third Part of a Treatise: Intituled of Three Conversions of England*, a Jesuit polemic written six decades later. As part of an attempt to reclaim England as a Catholic country still venerating the true saints of Catholic history rather than the invented martyrs of Foxe's *Actes and Monuments*, Persons describes Askew supplying Parr and her court with "hereticall books." The often quoted positive view of Askew's impact also appears much later in Bathsua Makin's 1673 assessment of Askew's influence on Parr: "Mris. *Ann Askue*, a Person famous for Learning and Piety, so seasoned the Queen, and Ladies at Court, by her Precepts and Examples, and after sealed her Profession with her Blood, that the Seed of Reformation seemed to be sowed by her hand."[30]

If the links between Askew and Parr are undocumented, who did make up Askew's community of faith? What is her "secte"? Who are her "fryndes"? Askew expresses a strong sense of her audience for *The Examinations*, perhaps a specific reformist community, beginning *The Firste Examinacyon* with the sentence, "To satisfie your expectation, good

[28] Askew, *The Examinations*, 121 and 122.
[29] Thomas S. Freeman, "One Survived: The Account of Katherine Parr in Foxe's *Book of Martyrs*," in Thomas Betteridge and Susannah Lipscomb (eds.), *Henry VIII and the Court: Art, Politics and Performance* (Farnham: Ashgate, 2013), 249.
[30] Robert Persons, *The Third Part of a Treatise, Intituled of Three Conversions of England* (St. Omer: English College Press, 1603/4), book 2, 494. See: Victor Houliston, *Catholic Resistance in Elizabethan England: Robert Persons's Jesuit Polemic* (Aldershot and Rome: Ashgate and Institutum Historicum Societatis Iesu, 2007), 107–8, and Makin, *Essay*.

people ... this was my first examynacyon" (19). Her teaching and preaching role begins immediately with her first question for her interrogators: "wherefore S. Steven was stoned to deathe?" (20). As Genelle Gertz-Robinson demonstrates, Askew follows the model of St Stephen, the preacher of Acts 7 "who transformed the occasion of trial into a platform for delivering a sermon." Rudolph Almasy concurs: "To have become Stephen was a sign to her community that her theology and her faith produced her behavior."[31]

Askew's connection to an evangelical network in London seems clear from the persona of teacher she adopts when addressing her audience of "good people" and from the reformist figures she calls upon for assistance. Megan Hickerson argues that Askew is best understood "as one of a community of persecuted Henrician heretics, whose example she followed in dealing with persecution ... and for whom she penned the account of her sufferings."[32] Askew addresses a "frynde" three times in *The Lattre Examinacyon*: "I do perceive (dere frynde in the lorde)," she writes, "that thou art not yet persuaded throughlye in the truthe concernynge the lords supper."[33] The parenthesis may not be Askew's, since Bale added this very phrase to the address to the reader in his edition of Elizabeth's *Glasse*; alternatively, this expression may have been an identifying locution among reformers. Askew then offers her persuasions about the Eucharist based in scriptural interpretation. Just after her account of her terrible racking by Wriothesley and Rich, Askew recounts that she is taken to a house and offered a choice between recanting and death by fire. She concludes that section with "Fare wele dere frynde, and praye, praye, praye." Finally, in a section addressed, "Oh frynde most derelye beloved in God," Askew responds to this friend's concern for her approaching death:

> I marvel not a little, what shuld move yow, to judge in me so slendre a faythe, as to feare deathe, whych is the ende of all myserye. In the lorde I desire yow, not to believe of me soch wyckednesse.[34]

[31] Genelle Gertz-Robinson, "Stepping into the Pulpit? Women's Preaching in *The Book of Margery Kempe* and *The Examinations of Anne Askew*," in Linda Olson and Kathryn Kerby-Fulton (eds.), *Voices in Dialogue: Reading Women in the Middle Ages* (Notre Dame, IN: Notre Dame University Press, 2005), 469; R. P. Almasy, "Anne Askew Constructing Her Text, Constructing Her Self," *Reformation*, 10 (2005), 1–20 at 11.

[32] Hickerson, "'Ways of Lying,'"51. Loewenstein, *Treacherous Faith*, 72, describes Askew as "a member of semi-clandestine reformist assemblies in London devoted to the free reading and exegesis of Scripture in English."

[33] Askew, *Examinations*, 88.

[34] Ibid., 132 and 133.

A heading, possibly Askew's own, but possibly provided by Bale, identifies this as "Anne Askewes answere unto Johan Lassels letter." Lassells was also accused of heresy and burned at Smithfield with Askew. Bale calls him "a gentylman whych had bene her instructour" and in *Actes and Monuments*, Foxe adds that he was a "Gentleman of the Courte and housholde of kynge Henry."[35] We might also wonder whether these three uses of "dere frynde" suggest someone else, a member of Askew's evangelical circle who experiences doubts and fears that require Askew's comfort and instruction in faith and fortitude. Just as likely, however, Askew may also be exploiting the rhetorical role of a listener to serve her purpose of teaching and preaching through her account of her experience.[36]

Askew does include some names in her account, noting who among her community might help her after her first arrest. When Bishop Bonner sends her to prison, Askew asks whether she might have her "suretees" to vouch for her, but Bonner denies the request until some days later her cousin, Christopher Brittayn, and Francis Spylman guarantee her court appearance. While in the Counter, Askew is allowed "no frynde admitted to speake with me"; instead, a priest is sent to question her and asks whether she has confessed and received absolution. Askew asks for the counsel of those she considers "to be men of wysdome" – "doctor Crome, syr Gyllam, or Huntyngton." Crome and Huntington were well-known evangelical preachers, and Bonner at one point appeared ready to summon them: "For she ded knowe them to be lerned, and of a godlye judgement."[37] However, perhaps fearing for their safety (as Bale claims in his commentary), Crome and Huntington did not come and Askew appears satisfied that "my cosyne Brittayne ... with diverse other, as Mastre Hawe of Grayes inne, and soche other lyke" arrive. Askew's link to the Inns of Court and to the lawyer, Member of Parliament, and historian, Edward Hall, is particularly intriguing, since Hall not only supported reformers, but was known to be writing his chronicle history in the mid-1540s.[38]

---

[35] Ibid., 154 and 192. See *ODNB* for John Lassells.
[36] For studies of Askew's rhetorical command, see: Patricia Pender, "Between 'Sygne' and 'Substance': Rhetorics of Figurality in *The Examinations of Anne Askew*," in Salzman (ed.), *Expanding the Canon*, 222–33; Susan Kirtley, "Anne Askew's Indirect *Ethos*," in Shane Borrowman et al. (eds.), *Rhetoric in the Rest of the West* (Newcastle: Cambridge Scholars, 2010), 155–71.
[37] Askew, *Examinations*, 65, 31, 33, and 38–9. For Crome's career, see Susan Wabuda, "Equivocation and Recantation during the English Reformation: The 'Subtle Shadows' of Dr. Edward Crome," *Journal of Ecclesiastical History*, 44 (1993), 224–42.
[38] Askew, *Examinations*, 44. McQuade, "'Except that they had offended the Lawe,'" notes Askew's "extensive legal connections," particularly Hall (6). For Hall's career, see Alan Harding, "Edward

The following year, Askew was again arrested and interrogated about her beliefs about the sacrament. Unshakeable in her insistence on the memorial nature of the bread and wine, Askew is threatened with death by fire and pressed hard to recant. She records various exchanges with religious and political figures until she becomes terribly sick, "thynkynge no lesse than to dye. Therfor I desired to speake with Latymer it wolde no be. Then was I sent to Newgate in my extremyte of syckenesse. For in all my lyfe afore, was I never in soch payne. Thus the lorde strengthen yow in the truthe. Praye, praye praye."[39] Whether Askew had heard Latimer preach or knew him through an evangelical network, her asking for him is both revealing and provocative. After a prominent presence in London as an advocate and preacher of reform, in 1539 Hugh Latimer, Bishop of Worcester, was deprived of his bishopric and rusticated; however, he appears to have returned to London before May 1546 when he was summoned by the King's Council "for having 'comforted Crome in his folly.'"[40] Mueller argues that "the homiletics of Hugh Latimer" were an important influence on Parr's Lamentation of a Sinner (1547) because of the "self-referential mode so conspicuous in Latimer's preaching."[41] Perhaps Askew names Latimer here as a source of clerical comfort in her illness, but his sermons may also provide an example for presenting her own story as the occasion for teaching and persuasion. Following the sentences about her extreme illness and pain, she addresses "yow," her audience; "thus" suggests that her bodily suffering leads to spiritual insight into "the truthe," and she wishes the same enlightenment for her audience, for which they must pray accordingly.

Bale's view of Askew as "thys godlye yonge woman" well describes her profound faith and courage in the face of death. But Bale's reason for choosing "godly" relates to his fundamental polemic and likely his reason for publishing Askew's work: he argues that she surpasses any Catholic saint in her "fervent and lyvelye faythe," and that her reformed faith is fully based in Scripture. As many readers have noted, the frontispiece woodcut features a female figure in classical garb holding the martyr's palm and displaying the Bible, connecting Askew's text to the first centuries of Christianity. In Actes and Monuments, Foxe describes Askew

---

Hall," www.historyofparliamentonline.org/volume/1509-1558/member/hall-edward-i-149697-1547.

[39] Askew, Examinations, 102.

[40] Allan G. Chester, Hugh Latimer: Apostle to the English (Philadelphia: University of Pennsylvania Press, 1954), 159.

[41] Parr, Katherine Parr, 437.

as "a singular example of Christian constancie," thus predicting the role she would continually play as an icon of the Reformation.[42]

Jane Grey, "An Exhortation to her Sister" (1554)

Lady Jane Grey moved in the same reformist milieu inhabited by Katherine Parr and Elizabeth Tudor. Like Elizabeth, she was a protégée of Katherine Parr. Parr's fourth husband, Thomas Seymour, acquired Grey's wardship, and she became a member of Parr's household in Chelsea and at Sudeley Castle for a year and a half (1547–8), possibly overlapping with Elizabeth. Also present was Parr's cousin by marriage and lady-in-waiting, Elizabeth Tyrwhit, whose reformist piety she shared.[43] In early 1548, Roger Ascham was appointed as Elizabeth's tutor in the Chelsea household and "it seems likely that, until Elizabeth left in May, he taught Jane as well."[44] The reformist preacher and translator of the Bible into English, Miles Coverdale, became Parr's almoner in March 1548, and his reformist friend, John Parkhurst, was Parr's chaplain. After Parr's untimely death in September 1548, Coverdale preached the funeral sermon and Jane Grey was the chief mourner. Mueller claims that by then she owned Parr's personal prayer book "almost certainly as a deathbed gift from Katherine." According to Mueller, Parr's book of 143 leaves, "entirely written in her hand and illuminated in red, blue, and gilt, comprises a sequence of prayers, meditations, and portions of Scripture taken from books of devotion issued, in large part, by English Lutheran translators, redactors, and printers."[45] However, James P. Carley and J. Stephan Edwards contest Mueller's conclusions, arguing that the prayer book is the work of a professional scribe and that Grey could have acquired it from a number of other sources.[46] If its provenance is unsettled, the prayer book nevertheless confirms Grey's immersion in Edwardian religion and politics. In her comprehensive study of Grey's reading persona, Edith Snook finds that Grey's letters to the Lord Lieutenant of the Tower, Sir John Bridges, and to her father written beneath particular prayers,

---

[42] Askew, *Examinations*, 133 and 192.

[43] See: Susan Felch, "Introduction" in Tyrwhit, *Elizabeth Tyrwhit's Morning and Evening Prayers*, Felch (ed.); see also Micheline White (Chapter 9) in this volume.

[44] Eric Ives, *Lady Jane Grey: A Tudor Mystery* (Chichester: Wiley-Blackwell, 2009), 51.

[45] Parr, *Katherine Parr*, 18.

[46] James P. Carley, "Italic Ambitions: The Works of Henry VIII's last queen and the problem of identifying exactly what Katherine wrote," *Times Literary Supplement*, 5644 (3 June 2011), 3–5; J. Stephan Edwards, "Guest Article by Stephan Edwards: Lady Jane's Prayerbook," January 6, 2016, www.ladyjanegrey.info/?p=10537.

show the extent of her agency as an evangelical reader. When Grey writes to and presents the prayer book to Bridges, "She does not openly dispute the lieutenant's earthly authority but contests his theological attachments, and with the placement of her words claims a place in a community of martyrs who see the Bible and not worldly governors as the source of the true law."[47]

The influence on Grey of Parr's own instructional voice seems clear; similarly, the example of the learned and prolific Elizabeth might have encouraged her. Possibly, the knowledge of the famous and widely admired Anne Askew might also have inspired her. Like Elizabeth, Grey possessed a precocious studiousness and an early commitment to reformist faith. Her family home at Bradgate tends to be remembered negatively from Ascham's *Scholemaster*, where he describes Grey as the admirable student who refused to join in family sports and resented her parents' discipline.[48] Yet it can also be described as "the principal aristocratic nursery of reform in England," particularly because her father, Henry Grey, Earl of Dorset, supported the lives and work of reformers like Ralph Skinner, John Willock, James Haddon, and John Aylmer, who was Jane's tutor, and funded international figures like John Ulm and Alexander Schmutz.[49] Dorset also supported Thomas Harding, whose apostasy is the occasion for Grey's "Epistle … to a learned man." In this text, Grey's strong language articulates her horror at Harding's return to Catholicism, which to her means abdicating the role of "imbassadour and messenger of his eternall Worde" to "follow the vaine tradicions of men."[50]

Such language suggests why, after Grey's execution for treason in February 1554, prominent reformers assisted in circulating a variety of printed versions of her writings and her scaffold speech. Two collections of Grey's works quickly appeared, probably printed in 1554, differentiated by the beginning of their title pages: *Here in this booke* and *An Epistle of the Ladye Jane*. Both include her four principal works: the epistle to the apostate Thomas Harding, the dialogue with the priest Feckenham, the letter to her sister Katherine, and her words on the scaffold. *Here in this booke* also includes "a godly prayer made by maister

---

[47] Snook, "Jane Grey, 'Manful' Combat," 57. For the texts, see Parr, *Katherine Parr*, 532 and 534. See also: Levin, "Lady Jane Grey: Protestant Queen and Martyr"; Ruth Ahnert, "Writing in the Tower of London during the Reformation, ca. 1530–1558," *Huntington Library Quarterly*, 72 (2009), 168–92.

[48] Ascham, *Scholemaster*, fols. 11ᵛ–12ʳ.

[49] Ives, *Lady Jane Grey*, 70 and 62.

[50] Grey, *An Epistle of the Ladye Jane*, [sig. A3ʳ].

Iohn Knokes," perhaps included because the compilers saw it implicitly defining Grey's role as an exemplary evangelical, for Knox concludes by praying that God will "suffer no papistry to prevaile in this realm" and will "illumynate the hert" of Queen Mary.[51] Coverdale included the letter to her sister in two different volumes, and importantly, Foxe included Grey's works in *Actes and Monuments*. As Snook asserts, "her militancy was useful" to the reformers' cause.[52] Foxe gives extensive coverage to Grey in the 1563 edition, printing the four texts from the 1554 collections, as well as "A certaine prayer of the Lady Iane in the time of her trouble" and "Certaine pretie verses wrytten by the said Lady Iane with a pynne." Predictably, Grey's texts differ in each of these printings, and once more, the source of the changes cannot be determined. Although the heading of the dialogue with Feckenham in *Here in this booke* adds "whiche she wrote with her owne hand" and in *An Epistle*, the heading reads "even Word for Word, her own hand being put therto," in the very first exchange of the dialogue, the two texts differ, with *An Epistle* adding words not found in *Here in this booke*. Foxe's 1563 version adds several lines of introductory dialogue and differs from both earlier versions.[53]

In her letter to her sister, Grey articulates the core of her faith and her predominant lesson. Beginning with "I have here sent you, good sister Katerine, a booke," as the instructor, she focuses on the value of the Bible itself, "more worth then precious stones," that will lead "us wretches" to salvation, "the path of eternall ioye."[54] Like Elizabeth and Parr, Grey verbalizes the doctrine of the miserable sinner saved by reading Scripture and God's grace. Her theme is, indeed, the essential reformist belief that Scripture is all-sufficient: "It will teache you to live and learne you to dye." Her own sentences seamlessly draw paraphrase of biblical texts into counsel, as she exhorts her sister to focus not on earthly inheritance, but by applying the Bible, to become "an inheritour of sutche riches, as neither the couetous shal withdraw from you, neither the theife shal

---

[51] John Knokes, "A Prayer of Mr. John Knokes" in Jane Grey, *Here in this booke ye haue a godly Epistle made by a faithful Christian* (London: Successor of A. Scoloker? 1554), [sig. B4ᵛ].

[52] Snook, "Jane Grey's 'Manful Combat,'" 60. Otto Werdmüller, *A moste fruitefull, pithie, and learned treatise, how a Christian man ought to behaue himselfe in the daunger of death*, trans. Miles Coverdale (London: Hugh Singleton, 1574); Miles Coverdale, *Certaine Most Godly, Fruitful, and Comfortable Letters of Such True Saintes and Holy Martyrs of God* (London: John Day, 1564).

[53] Ives, *Lady Jane Grey*, 20–6, assesses the authenticity of works bearing Grey's name, finding that the authenticity of the letters to Harding and Katherine and the dialogue with Feckenham are "beyond question" (23).

[54] Jane Grey, "An Exortation written by the Lady Iane the night before she suffered" in *An Epistle of the Ladye Iane* [sig. B6ʳ].

steale, neither yet the mothes corrupte." Here, the biblical paraphrase becomes the heart of Grey's sermon-like advice.[55] If the heading is correct and Grey sent the Greek New Testament to her sister "the night before she suffered," her imminent execution prompts a precise statement of her faith: "And as touching my death, rejoice as I do (good sister) that I shalbe delivered of this corruption, and put on uncorruption. For I am assured, that I shall for losing of a mortal life, winne an immortal life."[56]

Elizabeth, Askew, and Grey come together in Thomas Bentley's 1582 *Monument of Matrons*, although accorded varying degrees of prominence. As queen and dedicatee, Elizabeth dominates, and is heralded in the Epistle as a sign of God's love for England. In his "Second Lampe," Bentley publishes Elizabeth's *Glasse* as *A Godlie Meditation of the Inward Love of the Christian Soule Towards Christ our Lord*.[57] Following are Parr's *Lamentation or Complaint of a Sinner* and *Praiers and Meditations*, and Grey's "A certaine effectuall praier" (from Foxe's 1570 edition), "An Exhortation" to her sister, and the verses written with a pin, although not the letter to Harding. In "Certaine praiers made by godlie women Martyrs," including St Agnes and St Eulalia, Bentley prints Askew's prayer, "O Lord, I have mo enimies now than there be heares on my head." Each writer takes her place as an example of faith in a convergence of women's voices placed in a transhistorical community rather than in the specific community in which each wrote: Elizabeth as the great figurehead positioned among queens recent and biblical, Askew in the tradition of Christian martyrs, and Grey as a voice of piety rather than controversy. Each will continually reappear in adaptations of these roles, singled out as an exemplary Christian woman.

---

[55] "But lay up treasures for your selues in heauen, where nether the mothe nor canker corrupteth, and where theves nether digge through, nor steale," Matt. 6:20 (*GB*).

[56] Grey, "An Exortation" [sig. B6ʳ and B7ʳ].

[57] Bentley, *Monument of Matrons*. See Quilligan, *Incest and Agency*, 65–71, for a discussion of Bentley's inclusion of texts by and for Elizabeth; see also Katherine Narveson, "Traces of Reading Practice in Thomas Bentley's *Monument of Matrones*," *ANQ*, 21 (2008), 11–18.

8

Humanism, Religion, and Early Modern Englishwomen in Their Transnational Contexts

Julie D. Campbell

Dernièrement il a donné une leçon publique sur Thucydide, en présence de la femme de Guillaume Cecyl, trésorier de la reine et sécrétaire général d'état; les plus grands savants de l'Angleterre y ont également assisté. La femme de Guill. Cecyl écrit fort bien en grec et en latin.

Recently [Charles Utenhove] gave a public lesson on Thucydides, in the presence of the wife of William Cecil, treasurer for the queen and secretary of state; the most learned scholars of England also attended. The wife of William Cecil writes very well in Greek and Latin.

Charles Utenhove to Jean de Morel, London, July 26, 1564[1]

As the paradigm shift from study of learned women as isolated anomalies to study of them as numerous, vital participants in learned networks has taken place, the international influences and connections concerning English women have begun to garner notice. During the early modern period, humanists across the Continent and in England were certainly aware of such women's international cultural capital. Boasting about one's learned countrywomen became a feature of public discourse. John Coke announced to the humanists of France, "we have dyvers gentylewomen in Englande, which be not onely well estudied in holy Scrypture, but also in the Greke and Latyn tonges as maystres More, maystres Anne Coke, Maystres Clement, and others beynge an estraunge thing to you and other nations."[2] Continental humanists likewise advertised their learned

---

Thanks are due to Tara Peck, who, under the auspices of a summer research assistantship at Eastern Illinois University, helped to compile a bibliography of secondary sources for this chapter.

[1] Willem Janssen, *Charles Utenhove: sa vie et son oeuvre (1536–1600)* (Maastricht: Uitgevers-MaatschappiJ Gebrs. Van Aelst, 1939), 87–8. All translations are my own unless otherwise noted. This is Janssen's French summary of a Latin letter. The original may be seen in Bayerische Staats-Bibliothec, Munich. Ms. latin 10383, fol. 260ʳ.

[2] Coke is quoted in Stevenson, *Women Latin Poets*, 255.

female contenders. In *Orlando Furioso* (1532), Ludovico Ariosto praised powerful, learned women, including the poets, Vittoria Colonna and Veronica Gambara, "the darling of Phoebus and the choir of Muses," and the poet and Latinist, Ippolita Sforza.[3] When Sir John Harington, godson of Queen Elizabeth, translated *Orlando Furioso* into English in 1591, his glosses argued that Elizabeth and the Cooke sisters could easily outshine their Italian counterparts in virtue and learning.[4] In France, in *Les Éloges et vies* (1630), Hilarion de Coste takes his swing at the Italian competition: "If Italy has recently admired the knowledge of Catherine Cibo Duchesse de Camerin, our France boasts and celebrates among the learned ladies who have flourished in our history, Catherine de Clermont Duchesse de Rais, who for her capacity is praised not only by the French, but even by foreigners."[5]

This superficial boasting and cataloguing points to the international awareness of women humanists, but what of the transnational elements of their concrete and discrete experiences? The goal of this chapter is to explore and illustrate transnational contexts for elite early modern Englishwomen who not only dutifully studied with the humanist tutors their fathers provided but also participated in transnational communities of letters facilitated by mutual interests, most commonly of the religio-political variety. The travel to England of religious scholars such as Desiderius Erasmus, Bernardino Ochino, Pietro Martire Vermigli, and Robert le Maçon, as well as humanist tutors such as Charles Utenhove and Nicholas Denisot, along with women's own travels to the Continent and those of their fathers, brothers, and husbands, provided transnational contacts for elite Englishwomen. The circulation of continental books and manuscripts offered further exposure to transnational thought. The cases of the More sisters, the Cooke sisters, and the Seymour sisters provide examples of elite Englishwomen who participated in transnational intellectual contexts.

---

[3] Ludovico Ariosto, *Orlando Furioso*, trans. Guido Waldman (Oxford University Press, 2008), book 37, chapter 16; and book 46, chapter 10.

[4] John Harington, trans. *Ludovico Ariosto's Orlando Furioso*, Robert McNulty (ed.) (Oxford: Clarendon Press, 1972), 230 and 434.

[5] Hilarion de Coste, *Les Éloges et vies des reynes, princesses, dames et damoiselles illustres* (Paris: Sebastien Cramoisy, 1630), 147: "Si l'Italie a admiré ces derniers temps le sçavoir de Catherine Cibo Duchesse de Camerin, nostre France vante et celebre entre les doctes Dames qui ont fleury de nos jours, Catherine de Clermont Duchesse de Rais, laquelle pour sa capacité a esté loüée, non seulement par les François, mais mesme par les Estrangers."

Erasmus, the More Sisters, and English Catholic Exile

Possibly with Cicero's description of the friendship between Laelius and Scipio, in mind,[6] Desiderius Erasmus of Rotterdam (1466–1536) sought to create a *consensio studiorum* that united a wide circle of humanists, including the More sisters. Peter Iver Kaufman observes that Erasmus "nag[ged] friends to write or to read and approve authors of his choice" and "promised a belletristic revival" if scholars would "exchange letters of encouragement, circulate narrative assaults on barbarous educators, advertise each other's treatises and translations, share patrons, and fasten the friendship network with friendly dedications and favorable reviews."[7]

Margaret More Roper (1505–44) and her sisters (Elizabeth and Cecily, and foster sister Margaret Giggs) were part of Erasmus's network from their youth. They began their correspondence with Erasmus at their father's behest, as evidenced by Erasmus's often quoted letter to Guillaume Budé in 1521 conveying his positive impressions of their humanist accomplishments.[8] He states that the girls' Latin letters are not "inept or girlish" and that "the writing was such that you would think it was the work of someone improving every day."[9] The sisters continued their correspondence with Erasmus in earnest, and More Roper, especially, participated in his *consensio studiorum* through letters and translations. In 1523,[10] Erasmus sent More Roper, now married to William Roper, a Christmas gift of commentaries on two hymns by Prudentius (348 CE–413 CE), adding that "I have been put on my mettle so often lately ... by letters from you and your sisters ... that even if someone were to cut off the headings I should be able to recognize the 'offspring true-born' of Thomas More."[11] In his dedication of Ovid's *Nut-Tree* (1524) to John More, Erasmus encourages him:

---

[6] Robert Edwards and Vickie Ziegler, *Matrons and Marginal Women in Medieval Society* (Woodbridge: Boydell Press, 1995), 126; and see Cicero, *De senectute, de amicitia, de divinatione*, William Armistead Falconer (ed. and trans.), Loeb Classical Library 154 (Cambridge, MA: Harvard University Press, 1923), 124–5.

[7] Kaufman, "Absolute Margaret," 453.

[8] Ibid.; Ross, *Birth of Feminism*, 112–14. See Erasmus, "Letter to Guillaume Budé" in P. S. and H. M. Allen (eds.), *Opus Epistolarum Des. Erasmi Roterdami* (Oxford: Clarendon, 1922), 575–80.

[9] Ross, *Birth of Feminism*, 113–14; Erasmus, "Letter to Guillaume Budé," 577.

[10] Erasmus, "Erasmus of Rotterdam to the Virtuous Maiden Margaret Roper," in A. G. Rigg trans., Elaine Fantham and Erika Rummel, with Jozef Ijsewijn (eds.), *Collected Works of Erasmus*, 86 vols. (Toronto: University of Toronto Press, 1989), vol. XXIX, 173. The letter is dated 1524, but the editors point out that the year began at Christmas, so the date should be given as 1523 by the modern calendar (173n10).

[11] Erasmus, "Erasmus of Rotterdam to the Virtuous Maiden Margaret Roper," in *Collected Works*, vol. XXIX, 173. For commentaries on this letter, see Ross, *Birth of Feminism*, 111–12 and Anne M.

to share this *Nux* ... with your very charming sisters Margaret, Elizabeth, and Cecily, and with [Margaret] Giggs, who rejoices in their friendship. They keep on at me so often with their letters, and with such sound and acute arguments in such pure Latin, that I have difficulty in persuading my friends that the girls' letters were composed by their own efforts – though I know it for a fact.[12]

More Roper was touted as an exemplary female humanist to boast of England's place in the world of early modern humanism: Nicholas Harpsfield calls More Roper "our Sappho, our Aspasia, our Hypathia [sic], our Damo, our Cornelia ... Our Christian Fabiola, our Marcella, our Paula, our Eustochium."[13] Numerous contemporary comments and several documents illustrate how she interacted in learned circles and achieved such renown. In 1524, in keeping with the practices of Erasmus's *consensio studiorum*, she published *A Deuoute Treatise upon the Pater Noster*, a translation of his *Precatio Dominica*.[14] She also wrote on the "Four Last Things" in "friendly competition" with her father.[15] Her Latin letters and verses circulated abroad, thanks largely to Erasmus, and in England, among such figures as the Bishop of Exeter, John Veysey (c. 1462–1554), and the More family tutor, Richard Hyrde (d. 1528), both of whom, like her father, debated and supported contemporary Catholic interests in a period of turmoil.

Thomas Stapleton, author of the 1588 biography of Thomas More, writes of having seen Latin speeches "written as an exercise" by More Roper, and he also notes that she corrected "a very corrupt passage from St. Cyprian," which the Flemish Theologian Jacobus Pamelius (1536–87) acknowledged was an "emendation made by Margaret in his notes upon this passage."[16] Stapleton also states that in 1529 Erasmus wrote to Margaret "not only as to a gentlewoman, but as to an eminent scholar."[17]

O'Donnell, S. N. D., "Contemporary Women in the Letters of Erasmus," *Erasmus of Rotterdam Society Yearbook*, 9 (1989), 40–1.

[12] Erasmus, "Erasmus of Rotterdam to John More, a Young Man of Great Promise," in *Collected Works*, XXIX, 127. Subsequent citations of Erasmus's works are to this edition unless otherwise noted.

[13] Ross, *Birth of Feminism*, 117–18. See also Nicholas Harpsfield, *The Life and Death of Sir Thomas More, Knight*, Elsie Vaughan Hitchcock (ed.) (Oxford: Oxford University Press, 1932), 78–9.

[14] Erasmus, *A Deuoute Treatise*, trans. Roper; Erasmus, *Precatio Dominica*. See: Kaufman, "Absolute Margaret," 453; Demers, "Margaret Roper and Erasmus."

[15] Stevenson, *Women Latin Poets*, 256; Thomas Stapleton, *Life and Illustrious Martyrdom of Sir Thomas More* (1588), trans. Philip E. Hallett (London: Burns Oates & Washbourne Ltd., 1928), 113.

[16] See also Stevenson, *Women Latin Poets*, 256.

[17] Stapleton, *Life*, 113.

Anne O'Donnell points out that in Erasmus's dialogue, "The Abbot and the Learned Lady," the young matron "Magdalia" is More Roper.[18] More Roper, then, was an active participant in the Catholic humanist circles of her time, producing texts and influencing other humanist thinkers through her scholarly activities, correspondence, and conversations, as well as through her continuation of the intellectual household. Her daughter, Mary Roper Clarke Basset, translated Thomas More's *Of the Sorowe, Werinesse, Feare, and Prayer of Christ before hys Taking* (1557) from the original Latin and wrote a Latin version of the first book of Eusebius's Greek *Ecclesiastical History*, along with an English translation of the first five books.[19] Basset, a lady-in-waiting to Queen Mary, carried on the More family traditions of pro-Catholic scholarship.[20]

More Roper died in 1544,[21] three years before Edward VI came to the throne. Her sisters, Elizabeth More Dauncey (1506–64) and Cecily More Heron (b. 1507) married and had families; little more is recorded of their activities in humanist circles.[22] Margaret Giggs Clement (1508–70), however, continued her humanist pursuits in a transnational context largely because she fled England with her husband John Clement (c. 1500–72) and other members of the More circle during the reigns of Edward and Elizabeth. Clement, a Catholic physician and the More family's tutor, was renowned for his knowledge of Greek and was well connected in international humanist circles. In 1522, he traveled to Italy and helped with the editing of the Aldine Galen.[23] In 1526, Clement married Giggs,[24] and their fame in learned circles was such that they were the recipients of one of John Leland's *Epithalamia*.[25] Giggs Clement, then,

---

[18] O'Donnell, "Contemporary Women," 41. See also Ross, *Birth of Feminism*, 112. Similarly, Kaufman, "Absolute Margaret," 443–8, argues that a portrait of More Roper engaged in humanist/theological discourse may be seen in a dialogue about conformity and dissent that her father wrote in prison and sent to his stepdaughter, Alice Alington.

[19] Stevenson, *Women Latin Poets*, 258.

[20] For more on her life and experiences at court, see Jaime Goodrich, "The Dedicatory Preface to Mary Roper Clarke Basset's Translation of Eusebius' Ecclesiastical History [with text]," *English Literary Renaissance*, 40 (2010), 301–20.

[21] Margaret married William Roper (b. 1498) July 2, 1521; their children were Elizabeth, Mary, Margaret, Thomas, and Anthony. See Stapleton, *Life*, 100.

[22] Elizabeth married William Dauncey (1500–48), and Cecily married Giles Heron (b. by 1504–40). See Stapleton, *Life*, 100.

[23] Arthur Tilley, "Greek Studies in England in the Early Sixteenth Century," *English Historical Review*, 53.210 (1938), 237.

[24] Tilley, "Greek Studies," 237. He suggests that Giggs helped her husband "in making out difficult passages in Greek" and affirms that she "shared his knowledge of medicine as well as of Greek."

[25] John Leland, "Epithalamium Io. Clementis medici, & Margaretae" in *Principum, ac illustrium aliquot & eruditorum in Anglia virorum, encomia, trophæa, genethliaca, & epithalamia* (Londini: Apud

experienced transnational influence through her connections with the
Mores and Erasmus, as well as her early association with her husband as
her tutor, then, in adulthood during her years in exile in English Catholic
circles.

In 1549, two years after the new king's ascension, Giggs Clement
and her husband went to Bruges, then Louvain, part of the Spanish
Netherlands at this time.[26] Peter Marshall positions the Clements in the
larger exodus of English Catholics to Louvain:

> Louvain itself was certainly well established as a convenient and congenial
> refuge for English papal loyalists long before the Elizabethan "Louvainists"
> ... in the mid-1560s. The Dominican William Peryn retraced his steps
> there in 1547, along with John Christopherson, a friend of the established
> exiles [Richard] Brandisby and [Stephen] Tenhand [sic]. Another refugee
> was the London rector, and former Carthusian, John Foxe ... Two years
> later they were joined there by a further band of exiles, many of them fam-
> ily and associates of Thomas More: John and Margaret Clement, Thomas
> Roper, William and Winifred Rastell, John Story, John Boxall, Nicholas
> Harpsfield and others, including More's friend Anthony Bonvisi.[27]

Giggs Clement was thus part of this distinguished community of
Catholic humanist scholars at Louvain. Later, she and her husband
were also known for making their house in Mechlin a haven for English
priests.[28] The Clements returned briefly to England under the reign of
Mary to attempt to regain confiscated property but went into exile again
when Elizabeth came to the throne.[29] Both died in Mechlin.

The Clements had approximately eleven children, and among them
were five daughters, four of whom received international attention. An
account of their renown was published in Madrid in 1583, thirteen years
after Margaret Giggs Clement's death, in Juan Perez de Moya's *Varia historia de sanctas e illustres mugeres en todo genero de virtudes*. De Moya was
a priest, scholar of mythology, and well-respected mathematician – and
one must wonder if Giggs Clement's well-known mathematical abilities had brought her to his attention. De Moya's account is interesting,
as it enlarges our picture of Giggs Clement's, her daughters', and her

---

Thomam Orwinum, 1589; *USTC* 511263), 38–9. Note: page numbers 38 and 39 are reversed in
this edition.

[26] Martin Wood, *The Family and Descendants of Sir Thomas More* (Leominster, Herfordshire: Grace,
2008), 86.

[27] Marshall, *Religious Identities*, 260–1.

[28] C. S. Durrant, *A Link between Flemish Mystics and English Martyrs* (New York: Benziger Brothers,
1925), 186.

[29] See *ODNB* for Margaret Clement.

granddaughter's fame in Europe. He writes of "Margarita Gig, natural Inglesa," noting her fluency in Latin and Greek, and he records that she has four daughters "learned in the same languages": "Dorothea Clemente," a Poor Clare, "Margarita Clemente," an Augustinian nun, "Wenefreda," and "Elena Clemente," the wife of "don Thomas Prideaux, who lives in Madrid."[30] The nuns, Dorothy and Margaret, joined orders in Louvain, and Winifred, the wife of William Rastell, nephew of Sir Thomas More, also lived in Louvain. Helen, however, married Thomas Prideaux, and the two lived in Madrid where, De Moya writes:

> This lady, when she came to Spain, gave a speech in Latin before King Philip II, with much elegance. She has a daughter named Madalena Clemente, who in knowledge, virtue, and piety takes after her mother and her grandmother.[31]

Although in De Moya's account, he asserts that it was Helen, the mother of Madalena, who gave a speech in front of Philip II, a conflicting account is found in Pietro Paolo di Ribera Valentiano's work, *Le glorie immortali de'trionfi, et herciche imprese d'Ottocento quarantacinque donne illustri antiche, e moderne*. A Spanish priest and historian who wrote in Italian, Valentiano seems to have misread De Moya. After recording essentially the same praise about Giggs and her four daughters, he writes:

> when Margaret, mother of the aforementioned [daughters], arrived in Spain, she gave a Latin oration before King Philip II, with such rhetoric, doctrine, and elegance, that it won her no little admiration from the King and the other auditors in attendance, as has reported an Author.[32]

He does not mention Madalena, the granddaughter, but in his gloss beside this passage, Valentiano gives his source as "Joan. Perez" and his "variar. hist. de mulier"[33] While it would seem that Valentiano only cursorily read De Moya, it is clear that, like Margaret More Roper, Margaret Giggs Clement reared learned daughters, one of whom continued the

---

[30] Juan Perez de Moya, *Varia historia de sanctos e illustres mugeres in todo genero de virtudes* (Madrid: Francisco Sanchez, 1583), fol. 311ᵛ: "Esta senora luego que vino en Espana hizo un parlamento en latin al rey don Philippe, 2. deste nombre. n. s. con mucha elegancia. Tiene una hija llamada Madalena Clemente, que en saber, y virtud y Christiandad imita ala madre, y aguela."

[31] My thanks to Anne Cruz for help with this translation.

[32] Pietro Paolo di Ribera Valentiano, *Le glorie immortali de'trionfi, et herciche imprese d'Ottocento quarantacinque donne illustri antiche, e moderne* (Venice: E. Deuchino, 1609), fol. 306ʳ: "Margherita Madre delle suddette, poscia arrivata in Spagna, Fé un'Oratione Latina al Re Filippo 2. di questo nome, con tal Rettorica, dottrina, & eleganza, che diede non poca ammiratione al Re, & altri udifori assistenti, com'apporta un'Autore."

[33] Valentiano, *Le glorie immortali*, fol. 306ʳ.

tradition with Giggs Clement's granddaughter Madalena (or Madeleine). At least three generations of women of the More family achieved a measure of fame for their learning and piety in Catholic circles in England and on the Continent.[34]

Continental Reformists, the Cooke Sisters, and Queen Elizabeth

Around 1537, the Italian poet and Catholic courtesan Tullia d'Aragona (1501/5–1556) wrote a sonnet to Bernardino Ochino (1487–1564), the Franciscan friar and later Capuchin monk, famous for his reformist ideology. In it, she praises his "dolce dir," sweet speech, but excoriates his "arroganza," arrogance – that is, his Calvinist beliefs – which would deny "il libero arbitrio," the free will, that God gave humankind.[35] Other women, however, praised Ochino's theology and supported his reformist efforts. Vittoria Colonna (1492–1547) wrote a sonnet on Mary Magdalene in which she engaged with Ochino's language in his "Sermon preached ... on the Feast Day of St. Mary Magdalen."[36] Colonna and Caterina Cibo, Duchess of Camerino (1501–57), interceded for Ochino and the Capuchins with Pope Clement VII, who sought in 1533 to expel the monks from the Catholic Church. Later Ochino depicted Camerino as his "chief interlocutor" in his *Seven Dialogues* (1542),[37] a work that Diana Robin has argued influenced D'Aragona's *Dialogue on the Infinity of Love* (1547).[38] Colonna, Cibo, and Ochino all participated in the salon gatherings of Giulia Gonzaga (1513–66) at the convent of San Francesco delle Monache in Rome, along with other "leaders in the reform movement in Italy."[39] Ochino's reputation as an extraordinarily gifted reformist preacher spread throughout Europe and England, and his connections

[34] For a genealogical summary of Thomas More and his children, including Margaret Giggs Clement's family, see Wood, *Family and Descendants of St Thomas More*, 88–9.
[35] Tullia D'Aragona, "To the Preacher Ochino," in Julia L. Hairston (ed. and trans.), *Poems and Letters of Tullia d'Aragona and Others* (Toronto: CRRS/ITER, 2014), 97–9.
[36] Maria Galli Stampino, "Centrality and Liminality in Bernardino Ochino's 'Sermon Preached ... on the Feast Day of St. Mary Magdalen,'" in Julie D. Campbell and Maria Galli Stampino (eds.), *In Dialogue with the Other Voice*, 328–9. See the sonnet in Vittoria Colonna, *Sonnets for Michelangelo*, Abigail Brundin (ed. and trans.) (Chicago: University of Chicago Press, 2005), 76–7.
[37] Diana Robin, "Cibo, Caterina (Cybo: 1501–1557)," in Diana Robin, Anne R. Larsen, and Carole Levin (eds.), *Encyclopedia of Women in the Renaissance: Italy, France, England* (Santa Barbara: ABC-Clio, 2007), 79–80.
[38] Robin, *Publishing Women*, 163–4 and 176–80. See also Stampino, "Centrality and Liminality," 328.
[39] Robin, *Publishing Women*, 161. Robin points out that it "was in Cibo's house in Florence [in 1542] that Ochino took off his friar's robes and changed into lay clothes before he fled to Geneva" (163).

with powerful learned women who embraced reformed theology pro-
liferated. Such women were key agents in preserving and disseminating his work.[40] It stands to reason that Ochino would have spread the
fame of such worthy and loyal continental women during his sojourn in
England, and that he would continue to cultivate their admiration and
discipleship.

Ochino resided in England from 1547 to 1553. There, he continued
this pattern as he sought the support of women in the Cooke family and
the future Queen Elizabeth. Anne Cooke Bacon, second daughter of Sir
Anthony Cooke and Lady Anne Fitzwilliam Cooke, translated several of
his sermons into English while she was in her early twenties.[41] Anthony
Cooke's circle of Protestant friends included Ochino and Pietro Martire
Vermigli, among many other reformist thinkers close to Edward VI.[42]
Sir John Cheke, a tutor to the king, was introduced to Ochino by Celio
Secundo Curione at Basel,[43] and Sir John Abell was commissioned by
Archbishop Thomas Cranmer to invite Ochino and his fellow reform-
ist Vermigli to England in 1547. Vermigli, known as Peter Martyr,
was made professor of theology at Oxford;[44] Ochino was made preb-
endary of Canterbury, although he lived and preached in London.[45]
The publisher John Day, "as a means of making Ochino known to his
new countrymen," "issued in 1550 a selection of the 'Prediche,'" – the

---

[40] He was also a friend of and protected by Renée de France as her guest in Ferrara. See Christopher
Hare, *Giulia Gonzaga: A Princess of the Italian Reformation* (London: Harper & Brothers,
1912), 164.

[41] Valerie Wayne, "Introduction," in Betty S. Travitsky and Patrick Cullen (eds.), *Anne Cooke Bacon,
The Early Modern Englishwoman: A Facsimile Library of Essential Works* (Aldershot: Ashgate
Publishing, 2000), x. Wayne points out that the *Sermons of Barnardine Ochine of Sena* (London: R.
Carr for W. Redell, 1548; *STC* 18764) include five sermons translated by Anne, but do not name
her as the translator; the *Certayne Sermons of the Ryghte Famous and Excellente Clerke* (London:
John Day, c. 1551; *STC* 18766) include twenty-five sermons, nineteen of which are Anne's,
though she is not identified as the translator. Also, *Fouretene Sermons of Barnardine Ochyne,
Concerning the Predestinacion and Eleccion of God . . . Translated out of Italian and in to Our Native
Tounge by A. C.* (London: John Day and William Seres; *STC* 18767) includes the last fourteen sermons from *Certayne Sermons* plus a dedication from Anne to her mother and a preface in praise of
Anne's work. Finally, "around 1570, there appeared an edition ([London: John Day, c. 1570], *STC*
18768) that reprinted the same twenty-five sermons published around 1551 for which Anne was
the only translator named, although six of the translations were from R. Argentyne."

[42] See Ross, *Birth of Feminism*, 167; and Phillippy, "Introduction," in Russell, *Writings of an English
Sappho*, 15.

[43] Karl Benrath, *Bernardino Ochino of Siena*, trans. Helen Zimmern (London : J. Nisbet and Co.,
1876), 187; and Stevenson, *Women Latin Poets*, 261.

[44] He would incite the wrath of Richard Smyth, a member of the more family circle in Louvain, who
wrote polemical attacks against him. See Marshall, *Religious Identities*, 261.

[45] Benrath, *Bernardino Ochino*, 186–8. By this time, Ochino had a wife and small daughter; a son
would be born in England.

sermons – translated by Anne Cooke.[46] Ochino also cultivated the favor of Princess Elizabeth. In his dedication to Queen Elizabeth of his writings on predestination and free will, the *Labyrinthi* (c. 1561), he notes that the young princess, having read some of his *Prediche*, "summoned the author to discuss with him obscure points in this doctrine," and the "penetration she evinced, and her lively interest" convinced Ochino some ten years later to dedicate the work to her.[47] Clearly, Ochino assiduously sought out women with humanist learning and reformist beliefs wherever he traveled. His connections, as well as Vermigli's, with the Cooke family illustrates humanist women's participation in a reformist version of a *consensio studiorum*.

As Gemma Allen, Patricia Phillippy, Sarah G. Ross, Jane Stevenson, and others have recently explored, the Cooke sisters, Mildred (1526–89), Anne (c. 1528–1610), Margaret (c. 1533–58), Elizabeth (c. 1540–1609), and Katherine (c. 1542–83), were the products of a "household academy" that provided them with broad-ranging humanist study.[48] The catalyst for their education was their father, who educated his daughters and sons together, in both modern and classical languages, and seems to have had them "reading the same texts."[49] Cooke, who has been identified as a tutor for Edward IV, was more likely employed as a reader "after the retirement of Richard Cox in 1550," yet he would have had access to key humanist texts and teachings to pass along to his children.[50] Their mother, Anne Fitzwilliam Cooke, too, seems to have taken an active role in their education, especially their religious study; thus, Anne dedicates "her second set of translations of Ochino to her mother," extolling her mother's religious instruction and noting her disdain for Anne's study of Italian, possibly because she associated Italian with Catholicism.[51]

A prominent feature of this largely Protestant *consensio studiorum* was interest in the education of women. Allen points out that by the time of Mary's reign, Anthony Cooke had contacts among European humanists

---

[46] Benrath, *Bernardino Ochino*, 208.

[47] Ibid. See also Anne Overell, *Italian Reform and English Reformations, c. 1535–c. 1585* (Aldershot: Ashgate, 2008), 42 and 47 on Elizabeth's reaction to Ochino and double translation of his sermon *Quid sit Christus*.

[48] See: Allen, *Cooke Sisters*; Phillippy, "Introduction," in Russell, *Writings*, 1–40; Ross, *Birth of Feminism*, 166–86; Stevenson, *Women Latin Poets*, 261–8.

[49] Allen, *Cooke Sisters*, 1 and 21. See also Schleiner, *Tudor and Stuart Women Writers*, 34.

[50] Allen, *Cooke Sisters*, 1 and 21. Allen, 23, notes that some of the Cooke children's tutors included William Turner, Dean of Wells Cathedral, and John Thorne, a schoolmaster of Wells School.

[51] Allen, *Cooke Sisters*, 22–3.

in favor of humanist education for women, including Johann Sturm in Strasburg and Coelius Secundus Curio in Basel.[52] The latter educated his own daughters and edited the works of Olympia Fulvia Morata.[53] Morata, also educated by her father (Fulvio Pellegrino Morato), was exiled from her native Ferrara from 1532 to 1539. During that period she met Curio, who, according to Holt Parker, was largely responsible for her introduction to "the ideas of Erasmus, Melancthon, Zwingli, and Luther."[54] Morata's works would inspire a later generation of English women, adding yet another dimension to the notion of the international *consensio studiorum*.[55] For the Cooke women, however, the connections with male continental Protestant humanists were immediate.

Louise Schleiner writes, "In the 1550s and 1560s, the [Cooke] sisters moved in a circle of excited, internationally oriented Protestants who as yet had experienced little conflict among themselves, and they found the absorption in their cause highly energizing."[56] Anthony Cooke's continental connections may thus be seen to permeate his daughters' world, and they were clearly well known in his circle. Robert le Maçon, *sieur* de la Fontaine, also known as Robert Masson and R. Massonius Fontanus, minister in London's French Stranger Church (formerly minister at Orléans),[57] dedicated the 1576 and 1583 editions of Vermigli's *Loci Communes* to Anthony Cooke, and Allen notes that the prefatory letter in both "mentions the virtue and wisdom of Cooke's four daughters."[58] A copy of the 1583 edition was presented to Mildred Cooke Burghley by Maçon.[59] While less is known of the humanist activities of Margaret and Katherine, there is much extant material by and about Mildred, Elizabeth, and Anne.[60]

Mildred was involved in the publication of letters by Roger Ascham and Johann Sturm in which they praise humanist learning, with Ascham particularly arguing that study of scripture should be

[52] Ibid., 21.
[53] Ibid.; Stevenson, *Women Latin Poets*, 285–8.
[54] Holt Parker, "Fulvia Olympia Morata (1526/1527–1555)," in Robin, Larsen, and Levin (eds.), *Encyclopedia of Women*, 269.
[55] Bathsua Makin and Jane Weston were later influenced by her work. See: Parker, "Fulvia Olympia Morata," 271; Ross, *Birth of Feminism*, 185.
[56] Schleiner, *Tudor and Stuart Women*, 35.
[57] Joseph C. McClelland, "A Literary History of the *Loci Communes*," in Torrance Kirby, Emidio Campi, and Frank A. James, III (eds.), *A Companion to Peter Marty Vermigli* (Leiden: Brill, 2009), 489.
[58] Allen, *Cooke Sisters*, 22.
[59] Ibid.
[60] Ibid., 3–4.

of primary importance, but that "Plato, Aristotle, Demosthenes, and Marcus Cicero" should also be read to "profit and enrich human life."[61] Sturm supports the teaching of Homer and Virgil, along with those of the church fathers, and both are in favor of humanist education for women, with Ascham noting, "We now have many honorable women who surpass the daughters of Thomas More in all kinds of learning."[62] Allen notes that "Mildred's interest in the publication of these letters reveals that she wanted the two scholars' advocacy of female scholarship more widely disseminated."[63] Mildred, too, was well known for her erudition. In addition to her studies with her father and the tutors he provided, she studied Greek at Oxford with Giles Lawrence.[64] Moreover, she was acquainted with Karel [Charles] Utenhove, who would serve as tutor to the Morel family in France and the Seymour family in England. Utenhove met William Cecil, Lord Burghley, and his wife in 1561 or 1562, cultivated a friendship based on their mutual humanist interests, and sought to facilitate correspondence between Mildred and Camille de Morel, the most famous of the daughters of Jean de Morel, *sieur* de Grigny, friend of Erasmus, companion of the Pléiade poets, and "literary tutor" of Marguerite de Valois, Duchess of Berry.[65] There is no evidence that the correspondence took place, but Utenhove's attempt (see the epigraph to this chapter) shows his desire to draw Mildred Cooke Cecil further into the sixteenth-century Republic of Letters.

Elizabeth Cooke was reading the Bishop John Ponet's work, which probably included his translation of Ochino's *Tragedie or Dialog* (1549); in 1605 she would publish her translation of Ponet's *Diallecticon viri boni et literati* (1557), which her father had edited and published.[66] Her translation of this text, *A Way of Reconciliation of a Good and Learned Man*, allowed her, through Ponet's words, to engage in the debate over transubstantiation. Elizabeth dedicates the work to her daughter, Lady Anne Herbert, whose marriage Elizabeth had successfully arranged to Henry Somerset, Lord Herbert, interestingly, a wealthy scion of a Catholic

---

[61] Ascham, quoted in Allen, *Cooke Sisters*, 24.

[62] Ibid., 25.

[63] Allen, *Cooke Sisters*, 26.

[64] Ibid., 23.

[65] Seong-Hak Kim, *Michel de L'Hôpital*, Sixteenth Century Essays and Studies 36 (Kirksville, MO: Truman State University Press, 1997), 26.

[66] Schleiner, *Tudor and Stuart Women*, 254n4. For commentary on the contexts of the translation and publication of *Diallecticon*, see Russell, *Writings*, 318–416.

family.[67] Apparently, the desire for a rich match for her daughter enabled Elizabeth Cooke Hoby Russell to overlook her son-in-law's roots.[68]

Anne Cooke Bacon, as noted, engaged with Ochino's sermons, particularly those focusing on predestination, and she translated the *Apologia Ecclesiae Anglicanae* (1564) of John Jewel, a follower of Pietro Martire Vermigli. Jewel's *Apologie of the Church of England* includes a prefatory letter by "P. Martir."[69] As translated by Cooke Bacon, Vermigli calls the work "this felicity of your wit, this redification of the Church of God, this singular ornament of the estate of England," and he condemns the "champions and defendents of our times of Papisticall fictions."[70] Much earlier, in the prefatory letter of her 1548 translation of Ochino's sermons, Cooke Bacon wrote that she translated Ochino's sermons into English because "they truly conteyne moch to the defacying of al papistrie."[71] The keen disregard for "Papisticall fictions" shared by the Cooke sisters, Ochino, Vermigli, Maçon, Ponet, and Jewel clearly provided their connection – and a source of mutual admiration – in the Protestant *consensio studiorum* of the Cooke circle.

Mildred's ownership of Vermigli's *Loci Communes* along with Elizabeth's and Anne's translations serve as artifacts of the Cooke sisters' involvement in their father's transnational, reformist humanist circle; these examples represent, however, only a small part of these women's substantial contributions and influence. Documenting the extraordinary breadth and depth of the Cooke sisters' influence upon, and connections in, the scholarly, political, and religious networks of their time, Allen points out that the Cooke women stand as prime examples of the argument that humanist educations for girls were not simply for ornamental purposes.[72] She argues that the "act of translation offered the Cooke

---

[67] She became the wife of Henry Somerset, Lord Herbert, Marquess of Worcester, married June 1600. Regarding the Catholicism of Henry's father, Edward Somerset, 4th Earl of Worcester, see Roy Strong, *The Cult of Elizabeth* (Berkeley, CA: University of California Press, 1977), 27.

[68] Elizabeth Cooke's marriage to Thomas Hoby (1530–66), well-traveled humanist, translator of Castiglione's *The Courtyer* (1561) and short-lived ambassador to France, placed her briefly in Paris in 1566, but her husband's death there caused her swift removal of her family back to England. Her second husband, John Russell, also traveled in Italy and Germany in 1576, but Elizabeth remained in England. See Russell, *Writings*, 19.

[69] For a fuller discussion of Anne Cooke Bacon, see Jaime Goodrich (Chapter 2) in this volume.

[70] P. Martir, "To the right reverend Father in God, John Iuell," in John Jewel (ed.), *The Apologie of the Church of England* (London: I. R. for Thomas Chard, 1600), n. p.

[71] Bacon, "To Her 'Good Reader,'" in *Letters*, 51–3.

[72] Allen, *Cooke Sisters*, 7. Regarding the notion that humanist education for women was essentially ornamental, unless one was royal, see Lisa Jardine and Anthony Grafton, *From Humanism to the Humanities: Education and Liberal Arts in Fifteenth-and Sixteenth-Century Europe* (Cambridge, MA: Harvard University Press, 1986), 29–57.

sisters the chance not only to bolster their political networks, but also to contribute to strengthening the faith of their contemporaries, particularly with Cooke Bacon's widely disseminated 1564 translation of Jewel's *Apologia Ecclesiae Anglicanae*."[73] Of their relatively large number of extant letters, she writes that the sisters "used their humanist training as a means to legitimate their epistolary advice. In order to achieve this, they strategically utilized rhetorical appeals to their own political and religious experience, whilst they also demonstrated their classical and scriptural learning in their correspondence."[74] The letters, then, "allow a reconstruction of their political and religious networks, particularly their wide-ranging political activities as intermediaries for diverse clients," including a glimpse of how their interventions contributed to Elizabethan diplomacy, the question of the Queen's marriage, and other political initiatives.[75] Clearly, their correspondence, along with their translations, facilitated the Cooke sisters' wide acquaintance in international Protestant humanist circles.

Nicolas Denisot and the Political Commodification of the Seymour Sisters

Anne (b. c. 1532/34), Margaret (b. c. 1533/36), and Jane (1541–60), the eldest of the six daughters of Edward Seymour, Duke of Somerset, and his wife Anne Stanhope,[76] were tutored in French and Latin by the French humanist and spy Nicolas Denisot (1515–59), who also served as tutor to the children of Jean de Morel and Antoinette de Loynes in Paris.[77] Soon after Marguerite de Navarre died on December 2, 1549, Anne, Margaret, and Jane authored the *Hecatodistichon* (1550), an elegy in 104 distichs in her honor. The three young Protestant girls' verses resonate with admiration for Marguerite de Navarre's famous reform-leaning erudition and piety as they praise her beauty, her mind, her moderation, and her devotion to God.[78] Denisot, who had returned to

---

[73] Allen, *Cooke Sisters*, 7.

[74] Ibid., 7–8.

[75] Ibid., 8.

[76] See Hosington, "England's First Female-Authored Encomium," 121n11.

[77] Julie D. Campbell, "Crossing International Borders: Tutors and the Transmission of Young Women's Writing," in Julie D. Campbell and Anne R. Larsen (eds.), *Early Modern Women and Transnational Communities of Letters* (Farnham: Ashgate, 2009), 214–20.

[78] Ibid.," 217.

France in 1549, after being threatened with arrest in England for his espionage activities, learned of his former charges' work and requested that they send it to him. He then published it in Paris, accompanied by twenty-two poems in praise of the Seymour sisters in Latin and Greek by such figures of note in French literary circles as Antoine de Baïf, Pierre des Mireurs, Jean Dorat, Charles de Sainte-Marthe, Matthew Pac, and Valentina Alcinoia, the wife or mistress of Denisot.[79]

Sainte-Marthe writes that these three "Anglicae sorores" with their "Elegantibus ac pereruditis," elegant and learned, distichs have "put French poets to shame for abandoning their duty to Marguerite."[80] At Sainte-Marthe's behest, in 1551, the distichs were included in a volume entitled *Le Tombeau de Marguerite de Valois, Royne de Navarre. Faict premierement en Disticques Latins par les trois Soeurs Princesses en Angleterre. Depuis tracuiczt en Grec, Italien, & François par plusieurs des excellentz Poètes de la France.* In this work, the girls' verses are translated by poets such as Denisot, Dorat, Baïf, Joachim du Bellay, Jacques Peletier du Mans, Antoinette de Loynes, and several others, including Pierre de Ronsard, who wrote poems in praise of the sisters, here elevated to the status of "Princesses" by Sainte-Marthe's hyperbole.[81]

The political context for the circulation of the Seymour sisters' verses was largely influenced by the March 1550 Peace of Boulogne, a treaty meant to reinstate Anglo-French relations after England withdrew from Scotland and France took over Boulogne. The publication of the *Hecatodistichon* in 1550 and the *Tombeau de Marguerite de Valois* in 1551 underscores the desire of the English and French participants in these projects for peace and unity. In his dedication of the *Tombeau* to Marguerite, Duchesse de Berry, Denisot urges the duchess to accept "these divine verses" by "three virgin sisters" for the sake of Marguerite de Navarre who was loved and revered "by her own people and foreigners, not only for her royal condition but also for her incredible learning, Christian religion, and admirable piety," thus putting forth Marguerite

---

[79] Ibid.
[80] Charles de Sainte-Marthe, "Iur. Vtri. Doct. Ad Gallos," *Annae, Margaritae, Ianae, Sororum Virginum, Navarrorum Reginae, Hecatodistichon*, in Seymour Sisters (ed.), *Printed Writings, 1500–1640. Part 2: Anne, Margaret, and Jane Seymour* (Aldershot: Ashgate, 2000), n.p. Paraphrased by Hosington, "England's First Female-Authored Encomium," 118.
[81] Anne Seymour, Margaret Seymour, and Jane Seymour, *Le Tombeau de Marguerite de Valois*, n.p.

de Navarre herself as a unifying force, even in death.[82] This theme continues in Pierre de Ronsard's poem, "Aux trois Soeurs," which asserts that the girls' verses should be taken as a sign of unification:

> Thus then the spirits
> Of England and France,
> United together, have taken up
> The rod against Ignorance:
> And our Kings, once foes
> Now made perfect friends;
> End the cruel war
> Through a mutual peace.[83]

Antoinette de Loynes contributes a sonnet in which she addresses the deceased Marguerite and suggests she would call them "Mes Seurs," her sisters, further buttressing the idea of a unifying kinship between the French and the English.[84] The Seymour sisters, then, through the circulation of their *Hecatodistichon* by Denisot in France, became known among the leading French humanist poets of their day. Their fame was relatively brief: Jane died at nineteen, and Anne married John Dudley, son of the Earl of Warwick, on June 3, 1550. Margaret never married, and fell into obscurity.[85] Nonetheless, their poetry and their reputations as virtuous, learned young Englishwomen were broadly advertised by Denisot and his friends, suggesting to a French readership that the English and French could unite over the sacred memory of Marguerite de Navarre, as well as the newly minted peace between their countries.

As these three groups of elite English sisters illustrate, humanist, political, and religious forces in concert in the sixteenth century provided transnational contexts for female as well as male intellectuals. Continental figures such as Erasmus, Ochino, Martire, Maçon, Utenhove, and Denisot sought English women's acquaintance and

---

[82] Denisot, "A Tres Illustre Princesse," *Le Tombeau de Marguerite de Navarre*, in *Printed Writings*, n.p. He writes of "ces vers devins" by the "trois Soeurs vierges" and of Marguerite, who was loved and revered "des siens & des estrangiers, non tant pour sa condition royalle, que pour son incroiable doctrine, Chrestienne religion, & admirable pieté."

[83] Ronsard, "Aux trois Soeurs," *Le Tombeau de Marguerite de Valois* in *Printed Writings*, n.p.: "Doncques puis que les espritz/D'Angleterre & de la France,/Bandez d'une ligne, ont pris/Le fer contre l'ignorance:/E que noz Roys se sont faictz/D'ennemys, amys parfaictz:/Tuans la guerre cruelle/Par une paix mutuelle."

[84] Antoinette de Loynes (A. D. L.), "Que dirois-tu," *Le Tombeau de Marguerite de Navarre*, in *Printed Writings*, n.p.

[85] For overviews of their lives, see Hosington, "England's First Female-Authored Encomium," 119–25.

profited from it. Much more remains to be explored about the transnational activities of the women discussed here, as well as numerous others who lived abroad for political and religious reasons, but the present study makes clear, as Coke suggested, that the "dyvers gentylewomen in Englande" were indeed "well estudied in holy Scrypture" and "in the Greke and Latyn tonges," and they were, moreover, deeply engaged in international Catholic and Protestant networks.

9

Women in Worship
Continuity and Change in the Prayers of Elizabeth Tyrwhit and Frances Aburgavenny

Micheline White

Private prayer books were a popular and important genre in Tudor England. As Susan M. Felch has noted, around one hundred different prayer books were printed by 1600, and as Ian Green has observed, a few of these prayer books were bestsellers.[1] It has long been known that laywomen were consumers of prayer books, and we now know that some women were producers of devotional works, women including Lady Jane Wriothesley, Queen Katherine Parr, Anne Askew, Lady Elizabeth Tyrwhit, Lady Elizabeth Fane, Lady Jane Grey, the 'handmaid' from Wesel, Queen Elizabeth I, Anne Lock, Lady Frances Aburgavenny, Dorcas Martin, Anne Wheathill, and Elizabeth Grymeston. In approaching this body of texts, we must remember that they were produced during a time when ideas about the goals and forms of public and private worship were changing dramatically and when older materials were being reworked or replaced with new texts.[2] In England, lay Books of Hours (Primers) and prayer miscellanies began to change in the 1530s as reformers promoted the use of the vernacular and expressed hostility towards indulgenced or Marian prayers, and as new forms of public worship were promulgated on the Continent. Indeed, the reformation of public worship was of paramount importance, for as Felch notes, Books of Hours offered a simplified version of the eight canonical Hours of the

---

[1] Susan M. Felch, 'Introduction', in Tyrwhit, *Elizabeth Tyrwhit*, 30; Green, *Print and Protestantism*, 252 and 'Appendix 1'.

[2] Felch, 'Introduction', 19–23, helpfully suggests that Tudor prayer books can be grouped into six categories: traditional, transitional, reformist, occasional, authorized, and Elizabethan. The following discussion is indebted to her taxonomy. Primers are also discussed in the following: Duffy, *Marking the Hours*; White, *Tudor Books*; Charles C. Butterworth, *The English Primers (1529–1545): Their Publication and Connection with the English Bible and the Reformation in England* (Philadelphia: University of Pennsylvania Press, 1953).

Divine Office recited in monastic houses and large churches.[3] In 1549, public worship in England was transformed by the Book of Common Prayer (BCP), a book that introduced many new prayers, but that also preserved significant parts of the medieval liturgy.[4] When the BCP was revised in 1552, the Crown issued a new official *Primer or Book of Private Prayer* (1553), which sought to replace the eight Hours of prayer with Morning and Evening prayer from the BCP. When Mary came to power in 1553, the Catholic Mass and traditional Primers were reintroduced, but a newly revised BCP was printed in 1559 along with a new version of the Edwardian Primer. Under Elizabeth, devotional writers continued to produce new prayer books which contained both traditional and new material but which became increasingly diverse and increasingly divergent from the BCP.

Until recently, women's literary participation in this complex trajectory of Tudor devotional continuity and change was largely unmapped.[5] Several new studies, however, have begun to fill in this picture, and have offered detailed explorations of entire prayer books or of individual female-authored psalms, prayers, or hymns. Susan Felch, for instance, has noted that while traditional Primers involved the recitation of entire psalms, Tyrwhit, Lock, and Wheathill circulated creative Biblical 'Collages' and paraphrases; Janel Mueller has argued that BL Harley MS 2342 (a prayer book which she attributes to Parr) assembled traditional and reformist texts in ways that underscored their shared Christocentricity; and I have examined the circulation of innovative evangelical hymns by Elizabeth Cruciger and Elizabeth Tyrwhit.[6] This chapter seeks to further our understanding of women's responses to ongoing transformation of worship in Tudor England by focusing on two elite women: Lady Elizabeth Tyrwhit (before 1510–d. 1578), wife of Robert Tyrwhit and lady-in-waiting to Katherine Parr between 1543

---

[3] The Canonical Hours are Matins, Lauds, Prime, Terce, Sext, Nones, Vespers, and Compline. Felch, 'Introduction', 21, notes that although Primers were 'intended for private use, they were derived from the public liturgy and flowed smoothly back into the common pond of piety'.

[4] See Brian Cummings, 'Introduction', in Cummings, *Book of Common Prayer*, ix–lxiv.

[5] White (ed.), *English Women*, 6–7.

[6] Felch, '"Halff a Scrypture Woman"'; Mueller, 'Prospecting for Common Ground'; White, 'Women's Hymns in Mid-Sixteenth-Century England'. For other studies, see: Micheline White, 'Dismantling Catholic Primers and Reforming Private Prayer: Anne Lock, Hezekiah's Song, and Psalm 50/51', in Alec Ryrie and Jessica Martin (eds.), *Private and Domestic Devotion in Early Modern Britain* (Farnham: Ashgate, 2012), 93–113; Steven W. May, 'Queen Elizabeth's Performance at Paul's Cross in 1588', in Torrance Kirby and P. G. Stanwood (eds.), *Paul's Cross and the Culture of Persuasion in England, 1520–1640* (Leiden: Brill, 2014), 301–13.

and 1548, and Lady Frances (Manners) Neville Aburgavenny (before 1540–d. 1576), wife of Henry Neville, fourth Lord Aburgavenny.[7] These two women were both educated before the printing of the first BCP, they lived through several periods of dramatic religious change, and they both produced substantial prayer books that were reprinted in Thomas Bentley's *Monument of Matrons* (1582).[8] In what follows I will undertake a very close textual analysis of two prayers: Tyrwhit's 'A Confession to be said before Morning Prayer' and Aburgavenny's 'A Prayer to be said before the receiving of the Lord's Supper'. Both prayers belong to well-established genres of devotional writing for lay readers, and both prayers were tied to a liturgical service that was transformed, but not eliminated, by the BCP: the Mass/Communion service. As we shall see, both Tyrwhit's and Aburgavenny's prayers are deeply indebted to the BCP Communion service and we can discern the traces of their authors' creative labour as they tinkered with specific words and phrases. This creative intertextuality is instructive as it demonstrates the degree to which laywomen assimilated the new BCP services, and illuminates the ways in which laywomen used the BCP as a textual resource for the production of their own prayers. Of particular interest to us is that both prayers reveal that their authors were acutely aware of the ways in which the BCP had reworked material from the older, Catholic liturgy. Indeed, Tyrwhit and Aburgavenny responded to the retention or deletion of specific words from the Catholic Rite and either reproduced, recuperated, or resisted them in their household devotions.

'Save and Defend Me from Evil': Recalling the Misereatur in Tyrwhit's Morning 'Confession'

The textual history of Tyrwhit's *Morning and Evening Prayers, with divers Psalms, Hymns, and Meditations* is complicated. As Felch has demonstrated, the work was probably composed in the 1550s, was licensed for printing in 1569, and is extant in a shorter version printed by Henry

---

[7] Felch, 'Introduction', 1–16, offers a detailed account of Tyrwhit's biography. For Aburgavenny, see *ODNB*. It is unclear when Frances was born, but she is named as the second unmarried daughter in her father's will, which was written in November 1542. See Nicholas Harris (ed.), *Testamenta Vetusta: Being Illustrations from Wills*, 2 vols. (London: Nicholas and Son, 1826), vol. II, 719–21. She was married by 1554, when her daughter was born.

[8] Bentley, *Monument of Matrons* (*STC* 1892). The prayers by Tyrwhit and Aburgavenny are found in volume II.

Middleton in 1574 and in a longer version in Bentley's *Monument of Matrons* (1582).[9] Tyrwhit's books are eclectic works that include prayers, meditations, confessions, psalm paraphrases, hymns, collects, Biblical excerpts, anthems, a metrical psalm, and blessings, and while Tyrwhit compiled and edited material from other prayer books, she also appears to have written new prayers. Looking at the book as a whole, Felch concludes that it displays a 'cheerful ecumenicity' as it brings together material that is 'consistent with the new Protestantism and part of the ongoing, continuous tradition of Christian prayer'.[10] Here I will take a closer look at the interplay between the old and the new in one single prayer, 'A Confession to be said before Morning Prayer'. Both the 1574 and the 1582 editions of Tyrwhit's *Morning and Evening Prayers* begin with this piece: in the 1582 volume, it is the first item; in the 1574 volume it is the first prayer, following 'A Brief Exhortation unto Prayer'. In offering 'A Confession' to her readers, Tyrwhit was contributing to a long-established genre of penitential prayers for lay people. The traditional *Hore Beatissime Virginis Marie*, for example, concluded with a group of miscellaneous prayers, including a 'Form of Confession' that was organized around the seven deadly sins, Ten Commandments, five wits, seven works of mercy, eight beatitudes, etc.[11] This confession is clearly linked with the practice of auricular confession to a priest that occurred before taking Communion at Easter and that often involved a consideration of the Ten Commandments and the seven deadly sins.[12] The first Primer printed entirely in English, George Joy's *Ortulus Anime, the Garden of the Soul*, featured a different 'General Confession for every Sinner brought into the Knowledge of his Sins', which was also tightly organized around the Ten Commandments but found before (rather than after) the Hours.[13] The Henrician *King's Primer* (1545), first printed while Tyrwhit was Parr's lady-in-waiting, featured yet another form, 'A General Confession of Sins unto God' from Richard Taverner's

---

[9] Felch, 'Introduction', 50–64. Felch identifies Tyrwhit's sources in 'Appendix A', in Tyrwhit, *Elizabeth Tyrwhit*, 157–86.

[10] Tyrwhit, *Elizabeth Tyrwhit*, 33.

[11] *Hore Beatissime Virginis Marie ad legitimum Sarisburiensis Ecclesie ritum* (Paris: Regnault, 1527; STC 15951), fols. cxcviiᵛ–ccⁱʳ. See White, *Tudor Books*, 65.

[12] Duffy, *Stripping of the Altars*, 61.

[13] George Joye, *Ortulus Anime, the Garden of the Soul* ((Antwerp:) Argentine, 1530; STC 13828.4), J5v–J8v. This Confession was reprinted in many Primers throughout the 1530s and 1540s: it is in the Marshall Primer (1534; STC 15986), the Gough Primer (1536; STC 15992), and the Petyt Primer (1542; STC 16028).

Epitome of the Psalms.[14] This crown-sponsored Confession abounds with Biblical parables and also focuses on the Ten Commandments, and it had a long life as the Henrician Primer was reprinted many times under Edward and under Elizabeth.[15] In addition to these longer Confessions, some Primers and catechisms included the liturgical Confession (the Confiteor) that was used at the beginning of the Mass and during the Offices of Prime and Compline.[16] At the Mass, the priest said the Latin Confiteor and the clerks (or assistants) said the Misereatur, and then vice versa. The priest then recited the Absolution.[17] Late medieval lay Mass books encouraged (but did not require) the laity to say the Confiteor or a loose English verse translation along with the priest, and people were permitted to say it either quietly or out loud.[18]

With the advent of the BCP, these confessional practices were dramatically revised: Cranmer eliminated the recitation of the Confiteor and Misereatur at the beginning of the new Communion service; he made auricular confession before Communion optional; and he wrote new Confessions for public worship. For example, the 1549, 1552, and 1559 BCPs contain a new Exhortation, General Confession, and Absolution for the Communion Service. Importantly, these new texts contained phrases from the Sarum Confiteor, Misereatur, and Absolutionem as well as from a Confession from *A Simple and Religious Consultation*, a translation of a Lutheran church order issued by Hermann von Wied of Cologne and sponsored by the Duchess of Suffolk.[19] The laity were given a striking new role in this part of the 1549 service, for the Rubric indicated that the 'general confession' is to 'be made, in the name of all those, that are minded to receive this holy Communion, *either by one*

---

[14] *The Primer Set Forth by the King's Majesty* (London: Edward Whitchurche, 1545; *STC* 16034), KK1^v–KK4^r. Wolfgang Capito, *An Epitome of the Psalms* (*STC* 2748), Richard Taverner (trans.) (London: R. Bankes? for A. Clerke?, 1539), sig. A1^r–A4^r. Tyrwhit draws extensively on Taverner's book.

[15] The Henrician Primer was revised under Edward (*STC* 16053 ff) and reprinted under Elizabeth (*STC* 16087 ff).

[16] *Hore Beate Marie Virginis* (London: John Mayler, 1541; *STC* 16022), sig. B8^v–C1^r.

[17] For the Latin Confiteor, see F. H. Dickinson (ed.), *Missale ad usum ... ecclesiae Sarum* (Burntisland: Pitsligo Press, 1861–83), 580. For a translation, see Frederick E. Warren, trans. *The Sarum Missal in English*, 2 vols. (London: A. Moring, 1911), vol. I, 21–2.

[18] Thomas Frederick Simmons (ed.), *The Lay Folks Mass Book: or the manner of Hearing Mass* (London: EETS, 1879), 6–10.

[19] For Cranmer's sources, see F. E. Brightman, *The English Rite*, 2 vols. (London: Rivingtons, 1915), vol. II, 696–8. The Confession from Hermann von Wied is in his *A Simple and Religious Consultation* (London: John Day and William Seres, 1548; *STC* 13214), sig. Ddi^r. Cummings discusses Hermann in *Book of Common Prayer*, xxi.

of them, or else by one of the ministers, or by the priest himself'.[20] In 1552, Cranmer introduced a different, largely original, Exhortation, Confession, and Absolution to be recited at Morning Prayer.[21] This Confession demanded even greater lay participation as it was 'to be *said of the whole congregation* after the minister kneeling'.[22] This liturgical Confession entered into private use because the official Edwardian *Primer or Book of Private Prayer* included it as a prayer to be used in households 'before' the beginning of 'Morning Prayer'.[23] This Primer was reprinted at least five times between 1560 and 1580, meaning that some Elizabethan readers were familiar with the practice of saying the liturgical Confession from Morning Prayer in their homes.[24] In addition to this BCP Confession, Elizabethan readers had access to dozens of other penitential prayers and Confessions that appeared in private prayer books and that were completely independent from the BCP.

Tyrwhit's upbringing, her experiences at court in Parr's entourage, her use of materials from many different prayer books, and her experience of all three BCPs enable us to conclude that she was well aware of the evolution of Confessions from the 1530s through to the 1570s. It is thus fascinating that Tyrwhit did *not* simply transcribe an existing Confession into her prayer book; instead, she created an original collage prayer that 'mashes up' language from Cranmer's two Confessions, from the Latin Confiteor and Misereatur, and from Hermann's Confession. What we find, then, is a rich comingling of the old, the new, the English and the continental:

> A Confession to be said before Morning Prayer
>
> I Doo *acknowledge, and confesse* unto thee [Exhortation BCP MP; Hermann]; O most *mercifull* and heavenlie *father* [BCP MP], mine often and *grievous* offences [BCP Communion; Hermann] that I have *committed against thy divine Majestie* [BCP Communion], from my youth hitherto, in *thought, word and deed* [BCP Communion; Sarum Confiteor]; *leaving undone those things, which I ought and should have done; and dooing those*

---

[20] My emphasis. I cite from the 1559 Rubric, but it was the same in 1549 and 1552. See Cummings (ed.), *Book of Common Prayer*, 134.

[21] Brightman, *English Rite*, vol. I, 130–31. This Confession is composed mostly of Biblical passages.

[22] Cummings (ed.), *Book of Common Prayer*, 103. My emphasis.

[23] *A Primer or Book of Private Prayer* (London: William Seres, 1553; *STC* 20373), sig. C5ᵛ. Targoff, *Common Prayer*, 35, notes that the pronouns were adapted for private use so that the 'devotional *I* that the Primer puts forth is no more nor less than a singular version of the liturgical *we*'. She notes further that in contrast to medieval practice where the liturgical space was a site of private lay devotions, the 'home was now imagined as an additional site for common prayer' (34).

[24] *A Primer or Book of Private Prayer*, 1560; *STC* 20375, sig. C7ᵛ. See also: *STC* 20376 (1566); 20377 (1568); 20377.3 (c. 1570); 20377.5 (c. 1570); 20377.7 (c. 1580).

things which I ought not to have done [BCP MP]: *provoking thy wrath and indignation against me* [BCP Communion]. And now *lamenting* [Hermann] this my *wickednes* [BCP Communion], I appeale unto thy mercie, and saie with the Publicane, O Lord GOD be mercifull unto me a most wretched sinner [Luke 18:13], *forgive all that is past* [BCP Communion], *save and defend me from evill* [Misereatur], and *confirme me in good life* [BCP Absolution Communion; Misereatur], *to the glorie of thy name* [BCP MP; Hermann]: So be it.[25]

The rich intertextuality on display in Tyrwhit's prayer is valuable for several reasons. It suggests that the Reformers' goal of producing a new English liturgy that would be voiced, understood, and assimilated by the laity was successful (at least in some quarters), and it reveals how elite laywomen drew on liturgical works in creating their own, original prayers for domestic use. Tyrwhit's collage prayer is also interesting insofar as it demonstrates a familiarity with the Latin sources of Cranmer's work and recuperates language that Cranmer chose not to translate. For instance, we note that Tyrwhit cites Cranmer's adaptation of one phrase from the Confiteor very closely: in the Confiteor we find '*quia peccavi nimis cogitatione, locutione, et opere*' (that I have sinned greatly in thought, words, and deeds); in Cranmer's Communion Confession we find an acknowledgement of the sins that 'we ... grievously have committed, by thought, word, and deed'; and in Tyrwhit's prayer we find a confession of the 'grievous offenses' committed 'in thought, word, and deed'.[26] Later in Tyrwhit's prayer, however, she translates one tiny phrase from the Misereatur that Cranmer had jettisoned in his Absolution. So the Latin Misereatur asks: *Misereatur vestri omnipotens Deus, et dimittat vobis omnia peccata vestra; liberet vos ab omni malo; conservet et confirmet in bono* (May almighty God have mercy upon you and forgive you all of your sins, *deliver you from all evil*, preserve and confirm you in goodness, my emphasis in English text). Cranmer included most of this in his Absolution, dropping only the phrase *ab omni malo* (from all evil). Thus in the BCP, the priest says '[May God] have mercy upon you, pardon and deliver you from all your sins, confirm and strengthen you in all goodness'. Tyrwhit, I believe, remembered the petition to be delivered 'from all evil' and thus added it back in as she drew on Cranmer's adaptation: her prayer asks God to be merciful and to 'forgive all that is past, *save and defend me from evil,* and confirm me in good life' (my emphasis). This may seem like a small detail, but it is precisely in the literary minutia of the prayer that we catch a glimpse of Tyrwhit's participation in the ongoing evolution of England's devotional heritage. Tyrwhit obviously found that the BCP service was a compelling linguistic resource for her own devotional creativity, but she also retrieved a phrase that had been abandoned by Cranmer and reintroduced it into the world of private devotion.

'The Body of Our Lord Jesus Christ' (But Not Really): Aburgavenny's Resistance to the Words of Administration

In Bentley's volume, Tyrwhit's prayers are followed by the following title: 'The Prayers made by the right Honorable Lady Frances Aburgavenny, and committed at the Hour of her Death, to the right Worshipful Lady Mary Fane (her only daughter) as a Jewel of Health for the Soul, and a Perfect Path to Paradise, very Profitable to be used of every Faithful Christian Man and Woman'.[27] The long title (which calls the prayers a 'Jewel of Health' and a 'Perfect Path to Paradise') suggests that the prayers made their way to Bentley from Aburgavenny's daughter, Mary Fane. We must note, however, that in 1577 Hugh Jackson had been given a license to print 'Precious Pearls of Perfect Godliness to be used of every faithful Christian, begun by the Lady Frances Aburgavenny and finished by John Phillips'.[28] Unfortunately, this text is not extant so it is impossible to know the nature of the collaboration between Aburgavenny and Phillips or whether Fane played a role in transmitting the prayers to Jackson.[29] Two year later, Hugh Jackson printed *The Perfect Way [Path?] to Paradise* (1580), but the only extant books with that title are from 1588, 1590, 1617, and 1626.[30] These four editions are ascribed to Phillips with no mention of Aburgavenny (who had been dead since 1576). There is considerable overlap between the prayers printed under Aburgavenny's name by Bentley in 1582 and those under Phillips's name by Jackson in 1588,

---

[27] Bentley, *Monument of Matrons.* Aburgavenny's prayers cover vol. II, 139–213. All subsequent references are to Bentley's edition and will appear parenthetically.

[28] Edward Arber (ed.), *A Transcript of the Registers of the Company of Stationers of London, 1554–1640,* 5 vols. (1875–1894; reprint, New York: Peter Smith, 1950), vol. II, 321.

[29] For a brief biography of John Phillips see *ODNB.*

[30] The edition from 1580 is described, but no author is given in Joseph Ames (ed.), *Typographical Antiquities: or An Historical Account of the Origin and Progress of Printing in Great Britain,* augmented by William Herbert, 3 vols. (London: Printed for the editor, 1786), vol. II, 1133. Perhaps the volume was printed with no authorial ascription. The later editions are *STC* 19872, 19873, 19873.5, 19874.

but each volume also has unique prayers.[31] The Communion prayer that I will consider is in both the *Monument of Matrons* and *The Perfect Path to Paradise*, but there are two details that suggest that Aburgavenny was involved in its composition. The BCP, the Homily on the Sacrament, and all other male-authored Communion prayers from the 1560s, 1570s, and 1580s use only masculine or gender-neutral nouns to describe the Christian community – 'brothers' or 'neighbours'. By contrast, the prayer attributed to Aburgavenny by Bentley is unusual in drawing attention to the women in the congregation, warning about crimes committed against a 'widow' or against one's 'brethren and sisters' (vol. II, 165). The version of the prayer printed under Phillips's name in 1588 has quietly removed the word 'sister', referring only to crimes committed against 'our brethren'.[32] In light of this verbal clue, and since Bentley's text appears to have originated with Aburgavenny's daughter, I argue that it is reasonable to treat the prayer as 'Aburgavenny's' with the understanding that it may have been the result of a literary collaboration.

The Prayers Made by the Right Honorable Lady Frances Aburgavenny consists of forty-seven different compositions, and five of them are designed to prepare readers to participate in religious ceremonies found in the BCP: thus we find 'A godly prayer for the true worshipping of God, which may be used in the Church before common prayer', 'A Prayer to be said before or after the Sermon', 'A Prayer to be said before the receiving of the Lord's Supper', 'A Prayer or thanksgiving to be said after the receiving of the Communion', and 'A godly prayer to be said of every Christian, especially at burials' (vol. II, 158–9 and 162–9). In producing 'A Prayer to be said before the receiving of the Lord's Supper' (vol. II, 163–6), Aburgavenny was contributing to a long tradition of prayers related to

---

[31] Louise Horton addresses the complex issue of these shared prayers in '"Print therefore good Lord, and write these examples in my memory": the Forgotten History of Writing and Printing Lady Aburgavenny's Prayers'. (This is an unpublished paper presented at Women's Responses to the Reformation conference at Oxford University on 23 June, 2016. A podcast of the talk is available at https://podcasts.ox.ac.uk/series/womens-responses-reformation.) Horton further investigates this question in her thesis, '"A Doer of Thy Holy Word": Religio-Political Textual Production and Collaboration in Katherine Willoughby's Patronage Network, 1540–1600'. Jayne Elisabeth Archer has recently noted Jackson's 1577 licence but assumes that this was a different book and that there are no copies. Jayne Elisabeth Archer, 'Neville, Frances', in Garrett A. Sullivan, Jr. and Alan Stewart (eds.), *The Encyclopaedia of English Renaissance Literature: A–F, Volume 1* (Chichester: John Wiley and Son, 2012), 733. There are also similarities between the acrostic on Mary Fane's name in Bentley and a manuscript presented by John Phillips to John Lumley. See BL Royal MS 7 A xii, fols. 168ʳ–79ʳ, John Phillips, 'Christian and comfortable counsails for the health and preseruation of the boddy and the soule'.

[32] John Phillips, *The Perfect Path to Paradise* (London: H. Jackson, 1588; *STC* 19872), sig. K7ʳ.

the lay preparation for and experience of the sacrament. In the Catholic Mass, after the priest recited the words of consecration over the bread ('Take and eat ye all of this. For this is my body …'), he was instructed to 'incline to the host, and afterwards elevate it above his forehead so that it can be seen by the people'.[33] A bell was rung to warn lay people that the elements were about to be elevated, and candles were used to provide good visibility. The people were expected to 'adore' the host and the chalice when they were elevated, and as Eamon Duffy notes, Primers often had several 'elevation prayers' for lay people to use at these most sacred moments.[34] Catholic Primers also had prayers to help lay people prepare to receive Communion at Easter – prayers such as 'When thou shalt receive the sacrament' and 'When thou hast received the sacrament'.[35]

The 1549, 1552, and 1559 BCPs incrementally rewrote the Mass, which was called 'The Order for the Administration of the Lord's Supper, or Holy Communion' from 1552 onwards. For example, by 1559 the host and chalice were no longer elevated for adoration (but communicants still kneeled when receiving the sacrament); the service used reformed language to describe the sacrament, but retained some traditional formulations and gestures; and lay people undertook their own spiritual preparation and confessed together during the service.[36] In 1563, the Elizabethan Church issued 'A Homily of the Worthy Receiving and Reverend Esteeming of the Sacrament of the Body and Blood of Christ', a homily designed to help people understand the new service and presumably read to parishioners in the weeks leading up to a Communion service.[37] Interestingly, neither the Edwardian and

---

[33] The Chalice was also elevated as the wine was being consecrated: 'Here he [the priest] shall elevate the chalice as high as his chest, or above his head', Warren (trans.), *Sarum Missal*, vol. I, 45–6.

[34] Duffy, *Stripping of the Altars*, 119–20. Some primers have over ten such prayers. See, for example, *Hore Beatissime Virginis Marie* (Paris: Regnault, 1534; *STC* 15984).

[35] *The Primer in English and Latin, after the Use of Sarum* (London: Thomas Petyt, 1542; *STC* 16028), R6ʳ.

[36] This is a summary of the changes that are relevant to this paper, but there were many other changes as well. There is a lively scholarly debate about whether the eucharistic theology in the three BCPs reflects traditional, Lutheran, Zwinglian, Bullingerian, or Calvinist beliefs. For an overview of these issues see: James F. Turrell, 'Anglican Theologies of the Eucharist', in Lee Palmer Wandel (ed.), *A Companion to the Eucharist in the Reformation* (Leiden: Brill, 2014), 139–58; Timothy Rosendale, *Liturgy and Literature in the Making of Protestant England* (Cambridge: Cambridge University Press, 2007), 88–108; Horton Davies, *Worship and Theology in England, from Cranmer to Hooker, 1534–1603* (Princeton: Princeton University Press, 1970), 76–123 and 165–226.

[37] *The Second Tome of Homilies* (London: Richard Jugge, 1563; *STC* 13665), fols. 213ʳ–21ᵛ. Although the Elizabethan Church mandated that the laity should communicate three times a year, Communion services still only took place at Easter in many parishes.

Elizabethan Churches provided an official Communion prayer to replace those in the pre-BCP Primers, but this task was taken up by various clergymen and lay people, and we find lengthy Communion prayers in prayer books edited or written by Thomas Becon, James Chancellor, Henry Bull, John Day, Thomas Achelley, Richard Day, and John Field.[38]

Aburgavenny's prayer differs from those written by her peers in that it presents itself as a companion to the 1559 BCP Communion service and the Homily. In terms of its organization, it is clearly keyed to the structure of the Homily: it focuses on the correct 'understanding' of the sacrament, strong 'faith' in the sacrament, and appropriate preparation (repentance and social reconciliation).[39] In addition, Aburgavenny repeatedly echoes language from the Communion service, thus carefully preparing her readers for their actual encounter with the Eucharist.[40] For example, the second half of the prayer focuses on spiritual preparation and social reconciliation, and here she draws on the 'General Confession' in the BCP as well as on the Exhortations and Rubric that preceded it. So she asks:

> Indue us with love and *charity* to all men (Exhortation); make us *ready to forgive* (Exhortation), to love, and pardon our enemies, persecutors and slanderers ... give us grace to *make restitution* (Exhortation), and to ask with sorrowful plaints and floods of tears, from *the bottom of our hearts* (Rubric), pardon and free forgiveness of thee, for such and all other our offences whatsoever we have done, or *committed in thought, word, will and deed, against thy divine Majesty* ('General Confession'), or any other our brethren and sisters (vol. II, 165).[41]

Aburgavenny's prayer clearly supports and buttresses the approach to social reconciliation promoted by the BCP service, a detail that distinguishes her prayer from some other contemporary prayers which make no mention of social reconciliation. Moreover, as we saw in our discussion of Tyrwhit, this last phrase from the 'General Confession' is one that preserved language from the Latin Confiteor, and here (as in Tyrwhit's prayer) it is further disseminated in household devotions.

The first part of Aburgavenny's prayer, however, displays a more aggressive and interventionist response towards the language in the 1559 BCP. As we shall see, Aburgavenny works hard to ensure that one of

---

[38] See: *STC* 1720; 4558; 4028; 6428; 85a; 11555; 16429; 10846. Ironically, one of the most widely circulated Communion prayers in private prayer books printed in London was extracted from the Scottish Book of Common Order.

[39] The Homily has the same tripartite structure: see *Second Tome*, fol. 214ʳ.

[40] Many of the words and phrases from Aburgavenny's prayer are found in the BCP service.

[41] See Cummings (ed.), *Book of Common Prayer*, 133, 132, 124, and 134.

the BCP's adaptations of Catholic words of administration will *not* be interpreted in a traditional (Catholic) fashion, and she musters a range of literary techniques to make the reformed eucharistic language of the BCP more compelling. The first half of Aburgavenny's prayer deals with 'understanding' and 'faith', and it is notable that she begins by outlining the beliefs that must be rejected before introducing a more positive formulation. This is perhaps not surprising, for the English Communion service changed several times between 1548 and 1558, and the 1559 BCP is well known for including passages that allow for very different interpretations. Aburgavenny addresses the potential for a false interpretation immediately, asking for grace so that the English people will not 'build on the doctrine of men, who following their own imaginations, run headlong to the gaping gulf of danger and destruction' (vol. II, 164). She then gets right to the point, succinctly stating that 'pure knowledge' of the sacrament entails a rejection of Catholic ideas about Christ's corporal, 'real' or 'carnal' presence in the elements:

> Indue us plentifully with such pure knowledge, that we may not once think or say after any gross form or carnal manner, we *feed upon, or eat thy flesh really, or carnally*. (Vol. II, 164, my emphasis)

By means of this pithy sentence she positions her prayer in opposition to Catholic Communion prayers which would still have been in circulation in some circles. A popular Elevation prayer printed in 1557, for example, celebrated precisely the 'bodily' presence of Christ in the host: 'Hail very body incarnate of a virgin … At the point of death let us receive thee bodily, O sweet, O holy, O Jesu, son of Mary'. The next prayer, for 'receiving the sacrament', asked, 'have mercy upon me sinner, by the receiving of this thy body flesh and blood'.[42] A Communion prayer in Lady Jane Wriothesley's prayer book begins: 'Hail holiest body of our Lord Jesus Christ that art now faithfully contained here in this most excellent sacrament'.[43]

Aburgavenny is also, I believe, addressing the 1559 BCP and its controversial retention of traditional eucharistic language from the Mass. For example, as scholars have long noted, the editors of the 1559 BCP created new words of administration by combining two very different (and potentially incompatible) formulations from the 1549 and 1552 BCPs:

> The body of our lord Jesus Christ which was given for thee, preserve thy body and soul into everlasting life [from 1549 BCP; adapted from

---

[42] *Primer in English and Latin* (London: John Wayland, 1557; *STC* 16080), sig. M4ʳ.
[43] Bod MS Laud Misc. 1, fol. 33ʳ.

the Latin Rite]: and take and eat this, in remembrance that Christ died
for thee, and feed on him in thine heart by faith with thanksgiving
[from 1552].

  The blood of our lord Jesus Christ which was shed for thee, preserve thy
body and soul into everlasting life [from 1549 BCP; adapted from the
Latin Rite]: and drink this in remembrance that Christ's blood was shed
for thee, and be thankful [from 1552].[44]

In each case, the first clause has been re-introduced from the 1549 BCP
and is, in fact, derived from the Catholic Sarum form of Communion
for the Sick.[45] These clauses describe the bread and wine as the 'body'
and 'blood' of Christ, focus on their salvific power, and thus allow (but
do not require) a traditional Catholic interpretation. The second clause,
however, offers the words of administration from the 1552 BCP; they
offer a more reformed view by focusing on the communicants' remembrance, faith, thanksgiving, and spiritual feeding. Aburgavenny's insistence that her readers ask for grace so that they will not even 'once' think
that they 'feed upon, or eat thy flesh really, or carnally' can be read, I suggest, as an attempt to persuade her readers to reject a Catholic interpretation of the traditional Sarum words when they hear them at the crucial
moment of reception. She would certainly have known that others shared
her concern: in 1572, the Puritan agitators John Field and Thomas
Wilcox complained vehemently that in celebrating Communion 'we (the
English) borrow from papists, "The Body of our Lord Jesus Christ which
was given for thee", etc.[46]

  Aburgavenny's request that we 'not' believe that we eat Christ's body
'really' is immediately tied to a request that we 'constantly' believe that
Christ's 'glorious body is ascended up into heaven, and sitteth on the
right hand of thy Father ... and cannot be thence removed, till the time
that [he] shalt come with legions of Angels, to judge the quick and the
dead' (vol. II, 164). Importantly, this passage is drawn from the Creed,
a liturgical statement of faith that was part of the Communion service
and was frequently invoked by Reformers contesting the ideas of corporal
presence. In reciting the Creed, the Elizabethan priest asserted: '[I believe

---

[44] *The Book of Common Prayer* (London: Richard Jugge and John Cawood, 1559; *STC* 16292a), sig.
N1ʳ. I cite from this edition to preserve the original punctuation. I have modernized the spelling.
[45] The Latin words are: *Corpus domini nostri Jesu Christi custodiat corpus tuum et animam tuam in
vitam aeternam*. Davies, *Worship*, 170–1. Rosendale discusses the ambiguity of these words in
Liturgy and Literature, 100–1. See also G. J. Cuming, *A History of Anglican Liturgy* (London:
Palgrave, 1969), 122, and Cummings (ed.), *Book of Common Prayer*, 732–3n137.
[46] W. H. Frere and C. E. Douglas (eds.), *Puritan Manifestoes: A Study of the Origin of the Puritan
Revolt* (London: Society for Promoting Christian Knowledge, 1907), 13.

that on] ... the third day [Christ] rose again according to the Scriptures, and ascended into heaven, and sitteth at the right hand of the father. And he shall come again with glory to judge both the quick and the dead'.[47] Aburgavenny's rhetorical strategy, then, is remarkably compact and savvy: she does not overwhelm her readers with arguments against transubstantiation culled from the Church fathers or ecclesiastical councils (as the Homily does), but she uses one well-known piece of the Communion service (the Creed) to shape her reader's experience of another (the actual reception of the bread and wine). It may be worth noting that Aburgavenny's use of the terms 'thy flesh really' and her reference to Christ's ascension into heaven recall the famous 'Black Rubric' hastily added to the 1552 BCP as it was coming off the press. This rubric asserted that kneeling at the sacrament did not mean that people were engaged in adoration of the bread or wine or of any '*real* or essential presence there being of *Christ's natural flesh* and blood', which were, after all, 'in *heaven* and not here'.[48] The 'Black Rubric' was removed from the 1559 BCP, yet according to Bishop Grindal and Bishop Horne, the gist of the rubric was still being expounded by some ministers in 1567.[49] Aburgavenny, it would appear, was similarly working to disseminate its views.

Aburgavenny's prayer is next concerned with 'faith', asking God to 'confirm our faith' and providing readers with a positive definition of what the sacrament is. She writes:

> And since thou hast called us by thy word, as thy guests to this blessed banquet, wherein the mouths of our carnal bodies are fostered & fed with bread and wine: so Lord confirm our faith in thee, that the mouths of our souls may feed spiritually upon thy sweetest flesh, and drink thy dearest blood, and so be nourished to everlasting life, and heavenly blessedness. (Vol. II, 164–5)

She describes the 'blessed supper' again later, using many of the same phrases:

> Give us grace to come worthily, by the virtue of a true and fruitful faith, to this holy and blessed supper, that our souls feeding faithfully on thy sweetest flesh, and drinking thy dearest blood, we may both in body and soul be nourished by thee to everlasting and endless glory in heaven. (Vol. II, 165)

---

[47] Cummings (ed.), *Book of Common Prayer*, 127.
[48] Ibid., 667, my emphasis.
[49] Hastings Robinson (ed.), *Zurich Letters: Comprising the Correspondence of Several English Bishops ... During the Reign of Queen Elizabeth*, 2nd ed. (Cambridge: Cambridge University Press, 1846), 277.

In these passages Aburgavenny clearly develops a Cranmerian insistence that 'the manducation of Christ's body must be a figure, a metaphor' and that spiritual eating is 'believing, exercising faith in the Passion of Christ'.[50] Her metaphorical descriptions of 'souls' 'feed[ing] spiritually' and 'feeding faithfully' on Christ's flesh and blood noticeably echo three places in the BCP service: the Exhortation that stated that those with 'lively faith' would '*spiritually eat the flesh* of *Christ, and drink his blood*'; the post-Communion prayer that thanked God for having vouchsafed to '*feed* us … with the *spiritual food of the most precious body and blood of thy son*'; and the words of administration, '*feed* on him *in thine heart by faith* with thanksgiving'.[51]

I would argue, however, that these two positive Cranmerian descriptions of the sacrament also work hard to prevent a traditional interpretation of the Sarum words in the 1559 words of administration. As noted earlier, the first clause (from Sarum) asserted that the bread was 'the body of Christ' that would *preserve thy body and soul into everlasting life*, while the second clause suggested a purely spiritual feeding through faith. Aburgavenny has, of course, already vehemently denied any sort of corporal presence in the bread; here, she insists on this view again by asserting twice that it is through spiritual faith (not through the salvific power of the host and wine) that the 'body and soul' will be *nourished to everlasting life* and nourished 'to *everlasting and endless glory*'. In sum, Aburgavenny uses language from the second (more reformed) clause to prevent a Catholic interpretation of the first clause, a detail that reveals that she, like Tyrwhit, was acutely aware of the degree to which traditional language was preserved or abandoned by the successive versions of the BCP. Finally, it is worth noting that Aburgavenny goes beyond the 1559 BCP in insisting on the distinction between 'carnal' and 'spiritual' eating, and she uses metaphors, alliteration, and sensual language to make the idea of 'spiritual eating' appealing to readers. Thus, she contrasts the 'mouths of our bodies' with the 'mouths of our souls', and she stresses that while our carnal bodies are 'fostered and fed with bread and wine', the 'mouths of our souls' are 'feeding faithfully' on Christ's 'sweetest flesh' and 'dearest blood'. Her repetition of the phrases 'sweetest flesh' and 'dearest blood' are particularly interesting because the Catholic elevation prayers were replete with sensual language. As noted earlier, one such prayer asked, 'let us receive thee bodily, O sweet, O holy,

---

[50] Davies, *Worship and Theology*, 116.
[51] Cummings (ed.), *Book of Common Prayer*, 132, 138, and 137.

O Jesu, son of Mary'; another referred to Christ/host as the *angelorum panis* (bread of angels); and the one transcribed by Lady Wriothesley says, 'O thou sweetest manna, angel's food. O thou most liking ghostly drink, bring into mine inward mouth the sweetest honey of thine healthful presence'.[52] I suggest, then, that Aburgavenny may be looking backwards and forwards, drawing on the power of traditional eucharistic language as part of a larger rhetorical strategy to reject traditional eucharistic theology and to make an abstract 'spiritual' experience into something more appealing.

There is obviously much to be learned about Tudor women's devotional techniques and their participation in the evolution of devotional language across the sixteenth century. This chapter has examined only two prayers, yet it has yielded results that gesture towards a broader pattern. As we have seen, elite laywomen raised in the early to mid-sixteenth century were deeply familiar with traditional liturgical language and were attuned to every phrase that was translated, truncated, or transformed in the English BCPs. Both Tyrwhit and Aburgavenny engaged with the BCP with an intensity that distinguishes them from some of their peers, and in working with Cranmer's old-new text they invariably confronted the complex verbal web that accompanied the Reformation. On the one hand, they echoed key phrases from Cranmer's Communion Service, and in doing so they simultaneous reproduced 'new' material and perpetuated Catholic material that Cranmer had preserved. On the other hand, they both display an ambivalence or hostility to some of BCP's formulations, and while Tyrwhit recuperated traditional phrases that she valued, Aburgavenny resisted traditional language that she feared.

---

[52] *Primer in English and Latin*, sig. M4ʳ; *Hore Beatissime Virginis Marie* (*STC* 15984), fol. lxviiᵛ; Bod MS Laud Misc. 1, fol. 34ᵛ.

Spatial Texts
Women as Devisers of Environments and Iconographies

Peter Davidson

In early modern Europe, it was not uncommon to use the symbolic languages of the late Renaissance and Baroque to create temporary or permanent decorated environments, either designed as places of meditation and withdrawal or else as statements of the religious, philosophical or political position of an individual or community. Amongst these, there is a particularly interesting group made for and by early modern women in England, which demonstrate the degree to which women, sometimes as executants, sometimes as patrons or 'devisers', could create or commission complex adornments of spaces, cogent within current symbolic conventions and legible as verbal and visual texts. Many of these spaces involve the use of needlework, communicating in the discourses of emblems and iconographies. Some are painted with carefully articulated inscriptions and symbolic pictures: 'speaking rooms' with an apprehensible intellectual content are in a continuum with contemporary works for male or civic patrons, and manifestations of a phenomenon once widespread, which can be conjectured to have enjoyed a comparatively poor rate of survival. (The painted cloth, which was perhaps the most common form of room decoration in early modern Britain, has a very poor rate of survival indeed.)[1] Houses and gardens could be bearers of inscription and meaning. Meditation practices can also construct a symbolic space internally, a place made in the mind for prayer and contemplation, as Anne Bacon Drury's painted closet was an externally expressed place of thought and prayer.

---

[1] M. R. Pryor and J. C. Morrison, 'Caught in the Springe of the Kirke – For Covenant and King: Charles II 1650–51', in Peter Davidson and Jill Bepler (eds.), *Triumphs of the Defeated: Early Modern Festivals and Messages of Legitimacy* (Wiesbaden: Otto Harrassowitz, 2007), 191–225. This article discusses the most substantial survival in Scotland. In England there are painted cloths at Hardwick Hall, Derbyshire, and Owlpen Manor, Gloucestershire. Otherwise survivals are few. The author would like to acknowledge Jane Stevenson's assistance with this chapter.

The Painted Closet of Anne Bacon Drury (1572–1624), now in the Christchurch Mansion Museum, Ipswich, has recently been the subject of an exemplary book-length study, which prompts this survey and reconsideration of the activities of early modern British women as devisers and designers of environments.[2] This survey will re-visit the works of a diversity of early modern women, including Mary Queen of Scots (1542–87) and her gaoler and hostess, Elizabeth Countess of Shrewsbury (1527–1608). It will also consider Lady Anne Cooke Bacon (1527–1610) and her inscriptions at Gorhambury House, devised in collaboration with her husband Nicholas Bacon (1529–79), who was Anne Drury's grandfather, as well as the unrealised manuscript iconographies prepared in her circle, continuing with the carefully determined, and very verbal, word and image medium of the *Great Picture*, devised by Lady Anne Clifford (1590–1676). A considerable contrast is offered by the microcosmic garden layout made in her youth by the future Winter Queen, Elizabeth of Bohemia (1618–80), which offers an individual imagination of the world. The survey concludes by suggesting briefly some of the possibilities concerning the construction of interior space implied in the work of a major English visual artist, the recusant Catholic designer and maker of ecclesiastical textiles, Helena Wintour (c. 1600–71).

The Painted Closet: Anne Bacon Drury

The panels from Anne Bacon Drury's painted closet, now in Ipswich, have been relocated twice: at some point in Lady Drury's lifetime from Hardwick House, Hawstead, Suffolk, to Hawstead Place nearby, and then in 1924 to Christchurch Mansion in Ipswich (see Figure 10.1).[3] Professor Meakin's considered opinion is that Lady Drury designed the room for her own use, aware of Joseph Hall's 1606 *The Arte of Divine Meditation* but original in her adaptation of *imprese* and Latin *sententiae* to her own purposes. Whether she painted all or any of it remains uncertain: the design – with its unifying backgrounds of stylised trees and pale sky in the emblem panels – is elegant. The details, especially of human figures, are relatively unsophisticated, possibly the work of a member of a family which included an accomplished amateur painter, but equally plausible as the work of a regional professional painter.

[2] Meakin, *Painted Closet*.
[3] Ibid., 2.

Figure 10.1   Lady Elizabeth Drury's Painted Closet from Hawstead, Suffolk, before
1615, now at Christchurch Museum, Ipswich
© Dr Stephen Plunkett. This work is licensed under the Creative Commons Attribution-Share Alike
2.0 Generic Licence.

The room, as now constituted, consists of painted panels below a frieze
with inscriptions. There are a number of panels, now arranged together
with no inscription above, which may have changed their places in the
course of the move, possibly originally having been above windows or
doors,[4] otherwise, the forty emblem panels are grouped in sixes and nines
under the *sententiae* in an arrangement which Professor Meakin believes
to be close to their original arrangement. The lowest rank of painted
panels shows herbs (medicinal and symbolic). The sentences or mottos
are perfectly described as 'commonplaces re-calibrated'.[5] They seem to
function as headings below which the painted panels are grouped. These
sentences, in Latin, are adapted in terms of grammatical gender to be

[4] The evidence for the earlier arrangement of the panels comes from Rev Sir John Cullum, *The
History and Antiquities of Hawstead* (London: J. Nichols for the Society of Antiquaries, 1813).
[5] Meakin, *Painted Closet*, 8

Figure 10.2   Painted Gallery at Pinkie House, Midlothian, 1613
© Professor Michael Bath, reproduced by his kind permission.

apposite for a room owned and used by a woman. These *sententiae* are at once commonplaces and truths: 'warnings for one who must contend with the world and know it for what it is'.[6] They consider the limitations of mortality and the urgent need for prudence in the conduct of human affairs. To some degree, they offer the joint consolations of a learned Stoicism and Christian hope. In this, as Professor Meakin points out, the nearest parallel is the long gallery of inscriptions and emblems painted in 1613 for Alexander Seton, first Earl of Dunfermline, at his country villa (one of the first country houses in Scotland not to be fortified) Pinkie House in East Lothian (see Figure 10.2). The gallery emblems advocate prudence, reticence and temperance in dealing with a volatile body politic, and also offer the consolations of a Christian stoicism.[7]

[6] Ibid., 143.
[7] Michael Bath, *Renaissance Decorative Painting in Scotland* (Edinburgh: National Museums of Scotland, 2003), 79–94; Michael Bath, 'Alexander Seton's Painted Gallery', in Lucy Gent (ed.), *Albion's Classicism: The Visual Arts in Britain 1550–1660* (New York and London: Yale University Press, 1995), 79–109.

Lady Drury's *sententiae* include 'AMPLIOR IN COELO [there is a larger dwelling in heaven]', suggesting that the meditations undertaken in the restricted space of the painted closet could lead to Christian fulfilment in heaven, a sentiment echoed also in the reminder 'FRUSTRA NISI DOMINUS [in vain, without the Lord]'. 'PARVA SED APTA MIHI [small but fitting for me]' is partly a reflection of a commonplace about the felicity of a small landed estate. This sentence, originating with the Roman poet Horace, is partly a reflection on how a small room can contain so many thoughts and infinite permutations of trains of thought. It is also, as Professor Meakin says, a reflection on women and private spaces: 'These women and others like them used the spaces allotted to them to come to terms with [the] world and its restrictions, in often freeing ways'.[8] The inscription which has come to characterise the room is 'NUNQUAM MINUS SOLA QUAM CUM SOLA [Never less alone (feminine) than when alone]' – an adaptation to a specifically female environment of thoughts about the value of contemplation and the companionship of God.

The forty emblem panels cover a very large range of thought and devotion: from a mild satire of Catholics as blind moles unable to see in daylight, to the condemnation of ignoble retirement – a hibernating bear – with the motto that the obscure one is secure, albeit with the implication that no good can come of this course of action. The world is carried by a scuttling crab; thus the world's movement goes ('SIC ORBIS ITER'). There are endless reminders of the need for caution and negotiation, especially for an elite woman, as with the *impresa* of an unfinished woman's portrait on a painter's easel, with the motto 'DIC MIHI QUALIS ERIS [tell me what you will become]'.

The grouping of panels does not follow a particular sequence, one leading to its neighbour; so much so that it would seem that here, as elsewhere, the inscriptions in the frieze serve as headings under which to group ideas, intellectual fingerposts to the whereabouts of the ideas disposed about the room, labelled repositories under which ideas can be contained. A precise analogy is to be found in John Aubrey's life of the schoolmaster Ezreel Tonge:

> He afterwards taught at Islington at Sir Thomas Fisher's house, where was a long gallery and he had several printed heads of the Caesars etc: verbes under such a heade governed a Dative Case, under another an Ablative. The boyes had it as readie as could be.[9]

---

[8] Meakin, *Painted Closet*, 189.

[9] John Aubrey, *Brief Lives*, Kate Bennett (ed.), 2 vols. (Oxford: Oxford University Press, 2015), vol. I, 152–3.

So, as well as everything else, Lady Drury's room is a Theatre of Memory, ideas placed in physical (and also imaginary) space.[10] It is a microcosm, the world in one room, and also a paradise garden in its panels of herbs and flowers. As such it is a fitting point of focus for all subsequent thoughts about women and the texts of place: all of the constructed environments play one or more of these roles. The last word on the use of the closet should go to Professor Meakin:

> The closet presents us with another paradox, whereby we can discern ... an attempt on Lady Drury's part to order the external world – and yet it is also a kind of Narnian wardrobe into which one can step and find oneself undertaking different wanderings that may never be repeated or that will bring one back to the center, the still center of the *mediocre firma* of the Christian Neostoicism which the woman who sat in the centre of the closet embodied.[11]

Embroidery: Mary, Queen of Scots, and Elizabeth Talbot

Another way in which a small private space might be textualised is through embroidery. Mary, Queen of Scots had been taught how to make embroidered pictorial panels as a child at the Valois court, and continued to practice this skill throughout her life.[12] Such panels, appliquéd to larger textiles, of course lent themselves to the construction of personal iconographies. The Hardwick Hall inventory of 1601 suggests how they could be used to create a closet: there was a set of hangings in 'the little Chamber within the best bedchamber' which had

> Five peeces of hangings of grene velvet and Clothe of Golde and silver set with trees and slips and ciphers with long borders of stories in nedleworke and borders about all these hangings of Cloth of tissue silver and grene silk, everie peece being Eight foote deep.[13]

Embroidered slips would often be applied to bed-hangings. Other people normally shared a royal bedroom,[14] but a four-poster with its hangings makes a room within a room, the ultimate space for privacy and

---

[10] The best introduction to this vast topic remains Frances A. Yates, *The Art of Memory* (London: Routledge and Kegan Paul, 1966).

[11] Meakin, *Painted Closet*, 128.

[12] Patricia Wardle, 'The Embroideries of Mary, Queen of Scots: Notes on the French Background', *Bulletin of the Needle and Bobbin Club*, 64 (1981), 1–20.

[13] Lindsay Boynton (ed.), *The Hardwick Hall Inventories of 1601* (London: Victoria and Albert Museum, 1971), 26.

[14] Anna Whitelock, *Elizabeth's Bedfellows* (London: Bloomsbury, 2013), 29.

withdrawal. Mary created at least one politically charged set of emblematic hangings for a state bed, which suggests that she was shaping her immediate environment in a highly conscious way. One set was described at Fotheringhay after Mary's death and another was subsequently seen in Edinburgh in the early seventeenth century by Drummond of Hawthornden: these may or may not be the same.

The hangings which were found at Fotheringhay after the queen's execution were described in French in October 1587 (perhaps from an inventory made by a member of Mary's Francophone household).[15] The description includes more emblems than Drummond lists, but there is a great deal of overlap. However, according to George Mackenzie, the set of hangings seen by Drummond was actually sent by Mary to her son James in 1579. If this were so, then it would demand to be read both as a personal apologia and a lesson in statecraft. This might explain why along with Valois emblems, it includes the *impresa* of Henry VIII, a portcullis with '*altera securitas* [an additional security]', a reminder of common Plantagenet descent, and the consequent Stuart claim to the throne of England.[16] It is far from impossible that there were two sets: the duplication of motifs can be explained by the tenacity with which Mary maintained the same political position throughout her life.

The hangings described by Drummond were decorated with the *imprese* of Mary's mother, Henri II, François I, and the Cardinal of Lorraine, her uncle, among others, and also with more personal iconographies.

> Two Women upon the Wheels of Fortune, the One holding a *Launce*, the other a *Cornucopia*: which Impresa seemeth to glance at Queen Elizabeth and her self; the word *Fortunae comites* [companions of fortune] ... This is for her selfe and her Son, a big *Lyon* and a young *Whelp* beside her, the Word *unum quidem sed Leonem* [one, but he is a lion]. An Emblem of a *Lyon* taken in a Net, and Hare wantonly passing over him, the Word, *Et leopores devicto insultant Leoni* [hares insult the conquered lion].[17]

Other images – the camomile, all the sweeter for being trodden on, the palm tree, resisting the weight put on it through its innate virtue, the

---

[15] BL MS Cotton Caligula D. I., fol. 142ʳ. The description is dated to October 1587 by the State Papers.

[16] George Mackenzie, *The Lives and Characters of Eminent Scotsmen*, 3 vols. (Edinburgh: James Watson, 1711), vol. II, 328.

[17] Bath, *Emblems for a Queen*, 147. Appendix 6 contains information on Mary's bed of state collated from four early descriptions of bed-hangings no longer extant. Bath's chapter 3, 'Incriminating Emblems', is about the oppositional, political and religious iconographies in Mary's work (49–69).

caged bird – are all also read as self-representation. In these emblems, Mary not only expresses her sense of injury but her sense of her own worth and significance.

Similarly, the various emblems representing resistance against a stormy sea form part of a tradition of images particularly associated with royalty in adversity, such as 'A Porcupine amongst Sea Rocks, the Word, *ne volutetur* [lest she be tossed about]'. A rock in troubled sea was used with respect to her grandson, Charles I, in the frontispiece to *Eikon Basilike*, and by William of Orange in his motto '*Saevis Tranquillus in undis* [calm amid the raging waves]'. The illegal medal issued after the execution of Charles I also had the rock in a stormy sea and the motto '*Immota triumphans* [triumphing unmoved]'. The image of the pruned tree was used by the house of Orange and by the Medici – examples could be multiplied infinitely.

What is, however, important to realise is just how unequivocal the message of the lost state bed, or beds, is – and just how much of a confrontational statement is made by it, albeit made within the terms of a discourse which, though it may now seem remote, was wholly serious and comprehensible in the sixteenth century. It is worth observing the fascination with which Drummond of Hawthornden pores over its meaning(s), and that Ben Jonson evidently shared this interest. After plotting secretly to marry Mary, the Duke of Norfolk was beheaded on Tower Hill on 2 June, 1572: part of the evidence that he had conspired with her which was brought forward at his trial earlier that year was her gift to him of an embroidery, with the motif of the hand pruning the sterile branches of the vine (i.e. Elizabeth), and the motto '*virescit vulnere virtus* [its strength grows when it is wounded]'.[18] These draperies with their word-and-image statements about mistreated royalty and royalty in adversity would also appear to have been re-used as part of the furnishings prepared for the reception of Charles I in Edinburgh on his disastrous visit in 1633 – just as, with equal irony, the hangings made by Queen Claude, intimately familiar to the young Mary, were hastily pressed into service to decorate the St Germain apartments of her exiled great-grandson, James II.[19]

Also using needlework, but on an altogether grander scale, is the environment created in 1572 by Mary's sometime hostess (or gaoler) Elizabeth Talbot, Countess of Shrewsbury. Space does not permit a detailed examination of these here, but it is useful to reflect, in the light

---

[18] Bath, *Emblems for a Queen*, 58–9.
[19] Wardle, 'Embroideries of Mary, Queen of Scots', 11.

of her independent power and wealth, and her often adversarial relation to her husband, that the set of black-ground appliqué hangings which were made for Chatsworth in the early 1570s, and which were hung together in the Great Withdrawing Room at Hardwick by 1601, are a powerful statement about the power of heroines and the virtues which they embody.[20] On a black ground, she formed a complete textile equivalent of interior architecture: dado with pilasters, columns with bases, frieze or entablature with her and her husband's monogram, and in the intercolumnations of each panel a kind of Venetian window composed of three round-headed arches. In the central arch is a boldly designed female heroic figure worked in the appliqué of rich (probably mostly ecclesiastical) textiles: Artemisia. Zenobia, Cleopatra, Lucretia, Penelope. These are flanked in the lesser arches by two virtues which they could be said to embody: perseverance and patience for Penelope; Zenobia is flanked by magnanimity and prudence. As a whole, the scheme must have been very strong – the black and gold and gold-shot brocades and the monumental figures of great women and their virtues.

The *Sententiae*: Nicholas and Anne Cooke Bacon

A well-recorded instance of the extensive use of inscriptions in a domestic space is at Gorhambury. This house was built for Sir Nicholas Bacon, Queen Elizabeth's first Keeper of the Great Seal, and his wife, Anne, née Cooke (c. 1528–1610). It has long since been destroyed, though it survived long enough to be mourned by Horace Walpole.[21] The Long Gallery was built after 1572, when Queen Elizabeth commented on the smallness of the house, and before a second royal visit in 1577. Sir Nicholas was considered by contemporaries as 'a most eloquent man, and of rare learning and wisedome, as ever I knew England to breed'.[22] His second wife, Anne, was one of the four formidable daughters of Sir Anthony Cooke: a Latinist, a scholar and a translator.[23] Though Bacon was to describe the

---

[20] Santina Levey, *The Embroideries at Hardwick Hall, a Catalogue* (Swindon: National Trust, 2007); the 'set of five hangings depicting the noble women of the ancient world' are fully described on 74–9.

[21] See Horace Walpole, *Selected Letters*, W. S. Lewis (ed.) (Oxford: Oxford University Press, 1927–8), vol. I, 21: 'it is a most respectable and agreeable retirement, with an air of sober simplicity, yet calculated for great enjoyment, & evidently designed as such'.

[22] George Puttenham, *Art of English Poesie* (London: Richard Field, 1589), 117.

[23] See Allen, *Cooke Sisters*. See also Jaime Goodrich (Chapter 2) in this volume, on Anne Cooke Bacon's translations. Her translation of Jewel's *Apologia Ecclesiae Anglicanae* in 1564 was a significant undertaking since the volume was the official document defining the precise theological

texts as 'selected by Him owt of Divers Authors', given that Lady Bacon was one of the most learned women in England, and the marriage was one of close intellectual companionship, the collection of *sententiae* which were used to adorn the Long Gallery in the 1570s are probably the joint work of the couple.[24] It may be relevant to note a poem which Bacon wrote to his wife in 1558, on the occasion of his 'greate sicknes':

> Thinkeinge also with howe good will
> The Idle tymes whiche yrkesome be
> You have made shorte throwe your good skill
> In readeinge pleasante things to me
> Whereof profitte we bothe did se,
> As wittenes can if they coulde speake
> Bothe your Tullye and my Senecke.[25]

Cicero ('Tullye') and Seneca are the principal sources for the Gorhambury *sententiae*. From other evidence, such as letters, Lady Bacon was certainly familiar with Cicero's *De Officiis*, *De Amicitia* and *De Finibus*, and Seneca's *Epistulae morales* and *De Ira*, all of which are drawn upon.[26]

The inscriptions are preserved in the form of an illuminated manuscript on vellum which Bacon had made and sent to Jane, Lady Lumley 'at her desire', probably c. 1575: *Sentences Painted in sir Nicholas Bacons lorde Keepers gallerie at Goramburie, and by him sent to the la. Lumley.*[27] Its recipient was one of the several well-educated ladies of the Elizabethan court. Born Lady Jane Fitzalan (1536-76), she was the daughter of Henry Fitzalan, 12th Earl of Arundel, and married John, Baron Lumley in 1550, becoming Lady Lumley. She is listed as a lady of honour in 1558/9, and has left as translation exercises a translation of Isocrates from Greek to Latin, and a translation of Euripides' *Iphigeneia in Aulis* into

---

position of the Church of England, which the Convocation of 1563 had ordered to be placed 'in all cathedral and collegiate churches, and also in private houses'. See Ruth Hughey, 'Lady Anne Bacon's Translations', *Review of English Studies*, 10 (1934), 211. C. S. Lewis comments on her translation in his *English Literature in the Sixteenth Century, Excluding Drama* (London: Clarendon Press, 1954), 307, 'if quality without bulk were enough, Lady Bacon might be put forward as the best of all sixteenth-century translators'.

[24] Elizabeth MacCutcheon, *Sir Nicholas Bacon's Great House Sententiae*, English Literary Renaissance Supplement III (Amherst, MA: University of Hawaii, 1977).

[25] Nicholas Bacon, *The Recreations of His Age* (Oxford: The Daniel Press, 1919), 27.

[26] Allen, *Cooke Sisters*, 38.

[27] BL MS Royal 17 A xxiii, 'Sentences painted in the Lorde Keepars gallery at Gorhumbury' (1558–77). This manuscript merits study in its own right, as part of a group of particularly fine presentation manuscripts associated with the Cooke/Bacon/Cecil circle, including BL MS Royal 2 B X, 'Psalter, in Latin, preceded by a Calendar' (mid-fifteenth century); also Bartolo da Sylva's 'Giordano Cosmografico Cultivato', CUL MS Ii.5.37.

English, which she loved doing: 'ex huius lectione incredibilem semper cepi voluptatem'.[28] Both her husband and father were serious bibliophiles, and she shared their interests: we see here one seriously intellectual member of court circles reaching out to another.[29]

With this manuscript, which is now all that survives, instead of a house made to be read like a manuscript, we have a manuscript made to be read as a paper house (comparable to the 'paper triumphs' in which princes and prelates in adversity entered imaginary or occupied cities), made for the latinate Lady Lumley.[30] It is clear from this that the inscriptions formed part of a carefully worked-out decorative scheme. There were large windows of painted glass, 'every pane with severall figures of beast, bird, or flower'. The surviving fragments of glass suggest that each of the windows may have represented the flora and fauna of a different continent: this interest in creating a 'mirror of the world' in miniature is also found in the private paradise of Princess Elizabeth.[31] The walls were panelled in oak, with gilt in the compartments. The *sententiae*, never more than two lines long, were painted on the portals at both ends of the gallery, and on all four sides above the compartments of the wainscoting. Their spatial arrangements are an intrinsic part of their appeal.

The portal at the west end (which led to the private apartments) is dedicated 'De Summo Bono'. Perhaps unsurprisingly, quite a few inscriptions reflect on the nature of political life:

> SI HONORES PETITURI, CUM AMBITIOSIS, CULMEN DIGNITATIS
> ADEPTIS, DELIBERARENT: VOTA MUTARENT
> [If those who seek office were to consult the ambitious who had attained the highest honours, they might change their prayers.]
> QUANTO PLUS QUIS FORTUNAE SE DEDAT, TANTO MAGIS
> MATERIAM PERTURBATIONIS SIBI FECIT.
> [The more anyone gives himself to fortune, the more he has fashioned causes of anxiety for himself.]
> AMOR, INSANA AMICITIA: ILLIUS AFFECTUS: ISTIUS RATIO, CAUSA:
> AT EA SOLA AMICITIA DURAT, CUI VIRTUS BASIS EST

---

[28] BL Royal 15 A ix, 'Translations by Joan, Lady Lumley' (sixteenth century); Dorothy Gardiner, *English Girlhood at School* (Oxford: Oxford University Press, 1929), 180.

[29] Sears Jayne and Francis Johnson (eds.), *The Lumley Library: The Catalogue of 1609* (London: Trustees of the British Museum, 1956).

[30] For an example of a virtual or paper triumph, see Jelena Todorović, 'Spectacles in the Shadow: the Semi-Official Festivals of the Orthodox in the Habsburg Empire', in Davidson and Bepler (eds.), *Triumphs of the Defeated*, 55–76.

[31] Some glass was salvaged from Gorhambury before it was pulled down, and installed in a subsequent Gorhambury House constructed by the Grimston family in 1777–1784.

[Love is friendship gone mad: one arises from attraction, the other from reason: only that friendship lasts, whose foundation is virtue.]

All these, like most of the others, are adapted from Seneca; though other authors, notably Cicero, are also laid under contribution. Montaigne's house had a very similar scheme, as far as the actual *sententiae* go, though the inscriptions were (and are) painted along roof beams rather than decoratively deployed round the walls.

According to John Aubrey, when Francis Bacon eventually inherited Gorhambury (his mother had life interest in the house and clung tenaciously to it in her widowhood), the Long Gallery had become rather different from the impression given by the Lumley manuscript.

> Over this Portico there is a stately Gallerie, whose Glasse-windowes are all painted: and every pane wi[t]h severall figure, of beast, bird, or flower: perhaps his Lordship might use them as Topiques for Locall memo[rie]. The windowes looke into the Garden: the side opposite to them no window; but is hung all with pictures at length, as of King James, his Lordship, and severall Illustrious persons of his time. at the end you enter is no windowe, but there is a very large picture, thus. In the middle on a Rock in the sea stands King James in armour with his regall Ornaments; on his right hand stands (but whether or no on a Rock I have forgott) King Henry IV of France, in armour; and on his left hand the King of Spaine in like manner. These figures are (at least) as big as the life: they are donne only with umbre and shell-gold; all the heightning and illuminated part being burnisht gold and the shadowed umbre, as in the pictures of the Gods on the dores of Verulam-howse.[32]

It seems likely that it might eventually be possible to put together the *sententiae* and the surviving *ex situ* glass windows and make a reconstruction, as Aubrey hints, of a memory palace, with *loci memoriae*. Though the glass may go back to the Lord Keeper's day, the resemblance of the umber-and-gold kings to contemporary work at Verulam House suggest that they are a scheme superimposed on the inherited one after 1610. However, Aubrey additionally mentions mottoes and emblems in other rooms, notably the Hall, which he specifically says is 'of the auncient building': the Hall has 'an Oake with Akornes falling from it' on the wall over the chimney, 'the Word, *Nisi quid potius*, [unless something better turns up] and on the wall over the Table is painted Ceres teaching the Soweing of Corne, the Word, *Moniti meliora* [we now have better counsel]'.[33] These

[32] Aubrey, *Brief Lives*, vol. I, 217.
[33] Ibid., 218.

emblems do not seem to have the political charge of those deployed by
Mary, Queen of Scots. Gorhambury was a private house: unlike some of
the Queen's courtiers, Bacon and his wife were evidently using it primarily as an expression of their common, domestic concerns, rather than as a
location of theatrical displays of exaggerated loyalism.

Another set of manuscripts with a provenance from the circle of the
Bacons is also relevant to the idea of the inscribed house. BL Sloane MSS
1041, 1063, 1082 and 1096 all contain allegories for a painter.[34] Sloane
MS 1169 is something of an iconographer's handbook: it has extracts
from ancient and modern writers describing classical gods, personifica-
tions and allegories.[35] Sloane MS 1041 contains a remarkable ideal decorative scheme with *sententiae*, probably for large panel paintings, though
there is no evidence they were ever executed.[36] It describes a scheme with
'an allegory of the Tempest'. Jupiter is depicted sitting on a cloud of fair-
est azure; next comes 'Pietas', the Fates, Saturn and Mars, Orion (the star
associated with storms), 'the soonne in the tempest', 'the Queene within
a cloud'. The main text of the manuscript describes this characteristically
eclectic collection of images, with a set of marginal notes down the left-
hand side, which tell the painter to label the images and point out their
meanings by Latin and Greek tags and sentences in boxes, banners, scrolls
and other forms of label. Other paintings in what is conceived of as a
series are 'an allegory of Justice' and 'an allegory of Fortuna'. Thematically,
this more elaborate scheme is related to the subjects of the Gorhambury
sententiae. It would have looked – being very full of scrolls with very long
inscriptions – not at all unlike Lady Anne Clifford's *Great Picture*.[37]

The Great Picture: Anne Clifford

The Great Picture might be seen as another virtual closet.[38] It is very like
the kind of highly determined, very word-heavy representations urged in

[34] BL Sloane MS 1082, 'Directions for painting a table or picture containing allegorical and
other figures' (late sixteenth century). BL Sloane MSS 1041, 1063 and 1096 contain the same text.
[35] BL Sloane MS 1196, 'A collection of extracts in Latin and English, from ancient and modern writers, intended to serve for authorities in depicting mythological, historical or allegorical personages'
(seventeenth century).
[36] David Evett, 'Some Elizabethan Allegorical Paintings: A Preliminary Enquiry', *Journal of the
Warburg and Courtauld Institutes*, 52 (1989), 149–65.
[37] See Jessica Malay (Chapter 22) in this volume, on Clifford's *Great Books of Record*.
[38] Karen Hearn, 'Lady Anne Clifford's Great Triptych', in Karen Hearn and Lynn Hulse (eds.), *Lady
Anne Clifford: Culture, Patronage and Gender in Seventeenth Century Britain* (Leeds: Yorkshire
Archaeological Society, 2009), 1–24.

the Sloane manuscript iconographies – interesting for that alone, in its old-fashionedness and as an example of the realisation of a whole kind of visual/verbal imagination characteristic of the early seventeenth century. It is a triptych (unusual for a secular subject) and was commissioned to record Lady Anne Clifford's eventual succession to the inheritance she and her mother had always argued was rightfully hers.[39] It depicts her family history and personal accomplishments: her parents and dead brothers occupy the central panel, her youthful self is on the left, and herself at age fifty-six is on the right. Within the fictive space are carefully labelled portraits of other family members, together with her governess and tutor (in the left-hand panel), and shelves with labelled books significant to her intellectual development: there is a considerable quantity of 'writing' within the pictorial space, as there would have been in the Sloane pictures, had they been realised. *The Great Picture* is a remarkable statement of personal identity and formation, achieved in entirely visual terms.

The other, more public, message which Lady Clifford's works convey, apart from the careful heraldic management of family tombs at Skipton and Appleby, is expressed through the conservative style, and implicit claim of continuity with the past, of her numerous rebuildings of the castles on her inherited lands in the north of England.[40] As John Goodall writes, 'By owning and repairing castles, she was articulating her lordship over the lands attached to them'.[41] Thus her actions moved oddly in parallel to the conservative, even deliberately anachronistic, styles which had been adopted by some post-Reformation Catholic builders in the later sixteenth century, both in England and in Scotland, who are also articulating a religious connectedness to the past, albeit one born of the specifically Catholic antiquarianism of the Counter-Reformation.[42]

The Garden: Elizabeth of Bohemia

Lady Drury's painted closet existed in an intellectual territory between the Memory Palace and the Paradise Garden. The microcosmic gardens laid out

---

[39] Alice T. Friedman, 'Constructing an Identity in Prose, Plaster and Paint: Lady Anne Clifford as Writer and Patron of the Arts', in Gent (ed.), *Albion's Classicism*, 359–76.
[40] See Peter Sherlock (Chapter 16) in this volume, on Clifford's funeral monuments. See also John Goddall, 'Lady Anne Clifford and the Architectural Pursuit of Nobility', in Hearn and Hulse (eds.), *Lady Anne Clifford*, 76–7.
[41] Goddall, 'Lady Anne Clifford', 74.
[42] Examples of this phenomenon can be found at Samelsbury Hall in Lancashire and in the group of Aberdeenshire castles attributed to gentleman-masons of the family of Conn of Auchry.

under the direction of the future Elizabeth of Bohemia, in her childhood, at Lord and Lady Harrington's house at Coombe Abbey in Warwickshire, were both a paradise and a cabinet of wonders – that particularly late Renaissance and Baroque development of the epitome which is also a theatre of memory.[43] The overall setting sounds like something of an anticipation of the gardens of later centuries, with groves, water and concealed boundaries, but the princess's main focus of activity was an island in a small lake:

> Nothing took the Princess's Fancy so much, as a little Wilderness at the End of the Park, on the Banks of a large Brook, which ran winding along, and formed in one Place; a large irregular Bason, or rather a small Lake, in which, there was an Island covered with Underwood, and flowering Trees and Plants, so well mixed and disposed, that for nine Months in the Year, they formed a continual Spring. This Place, and the adjoining Thicket, my Young Mistress begged to have the Disposal of, during her Stay, which was granted with great Pleasure, by Lord and Lady Harrington, who made it their Study to render their Habitation agreeable to her ... she now formed the Design of collecting, in this little Paradise, all the different Kinds [of bird and fowl] that are in Nature; which, though she could not accomplish, yet she soon had a greater Variety than I ever saw.[44]

This paradise had also an aspect of museum or cabinet of rarities, with elements of the laboratory:

> Whoever had any Thing curious, or could procure it from any of their Acquaintances, in other Parts of the World, hastened to present it to the little Princess: Her Garden and Green house, were as well stored with Curiosities, and exotic Plants, as her Minagerie, with Creatures ... If a Butterfly or Glow worm took her Eye, some Account was given her of their Nature, and of the wonderful Changes, most of them go through; from Flies to Worms, and from Worms to Butterflies again; looking at these and smaller Insects, through the Microscope, which had been very lately discovered by Dribill, a Dutchman, was a frequent and favourite Entertainment.[45]

It seems possible that the formalised landscape in the background of Robert Peake's 1603 portrait of Elizabeth, painted for Lord Harington of Exton, shows some part of this contrived landscape of wood, waters and bridges. It certainly has some of the atmosphere of removedness and enchantment which Lady Erskine describes:

---

[43] This is described in some detail in Lady Frances Erskine, whose *Memoirs relating to the Queen of Bohemia, by one of her Ladies* were published privately, possibly in London and by her granddaughter, in 1772. It can be conjectured that they were written about 1670.
[44] Erskine, *Memoirs*, 113–14.
[45] Ibid., 115–16. There was also an astronomical telescope.

She was delighted with her Island, as I told you before, and the first Orders she gave about it were, to have a little thatched Building, which was in it, rendered commodious within, for the Dwelling of a poor Widow and her Children, who had been recommended commended to her Charity, and who, she intended should live in it, and take care of the different sorts of Fowls that were to be kept there; the Out-side of this House was to have some Alteration made in it, to give it the Appearance of an Hermitage, and near it a Grotto, the Adorning of which with Shells and Moss, was the Amusement of many of her leisure Hours, in which, as in every Thing else, she shewed a Genius above her Years. In the Wood, which I told you was on the other Side of the Brook, she had an Aviary made, like that she had heard Queen Elizabeth had admired so much, at the late Earl of Leicester's. The Top of this was round, with coloured Glass, that looked, at a little Distance, like rough Emeralds and Rubies, seemingly the Produce of a Rock, overgrown with Moss, which formed the Back and Roof of the Aviary; the rest was inclosed with a Net of gilt Wire: Within were many Bushes, for the Birds to perch upon, and Water falling continually from the artificial Rock, into a shallow Marble Bason, in which the pretty little feathered Inhabitants drank and bathed at Pleasure, and Recesses were made in the Rock for them to build their Nests in.[46]

To the zoological collection was added a museum of preserved specimens and something of an outdoor 'paper museum' of paintings of exotic specimens, interspersed with ideal and exotic buildings:

as there are many beautiful ones in other Countries, which cannot live in this, such as the Bird of Paradise, and humming Birds, their Feathers and Skins were stuffed, and hung about the Aviary. Representations of several other Creatures were placed in different Parts of the Wood, and the Pictures of such, whose Skins could not easily be had, adorned the little wooden Buildings, which were dispersed about, in all the different Orders of Architecture, which was a Science Lord Harrington thought a Princess ought to understand, and took this, Method of giving the Lady Elizabeth a Taste for it. Some of the Edifices were after the Draughts, given in Books of Travels, of those of India, and in them Figures drest according to the Manners of those Countries, so that this was a kind of World in Miniature.

This is an extraordinary construct altogether, probably best thought of as the outdoor laboratory, cabinet and architectural studio, designed for the education of a virtuosa, a future princess in an era of discovery and curiosity, in which the focus of Europe inevitably shifted outwards. It also would appear to have constituted an extraordinary anticipation of the exoticisms in garden building, and indeed the hermitages and aviaries of the eighteenth-century garden.

[46] Ibid., 120–1.

Conclusion

To conclude, there is only space to draw attention, very briefly, to an urgent and beguiling possibility: the corpus of ecclesiastical textiles designed and executed by the Worcestershire recusant gentlewoman (and daughter of one of the gunpowder plotters who had planned to snatch Elizabeth from her microcosmic paradise at Coombe Abbey and put her on the throne) Helena Wintour, made from the mid-1650s until her death in 1670. These textiles are ecclesiastical, vestment and altar-frontals, not designed to decorate a room or environment, but they are a fascinating instance of the use which an educated early modern woman made of the idea of symbolic and imaginary place. The meaning expressed by flowers, symbols and inscriptions on the various vestments and textiles from Helena Wintour's *atelier* indicate clearly the cultivation by her and her collaborators of an intense interior or imaginary space – the symbolically furnished paradise garden of the Blessed Virgin, as set out in the meditation treatise *Parthenia Sacra*, published in 1633 by the English Jesuit Henry Hawkins (1577–1646). Again and again the symbolic flowers of the Virgin from Hawkins's treatise appear in the needlework, especially on the white 'Alleluia' chasuble – tulips, irises, marigolds, lilies, roses and gillyflowers – on one vestment, the 'spangled sute' seen astonishingly in juxtaposition with the hedgerow campion, punning on the name of the great Jesuit martyr of the English mission, St Edmund Campion, executed in 1581.

These flowers, framed by the sweeping geometries of the parterres of a paradise garden, are illuminated by the sunburst and starburst monograms of the Society of Jesus, of the Jesuit saints, of the monogrammed Holy Names of Jesus and Mary. While they were constructing the embroidered garlands and sprays, it would seem wholly likely that Helena Wintour and her friends would have read and meditated on Hawkins, and thus would have created for themselves, a group of women in opposition to the state and its religion, an interior place of memory and devotion. As Anne Bacon Drury made her little world with painted panels and inscribed letters, so Helena Wintour and her companions made an invisible garden of symbolic flowers, an inviolable, mental paradise.[47]

---

[47] The most comprehensive account of Helena Wintour and her work is Janet Graffius (ed.), *Plots and Spangles, the Embroidered Vestments of Helena Wintour* (Stonyhurst: St Omers Press, 2015).

PART III

The Early Stuart Period (1603–1642)

Aemilia Lanyer's Radical Art
"The Passion of Christ"

Pamela J. Benson

Aemilia Bassano Lanyer's verse narrative "The Passion of Christ" is a discrete unit within her long poem *Salve Deus Rex Judeorum*. Its beginning and end are clearly indicated by marginal glosses and the story it tells gives it unity. Yet, despite this clarity, the topic of genre has been neglected. "The Passion" has been mined for evidence to support arguments about the volume as a whole without regard for the markers Lanyer set up indicating its integrity. This chapter focuses solely on "The Passion of Christ" in order to demonstrate the poet's radical reformulation of the ancient devotion, the Passion meditation.[1]

Traditional Passions have a single purpose. Whether aimed at a sole reader or a wider public, they attempt to present Christ's suffering to the readers' gaze in a manner that will lead them to reflect on their own sins and to rejoice that Christ's death has made it possible for them to be saved from damnation. The influential Calvinist theologian William Perkins describes Passions as "a looking glasse, in which we may cleerely behold the horriblenes of our sinnes, that could not be pardoned without the passion of the sonne of God."[2] Lanyer, too, presents Christ's suffering before readers' eyes, and she even describes her poem as a "mirror" and a "glasse" in her dedicatory letters.[3] Yet her mirror, though Calvinist, does

---

[1] For another reading of Lanyer's "Passion" in its theological context, see Longfellow, *Women and Religious Writing*, 59–91.

[2] William Perkins, *An Exposition of the Symbole or Creed of the Apostles* (Cambridge: John Legate, 1595), 179. He echoes Calvin, "Wee are too dull certeinely, unlesse we see clearly in this glasse, how greatly GOD abhorreth sinnes: and wee are more then stonie, unlesse we tremble and quake at such a judgement of his." John Calvin, *A Harmonie upon the Three Euangelists* (London: [Printed by Thomas Dawson] impensis Geor. Bishop, 1584), 420.

[3] Lanyer, "To The Queenes Most Excellent Majestie," lines 37 and 40; "To the Ladie Anne," lines 7–8; "The Author's Dreame," lines 209–12; "To the Ladie Margaret," lines 27–34. All references are to Lanyer, *Poems*; subsequent citations are given parenthetically. Wall, *Imprint of Gender*, 319–30, and Lynette McGrath, "Metaphoric Subversions: Feasts and Mirrors in Aemilia Lanier's *Salve Deus Rex Judaeorum*," *LIT: Literature, Interpretation, Theory* 3 (1991), 101–13, discuss the mirror but not in theological terms.

not fulfill the central spiritual mission of the genre. She does not prompt readers to inward reflection and discovery of their sinful selves but rather encourages self-satisfaction and urges anticipation of the joys of heaven.[4]

Lanyer used four techniques to accomplish this radical reorientation of the Passion away from introspection and remorse, while at the same time retaining a reformed Protestant orientation. First, she narrowed her audience to women by prefacing the poem with epistles addressed solely to women and by incorporating into the "Passion" itself direct address to her primary patron, Margaret Russell, Dowager Countess of Cumberland. Secondly, she took advantage of women's subservient social and political position to exempt them from responsibility for the Fall and the Crucifixion. Thirdly, she changed the story; she expanded some incidents, omitted others, added episodes and characters, featured heroic women characters, and diminished the heroism of men. In good Reformed fashion, she stressed women's open-heartedness and love, which connect them directly with their God and make them superior to men, who are separated from God by their commitment to religious and secular structures of power. Finally, she engaged in intertextual dialogue with two previously unrecognized Roman Catholic sources: the anonymous *S. Augustine's Prayers* and Antonio de Guevara's *The Mount of Calvarie*. Through manipulating words, phrases, and scenes from these texts, she refuted their interpretations of Passion events and put her poem squarely in the anti-Papist camp. In all these ways, Lanyer showed herself to be a far more sophisticated poet and thinker than has previously been demonstrated.

Literary Antecedents

Style associates Lanyer's "Passion" with a group of Passion narratives in verse published by Protestant and Catholic male authors in the 1590s and the first decade of the seventeenth century, and she may well have designed her volume to compete with them in the marketplace, as Kimberley Coles has argued.[5] Five such poems dedicated to patrons of high status, like Lanyer's, are especially relevant: Abraham Fraunce,

---

[4] Catherine Keohane, "'That blindest Weakenesse be not over-bold': Aemilia Lanyer's Radical Unfolding of the Passion," *English Literary History* 64.2 (Summer 1997), 359–89, interprets this difference as a "subversive feminist statement," part of Lanyer's "constituting, within the space of the Countess's breast a new church" (361 and 381).

[5] Coles, *Religion, Reform, and Women's Writing*, 149–78. On Robert Southwell's *St. Peter's Complaint* (1595) as the impetus for this style, see Shell, *Catholicism*, 57, 63, and chapter 2.

"The Passion, Buryall, and Resurrection of Christe" in *The Countesse of Pembrokes Emanuel* (1591); Samuel Rowlands, *The Betraying of Christ* (1598); Christopher Lever, *A Crucifixe: or, A Meditation upon Repentance, and, The Holie Passion* (1607); John Davies, *The Holy Roode* (1609); and Giles Fletcher, *Christs Victorie, and Triumph* (1610).[6] Joan Grundy explains that "this type of poem ... tells the story of the Passion ... lyrically and dramatically, and from the point of view of the particular speaker. It employs an excited emotional rhetoric, with stress on such figures as apostrophe, exclamation, rhetorical question, antithesis, paradox, and pun."[7] As does Lanyer in her "Preamble of the Author before the Passion" (gloss at line 265), they modestly speak of their craft and self-consciously defend their use of poetic techniques of high secular literature for their religious subject. They invoke the Muses, allude to classical mythology and learning, include extended speeches by characters, paint atmospheric descriptions of scenic elements such as the light of torches in the night, and invite readers to actively imagine scenes.[8]

Style links Lanyer to this group, but her discourse sets her apart. These authors, despite their radical application of the methods of secular literature to spiritual topics, have the age-old goals of Passion narratives: to praise God through representing the heroic suffering and sacrifice of his Son and to stimulate repentance and spiritual reform through leading readers to feel pity for his pain and recognize themselves in his persecutors. They do not jolt their readers by being inventive in the story they tell. They begin at different points, their emphases differ, and they develop and omit different elements, but they do not add events or characters to the scriptural account of the passion. They use their literary flourishes to intensify their readers' experience of the horror and terror of events.

[6] Nicholas Breton's manuscript *Countess of Penbrooke's Passion* (Sloane MS 1303; printed in 1599 as *The passions of the spirit*) is not a passion narrative, but it includes a brief mental encounter with the Crucifixion that is useful read alongside Lanyer's poem. See Coles, *Religion, Reform, and Women's Writing*, 163–6. Two other poems are more literal narrations of the story and stylistically distinct from Lanyer's: John Weever, *An Agnus Dei* (1603) and Robert Holland, *The Holie Historie of Our Lord and Sauiour* (1594). Lanyer may have known Thomas Lodge's *Prosopopea* (1596), also dedicated to the Countess of Cumberland and to Alice Spencer, Countess of Derby.

[7] Joan Grundy, *The Spenserian Poets: A Study in Elizabethan and Jacobean Poetry* (New York: St. Martin's Press, 1970), 194.

[8] Janel Mueller, "The Feminist Poetics of *Salve Deus Rex Judaeorum*," in Marshall Grossman (ed.), *Aemilia Lanyer: Gender, Genre and the Canon* (Louisville: University Press of Kentucky), 99–127; Kari Boyd McBride, "Gender and Judaism in Meditations on the Passion: Middleton, Southwell, Lanyer, and Fletcher," in Eugene Cunnar and Jeffrey Johnson (eds.), *Discovering and (Re)covering the Seventeenth Century Religious Lyric* (Pittsburgh: Duquesne University Press, 2001), 17–40, discuss Fletcher. Miller, *Engendering the Fall*, 54–5, mentions Holland, Fraunce, and Lever.

These authors include their patrons in their critique of humankind, but do not limit the reading experience to their patrons. Davies, for example, in his dedicatory letter, assumes that his dedicatees (Alice Spencer, Countess of Derby, and her daughters) need to be "clens'd" from "Siren-pleasures, that but Sense allure" and "runne to Helles impure" (sig. A2ʳ). Attending to his poem and being moved "'to minde [Christ's] paine" will cleanse them (A2ʳ). Yet, intimate as this approach is, once he begins his poem, Davies expands his audience to all humankind. He speaks to "Man," stating that "thy sinnes his Crucifiers were" (sig. A4ᵛ) and urges "carelesse Man thou worme, thou insect" (sig. B1ʳ) to read his poem. Like *The Holy Roode*, all these works succeed only if they can cause readers to recognize themselves in and identify with sinners who cause Christ's suffering and regret the role their personal sins have played in necessitating the Crucifixion.

Lanyer's "The Passion" is the only woman-authored text in this group of high-art poems, as the author herself is the first to tell us; other women, she asserts, have been "seldome seene" to write "of divinest things."[9] Given that meditative works on the Passion by Protestants Katherine Parr and Elizabeth Tyrwhit and Catholics Mary Basset and Elizabeth Grymeston had already been published and republished at the time *Salve Deus Rex Judeorum* was issued, Lanyer's claim seems an exaggeration. If considered in terms of style, however, Lanyer's poem is, indeed, a first. Even had she known of these women's works, she probably would not have found them to be engaged in projects similar to her highly literary one.

These other Passion-related texts by women are meditative works, not narratives like Lanyer's. Except for one hymn, they are prose compositions. They do not allude to classical deities, invoke the muse, or appeal for patronage. They are straightforwardly concerned with making their readers recognize the corruption of all humans, their own selves in particular, and the loving mercy of God who is willing to grant them salvation. Most use the first person and cite their authors' own sins as examples in order to prompt their readers to self-examination. Parr's Passion meditations do not constitute a unified formal unit in *The Lamentacion of a Synner*; rather, the topic of the usefulness of meditation on the Passion is woven in and out of a discussion of how justification by faith has operated in her life.[10] Tyrwhit's two Passion texts appear in the

---

[9] Lanyer, "To the Queenes," line 4.
[10] Katherine Parr, *The Lamentacion of a Synner* (London: Edward Whitechurche, 1547). Reprinted in Bentley, *Monument of Matrons*.

evening section of her *Morning and Evening Prayers* (1574; republished in Bentley's *Monument of Matrons*). Her brief prose "A Contemplation of Christes passion" is followed by the "The Hymne of the passion of Christ," a verse translation from the Divine Office of *The Hours of the Cross* with an added refrain in praise of the Trinity.[11] The former, a meditation prompted by Christ's suffering and death, examines the author's conscience and does not narrate events. The hymn is a thirty-line, barebones narrative from Judas's betrayal through the rising of the dead after the Crucifixion. Basset's "An exposicion of a parte of the passion," a close translation of the concluding sections of Thomas More's unfinished *Expositio Passionis Domini*, was published in More's English works. The text consists of an account of the events that occurred in the Garden of Gethsemane, followed by commentary that encourages introspection.[12] Grymeston's extended, formal prose meditation "A Good Fridayes Exercise, or a Meditation of the Crosse" in *Miscelanea, Meditations, Memoratives* does not recount events in chronological order but presents Christ's experiences on the day of the Crucifixion as discrete topics for meditation.

In the early days of research on writing by women, it was commonly assumed that texts by women such as these were permissible in their culture because their purposes and uses were private. But, despite their urgent personal tone, these works were not merely intended for private purposes. They are very sectarian in approach and probably were written to promote the interests of their parties. Their engagement with theological issues can be seen in their incorporation of words, sentences, ideas, and images from non-scriptural texts, usually without attribution, often in order to refute or modify them.[13] Parr borrows one of her key concepts, the crucifix as a "book," from the Catholic bishop John Fisher without crediting him and then uses his image to refute Catholic theology and practices. She looks into the "book," reads her own sinful soul, and denies the efficacy of "such riffraff as the Bishop of Rome." "I never knew my own wickedness," she writes, "neither lamented for my sins truly, until ... I looked in this book. Then I began to see perfectly,

---

[11] See Micheline White on Tyrwhit (Chapter 9) in this volume.

[12] Thomas More, "An exposicion of a parte of the passion," trans. Mary Basset, in *The workes of Sir Thomas More Knyght ... in the Englysh tonge* (London: John Cawod, John Waly, and Richarde Tottell, 1557), 1350–1404.

[13] At least one male author also used this technique. Thomas George labelled his intertextuality "plagiarism" in "Samuel Rowlands's *The Be-traying of Christ* and Guevara's *The Mount of Calvarie*, An Example of Elizabethan Plagiarism," *Notes and Queries* 14 (1967), 467–74.

that mine own power and strength could not help me, and that I was in the Lord's hand."[14] Protestant Tyrwhit "makes revisions that emphasize Reformation doctrines" in her translation from the "Hours of the Cross"; Catholic Grymeston borrows her vivid description of the crucified Christ word for word from martyred priest Robert Southwell's *An Epistle of Comfort* (1587) and, while keeping to Catholic theology, transforms his dark conclusion to hope.[15] He reminds his readers that they cause Christ's pain; she reminds hers that Christ's wounds bring mercy to sinners.

Like the male-authored narratives, all of these woman-authored texts address a mixed-sex audience, and in none of them does the author claim exceptional status as a female writer. Although the men, who in some cases write prefatory material, tend to call attention to their author's sex, they do not defend the women's right to write nor do they suggest that women have special insight on the topic by virtue of their sex. Instead of linking author and audience members with each other by interests they have in common as women, the male presenters and the female authors of these meditative works join authors and readers of both sexes as humans in a community of sin. They stimulate longing for grace and salvation by prompting readers to recall their sins and cultivate awareness of the possibility of damnation. Finally, every one of them is an intensely introspective spiritual work of universal appeal.

Lanyer's Difference: Exculpating Women

Unlike these works, Lanyer's "Passion" is neither universal in its appeal nor intensely introspective in nature. It is directed to women readers and prompts them to feel secure in their positive relationship with Christ. The dedicatory epistles gather an exclusively female community of readers for the volume in which "The Passion" appears, as many have noted, and Lanyer narrows the focus even further in *Salve Deus Rex Judaeorum*, the long poem in which "The Passion" is embedded. She addresses the first 328 lines preceding "The Passion" directly and solely to Margaret Russell, Dowager Countess of Cumberland, and at the narrative's conclusion, she invites her to meditate on the body of the crucified Christ.

---

[14] Parr, *The Lamentacion*, sig. A4ᵛ, 450, sig. D3ʳ; 466. Parr, *Complete Works*, Mueller (ed.), 430–9, identifies Fisher as the source of Parr's image.

[15] Tyrwhit, *Elizabeth Tyrwhit*, 37. Ruth Hughey and Philip Hereford, "Elizabeth Grymeston and her *Miscellanea*," *The Library*, 4th Ser., 15 (1934), 61–91 at 84, recognize that Grymeston "paraphrases to suit her own needs," but they do not identify Southwell as Grymeston's source.

Finally, in the last 503 lines, she describes Cumberland's charitable actions and praises her more generally. Throughout, Lanyer speaks of her as one of the elect. By doing so, she alleviates the need to urge her to introspective discovery of sin; as always already one of the elect, Cumberland has no need to be stirred to remorse.[16]

Having restricted her readership to a single elect woman and the community of women constructed in the dedicatory epistles, Lanyer tailored the narrative to make these readers feel secure in their sex's relationship with Christ and, therefore, feel no need for introspective meditation on sin. In selecting episodes to include, she took advantage of opportunities the Gospels offered to make women look good and men look bad, and she omitted almost all that make men look good and women bad. For example, she heightened Peter's aura of guilt by including Christ's prediction that the disciple will betray him and leaving out the scene of his denial in response to a servant girl's question. This has two effects: Lanyer's reader is not reminded of the negative role a woman played in the fall of a good man, and she does not hear Peter express his profound self-disgust and his recognition of his need for mercy, a high point of Fletcher's, Davies's, Rowlands's, and Fraunce's narratives. In Lanyer's narrative, Peter remains an unrepentant sinner. By contrast, Lanyer essentially omits Mary Magdalene, a traditional example of female sin; she mentions her only as one of the "Maries" who bring balms to the tomb, and we hear nothing of her repentant tears, much celebrated in other contemporary texts. By not including Mary Magdalene, Lanyer again avoids bringing up the topic of women's sin.

Lanyer's most substantial development of the positive virtues of women and their corollary, the vices of men, occurs in the three passages listed on the title page as items 2, 3, and 4 after "The Passion of Christ": "Eves Apologie in defence of Women" (lines 761–832, approximately), "The Teares of the Daughters of Jerusalem" (lines 969–1008), and "The Salutation and Sorrow of the Virgine Marie" (lines 1109–36). The equal billing of these sub-sections with the Passion on the title page indicates their importance to Lanyer's project and suggests that they form a group and should be considered together. All three are developed beyond their slim Gospel precedents or are entirely extra-Biblical. By means of them,

---

[16] Keohane, "'That blindest,'" 377, discusses the potential patronage problem this narrowing of address to a single patron might have posed. Longfellow, *Women and Religious Writing*, 71–5, discusses guilt in Passion exegesis, sermons, etc. and links Lanyer's omission of it with pleasing patrons.

Lanyer introduces female heroism into a narrative that had never before included it and identifies core reformed Protestant virtues with women and only women. Women have a positive relationship with God; their hearts are open to him and they follow them. Men have a flawed one; although their own hearts and their loving women direct them toward God and goodness, they seek their own "ease" by following the direction of their ever more corrupted reason and laws, which lead them first to eat the apple, then, to torture and execute Christ, and, then, to rule tyrannically over good, charitable, heart-driven, women.

"Eve's Apologie" and Christian Liberty

"Eve's Apologie" is a strikingly innovative addition to the Passion genre. Normally, in Passions the respective guilt of the two parties in the Fall is not discussed at any length, if at all, because the genre's goal is to inspire introspection in all readers, regardless of sex; all are guilty. In Lanyer's "The Passion," however, the greater guilt of Adam is an essential foundation for the specifically spiritual benefit that the Crucifixion offers to women. As Lanyer explains at the end of the "Apologie," this is the liberty to know God directly and follow their consciences.

Lanyer takes advantage of the traditional analogy of the Fall and the Crucifixion to introduce the origin story into her narrative. The narrator or Pilate's wife (critics do not agree about who is speaking) succinctly provides the link between the two events and suggests the core issue treated in "Eve's Apologie," the change in the power relationship between the sexes effected by the Crucifixion. The speaker draws a parallel between Pilate and Adam by referring to Pilate's impending decision to hand Jesus over to be crucified as "Mens fall" (line 759); and, to persuade him to desist, she appeals not to spiritual values – he has none – but to his pride and anxiety about dominance, warning him that his masculine "fall" will please women. "Let not us Women glory in Mens fall,/ Who had power given to over-rule us all" (lines 759–60). The rest of the "Apologie" unpacks the spiritual significance of this concise statement; it identifies men's power as the cause of the Fall and, then, in the now famous "let us have our Libertie againe" passage (line 825), explains what the second fall ought to have meant for women.[17]

---

[17] Critical commentary on "Eve's Apologie" along with the dedicatory "To the virtuous reader" in the context of the *querelle des femmes* is too extensive to cite here. My topic is limited to a neglected topic, the passage's function in the argument and structure of "Passion."

Lanyer's story of the Fall is based on the description of the creation in Genesis 2. In this version, the social and political hierarchical superiority of man is part of the fixed structure of creation. Eve was created after Adam, and God did not speak directly to her; her relationship with God was mediated by Adam. In Lanyer's narrative, everything follows from Eve's lack of intimate, direct contact with God; Adam is her source of information, and Adam, not the unknown God, is the object of her love. He proves an inadequate source and an unworthy object. The poet repeatedly emphasizes Eve's innocence of mind and loving heart. Contrary to centuries of popular misogyny that attributes her eating of the fruit and giving it to Adam to lasciviousness, Lanyer attributes her eating to a lack of knowledge and her giving to an abundance of love. Eve was "undiscerning" when she met the Serpent; "had she knowne," she would not have eaten; her heart was "harmelesse"; she gave "to Adam what shee held most deare"; her "fault was onely too much love" (lines 764–74 passim; 801). Clearly, Adam did not adequately inform her of God's prohibition; he had power and abused it by neglecting to use it for the good. Lanyer makes his unworthiness of Eve's love clear in his response to her gift; she points out that as her superior and guardian, he should have "reprove[d]" her "with those sharpe words, which he of God did heare" (lines 805–6), but he did not. Lanyer's Adam betrays God twice over – in eating the fruit and in not caring for the woman put in his trust – and he betrays Eve's love by not crediting her with having given him knowledge once he has gained it, the first of many men to fail to give women credit, the poet says.

Pilate is the second man in the poem to fail a woman who gives him knowledge. His wife "beg[s] her Saviours life" (line 752). and his failure to listen to her leads directly to his "fall," Christ's death, and the solution to women's problem. As a result of Christ's loving sacrifice, they have a worthy object for their love, Christ, and they have direct access to the three persons of God; the old hierarchy that required them to address God through their husbands has been abrogated. This idea is not original to Lanyer, of course; Calvin, among others, held this position.[18] But the emphasis on its benefits to women is hers.

---

[18] Calvin, *Harmonie*, 736. See also Abraham Fraunce, *Countess of Pembrooke's Emanuel* (London: (Thomas Orwyn) for William Ponsonby, 1591), sig. C4ᵛ: "Pilates wife in a dreame with Christ then greatly molested,/Perswades her good man for feare, that he might be released." As with the Genesis story, Lanyer had more than one version of Pilate's wife to choose from. Traditionally, her dream was sent by the devil and she warned her husband out of fear, but Calvin and others suggest that God sent the dream.

When she concludes her Apology and returns to the dramatic situation of Pilate about to judge Jesus, the poet writes stirring lines that have been taken as a radical demand for absolute equality of the sexes in the social and political realm. "If unjustly you condemne to die," she warns, you will be far more sinful than women are and will as a consequence have to "let us [women] have our Libertie again,/And challendge to yourselves no Sov'raigntie." She asks, "Your fault beeing greater, why should you disdaine/ Our beeing your equals, free from tyranny?" (lines 817–32 passim).

Lanyer does not follow these demands with an explanation of the nature of this "Libertie." I suggest that, as the text in which this appeal appears is a Passion narrative and it states that women's liberty ought to be restored as a result of their loving objection to and non-participation in the Crucifixion, it makes sense to look for the meaning of "liberty" in the Passion rather than in the secular realm. It is Christian Liberty. The concept derives from Galatians, where Paul says, "brethren, ye haue bene called vnto libertie: onely vse not your libertie as an occasion vnto the flesh, but by loue serue one another. For all the Lawe is fulfilled in one worde, which is this, Thou shalt loue thy neighbour as thy selfe" (Galatians 5:13–14, *GB*). Christian Liberty was of particular importance to reformed Protestants because it emphasized the individual Christian's direct contact with God through faith and grace, a tenet that lies at the heart of Lanyer's case for women throughout the "Passion." As George Downame, Calvinist and future chaplin of James 1, explained in a sermon preached at Paul's Cross in 1608, "Christian liberty is a spirituall liberty, freeing the true Christian from the servitude of sinne, and from all other yokes of spirituall bondage, wherewith sinne had intangled us … it is also positive, as being a liberty, power, right, and interest to the privileges of Gods children, who are also heires of God, and coheires with Christ."[19]

Lanyer's use of the word "again" in company with liberty suggests that this speech applies particularly to women of her own day. Women before Christ's death did not have this liberty and even Pilate's wife did not have it, as Christian Liberty only came into existence with his Crucifixion and women received it immediately upon his death. Yet, women no longer have this liberty. Men, deprived of legitimate power to govern women's spirituality, have tyrannically assumed that right. Women's liberty needs to be restored; thus, the implications of Lanyer's endorsement of Christian Liberty for her female readers are clear. They are free to act according to love. Loving

[19] George Downame, *A Treatise upon Iohn 8.36. Concerning Christian Libertie* (London: Felix Kyngston for Matthew Lownes, and William Welby, 1609), 8.

service of another is the highest virtue, and immediate contact with God without the mediation of husband or priest frees the faithful women in the narrative to this service. Pilate's wife has a dream and intervenes on Christ's behalf, the Daughters of Jerusalem know Christ himself and attempt to stop his execution, but the poem's supreme example of this liberty is Mary, the greatest biblical exemplar in the poem of women's capacity for virtue.

Lanyer's Protestant Intertextuality: Guevara's *Mount of Calvary* and Mary

Mary's very presence in Lanyer's Passion narrative is evidence of her radical rethinking of the genre. Protestant Passions very rarely included her, so merely including her is notable. Those that did include her place her at biblically sanctioned places, the foot of the cross or the tomb, but Lanyer daringly locates the meeting of mother and son on the Way of the Cross, distinctly Roman Catholic territory, and transforms Mary from the passive compassionate mother of the Gospel to an active proto-Protestant hero. This meeting is one of the mysteries of the Rosary and is read by Catholics as a sign of Mary's co-suffering with Christ and her future role as intercessor, and, quite remarkably, Lanyer's source for specific details of the encounter is a translation of a Spanish Roman Catholic prose account of the Passion, *The Mount of Caluarie, Compyled by the Reuerend Father in God, Lord Anthonie de Gueuara, Bishop of Mondonnedo, Preacher, Chronicler, and Councellor, unto Charles the Fift, Emperour.*[20] It might seem that Lanyer's use of Roman Catholic materials reveals Catholic sympathies, but it does the contrary. Lanyer cites Guevara's text to refute the most essential Roman Catholic beliefs about Mary and about the saving grace of Christ's blood.[21] Her Mary is an admirable, heroic "Servant, Mother, Wife and Nurse" whose actions are completely of this world.

---

[20] Antonio de Guevara, *The Mount of Caluarie* (London: A Islip for Edward White, 1595). Even before reaching the scene under discussion, Lanyer worked closely with Guevara's text. Her first use of it is at the moment when "Three feares at once possessed *Pilates* heart" and he chose to be cowed by the people's threatening (lines 913–20). Guevara also speaks of three fears and they are the same fears Lanyer cites (6–7). Then, her lovely description of the procession to Calvary (lines 961–8) is clearly indebted to Guevara's. He writes: "O who could have seen that procession from Hierusalem to Calvarie, should have seen goe before all the rest, the crier, crying and publishing the judgement, then the hangman with the nailes, then Christ with his crosse, then the theeves with their garments, then the sergeants which watched them, then the women which cried" (126).

[21] For a very different reading of this passage without the Guevara source text, see Theresa M. Di Pasquale, *Refiguring the Sacred Feminine: The Poems of John Donne, Aemilia Lanyer and John Milton* (Pittsburgh: Dusquene University Press, 2008), 136–7.

Lanyer closely paraphrases *Mount* to create a moving scene in which the grieving mother kneels in the street but she subtly adjusts Mary's actions to align them with Protestant beliefs. Guevara's Mary, "comfortlesse … everie where, where she found the tracke of his bloud shed … did also worship it upon her knees, and make it cleane with her teares … [Christ] lay [the dust] with the bloud which he shed … and the mother with the teares which she did weepe" (126–7). Lanyer's Mary neither worships nor clenses the blood. Her Mary "comfortlesse," kneels in the street and puts her tears to use to remove the blood entirely: "Her teares did wash away his pretious blood,/That sinners might not tread it under feet/To worship him"; she does this because she recognizes that Christ is "the Jesse floure and bud,/That must be gath'red when it smell'd most sweet" (lines 1010, 1017–19, 1021–2). The small differences between these two scenes are deeply significant. Guevara connects the historic events with future Catholic practices and beliefs. His reverent attitude toward the blood anticipates the attitude of Catholics who believe in transubstantiation, the notion that wine becomes Christ's blood every time the mass is celebrated, and who "worship" the blood in the form of relics, drops of Christ's blood that have been preserved across the ages. His analogy between the effect that Mary's tears had on dust and the effect of Christ's blood on it suggests that she can save souls by interceding with him on behalf of mortal dust. Lanyer undid these Catholic meanings and invokes the reformed Protestant understanding of the sacrifice of the Crucifixion as a historic and unrepeatable event by changing Mary's actions and omitting the effect of her tears on the dust. Her proto-Protestant Mary intervenes to prevent worship of the blood before it starts. She washes it away with her tears so that no one will be able to worship it in any form, thus preventing the desecration of the blood by sinners, that is, future Catholics. Lanyer makes this preemptive anti-Catholic motive clear when she attributes Mary's action to her recognition that Christ was to be sacrificed only once; this Jesse flower will not bloom again and again in the celebration of the mass. By intervening in this way, Lanyer's Mary preserves her sorrow, her son's loss of blood, and his death as one-time historic events, in keeping with reformed Protestant doctrine.

The witty intertextuality of this passage goes beyond the interaction with Guevara. In her key phrase, "That sinners might not tread it under feet," Lanyer realized the literal potential of an idiom the Geneva and other bibles used in translating Hebrews, "Of howe muche sorer punishment suppose ye shal hee be worthy, which treadeth vnder foote the Sonne of God, and counteth the blood of the Testament as an vnholie thing, wherewith he was sanctified, and doeth despite the Spirit of grace?" (*GB*, Hebrews 10:29). This passage was popular amongst reformers as a way of criticizing the Catholic belief in transubstantiation. For example, Anthony Anderson in his *The shield of our safetie*, after quoting the verse, identifies those who "treadeth under foote" as "the Papistes, for where God hath exalted him on high, no more subiect to death, they kill him every day at their Masse, and eate him (they say) in that cake."[22] Lanyer's Virgin, more Martha than Mary, actively intervenes to prevent this future cruelty to her son as Pilate's wife and the daughters intervened to attempt to prevent the Crucifixion.

Lanyer's representations of Mary's ingenious, active use of her tears to do pro-Protestant work stands in contrast to contemporary Passion-narrative writers' representation of her. Protestant Fletcher, for example, portrayed her helpless misery in a disturbing, Ovidian comparison of her to Philomela and Procne; weeping at the tomb, she is like a mother lark who "pittifully sings" her woe at the death of her "yet unfeather'd children," who died when a reaper mowed over her "warme nest."[23] In contrast to Fletcher's pathetic mother, Lanyer's is self-reliant and heroic; she takes risky, active action "Upon her knees, although in open street" (line 1020).

Mary and Eve: The Salutation

As was the scene of Mary's meeting with her son, "The Salutation," which represents the Annunciation, is a tissue of quotations, this time from the Gospels. The familiar language makes it seem that the passage is a close paraphrase of the biblical scene. Perhaps this is the reason it has gone almost unnoticed by critics, but this neglect is unwarranted. This scene, like the previous one, reinterprets Mary's role in a crucial event. Lanyer adds her "lowly mind" to the traditional definition of her character and stresses that it works in harmony with her loving heart. When the annunciate angel visits her, her simple Gospel question, "How shal this be, seeing I knowe not man?" (*GB*, Luke 1:34), becomes the substance of the scene. We follow the workings of her humble mind as, "on the knees of [her] submissive heart," she asks the questions that lead to her

---

[22] Anthony Anderson, *The Shielde of our Safetie* (London: H. Jackson, 1581), fol. N.i[r]. See also John Foxe, *Acts and Monuments*, 2 vols. (London: John Day, 1583), vol. II, 1445, quoting Ridley: "The Apostle playnely denieth any other sacrifice to remaine for him that treadeth under his feete the bloud of the testament by the which he was made holy. Christ will not be crucified againe, he will not his death to be had in dirision."

[23] Giles Fletcher, *Christs Victorie and Triumph* (Cambridge: C. Legge, 1610), 66.

all-important "humble answer which doth approove [her] Love [which means that] All these sayings in [her] heart doe rest" (lines 1091–2).

It was traditional to contrast Mary with Eve, and Lanyer followed suit. "The Salutation" forms a pair with "Eve's Apologie." But rather than contrast the two women on the basis of chastity and its lack, as was traditional, she compares their characters and she attributes the different effects of their actions to their relationship with men. Eve shares with Mary a desire to use her mind – that is why she eats the fruit – but, dependent on her husband for knowledge of God's wishes, she errs; whereas, extraordinary Mary, a virgin, "from all men free," attracts God to herself by the beauty of her mind and, through her openness of heart, is granted a direct, unmediated relationship with him; "the holy ghost .. come[s] on her" (lines 1078 and 1082). The first person in history to exercise Christian Liberty, a concept introduced into the poem by means of Eve, Mary models in an ideal form what women with liberty – free access to Holy Spirit – can do.[24]

Having located Mary on the Way of the Cross and dilated on the beauty of her acceptance of the Christ child, Lanyer does not place her at the foot of the cross. She empties that space of all biblical actors; the Virgin, Mary Magdalene, St John, Longinus, all are absent. Lanyer focuses our attention on Christ's crucified body, but with a difference. A reader of Parr, Davies, and the others would hear the author's self-excoriation for having caused Christ's suffering; however, in keeping with her omission of the topic of remorse and self-castigation throughout the poem, Lanyer shows Christ's pain without herself abjectly recollecting her sins or inviting her readers to do so.

That this radical omission is deliberate can be seen clearly because the essentials of the portrait are not original. Its model is *S. Augustines Praiers*, like Guevara's *Mount of Calvarie*, an English translation of a Roman Catholic source, this time Italian rather than Spanish.[25] As with *Mount*, Lanyer invokes the Catholic text in order to refute its central doctrines – in this case, the notion that God can be persuaded to change his mind about the eternal destiny of individuals. In lines 1153–76, Lanyer works closely with this text. She incorporates *verbatim* many words and phrases from it, such as "harlelesse hands," "his bowells drie," "members torne,"

---

[24] According to Calvin, the angel's words, "Haile Mary full of grace," are correctly employed as a salutation not as a prayer for intercession: see Calvin, *Harmonie*, 22.

[25] St Augustine of Hippo, *A right Christian treatise, entituled S. Augustines praiers*, trans. Thomas Rogers (London: Henry Denham, 1581), 24–6, passim.

and "his legges hang," but her poetic skill is most evident when she paraphrases and turns the prose into lyrical description. Concision is key. Where *St. Augustines Praiers* speaks of "undefiled feete, that have never stood in the way of sinners" (page 26), Lanyer creates a sense of real, heavy feet walking on the well-worn path created by others by speaking of "feet that never trode in sinners trace" (line 1154). In "His blessed blood watring his pierced feet" (line 1176), she reduces Augustine's "the streame of blessed blood watered his pierced feete" (page 27) to its essential elements, blessed blood and pierced feet. Her use of the participle, "watring," instead of the past tense, calls attention to the active life-giving nature of that blood by making it flow right now, before our eyes.

Lanyer very deliberately shifts the focus away from guilt and its corollary, the need for mercy. Nearly every line of *St. Augustines Praiers* links phrases describing Christ's pain to the human sin that caused it, and the speaker asks God, to whom the prayer is addressed, "for mercie, in respect of the bitter paines of his deere Sonne" (page 24). For example, he begs, "Behold his harmeles hands distilling foorth godlie blood; & being pacified, forgive the sins which mine hands have committed" (page 26). With strategic rewriting, Lanyer refutes this Catholic view of the relationship between sinful humans and God. She invites her reader to "behold" those same "harmeles hands" but does not link them with sins that her reader's hands have committed and, thus, obviates the need to move her to feel her need for mercy (lines 1169 and 1153).

As I said, Lanyer does not include biblical witnesses to the Crucifixion; she does, however, include a seventeenth-century one, the Dowager Countess of Cumberland. The description of Christ's body is three stanzas long and, in the midst of the third stanza, the poet interrupts her description, turns directly to Cumberland, and says, "This with the eie of Faith thou maiest behold/Deere Spouse of Christ (lines 1169–70). Then, in the following stanza, she expounds the personal meaning of the Crucifixion for Cumberland. Like Mary earlier, the Countess is isolated in an intense personal relationship with her "Love." We are told that in considering the image, she may understand the paradox Christ's death poses, "both Griefe and Joy thou maist unfold,/To view thy Love in this most heavy plight" (lines 1171–2), but we get no details of her emotional response. At this traditionally self-castigating, tearful moment, she is not prompted to weep and we are not told of her tears. The reason for this is revealed in the following stanza. Christ's death happened in the past (as Lanyer's Mary recognized); the "last" miracle, it "unit[ed] death, life, misery, joy, and care" once and for all (lines 1178–9). Joy lies ahead for "his deere elected" (line 1180), of whom, we have been often told, Cumberland is one. They "Shall find how deere they are of him respected ... Whose infinite dolours wrought eternall blisse" (lines 1182 and 1184). She looks upward, not inward. Tears of remorse have no practical purpose. The goals of the "Praier" have truly been reversed.

This appeal to Cumberland ends "The Passion," but one more related scene, representing the meditative interaction of the Countess with Christ, remains. After describing Christ's resurrected body in terms borrowed from the Song of Songs, Lanyer says, "in your heart I leave/His perfect picture, where it still shall stand ... environed with Love and Thoughts divine" (1325–8, passim). She suggests that Cumberland may embrace "his bleeding body" and "kisse his dying cheekes with teares of sorrow" (lines 1332–3) whenever she wishes in a sort of perpetual pietà. In this way, the Countess is able to complete the labor of mothering Christ begun by Mary, and she can do so because she, like Mary, is entirely open to the Holy Spirit. As Lanyer says in lines that might be about Mary in the "Salutation":

> These works of mercy are so sweete, so deare
> To him that is the Lord of Life and Love,
> That all thy prayers he vouchsafes to heare,
> And sends his holy Spirit from above;
> Thy eyes are op'ned, and thou seest so cleare,
> No worldly thing can thy faire mind remove;
> Thy faith, thy prayers, and his speciall grace,
> Doth open Heav'n, where thou beholdst his face. (Lines 1361–8)

The rest of the poem has nothing more to say about Christ and his Passion. It is devoted to demonstrating Christian Liberty in action. It recounts the Countess's "almes-deeds" (1335), the result of her election, it praises her superiority to famous biblical and secular women, and it suggests her similarity to the early martyrs of the Church. By "deliver[ing] the inestimable treasure of elected soules" (the crucified Christ) without attempting to stimulate remorseful self-reflection, Lanyer was able to achieve the goal she announced in her dedicatory epistle "To the Ladie Margaret"; she presented the Countess with "a mirrour of [her] most worthy minde" at work doing good in this world (page 35, lines 29–30). Lanyer's "The Passion of Christ" is not merely something "seldome seene" to be written by a woman. It is a remarkable achievement, an innovative, daring, and skilfull example of its genre.

Memory, Materiality and Maternity in the Tanfield/Cary Archive

Ramona Wray

Spanning the Stuart period, this chapter juxtaposes three generations of Tanfield/Cary women and three different forms of material and textual production. Central are the writings of Elizabeth Cary, Lady Falkland, in her time a well-known historian, translator, poet and dramatist, whose extant materials include a history of *Edward II*, translations from Jacques du Perron and Abraham Ortelius, and a rich store of letters and petitions.[1] Today, of course, Cary is best known as the author of the first original drama by a woman, *The Tragedy of Mariam*, a play that has attracted a substantial body of critical work and generated a new appreciation of the Cary *oeuvre*.[2] But still to be fully established is the extent to which Cary's textual legacy is imbricated with the memorializing endeavours of her close female relatives – her mother, Elizabeth (Symondes) Tanfield, and her daughter, Lucy Cary.

The later of these memorializing endeavours is well known and well used. Written in 1645 and completed in 1649, the *Life* – and its selective (and posthumous) recollection of the roles Cary played as mother and Catholic convert – is widely enlisted as the main source of information on Cary's life. A collaborative work involving several members of the family, the *Life* was written by Lucy (Cary's daughter) in the convent in Cambrai after she had taken orders; it was edited by three of Cary's other daughters, also at the convent, and by her son.[3] Despite a now widespread acknowledgement that the *Life* is a highly crafted and self-justifying production which needs to be assessed guardedly, it is difficult to overestimate its influence inside Cary studies. Following the editorial

---

[1] See Cary, *Tragedy*, Wray (ed.), 5–6.
[2] For summaries of critical tendencies in scholarship on the play, see Cary, *Tragedy*, Wray (ed.), 3–8, 32–4 and 45.
[3] These were, respectively, Elizabeth, Anne, Mary and Patrick. See Cary, *Elizabeth Cary/Lady Falkland*, Wolfe (ed.), 87–9.

example of Barry Weller and Margaret W. Ferguson, who combine an edition of the *Life* and *The Tragedy of Mariam* inside a single volume, scholarship over the past two decades has consistently probed the play, and to a lesser extent, the rest of Cary's extant works, in terms of a biographical approach, seeing as indissolubly linked this account of Cary's personal experience and her textual productivity.[4]

But there is a further text – another seventeenth-century biographical object and 'source', one which barely receives mention in the critical record. Conceived and commissioned by Cary's widowed mother, Elizabeth Tanfield, the Tanfield monument in Burford Church (St John the Baptist), Oxfordshire, has an interpretative potential equal to that of the *Life* (see Figure 12.1).[5] Begun in 1625, approximately twenty years before the writing of the *Life*, and completed in 1628, this Italianate monument marks the burial place of Cary's father, Sir Lawrence Tanfield, judge and Chief Baron of the Exchequer.[6] The monument is, as one historian of antiquities observes, 'remarkable for its size and elaboration' (a less kindly descriptor enlisted in guides to English heritage is 'ostentatious').[7] Constructed from Derbyshire alabaster, it boasts columns of black Italian marble and plinths of Purbeck marble.[8] Above the columns are figures of the classical 'virtues'; two heraldic emblems of the family adorn the upper canopy; and obelisks at the sides complement the whole. Recumbent painted figures of Elizabeth Tanfield and Lawrence Tanfield lie in postures of devotion on an enormous black marble tomb-chest, while at the Tanfields' feet is their kneeling grandson, Lucius Cary (born to Elizabeth Cary in 1610). At their head an effigy of Elizabeth Cary kneels in prayer, one of only two extant artistic representations of the writer. Underneath the family grouping – and in stark contrast to the colour and vivacity of the effigies above – lies a skeleton. Conventionally enough, as Jean Wilson notes, 'the monument celebrates Tanfield's achievements ... shows his posterity ... and yet reminds the viewer that for all the grandeur of

[4] Cary, *Elizabeth Cary, Lady Falkland*, Weller and Ferguson (eds.). See also note 2, above.
[5] The monument at Burford is not considered by Wolfe in her wonderfully full and scholarly edition, *Elizabeth Cary/Lady Falkland*. The only critical discussions are brief: see Raber, 'Introduction', in *Ashgate Critical Essays*, xiii, and Wynne-Davies, *Women Writers and Familial Discourse*, 112.
[6] See *ODNB* for Sir Lawrence Tanfield.
[7] Jean Wilson, 'Ethics Girls', 93–4. For the 'ostentatious' accusation, see, for example, Louise Simmons, 'The Hidden Churches of Oxfordshire', www.time-travel-britain.com (accessed 18 August 2016).
[8] Julian P. Guffogg, 'The Tanfield Tomb, Burford Church', www.geograph.org.uk (accessed 18 August 2016); and Jennifer Sherwood and Nikolaus Pevsner, *The Buildings of England: Oxfordshire* (Harmondsworth: Penguin, 1974), 506–7.

Figure 12.1   Tanfield Monument. St John the Baptist, Burford, after 1625
Editor's photograph.

the tomb, it is based on mortality'.[9] Less conventionally, it is possible to suggest that Elizabeth Tanfield, as well as assuming responsibility for the monument's design and construction, supplied inscriptions, epithets and verses. In fact, my argument goes further still, demonstrating how the content of the writings on the monument affirms its patroness's authorial credentials. The Tanfield monument, then, functions in a dual capacity as an artefact through which female composition is celebrated and as a secondary text that illuminates Elizabeth's Cary's life and work.

[9] Wilson, 'Ethics Girls', 94.

In this essay, I argue that the monument and the *Life* can be under-stood as interwoven texts that, representing competing attempts at memorialization, attest to the fraught processes of writing women's liter-ary history in the seventeenth century. Although each (the *Life* and the monument) privileges a sense of Cary as mother, each produces a very different – contradictory and competing – legacy. Intriguingly, neither the *Life* nor the monument references *The Tragedy of Mariam*, the play for which Cary has been celebrated in the modern era, although they implicitly – and perhaps explicitly – compete with letters authored by Cary which fashion a further (third) set of alternative forms of self-hood. Between her father's death in 1625, and the completion of the monument in 1628, Cary not only writes two histories of Edward II and begins her translation of Jacques du Perron's *Reply* but also crafts a series of letters relating to her separation from the family and penurious circumstances.[10] These variously protest, plead and cajole, agitating for a royal audience, for support, for access to her children and for redress of injustices; although critically under appreciated, they form a crucial part of any effort to contextualize Cary's achievement. Restoring occluded networks and praxes, this chapter investigates the significance of the intersections running between the Tanfield monument, the *Life* of Cary and Cary's extant *oeuvre*. It sees as fundamentally informing these three instances of textual production the shaping roles of, and relationships between, three generations of women. Teasing out the connections link-ing disparate materializations, the chapter illuminates the different and competing ways in which early modern women sculpted their own lives and their families' reputations.

Mortality, Misogyny, Money

Arguably the most striking feature of the Tanfield monument is the con-troversy surrounding its coming into being. Peter Sherlock notes that early modern women 'could and did design and commission [monu-ments] independently from men', yet few did so in such an antithetical environment as Elizabeth Tanfield.[11] Disallowed from erecting the monu-ment in Westminster Abbey, Elizabeth Tanfield sought support to place

---

[10] Jacques Davy du Perron, *The Reply of the Most Illustrious Cardinall of Perron* (Douai: Bogart, 1630; STC 1630).

[11] Sherlock, *Monuments and Memory*, 12. See Sherlock (Chapter 16) in this volume, for a discussion of women's commissions of funeral monuments.

and build it in the local Burford church. Thwarted here too, she forged ahead without permission, burying Sir Lawrence Tanfield at midnight and having the monument constructed around the corpse over the following three years.[12] Contemporary accounts suggest that Elizabeth Tanfield was refused permission because of Lawrence Tanfield's general unpopularity. Chief Baron of the Exchequer to James I, he was, according to an Oxfordshire guide, 'reviled locally for his ... interference in local affairs, and had a reputation for greed and corrupt practices in office'.[13]

One of the verses on the Tanfield monument alludes to the lack of co-operation from church authorities:

> Not this smalle heape of stones & Straightened Roome
> The Bench, the Court, Tribunall, are his tombe ...
> Pitty his memory ingaged should stand
> Vnto a privat Church, Not to the Land.

In view of the size of the monument (which dwarfs the chapel in which it is located), the first lines are richly ironic, and they work to prepare us for the final complaint that the tomb must reside in a local church rather than in a national landmark.[14] Taking much of their energy from barbed contrasts between public and private and between the city and the country, the doggerel rhymes reveal the resistance of their author to the monument's accommodation and present the background to its construction as a source of regret and injustice.

Locally accented popular accounts, taking their cue from the seventeenth-century objections, also associate the monument with its fraught conditions of origin and its female creator. Invariably the language of

---

[12] In an unreferenced transcription of the 1628 churchwardens' accounts, Raymond and Joan Moody note the contemporary complaint about the monument erected ... without consent (*A Thousand Years of Burford* [Oxford: Alden Press, 2006], 21). I am grateful to Alan Simpson, of the Oxfordshire Family History Society, who checked the 1625 Burford burial register for me; it specifies the precise time of interment.

[13] Slow Europe Travel, 'English Churches Oxfordshire: Church of St John the Baptist, Burford', http://wasleys.org.uk/eleanor/churches/england/cotswolds/oxfordshire/burford/index.html (accessed 2 September 2016). The murky details are that Lawrence Tanfield illegally obtained (through the court of the exchequer) the 'rights and privileges' belonging the town of Burford and imposed authority as lord of the manor (he had acquired Burford Priory in c. 1583) by buying up estates, increasing his demand for rents and extending his own leases: it is a classic tale of a conflict between a 'corporation' representing the interests of local traders and townspeople and a city-based aspirant bent on shoring up influence and capital. See: R. H. Gretton, *The Burford Records: A Study in Minor Town Government* (Oxford: Clarendon, 1920), 272–3; William J. Monk, *The Official Guide to Burford* (Cheltenham and London: Ed. J. Burrow, 1940), 16.

[14] Scodel, *English Poetic Epitaph*, 44, notes that, in its reflections on scale, the verse 'adopts a humanist topos'.

such descriptions is critical, with a standard example noting that the monument was conceived and executed by Elizabeth Tanfield 'despite [her] being refused permission by the church' – she 'peremptorily ... commandeered' St Catherine's chapel for her own memorializing purposes.[15] *The Official Guide to Burford* joins these detractions, detailing her 'high-handed procedure'.[16] As an effect of the construction of the monument, Tanfield's corruption was later visited upon his wife, with a typical local guide confirming that it is not so much her husband's greed as Elizabeth Tanfield's 'reputation for rapaciousness [that] remains embedded in Burford folklore [in] modern times'.[17] Local legend specifies a chariot of fire – driven by Elizabeth Tanfield – which, if spotted in the Burford skies, would bring bad luck to those who beheld it, and Ross Andrews notes that this visitation may have been connected to the tradition of burning effigies of the couple to celebrate their demise.[18]

Arresting is the misogyny underpinning these multiple accounts; it is impossible, for example, to imagine that a widower intent on memorializing his spouse would be recalled in such terms 400 years later. Nor are contemporary feminist critics immune from the arraigning tendency; hence, Marion Wynne-Davies writes of Elizabeth Tanfield's 'presumptuous erection of the Tanfield tomb [and] ... total disregard for any authority, be it municipal or religious, in the face of her own intentions'.[19] Critics averse to the mother's influence and keen to impugn Elizabeth Tanfield look to the *Life*'s antithetical characterizations and its suggestive anecdotes. The statement that '[Cary] freqvently redd all night; so as her mother ... was faine to forbid her servants to let her haue candles' has

---

[15] Simmons, 'Hidden Churches', n.p.; Slow Europe Travel, 'English Churches Oxfordshire: Church of St John the Baptist, Burford', n.p.; David Ross, 'Britain Express: Burford', www.britainexpress.com/counties (accessed 16 August 2016).

[16] Monk, *Official Guide*, 25.

[17] Guffogg, 'The Tanfield Tomb', n.p. For a fascinating discussion of the ghost stories surrounding Elizabeth Russell, another early modern monument-maker, see Phillippy, *Women, Death and Literature*, 179–210.

[18] See Ross Andrews, *Paranormal Oxford* (Stroud: Amberley Publishing, 2010), 95, and Monk, *Official Guide*, 16. Once a local clergyman had performed an exorcism, he trapped the spirit of Lady Tanfield in a bottle and cast it into the river, thereby reinstituting church authority, and the apparition no longer plagued the town. It was feared that if the bottle rose to the surface, the spirit would be freed; hence, during times of drought, the level of the river was regularly topped up to prevent this dreadful occurrence. See: Monk, *Official Guide*, 16; Joe Robinson, *Oxfordshire Ghosts* (Barnsley: Pen and Sword, 2000), 98–9; Marilyn Yurdan, *Unexplained Oxford and Oxfordshire* (Dunstable: Book Castle, 2002), 58.

[19] Wynne-Davies, *Women Writers and Familial Discourse*, 112. A similar view is expressed by Skura, 'Reproduction of Mothering', 38.

proved particularly irresistible.[20] Salutary here is the way in which the rhetoric of complaint of the early modern period filters unchecked into later constructions.

An alternative reading of the monument is that it represents a creative act, one willed into being inside proscriptive circumstances (that is, the ban on its being erected in the first place). Peter Sherlock observes that 'surviving evidence shows that a ... great deal of enthusiasm was required to see a monument through from its conception to installation', and this seems especially true in Elizabeth Tanfield's case.[21] While the undoubtedly wonderful artistry of the monument is attributed to Gerard Christmas, the agency is firmly female and defiant.[22] And no small part of Elizabeth Tanfield's resistant persona inheres in her articulation of herself as a writing subject. A poem on the monument, for example, injects a widow's perspective while explicitly raising questions about female authorship:

> In bliss is he
> Whom I lov'd best
> Thrice happy shee
> With him to rest
>
> So shall I be
> With him I loved;
> And he with mee
> And both us blessed,
>
> Love made me Poet,
> And this I writt
> My harte did doe y[t]
> And not my wit.

Notable alongside the conventional aspiration towards a contented afterlife is the apologia for a woman writing – only love has made Elizabeth Tanfield turn to verse. Marion Wynne-Davies is undoubtedly right to suggest that the text signals a 'late participation in a familial discourse of poetic composition that had been established by Elizabeth Cary', but the *effect* of Elizabeth Tanfield's contribution has never been properly

---

[20] Cary, *Elizabeth Cary/Lady Falkland*, Wolfe (ed.), 108. For descriptions of Cary's 'difficult and sometimes tyrannical mother', see Foster, 'Resurrecting the Author', 163.

[21] Sherlock, *Monuments and Memory*, 11.

[22] The attribution is suggested by Sherwood and Pevsner, *Oxfordshire*, 506.

considered.[23] Most immediately, given her daughter's significant literary reputation at this point in the 1620s, it is possible to suggest that there may be a barbed identification of Cary in the statement that it is appropriate for a woman to write only when she is emotionally pressed. More broadly, Peter Sherlock notes that inscriptions 'are crucial to an understanding of the precise intentions of tombs [and] their subjects', and his observation works to situate the ways in which the Tanfield monument endeavours to suppress, censor and efface memories of Lawrence Tanfield's imputed corruption by placing emphasis on, in Jean Wilson's words, its occupant's extended 'tenure as a judge, rather than any extraordinary forensic skills'.[24] The epitaph in question begins 'Here lyeth Interr'd Sr Lawrence Tanfield, Knight Sometime one of Ye Justices of his M^{aties} Bench & Late Lo Chief Baron of ye Excheq who continued those places of Judicature 20 yeares Wherein he survived all the Judges in Every Bench at Westminster'.[25] It is distinctive for specifying the occupation of several offices while endorsing a unique continuity if not tenacity.

If there is a suggestion of a public challenge (Lawrence Tanfield outlasts the petty squabbles of Burford), then this is clarified in one of the monument's inscriptions:

> Whose merits only raised him; and made good
> His standing there, where few so long have stood ...

Gesturing to the elevated placement of the effigy, the inscriptions echo the theme of longevity at the same time as they suggest his unimpeachable integrity: 'merits'. The theme is reiterated more assertively in a longer inscription which, because in Latin, can be seen as a more coded and extended appreciation intended for a different audience. A translation of that inscription reads:

> buried in this space rests one pre-eminent in English public life ... a famous judge. A prudent advocate, a dutiful legislator. Under his advocacy no innocent defendant was condemned; when he was judge no criminal dishonestly bought himself off ... [He] never took a bribe, nor ever made his court a source of income. His riches were virtuously acquired ... in his family affairs most attentively and strictly frugal ... A provident parent, the best of husbands, proven faithful in all his obligations.[26]

---

[23] Wynne-Davies, *Women Writers and Familial Discourse*, 113.
[24] Sherlock, *Monuments and Memory*, 13; Wilson, 'Ethics Girls', 98.
[25] The epitaph is transcribed in Nichols (ed.), *Progresses, Processions and Magnificent Festivities of King James the First*, vol. I, 321.
[26] The translation is taken from Wilson, 'Ethics Girls', 105n35.

Negatives are striking here – as judge, Lawrence Tanfield is defined for how he did not perform in office (he was not dishonest, did not accept bribes and did not make corrupt his practice). In this sense, the monument matches the *Life*'s favourable description of Lawrence Tanfield which is similarly indebted to negative phrasing.[27] Intriguing, however, is how quickly the terms of the inscription move from a defence of Lawrence Tanfield's public record into a defence of his financial conduct as *pater familias*. Here, details of his 'frugal' and 'provident' parenting echo William Gouge's 1622 treatise on family ideals ('the *head* [of] ... all the ... duties, which parents owe to their children ... is *A provident care*') and affirm that the chief duty of a father is financial circumspection.[28] In stark contrast, while privileging the same financial language as the monument, the *Life* argues for an improvident father, one financially neglectful of house and kin: Lawrence Tanfield, we are told, was so 'swallow[ed] ... vp' by his 'profession ... left the care of all his own affaires ... intirely to his wife and servants'.[29] There are two competing formulations, then: one which suggests prudent management and another which suggests a total abnegation of fiscal responsibility.

It is possible to read both interpretations as directly relating to Lawrence Tanfield's controversial will. The will disinherits Cary – the Tanfields' only child – skipping a generation and leaving the estate to her son Lucius instead. Thus, the monument, in its underscoring of financial futures, provides justification and rationale for the will (a provident father carefully secures the best outcome for his family and their future), while the *Life* denies paternal agency, suggesting that the will and its contents lie outside Lawrence Tanfield's sphere of responsibility (a work-obsessed father leaves financial planning for his family's financial future to his wife and staff). As Deanna Rankin notes, it was an earlier financial decision – Cary's 1622 decision to mortgage her jointure (in order to fund her husband's adventures in Ireland) – which 'displeased Cary's father ... so thoroughly' that she was immediately disinherited.[30] In Heather Wolfe's edition, the assumption is that Lawrence Tanfield disinherited his daughter for converting to Catholicism, but, aside from a brief angry reference

---

[27] For example, although we learn that 'many about him were sayd to be great bribe takers', Lawrence Tanfield distinguishes himself by not being cast in this mould. See Cary, *Elizabeth Cary/Lady Falkland*, Wolfe (ed.), 105.

[28] William Gouge, *Of Domesticall Duties* (London: John Haviland for William Bladen, 1622; *STC* 12119), fol. 505^r.

[29] Cary, *Elizabeth Cary/Lady Falkland*, Wolfe (ed.), 105.

[30] Rankin, '"A More Worthy Patronesse"', 204.

in a 1627 letter penned by Henry Cary, Viscount Falkland, there is no evidence for this.[31] Rather, the debates to which the *Life* and letters return are the very same debates as those carved in stone on the monument, and they centre on the subsequent – and material – consequences of disinheritance. Although there is one common theme, it is accessed and accounted for very differently across the Tanfield/Cary archive.

Letters, Mobility, Construction

When her father dies, Elizabeth Cary is in Ireland (where her husband was Lord Deputy and where she had been residing since September 1622).[32] She arrives in London with four of her children in July 1625. The general critical consensus is that Cary returned to England so as 'to further her husband's suits at court'.[33] However, it is possible to speculate that the spur to Cary's departure was precisely Lawrence Tanfield's death – the triggering of the will (at his death) means that a visit to her mother's becomes a priority.[34] Certainly, the move from Ireland is precipitous (Cary has only recently given birth to her last child, Henry), and, London formalities quickly over, she travels directly to her Oxfordshire family home. Moreover, as Meredith Skura notes, when Cary goes to Burford it is for 'a dual reunion … with her mother … and with her eldest daughter, Catherine, who was then about to give birth to her own first child'.[35] Had Cary wished only to press her husband's suit, it seems unlikely she would have organized these other familial encounters. In August of 1625, then, at precisely the time that Elizabeth Tanfield began erecting the memorial, Cary was staying in Burford, presumably at the Priory, where it is inconceivable that she would not have visited her father's tomb and possibly seen the monument beginning to take shape. There is evidence that, domestically, this was a traumatic period, far removed from the no doubt fondly imagined reunion – soon after arriving in Burford, Catherine died in childbirth along with her child. It is impossible to be categorical about the emotional effect of this episode on Cary's relationship with her mother; what is clear is that, a month or so afterwards, towards the end of 1625, Cary had left Burford for London.

---

[31] Cary, *Elizabeth Cary/Lady Falkland*, Wolfe (ed.), 293.
[32] See Rankin, "'A More Worthy Patronesse'", 203–21.
[33] See Raber, 'Introduction', 45.
[34] As Foster, 'Resurrecting the Author', 163, notes, in 1625, Lord Falkland was 'in danger of losing his entire estate … to pay off his enormous debts', his ventures in Ireland having come to nothing.
[35] Skura, 'Reproduction of Mothering', 45.

It is precisely in this post-Burford moment that her letters are inaugu-
rated and her bitter battle for financial survival is launched. In terms of
survival, both the *Life* and the letters express equivalent sentiments. Like
the *Life*, which describes conditions of great economic hardship, the letters detail want and impoverishment, and the tone can be melodramatic.
A letter of December 1626 is typical: Cary claims, 'I haue noe meate,
drinke, nor clothes, nor mony … to purchase any of them, and longe,
haue I bene, in this misery, I ly in a lodging, where I haue no meanes,
to pay for it', adopting an emotionally charged (rather than realist)
register.[36] As Karen Raber notes, the 'constructed status' of the *Life* 'cor-
relates to the crafted nature of the letters', meaning neither can be read
as unmediated biographical indexes.[37] The first group of letters (which
Wolfe dates c. October–December 1625) petition for financial recompense on Henry Cary's behalf, and it tends to be assumed that Cary and
her husband write them together as a concerted initiative.[38] However, the
fact that Cary travels with such haste to Burford, and that she only starts
writing after that trip, suggests the letters' impetus resides with a failed
mission to garner maternal support. These distinctively pleading epistolary productions may be less collaborative than individually constituted
by Cary – tracing their inception to a change in tactics once the anticipated familial reunion had foundered.

Such a hypothesis would make sense of Henry Cary's obvious irrita-
tion at his wife's interventions arguing for his case. For example, an April
1626 letter written to Edward Conway, the second Viscount Conway, a
soldier and politician, employs a characteristic construction in specifying how its author (Henry Cary) would 'take much more Compforte
to heare that shee [Cary] were quietly retyred to hir Mothers into the
Country, then that she had obteyned a greate suicte in the Courte'.[39]
The complaint mobilizes a tried-and-tested opposition between city
and country, public and private, retirement and achievement, court and
'home'. There is also much in 'quietly'; Cary, it is suggested, is both a
noisome and noisy presence in London, a source of unprofitable activity. This, it is implied, needs to be curtailed in favour of more productive
kinds of bargaining and negotiating in an alternative context. The point

---

[36] Cary, *Elizabeth Cary/Lady Falkland*, Wolfe (ed.), 275.
[37] Raber, 'Introduction', xvi. James Daybell and Andrew Gordon, 'Introduction', in *Cultures of Correspondence*, 2, note that the 'letter' is marked out as 'a highly artificial text, carefully fashioned for consumption'.
[38] Cary, *Elizabeth Cary/Lady Falkland*, Wolfe (ed.), 249.
[39] Ibid., 256.

is crystallized in a letter from slightly earlier in the month: 'I rather wishe shee [Cary] weare at home with hir Mother preuayling with hir Naturall Affection, then trauayleing to procure Courte fauers for me', Henry Cary writes.[40] In this instance, it is the contrast between *mother* and court that is most obviously visible; also, apparent in the plosive 'p' sounds ('preuayling … procure') is an emphasis on restoring the 'natural' order of things, namely, Elizabeth Cary's place in the inheritance chain. If there was shared design, it was to engineer a situation in which Elizabeth Tanfield reversed the father's earlier catastrophic financial renunciation of his kin.

As has often been noted, Henry Cary's letters change dramatically in tone in the wake of his wife's conversion (from affectionate and endearing to vitriolic and abusive). His desire for his wife to return to her mother's 'house', however, is a constant. Hence, a letter written to Charles I after the conversion becomes public (8 December 1626) sounds a familiar motif ('that shee may be nowe committed … with Commandment to hir Mother to receiue hir'), while another (July 1627) makes clear that maintenance will only be paid once the move to Burford is effected: 'the lawe Matrimoniall … doeth require that [Charles I] should remoue hir, and settle hir with hir Mother; where she shall receyue such allowance from me as is fitt for hir'.[41] As the repetition of the verb 'receive' suggests, a domestic welcome is inseparable from the prospect of a financial change of heart, pointing up a triangulated relationship around the word of the will in which mother, daughter and son-in-law strategically participate. An earlier (December 1626) letter, written to Sir John Coke, discovers Henry Cary demanding that his 'Apostat Wife' be 'instantly restrayned vnto the Custody of hir Mother', and distinctive here is how the language of retirement is replaced by rhetoric of incarceration.[42] Indeed, Henry Cary and his wife frequently have recourse to a similar discursive register, as when Cary herself takes up the prison metaphor in relation to Burford, bewailing an order that 'is to comand mee, to my mothers, in the nature of a prisoner'.[43] Particularly incapacitating for Cary was the simultaneity of a desire to alter her mother's conviction and a reluctance to be emotionally affiliated with her: the double-bind could only be lifted by a proverbial death-bed weakening of the mother's resolve. The idea is reflected upon most forcibly in a May 1627 letter to Charles I, which explains:

[40] Ibid., 254.
[41] Ibid., 269 and 294.
[42] Ibid., 270.
[43] Ibid., 273.

> I haue nothinge to trust to, hereafter, but my mothers bounty, at hir death … so if I offend hir, god knows, what may become of mee … if euer I come to hir either willingly, or by comand … shee will neuer, neither in hir life, or at hir death, either giue mee any thinge, or take any care for mee … to … goe downe to Burford … will bee the meanes to depriue mee, of all liuely hood hereafter.[44]

Powerfully enunciated is the suggestion that Cary stays away from Burford so as not to antagonize relations with her mother and jeopardize the prospect of reconciliation. The situation smacks of paradox, for, even as Cary is debating the likelihood of a thaw – a loosening of sticking-points – so was the monument establishing itself as a permanent fixture in the church at Burford, an enduring symbol of an unbridgeable family rift.

The notion that the conversion in 1626 amplified an *already existent friction* between mother and daughter (rather than precipitating a unique rift) is confirmed in the syntax of the *Life* ('her mother was never kind to [Cary], especially after her being a catholic') and in other contemporary materials.[45] Perhaps most importantly, the festering dynamic between Cary and her mother is adumbrated in Cary's movement – from the family seat in Burford to her mother's house in London and finally to another house. The various stages of mobility described with a remarkable equivalence in both letters and *Life* suggest a downward spiral:

> she retired to a little old house, that she tooke, in a little towne ten mile from London, the rather because her mother … in whose house she had hetherto lived … desired she would leave it, being so displeased with her.[46]

Discourses of diminishing scale ('little') and increasing age ('old'), as well as indications of parochialism and distance ('ten mile'), testify to Cary's growing isolation. And the accelerated nature of the falling out between mother and daughter – in addition to the stigma of conversion – are pointed out in the fact that Elizabeth Tanfield becomes unable to tolerate Cary's presence even in one of her own properties.

Despite being prevailed upon by Cary's husband, Charles I and, we can assume, Cary herself, Elizabeth Tanfield steadfastly refused her daughter assistance, rationalizing her decision in 1627 thus:

> I shall never haue hope to haue any comfort from you … my desiers wass I dout not [but] plesyng to god, to haue you to lyue with your husband,

---

[44] Ibid., 283.
[45] Ibid., 122. For further reflections on Elizabeth Tanfield, see Skura, 'Reproduction of Mothering', 69.
[46] Cary, *Elizabeth Cary/Lady Falkland*, Wolfe (ed.), 275 and 139.

and to lyue in that religeon wherin your war bred even the sam wherin by gods grace I will lyue and dy, as did your Dere father, but bes you repeted nayther him that most good man, nor me, for if you had, you cold never haue erred, nor falne into that myschef wherin you ar now.[47]

As Marion Wynne-Davies notes, Elizabeth Tanfield's epistle bristles with 'accusations of misdemeanours and disloyalties past and present'.[48] Proper observance of religion is aligned with the harmony of marital relations, while martyrological self-constructions aid the grief-stricken elaboration of the lost father. Perhaps most critically, financial failings ('erred') are identified as a prelude to Cary's abandonment of the Protestant religion ('myschef'). The conversion to Catholicism is regarded as both a continuation of perceived ill-conduct and a trajectory of disrespect; Cary, as the letter conceives of her, has long been a wandering soul lost to parental ministration.

Effigies, Impasses, Legacies

In contradistinction to the epistolary construct of a wilful and wayward daughter, Cary is represented via the monument's strategic imagining of her as an ideal daughter (see Figure 12.2). Peter Sherlock notes the way in which 'monuments could manipulate bodies – the bodies of the dead, [and] those of the living', with the Tanfield monument working to erase the very conflict that the *Life* and the letters affirm and underscore.[49] The Tanfield monument demonstrates this capacity through the effigies of Cary and Lucius (Cary's son and the beneficiary of Tanfield's will) and in its relational positioning of the two. Positioned kneeling, and hands locked in prayer in a Protestant church, Cary appears as sober, demure and matronly; the hair is flat and unadorned, the clothes simple and unflattering (a cloak and cord are the only ornaments).[50] Notably, the effigy differs markedly from the one other representation of the writer, a c. 1620 painting by Paul Van Somer (see Figure 12.3), in which she smiles, wears a sun-decorated dress and elaborate ruff, and sports a magnificent headpiece.[51] The effect is to present Cary as fully subscribing to religious orthodoxies and her part in a familial matrix. In view of the

---

[47] Ibid., 278. In a May 1627 letter, Elizabeth Tanfield requests 'no mor of thos tretnyngs [entreaties]': see Cary, *Elizabeth Cary/Lady Falkland*, Wolfe (ed.), 279.
[48] Wynne-Davies, *Women Writers and Familial Discourse*, 111.
[49] Sherlock, *Monuments and Memory*, 68.
[50] See plates 17–20 in Moody and Moody, *Thousand Years*.
[51] An engraving, c. 1621, in the Ashmolean Museum, Oxford, is a copy of this painting.

Figure 12.2   Tanfield Monument, effigy of Elizabeth Cary
Editor's photograph.

surrounding embitterment of controversy and correspondence, the envisioning of Cary in this way takes on almost parodic dimensions.

Cary's effigy is positioned directly opposite that of her son, Lucius, who also kneels (see Figure 12.4). While early modern funeral monuments often surround the deceased with kneeling family, grandchildren are not usually included. When they are (as with the sixteenth-century memorial to Robert Kelway at Exton Church), grandchildren tend to be imaged as miniatures of the mother. But, with the Tanfield monument, Cary and Lucius are of similar size, proportions and scale. Moreover, it is Lucius who occupies the better place, positioned, as he is, at the Tanfields' feet. Given the fact that, at the point of Lawrence Tanfield's

Figure 12.3   Paul Van Somer. *Portrait of Elizabeth Cary*, c. 1620
Reproduced by permission of the Sarah Campbell Blaffer Foundation, Houston.

death, there were ten living grandchildren, including three boys, it is striking that one grandchild alone is identified as so overwhelmingly significant.[52] Matching his singular position as privileged grandchild, Lucius's status is announced in the effigy's clothes and colours. It shows him in a richer palette of green, purple and gold and wearing attire decorated with heraldic motifs. Whereas the Cary effigy lacks any symbolic accompaniment, that of Lucius is flanked by, on the one side, a female

---

[52] Interestingly, Lucius is also singled out in the *Life*, but the other way around; here, he appears as anomalous and atypical (rather than wonderful and exemplary). Cary, we are informed, 'nursed' all her children 'herself [except] ... her eldest sonne (whom her father tooke from her to liue with him from his birth': see Cary, *Elizabeth Cary/Lady Falkland*, Wolfe (ed.), 113.

Figure 12.4   Tanfield Monument, effigy of Lucius Cary.
Editor's photograph.

demi-figure (Elizabeth Tanfield) and, on the other, a swan, thereby
affirming his immediacy to the family (the bird, signifying prosperity,
is part of the Tanfield crest). Via creative additions, Elizabeth Tanfield
doubles her own participation in the monument at the same time as she
downplays her daughter's significance. The effigy's prayer-like posture
signals Lucius's devotions, but his sword and armour mark him out as
a soldier accoutred for battle. In short, Lucius is envisaged as occupying a superior order of things; he is glamorous, ready for action, poised
in the present and in the world. The implication is that it is to Lucius
that power gravitates. Hence, the monument operates to naturalize the
process of transmission that omits the daughter, Cary, as inheritrix –
encountering the effigies, the transition seems stable, orderly and legitimate. Yet this is the opposite view to that which obtains in the *Life* in
which unnaturalness and aberrancy prevail; as it explains, 'that estate
(to *whi*ch [Cary] was naturall Heir) [was] giuen in present to her eldest
sonne'.[53] The crucial distinction here is between 'naturall' (the customary

[53] Cary, *Elizabeth Cary/Lady Falkland*, Wolfe (ed.), 141.

'next generation' pattern of inheritance) and 'in present' (that is, a gift that unfairly ruptures and usurps the lineal order of things). As so often in the Tanfield/Cary archive, texts contest and collide in contradictory if not self-cancelling combinations.

Remarkable in the monument, then, is a studied attention to continuity that prioritizes one family member at the expense of another. Lucius's effigy upstages that of Cary, for she is conceived of solely in terms of Lucius's birth and the biological achievement of motherhood. The notion is reinforced in the inscription, which records that Lawrence Tanfield 'left behind him *one onely daught*[e]r *& Heire*, who married wi[th] Henry Lord Viscount Falkland'.[54] In an unusually word-heavy monument, no adjectives interrupt the flow, and Cary is identified simply as 'Heire' (this is her function) and as a *married* woman (that is, she is identified but only insofar as her bodily presence is inseparable from her reproductive significance). Such a representation throws into relief the *Life*'s envisioning of an exemplary maternity based on a reification of Catholic doctrine; the monument's maternity is expressed in crude practical terms as preserving the family blood-line. Via these figurations, Cary, at least at the level of any role outside of motherhood, is essentially made redundant. In this connection, placement is again revealing. Whereas family members generally face in on monuments from the period (or are shown in profile), Cary is turned outwards, looking away from the rest of the family. In its discovery of a set of entangled relations, then, the monument articulates desire, projection and conviction in such a way as to suggest an impasse and a narrative of discord and division that, as the trajectory of Cary's life was to demonstrate, was to become increasingly and devastatingly self-evident. (There is an irony, then, in the way in which the Cary effigy currently faces the parclose screen separating the chapel from the church aisle: the decorative grille of the woodwork resembles bars, echoing the 'prisoner' metaphor of her 1627 letter.[55])

If the monument captures Cary's life trajectory, this is not to suggest prescience; rather, the Tanfield monument vitally contributes to Lucius's imagined assumption of familial responsibility by casting him in a heroic light and actively shaping future courses of action. And, in anticipating Lucius' role-to-be – and Cary's corresponding isolation – the monument accrues to itself power and agency beyond the grave. Cary's mother dies

---

[54] Nichols (ed.), *Progresses, Processions and Magnificent Festivities of King James the First*, vol. I, 321.
[55] See note 43 (above). See plate 114 in Llewellyn, *Funeral Monuments*, 160, for a revealing image of the monument in relation to the screen.

in 1629 and with her any hope that Cary might eventually accede to an inheritance. Unlike the ephemeral letter form, the monument remains, insisting upon its own active purchase in times to come. In particular, the Latin inscription reveals the ways in which the monument is envisaged as inserting itself in future courses of action and interpretation. It demands the viewer's involvement in the monument's own myth-making processes: 'Attend for a moment, passer-by, where this not undistinguished sepulchre asks your attention … you can complete his epitaph, traveller, yourself'.[56] The archetypal visitor, then, is asked to 'complete' the interpretive work of memorialization in the present-day, to be the judge of the Tanfield inheritance project. In her will, Elizabeth Tanfield left a house in Sheep Street, Burford, the rental for which was to be used for maintaining the monument; clearly, she envisaged the memorial performing familial work well into the future and beyond her own lifetime.[57]

As this chapter has argued, the monument is a vital part of an interwoven Tanfield/Cary archive in which various women memorialize, crafting rival narratives that jostle for prominence. The various texts involving the family differ in emphasis, detail and tone, making for a historical record that contradicts as much as it coincides. If the letters challenge the monument's vision, so does the *Life*, and, indeed, taken together, these multiple expressions of Cary point up overlapping efforts at achieving authority – at seeking to establish the dominance of a particular authorial initiative. Underpinned by a range of motivations, these narratives test, question and intervene in the process of representation, to the extent that it is the points of disagreement and discontinuity that make for the most lasting impression. Each of the productions explored here, then, attests to the complex mechanisms of writing women's literary history in the seventeenth century – and beyond.

There are broader lessons here as well. The elements comprising the Tanfield/Cary archive urge us to attend not only to the literary and the textual but also to the visual and the material. To understand Cary is both to engage with print and manuscript writings and with the familial/contextual environment of which she is so integral a part. It is also to grasp trajectories and travels that run across interlinked parts of the country; local and metropolitan points of connection are key to accessing the archive and its operations. Reappraising Cary in this fashion has implications for more familiar approaches to the Cary biography. Inserting

---

[56] The Latin inscription is translated in Wilson, 'Ethics Girls', 105.
[57] Moody and Moody, *Thousand Years*, 21.

the monument into the Tanfield/Cary archive means that Cary herself appears less as a Catholic convert and more as, in the words of Michael Drayton, 'sole Daughter and heire' to the family estate.[58] Much as her other roles are significant, Cary needs to be appraised as intricately implicated in systems of birth and privilege, as thoroughly ensnared in the ways in which capital circulates. By situating Cary anew in the practices of her moment, we may arrive at a richer and more revealing sense of how material pressures and maternal praxes inform the mnemonic work performed by early modern women, families and institutions.[59]

---

[58] Michael Drayton, *Englands Heroicall Epistles* (London: James Roberts for N. Ling, 1597; *STC* 7193), sig. G3ᵛ.

[59] I am extremely grateful to Patricia Phillippy, both for suggesting this topic and for meticulous, illuminating and energizing feedback.

13

Mary Wroth Romances Ovid
Refiguring Metamorphosis and Complaint in The Countess of Montgomery's Urania

Clare R. Kinney

It is stating the obvious to say that the early modern afterlife of Ovid is nowhere so visible, tenacious and polymorphous as in sixteenth- and seventeenth-century erotic poetics.[1] When Petrarch appropriates and inflects Ovidian myth in his own canzone of the metamorphoses (*Rime sparse* no. 23), he makes available in a particularly concentrated form a vocabulary for exploring the radical discontinuities between a former self and a self transformed by desire. In the centuries that follow, variations on this Ovidian discourse of rupture and self-estrangement seem to be indispensable not only to lyric but also to narrative and dramatic representations of the initiation into *eros*.[2] It is not only the Ovidian-Petrarchan *Metamorphoses*, however, that shape the early modern amatory imagination: the epistolary poems of Ovid's *Heroides* offer a resonant model for the representation of specifically female-voiced complaint. Variations on the heroic epistle foster dazzling rhetorical display, even as they rehearse and spectacularize the passionate and often intemperate utterances of the abandoned woman.

In 1567 Arthur Golding published his complete translation of the *Metamorphoses* (the first four books of his project had appeared in print

---

[1] On Ovid's influence on (and remaking within) the sixteenth- and seventeenth-century literature of desire, see e.g. Leonard Barkan, *The Gods Made Flesh: Metamorphosis and the Pursuit of Paganism* (New Haven and London: Yale University Press, 1986); Jonathan Bate, *Shakespeare and Ovid* (Oxford: Oxford University Press, 1993); Lynn Enterline, *The Rhetoric of the Body from Ovid to Shakespeare* (Cambridge: Cambridge University Press, 2000); Colin Burrow, "Re-Embodying Ovid: Renaissance Afterlives," in Philip Hardie (ed.), *The Cambridge Companion to Ovid* (Cambridge: Cambridge University Press, 2002), 301–19; Wiseman, "'Romes wanton Ovid'"; Paul White, *Renaissance Postscripts: Responding to Ovid's "Heroides" in Sixteenth-Century France* (Columbus: Ohio State University Press, 2009).

[2] For a very fine discussion of both the dynamics and the afterlife of the "canzone of the metamorphoses" in English love poetry, see Gordon Braden and William Kerrigan, *The Idea of the Renaissance* (Baltimore and London: The Johns Hopkins University Press, 1989), 157–90.

two years earlier); in the same year George Turberville published *The heroycall epistles of the learned poet Publius Ouidius Naso, in English verse.* Both translations would go through multiple editions over the next fifty years, making the Ovidian works newly accessible to readers who, like nearly all literate Englishwomen, had not enjoyed a humanist Latin education. This chapter explores one woman's provocative reshaping and reframing of two versions of the Ovidian dynamic.[3] In *The Countess of Montgomery's Urania* (1621), Mary Wroth offers a reappraisal of the metamorphic aesthetic within her romance's own "heroics of constancy," generating a revisionary dialogue with Ovid's Pygmalion narrative and foregrounding transformations which paradoxically ratify the "constant art" (and heart) of the female artist-lover.[4] (Her reinflection of meta-morphic narrative also interestingly revises its previous deployment in her uncle Philip Sidney's *The Countess of Pembroke's Arcadia* (1593).) At the same time, one of the *Urania's* embedded poems, a lengthy heroic epistle shot through with direct allusions to the *Heroides*, is positioned within Wroth's larger narrative in such a way as to suggest a striking reim-agination of both the framing and reception of female complaint. Wroth appropriates the mode for a woman artist, sets it in dialogue with her own innovatory prose romance, and in so doing – as is also the case with her reinvention of the metamorphic aesthetic – suggests new possibilities for both narrative beginnings and narrative endings within the *Urania's* garden of forking paths.

Wroth's *Metamorphoses*

In his canzone of metamorphoses, Petrarch represents the birth of his love for the unattainable Laura and the self-estrangement that accom-panies it by way of sometimes glancing, sometimes expanded, always idiosyncratic references to the stories of Daphne, Cygnus, Actaeon and others. The poet-lover desires and complains within an often threaten-ing dream landscape, enduring psychic transformation upon psychic transformation, reduced at one point to the disembodied voice of Echo.

---

[3] Robin Farabaugh, discussing Wroth's allusions to the Ariadne myth in *Pamphilia to Amphilanthus*, assumes that Wroth had read the *Heroides* in the original but offers no evidence for Wroth having received a Latin education. She does not mention the availability of the Turberville translation. See "Ariadne, Venus, and the Labyrinth: Classical Sources and the Thread of Instruction in Mary Wroth's Works," *Journal of English and Germanic Philology*, 96 (1997), 204–21.

[4] For the "heroics of constancy," see Lamb, *Gender and Authorship*, 163–7. "The constant art" is cele-brated in the third sonnet of Wroth's *Pamphilia to Amphilanthus*.

Eventually, as William Kerrigan and Gordon Braden have argued, the speaker-as-Actaeon is suspended in a perpetual present – "and still I flee the belling of my hounds" (*et ancor de' miei can fuggo lo stormo*) – trapped in the clamor of his own reiterations of undoing and remaking, dogged by his own desires.[5] The canzone's obsessive refiguring of traumatic metamorphosis regularly reappears, if on a smaller scale, in early modern English literature: Spenser's Britomart falls in love with the image of a knight in a magic mirror and fears that, feeding on shadows, she will suffer the fate of Narcissus. Shakespeare's Duke Orsino, invoking the Actaeon myth in a manner not dissimilar to Petrarch, declares that the first sight of Olivia transformed him into a deer: "And my desires, like fell and cruel hounds,/E'er since pursue me."[6]

The very first page of *The Countess of Montgomery's Urania* seems to usher us into familiar territory. A beautiful shepherdess laments in song:

> Unseene, unknowne, I here alone complaine
> To Rocks, to Hills, to Meadowes, and to Springs,
> Which can no helpe returne to ease my paine,
> But back my sorrowes the sad Eccho brings.

Only Echo answers and the singer's woes are "doubly resounded by that monefull voice."[7] We seem to be in the Ovidian space in which, as in *Rime sparse* 23, a lover-poet is reduced to a voice crying in the wilderness. There is, in fact, a comparable lyric moment in Philip Sidney's *The Countess of Pembroke's Arcadia*, when Pyrocles, trapped in his disguise as the Amazon Zelmane and despairing of winning the love of the princess Philoclea, utters a lament in which he complains that "The sound [of his song] to this strange air no sooner goes/But that it doth with Echo's force rebound,/And makes me hear the plaints I would refrain."[8] But as Maureen Quilligan points out, Urania, who has just learned that her supposed parents are only her foster parents and who indeed feels herself to be utterly "unknowne," is not confronting "the absence of a beloved but a lost

[5] Braden and Kerrigan, *Idea of the Renaissance*, 167. The translation quoted is that of Robert Durling, *Petrarch's Lyric Poems: The Rime Sparse and Other Lyrics* (Cambridge, MA: Harvard University Press, 1976), no. 23, line 160.
[6] Edmund Spenser, *The Faerie Queene*, A. C. Hamilton (ed.) (London: Longman, 2001), III.ii.44; and William Shakespeare, *Twelfth Night*, Roger Warren and Stanley Wells (eds.) (Oxford University Press, 1994), 1.1.18–22.
[7] Wroth, *First Part of the Countess of Montgomery's Urania*, 1. Subsequent citations of this work will be offered parenthetically.
[8] Sir Philip Sidney, *The Countess of Pembroke's Arcadia*, Maurice Evans (ed.) (Harmondsworth: Penguin, 1979), 326–7. Subsequent citations of this work will be offered parenthetically.

sense of self as a member of a family."[9] Wroth is wrong-footing her reader from the very beginning, suggesting that familiar discursive frameworks of representation and interpretation are being echoed with a difference.

To be sure, she misdirects us with her romance's very title. Urania, the eponymous fair unknown, will eventually take second place as heroine to Pamphilia, a character whose introduction into the narrative is by contrast relatively casual and whose own history of desire is oddly compressed.[10] Some sixty pages later, Prince Amphilanthus is escorting the recently rescued Princess Antissia to her own kingdom and engaging in a dalliance with her by the way; they break their journey at the court of his cousin Pamphilia's family. We are told, without further explanation, that Pamphilia is especially attentive to Amphilanthus's speech; we watch her take Amphilanthus to task when they are speaking in private and he extravagantly commends Antissia's beauty; we hear Amphilanthus jokingly accuse her of "womanish" envy (61–2). A sentence or so later, Pamphilia is alone and immediately beginning "to breath out her passions, which to none shee would discover," lamenting that the pain she now suffers in witnessing Amphilanthus with Antissia is undeserved, since *she* has "ever been a most true servant" to Love (62). The suggestion of duration in that "ever" implies that the birth of Pamphilia's desire has occurred in some unnarrated past; she will later grieve that in "so long time and so many yeares [she] could not make [Amphilanthus] discerne her affections," although conceding that she has never put them into plain words (91); she also admits that despite her woes she cannot "condemne [her] heart, for having vertuously and worthily chosen" (92).

Wroth never narrates the moment at which Pamphilia *chose*; the fiction presents her as always already in love with Amphilanthus: it is a narrative *donnée*. She is a lover, moreover, who does not represent herself as being the victim of a metamorphic force, but as an agent, one who chooses. (Wroth will reemphasize the importance of such agency at other moments in her romance: "I chose, and am forsaken," says another unhappy woman (437).) The author's unorthodox narrative treatment of her heroine erases the *unchosen* transforming initiation into love customarily foregrounded in both early modern lyric sequences and prose

---

[9] Maureen Quilligan, "The Constant Subject: Instability and Female Authority in Wroth's *Urania* Poems," in Elizabeth Harvey and Katharine Eisaman Maus (eds.), *Soliciting Interpretation: Literary Theory and Seventeenth-Century English* Poetry (Chicago: University of Chicago Press, 1990), 307–35 at 311.

[10] There is one fleeting preliminary reference to Pamphilia (as a touchstone of beauty) by the minor character Allimarlus (Wroth, *Urania*, 37).

romance; we do not seem to be in the same imaginative territory, for example, as the heroes of *The Countess of Pembroke's Arcadia*, who apostrophize the love that "disguisest our bodies and disfigurest our minds" and who emphasize the rupture between a former self and a desiring self when they consciously and very materially reinvent themselves as Zelmane the Amazon and Dorus the shepherd (174).[11] In the wake of transforming desire, Pyrocles and Musidorus write poems exploring the "hapless state of man in self-division" (188); Wroth is more interested in the consequences of choice for the constant female subject.

Wroth's narrative is in this sense anti-Petrarchan-Ovidian: Pamphilia's own sonnet sequence may begin with a conventional vision of Venus and Cupid acting upon the speaker, suppressing her agency as they place a burning heart inside her breast, but there is no narrative equivalent to that scene within the *Urania* itself.[12] This emphasis upon a conscious choice also offers a challenge to the erotic fictions in which the responsibility for the more crooked shifts adopted by a male protagonist in the name of love is slyly displaced upon the female object of desire. Revealing his true identity to Philoclea, the disguised Pyrocles declares: "You shall see ... a living image and a present story of what love can do when he is bent to ruin ... Behold here before your eyes, Pyrocles, prince of Macedon, whom you only have brought to this game of fortune and unused metamorphosis, whom you only have made neglect his country, forget his father and lastly, forsake to be Pyrocles" (328).

Pyrocles constructs a metamorphosis of his own here, sliding away from the "present story of what love can do" to turn Philoclea into the goddess responsible for his "unused metamorphosis" and subsequent errancy. Wroth perhaps glances at and critiques this displacement of agency – echoed elsewhere in the *Arcadia* in the rhetoric of other impassioned male characters – in a darkly comic episode in which the willful Princess Nereana, separated from her entourage and lost in a forest, is tied to a tree and forcibly tricked out as a goddess of the woods by the madman Alanius (196–200).[13] Tellingly, Nereana is so horrified by the reflection of

---

[11] For a detailed discussion of Sidney's interest in Ovidian metamorphosis in the *Arcadia*, see Kinney, "The Masks of Love."

[12] Little work has been done on Wroth's relations with the *Metamorphoses*, with the exception of a short study focusing on her pastoral drama; see Joyce Green MacDonald, "Ovid and Women's Pastoral in Lady Mary Wroth's *Love's Victory*," *Studies in English Literature, 1500–1900*, 51 (2011), 447–63.

[13] For other instances of the displaced agency phenomenon, see, for example, Sidney, *Countess of Pembroke's Arcadia*, 439 (Musidorus to Pamela) and 451 (Amphialus to Philoclea).

her transformed self in a stream that "she would not goe so neere unto her metamorphos'd figure" (198) – turning away from the "self" that has been created for her by the masculine artist, she refuses to look again in the mirror. But Wroth goes beyond this critique of manmade metamorphosis to offer her own metamorphosis of transforming desire.

Book I of the *Urania* concludes with Pamphilia's rescue of several characters from imprisonment within the Cyprian "Palace of Venus." This magical edifice has been previously described at some length: its three towers are graced, respectively, with images of Cupid, Venus and Constancy. Cupid's right hand points to the white marble statue of Venus on the second tower, a statue which

> might for rarenesse and exquisitenesse haue beene taken for the Goddesse her selfe, and have caused as strange an affection as the Image did to her maker, when he fell in loue with his owne worke ... her left hand holding a flaming Heart, her right, directing to the third Tower, before which ... was the figure of *Constancy*, holding in her hand the Keyes of the Pallace; which shewed, that place was not to be open to all, but to few possessed with that vertue. (48)

When Pamphilia eventually enters the third tower, she takes from the hands of Constancy the keys that will free the palace's captives, "at which instant *Constancy* vanished, as metamorphosing her self into her breast" (169). The gestures of the statues direct the onlooker's gaze from Cupid to Venus and thence to Constancy, as if the powers of love are ultimately invested in or must defer to the virtue which will in its turn be subsumed by Pamphilia. Although a putative metamorphosis takes place when Constancy vanishes into Pamphilia (as if she has, at this instant, wholly come to represent that quality), Wroth's narrative has made it perfectly clear that Pamphilia already embodies constancy: indeed it is her fidelity to her still concealed and unrequited love for Amphilanthus that permits her to resist the palace's enchantments and free its captives. Having turned love into constancy, she is the author, not the object, of the metamorphosis – a metamorphosis which is anti-metamorphic in that it announces an end to all further changes of state.

Wroth's account of the palace's artworks further complicates her challenge to a more familiar metamorphic aesthetic. She proposes that the statue of Venus might have "caused as strange an affection as the Image did to her maker, when he fell in loue with his owne worke," and her oddly unspecific invocation of *another* image may, as Josephine Roberts suggests, echo a stanza in Book IV of *The Faerie Queene* in which Spenser invents his own myth of the sculptor Phidias languishing over the Venus he has made.[14] But the reference to "the Image" is sufficiently vague (why not just say "the Venus of Phidias"?) that the reader may as easily recall Ovid's Pygmalion, another artist who fell in love with his own artifact. If, however, Wroth's Venus is comparable to, or perhaps even exceeds, the beloved created by the desiring male artist, she is not a statue who can be animated (as in the Ovidian narrative) to fulfill a male maker's solipsistic fantasy. In Wroth's house of fiction, Venus defers to and is displaced by the sculpted representation of Constancy, who will, upon Pamphilia's achievement of her quest, herself be embodied – or brought to life – by a desiring woman.

That climactic moment of Pamphilia's revisionary metamorphosis feels as if it should be a moment of conclusion, of closure, but it occurs when we are only a quarter of the way into the 1621 text. It is a text that is as labyrinthine as the *Metamorphoses*, but its own privileged metamorphosis – dilated upon so often in the many interpolated narratives which reconsider the situation of the constant woman who, once transfigured by love, can never break faith with a changeable lover – brings no sense of an ending.[15] Wroth's own *carmen perpetuum* proves, moreover, to be capacious and complex enough to refigure the Pygmalion narrative in a considerably darker vision of the anti-metamorphic metamorphosis of the female lover. Towards the end of Book 4 of the *Urania*, the Duke of Florence hears the history of the lady of the Forrest Champion, whose beloved was first unfaithful to her and finally "made it appeare that hee loath'd her" (632). She

> so grievously tooke this curst hap, as shee melted into griefe, as Virgins waxe with the heate of fire will into water, and yet thereby the coldnesse of that Element grow hard, as frozen by coldnesse: So was shee clos'd in cold despaire; yet not hardened, but with that, not with hate, or dislike, suffering as patiently, as a dead body permits handling, by any rude standers by; she onely felt paine of love, and into that was metamorphosed. (632)

Loved by many other men, the bereft lady refuses them all: "'never any more belov'd woman breath'd, nor ever will or can breath so true a loving woman'" (633).

Wroth offers two striking figures for the lady's emotional transformation; her first dissolution into grief evokes the comparison to "Virgins

---

[14] See Roberts's note, Wroth, *Urania*, 722 and Spenser, *Faerie Queene*, IV.X.40.
[15] For a suggestive discussion of Wroth's recursive use of narrative counterpoint and of her obsessive retelling of one particular narrative, see Jennifer Lee Carrell, "A Pack of Lies in a Looking Glass: Lady Mary Wroth's *Urania* and the Magic Mirror of Romance," *Studies in English Literature 1500–1900*, 34 (1994), 79–107.

waxe" – absolutely pure and unused beeswax – that has been warmed and liquefied only to be "frozen by coldnesse"; the despairing endurance and "hardening" which follows is likened to a corpse's impassivity. The passage hauntingly rewrites Ovid's striking description of the metamorphosis of Pygmalion's statue – I offer here the Golding translation that would have been available to Wroth:

> ... the Ivory wexed soft: and putting quyght away
> All hardnesse, yielded underneath his fingers, as we see
> A piece of wax made soft against the Sunne, or drawen to bee
> In diverse shapes by chaufing it betweene ones hands ...
> [...]
> He felt it verraye fleshe indeed.[16]

Instead of the wax that softens and warms and holds the possibility of multiple metamorphoses, instead of a marmoreal hardness being replaced by living flesh, instead of a woman made pliable at the touch of her lover, Wroth offers us softened wax freezing, a live woman turning into a corpse. The cruel lover is by implication an anti-Pygmalion: he is not the animating but rather the destroying artist of his lady's change. He is placed in the same position that Pyrocles rather dubiously conferred upon Philoclea: he becomes the author of another's "unused metamorphosis" – but his metamorphic powers do not, at last, introduce the kind of radical alienation from a previous identity that Pyrocles blames upon Philoclea. The lady is "metamorphosed" into "paine of love," but love's pain cannot change her nature as a true lover. Her constancy preempts, in effect, her false beloved's destructive power.

Wroth's *Heroides*

Wroth's idiosyncratic reappraisal of the metamorphic aesthetic acquires especial resonance because it is in perpetual dialogue with the narratives of inconstancy and abandonment that populate her romance, and it is one of these that triggers her equally fresh reappraisal of the Ovidian heroic epistle.[17] In Book 3 of the *Urania*, the Queen of Naples and

---

[16] Nims (ed.), *Ovid's Metamorphoses: The Arthur Golding Translation 1567*, book X, lines 308–311 and 315. The Ovidian lines are: *temptatum mollescit ebu positoque rigore/subsidit digitis ceditque, ut Hymettia sole/era remollescit tractaque pollice multas/flecitur in facies ipsoque fit utilis usu./... corpus erat!* See Ovid, *Metamorphoses: Volume II*, trans. Frank Justus Miller, 2nd ed. rev. G. P. Gould, Loeb Classical Library no. 43 (Cambridge, MA: Harvard University Press, 1984), book X, lines 283–6 and 289.

[17] For an overview of the reading and reception of the *Heroides* in the early modern period, see Wiseman, "'Rome's wanton Ovid.'"

Limena of Sicily, walking in the woods, encounter a distraught woman railing at her fate; this lady, Dorolina, tells them a familiar story of love consummated, followed by a beloved's fickleness (492). In a final attempt to recall her lover to fidelity, Dorolina had sent him some verses which she is prevailed upon to share with the other ladies. What follows is a long poem in heroic couplets (492–5), very obviously modeled after the epistles of the *Heroides* and explicitly invoking the vicissitudes of five Ovidian letter-writers – Dido, Ariadne, Phyllis, Medea and Penelope.[18] Its more epigrammatic moments anticipate the later Augustan translations of the Ovidian epistles: of Ulysses's detainment by Calypso and Circe; for example, Dolorinda notes snappily, "Against his will, he oft his will enjoyed,/And with variety at last was cloy'd" (494, lines 31–2).[19] The governing conceit of the poem, however, is that Dorolina's trials both parallel and exceed the suffering and the fidelity of the Ovidian heroines. She has been deprived of a more powerful experience of love than Dido ever enjoyed: "she lost less than I" (493, line 5). Ariadne saved the faithless Theseus with her thread; Dorolina likens that "thrid" to her very life, offered to "draw [her beloved] from harme,/My study wholly how I might all charme/That dangerous were" (495, lines 11–12). Noting that Phyllis hanged herself when Demophoon failed to return to her, Dorolina suggests that such an action would be otiose in her own case: "I strangled am, with your unkindnes choak'd" (493, line 35). (Dorolina's allusions to the Phyllis story, incidentally, offer evidence that Wroth was indeed familiar with Turberville's translation. When Dorolina describes Phyllis as "Making ... a Cord/The end of her affections" (493, lines 33–4), Wroth follows Turberville's rendering of "laqueus" [noose] as cord.)[20] In conclusion, Dorolina positions herself as a Penelope who, ever

---

[18] Barbara Lewalski briefly notes the echo of the *Heroides* in her chapter on Wroth, *Writing Women in Jacobean England* (Cambridge, MA: Harvard University Press, 1993), 279. Danielle Clarke, "Formed into Words," 81–5, and Lorna Hutson, "The 'Double Voice,'" 158–60, have both discussed Dorolina's poem in relation to the Ovidian model and to early modern gendering of voice, but neither of their insightful essays considers the reframing of the poem within Wroth's larger narrative project.

[19] See Ovid, *Ovid's Epistles Translated by Several Hands* (London: Jacob Tonson, 1680); the project was supervised by Dryden and Tonson.

[20] The Ovidian text reads: *colla quoque, infidis quia se nectenda lacertis/praebuerunt, laqueis inplicuisse iuvat* ("my neck, too, because once offered to your false arms, I could gladly ensnare in the noose"). Ovid, *Heroides and Amores*, trans. Grant Showerman, 2nd ed., Loeb Classical Library no. 41 (Cambridge, MA: Harvard University Press, 1977), *Heroides* II, lines 141–2. Subsequent non-Turbervillian references to the *Heroides* refer to this text and will be cited parenthetically. Turberville, *Heroycall Epistles*, sig. 11ʳ, renders this passage (extremely freely) as: "Then with a string to stoppe my breath,/I thinke it passing fit: /And with a ruthlesse hande, a corde/about my throte to knit." Subsequent quotations from Turberville will be noted parenthetically.

steadfast in the face of his absence, begs her lover to flee the "powerfull charms" of strangers and sirens and find in her "A minde of beauteous faith, fit for the name/Of worthy Constancy" (494, lines 41 and 37).

Ovid's own heroines explicitly compare their plights to other women's misfortunes. In *Heroides* II, for example, Phyllis accuses errant Demophoon of being heir to his father Theseus's history of philandering and recalls the latter's abandonment of Ariadne.[21] Dorolina, having invoked Ariadne's story and moved on to Phyllis's sufferings, reinscribes that indictment of Demophoon: "For Theseus was his Sire that King of spight/Thus did he both inherit state, and ill" (493: 30–31). The effect is of an echo chamber in which variations on the traumatic story of abandonment reverberate *ad infinitum*: Dorolina joins the members of an epistolary community who rehearse unhappy histories, play out their roles in the same old plots. But in Wroth's *Urania*, Dorolina, as both a character within a larger narrative and a woman whose voice does not fall silent as her poetic epistle ends, is ultimately freed by her creator from this community of impotent woe (and from the fruitless revolt against the conclusion of an already written tale).[22]

In the *Heroides*, Dido and Phyllis and Ariadne offer their words to the empty air and receive no reply; the reader becomes the privileged voyeur of the spectacle of grief, eavesdropping, as Laurel Fulkerson remarks, "on a conversation clearly marked as private" – although in the case of those heroines it is no conversation at all.[23] By contrast, when Wroth borrows the Ovidian epistle and embeds it in her romance, her narrative reframes the mode in a manner that lets the lyric speaker wear her rue with a difference. Dorolina has *written* her poem to no end, but she does not now speak to her betrayer, nor, to what John Kerrigan, discussing the related lyric subgenre of female complaint in medieval and Renaissance poetry, has described as "a landscape that yields nothing but [her] voice."[24] In the *Urania*, sympathetic female listeners replace an anonymous and uncaring lover – or an unseen male witness who simply transcribes the lamentation. Telling her story, Dorolina had described her increasingly distant

---

[21] Ovid, *Heroides* II, lines 75–8.

[22] Raphael Lyne, *Ovid's Changing Worlds: English Metamorphoses 1567–1632* (Oxford: Oxford University Press, 2001), 15, notes apropos of the *Heroides* that the encompassing larger narratives within which the heroines are trapped become "contentious accounts against which the subjects complain."

[23] Laurel Fulkerson, *The Ovidian Heroine as Author: Reading, Writing and Community in the Heroides* (Cambridge: Cambridge University Press, 2005), 10.

[24] John Kerrigan (ed.), *Motives of Woe: Shakespeare and "Female Complaint": A Critical Anthology* (Oxford: Clarendon Press, 1991), 1.

lover as receiving other poems she had given him "like a King, that takes
a Present and likes it, but thinks it was his Subjects due to present it, and
so meanes not to reward the bringer, scarse the giver" (492); these new
listeners, having pitied her plight, "promised their helps to assist her"
(495). Most importantly, Dorolina's poem does not fully contain or cir-
cumscribe her, it does not fix her forever in the position of lamentation
or of pleading or solipsistic grief: Wroth does not abandon the abandoned woman.

Before inspecting the new story Wroth creates for Dorolina, it might
be useful to consider the very different practice of George Turberville
in his translation of the *Heroides*. Each of the epistles in Turberville is
prefaced by an "Argument" in which the translator summarizes the narrative events leading up to the writing of the letter, framing the speaker's
situation in his own moralizing rhetoric and often directing in advance
the interpretation of her woes. Thus we read of Phaedra's passion for the
disdainful Hippolytus:

> She naythelesse attacht with glowing gleede,
> To winne the chastfull youth to filthie lust:
> In subtile sort his humors sought to feede,
> Perswading him hir sute to be but iust.
> With sundrie sleightes she went about to winne
> The retchlesse youth, that minded nothing lesse
> Than shamefull lust and filthie fleshly sinne. (Sig. 18ᵛ)

The heavy-handed description of Phaedra's "filthie lust" and the emphasis upon Hippolytus's abhorrence of "fleshly sinne" preemptively passes
judgment on the heroine before the reader scans a single word of her
complaint. In another example of this phenomenon, Sappho is labeled
"wanton Sappho" (sig. 108ʳ) in the Argument to her epistle (with no
mention at all of her identity as a poet). Moreover, the translations
themselves – often very free – demonstrate Turberville's willingness to
recalibrate the empathy created by the Ovidian text. Ovid's Dido concludes her letter to Aeneas by imagining her own epitaph: *Praebuit Aeneas
et causam mortis et ensem;/ipsa sua Dido concidit usa manu* ("From Aeneas
came the cause of her death and from him the blade; from the hand of
Dido herself came the stroke by which she fell") (*Heroides* VII, lines 195–
6). Turberville renders these lines:

> Aeneas gaue the cause
>   and sworde wherewith I dyde:
> But desperate Dido on hir selfe
>   hir ruthlesse hande hath tryde. (Sig. 47ʳ)

The supplementary adjectives "desperate" and "ruthlesse" brusquely co-opt Dido's own voice to prejudge the abandoned woman, suggesting an irrational frenzy quite at odds with the chilly misery of the Latin text. Turberville similarly expands upon Phyllis's description of how she loiters on the seashore, imagining that every ship she sees heralds Demophoon's return. Ovid writes: *in freta procurro; vix me retinentibus undis* ("I run into the waters, scarce halted by the waves," 127); Turberville translates: "Then lyke a Bedlam wight to waues/and drenching seas I ronne" (sig. 10ᵛ). His Phyllis proclaims her own insanity. As Turberville reimagines and recontains Ovid's heroines through his framing glosses and his interpretive translations, his invasive commentary intermittently undermines even the limited authority to record, uninterrupted, their own version of history – or to fantasize alternative futures – offered them by Ovid's own acts of ventriloquization.[25]

Wroth, by contrast, sidesteps moralizing gloss to offer a new sense of an ending. Dorolina's re-spoken epistle concludes conventionally enough with its author taking an absolutist stance: "Come and give life, or in your stay send death/To her that lives in you, else drawes no breath" (495, lines 9–10). But the very fact that the bereft Dorolina is still alive, angry and in a position to recite the poem within Wroth's larger narrative suggests that she may have other options than her verses concede. Dorolina does not kill herself (like Dido and Phyllis). Nor does she kill the woman who displaces her (like Medea) or get her beloved back after twenty years (like Penelope) or exchange him for a deity (like Ariadne). She resolves instead to go to Pamphilia and offer her services to that lady (495). Wroth's conspicuous sidestepping of familiar Ovidian outcomes tempts one to leap across a few centuries and anachronistically juxtapose her practice with Virginia Woolf's fantasy of a novel written by a woman which resists the conventional teleologies attached to fictions about women (i.e. marriage or death), a novel which breaks the sequence, has designs of its own.[26] Dorolina, it turns out, now sees, "as if she lookt into a glasse," the abuses of the past: "never to be righted or cleered, if not by death, forgetfulnes, or charity" (495). Death has been rejected,

---

[25] For an extended discussion of Turberville's practice as a translator, see Deborah S. Greenhut, *Feminine Rhetorical Culture: Tudor Adaptations of Ovid's Heroides* (New York: Peter Lang, 1988). Patricia Phillippy, "'Loytering in Love': Ovid's *Heroides*, Hospitality, and Humanist Education in *The Taming of the Shrew*," *Criticism*, 40 (1998), 27–53 at 31–5, has argued, by contrast, that Turberville's interventions are significantly less pronounced than those of sixteenth-century continental translators who offer a much more extended moralizing apparatus and commentary.

[26] Woolf, *A Room of One's Own*, 62–9.

but forgetfulness and charity still seem to be possibilities; in Pamphilia's service Dorolina lives "as in her former daies in much respect, and us'd with all courtesie" (495). The reader of an Ovidian epistle cannot intervene to affect the writer's destiny, but in Wroth's narrative reframing of an Ovidian epistle it seems that the purgative experience of re-speaking the text of grief to a new and sympathetic audience and arousing the "charity" – or caritas – offered by Dorolina's listeners nurtures a reflective process that undoes the paralysis of grief and gives Dorolina the agency to seek out Pamphilia's kindness.[27]

One might compare Wroth's repositioning of Dorolina to the rather different endgame offered by Isabella Whitney in *The Copy of a Letter* (1567). Complaining to the lover who has married another woman, Whitney's speaker likens his betrayal to the infidelities of Aeneas, Theseus and Jason, and thus aligns herself with the epistolary heroines Dido, Ariadne and Medea.[28] Her letter, as is typical in the *Heroides*, concludes with a flurry of attempts to control a future that is no longer in her power to alter: she suggests that her lover may come to "wish you had *me* taken" (line 88, emphasis mine); she reverses herself to hope that his wife may be a Penelope rather than a Helen (lines 93–100); she wishes she had had the gift of prophecy to foresee her ill-fortune (lines 113–16); she asks God to be her guide and nobly wishes long life and good fortune to the "unconstant lover" (lines 121–32); she commands him to keep her letter "in store" as it will be her last (lines 133–6) – and then she concludes:

> And now farewel, for why at large
>   my mind is here exprest?
> The which you may perceive, if that
>   You do peruse the rest? (137–40)

The false beloved is redirected to understand the expression of her mind by perusing "the rest" of the letter; Whitney's poem "resets," as it were, in the mode of its original complaint – as if there were nowhere else to go. If Whitney reclaims female complaint, some decades before Wroth, from the "transvestite ventriloquism" (to borrow Elizabeth Harvey's felicitous

---

[27] For a rather different account of Renaissance representations of women in the act of asserting their identity both through and against intertextual invocations of the *Heroides*, see Lyne, "Intertextuality and the Female Voice."

[28] Whitney, *The Copy of a Letter*, lines 33–52. Subsequent quotations from this work will be indicated parenthetically by line number. Danielle Clarke discusses Whitney's appropriation of Ovid (although with rather different emphases to my own) in *Politics of Early Modern Women's Writing*, 193–7.

phrase) of the male poets, she nevertheless does not quite breach its familiar parameters.[29]

Wroth's appropriation and reframing of Ovidian epistle is a far more complex matter. She does not simply revoice female complaint: she moves it from the closed circuit of the letter that receives no response into a more dialogic universe; she imagines for it a new reception history, a different audience – and she opens up the possibility of a different ending for its author. In Ovid's poems, as Duncan Kennedy notes, the heroines speak from within a well-known narrative with a fixed conclusion. *They* may experience their circumstances as "open and contingent," but however much they attempt to imagine alternative outcomes, their pleas and hopes are inevitably rendered ironic or pathetic or fantastic by the superior knowledge possessed by the readers looking over the shoulder of the poem's official addressee.[30] Dorolina is not, however, a figure locked in the canon of myth: she participates in a narrative whose ending is unknown; she has a future within the larger romance that reaches beyond the letter that she recites to her sympathetic audience. Wroth's embedding of the heroic epistle within a quite different genre interrogates the limitations of complaint, obliges it to figure differently – she breaks the sequence, breaks the sentence. Her poet-speaker is not defined and circumscribed by the act of complaint: she can make choices which allow her to walk out of the end of her lyric performance, to recalibrate her identity. Indeed she can now take on a new role as a sympathetic listener herself.

This last aspect of Dorolina's reinvention combines a linear progression into new narrative territory with a recursive confirmation that the voicing of and listening to complaint is a structuring dynamic of Wroth's romance. Pamphilia receives Dorolina all the kindlier because she is herself suffering the miseries of an abandoned woman: the errant Amphilanthus has forsaken her for one of his former flames. Dorolina now seeks to comfort her suffering mistress and although she cannot persuade Pamphilia to share any of her own poems (498), she does become the charitable and loving confidante, the understanding audience, to whom Pamphilia relates the supposedly imaginary "French" history of Lindamira, which Dorolina quickly realizes is "more exactly related than a fixion" (505). It is a history that does not only "shadow" a version of Pamphilia's own woes but also represents one of those episodes in which,

[29] Harvey, *Ventriloquized Voices*, 16.
[30] Duncan F. Kennedy, "Epistolarity: The *Heroides*," in Philip Hardie (ed.), *The Cambridge Companion to Ovid* (Cambridge: Cambridge University Press, 2002), 217–32 at 225.

as many commentators have noted, Wroth's own erotic history comes very close to the surface of her text.[31] When Pamphilia, speaking of Lindamira's faithless beloved, declares "'I will with the story conclude my rage against him'" (502), the "him" might as easily be Amphilanthus – or for that matter, Wroth's own philandering lover, William Herbert. The particular freight that the episode bears within the *Urania* is underlined, furthermore, by the fact that this "micro-narrative" in prose with its appended lyric sequence (the seven sonnets of "Lindamira's Complaint") replays, on a small scale, the romance narrative + lyric sequence offered, thanks to the appended *Pamphilia to Amphilanthus* sonnets, by the 1621 *Urania* itself.

I began by suggesting that Wroth's revisions of both the Petrarchan-Ovidian narrative of transforming desire and the Ovidian aesthetic of epistolary female complaint have potentially interesting consequences for narrative endings and beginnings in Wroth's reshaping and re-gendering of the protocols of romance. What does the history of a desiring subject look like if it does not begin with a moment of rupture or of estrangement from one's very self ("yet was her choice *like her selfe* the best," the *Urania*'s narrator says of Pamphilia (64)). What happens to a whole history of female complaint if a lyric speaker can move on to a future that leaves the faithless beloved behind (Dorolina does not even grant her betrayer the honor of a name to be inserted within the historical record)? And yet, as is always the case when one recognizes and even delights in Wroth's more contestatory experiments with the literary discourses available to her, one must be wary of overstating one's claims. If Wroth privileges the heroic constancy of the loving woman over the metamorphic initiation into love and makes it almost a precondition of her stories of desire, she nevertheless recounts again and again that other rupture produced by a beloved's faithlessness, a rupture that wreaks its own havoc on the constant lover's psyche, if not on her constancy. And it seems telling to me that Dorolina walks out of her lyric impasse only to participate, as charitable audience, in an episode of storytelling that functions as a kind of *mise en abîme* in which Pamphilia's not quite fictional tale of Lindamira and her translation of Lindamira's woes into a miniature

---

[31] On the *Urania*'s topicality and autobiographical "shadowing," see Roberts's introduction to her edition of the 1621 text (lxix–lxxi); I borrow her very useful term in my own discussion. For some of the earliest and best discussions of the Lindamira episode, see: Lamb, *Gender and Authorship*, 187–8; Naomi J. Miller, *Changing the Subject: Mary Wroth and the Figurations of Gender in Early Modern England* (Lexington: University Press of Kentucky, 1996), 138; Quilligan, "The Constant Subject," 326–7.

sonnet sequence rehearse on a small scale and in a supremely charged manner both the 1621 *Urania*'s larger design and Wroth's recursive shadowing of her own erotic vicissitudes. To put it another way, Dorolina abandons her own echo chamber to enter another one, glancingly inhabiting the position of the extradiegetic reader of the romance that weaves and reweaves narratives of abandonment, the unfinished romance that is also, in some sense, Mary Wroth's own heroic epistle: the never-ending, never-answered letter of both love and complaint to William Herbert.[32]

---

[32] Mary Ellen Lamb, in "Classical Precedents for Author Figures in Wroth's *Urania*: Pamphilia, Sappho, and Ovid," an unpublished paper delivered at the 2016 Renaissance Society of America conference, proposes that Ovid's representation of Sappho in the *Heroides* XV offers a model of female authorship that may shape Wroth's presentation of Pamphilia in her romance My argument here extends her argument extradiegetically and perhaps (with respect to the range of voices in the *Heroides*) more generally.

14

Nuns' Writing
Translation, Textual Mobility and Transnational Networks

Marie-Louise Coolahan

From the dissolution of the monasteries in the 1530s, British and Irish women who wished to enter religious life were forced abroad. The decision to leave worldly concerns behind now entailed, paradoxically, a process of engagement with other countries and languages. The first exiled English convent was founded in Brussels in 1598 by recusants (Mary Percy, Dorothy and Gertrude Arundell) fleeing persecution in England. To enter religious life was also to engage with the writing culture of Counter-Reformation Catholicism. Dorothy Arundell composed a martyrological life of her spiritual mentor John Cornelius, who had been executed in 1594 following a raid on the Arundells' Chideock Castle, Dorset. This document was testament to his fortitude and the signs of divine approbation; recounting two miraculous events, her life of Cornelius was incorporated into Jesuit collections that aimed to buoy the faithful across Europe. It was translated into Spanish, Italian and Latin. The Catholic religious orders created and sustained textual as well as personal networks; indeed, for enclosed women religious,[1] it was textual exchange that facilitated their contributions to devotional currents, spiritual controversies and worldly developments. Exposure to the channels of communication available to the religious orders – institutions that transcended the national – opened up the means of textual mobility and exchange, although not necessarily the markers of female authorship. As Elizabeth Patton has shown, Arundell's text was usually integrated into Jesuit histories without attribution.[2] Authorial credit is a complex

---

[1] 'bound by monastic vows'; see *OED*, 'religious' B *n*. 1.
[2] See Elizabeth Patton, 'From Community to Convent: The Collective Spiritual Life of Post-Reformation Englishwomen in Dorothy Arundell's Biography of John Cornelius', in Bowden and Kelly (eds.), *English Convents in Exile*, 19–31.

issue for writers who were nuns; convent identity prized the collective and collaborative over individual authorship. But the failure of the male orders to acknowledge Arundell points also to the wider social leeriness of women's writing. Moreover, their control over the means of circulation highlights the layers of mediation at play in nuns' textual production.

Not only their experiences of persecution but also their devotional activities impelled nuns to produce texts of all kinds in post-Reformation Europe. The emphasis on vernacular texts of instruction impacted on the religious orders, and translations of convent rules and constitutions were increasingly necessary for women who travelled to join foreign convents or establish their own foundations. The kinds of writing produced in convents ranged from obituary and chronicle history to religious rules and devotional translations, as well as profession and financial records. These were texts required by the community; they addressed, documented and shaped that female readership. They were vital sources of authority when controversies arose – which happened frequently. But these texts also participated in the Counter-Reformation effort and therefore sustained interest beyond their initial audiences. The religious orders, with their pan-European reach, functioned as transnational networks for the transmission and distribution of nuns' writings.

The challenges of accessing writing by women religious – often in continuous use by convents, sometimes suppressed by church authorities, and always problematic for the hegemonic narrative of Protestant England – has meant that the study of writing by women religious has languished behind other forms of early modern women's writing. Enclosure as well as the ongoing value of the texts have militated against public access to archival holdings. As Jaime Goodrich has observed, the lack of fit with the single-author paradigm may also account for this omission from the feminist recovery project.[3] However, scholarship in this area has burgeoned in the twenty-first century. The groundbreaking *Who were the Nuns?* project, led by Caroline Bowden, has established the membership of all the exiled English convents, spearheading a publication programme that has so far amassed six volumes of edited texts and one essay collection.[4] The thriving hub of devotional writing produced

---

[3] Goodrich, *Faithful Translators*, 109.

[4] *Who were the Nuns? A Prosopographical Study of the English Convents in Exile 1600–1800* http://wwtn.history.qmul.ac.uk/index.html (accessed 25 July 2016); Bowden and Kelly (eds.), *English Convents in Exile*.

by the English Benedictines in Cambrai and Paris, stimulated by their confessor Augustine Baker, and the writings of the Carmelite order have been edited and analysed. Scholars have directed attention to reading and writing practices in the convents, as well as spirituality and devotional exercise, visual and musical culture, life writing and translation, enclosure and the perception of nuns in mainstream English culture. This growth complements the wealth of scholarship on women religious in France, Germany, Italy, Spain and the New World.[5]

This chapter focuses on the conditions of exile and mobility that informed the production and circulation of nuns' writing. Translation was a prerequisite for textual exchange, the means of knowledge transfer. The translator was creator and adaptor as well as mediator of the original for new readers. Women religious were highly attuned to their audiences, retooling the texts they translated in order to serve their own, often polemical, purposes. But this was not solely a female preserve. Male confessors and spiritual directors – as well as fellow travellers outside the convent – collaborated with the nuns and mediated their texts. The study of nuns' writing inevitably provokes questions about the nature of authorship (individual, plural, collaborative), the idea of 'authentic' texts, the layering of identity, the gendering of spirituality and power, as well as translation and transmission. This discussion begins with Mary Ward, whose radical proposal for a non-enclosed order thrust her into conflict with the authorities. The centrality of texts to the struggle of her 'institute' is evident from their translation and suppression. The battle over Ward's reputation is complemented by consideration of the life of the Benedictine Lucy Knatchbull, whose original writings were reproduced by her biographer as proofs of piety that also reveal the immersion of women religious in a writerly devotional culture. The analogy drawn between Knatchbull and St Teresa elevates the former, but founding saints were equally important as models of behaviour in testing times, as is evident from writings of the English and Irish Poor Clares. The appeal of the religious order as sanctuary from such insecurity lies at the heart of the advertisement for the Sepulchrine lifestyle at Liège, published in the early Interregnum.

---

[5] Space constraints forbid citation here of all but the most recent studies. For examples, see: Lay, *Beyond the Cloister*; Jennifer Hillman, *Female Piety and the Catholic Reformation in France* (London: Routledge, 2015); Nicky Hallett, *The Senses in Religious Communities, 1600–1800* (Farnham: Ashgate, 2013).

Mary Ward, Institute of the Blessed Virgin
Mary/Congregation of Jesus

Mary Ward (1585–1645) is a unique figure of the period, whose inspiration of controversy, admiration and hostility across Europe makes her an extreme but all the more illustrative case that highlights the conflict between gender and authority and, consequently, the importance of reputation management. Ward was a Yorkshire recusant who left home in 1606 for the Walloon town of Saint Omer, then under jurisdiction of the Spanish Netherlands and consequently a hive of exiled Catholic activity. Ward was accepted only as a lay sister rather than choir nun; the latter were retired from the world in order to dedicate themselves wholly to devotion, whereas the former liaised between convent and outside world, combining spiritual with manual work (sometimes begging). She was inspired to found the first English convent of this order, ultimately located at Gravelines, in 1607. Prior to full profession in May 1609, Ward received divine direction that this was not to be her vocation. Returning to England for missionary work, she experienced a vision (known as the 'Glory Vision') assuring her of a different path, which was finally revealed to her in another vision in 1611. She was to establish a non-enclosed order, grounded in the principles of the Jesuit constitutions and pedagogical mission.

Ward's absolute insistence on fulfilling this vision led her into conflict with Church authorities, including the various popes of her time. Initially well received by Bishop Blaes of Saint Omer, the project was a success and her institute expanded quickly to Liège, Cologne, Trier, Rome, Naples, Perugia, Munich, Vienna and Pressburg (Bratislava) despite periods of arrest in England and worsening health. In pursuit of her mission, Ward criss-crossed Europe, often travelling on foot with her companions, sometimes offered coaches by aristocratic supporters. The flurry of expansions hit a brick wall at Prague, where local opposition prevented a new house opening.

Many of these foundations were short-lived; opposition to her radical project mounted as fast as her new houses. The sticking points were significant, and gendered. Ignatius Loyola had prohibited the Jesuits from cultivating a women's order, and the directive of convent enclosure had been retrenched at the Council of Trent (1545–63).[6] The Ursuline order, whose founder Angela Merici proposed a similar mission, was formally enclosed

---

[6] See Elizabeth Makowski, *Canon Law and Cloistered Women: Periculoso and its Commentators, 1289–1545* (Washington, DC: Catholic University of America, 1997).

in 1572. More importantly, Jesuits were not subordinate to local bishops; Ward's proposal was for a community of women who would take vows but operate in the world under a female superior, directly under the authority of Rome. This was unacceptable to the hierarchy. Pope Urban VIII finally ordered the suppression of Ward's institute via a papal bull in 1631.[7]

Texts were central to the institute's battle for survival. Ward's letters and petitions to members of the Church hierarchy made the case time and again for the integrity of her vision and its divine sanction. During her imprisonment in Germany in 1631, she smuggled out instructions to her followers by writing letters in lemon juice. Her ingenuity in textual communication also extended to glass. In London in 1618, she called on Lambeth Palace (home to the Archbishop of Canterbury): 'she left her Name, and that she had beene there to see him written in the glasse Window with a Diamond'.[8] In doing so she joined such exalted company as Elizabeth I, Lady Jane Grey and Mary, Queen of Scots, whose window verses were made during their incarcerations. There are allusions to window poems throughout the seventeenth century, although the only surviving early modern examples in England are the quatrains by Katherine Philips at Haddon Hall, Derbyshire, recently discovered by Elizabeth Hageman.[9] All Ward's texts were preserved, translated and circulated by her female followers. Their transmission was an act of defiance. Church authorities did their utmost to suppress relevant documentation: the Vatican archives concerning Ward were not accessible until the 1980s. Moreover, the key texts themselves have only recently emerged in the public domain. The first edition of the multilingual Ward's writings, in German, was published in 2007, followed by a selective English edition of the major works in 2008.[10] Despite her international notoriety, then, Mary Ward is representative of the tardy arrival of nuns' writings to scholarly debates about early modern women.

Autobiographical Fragments

Ward's consciousness of a public audience for her story is clear from the survival of seven autobiographical fragments. None are finished; these

---

[7] Immolata Wetter, *Mary Ward Under the Shadow of the Inquisition 1630–1637*, trans. Bernadette Ganne and Patricia Harriss (Oxford: Way Books, 2006), 129–40 and 213–18.

[8] Ward, *Mary Ward*, 22.

[9] Hageman, 'Afterword', 314–17.

[10] Ursula Dirmeier (ed.), *Mary Ward und ihre Gründung: Die Quellentexte bis 1645*, 4 vols. (Münster: Aschendorff Verlag, 2007); Ward, *Mary Ward*.

are drafts toward a fuller narrative of her life. In an introduction, Ward makes a rhetorical move that is typical of nuns' writing (and not unlike the modesty topos employed more widely by early modern women): legitimacy and authority are located in the male superior.[11] Self-assertion is masked by apparent deference to male direction. Father Robert Lee charged Ward to write her story, to do so before any trip to England, where 'my life or liberty might be endaingered' and to 'leave yt sealed upp with our company' for safekeeping.[12] The longest and most cohesive of these fragments was composed in Italian, 1624–26. The fragments focus on her childhood, reworking specific episodes that illustrated her spiritual awakening and evolution; they resemble drafts toward a *bildungsroman*. Her family's recusant credentials are the starting-point, her parents and grandmother having been imprisoned on various occasions for their beliefs (two relatives were convicted gunpowder plotters).[13] Deliveries from adversity – such as arranged marriage or a house fire – are presented as signs of divine providence (another trope that was not limited to Catholic women's life writing).[14] The Italian fragment relates in affective terms her emotions and shifting motivations in deliberating over leaving the Walloon convent, founding and then leaving the English Poor Clare convent, and her 'Glory Vision'.[15] This latter revelation – the foundation of her driving mission – was consistently rewritten in her letters and petitions.

'A Briefe Relation'

For the women who took up Ward's vision, there was an imperative to defend and vindicate their founder, who had been vilified at the highest levels of the Church. 'A Briefe Relation. Of the holy Life, and happy Death, of our dearest Mother, of blessed memory, Mistress Mary Ward' was a biography composed in the years immediately following her death, between 1645 and 1650, by her companion Mary Poyntz with the assistance of Winefried Wigmore. As with Ward's autobiography, the spur to

---

[11] Nicky Hallett cites Teresa of Avila (1515–82) as an influential model for this; see 'Shakespeare's Sisters: Anon and the Authors in Early Modern Convents', in Bowden and Kelly(eds.), *English Convents in Exile*, 140.

[12] Ward, *Mary Ward*, 104.

[13] Wallace, *Strong Women*, 155–6.

[14] See, for example, the spiritual autobiography of Mary Rich, Countess of Warwick, whose refusal to marry her father's choice is presented as providential; BL Add. MS 27357, fol. 4[r].

[15] See Ward, *Mary Ward*, 121–40, for an English translation.

composition is attributed to male authority: the Spanish Carmelite and supporter, Dominicus a Jesu Maria, 'wou'd often Times tell us, we must not be so ungratfull, as to let her Life and Example passe without note, not onely for our owne, but others their profit'.[16] From the outset, then, this life-writing project was intended for wider circulation. Wigmore translated it into French before 1657. Another seventeenth-century French copy survives, as does a German translation dating from the early eighteenth century. Their recent editor, Christina Kenworthy-Browne, argues that the two earliest manuscripts of the English text derive from an earlier copytext. In addition to these three English manuscripts, one German and two French translated copies, an *Italian Life*, possibly also written by Mary Poyntz when superior of the institute and based in Rome between 1654 and 1662, is extant.[17]

The struggle to implement her ideas played out as a contest over Ward's public reputation. As early as 1617, she was perceived to be dangerous as much as pious. The Archbishop of Canterbury reportedly stated that 'she did more hurt then 6 Jesuits'.[18] Technically not nuns, as their institute was denied papal approbation, Ward and her followers attracted a range of popular epithets, from 'English Ladies', through to the more derogatory 'Jesuitesses' and 'galloping girls' – the latter capturing the threat of women operating independently in the world.[19] On her final return to England in 1639, her reputation preceded her; her 'Ennemyes had beene so bold as to make it passe for an undoubted truth that she was a condemned prisoner for Life in the Inquisition, and nothing but her presence cou'd have cleared this thruth [sic]'.[20] She was subjected to surveillance as she travelled Europe – spies were appointed by the Vatican, the English government and the Inquisition. This very public notoriety is balanced in the biography by naming her champions: among others, the rulers of the Spanish Netherlands Isabella of Spain and Albrecht VII of Austria, Elector Maximilian I and Elisabeth of Bavaria, and Emperor Ferdinand II. This alignment of forces has led David Wallace to interpret the clash as one of northern versus southern European worldviews and temperaments.[21]

---

[16] Ward, *Mary Ward*, 29–30.
[17] Ibid., 1–2; Wallace, *Strong Women*, 140.
[18] Ibid., 21.
[19] Wallace, *Strong Women*, 170–1; see 180–3 for discussion of the Ward-figure in contemporary English drama.
[20] Ward, *Mary Ward*, 65.
[21] Wallace, *Strong Women*, 134.

Ward's determined, unshakeable persistence makes her story one of gender, power and resistance. Her first papal audience in 1622 is described in explicitly gendered terms in the 'Briefe Relation'. Gregory XV 'received her with all fatherly and benigne expresssions', averring that 'much good can come by woemen'.[22] The dissimulation of church authorities in their solicitous reception of Ward in person but implacable hostility to her ideas is resolved in the text by emphasizing Ward's own recourse to divine will. Her insistence on her personal vocation and its divine sanction allowed her to position herself as simultaneously subordinate and unyielding: 'to desist if his Holynes and their Eminencyes thought good she cou'd, but alter or take other she cou'd not'.[23] This dogged refusal to give up on her goal is reiterated throughout the narrative. The assertion of qualities of modesty, obedience and submission is a crucial part of her biographer's strategy. Without fail, Ward's response to all opposition is generous and magnanimous – at no point is she tempted to descend to criticism of her male superiors. The biographer foregrounds episodes of the life that present compliance as characteristic. For example, when her spiritual advisors regret having directed her toward the Walloon convent, Ward insists on submitting to the order's authorities (subsequently, their General Visitor confirms to her that she is free to choose).[24] There is an element of having one's cake and eating it here: her advisors suffer torments of conscience for their misguided counsel; Ward is obedient to all, yet she leaves the convent without blemish. This apparently oxymoronic submission to Church ruling and commitment to her (transgressive) vision is held in tension, even at the moments of starkest conflict – as, for example, when her schools were closed in 1628, 'the true Servant of Christ having long since learned the value of Obedience, humbly submitted, and enjoyed as much peace as if the thing had beene of her owne procuring'.[25]

Like many accounts of pious lives in the period, the 'Briefe Relation' identifies signals of divine approbation. The biographer is careful not to tip into forthright claims to sanctity but she ensures they hover over her narrative. For example, Ward's first word as a child, 'Jesus', is represented as prodigious: 'as it were marked out for heaven, before the time Babes use to speake'. As in other Catholic lives, the groundwork is laid

---

[22] Ward, *Mary Ward*, 24–5.
[23] Ibid., 38.
[24] Ibid., 10–11.
[25] Ibid., 27.

for future beatification by recounting putative miraculous occurrences. Reportage distances the biographer from such imputations. An English Protestant convert, rather than the narrator, remarks of Ward that 'there never was such a Woman but the sacred Mother of God'. Her delivery from seemingly fatal illness in 1631 causes her physician to exclaim that 'to recover in any place had been miracle playne enough, but to recover in that place ... was that God wou'd make it more then playne to be seene to the confusion and reprehension of her Ennemyes'. In a perfect about-face, the double agent assigned to spy on her by the Inquisition, posing as her confessor in Italy, 'by occasion of seeing her admirable Life and conversation, wrott such an Information as they said was not onely sufficient for a Justification, but even a Canonization'.[26] Such accounts of her impact abound, functioning as third-party corroboration of Ward's extraordinary piety and sanctity.

Reliable testimony is the foundation of successful Catholic biography. Poyntz, who was born in 1604, was too young to have been present during the events of her subject's childhood and time in Saint Omer. Nevertheless, she deployed the first-person narrative voice from the out-set, in order to secure her text's status as eye-witness documentation – if not witness to the event described, then at one remove. For example, the generosity of Ward's father is attested: 'and my selfe have heard it spoken of'. Her visit with Ward to the latter's childhood home allows for the fusion of memory, reportage and eye-witness testimony: 'I being at Newby with [Ward] ... the Lady Blakestone recounted with great feeling, the memory was to that Day kept in that Towne'. Her proximity renders credible the use of direct speech in accounts of Ward's various meetings with clerical authorities and it licenses statements such as 'she was wont to recount'.[27] These devices gloss over the moments of slippage between authenticated and recounted speech. Hence, the layers of testimony and reportage, of first- and third-person account, of memory and invention, sustain each other to form a narrative that is equal parts defence, vindication, counter-propaganda and record for the canonization process.

In important ways, this biography is an example of civil war writing by women. Residing in London in 1639, the heightened tensions of imminent war render Ward's earlier clandestine recusant lifestyle impossible; the concluding episodes of the life relate the women's removal to Yorkshire and experiences of the siege of York in 1644. The narrative

[26] Ibid., 22, 52, and 57.
[27] Ibid., 3 and 12.

remains on-message. Their safe passage, first to the remote Hutton Rugby, then Heworth, thence the city of York, and then out of York again following the successful parliamentarian siege, is attributed to providence. In particular, their evasion of the soldiers' notice as they pass within and without the city walls and the 'very remarquable' preservation of the chapel and Ward's own chamber from destruction at Heworth are presented as signs of God's protection.[28] The perspective on events offered here is neither parliamentarian nor royalist. The imperative to reiterate and reinforce Ward's piety and sanctity renders secondary the political allegiances at stake in the civil wars. But it is warfare that jeopardizes the community and forces its evacuation. Mobility and enclosure – apparent opposites – are reconciled, as Wallace observes, through Ward's presence: the various lives 'record Mary Ward's charismatic transformations of a carriage, a bedroom, or alehouse lodgings into sanctified space, suggestive of religious enclosure'. The 'crucial point', he argues, 'is that a female community be allowed to impose and regulate *an enclosure of one's own*' (his italics). If the 'Briefe Relation' is, as Wallace has argued, part hagiography and part romance, it is also a rebuttal and a conduct book.[29] Born of the same moment as narratives that processed the civil wars but also such bestselling guides as Jeremy Taylor's *Rules and Exercises of Holy Living* (1650) and *Holy Dying* (1651), the lives of divinely noticed women offered models of good behaviour in times of adversity.

Ward was an outlier – this is why she was so troubling to the hierarchy. The circulation and transmission of her story were vital in the face of suppression. It was necessary to produce and exchange texts in order to counter derogatory appellations and uphold the institute's good name. But more broadly, the particular value of the religious life (whether Catholic or Protestant) to inspire others required that it be distributed. The community did not confine themselves to the written word. A series of fifty paintings, known as *The Painted Life*, were commissioned by Ward's companions in the seventeenth century. They are now held in Augsburg, by the Congregation of Jesus – the name intended for her institute by Ward, and formally permitted only as recently as 2004 (known as the Institute of the Blessed Virgin Mary from 1749).[30] The promulgation of her reputation in the face of such hostility has been as resolute as Ward herself.

---

[28] Ibid., 71.
[29] Wallace, *Strong Women*, 174 and 140.
[30] See www.congregatiojesu.org/en/maryward_painted_life.asp (accessed 25 July 2016).

Lucy Knatchbull, Benedictines

Although the preservation and transmission of many texts authored by women religious was mediated by women, their genesis was often presented as collaborative with the male confessor, as we have seen. Yet the agents involved in the production of nuns' writings could also be more hands-on. With collective authorship, the boundaries between individual contributions are often indistinct and the limitations of the single-author model of authorial credit become apparent. Such is the case with the writings of Elizabeth (in religion Lucy) Knatchbull (1584–1629), who left England at the age of seventeen to join the exiled Benedictine convent at Brussels, subsequently becoming first abbess of the same order's community at Ghent.[31] Like Ward, Knatchbull was urged by her confessor to write her own life. The autobiography that survives covers her time in Brussels. It is the first part of Toby Matthew's life, on which he worked between 1642 and 1651. Matthew was a prolific devotional writer, translator and polemicist. Son of the Protestant Archbishop of York, he was exiled three times from England due to his conversion to Catholicism and proselytizing activities. His biography of Knatchbull, based on her own writings, circulated in at least two manuscript versions.[32] However, its tenor is markedly more focused on interior spirituality than that of Mary Ward.

'The relation of the holy and happy life and death of the Ladye Lucie Knatchbull' is framed by Knatchbull's own writings. The first section is comprised of her autobiography; the second, Matthew's account of her spiritual life; the third, his selection of her letters. Hence, the text is a generic amalgam: a biography that is also an edition, comprising autobiography, letters and meditations. The drama of her autobiography lies in its access to Knatchbull's acute experience of faith. Beginning with her realization of her vocation and continuing into her profession and early years in Brussels, the paradigm is one of extremes: periods of crisis alleviated by 'Comforts', moments of intense, mystical assurance that result from the application of the Ignatian model of spiritual meditation (itself controversial within many communities).[33] Her own accounts are

---

[31] All professed names are supplied; however, individuals are cited here according to the name by which they are currently best known.

[32] See Nicky Hallett (ed.), 'The Life of Lucy Knatchbull', in Bowden and Kelly (eds.), *English Convents in Exile*, vol. III, 159.

[33] Hallett (ed.), 'Life of Knatchbull', 163. For discussion of debates over Ignatian spirituality, see Goodrich, *Faithful Translators*, 145–83.

recycled by Matthew in the biography that follows. Knatchbull describes a particular vision as occurring on St Teresa's feast day; the experience is similar to 'Comeing out of a most delightful trance'. She describes 'our Lords drawing my affections to him, and & [sic] the Sunnes drawing of vapours from the earth; and the eye of understanding ... as a beame of Moates to pass from mee to our Lord with this my Soule beganne to be wise; for now she was made soberly drunke'. In his summary account of her six visions, Matthew retells this story, revising her description and reiterating her words: 'he was pleased to draw her then as some beam of Moates might passe, or as the Sunne drawse vapours up from the earth, and she sayth, this favour made her become wise, and Soberly Drunk ... as out of a most delightfull Trance'.[34] Repetition drives home the language for the reader, ensuring that its significance is not lost. The autobiography is presented as evidence of her mystical experience both on its own terms and reworked for conventional biography.

Both versions draw attention to the occasion: the feast day of St Teresa. Matthew's penultimate publication in his lifetime was a translation of Teresa's autobiography, *The Flaming Hart* (1642), and its influence is evident throughout his biography of Knatchbull. In this particular instance, as Nicky Hallett has noted, the image of the vapours of the sun echoes Teresa's description of spiritual understanding as a light that is 'more cleare then the Sunne'. Knatchbull had considered founding an English Teresian house and echoes Teresa's *The Interior Castle* elsewhere in her autobiography, when she compares her revelations to 'flashes of Lighting'. Matthew's biography regularly draws attention to the parallels between his two biographical subjects, even quoting extensively from his *Flaming Hart* to illustrate their similarity.[35]

The life of St Teresa offered an approved, influential model of behaviour for women religious. It performed a dual function when applied to the life of another, as here, suggesting both the biographical subject's aspirational model but also a homologous exaltation of the subject herself. Mary Ward's biographer was careful to place overt terms of sanctity in the mouths of her protagonists; Poyntz herself did not argue straightforwardly for the miraculous effects of her subject. Similarly, Matthew attempts to disavow the suggestion of equivalence. 'Nott yett that I am so foolish, as to Compare this Blessed Creature with those Saincts', the biographer states in one breath yet in the next says:

[34] Hallett (ed.), 'Life of Knatchbull', 169 and 178.
[35] Ibid., 169; 387n24; 166, 387n12; 163, 386n5; and 187–8.

But I thinke I may safely affirme, that certainly both these and those were
of the self-same kind, in the supernaturall way though yet different as
much as you will in the degree, and who soever will take the paines, and
pleasure to read of Saint Teresas [sic] Life of the flaming hart; will clearly
find the truth of that which I am delivering here.[36]

A tangle of qualifications, this sentence both asserts and denies the parallel being drawn, leaving the ultimate judgement to the reader (and conveniently signalling his own recent work in the process). Moreover, the
reader's response surely rests on assessment of Matthew as editor. If the
autobiography is faithfully transcribed, the origin of the Teresian influence rests with Knatchbull herself. But if Matthew's editorial approach
was interventionist, it would have implications for our understanding
of collective authorship in this instance, as well as for the feminist goal
of recovering a woman's writing. Such suspicions might be allayed by
Matthew's determination, in the third part, to have Knatchbull speak for
herself by publishing a range of letters and fragments.

The limitations of biography led Matthew to experiment with a different kind of narrative. Seeking the best way to represent her virtues,
he resolved on 'a different, and perhaps fitter way'. The reader remains
central and the promise of the 'authentic' text lies in intimate access:
'Namely by letting you see, what passed even between God and her
self in that kind; as also between her & her Ghostly Fathers, and other
Spirituall frinds, to whome she gave inward notice of her self, for this
in fine will amount, to be also a kind of history of her life'.[37] The mid-
dleman-biographer aims to disappear. For the vanishing trick to work,
the reader must accept his editorial scrupulosity (and ignore her/his
now-voyeuristic position). Seven of Knatchbull's letters to her confessor
are reproduced expressly as 'Evidence … which proves the Spiritt, and
the Sanctitie of her Soule … all of them written with her owne hand'.
Further proofs of her piety are selected from her 'Scattered Papers'.
Matthew claims these quotations to be verbatim: 'they beginne as fol-
loweth word, for word'.[38] Two examples of her spiritual exercises – 'Her
Contemplation upon the Circumcition' and 'Her Contemplation upon
the Ecce home [John 19:5]' – are also printed. These are representative,
Matthew writes: 'the account … of every Meditation is written, and is
still remaining, and declared in her owne hand) they are soe very many

---

[36] Ibid., 194.
[37] Ibid., 193.
[38] Ibid., 202–3.

and would take up soe much roome, as that it would make this discourse
to bigg' – recalling the decision-making process of Anthony Walker, editing his wife's Protestant meditations half a century later.[39] This editorial
self-reflexivity in itself suggests fidelity to Knatchbull's originals and,
by extension, that Matthew elaborated upon rather than initiated the
Teresian analogies. This is further supported by his concern to validate
the text by consulting Knatchbull's confessor – an action which causes
Knatchbull's literary legacy to run almost out of control. Matthew's motivation was 'to learne of him, as an eye witness who was likely to know
most of the matter; whether al that which I had sett downe and shewed
to him, had bine rightly conceaved, and well declared by me Concerning
her'. Not only does the confessor confirm its accuracy but he produces
additional texts written by Knatchbull, which Matthew cannot resist
reproducing consecutively, 'without any intermixed discourse' of interpretation.[40] Ten more meditations follow.

Knatchbull's writing is presented as proof of her sincerity and piety –
but most of all, as evidence of the profundity of her mystical experience.
Rather than the persistent conflicts with Church hierarchy experienced
by Mary Ward, inner spiritual struggle is the hallmark of Knatchbull's life
and writing. The lives and writings of both women were composed and
circulated as models for imitation. Their points of difference from each
other demonstrate how varied the models of exemplary Catholic womanhood could be in the seventeenth century. Like many life narratives of
exemplary Protestant women, the signs of divine providence abound in
these biographies. But the potential for sainthood lends Catholic biographies an edge that fuels their embrace of the miraculous.

Elizabeth Evelinge and Mary Bonaventure Browne, Poor Clares

For particular orders, their founding saint's life was paradigmatic. It tra-
versed houses and orders as well as languages. The English Poor Clares
at Aire, for example, printed *The History of the Angelicall Virgin Glorious
S. Clare* in 1635. This was an English translation from the French version by the Franciscan priest François Hendricq – itself an extracted

---

[39] Ibid., 202; Marie-Louise Coolahan, 'Literary Memorialization and the Posthumous Construction
of Female Authorship', in Andrew Gordon and Thomas Rist (eds.), *The Arts of Remembrance in
Early Modern England: Memorial Cultures of the Post Reformation* (Farnham: Ashgate, 2013),
172–5.
[40] Hallett (ed.), 'Life of Knatchbull', 207.

translation from the Latin history of his order by the Irish Franciscan Luke Wadding, *Annales ordinis minorum*, the first two volumes of which were published in 1625 and 1628. These were not straightforward translations: Hendricq's version modified the text to suit his community at Saint Omer; and the Poor Clare version further alters the original, even to the extent of inserting a new chapter, as an intervention into a controversy over whether to follow local episcopal or Franciscan authority.[41] The Franciscan order had a particular interest: St Clare had been inspired to establish her community by St Francis, her contemporary (this was exactly the kind of arrangement common among the religious orders and expressly prohibited by Loyola in his Jesuit constitutions). Their common heritage and shared goals meant that defined channels of circulation were in place and that textual interactions were mutual, multilingual and multidirectional.

Translation and adaptation were conditions of textual exchange among the religious orders, and this muddied the waters of attribution and authorial credit. Where communities of women religious produced translations of saints' lives, as well as chronicles and obituaries, individual writerly contributions were often subsumed by the collective. As Hallett observes, such self-effacement was an inevitable corollary of subjugation to the collective as well as the divine, a product of doctrinal humility as well as strategic 'positioning ... against inquisitorial review'.[42] What's more, as Jaime Goodrich has shown, anonymity in itself could enable individual nuns to align their personal views with those of the corporate body, 'transforming their publications from the work of one nun into representations of English monasticism'.[43] A culture in which foundational texts are exchanged, translated, adapted and repositioned for local use embraced fluid concepts of authorship. Hence, the attribution of the *History of ... S. Clare* is ambiguously presented. The dedication is signed by the collective but the title page identifies Catherine Bentley (in religion Magdalen Augustine; 1592–1659). Other authoritative sources, however, attribute this work (and the 1621 *Life of St. Catherine*

---

[41] See: Marie-Louise Coolahan, 'Identity Politics and Nuns' Writing', *Women's Writing*, 14 (2007), 308–11; Jaime Goodrich, '"Ensigne-Bearers of Saint Clare": Elizabeth Evelinge's Early Translations and the Restoration of English Franciscanism', in White (ed.), *English Women*, 83–100.

[42] Hallett, 'Shakespeare's Sisters', 142.

[43] Goodrich, *Faithful Translators*, 183. See also Victoria Van Hyning, 'Naming Names: Chroniclers, Scribes and Editors of St Monica's Convent, Louvain, 1631–1906', in Bowden and Kelly (eds.), *English Convents in Exile*, 88.

of Bologna) to Elizabeth Evelinge (in religion Catherine Magdalen; 1597–1668).

Further extending the chain of textual transfer, Evelinge's translation was appropriated by the Irish branch of the order in a translation of *their* foundational text, the chronicle history composed by Mary Bonaventure Browne. The Irish Poor Clares had been founded in 1629 by five nuns who had themselves professed in the exiled English convent at Gravelines, founded by Mary Ward. They carried with them the English vernacular texts that had been produced on the Continent: the *Rule* and revised constitutions, which had been printed in Flanders in 1621 and 1622, and also the life of their founder. Composed in the Irish language from her exile in Spain, Browne's chronicle was carefully researched, the product of collaboration with the various host convents where her sisters had ended up after the banishment of all religious from Ireland in 1653 (ordered by Cromwell). It was sent to the Poor Clare convent in Galway when it was re-founded in 1672. The extant version is a late seventeenth-century translation from Irish to English, made in that convent (the original was destroyed during the Williamite Wars).[44] Either Browne or her translator was familiar with Evelinge's life of St Clare. The description of a military attack on the Bethlehem convent in 1642 echoes that text, suggesting that its model of exemplary response to calamity was internalized by the nuns. Unlike the case of Knatchbull, whose own exemplarity is reinforced through her similarity to Teresa, here St Clare provides a model for how to cope with siege.

The religious order was the site of textual production, translation and exchange, and the mobility of texts facilitated the transhistorical modelling of exemplary female devotion as well as situational flexibility in dealing with circumstances of warfare. The ideal of enclosure could be challenging even for those who sought to meet it fully. The chronicle articulated and bonded communal identity. As a means to shape and claim ownership of the community's story, it embraced collective rather than individual authorial credit. But the Church's insistence on enclosure – so great a problem for Mary Ward and her companions – is revealed as aspirational rather than always realistic in these texts. External events unavoidably impinge on these histories. They are not simply stories of enclosed, sealed-off devotional communities but also, inevitably, reflections of the experience of living through difficult times and religious

---

[44] See Coolahan, *Women, Writing, and Language*, 63–101.

persecution. The Irish Poor Clares, for example, were constantly on the move – from Dublin to Lough Ree and thence to found sister convents, to Galway as a consequence of the wars of the 1640s, and to exile on the Continent thereafter. As Hallett has shown of the exiled Carmelite convents, 'Enclosure was often breached, sometimes for building work, or when the nuns gave hospitality to influential visitors' such as exiled royalists.[45] Given the volatile and insecure political circumstances of early modern Europe, worldly events often forced communities of women religious out of the cloister.

Susan Hawley, Sepulchrines

Notwithstanding that reality, it is likely that this very instability drove women to join convents in the first place. The appeal of order, security and seclusion in times of strife was exploited by Susan (in religion, Mary of the Conception) Hawley (1622–1706) in her *Briefe Relation of the Order and Institute, of the English Religious Women at Liège*, printed in 1652, the year she became first prioress of that convent. Directly addressed to an English audience, this narrative is an advertisement for religious life. The text was explicitly pitched in terms of public relations, at an exhausted populace:

> These English Religious Women at Liège reflecting how little their Order is known in England, because this their only House of our Nation is but lately begun, have desired this short Paper should be publish'd. For they conceive their Institute to be so exceedingly agreeable and sutable to our English natures, that many by the knowledge of it, may be invited to serve God in it, who otherwise in the world may perish most miserably.[46]

There was a real audience for this kind of material. It filled a vacuum lamented by Mary Ward, for whom the absence of information about religious orders meant that she could not choose which to enter: 'for I had noe instructions tuchinge anie perticuler Order, nor any means to inform my self in that living in a cuntrie infected etc. nether had I the curredg to aske anie one the difirence betwixt them'.[47]

These were Sepulchrine nuns, so called (as their pamphlet explains) because they were originally founded at the Holy Sepulchre in Jerusalem.

---

[45] Nicky Hallett, 'Philip Sidney in the Cloister: The Reading Habits of English Nuns in Seventeenth-Century Antwerp', *Journal for Early Modern Cultural Studies*, 12 (2012), 92.
[46] Hawley, *Briefe Relation*, n.p.
[47] Ward, *Mary Ward*, 118.

They were the only exiled English house of this order, founded from the Flemish convent at Tongres in 1644, and therefore needed to pursue recruits more aggressively than well-established orders such as the Benedictines, who had seven English convents in France and the Low Countries. The *Briefe Relation* builds on the allure of retirement from the world by setting out in detail their origin narrative, citing such authorities as Saints Augustine, Ambrose and Basil. The emphasis on the order's antiquity is designed to conjure up a nostalgic conservatism, stressing the roots of the community (which had, after all, only recently been founded).

Its Englishness was a key feature of the sales pitch. St Helena is claimed as 'Patroness of our Monastery, and a most noble Empress of our Nation'; her adoption of the Sepulchrine habit neatly aligning her (legendary) national identity with that of the order.[48] A typical day in the convent is described in order to give the reader a sense of the routine and regularity involved in convent life, making it resemble 'a handbook for potential members'.[49] Five different levels of membership are described. In addition to choir and lay sisters, common to all convents, circumscribed admission is open to three further categories: the disabled, 'young Gentlewomen desirous of good breeding' and – an option recommended particularly to her English audience as 'A most happy state to be found no where else in our Nation' – retired dames:

> These must be ancient Gentlewomen of Quality, or Ladies who desire to live a quiet, devout, retired life. They are not oblig'd to make any vow, tho' it be commendable in them, if they make Vows obliging only for the time they stay in the Monastery. They live within the Inclosure in chambers apart, observing certain Rules very sutable to that devout state, as long as they continue in the Monastery … They may wear any modest and grave Habit … If they desire it, they may keep a maid.[50]

This is the convent as sojourn, as temporary retreat from the world, and it was potentially lucrative. The penultimate paragraph sets out the tariffs, competitively ('no. where more moderate then here'): £300 for a choir sister; £400–500 'for a defective Sister', depending on her disability; £26 per annum for a retired dame; and £15–20 for a student – 'All these foresaid summs to be paid at London', upfront and in advance.[51] The text's

---

[48] Hawley, *Briefe Relation*, 37–8.
[49] Caroline Bowden, '"A distribution of tyme": Reading and Writing Practices in the English Convents in Exile', *Tulsa Studies in Women's Literature*, 31 (2012), 101.
[50] Hawley, *Briefe Relation*, 53–4.
[51] Ibid., 54.

promotional function is copper-fastened, finally, by geographical directions: 'The best and shortest way from England to Liège, is by Holland to Rotterdam, thence to Boisleduc, then to Maestricht, so to Liege'.

Conclusion

Convent membership nurtured as co-extensive a set of identities that in other contexts were perceived as conflicting: nuns gave up their individual worldly identities when they took names in religion; they belonged to the particular house as well as to their nation; they belonged above all to the order, an affiliation that transcended country boundaries and allegiances in favour of commitment to the form of life and prayer prescribed in the order's rule. These identities dovetailed together, ideally complementing each other. They facilitated textual translation and exchange, and informed a fluid, open-minded attitude to authorial attribution. Texts were central to these women's vocations and practice, especially when controversy arose. The orders were transnational networks that facilitated the transmission of texts. Such exchanges depended on translation, and translation involved degrees of adaptation and transformation. Translation is also an act of mediation; the shepherding of nuns' writing to wider circulation, by women and men, opens up new ways of understanding collaborative composition just as the priority of communal identity compels us to probe the distinction between individual and collective credit. The study of nuns' writing requires a capacious approach to authorship and the text. Finally, it is clear that if enclosure meant that textual mobility was essential, then forced evacuation and travel equally found their way into the texts produced by women religious. Writing generated in early modern convents – increasingly and exponentially available to modern scholars – warrants investigation for its perspectives on historical events as well as for the negotiation of internal politics and spirituality.[52]

[52] Research for this chapter was funded by the European Research Council under the European Union's Seventh Framework Programme (FP/2007–2013/ERC Grant Agreement no. 615545).

15

Motherhood and Women's Writing in Early Seventeenth-Century England
Legacies, Catechisms, and Popular Polemic

Paula McQuade

In a letter to her daughter likely written in 1668, Lucy Hutchinson suggests that motherhood had a considerable influence upon her development as a writer and thinker. Describing her instruction of her children and servants, she "assures" her daughter: "I have by that means learnt more then by all my hearing and study, having found the Lord to open my owne understanding and to warme my heart while I have conscientiously labored to communicate the light he gave me."[1] Hutchinson's remarks, which connect domestic religious instruction with the growth of her "understanding," suggest that we might need to think more deeply about the relationship between maternity and women's writing in early modern England. As mothers, women were responsible for the religious education of their household. This responsibility encouraged women to deepen their religious knowledge and to develop their interpretive skills. It also provided them with a creative way to show their loving concern for their children's spiritual development. Drawing upon print and manuscript sources, I explore in this chapter how maternity fostered women's literary engagements in three of the most popular early seventeenth-century genres: legacies, catechisms, and polemics. Early modern women bequeathed legacies to their children as testimonies of their love and concern; they composed original catechisms tailored to

---

Original spelling and capitalization have been retained in quotes from manuscripts and printed texts, although contractions have silently been expanded. I have modernized conventions such as long "s" and archaic uses of "i," "j," "u," and "v." Thorns are rendered "th" and yoghs "y." I have regularized the spelling of Biblical books and modernized the names of Biblical places.

[1] Hutchinson's legacy was published in 1817 together with her translation of a Latin treatise by John Owen as Lucy Hutchinson, *Principles of the Christian Religion*, 7. Elizabeth Clarke, who is preparing a modern edition of the text as part of *The Works of Lucy Hutchinson*, suggests 1668 as the most likely date of the manuscript's composition: see Elizabeth Clarke, "Preparationism in Lucy Hutchinson's 'Principles of the Christian Religion'" in Jonathan Willis (ed.), *Sin and Salvation in Reformation England* (London: Routledge, 2015), 191–206 at 191.

the interests and abilities of their children; and they appealed to loving motherhood as a defense against anti-women sentiment. I argue that, for some women, motherhood offered both a culturally sanctioned space for authorship and a defense against popular misogyny.

Maternal Legacies: Desire and Motherly Advice

One of the most frequently reprinted genres in seventeenth-century England, the maternal legacy has been traditionally defined in terms of its purpose: writing that a mother composes or compiles to instruct her children.[2] Like other kinds of miscellanies, (a popular genre in the period), the maternal legacy is a compilation of diverse textual forms, both original and transcribed, with a mother's dedication of the work to her children and also including letters, poetry, prayers, transcriptions or translations of devotional works, confessions of faith, and catechisms. Twenty maternal legacies survive in manuscript and print; there were likely many more.[3] Manuscript maternal legacies were often family heirlooms, treasured as textual representations of a female relative's piety and devotion. This may help to explain the relatively high survival rates of these texts.

The different genres that a mother includes in her legacy reflect her concerns, just as the works transcribed in a manuscript miscellany reflect the compiler's preoccupations and aesthetic judgments.[4] In *The Mother's Blessing* (1616), one of the earliest printed mother's legacies, the evangelically minded Dorothy Leigh includes a poem, "A Counsell to My Children," as well as practical and spiritual advice in prose. Elizabeth Joscelin's *The Mother's Legacie to her Unborne Child* (1622; 1624, second edition) includes advice on avoiding sloth, pride, and drunkenness, and keeping "holy the Sabbath day" but few prayers, urging her unborn child to use "Dr. Smith's morning prayer; then which I know not a better." In contrast, the conservative Protestant Lady Elizabeth Richardson's *A Ladies Legacie to her Daughters* (1645) consists almost entirely of prayers and spiritual meditations. The Catholic Elizabeth Grymeston's *Miscelanea, Meditations, Memoratives* (1604) is one of the more generically diverse of the printed mother's legacies: it includes poetry, meditations, a

---

[2] Heller, *Mother's Legacy*, 2.
[3] Ibid., 6.
[4] See Burke, "Miscellanies." See also Joshua Eckhardt and Daniel Starza Smith, "Introduction: The Emergence of the English Miscellany," in Joshua Eckhardt and Daniel Starza Smith (eds.), *Manuscript Miscellanies in Early Modern England* (Aldershot: Ashgate, 2014), 1–16.

"pathetical speech in the person of Dives in the torments of hell," and even a madrigal.[5] Manuscript legacies display a similar generic diversity. Katherine Thomas, a conformist Protestant widow residing in a small village in Herefordshire, includes prayers, verse elegies (both original and transcribed), catechisms, and transcriptions of Church of England and Catholic devotional works. The godly Protestant Lady Ann Montagu includes a letter to her stepchildren, prayers, a copy of a catechism by Joseph Hall, and a 160-stanza poem, written in ballad meter.[6] Lucy Hutchinson's maternal legacy includes a letter to her daughter and a treatise, *On the Principles of the Christian Religion*, and may also have originally included Hutchinson's translation of John Owen's *On Theology*.

Authors of print legacies draw upon their positions as domestic religious instructors to legitimize their textual productions. Leigh recognizes that her children may "marvell" at her decision not to follow "the usuall custome of Women" and "exhort you by word and admonitions, rather than by writing," but she defends her decision in terms of the "motherly affection that I bare unto you all, which made me now (as I hath done heretofore) forget my selfe in regard of you."[7] Demonstrating her scripturalism, Joscelin draws upon Psalm 69.9 ("For the zeale of thine house hath eaten me") when she observes that she writes because she could find "no other means" to express her "motherly zeale." The allusion invites the reader to compare Joscelin's maternal love with the psalmist's fervent desire to serve the Lord.[8] Echoing a Jacobean commonplace, Elizabeth Grymeston equates maternal instruction with love, remarking that "there is no mother can ... more naturally manifest hir affection, than in advising hir children our of her owne experience."[9]

Women who composed legacies believed that they could most fully express their maternal love by contributing to their children's spiritual welfare. Katherine Thomas includes in her manuscript a letter addressed to "my Deare Children wch Survive." The phrasing is poignant, since we know that three of Thomas's five children died young. Her letter simultaneously memorializes her dead children and acknowledges that

---

[5] Leigh, *Mother's Blessing*; Joscelin, *Mother's Legacie*, 77 and 45–6; Richardson, *A Ladies Legacie*; Grymeston, *Micelanea*. sig. A3ᵛ.

[6] NRO Montagu MSS .3, fol. 241, MS 4340A, The Loose Papers of Lady Ann Montagu; National Library of Wales, Aberstwyth, Katherine Thomas, Commonplace Book. Neither manuscript includes page numbers consistently. Thomas's manuscript can be found in *Perdita Manuscripts, 1500–1700*.

[7] Leigh, *Mother's Blessing*, 3–4.

[8] Joscelin, *Mother's Legacie*, sig. B1ʳ. All scriptural quotations are from *GB*.

[9] Grymeston, *Miscelanea*, sig. A3ʳ.

her surviving children will read this after their mother's death. She then provides six precepts reflecting her "desire and motherly advice." These precepts join with the other material contained in her legacy to create an image of a devout, literate, and loving mother, whose concern for her children does not end with physical death. Similarly, Joscelin describes her legacy as a textual representation of her love and concern for her children's spiritual welfare, explaining to her child that nothing can "stay my hand from expressing how much I covet thy salvation. Therefore deare childe, reade here my love."[10] Expanding and elaborating upon the popular description of mothers' writings as a legally binding bequest, Hutchinson urges her "deare" daughter to consider her treatise as "a testimony of my best and most tender love for you."[11]

Because they often include transcribed materials, maternal legacies can tell us a great deal about early modern women's reading practices. The recusant Elizabeth Grymeston includes poems by the Catholic poets Richard Rowlands and Robert Southwell, as well as paraphrases of Patristic sources and selections from the Vulgate in her *Miscelanea*.[12] Katherine Thomas lived in a small village near the Welsh border. Despite her distance from the bookselling capital, she includes material from a wide variety of printed sources, including, for example, funeral inscriptions found within St Paul's Cathedral in London. Thomas obtained these inscriptions from William Dugdale's *The History of St. Paul's Cathedral* (1658), demonstrating that the circulation of books in early modern England could counter the geographical isolation of rural women. She also transcribes passages from a prohibited Catholic devotional text, John Heigham's *The Life of Our Lord and Savior Jesus Christ* (1622), suggesting the continuing popularity of early seventeenth-century Catholic devotionals among late seventeenth-century Protestant readers.

The legacies of Leigh and Joscelin include few non-scriptural sources, instead relying almost wholly upon the Geneva Bible. The Geneva Bible's extensive annotations and cross-references made it a logical choice for godly women readers.[13] As we shall see, it was also relied upon or consulted by the female catechists Katherine Fitzwilliam and Dorothy Burch, as well as by the polemicist Rachel Speght. Leigh is a competent exegete, unafraid to paraphrase a verse's meaning or comment upon its

---

[10] Joscelin, *Mother's Legacie*, 11.
[11] Hutchinson, *Principles of the Christian Religion*, 8.
[12] Snook, *Women, Reading*, 87–8.
[13] Molekamp, *Women and the Bible*, 28.

implications.[14] Joscelin's scripturalism is remarkable.[15] Educated by her grandfather William Chaderton, Bishop of Chester and Lincoln, and Lady Margaret and Regius Professor of Divinity at Cambridge, Joscelin ranges among the Old and New Testaments with equal facility.[16] When urging her child to seek to serve God above all else, Joscelin quotes from the Psalms, likely by memory: "if thou covet pleasure, set David's delight before thine eies: I have had more delight in thy testimonies then in all manner of riches Psalm 119."[17] The wide-ranging citations, elegantly integrated into her text, support her claim concerning the superiority of spiritual pleasures, just as her final citation urges further reading and contemplation.[18]

Trained from birth to avoid publicity, most early modern women composed and exchanged legacies in manuscript in order to cultivate friendships among like-minded readers. As Margaret Ezell has remarked, manuscript circulation "permitted and encouraged participation in literary life of people whom print technology effectively isolated and alienated."[19] Grymeston's manuscript legacy was dedicated to her son, Bernye, and printed only after her death; Joscelin's legacy includes letters to her husband and unborn child, suggesting that she envisioned primarily a familial audience. It breaks off before completion and was printed posthumously. Elizabeth Richardson published her manuscript in 1645, but Victoria Burke has shown that Richardson prepared at least two manuscript versions of her legacy, the first as early as 1606.[20] Leigh, who printed her own text, is unusual, but she plausibly claims that she determined to print her legacy because it was the most economical way for her to obtain copies for all of her children.[21]

[14] Sylvia Brown, *Women's Writing in Stuart England: the Mother's Legacies of Dorothy Leigh, Elizabeth Joscelin, and Elizabeth Richardson* (Thrupp: Sutton Publishing Ltd, 1999), 11.
[15] Narveson, *Bible Readers*, 178–9, cautions against dismissing a woman's internalization of scripture as "a cooptation by masculine discourse" and instead urges us to "recognize the range of intersecting forces, both conscious and unconscious, that contribute to the remarkable confidence and authority of her rhetoric."
[16] Brown, *Women's Writing in Stuart England*, 98.
[17] Joscelin, *Mother's Legacie*, 49.
[18] Brown, *Women's Writing in Stuart England*, 98.
[19] Ezell, *Social Authorship*, 12.
[20] The first is Folger MS. V. a 511; the second is ASH 3501, held by the East Sussex Record Office. See Burke, "Elizabeth Ashburnham Richardson."
[21] Concerning Aemilia Layner's decision to print, rather than prepare manuscript copies of *Salve Deus Rex Judaeorum* (1611), Longfellow, *Women and Religious Writing*, 66, remarks: "whether she paid or was paid, printing would have been a considerably cheaper option than hiring a scribe."

If, as these examples suggest, print publication was neither a preferred nor a default choice for early modern women, why were so many maternal legacies printed? Economics certainly played a role, but politics may have been a more frequent motivation. Patricia Phillippy has urged scholars to consider the "cultural work" done by the "performative concept of maternity" in early modern England.[22] By printing a maternal legacy, a man (or woman) could harness the power and authority of virtuous maternity to his or her political or religious agenda. The best recent work on maternal legacies has documented how printed maternal legacies engage with ongoing political and religious controversies: Sylvia Brown demonstrates that Leigh's legacy advocates for vernacular Bible reading and the establishment of Protestant lectureships. Brown further observes that while Joscelin's manuscript legacy urges a strict Sabbatarianism, the chaplain Thomas Joad toned down this discussion when he edited her text for publication.[23] Megan Matinchske has persuasively shown that the second edition of Grymeston's *Miscelanea* was substantively revised to address issues of concern to politically conservative Catholics. These included oath-taking and the nature of royal authority.[24] Drawing upon Victoria Burke's discovery of multiple manuscript versions of Lady Richardson's published legacy, Elizabeth Clarke suggests that the published version was intended to intervene in contemporary Laudian-inspired debates concerning the validity of set prayers.[25] Notably, in almost every case, it is the revisions to the manuscript or printed text that indicate its cultural and political ramifications.

We should not, however, conclude that manuscript legacies, unlike printed ones, were necessarily apolitical. If one's audience were local, manuscript circulation, with its emphasis upon community and exclusivity, might be preferable. The manuscript legacy of Lady Ann Montagu, for example, which emphasizes the godliness of the Montagu household, could have been intended to shore up support for the Montagu family – and their political commitments. But in the absence of additional evidence, we cannot be certain. A stronger case can be made for

---

[22] Phillippy, *Women, Death, and Literature*, 149.
[23] Sylvia Brown, "The Approbation of Elizabeth Joscelin," in Peter Beal and Margaret Ezell (eds.), *English Manuscript Studies, 1100–1700*, vol. IX (Oxford: Blackwell, 2000), 129–64 at 136–7.
[24] Megan Matchinske, "Gendering Catholic Conformity: The Politics of Equivocation in Elizabeth Grymeston's Miscelanea," *The Journal of English and Germanic Philology*, 101.3 (2002), 329–57.
[25] Elizabeth Clarke, "The Legacy of Mothers and Others," in Chistopher Durston and Judith Maltby (eds.), *Religion in Revolutionary England* (Manchester: Manchester University Press, 2006), 69–90 at 70.

the political import of the "legacy" of Barbara Slingsby Talbot. Held by the Huntington Library, this handwritten devotional text contains a preface in which Talbot directly addresses her readers. She explains that the manuscript is an edited copy of a Catholic devotional text, which had been sent to her by her father, Henry Slingsby, shortly before his execution on charges of treason in 1658. In the preface, Talbot identifies herself as a practicing member of the Church of England and explains that she has revised her late father's Catholic devotional so that it conforms with Protestant doctrine. After characterizing the text as her father's "last legacie," she explains that she has kept "ye best of it." The preface is dated 1687, so it was composed and circulated during the reign of the Catholic James II. Talbot arguably intended the manuscript, with its emphasis upon doctrinal common ground, as an intervention in public discussions concerning cross-confessional tolerance.

Catechisms: Childish Rudiments and the Misterie of Learning

Like maternal legacies, catechisms were significant sites of female textual production in early modern England.[26] Broadly defined, a catechism is any work on a religious subject in question-and-answer form.[27] Often included in maternal legacies, catechisms were popular in early modern England, with over 250,000 catechisms published between the years 1540 and 1640.[28] Originally designed to provide basic religious instruction or, "milke for babes," ministerial catechisms evolved to serve a variety of functions in seventeenth-century England, including advanced scriptural interpretation, historical biblical education, and the summary of complex material. Women's catechetical compositions amplify this diversity. Mothers were largely responsible for domestic catechesis, and many published catechisms were designed to appeal to them, including *The Manner How to Examine* (1582), *The Mother and The Child* (1611), *Milke for Babes* (1646), *The Mother's Catechism* (1707), and *The Mother's Catechism for the Very Young Child* (1735).[29]

---

[26] I discuss the relationship between maternal catechesis and female authorship, as well as the catechisms of Lady Fitzwilliam, Lady Montagu, Katherine Thomas, Barbara Slingsby Talbot, and Dorothy Burch more extensively in McQuade, *Catechisms and Women's Writing*.

[27] I adapt this definition from Ian Green, *The Christian's ABC: Catechisms and Catechizing in England, 1530–1740* (Oxford: Oxford University Press, 1996), 52.

[28] Green, *Christian's ABC*, 65–6.

[29] These catechisms can be found in Paula McQuade (ed.), *Catechisms*.

Catechisms are textual representations of oral practice. Introductory catechisms were designed to be rehearsed communally and often include advice on elocution, "Saie it with a high voice, and pronounce it well," urges the mother in *The Manner How to Examine*.[30] In the early twentieth century, educational theorists rejected catechesis as a form of rote-learning, but early modern accounts suggest that catechetical rehearsal resembled a dynamic, student-centered classroom. George Herbert suggests that if catechesis is to be effective, men and women must be prepared to go off script, to use the written words as guide, but extemporize, so that they can tailor instruction to the catechumen's abilities.[31] Perhaps reflecting the cultural importance accorded to maternal catechesis, as well as the knowledge and creativity catechesis required, the catechism seems to have been a favorite genre of early modern women: we know of at least ten early modern women who composed, transcribed, or translated catechisms in manuscript or print.

The household devotional of Lady Katherine Fitzwilliam (b. 1579) exemplifies both the variety of catechesis that took place in a godly household and the creative ways a mother might adapt her instruction to the interests of her children.[32] Born Katherine Bridges, Lady Fitzwilliam married William Fitzwilliam V (later Baron Fitzwilliam) in 1603. They resided at Milton in Northampton, not far from their godly neighbors (and relatives) the Mildmays.[33] Held by the Northampton Record Office, Lady Fitzwilliam's devotional, FH 246, contains multiple catechisms, including one designed for very young children, *A Child's First Lesson*, and another, *Can It Be Otherwise*, intended to test more advanced learners. *A Child's First Lesson* consists of simple, interlocking questions and answers: "Q. How came you in to ye worlde? A. By God's mighty power and working. Psalm 22.9. Q. Who preserveth you in ye worlde? A. God is preserver of all men but specially of ye faithful. 1. Timothy 4.10." The answers are largely scriptural verses, but they are neither glossed nor cross-referenced. *Can It Be Otherwise*, in contrast, contains

---

[30] Dorcas Martin, *The Manner How to Examine*, in McQuade (ed.), *Catechisms*, 235. For more on Martin, see Micheline White, "A Biographical Sketch of Dorcas Martin: Elizabethan Translator, Stationer, and Godly Matron," *Sixteenth Century Journal*, 30.3 (1999), 775–92.

[31] George Herbert, *A Priest to the Temple, or The Countrey Parson* (London: T. Maxey for T. Garthwait, 1652), 83–5.

[32] NRO MS FH246, Devotional Notebook of Lady Katherine Fitzwilliam. I provide page numbers when they are available.

[33] Fitzwilliam's mother-in-law, Winifred Mildmay, was the sister of Anthony Mildmay, husband of Lady Grace Mildmay (1552–1620), a prolific author of manuscript works; Apethorpe, the ancestral manor of the Mildmay family, was approximately fourteen miles from Milton.

highly sophisticated question-and-answer sequences and concludes with
a challenge for advanced students in which Lady Fitzwilliam provides
a topic, such as "Faith in Christ," and a scriptural verse, "Colossians
2.6.7." She then invites her pupil to construe or "reckon" the relationship between the topic and verse independently and so demonstrate her
knowledge and interpretive ability. *Can It Be Otherwise* concludes with
what is arguably a playful exchange between mother and child. "Be these
few all?" asks the child. "Not so," the mother gently replies.[34]

Through catechizing their children and servants, early modern women
developed their religious knowledge, authorial confidence, and linguistic prowess. The questions and answers included in *Can it Be Otherwise*
reveal Lady Fitzwilliam's mastery of Scripture and doctrine, as well as
her exegetical subtlety. In response to the question, "what need preaching," Fitzwilliam provides three nuanced responses: the preacher is a
"guide" who "divideth the worde aright," comforts the "feeble minded,"
and provides a "ministration of ye spirit." Each is carefully supported
by a different scriptural verse; answer and verse elaborate and expand
upon each other.[35] Sarah Henry, daughter of the minister Phillip Henry,
participated in weekly domestic catechesis. A family notebook, held by
Chetham's Library, is titled "Questions of Conference in the Family."
On July 13, 1678, the question reads: "What are the Scripture Names,
titles, and attributes of God the son?" The answer reveals the respond-
ent's skill in interpretation and argumentation: like the answer provided
in Lady Fitzwilliam's catechism, it provides three answers and supports
each with a scriptural reference: "It is Jesus. Mathew 1.21. A savior.
Hebrews 7.25 ... He is Christ anointed. Luke 2.26. Psalm 2.2. Hebrews
1.9."[36] Dorothy Burch, a mother of five children who lived in Stroud,
Kent, precisely distinguishes in her catechism between the Old and New
Covenants, as well as "the three sorts of services [servitude] in the world."
Her catechism displays her scriptural knowledge: "How hath Christ
redeemed his people from the Law," reads one question. "By fulfilling it
for them in his own person, Romans 5.19.20, Romans 8.2.3." Here, the
scriptural verses constitute part of the answer: the first reads, "For as by

---

[34] NRO MS FH 246, Fitzwilliam, *Can It Be Otherwise*, 43.
[35] NRO MS FH 246, Ibid., 13.
[36] Chethams Library, Manchester, UK. Bailey Collection A.2.125. Commonplace Book and
Catechetical Instructions on Sabbath Evenings.

one man's disobedience many were made sinners, so by that obedience of that one, shall many be made righteous."[37]

Like maternal legacies, many published female-authored catechisms indicate their origin in household practice. Dorothy Burch explains that she wrote by "asking myself questions and answering them." She dedicates the work to her children "whose good," she wrote, "I must and will consider as my own."[38] The Fifth Monarchist Mary Cary includes multiple catechisms in *The Resurrection of the Witnesses (1653)*; her phrasing – "some might say," "if it be queried" – suggests the origin of her text in oral, communal, scriptural study. Lucy Hutchinson suggests that childhood catechesis is invaluable both because it provides a thorough grounding in "the principles of religion" and because it encourages women's textual production. She underlines the pedagogical value of such instruction for one's lifelong spiritual development: in these "childish rudiments," she concludes, "there is more misterie of learning then every common reader is capable of understanding."[39]

One popular catechetical subgenre produced by ministers was the historical catechism. Designed for children between the ages of 7 and 12, the genre aimed to familiarize students with scriptural stories, while at the same time it encouraged them to read through the Bible independently.[40] Popular examples of historical catechisms include Eusebius Pagit's *Historie of the Bible* (1628), *The Way to True Hapiness* (London, 1642), and Ambrose Rigge's *Scripture Catechism for Children* (London, 1672). Elaborating upon this ministerial production, Katherine Thomas includes a historical catechism in her manuscript miscellany. Her questions range from the simple, "Whoe was the strongest man____Samson," to the more complex, "who prayed that it might not raine 3 years and 6 month____Elijah." Her formatting resembles a household account book: unlike printed catechisms, which are organized vertically, she lays out the catechism horizontally, placing the questions on the left side and the answers on the right. This format may suggest its use in Thomas's household: it would have been easy for Thomas to cover the answers with her right hand while going over the catechism with her children.

---

[37] Burch, *Catechisme*, sig. B3ᵛ and sig. A8ᵛ.
[38] Ibid., sig. A3ᵛ.
[39] Hutchinson, *Principles of the Christian Religion*, 7.
[40] On historical catechisms, see Eamon Duffy, "The Godly and the Multitude in Stuart England," *Seventeenth Century*, 1.1 (1986), 31–55.

Protestant ministers also used the catechetical form to provide abstractions of longer, more complex devotional works. Stephen Egerton, minister at St Anne's Blackfriars, composed a catechetical version of the godly divine Richard Rogers's devotional work *Seven Treatises* (1603) which Egerton published in 1618 as *The Practice of Christianity: Or, An Epitome of Seven Treatises*. In a preface, Egerton explains that he composed this catechism in manuscript in 1604 because he realized that many of his parishioners lacked the time or motivation to read Rogers's work in its entirety.[41] While residing at her family's estate in Milton, Northamptonshire, Lady Fitzwilliam similarly composed a catechetical redaction of Rogers's *Seven Treatises* (1603), likely for use in domestic religious instruction. This catechism, *The First Treatise Teacheth*, provides a sophisticated, nuanced abstract of Rogers's devotional writings. Fitzwilliam condenses and arranges Rogers's prose so that it reflects her interests as a wife and mother. Like her ministerial counterpart, Fitzwilliam was aware of the need for an abstracted account of Rogers's treatise. That she decided to write one herself testifies to her intellectual and authorial confidence – a confidence that she arguably developed through domestic catechesis.

Some early modern women drew upon the generic knowledge and interpretive skills they gained in domestic catechesis to publish catechisms that intervened in Civil War politics, just as some legacy writers published their works to engage in ongoing political and liturgical debates. Burch composed her catechism in response to a conflict with her newly installed Laudian minister. A godly, scripturally literate Christian, Burch bristled when this new minister insulted her fellow townspeople with a common slur on lower-class evangelicals: "Myself heard him say," writes Burch, "that wee were poore, ignorant, simple people, and as concerning God we knew nothing (which thing I desire God to pardon in him!)."[42] Mary Cary published *The Resurrection of the Witnesses* in support of the Fifth Monarchist movement. She argues that Revelation 11:11, which narrates the rebirth of the two witnesses, refers to the revitalization of the New Model Army in 1645. Her text also seeks to intervene in contemporary religious debates by making communal catechesis the basis for an alternative Christian ecclesiology in which all of the godly, regardless of gender, serve the community as prophets, teachers, evangelists, or teachers.

---

[41] Stephen Egerton, *The Practice of Christianity* (London: Felix Kingston for Thomas Man, 1618), sig. A4ʳ.
[42] Burch, *Catechisme*, sig. A3ᵛ.

The Early Seventeenth-Century Gender Debate

In 1615, one year before the publication of Dorothy Leigh's *The Mother's Blessing*, the bookseller Thomas Archer published *The Arraignment of Lewd, Idle, Froward, and Unconstant Women*. The first edition was only signed "Thomas Tell-Troth," but subsequent printings identified the author as Joseph Swetnam, a non-university-educated layman whose only other publication seems to have been a fencing manual.[43] Reprinted nearly a dozen times before 1650, *The Arraignment* rehashes longstanding misogynistic tropes: it juxtaposes classical and scriptural stories of unchaste or immoderate women such as Clytemnestra with popular anti-woman adages such as "marry in haste, and repent by leysure."[44] Swetnam offers avuncular advice on the dangers of lust: "women know their time to worke their craft, for in the night they will worke a man like waxe," and asserts his independence from maternal authority: "I am weined from my mother's teat, and therefore never more to bee fed with her pap." But his main concerns are economic. He warns that women will "account thee pinch-penny" and that a man's labor with a woman "is all cast away, for shee will yeelde thee no profit at all." He concludes with advice on how to choose a good wife, but he has little confidence that one will be able to do so. "Women," he observes, "will spend all thy gains."[45]

The popularity of Swetnam's text derived at least in part from its mixture of oral and literate forms. Like the bestselling, *Crossing of Proverbs* (published in 1616 by Archer's competitor John Wright), *The Arraignment* includes such sententious lore as "There is an old saying goeth thus, that he which has a faire wife, and a white horse, shall never be without troubles" and "It is said, and olde dog and a hungry flea bite sore."[46] The wisdom is traditional and distinctly oral: when Swetnam introduces a "Countrey man's proverb," he specifies that "you have it as I heard it." Such sayings place Swetnam's text in an oral, convivial community, where one can be "honest" about women's shortcomings without worrying about courtly decorum. Swetnam concludes his epistle, "Yours in the way of honesty."[47]

---

[43] Joseph Swetnam, *The School of the Noble and Worthy Science of Defense* (London: Nicholas Oakes, 1617).

[44] Swetnam, *Arraignment*, 34.

[45] Ibid., 11–12, sig. A3^r, 28, 29, and 15.

[46] Ibid., 4 and 12. On orality in early modern print culture, see Tessa Watt, *Cheap Print and Popular Piety, 1550–1640* (Cambridge: Cambridge University Press, 1991). Watt, 288, discusses Breton's aphoristic *Crossing of Proverbs* (London: John Wright, 1616).

[47] Swetnam, *Arraignment*, 9.

Three women responded in print to Swetnam's claims.[48] Esther Sowernam, writing from London, where she has been "this last Michaelmas term," places her pamphlet, *Esther Hath Hanged Haman* (1617), within the tradition of academic (and perhaps legal) debate by including a fictive "arraignment" and "indictment" of Swetnam – juridical forms that Megan Matchinske argues indicate Sowernam's interest in institutional reform.[49] Analyses of Eve's exemplarity are conventional within the early modern gender debate. Sowernam uses them to her advantage, as Shannon Miller has observed, by arguing that Eve's paradisal birth guarantees her unalienable virtue – and that of her daughters. Eve, Sowernam explains, "was framed in Paradice, a place of all delight and pleasure" so "that woman neither can nor may degenerate in her disposition from that natural inclination of the place in which she was first framed, she is a Paradician."[50]

The daughter of a Calvinist minister, Rachel Speght also offers a spirited defense of Eve in *A Mouzell for Melastomus* (1617).[51] Where Swetnam's citations are haphazard, Speght refers with precision to Swetnam's text when advancing her critique: "You affirme (Page 10, line 18)" and "Page 11, line 8, you count it."[52] These references demonstrate Speght's assured literacy. She also uses sophisticated methods of scriptural interpretation, methods that, like Joscelin and Fitzwilliam, she likely learned through domestic scriptural study. Like Joscelin, Speght interweaves passages of scripture with her own voice, so that the line between them is seamless. In her account of creation, she weaves together three different scriptural texts – Ephesians 2.4, John 1.3, and 1 Corinthians 1.30 – into a coherent account: "Almighty God, who is riche in mercie, having made all things of nothing, and created man in his own image

---

[48] Two of these women, Esther Sowernam and Constantia Munda, used pseudonyms. This does not necessarily indicate that they were "really" men. Marcy North, "Women, the Material Book, and Early Printing," in Knoppers (ed.), *Cambridge Companion*, 79, observes that a noblewoman might be just as likely to write under an assumed name. I also agree with Matchinske, *Writing, Gender, and State Formation*, 195n3, that "regardless of gender," both Sowernam and Munda "construct themselves as female and as such establish themselves in those terms." Consequently, I assume female authorship.

[49] Megan Matchinske, "Channeling the Gender Debate: Legitimation and Agency in Seventeenth-Century Women's Tracts and Women's Poetry," in Suzuki (ed.), *History*, 48–64 at 50.

[50] Esther Sowernam, *Esther hath Hang'd Haman* (London: (Thomas Snodham) for Nicholas Bourne, 1617), 6; Shannon Miller, "All About Eve: Seventeenth-Century Women Writers and the Narrative of the Fall," in Suzuki (ed.), *History*, 64–79 at 65.

[51] Rachel Speght, "A Mouzell for Melastomus," in Barbara Lewalski (ed.), *The Polemics and Poems of Rachel Speght* (Oxford: Oxford University Press, 1996), 14–15.

[52] Speght, "Certaine Quaeres to the Bayter of Women," in *Polemics and Poems*, 35.

(that is, as the Apostle expounds it) In wisedome, righteousnesse and true holinesse; making him Lord over all."[53] By using a verse from 1 Corinthians to "expound" the meaning of previous scriptural citations, Speght deploys a type of scriptural exegesis characteristic of advanced catechesis – and ministerial practice.

Swetnam's lack of education is Speght's primary focus. She criticizes Swetnam's grammar, claiming he has been so quick to "botch up" his "mingle-mangle invective against women" that he has not observed "grammar sense." His text is "altogether without methode, irregular and without Grammatical Concordance."[54] To Speght, these grammatical errors are significant because they reflect Swetnam's weakness as a scriptural interpreter. Because Swetnam does not understand irony, he "misconster[s]" a passage from Job; "a true construction thereof," urges Speght, "will shew it to be a Sarcasmus or Ironicall speech, not an instigation to blasphemy." Nor does Swetnam understand genre: he misreads a passage in Hosea 1 as a case where a prophet was brought unto Idolatrie by marrying with a lewd woman – an interpretation which is, as Speght remarks with some asperity, "as true as the sea burnes."[55] Speght imaginatively connects Swetnam's misogyny with his lack of instruction: he criticizes women because he is a poor interpreter of scripture, whose "brainsick exhalation against women," she concludes, is "a perverting of a part of holy Writ."[56]

Near the end of her careful refutation, Speght pauses to address her opponent directly: you "defame and exclaim against women," she urges, "as though your self had never had a mother, or you never been a child."[57] Speght does not pursue her remark's implications, but Constantia Munda uses the cultural prestige of maternity as the basis for her argument in *The Worming of a Mad Dogge* (1617). Playfully gesturing to her title, she remarks that Swetnam's attack does not spare "the mother that brought forth such an untoward whelp into the world as they selfe."[58] Where Speght's analysis demonstrates her familiarity with the Christian Bible, many of Munda's examples derive from Roman history: she remarks that Coriolanus stopped fighting because of the "natural"

---

[53] Speght, "Mouzell," 12.
[54] Ibid., 7; Speght, "Certain Quaeres," 31.
[55] Speght, "Mouzell," 35 and 36.
[56] Speght, "Certain Quaeres," 32.
[57] Ibid., 35.
[58] Constantia Munda, *The Worming of a Mad Dogge* (London: (George Purslowe) for Laurence Hayes, 1617), 6.

love all men have for their mothers. Swetnam, in contrast, is a marauder, whose "barbarous hand will not cease to ruin the senses and beleaguer the forces of Gynacia."[59] Again drawing upon Roman history, Munda compares Swetnam to the Emperor Nero, well known in the early modern period as a matricide: "Your wits gon a wool-gathering," she observes, since "you had forgot yourself (as I think) Nero-like in ripping up the bowels of thine owne Mother."[60] Gesturing to Swetnam's boast that he has been "weaned from his mother's teat," Munda pointedly queries: "is there no reverence to be given to your mother because you are weaned from her teat, and never more shall be fedde with her pappe?"[61]

Munda frames her "redargution" of Swetnam's pamphlet with a prefatory poem, which she dedicates to her "most deare mother, the Lady Prudentia Munda, the true pattern of pietie and Vertue." In the poem, Constantia thanks her mother for both her physical birth and for her education, which she describes as a "second birth" that has "perfect [ed]" her.[62] Like the legacy authors and catechists, Constantia suggests that her mother has been primarily responsible for her education, a responsibility which Constantia describes as "travail" but also as evidence of her mother's love. Constantia describes her pamphlet as a partial "recompense" or "requital" of her mother's efforts, affirming the importance of maternity to multiple types of early modern women's writing: "although this be a toy scarce worth your view/Yet deigne to reade it, and accept in lieu/Of greater dutie, for your gracious looke/Is sufficient Patrone to my booke."[63]

Underpinning Munda's analysis is the conviction – shared by the legacy authors and catechists – that most mothers cherish their children and that most adult children love and respect their mothers. In one of her most rhetorically effective moves, Munda mobilizes these emotions by collecting Swetnam's most virulent anti-women comments, condensing them into a single paragraph, and replacing all of Swetnam's references to "woman" with "my mother."

> My mother in her furie was worse than a Lion being bitten with hunger ... No spur would make my mother go, nor no bridle would hold her back: tell her of her fault, she will not beleeve she is an any fault: give her good counsel, but she will not take it ... tis a wonderful thing to see the madde feates of my mother, for she would pick thy pocket, empty thy

[59] Ibid.
[60] Ibid., 17.
[61] Ibid., 18.
[62] Ibid., sig. A2r.
[63] Ibid., sig. A3v.

purse, laugh in thy face and cut thy throat. She is ungratefull, perjured, full of fraud, flouting, and deceit, unconstant, waspish, toyish, light, sullen, proud, discourteous and cruel.[64]

The substitution draws upon the reader's own (presumably happy) relationship with his or her own mother to urge a reconsideration of the implications of Swetnam's argument against all women. "Is it not a comely thing," Munda urges sardonically, "to hear a sonne speak thus of his mother?"[65]

Conclusion

Maternal legacies, catechisms, and gender debates – these varied genres all attest to the importance of motherhood to the textual production of early modern women. In early modern England, mothers were largely responsible for domestic religious instruction; by teaching their children, women nourished their creativity and developed their linguistic competence. This encouraged these women to compose their own works, in print and manuscript. Some women expanded and elaborated upon this training to compose legacies and catechisms to intervene in contemporary political and religious controversies, leveraging the cultural capital of motherhood for their own purposes. As adults, children remember maternal instruction as evidence of a mother's love; this memory, in turn, provides powerful ammunition for those seeking to counter anti-women rhetoric. Taken together, these examples demonstrate that although some early modern women were economically and physically disadvantaged by their maternity, others discovered in motherhood a culturally sanctioned role for expressing their love, creativity, and authorial competence.

[64] Ibid., 17.
[65] Ibid., 17.

16

Monuments and Memory

Peter Sherlock

In 1559 Queen Elizabeth famously declared to the Commons that 'in the end this shalbe for me sufficient that a marble stone shall declare that a queen having reigned such a time lived and died a virgin'. This was one of Elizabeth's earliest interventions into the great debate about her marriage and heir. Her memorable pronouncement on her destiny is not as remarkable as it may seem, for self-representation was not a privilege restricted to royal women. The queen was one among many sixteenth- and seventeenth-century Englishwomen who publicly expressed their identity and sought to shape how they would be remembered through the authorship of epitaphs and the patronage of monuments. Elizabeth's proposed epitaph, delivered in a rhetorical flourish at the beginning of her reign, was never engraved on a memorial. The queen made no preparations for her own monument, and her successor James had other plans for her tomb.[1]

This chapter demonstrates that by writing epitaphs and commissioning funerary monuments, early modern Englishwomen participated in the creation of collective memory as authors and patrons. By determining the images, inscriptions, heraldry, architecture and places through which they would be remembered, they wrote history for posterity. Through monuments, women fashioned their identity, defined their place in political and religious terms, and established circles of female commemoration.

Reading Women's Voices

Tombs commissioned by women are ubiquitous – from parish churches to Westminster Abbey to the monument now in the Victoria and Albert Museum built by Elizabeth, Countess of Winchilsea. Medieval women were frequently patrons of funerary monuments. Alice Chaucer, the fifteenth-century Duchess of Suffolk, is one of the most well known, through

---

[1] Peter Sherlock, 'The Monuments of Elizabeth Tudor and Mary Stuart: King James and the Manipulation of Memory', *Journal of British Studies*, 46.2 (2007), 263–89 at 266.

the double-effigy monument she created for herself as the focus of her charitable works at Ewelme. Prior to the mid-sixteenth century, however, there is little secure evidence of female patronage through which to explore the motivation and self-representation of women who 'wrote' monuments.[2]

Patricia Phillippy has established that the patronage of a significant number of early modern English monuments can be securely attributed to women. Sixteenth- and seventeenth-century monuments 'offer a unique site for women's writing and a means for women to represent themselves and to forge and preserve female alliances'.[3] By commissioning monuments and writing epitaphs, women engaged in self-portraiture. Women were agents of their own representation, expressing their identities, affections and beliefs to themselves, to contemporaries and to posterity. The activity of women as patrons of funerary monuments demolishes the stereotype that the portrayal of women in early modern England was the work of men alone.

Most early modern English monuments sought to demonstrate and promote the ancient lineage and present virtues of the gentry and nobility. As the Reformation altered the relationship between the commemoration of the dead and the afterlife, so monuments began to discuss piety and charity in new ways, either reflecting the dominant theology of the reformed Church or expressing traditionalist or radical alternatives. Monuments used conventional forms, images and words inherited from medieval practice, imitating European innovations in design, or developed by local workshops. They were almost invariably patriarchal objects, representing the power of men over women, monarch over kingdom, aristocracy over people. Even where a woman's effigy was placed above that of a man, such as on the Earl of Hertford's tomb at Salisbury Cathedral, this was simply a device for illustrating the precedence of a father's lineage over a husband's. Women as well as men participated as patrons in the promotion of patriarchal culture, emphasising their superior lineage, honour and power over others. As Anthony Fletcher writes, 'Upper-class women were, it could be said, coopted into the gender system'.[4]

Nevertheless, in an age characterised by female rule, censored plays and republican revolution, cultural and political challenges to patriarchy were more than mere possibilities. Susan James argues that on

---

[2] Nigel Saul, *English Church Monuments in the Middle Ages: History and Representation* (Oxford: Oxford University Press, 2009), 290–9.

[3] Phillippy, '"Herself living, to be pictured"', 130.

[4] Anthony Fletcher, *Gender, Sex and Subordination in England 1500–1800* (New Haven, CT: Yale University Press, 1995), 409.

monuments commissioned by women, epitaphs played down the values of obedience and chastity in favour of balance: 'epitaphs chosen by women for themselves generally bore a closer relationship to their male counterparts than epitaphs chosen for them by male relatives'.[5] To assess such a claim, monuments commissioned by women must ultimately be compared with those erected by men. In commemorating the dead, gender difference emerges in two ways. First, monuments commemorating men spoke wherever possible of their participation in battle, in chivalrous fiction as knights of the realm, or in the brutal reality of war. Monuments to men might include sculpted details of drums, shields, banners, spears and guns, present the effigy in armour, or reference specific battles in reliefs and epitaphs.[6] Such imagery was not used by or for women. Second, monuments to women who died in childbirth represented maternal death through sorrowful epitaphs and poignant images of loss, such as a tiny statue of a child clasped to its dead mother's chest.[7]

More subtle approaches are required to see past the starkly gendered distinctions of death in battle and death in childbirth. Reading monuments to tease out identity, beliefs and ideals is a complex task, requiring attention to location, selection of design and mason, cost, architecture, imagery, inscriptions and heraldry. Frequently, nothing survives apart from the monument itself, requiring investigation of antiquarian readings or imitation by other monuments. The growing body of scholarship on women as patrons of funerary monuments has illustrated two further points applicable to the interpretation of monuments. First, monuments need to be read in the widest possible context, including printed epitaphs and manuscript elegies, biographical, genealogical and antiquarian records, even architecture such as houses and chapels. These forms illuminate each other and the identities and intentions of their authors. Second, the monuments commissioned by female patrons represented a surprisingly wide range of political, cultural and religious identities. Susan Wiseman's study of Lucy Hutchinson shows how in the mid-seventeenth century a Puritan woman created sophisticated elegies and a funerary monument sympathetic to the landscape of her home and refuge. Her interventions presented an integrated commemorative scheme for her

---

[5] James, *Feminine Dynamic*, 13.

[6] Peter Sherlock, 'Militant Masculinity and the Monuments of Westminster Abbey', in S. Broomhall and J. van Gen (eds.), *Governing Masculinities in the Early Modern Period: Regulating Selves and Others* (Aldershot: Ashgate, 2011), 131–52.

[7] Judith W. Hurtig, 'Death in Childbirth: Seventeenth-Century English Tombs and Their Place in Contemporary Thought', *Art Bulletin*, 65.4 (December 1983), 603–15.

husband that set out their shared political and religious ideals in a hostile environment.[8] Constance Lucy created several monuments that testify to her identity as a widow, and to her affective relationships, especially with her grandchildren. Phillippy has demonstrated how these public, material memorials are further elucidated by manuscript accounts of Lucy's life.[9]

In the wake of the Reformation, the dead no longer called on the living through epitaphs to pray for them. Instead monumental inscriptions offered advice to the reader from beyond the grave. The writers and engravers of epitaphs, whether male or female, recognised that the female first-person voice was a powerful vehicle. Some monuments presented a 'sacred conversation', as in the tomb of Elizabeth Cecil (d. 1591), erected at Westminster Abbey by her grieving husband Robert. Here a Latin epitaph allowed Elizabeth to speak to both reader and husband of her great marital union: 'One love was ours, one indivisible will/There was one heart, one inviolable faith'. The 'husband' replied, affirming their mutual love but also pointing towards the triumph of hope over sorrow, for 'Christ draws you to himself with a greater love ... [and] gives hope to me that I may share your peace'.[10]

The power of the female voice was nowhere more prominent than in monuments for women who died in childbirth.[11] While these inscriptions were rarely (if ever) written by the deceased subject, they accentuated the shock and grief of this all-too-common form of death.[12] The monument of Penelope Mohun, wife of William Drew, was erected at Boconnoc, Cornwall, shortly after her death in 1637 at the age of just twenty-eight years (see Figure 16.1). Its decoration and position establishes conventional themes of honour, lineage and piety: the young woman kneels at prayer under a triumphal arch bearing her heraldic lozenge, with an inscription locating her as a daughter and wife. But the second part of her epitaph is placed directly beneath the effigy, and, written in the first person, speaks directly to the visitor:

> My name was Mohun, my fate like various weare
> My short lifes often changes makes it cleare

---

[8] Wiseman, 'No "Publick funeral"'.

[9] Phillippy, '"Herself living, to be pictured"', and Patricia Phillippy, 'A Comfortable Farewell: Child-loss and Funeral Monuments in Early Modern England', in Naomi J. Miller and Naomi Yavneh (eds.), *Gender and Early Modern Constructions of Childhood* (Farnham: Ashgate, 2011), 17–38.

[10] Phillippy, 'Living Stones', 31.

[11] See Paula McQuade (Chapter 15) in this volume, for a discussion of the maternal voice in early modern mother's legacies.

[12] Llewellyn, *Funeral Monuments*, 287–9.

Figure 16.1   Monument of Penelope Mohun (d. 1637), Boconnoc, Cornwall
© Mike Searle. This work is licensed under the Creative Commons Attribution-Share Alike 2.0
Generic Licence.

> A virgin starre on earth a while I shind
> With noted splendour, cheifly of the mynd
> Till my Will: Drew me to his nuptiall bed
> Thence soone by Gods high call to heaven I fled
> Not without hope in Christ, to be a gemme
> Set in the walles of new Jerusalem.[13]

---

[13] A variant of the present-day inscription is found in Richard Symonds, *Diary of the Marches Kept by the Royal Army during the Great Civil War* (Camden Classic Reprints vol. 3, Cambridge: Cambridge University Press, 1997), 52.

The playful use of William Drew's name in the epitaph does nothing to mark its stark message: Penelope tells us that the primary cause of her death was the sexual relations of marriage. The text is bold in positing that marriage leads to death, and that Penelope's shining virtues were only visible in her virgin youth on earth or in the eternal city of heaven.

Women as Patrons

Women's voices are more readily heard in the tombs they commissioned. To date no female tomb sculptor has been identified in early modern England. Monuments were carved, transported and erected by male masons.[14] Yet, like male patrons, women controlled the design of monuments, including their size, position, architecture and imagery. Patronage constitutes evidence of the power wielded by some women, through access to privileged spaces such as family aisles and chancels, and possession of sufficient wealth to commission and erect a tomb. The duty of commemoration frequently fell to widows, who used monuments to express their grief, take responsibility for the continuity of their lineage, and, sometimes, put to right matters left unfinished by their late husbands.[15] These women's deeds were prominently recorded in epitaphs and inscriptions, using a variety of formula such as the classic Latin phrase '*hoc monumentum posuit* [she placed this monument]'. Although the monument of Edward Burnell (d. 1589) at Sibthorpe, Nottinghamshire, included only one, male effigy to represent its subject, a large inscription stated assertively, 'By me Barbara Burnell'. This authorial statement credits a woman with the creation not only of effigy and epitaph, but also the tomb's striking variations on Renaissance architecture, decoration, and heraldry. Everyone is then included in a further petition, 'God graunt us all a joyfull resurrection'. Barbara was not new to monumental commemoration, having already built a tomb for her previous husband, Robert Whalley (d. 1583) at Screveton, Nottinghamshire, similarly declaring there that 'this Tomb erected she, For him who well deserv'd the same'. Through her husbands' monuments, Barbara Burnell boldly tells visitors, 'I made this' and 'we shall rise'.

---

[14] Adam White, *A Biographical Dictionary of London Tomb Sculptors, c. 1560–c. 1660: The Sixty-First Volume of the Walpole Society* (London: Walpole Society, 1999).

[15] Peter Sherlock, 'Patriarchal Memory: Monuments in Early Modern England', in Megan Cassidy-Welch and Peter Sherlock (eds.), *Practices of Gender in Late Medieval and Early Modern Europe* (Turnhout: Brepols, 2009), 279–99.

In 1617 Anne Drury paid Nicholas Stone £140 to complete the monument at Hawstead, Suffolk, for her husband Sir Robert Drury.[16] The memorial did not depict Robert or Anne, but presented a pair of arches, each framing an epitaph for the husband or wife above a grand sarcophagus. Robert's father William Drury's bust was placed above the arches in a niche, with a Latin text reporting William's death in France in 1589, and Anne's fulfilment of Robert's request that the monument be erected. The tomb argued for lineal honour, giving William Drury status as a patriarch, and reminding visitors of Anne's own esteemed descent. It also struck a poignant tone, for Robert and Anne's two children predeceased them. Yet, as H. L. Meakin has argued, 'Lady Drury's epitaph and monument give us access to the person Lady Drury wanted to project in public'.[17] Anne was presented neither as a vehicle merely carrying out the desires of men nor as wholly a failure in her barrenness. Robert Drury's Latin epitaph was presented in the genitive case while Anne's used the nominative, subtly indicating her agency as the monument's author. Less subtle was the inscription's conclusion: 'having faithfully discharged her duty to him who faithfully discharged his, she leaves this space on the stone table, to be filled in with those things which should be said of her (as God wills, and as they will) by those who come after'.[18] In a brilliant interpretation, Meakin suggests that the choice of the word *infæcunda* in the epitaph allows for a double-reading of Anne's awkward state as a woman who had raised children but was survived by none. This word spoke of the fruitfulness of the literary achievements of this grieving mother and published author: read as *infecunda*, she was 'neither barren nor a mother', but read as *infacunda* she was 'not ineloquent nor a mother'.[19]

Catherine Roper commissioned Epiphanius Evesham to produce a magnificent monument for her husband Christopher Roper, Lord Teynham, at Lynsted, Kent after she was widowed in 1622 (see Figure 16.2). Lady Teynham had herself represented as a widow kneeling at prayer alongside her husband's effigy, faithfully watching by him for all time. Like many seventeenth-century tomb patrons, she would worship alongside her own effigy until her own death in 1625. The formal architecture of the tomb and its heraldic display contrast with the depictions

[16] W. L. Spiers (ed.), *The Note Book and Account Book of Nicholas Stone: The Seventh Volume of the Walpole Society* (London: Walpole Society, 1919), 45. See Peter Davidson (Chapter 10) in this volume on Lady Anne Drury's Painted Closet
[17] Meakin, *Painted Closet*, 77.
[18] Ibid., 88.
[19] Ibid., 97.

Figure 16.2   Monument of Sir Christopher Roper (d. 1622), Lynsted, Kent
© Julian Guffogg. This work is licensed under the Creative Commons Attribution-Share Alike 2.0
Generic Licence.

of the mourning widow and images of her overtly weeping daughters and praying sons. The primary emotional register of the tomb is the sorrow and grief of a widow and her family at the death of a father and husband. The epitaph identified Catherine as patron, concluding, *Catherina uxor posuit* (Catherina his wife erected this). Through it she boldly proclaimed the family's religious adherence, describing her husband as '*in fide ac religione Catholica constantissimo* (most constant in faith to the Catholic religion)', while reassuring the reader that he was a loyal subject of king and country.

Monuments borne of affection were not restricted to widows alone. A brass inscription at Ditton, Kent beguilingly records a woman's commemorative deed, perhaps for her intended husband:

> Here lyethe the bodye of Rowland Shakerly, gent. sonne and heyre of Frauncis Shakerly of Brooke Court, within this paryshe of Dytton, esquyer, which Rowlande, beynge fellowe of Grays Inne, deceased the XXII. day of June, in the yeare of our Lord 1576. and hadd this memoriall of his deathe made by a young gentlewoman, as an argument of her unseparable good meanyng towardes him.[20]

Women made preparations for their own monuments during their lifetimes, a common practice, and created tombs for relations other than their husbands. Alice Spencer, Countess of Derby, prepared a lavish tomb for herself at Harefield, Middlesex, prior to her death in 1637. This depicted her effigy under a canopy with her daughters kneeling on the monument's base. Her extravagant self-commemoration contrasted starkly with the attitude of her first husband, Sir Thomas Egerton, who wished to be buried like Seneca, it was said, without either funeral or monument.[21] Elizabeth Carey (d. 1630) commissioned her own monument from Nicholas Stone in 1617 for the sum of £220.[22] The tomb rendered her white marble effigy in a relaxed pose with the head turned slightly to one side, one hand at the bosom, and the other at the side, as if she were taking a daytime nap. The inscription recounted how her grandfather was the Earl of Worcester, her first husband a knight, her second husband the son of a baron, and she the mother of ten children, before concluding that 'in this her Manor of Stowe (which had continued long in the familie of her father) she erected this monument in remembrance of her and her children'. A Latin epitaph pronounced that 'Sic Familia praeclara/Praeclarior prole/Virtute praeclarissima [she is distinguished by her family, more distinguished by her descendants, and even more distinguished in virtue]'.[23] There was little subtlety in this proud narrative of a distinctly fruitful lineage and the heavenly honours brought by virtue.

The monument erected at St Leonard's Shoreditch in 1591 by Adeline Neville in accordance with the will of her sister, Katharine Constable, is

---

[20] John Thorpe, *Registrum Roffense* (London: printed for the author by W. and J. Richardson, 1769), 795–6.
[21] Llewellyn, *Funeral Monuments*, 294.
[22] Spiers (ed.), *Notebook of Nicholas Stone*, 46–7.
[23] Mary Catherine Wilheit, 'Virtuous Wives and Loving Mothers: Early Modern English Women's Epitaphs,' *Explorations in Renaissance Culture*, 27 (2001), 89–111 at 93.

one of the most lavish examples of a tomb by a woman to commemorate a group of women. The monument presented a monumental circle of commemoration composed of the effigies of four women from two generations kneeling at prayer. Although the epitaph reported that two male relations were also buried at the site, they were not visually represented.[24]

Women as Authors

Women not only commissioned tombs but also composed the monumental inscriptions carved or painted on them.[25] Elizabeth Russell is the most renowned author of such epitaphs, but she was by no means alone.[26] The new opportunities created by sixteenth-century humanist approaches to the education of girls and women, combined with the desire for fame in posterity and reformed attitudes towards the memory of the dead, meant that it was not only possible but perhaps even desirable for women to write epitaphs for themselves, their relatives and friends. Some of these were transferred from manuscript to monuments.

Female authors included women who instructed their executors as to what should be included in their epitaphs and women who drafted and finalised texts themselves. Frances Sidney, Countess of Sussex, left detailed instructions in her will for her monument at Westminster Abbey, perhaps because she had no children to commemorate her (see Figure 16.3).[27] Her will specified that her body should be buried 'decently and orderly without vayne pompe or chardge, but only havinge respect to my dignitie and estate'. Her monument, should she fail to complete it herself, was to include 'my pitture in Allabaster stone and other garnishinge as shall be meete for my degree and callinge to be placed and sett upp in the sayd mynster as soone as conveniently maye be after my decease withe a superscription thereuppon to be engraven declaringe my name and pettigree and that I was the wife of the sayd late Earle'.[28] The monument was duly completed in St Paul's Chapel with her effigy and two lengthy epitaphs in Latin and English that paid especial

---

[24] Sherlock, *Monuments and Memory*, 59–60; James, *Feminine Dynamic*, 16–17.

[25] White, 'Women Writers and Literary-Religious Circles'.

[26] For Russell's tombs, see Phillippy, *Women, Death and Literature*, 179–210; see also Seeal and Helen C. Gladstone, 'Building an Identity: Two Noblewomen in England, 1566–1666' (unpublished PhD dissertation, Open University, 1989). For a scholarly edition and translation of Russell's epitaphs, see Russell, *Writings*.

[27] James, *Feminine Dynamic*, 21.

[28] TNA PROB 11/74, Will of Frances Sidney, Countess of Sussex, 6 December 1588.

Figure 16.3 Monument of Francis Sidney, Countess of Sussex (d. 1589),
Westminster Abbey
© Dean and Chapter of Westminster Abbey.

tribute to her 'many and most rare gifts both of minde and body' and her endowment of Sidney Sussex College, Cambridge.

Susanna Hall, William Shakespeare's daughter, was the implied and possibly the actual author of the epitaph of her mother Anne (d. 1623), Shakespeare's widow, at Stratford upon Avon, Warwickshire. In this Latin inscription, a child praises its mother, laments the separation imposed by death, and anticipates the resurrection of the dead:

> Thou, my mother, gave me life, thy breast and milk; alas ! for such great bounty to me I shall give thee a tomb. How much rather I would entreat the good angel to move the stone, so that thy figure might come forth, as did the body of Christ; but my prayers avail nothing. Come quickly, O Christ; so that my mother, closed in the tomb, may rise again and seek the stars.[29]

Susanna may also have written an epitaph of her husband John Hall after his death in 1635. This Latin text conjures up the presence of the widow perpetually waiting by the grave:

> Here is the dust of Hall, most famous in medical art, awaiting the glorious joys of the Kingdom of God. Worthy was he to have surpassed Nestor in well-earned years, in every land, but impartial Time has snatched him away. Lest anything be wanting to the tomb, his most faithful spouse is there, and he has the companion of life now also in death.[30]

Furthermore, Susanna's daughter Elizabeth Barnard is very likely to have commissioned the famous engraving of her grandfather Shakespeare's tomb in William Dugdale's *Antiquities of Warwickshire*, revealing how women sponsored the dissemination of monumental images.[31]

Jane Purefoy Wright was the author of an epitaph on the unusual tomb of her husband Christopher (d. 1602), originally in the chancel at Withybrook, Warwickshire. Christopher and Jane's images were incised on the top of a tomb chest, with a standard inscription identifying Christopher as a Justice of the Peace. Above, the Wright and Purefoy heraldic bearings were prominently displayed with a further inscription

---

[29] For the Latin epitaph, see William Dugdale, *Antiquities of Warwickshire* (London: Thomas Warren, 1656), 518. Translation from Lachlan Mackinnon, 'His daughter Susanna Hall', in Paul Edmondson and Stanley Wells (eds.), *The Shakespeare Circle: An Alternative Biography* (Cambridge: Cambridge University Press, 2015), 71–85. Mackinnon also proposes Susanna Hall as the author of her father's epitaph. Germaine Greer, *Shakespeare's Wife* (London: Bloomsbury, 2007), 343, more conventionally suggests Anne's epitaph was by John Hall, 'ventriloquising for Susanna'.

[30] Translation from Mackinnon, 'His daughter Susanna Hall', 80.

[31] Tom Reedy, 'William Dugdale on Shakespeare and His Monument', *Shakespeare Quarterly*, 66.2 (Summer 2015), 188–96.

'Erected by Jane wife of Christopher Wright'.[32] Three panels on the tomb chest displayed verses in Greek and English:

> [*Greek, now illegible*]
> Begone Thalia with thy Comick Jests,
> Approach Melpomene dignify these Hests,
> Pale Death prov'd Nothing, Lethes Muddle groome
> Hath laid this Rightfull Wright in deadly tombe;
> His justice, valour, bounty, well-led life,
> Could not keep back the fatal sisters knife.
>
> His place of Justice he forc'd was to resign
> To his dispose, whose power is divine.
> And though his noble gifts, faith, love, and pitie,
> Did pierce the Clouds, and entred heavenly citie;
> Yet Jove his palefaced messenger did send,
> To tell this Saint which way to Joy did tend:
> His message done, he streight resolv'd to die,
> And now enthronis'd lives aeternally.
>
> Death, Angels, grave, did slay, did take, doth hold
> The man, his soul, the corps, with shaft, with hand, with gold.
> Death slew the man, the angels convey'd him slain,
> The grave, whom they conveyed, doth still retain
> Sleepe, tho' his corps secure, his soul lives still,
> The angels conducted it to Sion Hill.
> This only comfort still remains for me,
> Thou trodst the path by which I come to thee.
>
> JANE WRIGHT.

The prominent signature to this epitaph performs a double act. It is a token of a widow's grief and a proud statement that leaves no doubt about its authorship.

In this remarkable inscription a woman of whose education and other writing we know nothing displays her erudition and theology. The first section invokes tragic Melpomene to set aside Thalia's 'Comick Jests', before deriding 'Pale Death'. In the second part, the dead man's virtues are said to have entered the heavens before 'Jove his palefaced messenger

---

[32] Llewellyn, *Funeral Monuments*, 121. The epitaph is first recorded in William Dugdale, *The Antiquities of Warwickshire* (London: J. Osborn and T. Longman, 1730), 217. Jane Wright directed 'my body to be buried in the Chauncell of the parish church of Withebrooke aforesaid neere unto the Monument of my late husband Christopher Wright Esqr', in her will, dated 19 November 1626: see TNA PROB 11/151.

did send,/To tell this Saint which way to Joy did tend'. The final verse apportions Wright's identity in classic seventeenth-century terms, with Death separating soul from body, the mortal remains being held in the grave while the soul ascended to heaven. Jane shows her readers the way to salvation and assures herself of a happy reunion in the world to come. She combines ancient Greek and Roman mythology with Protestant doctrine to assert that Christopher Wright has won eternal life.

Women Changing History

Anne Clifford is, after her aunt Elizabeth Russell, the best known female patron of monuments in early modern England.[33] She inherited an aptitude for commemoration from her mother, Margaret Russell Clifford, who had commissioned at least one monument, at Hornsey, Middlesex for her associate in a lead-mining business, Richard Cavendish. This displayed an English verse with the attribution 'Promised and made by Margaret, Countess of Cumberland', justifying its creation on account of how Cavendish was 'Beloved of great and Honourable Peeres/Of all estemed embraced and desired'.[34]

Anne spent virtually her entire life either in battle for the inheritance of her father's ancestral titles and estates or, after she finally received them in 1643, asserting that they had always belonged to her. Anne Myers has persuasively argued that Anne should be seen as an antiquary, who created, preserved, and disseminated history, genealogy, law, epigraphy, and topography in staking her ancestral claims for posterity.[35] Anne prosecuted her case through interdependent media including manuscript and monument, book and building, engaging in what Susan Wiseman has described as the 'textualisation of land, buildings and life'.[36] Anne understood the power of speaking to posterity, not only through material artefacts strategically positioned in the early modern landscape, but also

---

[33] Adam White, 'Love, Loyalty and Friendship, Education, Dynasty and Service: Lady Anne Clifford's Church Monuments', in Karen Hearn and Lynn Hulse (eds.), *Lady Anne Clifford: Culture, Patronage and Gender in Seventeenth Century Britain* (Leeds: Yorkshire Archaeological Society, 2009), 43–71. On Anne Clifford's monumental *Great Books of Record*, see Jessica L. Malay (Chapter 22) in this volume.

[34] John Hassell, *Picturesque Rides and Walks*, 2 vols. (London: J. Hassell, 1817), vol. I, 36.

[35] Anne M. Myers, *Literature and Architecture in Early Modern England* (Baltimore and London: The Johns Hopkins University Press, 2013), 132–59.

[36] Susan Wiseman, '"Knowing Her Place": Anne Clifford and the Politics of Retreat', in Philippa Berry and Margaret Trudeau-Clayton (eds.), *Textures of Renaissance Knowledge* (Manchester: Manchester University Press, 2003), 207.

through their dissemination by other antiquaries and historians in manuscript and print.[37]

As author of these myriad texts, she attempted to ensure maximum control over posterity, vindicating her life's work and her eventual victory.[38] Restorative justice was not her sole passion; she erected monuments for the poet Edmund Spenser at Westminster Abbey and her tutor Samuel Daniel at Beckington, Somersetshire. Even in praising erudition, she promoted her own claims; the major part of Samuel Daniel's epitaph speaks about Anne, described as 'sole Daughter & heire to George Clifford Earle of Cu[m]berland'. The affections of grief and love were also prominent, nowhere more so than in the 'Countess Pillar' she erected in 1656 on the site of her last physical encounter with her mother some forty years earlier.

Illustrative of these passions is the monument Anne created for her mother Margaret, Countess of Cumberland, after her death in 1616. Like Anne's famous 'Great Books', this monument presented a record for posterity.[39] She was unable to see to her mother's burial in the Clifford family church at Skipton because it was under the control of her uncle and arch-enemy. Her diary records that 'when I consider'd her Body should be carried away & not interr'd at Skipton; so as I took that as a sign that I should be dispossessed of the Inheritance of my Forefathers'.[40] Instead the Countess was interred at Appleby, Westmorland, where in 1617 Anne supplied an elegant but conventional monument comprised of a tomb chest surmounted by a finely sculpted effigy, hands clasped in prayer and clothed in a widow's cloak, her head surmounted by a coronet. One inscription detailed the Countess's ancestry, marriage and issue, recording that it was Anne 'whoe in memorye of her Religious Mother Erected this'. A second, verse epitaph on the side of the tomb was displayed in easily read capitals:

> Who fayth, love, mercy, noble constancie
> To God, to virtue, to distress, to right,
> Observd, exprest, shewd, held religiously,
> Hath here this monument thou seest in sight
> The cover of her earthly part, but passenger
> Know heaven and fame contaynes the best of her.

[37] Myers, *Literature and Architecture*, 154–5.
[38] Salzman, *Reading Early Modern Women's Writing*, 220.
[39] Ibid., 95
[40] D. J. H. Clifford (ed.), *The Diaries of Lady Anne Clifford* (Stroud: Sutton Publishing, 1990), 36.

In this epitaph it is possible to read the ideals by which Anne herself would wish to be judged by God and by posterity. Throughout runs the theme of constancy, holding fast to the attributes of faith, love, and mercy in good times and bad.

Apart from the 'Countess Pillar', Anne's later family commissions are less intimate as she strove to fix her image for posterity. The monuments she erected for herself and her father in the 1650s displayed no effigies and instead rehearsed the Clifford family titles through a maze of heraldic shields. The lengthy inscriptions zealously promoted Anne's version of the past, describing her father as 'the last Heyre male of the Cliffords that rightfully enjoyed those ancient lands of inheritance', the word 'rightfully' a refutation of her uncle's claim to the Clifford titles and estates. In her own monument's inscription, erected two decades before her death, she listed in detail the titles she claimed as a birth-right: 'Baronesse Clifford Westmerland & Vescy High Sheriffesse of ye County of Westmerland & Lady of ye Honor of Skipton in Craven'.[41]

Women Making Memory

One of the outcomes of the Reformation was the creation of a new class of persons, the wives of the clergy. Clerical marriage was a symbol of the reformers' challenge to traditionalist doctrines on the nature of ministerial priesthood and the exercise of authority in the church. While patriarchal patterns of social and political order survived the religious upheavals of the sixteenth century, able to accommodate both Catholic and Protestant queens regnant, clerical wives presented a unique problem. Were the marriages of clergy and bishops to be equated with those of the gentry and nobility? Were the wives of bishops to be accorded the dignity and rank of a lady, as wives of members of the House of Lords? Frances Matthew, daughter of the Bishop of Chichester and wife of Toby Matthew, Bishop of Durham and Archbishop of York, addressed these issues directly through commissioning funerary monuments. Her patronage demonstrates how women created potent self-representations through monuments and epitaphs that shaped new identities and spoke directly to Protestant contexts.

Frances was a prolific patron of monuments to her birth family, the Barlows. Her patronage began in 1595 following the death of her mother Agatha and the elevation of her brother-in-law William Day

---

[41] Jean Wilson, 'Patronage and Pietàs: The Monuments of Lady Anne Clifford', *Transactions of the Cumberland and Westmorland Antiquarian and Archaeological Society*, 97 (1997), 119–42.

to the episcopate. The first event offered an opportunity to celebrate the extraordinary life of an aged matriarch who was a bishop's widow. The second created the stuff of legend: five husbands of the five Barlow daughters had become bishops in the Church of England. Frances and her siblings exploited this remarkable occurrence to win recognition of their godly piety and learning and to establish the bishop's wife as an honourable role in contrast to the vicious caricatures of mid-sixteenth century debates about clerical marriage.[42]

Frances erected her mother's monument at Easton, Hampshire. Her brother William Barlow was rector of Easton, and Agatha had lived here for many years. Chichester Cathedral, where Agatha's husband Bishop Barlow was buried, must have seemed an obvious alternative, but would have required significant negotiation and cost, and opportunities for self-expression may have been more limited. Agatha's mural monument focused attention on a lengthy epitaph, surmounted by a small coat of arms and the date, 1595. The heraldry was that of Agatha's birth family, the Wellesbournes, evidence that Bishop Barlow's marriage was comparable with those of the gentry and nobility. Perhaps the heraldry also reflected a sore point: convention would normally require the display of Agatha's husband's arms, yet the union of William Barlow and Agatha Wellesbourne must have occurred in utmost secrecy in the reign of Henry VIII, its existence not revealed until after the accession of Edward VI in 1547; moreover, in 1553 the marriage was one of the causes of William Barlow's deprivation from the see of Bath and Wells and the family's exile from England for fear of persecution by Philip and Mary.[43]

The monument presented three inscriptions, beginning with a quotation from Psalm 112, 'The righteous shall be had in everlasting remembrance'. This was a classic English Protestant rationale for funerary monuments, drawing on the principle of *sola scriptura* to justify the commemoration of the dead. In this case, it immediately positioned Agatha Barlow as one of the righteous. Second was the long text that was the focus of the monument. This ended with a few Latin words identifying Frances as the patron: '*rogatu et sumptibus filie delectae Franciscae Mathew* [by request and at the expense of her esteemed daughter Frances Matthew]'. It began conventionally by establishing Agatha as a daughter,

[42] Sherlock, 'Monuments, Reputation'.
[43] Ibid., 63–4. See also Mary Prior, '"Reviled and crucified marriages": The Position of Tudor Bishops' Wives', in M. Prior (ed.), *Women in English Society 1500–1800* (London: Routledge, 1991), 119–48.

wife and mother, before revealing that 'shee had seven children unto men and wemens state too sunnes and five daughters' and explaining how she came to have five episcopal sons-in-law. The inscription continued:

> shee being a woman godly wise and discreete from her youthe most faithfull unto her husband bothe in prosperite and adversite and a companione with him in banishmente for the gospell sake moste kinde and loving unto all her children and dearly beloved of them all for her ability of a liberall mynde and pitifull unto the poore shee haveing lived aboute LXXXX yeares died in the Lorde whom shee dayly served the XIII of Iune anno domini 1595.

Through these words Frances not only honoured her aged mother but also established the attributes of a good bishop's wife, attributes she herself might then display. A bishop's wife was to be godly, discerning, faithful, loving and beloved of her children, charitable to the poor, daily serving God, and willing to suffer for the sake of the gospel.

The final epitaph was a Latin verse, not part of the mural monument itself, but engraved in capitals on a brass plaque immediately beneath. The verse was widely disseminated in print and manuscript, as in Thomas Fuller's English translation of 1662:

> Barlow's wife, Agatha, doth here remain;
> Bishop, then exile, bishop again.
> So long she lived; so well her children sped,
> She saw five bishops her five daughters wed.[44]

This text attributed Agatha with a directing hand in the family's remarkable marital achievements.

In the next five years Frances created at least two other family monuments. One was for her sister Elizabeth Day, who died in 1575 and was buried in Eton Chapel, jointly commissioned with her nephew Richard Day. The other was for Bishop William Wickham (d. 1595), who was married to Frances's favourite sister, Anthonine. This monument no longer survives, but was described in 1633 as 'a very faire stone by the Communion Table' in the chancel of St Mary Overies, Southwark. This bore a Latin inscription and verse, certainly commissioned and probably written by Frances herself:

> William Wickham died 11 June 1595 being the Bishop of Winchester, shortly after his translation from the seat of Lincoln in the month of

---

[44] *Hic Agathae tumulus Barloi praesulis inde/Exulis inde iterum praesulis uxor erat/Prole beata fuit plena annis quinq. suarum/Praesulibus vidit praesulis ipsa datas.* Thomas Fuller, *History of the Worthies of England*, 2 vols. (1662; repr. London: J. Nichols, 1811), vol. II, 389.

March. He left a most praiseworthy wife who is buried in Alconbury, county Huntingdon. Near the table by your hand is a bishop outstanding in learning and of an equal character, solemn in eloquence and piety. Here he lies neglected, not on account of thrift, in the honour of an upright tomb. O unwise age, truly the man now dead is more than equal to such a tomb. May God allow the winged messengers to bear his departing soul across the threshold of Heaven. F[rances] M[atthew] placed this 10 June, in the year of the Lord 1600.[45]

As she remedied the neglect of her brother-in-law's grave five years to the day after his death, Frances affirmed the dignity of the office of bishop's wife. She offered her opinion on the conduct of monumental commemoration, arguing that Bishop Wickham deserved something more than the modest stone she had created.

Frances's own monument was erected at York Minster in 1629. The inscription rehearsed the themes of her mother's epitaph, enhanced by praise of her erudition, and casting her as a great ecclesiastical benefactor:

> One exemplary Act of hers first devised upon this Church, and through it flowing upon the Country, deserves to live as long as the Church itselfe: The Library of the deceased Archbp. consisting of above 3000 Books she gave entirely to the publick Use of this Church; a rare Example that so great care to advance Learning should lodge in a Woman's Breast.[46]

Conclusion

Patricia Phillippy has asked whether early modern women made use of monuments 'to record their own perceptions of their life's work and meaning and to transmit these self-authored images to contemporaries and posterity'.[47] I maintain in this chapter that they did. Monuments created by women are a major source for women's writing in early modern England. They offer invaluable insights into how elite women wished to represent themselves to the readers of the future. Further research is likely to reveal other women who wrote epitaphs or took an active hand

---

[45] John Stow, *The Survay of London*, Anthony Munday (ed.) (London: Nicholas Bourne, 1633), 452. *Gulielmus Wickham, translat. à sede Lincoln. & Mense Martii, 1595. existens Episcopus Winton. Obijt 11. Iunii, prox. sequent. Reliquit uxorem laudatiss. quae sepelit in Awkenbery, Com. Hunt. Doctrina Antistes praestans/& moribus aequis,/Eloquio & pietate gravis,/mensaque manuque./Non parcus, justi neglectus/honore sepulchri,/Hic jacet. O seculum/insipiens, verum aequior illi,/Dum moritus,Deus Aligeros/dat cernere missos,/Qui migrantem animam/Coeli ad sublimina ferrent./ F.M. posuit 10. Iunii, Anno Domini 1600.*

[46] John Le Neve, *Lives of the Protestant Bishops* (London: W. Bowyer, 1720), part 2, 114–15.

[47] Phillippy, "'Herself living, to be pictured'", 129.

in the design of monuments. The scholarship on women, literature and monuments has created new avenues for the exploration of the self-representation of male monumental patrons.

What, then, does women's monumental writing tell us? Women were proud of their role as patrons and authors. They signed their monuments and epitaphs, sometimes boldly, sometimes with their initials alone. They demonstrated erudition and literacy in multiple languages from English and Latin to Greek and heraldry. They sought the recognition of contemporaries and the attention of posterity. Some were bold in their patronage, commissioning innovative and influential designs. Others were forthright in creating new political and religious identities through serial use of monuments. Nevertheless, monuments commissioned by women shared much with those created by men. They used the same devices of location, architecture, words, images and heraldry to convey their messages. They valorised lineage, honour, and piety, expressed grief at the loss of loved ones, and sought comfort in the hope of resurrection of the dead. On the whole women represented themselves as virgins, mothers, wives, and widows, and men as learned, grave, and noble. In a world that had experienced female monarchy and religious reformation, and into which revolutionary politics were about to be unleashed, women as patrons and authors might well have used funerary monuments in ways that shook the foundations of patriarchal authority in politics, family, and religion. In commissioning monuments and writing epitaphs, women did not transform or challenge monumental commemoration. Rather, they demonstrated the surprising extent to which elite women could raise their voices and be seen, heard, and read in a patriarchal society.

PART IV

The English Civil War, Interregnum, and Restoration (1642–1676)

17

Prophecy, Power, and Religious Dissent

W. Scott Howard

"Triumphing Expressions": Sects, Texts, and the Temper of the Times

> Every Saint in a sence, may be said to be a Prophet ... for when the Lord hath revealed himself unto the soul and discovered his secrets to it ... the soul cannot choose but declare them to others ... though some Saints can doe it farre more excellently then others, yet he that speaketh ... though with much weaknesse, doth as truly prophesie as he that hath greatest abilities.[1]

By way of this passage (which cites I Corinthians 14:3), Phyllis Mack argues that "Mary Cary formulated a new, moral definition of prophecy that universalized the experience of communication with the divine" for women writers who were religious visionaries and social reformers.[2] There were forerunners, of course, from earlier centuries and decades, including Anne Askew, Lady Russell, Sister Joan Seller, and Alice Sutcliffe.[3] However, as Mihoko Suzuki reasons, "a public did not [yet] exist in early seventeenth-century England ... for the imaginary of political equality for women."[4] The combined influences of self-motivation, economic independence, and self-education directed toward rigorous engagements with public discourse (through speech and print) distinguished the visionary women of the Civil War and Interregnum. Mack positions Cary's defense of prophecy within and against the gendered discourse of seventeenth-century England and also in opposition to twentieth-century historical research that would trope "women's spirituality as a metaphor

---

[1] Cary, *Resurrection*, 65–7.
[2] Mack, *Visionary Women*, 90.
[3] Anne Askew, *The Lattre Examinacyon of Anne Askewe* (1547); Elizabeth (Cooke), Lady Russell, *A Way of Reconcilitation* (1605); Sister Joan Seller, *English nun's oath of obedience* (1631); Alice Sutcliffe, *Meditations of man's mortalitie* (1634). Photographic facsimiles from and discussions of these texts may be found in Ostovich and Sauer (eds.), *Reading Early Modern Women*, 138–49. On Askew, see Elaine Beilin (Chapter 7) in this volume.
[4] Suzuki, *Subordinate Subjects*, 131.

for something else."[5] Numerous invaluable works in this field since the 1980s, including *Visionary Women*, have established the foundation for a more capacious and dynamic historical perspective.[6]One of the methodological principles at work throughout the chapters in this volume concerns the quest for an "inclusive view of literate practice[s] in early modern England."[7] Indeed, within context of her tract, which was republished in 1653, Cary claims prophecy as a moral, universal, and transhistorical right for anyone (man or woman) who would "speak the word of exhortation, and information, to the confirming of Saints in the truth."[8] Cary cites Revelation 19:10 with definitional authority, "for the testimony of Jesus is the spirit of prophecy" (KJV). Such rhetorical, exegetical, and millenarian principles are consistent in Cary's other pamphlets as well as in the numerous works from her contemporary nonconformists, who also expounded the Scriptures as the basis of their search for truth. These include, for example: John Saltmarsh's *The Smoke in the Temple* (1646); Elizabeth Avery's *Scripture-prophecies Opened* (1647); Laurence Claxton's *A Single Eye* (1650); John Rogers's *Ohel, or Beth-shemesh* (1653); Anna Trapnel's *The Cry of a Stone* (1654); and Margaret Askew Fell Fox's *Womens Speaking Justified* (1667), which concludes by celebrating the example of Deborah (from Judges 4 and 5) who "Preacht and sung ... glorious triumphing expressions."[9] These mid-century exegetical prophets used "Biblical language and allusion [in order to articulate] radical critiques of state structures and the politics of education."[10] They did not speak in conventional English, but in the language of sacred poetry because "they assumed the existence of a shared mnemonic culture, a range of symbols

---

[5] Mack, *Visionary Women*, 88.

[6] See, for example, Thomas N. Corns, *A History of Seventeenth-Century English Literature* (Oxford: Blackwell, 2007); Susan Staves, *A Literary History of Women's Writing in Britain, 1660–1789* (Cambridge: Cambridge University Press, 2006); Marcus Nevitt, *Women and the Pamphlet Culture of Revolutionary England, 1640–1660* (Aldershot: Ashgate, 2006); N. H. Keeble (ed.), *The Cambridge Companion to Writing of the English Revolution* (Cambridge: Cambridge University Press, 2001); Nigel Smith, *Literature and Revolution in England, 1640–1660* (New Haven and London: Yale University Press, 1994).

[7] Phillippy, Introduction: "Sparkling Multiplicity," 15, in this volume.

[8] Cary, *Resurrection*, 67.

[9] Margaret Askew Fell Fox, "Womens Speaking Justified," in Moira Ferguson (ed.), *First Feminists: British Women Writers 1578–1799* (Bloomington: Indiana University Press, 1985), 126. These lines are from the "Postscript" to the 1667 second edition that is absent from the 1666 pamphlet; the latter concludes: "the Lamb and the Saints shall have the Victory, the true Speakers of Men and Women over the false Speaker" (Fox, *Womens Speaking Justified* (1666), 8).

[10] Elaine Hobby, "The Politics of Women's Prophecy in the English Revolution," in Helen Wilcox (ed.), *Sacred and Profane: Secular and Devotional Interplay in Early Modern British Literature* (Amsterdam: VU University Press, 1996), 295–306 at 295.

and stories derived from the Old and New Testaments whose meanings would be universally understood and whose power, they hoped, would be universally acknowledged."[11] Cary, Avery, Rogers, and Trapnel were Fifth Monarchists. Saltmarsh was a Seeker, Claxton a Ranter, and Fell Fox a Quaker. Although these separatists embraced different principles, their distinctive beliefs and communities were intertwined, as Nigel Smith discerns:

> While Seekers, Ranters, and Quakers generally looked to an inner reappearance of Christ, the Fifth Monarchist movement of the 1650s expected the bodily return of King Jesus ... Though the Fifth Monarchists were literalists in their interpretation of the Second Coming, they still found support from some Quakers, while some Fifth Monarchists [also] believed in both an inward and an outward return.[12]

Beyond the groups already noted here, there were numerous early modern dissenting religious communities, all of which, though discretely differentiated, were united in their protest against the Church of England's dominance and destabilizing transition from Episcopalism to Presbyterianism to Anglicanism.[13] This transition was underscored, for example, by: successive Acts of Uniformity (1549, 1552, 1559, 1662) that enforced liturgical conformity in Books of Common Prayer; the Solemn League and Covenant (1643), which accommodated Presbyterianism to Parliamentary control; and the Westminster Assembly (1643), which was appointed by the Long Parliament to write and publish the *Directory for Public Worship* (1645) as a replacement for the Book of Common Prayer. Although the authors imagined a reformed national church, sectarians immediately rejected the *Directory* "as confining and intolerable."[14] An anonymous single-sheet broadside publication, *A Catalogue of the Several Sects* (1647), offers twelve engravings with accompanying poems that satirically portray members of dissenting groups (including Arminians, Familists, and Seekers). One caricature even portrays the "Divorcer" who threatens his wife with a cane: "To warrant this great Law of Separation,/ And make one two, requires high aggravation." Following the poems, a

---

[11] Mack, *Visionary Women*, 137.
[12] Smith, *Perfection Proclaimed*, 9–10.
[13] Some of these dissenting groups include: Adamites, Anabaptists, Anglicans, Antinomians, Arians, Arminians, Baptists (general and particular), Barrowists, Behmenists, Brownists, Catholics, Congregationalists, Diggers, Enthusiasts, Familists, Fifth Monarchists, Grindletonians, Jesuits, Levellers, Libertines, Lollards, Methodists, Muggletonians, Pelagians, Puritans, Philadelphians, Quakers, Ranters, Sabbatarians, Seekers, and Socinians.
[14] This discussion of religious and political reform draws upon the rich collection of excerpted documents in David Cressy and Lori Anne Ferrell (eds.), *Religion and Society in Early Modern England: A Sourcebook* (London: Routledge, 1996), 40–195, at 186.

prose manifesto defends "an Ordinance for preventing of the growing and spreading of heresie" (January 19, 1646/7).[15] Although no explicit reference either to John Milton or to his five divorce tracts (1643–45) appears in this broadside per se, the sarcastic elevation of divorce to the status of a fanatical sectarian movement highlights the charged social context and rhetoric of the times with which the first edition of *The Doctrine and Discipline of Divorce* (1643) would have been readily associated.[16] Indeed, Milton was sometimes mocked as "the spokesman" for the Divorcers.[17]

Prophecy and dissent were common currency among all Independents during these tumultuous years from 1642 to 1676 – that is, roughly from the battle of Edgehill (October 1642) to the completion of the Monument to the Great Fire of London. In terms of literary history, this era includes a vast array of documents, from Sir Thomas Browne's *Religio Medici*, and Jane Jackson's *A very shorte and compendious Methode of Phisicke and Chirurgery* (both published in 1642) to Anne Wentworth's *A True Account of Anne Wentworths Being Cruelly, Unjustly, and Unchristianly Dealt With by Some of those People Called Anabaptists* and Lodowick Muggleton's *A Brief and True Account of the Notorious Principles and Wicked Practices of that Grand Imposter, Lodowick Muggleton, who has the Impudence to Stile Himself One of the Two Last Commissionated Witnesses and Prophets of the Most High God Jesus Christ* (both printed in 1676). Most of the separatists, with the exception of the Baptists and Quakers, flourished sporadically at best during the 1640s and 1650s until the promise for sectarian toleration ended abruptly when King Charles II and Parliament implemented the 1662 Act of Uniformity (which mandated Anglican liturgy following the 1661 Prayer Book) and also began relentlessly persecuting nonconformists until the Toleration Act of 1689, which, despite the title, did not grant universal toleration. Those who would not "accept Anglican liturgy were permitted to worship in *unlocked* meeting houses, licensed by the bishop, provided that the minister subscribed to the Thirty-Nine Articles [1563] except on baptism and church government."[18] The Quakers benefited from this and, in 1696, were permitted to affirm rather than take an oath.

[15] Anon., *A Catalogue of the Several Sects and Opinions in England and Other Nations With a Briefe Rehearsall of Their False and Dangerous Tenents* (London: R. A., 1647).

[16] van den Berg and Howard, "Milton's Divorce Tracts."

[17] William Riley Parker, *Milton: A Biography*, 2nd ed., 1968, rev. ed. Gordon Campbell (Oxford: Clarendon Press, 1996), 287.

[18] John Cannon (ed.), *The Oxford Companion to British History* (Oxford: Oxford University Press, 1997), 923.

This chapter engages a robust body of religious and political writings that emerged during the Civil War and Interregnum, locating key publications by women and men within networks of devotion and dissent, prophecy and protest. Authorship, in this regard, concerns interventions into converging and diverging fields of reform, where identities and texts are shaped according to the exigencies and materials suited to forms of expression ranging from prayers and meditations to conversion narratives, true relations, and political tracts – among other modes of textual production and exchange. Writers in this diversified tradition are not only autobiographers, essayists, and poets, they are social reformers; their texts, positional catalysts imbricated in processes of religio-political and literary change. This chapter considers selected works by Eleanor Davies, Susanna Parr, Katharine Evans and Sarah Cheevers, Margaret Askew Fell Fox, Jane Withers, and Anna Trapnel, thereby illustrating forms of individuality and interpretation that were distinctive to the prophetic experiences and texts of writers from Baptist, Quaker, and Fifth Monarchist communities. The chapter's concluding section situates, within and against that context, elegiac and prophetic self-fashioning in An Collins's *Divine Songs and Meditacions* (1653) among other contemporary works of devotional poetry and political dissent. The publications of these representative writers illuminate their singular constructions of radical personae shaped by contingent and contrary social contracts for reform in seventeenth-century England. The chapter addresses significant works by men and women within an expansive, integrated context, thereby presenting an inclusive view of religious and political writings that embrace multiple voices and visions – a matrix of texts inseparable from their historical moments, social functions, and sectarian spirits.

"Awakened *by a Voice*": The Liberty of Prophesying

> It hath ever been charged on the *English*, as if they always carried an old Prophesie about with them in their pockets, which they can produce at pleasure to promote their designes, though oft mistaken in the application of such equivocating Predictions.[19]

As Thomas Fuller observed in 1655, prophetic writings were ubiquitous during the years of the Civil War (1642–51). Their popularity continued through the Interregnum (1649–60) and into the Restoration and reign

---

[19] Thomas Fuller, *The Church-History of Britain* (London: John Williams, 1655), book II, 396.

of Charles II (1660–85). Christopher Hill asserts that "the revolutionary decades gave wide publicity to what was almost a new profession – the prophet, whether as interpreter of the stars, or of traditional popular myths, or of the Bible."[20] Within the scope of the thirty-four years covered by this chapter, several hundred ephemeral pamphlets proclaimed visionary agency, many of which were published pseudonymously or anonymously. Thomas Hobbes worried, in *Behomoth, or, An Epitome of the Civil Wars of England* (1679), that "there is nothing that renders human counsels difficult, but the uncertainty of future time ... prophecy being many times the principal cause of the event foretold."[21] There was widespread belief (from radicals to rationalists) that the end of the world was nigh. Millennialism sparked the arguments of Mary Cary and Anna Trapnel, John Milton, and Sir Isaac Newton.[22] Cary and Trapnel both foresaw the imminent arrival of King Jesus in the 1650s; Milton, of a rightful Protestant kingdom following upon the execution of King Charles I; Newton, of the establishment of Paradise by The Kingdom of God on Earth sometime in the twenty-first century (in either 2034 or 2060). The Fifth Monarchists predicted that the final apocalyptic battle and the destruction of the Antichrist were to take place between 1655 and 1657. William Aspinwall (an Antinomian who later embraced Fifth Monarchism) proclaimed[23] that the Millennium would begin in 1673.

There were several major factors contributing to this unprecedented wave of prophetic literary production – not the least of which were the traumatizing and far-reaching influences of the trial and execution of King Charles I, decades of religious and political instability, several international wars, two major outbreaks of plague (1645 and 1665), and the Great Fire of London (1666). The demise of government control over the book trade from 1637 until the 1662 Licensing Act also energized this culture of dissent. In June of 1643, Parliament issued *An Ordinance for the Regulating of Printing*, which Milton attacked in his unlicensed

---

[20] Christopher Hill, *The World Turned Upside Down: Radical Ideas During the English Revolution* (New York: Viking, 1972), 73.

[21] Thomas Hobbes, "Behemoth," in Sir William Molesworth (ed.), *The English works of Thomas Hobbes of Malmesbury*, 11 vols. (London: John Bohn, 1839–45) vol. VI, 399.

[22] Mary Cary, *The Little Horns Doom & Downfall* (London: printed for the author, 1651); Anna Trapnel, *Strange and Wonderful Newes from White-Hall* (London: Robert Sele, 1654); John Milton, *The Tenure of Kings and Magistrates* (London: Matthew Simmons, 1649); Sir Isaac Newton, *Observations upon the Prophecies of Daniel, and the Apocalypse of St. John* (London: J. Darby and T. Browne, 1733).

[23] William Aspinwall, *A Brief Description of the Fifth Monarchy or Kingdome that Shortly is to Come into the World* (London: M. Simmons, 1653), 14.

pamphlet, *Areopagitica* (1644). Although this ordinance reclaimed most of the provisions in the 1637 Star Chamber Decree, Parliament ultimately could not control the torrent of texts that swiftly generated an unregulatable trade. More works were published between 1642 and 1662 than in the entire history of English printing.[24] To illustrate just one of these cases, the King's Book stands out. *Eikon Basilike* (i.e. royal image) (1649) invited prophetic readings after the King's death through this textual *pourtraicture of His Sacred Majestie in his solitudes and sufferings*: "Yet since providence will have it so, I am content so much of My heart ... should be discovered to the world."[25] Assembled by Charles I and his defenders during the months of his captivity (March 1648–January 1649) and containing passages purportedly written by the King with his own blood, the book was released on the day of his execution (January 30), swiftly transforming him into a martyr "whose spilt blood was capable of healing the sick of scrofula and blindness."[26] In 1649 alone, thirty-five editions were published in England, twenty-five elsewhere in Europe. Printers were hunted down, presses and volumes, destroyed. In March, the Council of State appointed Milton to the post of Secretary of Foreign Tongues. His first assignment was to demolish the credibility of the King's Book. Milton's vituperative pamphlet, *Eikonoklastes* (i.e. image breaker), mocks prophetic interpretations of *Eikon Basilike* as "the cunning drift of a factious and defeated Party."[27]

Within this vexed and vibrant context of competing print cultures, Eleanor Davies (Lady Douglas) may have been the first Englishwoman who actively appropriated "the printing press for the public expression of her vision of herself in her world."[28] Lady Douglas (among the Baptists who became sympathetic toward the Fifth Monarchist cause during the 1650s) experienced a vision in 1625 that revealed a prophecy spoken to her by Daniel, which she relates in third person: "Shee awakened *by a voice from HEAVEN*, in the FIFTH moneth, the 28. of *July*, early in the Morning, the Heavenly voice uttering these words. 'There is Ninteene

---

[24] David Scott Kastan, "Print, Literary Culture and the Book Trade," in Loewenstein and Mueller (eds.), *Cambridge History of Early Modern English Literature*, 107.

[25] Charles I, King of Great Britain, *Eikon Basilike* (London: Thomas Paine, 1649), 190.

[26] Jim Daems and Holly Faith Nelson, "Introduction," in Jim Daems and Holly Faith Nelson (eds.), *Eikon Basilike with Selections from Eikonoklastes* (Peterborough, Canada: Broadview Press, 2006), 15.

[27] Milton, *Eikonoklastes*, 2.

[28] Beth Nelson, "Lady Elinor Davies: The Prophet as Publisher," *Women's Studies International Forum*, 8 (1985), 403.

yeares and a halfe to the day of *Judgement*."[29] Davies believed in an unbroken legacy of prophecy from the Old Testament to her own day in which she directly participated; in fact, she accurately predicted a series of future events, including: the death of her first husband, Sir John Davies (1626); the assassination of George Villiers, Duke of Buckingham in 1628; the 1639 London fires; and the executions of Archbishop Laud (1645) and of Charles I (1649). Arrested and imprisoned (1633–35) for her political writings, and later committed to the asylum of Bedlam (1637–39) for her protests against Church government in Lichfield, Davies "spent the rest of her life composing apocalyptic, antigovernment tracts that were handed personally to members of Parliament, which she may have visited almost daily during the 1640s."[30] Lady Eleanor died in 1652 and was honorably buried in her family's chapel.

In her manuscripts and printed works, Davies constructs a complex, cross-gender identity by imbricating multiple subjectivities, intertextual references, personal experiences, and deft allusions to the Scriptures. She identified many of her publications as her *Babes*. In "Bathe Daughter of Baby London" (c. 1630), for example, Davies aligns verses from the book of Revelation with local details, such as: "And I heard the Angell of the waters saye Lord &/And the fourthe angell powred his vial out/ on the sunn &" (16:1–19); and "some noteable/Judgement observed &c/ then/a drye summer & c ... By her Beware/before too Late/repent."[31] The manuscript ends with the signature of "Elea Tichet" that playfully signifies Tuchet or Touchet, which was her family name. Davies frequently puns, in her many pamphlets, "on the other surnames that she claimed: Audley (her father's barony), Davies (her first husband, the jurist and poet Sir John Davies); and Douglas (her second husband, Sir Archibald Douglas)."[32] Esther Cope arranges Davies's publications into three phases: court prophecies (1625–33), years in the Netherlands (1633–40), and apocalyptic works (1640–52).[33] Between 1642 and 1652, Davies published at least fifty works, including *The Star to the Wise* (1643), and *The Benediction* (1651), which she addressed to Oliver Cromwell. The title page cites

---

[29] Eleanor Davies (Lady Douglas), *The Lady Eleanor, her appeale to the high court of Parliament* (S. I., [s. n.], 1641), 14.

[30] Mack, *Visionary Women*, 16–17.

[31] Eleanor Davies (Lady Douglas), "Bathe Daughter of Baby London," in Ostovich and Sauer (eds.), *Reading Early Modern Women*, 142.

[32] Mark Houlahan, "Commentary," in Ostovich and Sauers (eds.), *Reading Early Modern Women*, 144.

[33] Eleanor Davies (Lady Douglas), *Prophetic Writings of Lady Eleanor Davies*, Esther S. Cope (ed.) (Oxford: Oxford University Press, 1995).

2 Kings 9:5, *I have an Errand to thee O: Captain*. This two-page apocalyptic pamphlet uses anagrams, initials, and symbols to associate Cromwell with the sun and moon, eyes and horn of the lamb of Revelation: "*as much to say*, O: Cromwell, Renowned, be Victorious so long as Sun Moon continues or livever."[34] Davies often coded her prophecies within anagrams, and she ciphered her own name, Eleanor Audelie, as *Reveale O Daniel*.

These rhetorical, political, and hermeneutic strategies – combinations of hybrid subjectivities, intertextuality, autobiographical vignettes, Scriptural citations, and prophetic revelations – were common in works of prose and poetry among Baptists, Quakers, and Fifth Monarchists during the 1640s and 1650s. The activities of these groups converged until Cromwell's expulsion of the Rump Parliament on April 20, 1653 and the subsequent dissolution of Praise-God Barebone's Parliament on December 12, 1653 – after which the Fifth Monarchists never fully recovered. The first English Baptists were dissenters from the English Separatist church in Amsterdam who had adopted the belief (under the influence of the Mennonites) that because Christ had died for all, not just an elect number, universal redemption was a prevenient gift symbolically confirmed through baptism. These so-called General Baptists established their first community in London in 1612, and their movement gathered momentum but also division from within. A Calvinist faction (led by Henry Jacob's Independent church in Southwark) opposed the practice of infant baptism, emphasizing instead more strident beliefs in restricted atonement, voluntary baptism, and salvation for the elect – hence, the emergence of the Anabaptists (also known as Particular Baptists) first organized under the leadership of John Spilsbury in 1633.[35] While these two communities were divided concerning this point of doctrine, and although their individual congregations were self-governing, both groups communicated by way of messengers and also held general meetings. Baptist communities usually followed democratic principles: men and women were allowed what Jeremy Taylor called the "liberty of prophesying."[36] Officers were elected by congregational votes; any member of the congregation could be chosen as deacon, but election to eldership was reserved for those who were believed to possess special talents for pastoral duties.

---

[34] Davies, *Benediction*, 2.
[35] Louise Fargo Brown, *Political Activities of the Baptists and Fifth Monarchy Men in England during the Interregnum* (New York: Franklin, 1911), 1–43.
[36] Jeremy Taylor, *Theologia eklektike. A Discourse of the Liberty of Prophesying* (London: R. Royston, 1647).

Susanna Parr attests to these inherent contradictions and the suppression of women's opinions in Lewis Stuckley's congregation from which she was excommunicated in 1658:

> Thus I did from time to time, whilst we were without Officers and Ordinances, partly through the great desire I had to promote the work of Reformation among us ... reprove them for their indifferency of Spirit, stir them up to that which I conceived was their duty ... But after the officers were chosen, I never medled (to my remembrance) with Church affaires, nor spake in the meetings, after I heard by Mr. *Stucley* my speaking was disrelisht; unless a Question was proposed, and I was desired to give my Answer unto it.[37]

The title page notes that Parr composed and published this pamphlet "by her selfe, for the clearing of her own innocency, and the satisfaction of all others, who desire to know the true reason of their so rigorous proceedings against her" – thereby signaling the work's participation in the emerging literary forms of the conversion narrative and the true relation, which overlap with prophetic texts published by women and men within and across these three dissenting groups during the 1640s and 1650s. In their vigorous contextualization of these various writers and genres, sects and texts, Elspeth Graham, Hilary Hinds, Elaine Hobby, and Helen Wilcox argue that Parr's rebuttal – "poised between rebellion against the church and affirmation of her understanding of correct Christian behaviour" – demonstrates "the independence women could construct, even whilst occupying what seem to be 'conservative' positions."[38]

Although the *liberty of prophesying* was permitted among Baptists, Quakers, and Fifth Monarchists, the Quakers held a singular understanding about the individual's relationship to God's embedded presence – the light, or the seed – within the self that transcended contemporary notions of subjectivity. For example, whereas Parr would assert that she "had to promote the work of Reformation" and "was desired to give [her] Answer," Katharine Evans and Sarah Cheevers would affirm they "must wait to know the mind of God, what he would have [them] to do [for] the Lord would make it manifest."[39] Founded by George Fox – a Leicestershire man of Puritan background who began itinerant preaching in 1647, rallying various nonconformists (including Seekers, Ranters, and Baptists)

---

[37] Parr, *Susanna's Apologie*, 12–13.
[38] Graham et al. (eds.), "Susanna Parr," in *Her Own Life*, 102.
[39] Katherine Evans and Sarah Cheevers, *This Is a Short Relation of Some of the Cruel Sufferings (for the Truths Sake)* (London: Robert Wilson, 1662), 23–4.

around principles that rejected political hierarchy, organized church government and tithes, and all restrictive devotional practices in favor of *the
inner light* – the Friends of Truth (also known as the Society of Friends)
grew in membership and influence, ultimately numbering between
30,000 and 40,000 by 1660.[40] Quakerism, as Margaret Ezell observes,
"offered women an important position in the literary life of the movement which far exceeded the range of activities of women publishing"
in other Independent communities. Instead of "being subordinate to the
external, masculine institutions of academia and the church, the [Quaker]
woman sought knowledge residing in her; she, and she alone, became
the 'authority' through the Light."[41] In 1659, for example, *above seven
thousand* Quaker women presented to Parliament a petition against *the
oppression of tithes*, which Mary Forster proclaimed as a *matter of so great
concernment ... the work of the Lord at this day*.[42] George Fox was imprisoned eight times, and the Quakers were widely persecuted until 1689.

Margaret Fell met George Fox at Swarthmore Hall in Lancashire in
1652 and was immediately convinced that "what he spoke was the truth
the first time she heard him, and was even more moved when [he] stood
up in her local church and (with the rector's permission) spoke to the
congregation, upon which [she] first stood up in acknowledgement of
what Fox was saying."[43] Margaret soon thereafter became the primary
organizer of Quaker women's meetings, and was imprisoned in 1664 for
permitting illegal gatherings at her home and for refusing the 1663 Oath
of Allegiance. During this imprisonment, she wrote *Womens Speaking
Justified* (1666, revised and reprinted in 1667), the first published defense
of women's public preaching, which delivers a powerful interpretation
of Genesis 3:15 – "if the Seed of the Woman speak not, the Seed of the
Serpent speaks; for God hath put enmity between the two Seeds, and it is
manifest, that those that speak against the Woman and her Seeds Speaking,
speak out of the enmity of the old Serpents Seed."[44] In 1669, George Fox
and Margaret Fell were married. Margaret published at least twenty works
between 1642 and 1676, including, for example: *False Prophets, Antichrists,
Deceivers which are in the world* (1655); *To the Generall Councill of Officers
of the English Army* (1659); and *A Touch-stone* (1667).

---

[40] Cannon (ed.), *Oxford Companion to British History*, 391.
[41] Ezell, *Writing Women's Literary History*, 137.
[42] Mary Forster, *These Several Papers was Sent to the Parliament the Twentieth Day of the Fifth Moneth,
1659* (London: Printed for Mary Westwood, 1659), 1.
[43] Salzman, *Reading Early Modern Women's Writing*, 125.
[44] Fox, *Womens Speaking Justified*, 4.

Compared with the catatonic trance states of what Mack describes as the "traditional visionary" – as illustrated, for example, by the experience and writings of the Fifth Monarchist, Anna Trapnel – the Quaker prophet endeavored to suspend the ego in order to release the inner light "from the depths of the soul, through layers of temperament, appetite, and habit, finally bursting through the individual's outer husk – her physical shape, her gender – to unite with the voices of other Friends in prayer or to enlighten strangers in the public arena."[45] In a remarkable passage, Jane Withers documents this paradoxical and contradictory process of sensible self-abnegation:

> When these words came to me, the power of the Lord seized upon me; but the deceit prevailed so over me, that I did not obey at the first movings; but the power of the Lord so seized on me again, that I was bound about my body above the middle, as if I had been bound with chains, and it was said to me, *That if I went not I should repent it, and he should know it*; and in the afternoon I was forced to go, and as I sent in at the door, I should have said, *The plagues of God must be poured upon thee*, but I did not speak the words then; and then the power of the Lord came upon me: but in that Priest Moor saies, I was in a trance, it is a lye, for I was as sensible all the while ever I was; and for foming at the mouth I did not, that is a lye; but for the working of the power of the Lord in my body I deny not; and two of the Priests own hearers which were close by me, we sent for, hearing this lying slander was sent to be printed, being examined whether or no they saw her fome at the mouth, the one of them did affirm that it was a lye, and she laid me on her lap; and the other said, She saw no such thing; but the Priest went his way, and I went after him & then I spoke the words that was commanded, and as soon as I had spoken them, the power ceased.[46]

Withers recalls a sequence of alternating impulses, physical constraints, and contested accounts of her actions – "sensible all the while"– and subverts the printing of slanders against her. As this astonishing and true relation reveals, and as Mack insightfully argues, Quaker women "were not being assertive when they preached; on the contrary, they were actually preaching against their own wills and minds."[47]

During Anna Trapnel's attendance at the January 1654 Council of State examination of Baptist/Fifth Monarchist Vavasour Powell, she "fell

---

[45] Mack, *Visionary Women*, 136.
[46] Jane Withers's testimony in James Naylor, *A Discovery of the Man of Sin, Acting in a Mystery of Iniquitie, Pleading for His Kingdom, Against the Coming of Christ to Take Away Sin* (London: Giles Calvert, 1654), 45.
[47] Mack, *Visionary Women*, 137.

into a trance which lasted twelve days," during which time "her extempporary and prophetic verses and prayers were recorded by a friend."[48] Two of these accounts were subsequently published in 1654: *Strange and Wonderful Newes from White-Hall* and *The Cry of a Stone*. These two works were co-written with an amanuensis, who calls himself "the relator" and conveys Trapnel's statements, prophecies, and songs (printed in verse), providing context and occasional explanations. As Paul Salzman reflects, these collaborative transcripts contrast with the highly personalized texts of Eleanor Davies. Whereas Davies channeled her prophecies through an idiosyncratic (sometimes cryptic) style of writing, Trapnel embodied her prophecies in these two works by foregrounding her testimony – that is, the truth of her experience – rather than her narrative's form.[49] An ardent critic of Oliver Cromwell, Trapnel traveled to Cornwall to preach her apocalyptic visions and was arrested, then imprisoned in Plymouth in March 1654 for denouncing the Protectorate. In *The Cry of a Stone* she protested that Cromwell had betrayed the Fifth Monarchists; rather than "blowing the trumpet of courage and valour," he had "on a suddain" transformed into a Beast, who ran at her "with his horn to [her] breast" and who also charged "at many precious Saints that stood in the way of him, that looked boldly in his face."[50]

While in captivity, she wrote *Anna Trapnel's Report and Plea* (1654). Compared with the collaboratively written pamphlets, this text reveals Trapnel's impressive command of testimony and experience, substance and style, as she writes meta-discursively, weaving together autobiographical vignettes, political commentary, prophetic utterances, and courtroom drama from her trial at which she vindicated her true relation of how and why the Lord "told [her] what [she] should say."[51] Trapnel's other publications include *A Legacy for Saints* (1654), and "[A] voice for the king of saints and nations" (1657). Following the collapse of Praise-God Barebone's Parliament, the split between Cromwell and the Fifth Monarchists intensified. The militants attempted uprisings against the Protectorate in London in 1657 and 1661, but their group became increasingly splintered. Trapnel nonetheless continued her visionary work during these later years, as attested by the existence of what Erica

---

[48] Graham et al. (eds.), "Anna Trapnel," in *Her Own Life*, 73.
[49] Salzman, *Reading Early Modern Women's Writing*, 116–17.
[50] Anna Trapnel, *The Cry of a Stone* (London: [s. n.], 1654), 6 and 13.
[51] Trapnel, *Anna Trapnel's Report and Plea*, 80.

Longfellow describes as "a new Fifth Monarchist Bible"[52] – a 990-page folio collection of Trapnel's writings that survives in just one copy without title page.[53] Salzman surmises that this single volume signifies "a certain popularity that Trapnel still maintained" and that "other copies may have been hoarded and read until they disintegrated."[54] The last entry in this folio is August 7, 1658, which suggests the volume may have been published near the time of Cromwell's death on September 3, 1658.

"Twere Joy to Sing": Of Devotion and Dissent

> Wherein it pleased God to give me such inlargednesse of mind, and activity of spirit, so that this seeming desolate condicion, proved to me most delightfull: To be breif, I became affected to Poetry, insomuch that I proceeded to practise the same; and though the helps I had therein were small, yet the thing it self appeared unto me so amiable, as that it enflamed my faculties, to put forth themselvs, in a practise so pleasing.[55]

The sole extant copy of An Collins's *Divine Songs and Meditacions* (1653) resides at the Huntington Library, shelfmark RB 54047. Compared to Trapnel's rare folio, which charts a legacy in-progress, the singularity of Collins's volume has informed the mistaken notion that she had no audience outside of London.[56] Collins's book is a collection of devotional poems with two prefaces – one in prose, the other in verse – each intimating very little about the author. Even her most autobiographical texts (such as "The Discourse") continue to yield only provisional accounts of Collins's personal life; she has often been portrayed as a quietist writer who held little or no concern for either religious or political conflicts.[57] The book's first preface, "To the Reader," supports such interpretations, recounting the consequences of suffering: "I inform you, that by divine

---

[52] Longfellow, *Women and Religious Writing*, 171.
[53] This volume is Bod Arch. A c.16.
[54] Salzman, *Reading Early Modern Women's Writing*, 119.
[55] Collins, *Divine Songs and Meditacions*, sig. A1ʳ; Gottleib (ed.), *An Collins: Divine Songs and Meditacions*, 1. All subsequent references to the poetry and prose of An Collins follow Gottleib's edition, hereafter identified parenthetically by either page or line numbers.
[56] Recent scholarship has found evidence of an audience for Collins in Edinburgh. See Howard, "Introduction: Imagining An Collins," in Howard (ed.), *An Collins and the Historical Imagination*, 6–7.
[57] For example, Helen Wilcox, "An Collins," in Graham et al. (eds.), *Her Own Life*, 54–7, tentatively introduces An Collins as "a middle-of-the-road believer who interpreted and found purpose in her uncomfortable and withdrawn life by means of biblical precedent and a vocation to poetry" (55).

Providence, I have been restrained from bodily employments, suting with my disposicion, which enforced me to a retired Course of life" (1). Following this poignant articulation, however, Collins acknowledges an indwelling force shaping the crux of her situation – the gift of poetry, which, as she reflects in the passage above, "enflamed [her] faculties, to put forth themselvs, in a practise so pleasing." The second preface (and first poem) in *Divine Songs and Meditacions*, "The Preface" (19 stanzas, 133 lines), establishes relationships among physical affliction, spiritual knowledge, and social criticism that are central to Collins's devotional and political poetics. This experiential and rhetorical progression – from suffering to reflection to praxis – turns upon a principle of conversion: through saving faith, Collins extends to her readers a defense of knowledge that yields (in a majority of her poems) religious and political critiques as well as historical prophecies. Through the modalities of poetic elegy, Collins fashions her own *politics of mourning*[58] as a model for her reader's spiritual conversion and social commitment to the ongoing work of Reformation. Such priorities suggest Collins's affiliation with either Particular Baptists (sympathetic toward the Fifth Monarchists) or Quakers.

Collins's more overtly political poems – especially the elegies, "A Song composed in time of the Civill Warr"[59] and "Another Song. Time past we understood by story"[60] – have been recognized as significant texts, not only for their deft critiques of the Rump Parliament's acts and policies between 1649 and 1653 but also for their apt figurations of Collins's autobiographical, devotional, and prophetic personae.[61] After distinguishing herself from false prophets and poets in "A Song composed in time of the Civill Warr," Collins boldly invokes Deborah of Ephraim[62] from Judges 4 and 5. Collins subtly qualifies her alignment with this figure – "twere joy to sing" – at the same time as she analogically

---

[58] See Howard, "An Collins and the Politics of Mourning."
[59] Helen Wilcox, "Literature and the Household," in Loewenstein and Mueller (eds.), *Cambridge History of Early Modern English Literature*, 737–62, offers a compelling reading of this poem as a defense of the positive qualities of home life threatened by the Engagement Controversy.
[60] Clarke, "The Garrisoned Muse."
[61] Howard, "Imagining An Collins," 1–22.
[62] Deborah of Ephraim (c. 1200–1124 BC), prophetess of Yahweh and fourth Judge of pre-monarchic Israel; counselor, warrior, and wife of Lapidoth. See Michael D. Coogan, *The Old Testament: A Historical and Literary Introduction to the Hebrew Scriptures* (Oxford: Oxford University Press, 2011), 214–19.

appropriates[63] Deborah's song of triumph for Israel over Sisera (leader of Jabin's Canaanite forces) as a remedy for England's turmoil:

> With *Deborah* twere joy to sing
>   When that the Land hath Rest,
> And when that Truth shall freshly spring,
>   Which seemeth now deceast,
> But some may waiting for the same
>   Go on in expectation
> Till quick conceipt be out of frame,
>   Or till Lifes expiracion. (Lines 9–16)

Just as Deborah's song – a remarkably outspoken voice from the only female judge in the entire history of pre-monarchic Israel – praises triumphant godly acts in times of religious and political crisis, Collins's own "quick conceipt" defends God's Truth in the schismatic public sphere.[64] Collins's affirmation of redemptive spiritual knowledge – the "fruit most rare" (28) of her *Divine Songs and Meditacions* – links the prophetic charge of Deborah's song to this poet's private apprehension of public urgency.

Deborah's namesake is *Bee* and Collins figures herself, in "The Preface," as a Bee who converts spiritual and social sufferings into "sweetnesse, fit for some good end," thereby countervailing the "vennom so compacted" of a "spider generacion" (lines 115 and 114).[65] The bee was a common conceit in devotional writing of the sixteenth and seventeenth centuries, signifying the manner by which a pure meditative soul extracts the essence of spiritual wisdom from either sacred or secular exemplars, improving those sources of inspiration through the process of reflection.[66] In such instances, Collins skillfully employs the rhetoric of the enclosed garden topos to political ends. Other connotations of the bee conceit hover

---

[63] Some scholars might object that Collins's personal relationship with Christ precludes her prophetic role. See, for example, Miriam Beth Garber, *Gender and the Authority of Inspiration* (Ann Arbor, MI: University of Michigan Press, 1996), 42. More recently, others have connected An Collins to an early modern visionary/prophetic tradition including a diversity of writers, such as Eliza, Margaret Fell, Sarah Jones, Morgan Llwyd, Elizabeth Major, Elizabeth Poole, Anna Trapnel, Henry Vane, and Elizabeth Warren. See Clarke, "The Garrisoned Muse," and Gray, *Women Writers and Public Debate*.

[64] Deborah led a successful counterattack against Jabin, King of Canaan, and his military commander, Sisera (Judges 4:1–24): "And Deborah said unto Barak, Up; for this *is* the day in which the Lord hath delivered Sisera into thine hand: is not the Lord gone out before thee?" (4:14) (KJV).

[65] Walter B. Fulghum, Jr, *Dictionary of Biblical Allusions in English Literature* (New York: Holt, Rinehart and Winston, 1965), 54–5.

[66] See Greer et al. (eds.), *Kissing the Rod*, 151 n114.

with particular resonance for An Collins. While Collins clearly alludes to Deborah through these metaphors, the bee motif also signals her deft tribute to Aemilia Lanyer's "Authors Dreame" that praises the "finer, higher priz'd" sugar of Mary Sidney Herbert's completed *Psalmes of David* (c. 1599), which circulated widely in manuscripts throughout the seventeenth century. Lanyer figures the Countess of Pembroke as the Queen Bee/poet for whom she, "the painefull Bee," strives to gather her own fruits/verses.[67] Many scholars (including Margaret Hannay) have demonstrated the significance of the Sidney-Pembroke psalter for the development of the seventeenth-century religious lyric, while others (including Debra Rienstra) have explored the richness of Lanyer's tropes for the Countess of Pembroke throughout *Salve Deus Rex Judaeorum* (1611).[68] Helen Wilcox and Lynette McGrath include Collins's *Divine Songs and Meditactions* (1653) in a tradition of devotional poetry inspired by Mary Sidney Herbert and the works of other contemporaries, such as Diana Primrose's *A Chaine of Pearle* (1615), George Herbert's *The Temple* (1633), Anne Bradstreet's *The Tenth Muse* (1650), and *Eliza's Babes* (1652).[69]

Within such a rich field of poetics and praxis, An Collins's *Bee* lights upon her own connection to a distinctive community of women's readership and authorship[70] that would also include Margaret Fell Fox's *Womens Speaking Justified* (1666–7) and Bathsua Makin's *Essay to Revive the Antient Education of Gentlewomen* (1675), which praises Deborah as "without all doubt a learned woman, that understood the law."[71] Following her relative obscurity throughout the nineteenth century, then her intermittent visibility throughout much of the twentieth, An Collins – the mid-seventeenth-century English poet of devotion and dissent – has once again reached a horizon of critical expectation that continues to unfold.

---

[67] Aemilia Lanyer, "The Authors Dreame to the Ladie *Marie*, the Countesse Dowager of *Pembroke*," in Lanyer, *Poems*, line 199.

[68] Margaret P. Hannay, "'Princes you as men must dy': Genevan Advice to Monarchs in the Psalmes of Mary Sidney," *English Literary Renaissance*, 19 (1989), 22–41; Debra Rienstra, "Dreaming Authorship: Aemilia Lanyer and the Countess of Pembroke," in Eugene Cunnar and Jeffrey Johnson (eds.), *Discovering and (Re)Covering the Seventeenth Century Religious Lyric* (Pittsburgh: Duquesne University Press, 2001), 80–103.

[69] Wilcox, "The 'finenesse' of Devotional Poetry"; Lynette McGrath, *Subjectivity and Women's Poetry in Early Modern England* (Burlington: Ashgate, 2002).

[70] Mary Morrissey, "What An Collins Was Reading," *Women's Writing*, 19 (2012): 467–86. On the bee motif as a trope for women's literacy, see Snook, *Women, Reading*, 57–82.

[71] Joy A. Schroeder, *Deborah's Daughters: Gender Politics and Biblical Interpretation* (Oxford: Oxford University Press, 2014), 113; and Makin, *Essay*, 25.

18

Coteries, Circles, Networks
The Cavendish Circle and Civil War Women's Writing

Sarah C. E. Ross

I *Saw your* Poems, *and then Wish'd them mine,*
Reading the Richer Dressings *of each Line*;
Your New-born, Sublime Fancies, *and such store,*
May make our Poets *blush, and Write no more*:
Nay, Spencers Ghost *will haunt you in the Night,*
And Johnson *rise, full fraught with* Venom's Spight;
Fletcher, *and* Beaumont, *troubl'd in their* Graves,
Look out some Deeper, and forgotten Caves;
And Gentle Shakespear *weeping, since he must*
At best, be Buried, now, in Chaucers Dust:
Thus dark Oblivion *covers their each* Name,
Since you have Robb'd them of their Glorious Fame.[1]

Margaret Cavendish's desire for public literary fame was actively encouraged and cultivated by her husband, William Cavendish, Duke of Newcastle. William's dedicatory poem to the second edition of her *Poems, and Phancies* (1664) elevates his wife to the 'Glorious Fame' of print-published poets and playwrights from Chaucer to Jonson, encouraging and supporting Margaret's oft-articulated desire that she might achieve the profile and longevity of the 'straight poet'.[2] Her own prefatory letter to the volume, addressed 'To all noble, and worthy Ladies', declares boldly, 'all I desire is *Fame*, and *Fame* is nothing but a *great Noise*, and *Noise* Lives most in a *Multitude*; Wherefore I wish my *Book* may set awork every *Tongue*'.[3] Margaret Cavendish is unusual among early modern women writers in her explicit cultivation of literary fame, and in embracing print culture as the medium through which to achieve it. William Cavendish's endorsement of her canonical ambitions and her forays into

---

[1] William Cavendish, 'To the Lady Marchioness of Newcastle, On Her Book of Poems', in Cavendish, *Poems, and Phancies* (1664), sig A2ʳ. A draft of the poem is in Hallward Library, University of Nottingham, Portland MS PwV 25, fol. 13ʳ.
[2] Cavendish, 'The Purchase of Poets', in *Poems, and Phancies* (1664), line 4.
[3] Cavendish, *Poems, and Phancies* (1664), sig A3ʳ.

print is, similarly, unusual, but his encouragement of her writing per se is less so. Husbands, as well as fathers and other male associates, were often instrumental in encouraging and supporting the early modern women writer, and in producing her for posterity, as Gillian Wright has shown.[4] Henry Sibthorpe, for example, compiled the manuscript writings of his wife, Anne Southwell, after her death in the 1630s, preserving her as an exemplar of piety, wit and learning.[5] John Egerton, the second Earl of Bridgewater, took an active role in transcribing and curating the devotional writing of his wife Elizabeth – William Cavendish's daughter – after her death.

While William Cavendish promoted his wife's ambitions to enter the annals of the nascent English literary canon, he also cultivated the 'far more conventional' literary activities of his daughters, Elizabeth and her older sister Jane, whose writings remained more discreetly contained in manuscript networks.[6] William was himself a prolific author of poems and collaborative dramas, and he was one of England's most important literary patrons. He encouraged his daughters (Margaret's stepdaughters) to write, and the elder two produced an important body of manuscript work: there is poetry by Jane, two collaborative dramas – *A Pastorall* and *The Concealed Fancyes* – co-authored with Elizabeth, and an extensive array of devotional writing penned by Elizabeth during her marriage to John Egerton. Margaret Cavendish expressed scorn for devotional writing of this kind, and Elizabeth's daughter in turn wrote tartly of her step-grandmother: 'Mongst Ladyes let Newcastle weare ye Bayes,/I onely sue for Pardon, not for Praise'.[7] Such intra-familial contestation over versions of female authorship suggest a sharp divide between literary ambition and modesty, print and manuscript publication, but both versions of female authorship were endorsed by William Cavendish, and practised in his circle. The writings of the Cavendish women, and those around them, illustrate the complexity of literary culture, its values and its material textuality, in the elite circles and networks of mid-seventeenth-century England. Jane and Elizabeth Cavendish's poems, plays and devotional

---

[4] See Wright, *Producing Women's Poetry*, 18–19.
[5] Sibthorpe appends encomiastic poems to Folger MS V b 198, *The Works of the Lady Anne Southwell*.
[6] Travitsky, *Subordination and Authorship*, 29.
[7] Cavendish, *Sociable Letters*, 225–6; and for the younger Elizabeth Egerton, Hunt MS EL 8367. Jane's and Elizabeth's husbands, Charles Cheyne and John Egerton, Earl of Bridgewater, praise Margaret Cavendish's writings effusively in a volume honouring her (*Letters and Poems in Honour of the Incomparable Princess, Margaret, Dutchess of Newcastle*, 1666), but Betty S. Travitsky, following Victoria Burke and Marie-Louise Coolahan, regards this praise as 'patently insincere' (Travitsky, *Subordination and Authorship*, 47–8).

writing exemplify a mode of elite literary sociality and aristocratic household cultural production that was both alternative to and continuous with the print aspirations of their more famous stepmother.

This chapter explores the Cavendish sisters and their associates as one node in an extensive, and at times elusive, network of elite early modern women's literary production that yet has much to tell us about coteries, circles and networks as the loci of much early modern women's writing and cultural performance. Jane and Elizabeth penned their collaborative dramas, and Jane wrote her poetry, at Welbeck Abbey in the early 1640s, when Elizabeth had already married, but had not taken up residence with, John Egerton. Living with John at the Bridgewater home of Ashridge, Hertfordshire, at this time was his older sister Alice, who had played the role of the Lady in Milton's masque *Comus* when it was performed at Ludlow Castle in 1634. Jane's verse includes at least one instance of poetic engagement with her new sister-in-law, an eminent pupil of the court musician Henry Lawes, a woman performer whose post-*Comus* cultural afterlife is not only little-explored, but often elided or erased. Alice Egerton's association with Lawes through the 1650s is likely to have brought her into contact also with Katherine Philips, another royalist poet and lyricist, although one of less elite standing. Each of these women writers and performers illustrate, in different ways, the centrality of marital and familial circles, of household coteries and extended social networks, to elite women's literary production in the mid-seventeenth century. Their texts and performances illustrate the complex relationships in these decades between manuscript and print, familial and 'public' modes of authorship and cultural production, and competing models of women's writing and female fame.

Power Couple

William Cavendish (1593–1676), Duke and Marquess (from 1643) of Newcastle, was one of early modern England's most extensive and influential literary patrons. He occupied the most elite echelons of Stuart society,[8] and he presided in the decades before the English Civil War over a large and vital literary circle, as well as a scientific network – exploring the new philosophy – of considerable note. Ben Jonson wrote masques for the christening of his son Charles (to whom the future

---

[8] When he was created a marquess in 1643, there were only six Englishmen and two Scots, apart from Charles I and his children, who took precedence over him in all of Great Britain.

Charles I was godfather) in 1620, and for extravagant entertainments for King Charles I in 1633 and 1634 which took place at Welbeck Abbey and Bolsover Castle, the lavishly decorated Cavendish family homes.[9] William Davenant, Robert Davenport, James Shirley, Richard Brome, John Dryden, van Dyck, Fanelli, Hobbes and Descartes were among the poets, dramatists and philosophers patronised by him; and his compendious manuscript miscellany of poetry, the Newcastle manuscript, contains extensive tracts of verse by Donne, Thomas Carew, Richard Andrews and others.[10] Forced into exile on the Continent after defeat at Marston Moor in 1644, he presided in Paris and then Antwerp over a busy literary salon, composing several dramatic and musical entertainments. Timothy Raylor has explored the conceptual and terminological distinctions between the literary 'circle' (closed, tightly knit) and the 'network' (open, large), suggesting that 'the so-called Cavendish, Newcastle, or Welbeck circle' revolving around William Cavendish in the 1630s 'is really best understood as an extension of the aristocratic household'.[11] William Cavendish presided at Welbeck and on the Continent over a literary culture that had its heart in the most aristocratic of households, and that extended into the royal court and beyond, in household and public performances, and in manuscript culture and in print.

William Cavendish's own literary writings run the gamut from social and occasional verse in manuscript, to household and court dramatic productions, to collaborative plays performed in the commercial theatre. He wrote a wide range of social and devotional occasional poetry embedded in seventeenth-century cultures of literary sociality, and of the easy exchange of verse within elite households and networks. Poems addressed to members of the royal family celebrate and display his close connection to them (he was governor to Prince Charles, later Charles II, for three years from 1638), and others instantiate networks of slightly less elite sociality in very similar ways. Encomia and elegies on Ben Jonson,

---

[9] Travitsky, *Subordination and Authorship*, 25; see also Timothy Raylor, '"Pleasure Reconciled to Virtue": William Cavendish, Ben Jonson, and the Decorative Scheme of Bolsover Castle', *Renaissance Quarterly*, 52 (1999), 402–39.

[10] See Raylor, 'Newcastle's Ghosts', 93–4, and David M. Bergeron, *Textual Patronage in English Drama, 1570–1640* (Aldershot: Ashgate, 2006), 185–91. The Newcastle manuscript is BL Harleian MS 4955; see Hilton Kelliher, 'Donne, Jonson, Richard Andrews and the Newcastle Manuscript', in Peter Beal and Jeremy Griffiths (eds.), *English Manuscript Studies 1100–1700*, vol. IV (London: British Library, 1993), 134–73.

[11] Raylor, 'Newcastle's Ghosts', 93 and 114. Peter Beal – see *A Dictionary of English Manuscript Terminology 1450–2000* (Oxford: Oxford University Press, 2008) – defines a literary coterie as a 'circle ... of a somewhat exclusive nature'.

Endymion Porter, Sir Kenelm Digby and his own family members trace the outlines of his rich socio-literary environment and a shared poetic discourse of praise. *The Phanseys of the Marquesse of Newcastle, sett by him in verse att Paris* are for the most part verses addressed to Margaret Lucas in their courtship, of a highly conventional kind. Newcastle also wrote numerous dramatic interludes and plays, some of which made their way onto the commercial stage and into print publication. *The Country Captaine* and *The Varietie*, for example, premiered in London in 1641, and were published together, anonymously in 1649.[12] The *Triumphant Widow*, published in 1677, derives from two earlier dramatic compositions by him: 'A Pleasant and Merrye Humor off a Roge', which exists in an autograph manuscript, and 'The King's Entertainment', believed to have been written during Newcastle's period in Antwerp for a private function to celebrate Charles II's triumphal return to London.[13] The commercial and published reworkings of these salon dramas are widely acknowledged to be a collaboration between Newcastle and Thomas Shadwell.[14]

Margaret Cavendish's quest for literary fame is one mode of female literary engagement to emerge from this literary circle. Margaret met and married William Cavendish in 1645 in Paris, where she was a twenty-two-year-old lady in waiting to Queen Henrietta Maria. Her poems are wide-ranging in genre and focus, including occasional poems on the death of her brother and on the sacking of Bolsover castle, alongside philosophical dialogues and explorations of atomic theory, reflecting the rich intellectual environment of the Cavendishes' exile community in Paris and Antwerp. *Poems, and Fancies* appeared in 1653 (with a second edition, heavily revised by her, in 1664), as did *Philosophical Fancies*; numerous volumes of poetry, philosophical observations, and letters followed. Margaret's works include collaborative dramas co-authored with her husband, also composed during their exile and printed in *Playes Written by the thrice Noble, Illustrious and Excellent Princess, the Lady Marchioness of Newcastle* in 1662. In a prefatory poem to the volume, she draws a self-denigrating comparison between herself and Jonson, Shakespeare, Beaumont and Fletcher, recasting the laudatory language

[12] *The Phanseys of the Marquesse of Newcastle* is BL Add MS 32497. A manuscript version of *The Country Captaine* is BL Harleian MS 7650.
[13] Hallward Library, University of Nottingham, MS PwV 24/35, fols. 18ᵛ–31ᵛ and MS PwV 23.
[14] Sally Ann Hoare, 'A Critical Edition of *The Triumphant Widow, or the Medley of Humours*, by William Cavendish and Thomas Shadwell', unpublished doctoral thesis, University of Auckland, 2009; see also William Cavendish, *Dramatic Works*.

of her husband's celebratory poem in modest terms. She nevertheless concludes, '*I covet not a stately, cut, carv'd Tomb,/But that my Works, in Fames house may have room*'.[15] And it is her enthusiasm for print publication that differentiates her most sharply from her contemporary women writers, as she embraced the possibilities of print for promulgating her literary fame. Many of her volumes are prefaced with frontispieces featuring elaborate pillars and busts that marmorealise her as a poet, enacting a model of literary publication in the vein of Jonson's self-published folios.

Welbeck and Beyond

The authorial practices of William Cavendish's eldest daughter, Jane, take their cue from the more 'amateur' end of the spectrum of William's household literary and dramatic productions. Jane's poetry was penned at Welbeck Abbey in the 1640s, after her father and brothers' departure for royalist military action and, after July 1644, exile on the Continent. Jane, as the eldest daughter, remained at Welbeck under siege, in residence with her sisters Elizabeth and Frances, and she authored there a volume of social and religious poetry that she addressed to her father, written 'When that shee heard the drumms and cannon play' (77).[16] Jane's verses, like her father's, are a blend of social and religious occasional pieces, addressing – invariably as the epitome of all that is good – her own two sisters, her absent father and brothers, and familial figures from a servant to her great-grandmother, Bess of Hardwick. Jane wishes in very many of these poems for her father's return, fusing her desire for her heavenly and earthly fathers, and repeatedly envisaging William Cavendish landing safe on English soil: 'Wee pray, wee wish, and hope to see,/Your selfe againe in Welbeck bee'.[17]

Jane and Elizabeth's co-authored pastoral dramas, *A Pastorall* and *The Concealed Fancyes*, also imagine their father in his absence. In *A Pastorall* the authors' father is the focus for the sister-shepherdesses' lament, while in *The Concealed Fancyes*, Luceny and Tattiney are two sisters who mourn their exiled father, Lord Calsindow. These dramas have been explored extensively as participating in a shared 'Cavendish familial discourse',

---

[15] M. Cavendish, 'A General Prologue to all my Plays', in Cavendish, *Playes*, sig. A7r.
[16] There are two manuscripts of Jane Cavendish's poems: Beinecke Rare Book and Manuscript Library, Yale University, MS Osborn b. 233, and Bod MS Rawl. poet 16. Quotations in this chapter are from the Yale manuscript.
[17] J. Cavendish, 'A Songe', 12.

following as they do in their father's mode of household dramatic interludes and entertainments, and collaborative manuscript production.[18]
In their pastoral form and elite, extended household context, they could
also be seen to echo the pastoral dramas of the courtly salon over which
Queen Henrietta Maria presided in the late 1620s and 1630s.[19] Nathan
Starr and Betty Travitsky have speculated that the Cavendish sisters
may have performed *The Concealed Fancyes*, perhaps for the elder Earl
of Bridgewater at Ashridge in 1646 (Starr) or for Charles I at Welbeck
in August 1645 (Travitsky), and while there is no evidence of a performance, it is by no means out of the question for two girls raised in the
masquing culture of the elite 1630s household.[20] Their father's manuscripts describe 'a Countrie maske, a Christmas toye' made by him for
his daughters 'Att your desiers', and which they have now asked him to
record in a book.[21] No text of this masque survives, but the record of it
points to household dramatic performances in which the girls took instigating roles.

    Few family coteries illustrate so clearly as the Cavendishes' the way
in which the elite 1630s household expands outward into wider social
circles and networks of authorship, readership and shared cultural production in the period. Jane Cavendish's intra-familial poetic authorship
is, certainly, a centre from which she cultivated what can be seen as a
feminised version of her father's literary activity, reaching out into other
overlapping household and courtly circles. She describes a domestic,
female reading circle in a poem titled 'The Carecter', gently satirising
a long list of various servants before describing 'Now for the Ladyes in
good faith they sitt/All day to giue their Carecters of witt' (25). Katherine
Larson has associated the witty, conversational interchange central to the
Cavendish sisters' literary output with salon culture of the 1630s, and
Jane's poetic conversation addresses central figures in that cultural milieu.[22]
She writes an answer poem to Thomas Carew's lines on the Countess
of Carlisle, a renowned beauty who was deeply involved in literary and

---

[18] Wynne-Davies, *Women Writers and Familial Discourse*, chapter 7.
[19] Sanders, 'Caroline Salon Culture and Female Agency', 449. Of the Cavendish sisters' dramas, Jane
    Milling also suggests that they 'function as a reclamation and valorisation of the dramatic form
    itself, once popular at Henrietta-Maria's court' ('Siege and Cipher', 414).
[20] See Travitsky, *Subordination and Authorship*, 64–8, and Starr (ed.), 'The Concealed Fansyes', 836.
    Deanne Williams believes the Cavendish sisters may well have performed in court and household
    masques (*Shakespeare and the Performance of Girlhood*, 192–3).
[21] Hallward Library, University of Nottingham, Portland MS PwV 25, fol. 16ʳ.
[22] Katherine R. Larson, *Early Modern Women in Conversation* (Basingstoke: Palgrave, 2011),
    chapter 5.

theatrical production at the 1630s court, and who has been recuperated by Julie Sanders as a 'chief rival' to Queen Henrietta Maria in her sponsorship of court masques and theatricals.[23] She addresses another answer poem, a form central to coterie culture and its 'complex dynamic of audience',[24] to Lady Alice Egerton, as I will discuss below. And William Cavendish's Newcastle manuscript also contains a poem written *to* Jane in 1629, when she would have been eight years old, by Francisca Andrews, the daughter of Richard Andrews, the Cavendish family physician and a coterie poet.[25] This latter poem is an intriguing early fragment of Jane's poetic conversations from the other side, and from a less elite associate of her household. It is indicative of a feminised Cavendish 'sub-coterie' or 'counter-coterie' held together by poetic exchange, and of specifically female authorial affiliations within the overlapping coteries and networks associated with the Duke of Newcastle.

Unmasking Alice Egerton

Elizabeth Cavendish's marriage in 1641, at the age of fifteen, to John Egerton, later second Earl of Bridgewater, brought the Cavendish sisters into a formal alliance with another of England's most influential elite literary families. Elizabeth was regarded as 'too young to be bedded', in the famous words of her later stepmother Margaret,[26] and so she remained at first at the Cavendish family home of Welbeck, residing there with her sisters during her father's absence in the early 1640s. Jane's social verses include several gentle references to her sister's husband and her marital status: one short poem on John Egerton opens 'You are a Husband iust as one would wish,/For you desire but your wife to kiss'; and a witty vignette on 'The Peart one, or otherwise my Sister Brackley' (Elizabeth) describes 'for wives, you are the only size;/And what then can bee better wished,/Then pritty, faire, & witty, to bee kis'd' (21 and 13). But Jane's answer poem to Alice Egerton is perhaps the most suggestive of socio-literary and cultural exchange between the two households, titled as it is 'An Answeare to my Lady Alice Egertons Songe of I prethy send mee back my hart' (18). Jane describes as 'Alice Egerton's' an enormously

[23] Sanders, 'Caroline Salon Culture', 451; Burke and Coolahan, 'The Literary Contexts of William Cavendish and his Family', 135–6; Ross, *Women, Poetry, and Politics*, 107–8.
[24] Jerome de Groot, 'Coteries, Complications and the Question of Female Agency', 197.
[25] BL Harleian MS 4955, fols 86ᵛ–87ʳ; see also Kelliher, 'Donne,' 141.
[26] Margaret Cavendish, *The Life of William Cavendish, Duke of Newcastle, to Which Is Added the True Relation of My Birth, Breeding and Life*, ed. C. H. Firth (London: John C. Nimmo, 1886), 141.

popular lyric that has been variously attributed to Sir John Suckling
and to Henry Hughes, and that was published in a musical setting by
Henry Lawes in his third book of *Ayres and Dialogues* (1658).[27] Alice
Egerton enjoyed a long and celebrated relationship with Lawes, as his
musical pupil in the 1630s and 1640s; and so it seems most likely that
Jane's poetic 'Answeare to my Lady Alice Egertons Songe' is a response
to a household musical performance, in one of the Egerton or Cavendish
family homes.

   Alice Egerton had a considerable pedigree as a young female performer
in a coterie and elite household context. She is best known to literary
history as the Egerton daughter who performed the role of the Lady in
Comus, the masque written by Milton for the Egerton children and performed by them at Ludlow Castle on the Welsh marches on Michaelmas
night, 1634. The masque centres on the Lady who gets lost in the woods
with her two brothers, and who must defend her virtue against her
would-be seducer, Comus. Alice spoke as well as sang in her role as the
Lady, her younger brothers John (aged eleven, the future second Earl of
Bridgewater) and Thomas (aged nine) taking lesser roles. Henry Lawes, as
the children's music teacher, played the role of the Attendant Spirit, and
it is almost certainly through Lawes that Milton received the commission to write the masque, as the musician was a friend of Milton's father.
Comus exemplifies a rich culture of masquing and musical performance in
the Egerton family, including its women and girls: several of the Egerton
girls, including Alice, performed in court masques.[28] *Comus* is frequently
read as a recuperation of familial purity in the face of the Castlehaven
sex scandal, involving the Earl's brother-in-law Mervyn Touchet. In the
Egerton family, it seems, a rite of purification was not inconsistent with
spoken and sung performance on the part of a fifteen-year-old girl.

   According to canonical literary history, the story of Alice Egerton
ends with her performance in *Comus*, poised at the point of marriage-
ability, her chastity saved and celebrated.[29] Egerton's story, however, is

---

[27] Henry Lawes, *Ayres and Dialogues* (London: W. Godbid for John Playford, 1658), 48; see also
Ross, *Women, Poetry, and Politics*, 108.

[28] Williams, *Shakespeare and the Performance of Girlhood*, 153.

[29] Stephen Orgel suggests that 'Alice Egerton's story, like most women's stories throughout history,
ends with marriage. In fact, for our purposes, it ends sixteen [sic] years before her marriage, with
Milton's masque' ('The Case for Comus', 44; Orgel misdates the marriage to 1650). Alice's
descendent and early editor of *Comus*, Alix Egerton, is more nuanced: 'Here, so far as "Comus" is
concerned, the history of the three children ends; for the after lives of Lord Brackley and Lady
Alice another place must be found' (Alix Egerton [ed.], *Milton's Comus, being the Bridgewater
Manuscript. With Notes and a Short Family Memoir* [London: J. M. Dent, 1910], 31).

long – and only one of its intriguing aspects is that she did not marry for another eighteen years until, at the age of thirty-three in July 1652, she became the third wife to Richard Vaughan, second Earl of Carbery. Her protracted maidenhood has often been noted,[30] and is striking in comparison to her sister-in-law Elizabeth Cavendish's marriage to John Egerton at the age of fifteen. Fifteen is the age at which young women were driven to 'pushes' (or extremities) in love, according to the Jailer's Daughter in Fletcher and Shakespeare's *The Two Noble Kinsmen* (2.4.6–7); and the Jailer's Daughter is 'cured' via wooing (and sexual consummation) at the age of eighteen (5.2.31). And like the Jailer's Daughter, it seems, Alice Egerton was treated for a 'disease of chastity' from October 1632 to August 1633, her treatment concluding less than a year before the performance of *Comus*: extended records in the casebook of the family physician Richard Napier document her symptoms, and uncertainty as to whether they arise from natural causes or witchcraft.[31] Alice's sister Magdalen, also treated for similar symptoms in the same time period, married Gervase Cutler at the age of eighteen in 1633.[32] Of Alice, Brogan Boyd reflects that her mother died in 1636 and her ailing father needed care; and that 'later, the civil war decimated the stock of potential husbands, as well as damaged the family finances'.[33] It may simply be that the disruption of the Civil War 'condemned' Alice Egerton to 'a kind of protracted girlhood', as Deanne Williams has written of the Cavendish sisters.[34] Jane Cavendish, certainly, did not marry until 1654, at which time she was also thirty-three. But whatever the reason for Alice Egerton's prolonged unmarried state, her story ends neither with *Comus* nor with marriage alone: for the intervening years there are several scattered but suggestive records of her ongoing engagement in musical and performance activities at home and beyond.

Alice Egerton continued to live at Ashridge through the 1640s, after Elizabeth Cavendish moved there to join her husband in mid to late 1645. (Jane Cavendish may also have spent some time there after the Cavendish sisters' departure from Welbeck and before her marriage in

---

[30] See, for example, William Riley Parker, *Milton: A Biography*, 2nd ed., 1968, rev. ed. Gordon Campbell (Oxford: Clarendon Press, 1996).

[31] Boyd, 'The Masque'. Boyd has examined records more extensive than the single letter transcribed by Barbara Breasted in her influential article, 'Another Bewitching of Lady Alice Egerton, the Lady of *Comus*', *Notes and Queries*, 17 (1970), 411–12.

[32] Boyd, 'The Masque,' suggests that the Egertons regarded eighteen as a suitable age for marriage, based on the examples of Alice's sisters (41).

[33] Boyd, 'The Masque', 42.

[34] Williams, *Shakespeare and the Performance of Girlhood*, 189.

1654.)[35] Alice continued to perform – and almost certainly to study – music with Henry Lawes until her marriage,[36] and there is among the records of the Bridgewater family a song performed by her and Lawes, celebrating Elizabeth and John Egerton after the birth of their first child. 'A Hymneall Songe On a celebration of the Nuptials, of the Right Ho[ble] John, Lord Brackley, and his virtuous Lady, After the Byrth of their First Sone' is in two parts, the voices attributed to 'La[dy]', performed by Alice Egerton, and 'H[enry] L[awes]'. Lawes's voice is 'an Eccho' to the Lady's celebration of 'this happye daye', of the birth of an heir, and of 'our Brydegroome, and our Bryde'.[37] Lawes's figure of echo may be a 'witty allusion to his Echo song from *Comus*', as Deanne Williams argues,[38] but more generally, the sung dialogue realizes in formal terms the reiteration of celebration and praise, as the voice of echo repeats and endorses the Lady's expressions of joy. Several further anniversary songs are included in the Egerton papers, including another 'Aniversary on the Nuptials of the Right Ho[bles] The Earle and Countess of Bridgewater', signed by Lawes and dated 22 July 1651.[39] This is another two-part song, 'set into Musique for 2 voices', and while the performers of the voices are not in this case specified, it is possible Alice Egerton was called on again.

Alice's prolonged residence at Ashridge coincided with the more circumspect devotional writing of her sister-in-law Elizabeth, who marked her years of childbearing in the voluminous production of religious prose and poems.[40] Elizabeth bore at least nine children between 1646 and her death in childbirth in 1663,[41] and her hopes and fears for herself and

---

[35] Betty Travitsky notes Jane's description in a later document of '2 pare of holland sheets which I used to lie in at Welbeck, I brought with mee to Ashridge, & from thens to Chellsey' (*Subordination and Authorship*, 65). Chelsea was Jane's home after her marriage in 1654.

[36] Willa McClung Evans, *Henry Lawes: Musician and Friend of Poets* (New York: Modern Language Association of America, and London: Oxford University Press, 1941), 191, suggests that 'until her marriage Lady Alice Egerton probably continued to study with her old master'.

[37] Hunt MS EL 8342. Elizabeth and John's first child, John, was born on 9 November 1646 (Hunt MS EL 8348).

[38] Williams, *Shakespeare and the Performance of Girlhood*, 169.

[39] Hunt MS EL 8343. The same lyric is published, with its musical setting, in Lawes's first book of *Ayres and Dialogues*, 33. It is dated 1652 in the published version, but that is incorrect. The song celebrates the couple's tenth wedding anniversary (1651).

[40] Elizabeth's religious 'loose papers' were collected and transcribed in multiple manuscript copies after her death, 'examined' and signed by her husband, John Egerton. One of her volumes is BL Egerton MS 607, from which quotations below are taken. Two other copies are at the Huntington Library, one of which is the basis of Travitsky's edition in *Subordination and Authorship*.

[41] Nine children, living or deceased as infants, are listed in her death certificate, although this does not mention the stillborn infant whose birth led to her own death (Hunt MS EL 8348). Among the Egerton papers is a poem on her death by her sister Jane, 'On the death of my Deare Sister the

her infants are charted in these writings. She writes simple but moving prayers on her multiple pregnancies and confinements, and brief memorials on the deaths of 'my Boy Henry' and 'my Deare Girle Kate'.[42] It is rare for Elizabeth to move beyond these maternal subjects of piety and loss, but in one short poem, she adopts an ekphrastic posture, composing a poem 'Made on a Sight of ye Countesse of Bridgewaters Picture'.[43] She celebrates her husband's mother, Frances, the first Countess of Bridgewater, in conventional language: 'On thy true Picture all may looke,/And make of thee a perfect vertuous Booke', and 'So rest y^u happy Soule, 'twas such,/Thy Children cannot giue thee praise too much'.[44] Her praise of the first Countess as a 'vertuous Booke' is apt: Frances was renowned for her piety and her learning, and the Bridgewater manuscripts include a list of more than 200 books owned by her.[45] One of these books brings her daughter Alice and her daughter-in-law Elizabeth together in the record of women's household reading. Frances's *Elizabethan Book of Homilyes* contains Alice Egerton's signature, as well as an inscription by John Egerton, third Earl of Bridgewater (1646–1701), indicating that it was a gift from his mother – that is, Elizabeth.[46]

While Alice Egerton is associated with household pious reading in the record of her mother's library, she also engaged in the early 1650s in more public lyric performances, in music meetings held at Henry Lawes's London home. Lawes's music meetings have received attention as a site of female public performance in the years of the Commonwealth, and for their enactment of a displaced royalist court culture.[47] Edward Phillips, Milton's nephew, describes 'brightest Dames, the splendour of the court' in attendance, and the audience seems to have been 'a mix of aristocrats, literati, and personal friends'.[48] Margaret Cavendish made several visits to Lawes's house during her trip to London between November 1651 and March 1653, and Sophie Tomlinson and Hero Chalmers suggest that the

---

Countesse of Bridgewater dying in Childbed, Delivered of a dead Infant a Son, the 14th day of Iune 1663' (Hunt MS EL 8353).

[42] BL Egerton MS 607, fols. 119^r–126^v.

[43] Her sister Jane Cavendish's occasional poems include several comparable ekphrastic poems, composed on portraits of her absent, exemplary father and brothers; see Ross, *Women, Poetry, and Politics*, 115 and 119.

[44] BL Egerton MS 607, fol. 127^r.

[45] See Hackel, 'The Countess of Bridgewater's London Library'.

[46] The book is Hunt HUL RB473000, described in Molekamp, *Women and the Bible*, 88–9.

[47] Chalmers, 'Dismantling the Myth of "Mad Madge"', 324–5; Sophie Tomlinson, *Women on Stage in Stuart Drama* (Cambridge: Cambridge University Press, 2005); Catharine Gray, 'Katherine Philips and the Post-Courtly Coterie', *ELR* 32 (2002), 426–51 at 430.

[48] Austern, 'The Conjuncture of Word, Music, and Performance Practice', 233.

'support of female musical achievement propagated by Lawes' may have 'helped galvanise' her determination to publish her own dramatic and poetic writings.[49] Lawes's valorisation of women's musical achievement – most famously in Alice Egerton – is illustrated in his dedication of his first book of *Ayres and Dialogues* (1653) to her and her sister Mary, both then married. Lawes's dedication looks back to his years of employment by their parents, and to their outstanding musical achievements:

> no sooner I thought of making these Publick, than of inscribing them to Your *Ladiships*, most of them being Composed when I was employed by Your ever Honour'd Parents to attend Your *Ladishipp's* Education in *Musick*; who (as in other Accomplishments fit for Persons of Your Quality) excell'd most Ladies, especially in *Vocall Musick*, wherein You were so absolute, that You gave Life and Honour to all I set and taught You. (Sig. aʳ)

That Lawes's circle provided a rare and rarified site of women's lyric agency is also evinced in the dedication of his *Second Booke of Ayres and Dialogues, for One, Two, and Three Voyces* (1655) to Mary Harvey, Lady Dering, which highlights her own composition:

> those Songs which fill this Book have receiv'd much lustre by your excellent performance of them; and (which I confess I rejoice to speak of) some which I esteem the best of these *Ayres*, were of your own *Composition*, after your Noble Husband was pleas'd to give the *Words*. For (although your *Ladiship* resolv'd to keep it private) I beg leave to declare, for my own honour, that you are not only excellent for the time you spent in the practice of what I *set*, but are your self so good a *Composer*, that few of any Sex have arriv'd to such perfection. (Sig. aʳ)

The same *Second Booke of Ayres and Dialogues* that celebrates Mary Harvey, Lady Dering, also features a prefatory poem by another likely attendee of Lawes's music meetings: the poet Katherine Philips. Philips was a school friend of Mary Harvey, and her poem 'To the much honoured Mr Henry Lawes, On his Excellent Compositions in Musick' praises him as a 'Great Soule of Nature' who lives to 'asswage/The savage dulness of this sullen Age' (sig. bʳ). Philips's own musical training is uncertain, although Linda Phyllis Austern reflects that women of Philips's class, 'children of successful merchants whose religious convictions led them to emphasize access to the written word', were often trained in vocal and instrumental music. Mary Harvey's achievements suggest that Mrs Salmon's boarding school in Hackney, attended by Philips and

---

[49] Chalmers, 'Dismantling the Myth of "Mad Madge"', 324.

Harvey, offered a musical education.[50] Certainly, Henry Lawes set at least four of Philips's poems to music. One of these, a musical setting of 'Friendship's Mystery, to my Dearest Lucasia', is printed in Lawes's *Second Booke of Ayres and Dialogues*; another, his sarabande setting for Philips's lyric 'On the death of my first and dearest childe, Hector Philips', is preserved in a later manuscript miscellany. At least two further settings have been lost.[51]

Katherine Philips's likely presence at Henry Lawes's socially elite music meetings suggests a new configuration of overlapping royalist literary and cultural circles in Civil War and republican England. Philips is of course renowned for her own poetic coterie, her Society of Friends, cultivated and sustained through the circulation of her manuscript poetry among her social and literary associates. Mary Harvey's husband, Sir Edward Dering, was an intimate member of this coterie, known by the pastoral name of 'Silvander'; his manuscript volume of Philips's poems, compiled in the early 1660s, is one of the important witnesses of her work.[52] One of the poems he records is an occasional verse written by Philips to Alice Egerton, with whom she had presumably come into contact at Lawes's music meetings. Philips writes to Egerton on the occasion of her arrival in Wales, where Philips also resided, on her marriage to Richard Vaughan, Earl of Carbery, in July 1652. 'To the Right Honourable Alice, Countess of Carberry, on her enriching Wales w^t her presence', addresses Alice in an encomiastic conceit, figuring her as a sun who will bring a welcome lustre to dull Welsh obscurity. She goes on to praise Egerton's 'great splendours' that, 'like eternall spring/To these sad groves such a refreshment bring/That the despised countrey may be growne/And justly too the envy of the Towne' (23–6). Philips's poetry of the early 1650s has been explored extensively for its politically charged articulation of friendship,[53] but this poem's formal, fulsome praise suggests that she may not have known Egerton well. Egerton was not a member of Philips's Society of Friends (she has no pastoral pseudonym); and in comparison to Jane Cavendish's earlier answer poem on Egerton's musical

---

[50] Austern, 'The Conjuncture of Word, Music, and Performance Practice', 214–15.

[51] Henry Lawes, *Second Booke of Ayres and Dialogues* (London: T. H. for John Playford, 1655), sig. H^r; see also Joan Applegate, 'Katherine Philips's "Orinda upon Little Hector": An Unrecorded Musical Setting by Henry Lawes', in Beal and Griffiths (eds.), *English Manuscript Studies 1100–1700*, vol. IV (1993), 272–80. Settings for 'A Dialogue between Lucasia and Orinda' and 'To Mrs M. A. upon absence, 12 December 1650' are at present unlocated.

[52] The Dering Manuscript, containing seventy-four of Philips's poems, is HRC Pre-1700 MS 151 (available on the Adam Matthews Perdita Manuscripts database).

[53] See, for example, Chalmers, *Royalist Women Writers*, and Anderson, *Friendship's Shadows*.

performance, Philips's poem seems to enact a relatively aspirational socio-poetic address.[54]

Katherine Philips and Alice Egerton both spent the 1650s in Wales, Philips in Cardigan and Egerton, now the Countess of Carbery, at Golden Grove in Carmathenshire. Whether they became more closely acquainted is unknown, at least for now. Coteries, circles, and networks of literary and cultural production often leave only ephemeral records – especially where women are concerned – and much work remains to be done on the extended literary lives of the Cavendish sisters, Alice Egerton and their poetic and musical associates. Other circles or apparently iso-lated writers may yet be found to have overlapped or intersected with them. Hester Pulter, the daughter of James I's Lord Chief Justice and a staunchly royalist poet, spent the 1640s only twenty-five miles away from Ashridge, at Broadfield in Hertfordshire; it seems that the self-professedly isolated Pulter, 'shut up in a Country grange', did not associate with the extended Cavendish circle. Her witty poem on William Davenant's loss of his nose indicates that she is 'unknown' to him, while Davenant was supported by William Cavendish and wrote a celebratory poem on Jane Cavendish's wedding to Charles Cheyne in 1654.[55] Pulter's elegy on the death of Margaret Cavendish's brother, Sir Charles Lucas, in 1648, inti-mates no personal connection. Pulter, it seems, moved in very different circles despite her royalism – and indeed, her sharp poetic criticism of Hyde Park, Spring Garden, and of duchesses eating 'scurvy Cheesecake' is at odds with the fashionable pre-Civil War lifestyle of Margaret Cavendish and her types.[56]

Conclusion

Coteries, circles and networks have been thoroughly explored as 'essential material conditions' for literary production in early modern England, and the elite 1630s household was a nucleus of rich and elaborate poetic

---

[54] Another manuscript copy of the poem is contained in the papers of the third Earl of Bridgewater (Alice Egerton's nephew); in this copy, the poem is written 'On the Right Honourable Alice' rather than 'To' her: see Elizabeth H. Hageman and Andrea Sununu, 'New Manuscript Texts of Katherine Philips, the "Matchless Orinda"', in Beal and Griffiths (eds.), *English Manuscript Studies 1100–1700*, vol. IV (1993), 172–219.

[55] Eardley (ed.), *Lady Hester Pulter*, 172–4; A. M. Gibb, 'Upon the Marriage of the Lady Jane Cavendish with Mr Cheney', in A. M. Gibb (ed.), *The Shorter Poems, and Songs from the Plays and Masques* (Oxford: Clarendon Press, 1971), 131–2.

[56] See Pulter's twentieth emblem poem, in Eardley (ed.), *Lady Hester Pulter*, 210–13.

and dramatic production, including that of women.[57] Jane and Elizabeth Cavendish and Alice Egerton operated at the centre of elite household coteries, and in the wider and overlapping literary circles that emanated from them. Katherine Philips presided over a literary coterie of her own, and her Society of Friends illustrates the changing nature of the literary coteries, circles and networks in which women wrote and performed, alongside the changing nature of the literary women.[58] Philips emerged from a relatively new class of literate and literary woman in the mid-century, as did her friend Mary Harvey, and their eminence in the circles of Henry Lawes is manifest in manuscript as well as print publication. Of all the women discussed in this chapter, it is Philips whose work was first produced on the public stage: her translation of Corneille's *La Mort de Pompée* was performed at Smock Alley theatre in Dublin in 1663. And notwithstanding Margaret Cavendish's quest for fame and canonicity, it was Philips who became a model for female authorship in the later seventeenth century, after the print publication of her *Poems* in 1664 and 1667, and after her untimely death from smallpox. Like Margaret Cavendish, Philips was a printed poet; unlike Cavendish, her identity and mode remained firmly associated with the coterie and manuscript network culture that has been explored in this chapter. Even in mid-seventeenth-century England, authorship in manuscript circles and networks remained more acceptable for women than Margaret Cavendish's brand of printed self-promotion. Indeed, the 'material condition' of the literary circle is not only essential to Philips's writing but to the image of the female author that it enabled, at once retiring and strategic in her circulation of verse, and discreet yet purposefully prolific in the circulation of her work.

---

[57] Summers and Pebworth (eds.), *Literary Circles and Cultural Communities*, 1.

[58] A further extension of such social change is represented in the country house poem 'The Vision. Or a Poeticall View of Ashridge', penned in 1699 by the daughter of the third Earl of Bridgewater's chaplain, Marie Burghope (Hunt MS EL 35/B/62; available in Millman and Wright (eds.), *Early Modern Women's Manuscript Poetry*, 194–213).

19

Inventing Fame

Jane B. Stevenson

Applying the concept of fame to women has been problematic. Thucydides put in Pericles's mouth the truism that she 'of whom there is least talk among men whether in praise or in blame', enjoys the appropriate form of female glory.[1] Two thousand years later, in seventeenth-century England, fame and infamy still ran close together for women, because public presence was so readily linked with sexual incontinence.[2]

Martha Moulsworth, in her autobiographic poem written in 1632, claimed with pride that her father (a clergyman and tutor of Christ Church, Oxford, who died when she was two and a half) 'was a Man of spottles ffame'.[3] But for people whose gender, class or religious affiliation put them at odds with the dominant elite, spotless fame was hard to achieve. By contrast, the Bishop of Lincoln wrote of one Jane Hawkins, a beggar-woman who had got into trouble for prophesying, 'the weoman is not yeat (Generallye) of any good; and hath beene of very badd fame'.[4] To acquire fame is to risk defamation: Hawkins's 'badd fame' derived from being a puritan in the age of Archbishop Laud, though to fellow-puritans, including her vicar, Hawkins was virtuous, even holy.

However, the early modern world had a particular idea of fame as it applied to women. Though Mary Evelyn wrote in 1672 that 'a heroine is a kind of prodigy; the influence of a blazing star is not more dangerous or more avoided',[5] in her *Doctrine for the Lady of the Renaissance*, Ruth Kelso assembled 891 treatises on women, the vast majority of which hold up heroines for admiration, if not direct emulation.[6] *An Essay to Revive*

---

[1] Thucydides, *History of the Peloponnesian War, Volume I: Books 1 and 2*, trans. C. F. Smith, Loeb Classical Library 108 (Cambridge, MA: Harvard University Press, 1919), book II, 45.

[2] Gowing, *Domestic Dangers*.

[3] He was Richard Dorsett: see *ODNB* for Martha Moulsworth; see also Stevenson and Davidson (eds.), *Early Modern Women Poets*, 127.

[4] Stevenson and Davidson (eds.), *Early Modern Women Poets*, 226.

[5] Letter to Ralph Bohun, printed in John Evelyn, *Diary and Correspondence*, William Bray (ed.), 4 vols. (London: H.G. Bohn, 1862–3), vol. IV, 8–9.

[6] Kelso, *Doctrine for the Lady of the Renaissance*, 327–424.

the Antient Education of Gentlewomen, dubiously attributed to Bathsua Makin, is typical of the genre in its derivativeness, carelessness about details, and absence of any concern for primary evidence.[7] What we see here is contentless fame, the perpetuation of names copied from book to book, often shedding details along the way and frequently acquiring error. Thus 'fame' for a woman, could not only be double-edged, it could also be utterly detached from an attempt to evaluate, or even value, what a famous woman had actually achieved.

Katherine Philips

Competing concepts of worth coexisted in mid-seventeenth century England, and noble rank was not a universal currency. Mary Evelyn was scandalised by the Duchess of Newcastle on her visit to London in 1667. She judged her 'amasingly vain and ambitious', and continued:

> What contrary miracles dos this Age produce, This Lady and Mrs Phelips, the one transporded with the shadow of reason the other possessed of the substance and insensible of her treasure, yet men who pass for learned and wise not only put them in iquall balance but make the greatness of the one wheigh down the certaine and reall worth of the other.[8]

As Mary Evelyn implies, ideas about honour, status, worth and fame were variously defined in the mid-century. Women might also be judged for professionalism and talent. In Edward Phillips's list of 'women among the moderns eminent for poetry', Katherine Philips (no relation) is discussed.

> *Catherine Philips*, the most applauded, at this time, Poetess of our Nation, either of the present or former Ages, and not without reason, since both her Fame is of a fresh and lively date from the but late publisht Volume of her Poetical works, and those also of a style suitable to the humour and Genius of these times.[9]

---

[7] Noel Malcolm, 'The Lady Vanishes', *TLS* (5 November, 1999), 28; Makin, *Essay*. Sources drawn on verbatim include Thomas Heywood, *Gynaikeion: or, Nine bookes of various history. Concerninge women* (London: Printed by Adam Islip, 1624), 398 on Laurentia Strozza; and Samuel Torshell, *The Womans Glorie: A Treatise* (London: for John Bellamy, 1650), 256 on Margarita Sarocchia, both found in *An Essay*. See Teague and Ezell (eds.) and Walker (assoc. ed.), *Educating English Daughters*, 36–42, for a recent discussion of the attribution of the work to Makin.
[8] Mary Evelyn to Mr Bohune, Fellow of New College (Dr Ralph Bohun), quoted in Beal, *In Praise of Scribes*, 154.
[9] Edward Phillips, *Theatrum Poetarum, or a Compleat Collection of the Poets* (London: Charles Smith, 1675), 157 [=257].

As Peter Beal has shown, during her lifetime, Philips had a public identity as a manuscript poet, even though the circulation of manuscripts was
risky.[10] Katherine Philips's friend Henry Lawes issued his 1653 collection
of songs, *Ayres and Dialogues*, as a counter to John Playford's 1652 volume which contained, he claimed, twenty of his songs.[11] In many cases,
the sequence of publications supports the view that piracy was a genuine
problem.

The popularity of Philips's poems similarly led to her writings being
pirated.[12] She wrote to the Earl of Orrery,

> I intend to send you by the first Opportunity a Miscellaneous Collection
> of Poems, printed here, among which, to fill up the Number of his Sheets,
> and as a Foil to the others, the Printer has thought fit, tho' without my
> consent or Privity, to publish two or three Poems of mine, that had been
> stolen from me'.

Her reaction was less insouciant when a whole collection of her work,
based, as Peter Beal has demonstrated, on a manuscript which she had
put into circulation,[13] was published by Richard Marriott, a known
pirate who also published unauthorised editions of Donne's *Poems* in
1633 and Henry King's in 1657.[14] Since the format (small quarto)
allowed the reader to assume that Philips had published the collection for
money, she was acutely embarrassed, and put enormous effort into getting it withdrawn.[15]

The implication of Mary Evelyn's contrast between Cavendish and
Philips is that, in the judgement of many contemporaries, fame might
be *awarded* to women but not sought. Similarly, Philips's 'Friendship in
Emblem', for her friend Anne Owen, represents fame as the judgement
of posterity – and, interestingly, raises the possibility of her work drawing down infamy instead, if later readers impute a sexual aspect to their
mutual devotion.

---

[10] Beal, *In Praise of Scribes*, 147–91.

[11] Ezell, *Social Authorship*, 47–8. As Ezell also points out, the improved text might, however, circulate
only in manuscript (48–55).

[12] Katherine Philips, letter 'Orinda to Poliarchus', 15 May, 1663, in Katherine Philips, *The Collected
Works of Katherine Philips, the Matchless Orinda* Patrick Thomas (ed.), 2 vols. (Saffron Walden,
Essex: Stump Cross Books, 1990), vol. II, 88, referring to *Poems by Several Persons of Quality and
Refined Wit* (Dublin: John Crooke for Samuel Dancer, 1663).

[13] Beal, *In Praise of Scribes*, 165.

[14] Katherine Philips, *Poems by the Incomparable Mrs. K.P.* (London: J. G. for Rich. Marriott, 1664).

[15] Stevenson, 'Women and the Cultural Politics of Printing', 220–4.

> But as there is degrees of bliss
> So there's no friendship meant by this,
> But such as will transmit to fame
> *Lucasia's* and *Orinda's* name.[16]

'Philo-Philippa' similarly writes of Philips in terms of a fame awarded rather than sought, and consequently, authentic.[17]

After Philips's death, the 'Rosania Manuscript', a 400-page quarto memorial volume, was written in a neat, possibly professional, hand, for presentation to her then closest friend, Mary Aubrey, whom Philips regularly addressed as Rosania.[18] This calls for Philips's work to be printed posthumously, though it acknowledges, and endorses, her reluctance to be printed during her life.

> To appear in print, how unenclined she was? (I confess an Edition now, would gratify her Admirers, and 'twere but a just remeriting that value which (in hers, & in their own Right) was y[e] Universall consent).[19]

Such a posthumous edition was indeed set in motion.[20] Fame, these writers imply, came to Philips deservedly, the more so for being unsought.

Lucy Hutchinson

To paraphrase Shakespeare, some were born famous: members of the royal family and nobles. Some achieved fame, as did Philips, and some had fame thrust upon them, which appears to be the case with Lucy Hutchinson, since most of her work survives either as family papers or in nineteenth-century editions by her descendant Julius Hutchinson. However, though her self-representation in most of her writing is reclusive, she was known to be a writer by contemporaries, and like Philips, she circulated some verse. Her reply to Waller's panegyric on Cromwell

---

[16] Since the poem borrows its central image from Donne's poem to his future wife, 'A Valediction, forbidding mourning', the imputation of a lesbian connection is potentially there to be raised: see Stevenson and Davidson (eds.), *Early Modern Women Poets*, 327–9.

[17] Stevenson and Davidson (eds.), *Early Modern Women Poets*, 402.

[18] Aberystwyth, National Library of Wales MS 776. The close resemblance of the sometimes idiosyncratic orthography of this MS to that of MS A would suggest that the poems which it contains were copied from autograph papers, an indication of concern to get as close as possible to Philips's original intentions.

[19] Beal, *In Praise of Scribes*, 170.

[20] Katherine Philips, *Poems by the most deservedly admired Mrs. Katherine Philips, the matchless Orinda* (London: Printed by J.M. for H. Herringman, 1667).

survives in Hyde family papers, and she gave her cousin Ann Wilmot, Countess of Rochester, a copy of her long poem *Order and Disorder*.[21]

When she was a young mother in the 1650s, Hutchinson translated the Epicurean philosopher Lucretius: 'I turnd it into English in a roome where my children practizd the severall quallities they were taught with their Tutors, and I numbred the sillables of my translation by the threds of the canvas I wrought in, & sett them down with a pen & inke that stood by me'.[22] Since she used at least two different editions of her original, the translation cannot have been quite this casual, but in 1675, when she wrote this description, she was distancing herself from the entire enterprise. Why she embarked on it in the first place is a question. There was considerable interest in Lucretius in the 1650s.[23] John Evelyn published a translation of the first book in 1656, known to Hutchinson, and the scholarly recusant Sir Edward Sherburne also produced an unpublished translation.[24] The royalist playwright and pamphleteer Alexander Brome was working on a version in 1658. Hutchinson's was finished by then, and in circulation, since Sir Aston Cokain mentions it in a poem encouraging Brome to persevere with his own translation.[25]

One problem with assessing Hutchinson's work is that so much of what we see of her life and achievements is from the perspective of the 1670s, after years of widowhood, disappointment and loss. The intellectually curious young woman she had once been is glimpsed from a distance, rejected by her later self.[26] However, it would seem from various writings of Hutchinson that her study of Classical texts had left her fascinated by people who had had to make sense of their lives in a pre-Christian universe. This shapes her interest in Lucretius, who argued for the gods' indifference to human lives. From Hutchinson's Christian perspective, this was true. Before Christ, there was no interaction between the gentiles and God, so Lucretius's Epicurean rejection of superstition was

---

[21] Hutchinson, *Works, Volume I*, xci and cxiii.

[22] Ibid., 7.

[23] Kroll, *Material Word*, 85–179.

[24] John Evelyn, *An Essay on the First Book of T. Lucretius Carus De rerum natura. Interpreted and Made English verse by J. Evelyn Esq* (London: for Gabriel Bedle, and Thomas Collins, 1656); Edward Sherburne, *The Poems and Translations of Sir Edward Sherburne (1616–1702)*, ed. and intro. F. J. van Beeck (Assen: van Gorcum, 1961).

[25] Sir Aston Cokain, *Small Poems of Divers Sorts* (London: William Godbid, 1658), 204. Cokain moved in circles which overlapped with Hutchinson's own family and connections, but that did not mean he was sympathetic to her: he was a royalist, and a Catholic (Hutchinson, *Works, Volume I*, xxiii).

[26] See Goldberg, 'Lucy Hutchinson'.

the best that mere human reason could achieve. Conversely, if one had been lucky enough to be born in the Christian era, and offered salvation, Epicureanism would be a wicked rejection of God's mercy.

However, a second upsurge of interest in Lucretius after the Restoration was associated with secularistic, hedonistic and atheistic reaction against the puritan piety of the Interregnum. When Thomas Creech's translation was published in 1682, it opened up Lucretius's text to a new and interested audience. Aphra Behn's long poem in Creech's praise suggests something of the excitement it generated.[27] In the 1670s, Hutchinson found to her horror that an unauthorised copy, or copies, of her translation was circulating. This in turn suggests that, like Philips, she found that her text had escaped out of her control. What made things worse was that she feared her translation was feeding the new, neo-Epicurean, interest in Lucretius, which to her was pernicious madness.

Her reaction was twofold. She published *Order and Disorder* anonymously in 1679, explaining in its Preface that it had been written as a sort of antidote to her Lucretius translation:

> These meditations were not at first designed for public view, but fixed upon to reclaim a busy roving thought from wandering in the pernicious and perplexed maze of human inventions; wherein the vain curiosity of youth had drawn me to consider and translate the account some old poets and philosophers give of the original of things ... it filled my brain with such foolish fancies, that I found it necessary to have recourse to the fountain of Truth, to wash out all ugly wild impressions.[28]

She seems to have hoped that her Genesis poem would militate against potential damage done by her Lucretius translation: 'lest that arrive by misadventure, which never shall by my consent, that any of the puddled water my wanton youth drew from the profane Helicon of ancient poets should be sprinkled about the world, I have for prevention sent forth this essay'. She also had a new copy made from her own manuscript, which she had evidently kept by her, in 1675, and presented it to her friend Arthur Annesley, Earl of Anglesey, with a dedication which denounces modern atheists and hedonists as even more pernicious than the pagan Lucretius.[29] Thus, like other early modern writers, she creates

---

[27] Thomas Creech, *T. Lucretius Carus the Epicurean Philosopher His Six Books De natura rerum* (Oxford: L. Lichfield for Anthony Stephens); and Behn, *Works*, vol. I, 25–9.

[28] Hutchinson, *Order and Disorder*, 3.

[29] BL Add. MS 17018, Lucy Hutchinson, 'To Mr: Waller vpon his Panegyrique to the Lord Protector', fols. 214ʳ–15ʳ.

an authorised version in order to keep some control over her text. It is also clear that she was attempting to manage her reputation.

The Hutchinson who was a young woman married to a leading Parliamentarian, on the winning side in the Civil War, was a very different person from Hutchinson in the 1670s. After the Restoration, she was the wife, then widow, of a regicide, and herself a Dissenter in an England in which episcopal control had been effectively re-established. While the *Indemnity and Oblivion Act* (1660) attempted, as far as possible, to heal national divisions after the Restoration, it specifically excluded the regicides, who as a group were the focus of orchestrated infamy. Colonel Hutchinson escaped a traitor's death, either, as Hutchinson claims, due to the efforts of his wife and her royalist relations, or as other evidence suggests, by suing humiliatingly for mercy.[30] She wrote his biography for her children, both to clear his name and to give his descendants a highly tendentious version of his history (and hers). This was perhaps suggested to her by Cavendish's published biography of her husband and autobiography, both of which are, similarly, extremely partisan documents.[31]

The *Memoir*'s existence was known outside the family in the eighteenth century. Catherine Macaulay, author of an eight-volume political history of the seventeenth century (published 1763–83), was interested in it and attempted to persuade Thomas Hutchinson, who owned it, to allow it to be published, without success.[32] It was eventually published in 1806 by Thomas Hutchinson's nephew Julius, and was a considerable success; editions of 1808, 1810 and 1822 followed. It was re-edited by C. H. Firth, appeared in Bohn's Standard Library and Everyman's Library, and edited again by Harold Child in 1905, James Sutherland in 1973, and Neil Keeble in 1995.[33] Part of its interest for the nineteenth century was the vivid impression it gives of the experience of civil war, but its great attraction was the portrait of a marriage which seemed to nineteenth-century critics to express a perfect ideal of conjugality, from

---

[30] Derek Hirst, 'Remembering a Hero: Lucy Hutchinson's Memoirs of Her Husband', *The English Historical Review* 119, 482 (June 2004), 682–91 at 683 and 687–8.

[31] On the biography, see Douglas Grant, *Margaret the First: A Biography of Margaret Cavendish, Duchess of Newcastle, 1623–1673* (London: Hart Davis, 1957); and on the autobiography, Whitaker, *Mad Madge*, 199.

[32] Lucy Hutchinson, *Memoirs of the Life of Colonel Hutchinson* Julius Hutchinson (ed.) (London: Longman, Hurst, Rees and Orme, 1806), i.

[33] Lucy Hutchinson, *Memoirs of the Life of Colonel Hutchinson* James Sutherland (ed.) (Oxford University Press, 1973), xxvi.

Francis, Lord Jeffrey, in the *Edinburgh Review*,[34] to Sarah Josepha Hale in 1860, who summed up Hutchinson in her own words: 'she was but a faithful mirror, reflecting truly, but dimly, his own glories upon him'.[35]

By contrast, Hutchinson's Lucretius translation was not published until 1996. Because the surviving copy belonged to the Earl of Anglesey, the manuscript travelled separately from the Hutchinson family papers, and ended up in the British Library. It first came to light via H. A. J. Munro, editor of Lucretius, in 1858, and his view was that it 'would hardly increase the reputation of the author of the *Memoirs*'.[36] He printed the Preface, which was picked up by C. H. Firth, who added it to his edition of the *Memoirs*, but the translation could not readily be assimilated with the established view of Hutchinson as pious reflector of her husband's glory. Myra Reynold, in her pioneering *The Learned Lady in England* (1920), was evidently aware, thanks to Firth, of the existence of the translation, but it failed to influence her representation of Hutchinson, which is dominated by the latter's exemplary wifehood.[37]

Elizabeth Melville, Lady Culross

A Scotswoman whose relation to print forms a comparandum with that of Hutchinson is the most successful published woman poet of the English-speaking world in the early modern period, Elizabeth Melville, Lady Culross. Her long poem, *Ane Godlie Dreame*, was not published in England, but she was the *only* seventeenth-century Scots poet, of either gender, whose work was printed and reprinted in her native land.[38] *Ane Godlie Dreame* was issued at least thirteen times between 1603 and 1737. This is surprising, since only two other women published in Scotland before 1700: Anna Hume, whose Petrarch translation, *The triumphs of: love: chastitie: death* came out in 1644 (she also edited her

[34] Francis Jeffrey, 'Memoirs of the Life of Colonel Hutchinson', *Edinburgh Review* 25 (October 1808), 1–23 at 4: 'we do not know where to look for a more noble and engaging character than that under which this lady presents herself to her readers; nor do we believe that any age of the world has produced so worthy a counterpart to the Valerias and Portias of antiquity'.
[35] Sarah Josepha Hale, *Women's Record* (New York: Harper & Sons, 1860), 359–60. See also Looser, *British Women Writers*, 28–60.
[36] H. A. J. Munro, 'Mrs Lucie Hutchinson's Translation of Lucretius', *Journal of Classical and Sacred Philology*, 4 (1858), 128–39.
[37] Myra Reynold, *The Learned Lady in England* (Chicago and New York: Houghton Mifflin, 1920), 72.
[38] For further discussion of the peculiarly small, archaic and rigid canon of printed literature in early modern Scotland, see Stevenson, 'Reading, Writing and Gender', 338.

father's *History of the Houses of Douglas and Angus*); and an unidentified 'Lady of Honour' who published a broadsheet poem puffing the Darien Scheme in 1699, *The Golden Island*.[39] Additionally, women's spiritual journals were circulated in manuscript, as was the case in England, Lucy Hutchinson's among them.[40] For example, Henrietta Lindsay's journal was scribally published with her permission, since it was copied by Robert Wodrow from a version 'in the hand of Mr J. Anderson, who had it from my lady'.[41]

Melville was the daughter of the courtier and ambassador Sir James Melville of Halhill, himself the author of a highly readable memoir, written for his son, but published in London in 1683. The family was part of a group of intellectual Fife lairds; Sir James's mother was an aunt of the mathematician John Napier. Sir James's own social formation took place in France, where he went, aged fourteen, as a page to Mary, Queen of Scots. Though he was loyal to his queen, he embraced Calvinism, and was adopted as heir by John Knox's associate Henry Balnaves. However, his reading was more extensive than was usual with 'the godly', and, due to his sojourn in the verse-loving Valois court, more literary. When Elizabeth I questioned him about his reading habits, 'and would know what sort of books I most delighted in, whether Theology, History, or Love matters? I said, I liked well of all the sorts'.[42] It is entirely reasonable to guess that his library, for which there is no direct evidence, contained books in French and English (he admits to being a less than confident Latinist),[43] and verse of various kinds, not all of it religious. This would help to account for Melville's confidence as a writer, and the fact that she was familiar with English lyrics, including the sonnets of Sir Philip Sidney.[44]

---

[39] Additionally, the probate inventory of the printer/publisher Thomas Bassandyne in 1579 lists another printed book apparently by a woman, 'tua of Lady Lettins prayaris, price of the pece, xl d' (3s 4d (Scots)). See Robert Dickson and John Philip Edmond, *Annals of Scottish Printing From the Introduction of the Art In 1507 to the Beginning of the Seventeenth Century* (Cambridge: Cambridge University Press, 1890), 298.

[40] The Earl of Anglesey owned a copy of Hutchinson's journal: 'The diary of the Earl of Anglesey, 1675–1684', BL Add. MS 18730, fol. 100^{r-v}. Scots examples include Anon., *The Exercise of a Private Christian, or Barbara Peebles' Trance* (dated 20 July 1660), which survives in three copies, as does Jean Collace's *Some Short Remembrances of the Lord's Kindness to me*; similarly, there are two copies of Margaret Cunningham's autobiographic writings. See Trill, 'Early Modern Women's Writing', 204.

[41] National Library of Scotland NLS Wodrow MSS Octavo xxxi/8 (colophon). See Mullan (ed.), *Women's Life Writing*, 351. There is another copy in the Lindsay collections, NLS Acc 9769 84/1/3.

[42] James Melville, *Memoires of Sir James Melville of Hal-Hill* George Scott (ed.) (London: E. H. for Robert Boulter, 1683), 50.

[43] Melville, *Memoires*, 178.

[44] Baxter, 'Elizabeth Melville', 151.

Melville first appears in Scottish literature as the dedicatee of the Presbyterian minister Alexander Hume's *Hymnes or Sacred Songs* (1599), written when she was perhaps twenty-one. He praises her 'compositiones so copious, so pregnant, so spirituall', indicating that her poems were already circulating in manuscript. *Ane Godlie Dreame* was first published as 'be M. M. [Maistres Melville] Gentelwoman in Culros at the requeist of her freindes'; by the second edition (1604), her name appears on the title-page as 'Eliz. Melvil, Lady Culros yonger'.[45]

Her poem is a Calvinist spiritual journey, an elaboration of the verse quoted (in Latin) on the title page, Matthew 7:13: 'Enter ye in at the strait gate: for wide *is* the gate, and broad *is* the way, that leadeth to destruction, and many there be which go in thereat'. After a day of meditation on the vanity of the world, strongly influenced by the Psalms, Melville goes to bed and dreams of a smiling 'Angell', who turns out to be Christ. Clinging to his arm, she sets off on an arduous journey, over mountains, seas and a field of iron spikes, with his constant encouragement and help, until heaven is in sight. After these stupendous labours, she sees 'staitlie steps' up to the heavenly citadel, and begins to run up them. Christ pulls her back, warning that they are too steep for her. Instead, he takes her into hell, flying over a lake of fire, assuring her that if she keeps hold of him, she will reach her goal. She wakes in a moment of pure fear when a damned soul clutches at her, her shaking hands lose their grip, and she almost falls into the fire. Melville then proceeds to expound the meaning of her dream, in orthodox Calvinist terms, for approximately the last third of the poem. It is a purely Protestant version of an otherworld journey, dramatising the view that faith in Christ is the only key to salvation, and as such, it was widely read. The poem has no obvious antecedents, though dream-narratives are common in early modern Scottish writing;[46] and in some ways, the work most like it is the much later *Pilgrim's Progress* (1678), which is also cast as a dream. Since the second and subsequent editions of *Ane Godlie Dreame* were printed in an Anglicised text, it is possible that it fell into Bunyan's hands, part of the underground river of Puritan nonconformist literature which flowed between England and Scotland.

---

[45] Scotswomen did not take their husbands' names but did use their titles; she was Mistress Melville, or Lady Comrie (when she and her husband lived on a small estate called Wester Comrie), or later, Lady Culross, but never Elizabeth Colville.

[46] Sir David Lindsay's the *Dreme* and *Ane Dialogue betuix Experience and ane Courteour* both include a journey to hell; no Scottish poet was more widely read. James Melville, John Burel and Alexander Montgomerie all published dream-vision poems between 1590 and 1597.

Melville's publication occasioned no comment, despite the fact that half the poem is direct exhortation to the reader, of a kind not always thought appropriate to women. Weakness is womanly, strength manly, in Scotland as elsewhere. Thus Christ tells Melville (as they confront hell), 'now play the man, thou neids not trimbill so' (line 275). Within the terms of orthodox Calvinist theology, the posture of abject dependence which Melville assumes relative to Christ was equally relevant to a male or female reader: both men and women were encouraged to conceptualise themselves, or the Church collectively, as wives of the bridegroom Christ.[47] The requirement to exhibit manly strength was also appropriate to both genders: similarly, Lady Jane Grey, as reported by Foxe and others, wrote of the need to engage in 'manful combat'.[48]

Melville was thus writing in a context where women were spiritually equal, though socially subordinate. The role of elite women in the Scottish Reformation was considerable, but has been little studied.[49] One of the attractions of Calvinism, in its earliest phase, for educated women was the capacity to teach, which was opened up by Calvin's rejection of sacramental authority.[50] Melville was part of a group who perceived themselves as completing and perfecting the Reformation in Scotland in opposition to James VI, and was distantly related to Andrew Melville, their leader. After 1596, they were on the back foot, a dissident minority, and in their view, a persecuted one.[51] Her poems, 'A sonnet sent to Blackness to Mr John Welsh',[52] and 'My lady Culros to Mr Andro Meluill' show her links with these embattled Presbyterians, since both

---

[47] David George Mullan, 'A Hotter Sort of Protestantism? Comparisons between French and Scottish Calvinisms', *Sixteenth Century Journal*, 39.1 (Spring 2008), 45–69 at 67.

[48] Snook, 'Jane Gray, "Manful" Combat', 52: 'the rhetorical presentation of militant Protestantism [in Gray's dialogue with the Catholic Feckenham] as masculine and Jane Gray as its defender ensures that masculinity is not the exclusive preserve of men'.

[49] See David George Mullan, *Scottish Puritanism, 1590–1638* (Oxford: Oxford University Press, 2000), 154–60. Paul J. McGinnis and Arthur Williamson, 'Politics, Prophecy, Poetry: The Melvillian Moment, 1589–96, and Its Aftermath', *The Scottish Historical Review*, 89.1, no. 227 (April 2010), 1–18, argue the particular importance of Jean Fleming, Lady Maitland, among Melville's contemporaries as a Presbyterian activist (12). The extent to which John Knox regards women as equal in some ways and subordinate in others is explored by Susan M. Felch, 'The Rhetoric of Biblical Authority: John Knox and the Question of Women', *Sixteenth Century Journal*, 26.4 (Winter 1995), 805–22.

[50] Nancy L. Roelker, 'The Role of Noblewomen in the French Reformation', *Archiv für Reformationsgeschichte*, 63 (1972), 168–95 at 194; John L. Thompson, *John Calvin and the Daughters of Sarah: Women in Regular and Exceptional Roles in the Exegesis of Calvin, His Predecessors, and His Contemporaries* (Génève: Librairie Droz, 1992).

[51] Julian Goodare, 'The Scottish Presbyterian Movement in 1596', *Canadian Journal of History*, 45 (2010), 21–48.

[52] Greer et al. (eds.), *Kissing the Rod*, 33.

men were imprisoned at the time, the one in Blackness Castle, the other in the Tower of London.[53] She also wrote elegantly to another minister, William Ridge, in Blackness, 'that the darkness of Blackness was not the blackness of darkness'.[54] All these texts survive in hands other than Melville's own.

In the dedication to his *Hymnes*, Alexander Hume wrote that she was an example to the women of Scotland, due to her intensely religious temperament, adding:

> I know ye delite in poesie your selfe, and as I vnfainedly confes, excelles any of your sexe in that art, that euer I hard within this nation ... I doubt not but it is the gift of God in you.[55]

Hume considered her writing unproblematic, because it was linked with the religious agendas they shared: he was fiercely antagonistic towards secular poetry, but the Scottish reformers did not despise verse, provided it was written in the 'plain style' of the metrical psalter and made no reference to classical mythology.[56]

As Hume's Dedication states, Melville circulated her verse in manuscript. Much of it is preserved in a single copy written on the last thirteen leaves of a volume of sermons preached by Robert Bruce (another associate of Andrew and James Melville), between autumn 1590 and spring 1591, and presumably copied by a sympathiser in the early 1600s, when the king was attempting to impose episcopacy.[57] It is in the same neat hand as the rest of the manuscript, suggesting that the poems and the sermons are linked in the mind of the person who commissioned it.

It is a question in what sense Melville was 'famous'. She certainly did not enjoy the 'fame' sought by the Duchess of Newcastle, since she never appears in early modern catalogues of learned women, or poets.[58]

---

[53] Melville, *Poems*, 67–8.

[54] John Livingstone, 'Memorable Characteristics, and Remarkable Passages of Divine Providence', in W. K. Tweedie (ed.), *Select Biographies* (Edinburgh: printed for the Wodrow Society, 1845), VII. 1, vol. I, 293–348 at 312.

[55] Alexander Hume, 'The Epistle Dedicatorie', in *Hymnes, or Sacred Songs* (Edinburgh: Robert Waldegrave, 1599), sig. A2ᵛ.

[56] Peter Auksi, *Christian Plain Style: The Evolution of a Spiritual Ideal* (Montreal and Kingston: McGill-Queen's University Press, 1995). Zachary Boyd, *The Garden of Zion* (Glasgow: George Anderson, 1644) argues that the General Assembly of the Church should 'banish out of the land all the names of the pagan gods and goddesses' (preface, unpaginated, sig. A6ʳ).

[57] Melville, *Poems*, 106–7, for discussion of the manuscript. See also Baxter, 'Presbytery, Politics and Poetry'.

[58] See Mihoko Suzuki (Chapter 20) in this volume, on Margaret Cavendish's transnational models for her crafting of a public persona.

Her one published work enjoyed a success unparalleled by any English woman writer, because it spoke directly to a set of beliefs shared with many of her countryfolk who, like herself, had the Scottish metrical psalter more or less by heart, and were devoted readers of the Geneva Bible.

This did not make her a public figure. Despite her association with the leading lights of Scottish Presbyterianism, none of them ever contributed a biography to an edition of her poem, or wrote up her life in any other context. The minister John Livingstone was a close friend (a number of her letters to him survive), but, though she features several times in his 'Memorable Characteristics, and Remarkable Passages of Divine Providence', he is interested in nothing but her witness to the spiritual lives of herself and others.[59] The very real success of *Ane Godlie Dreame* is an example of public demand for a text, unconcerned with its authorship. This can be paralleled by an egregious example, the *Booke of Christian Exercise*, written by the outlawed Jesuit controversialist Richard Parsons, which was revised for Protestant use two years after its first appearance in Rouen by one Edmund Bunny and went through forty-four Protestant editions before 1700, to Parsons' fury.

Melville's name would probably have been recognised by many Scots, but her personal life remained private, with the result that much of it is now completely obscure, starting with her date of birth. Anecdotes recorded by Livingstone and others show that she was honoured and respected for her religious commitment within her community; surviving letters reveal a concerned mother, and a supporter of exiled and suffering ministers.[60] In this, her profile somewhat resembles that of Lucy Hutchinson, though there is no indication that she sought to control or manage her reputation – or that she needed to.

Melville and her work suggest that a woman appearing in print did not inevitably provoke intrusive interest. She wrote supported by a religious peer-group, and it is clear from an occasion recorded by John Livingstone, at a devotional meeting in Shotts in June 1630, that she was considered able and entitled to instruct others:

> William Ridge of Adderny [a minister] coming into the room, and hearing her have great motion upon her, although she spake not out, he desired her to speak out, saying, that there was none in the room but him

---

[59] Livingstone, 'Memorable Characteristics', 293–348.
[60] 'Letters from Elizabeth, Daughter of Sir James Melvill of Halhill, and Wife of John, Lord Colvill of Culross, to Mr John Livingstone', in Tweedie (ed.), *Select Biographies*, vol. I, 349–70.

and her woman … She did soe, and the door being opened, the room filled full. She continued in prayer, with wonderfull assistance, for large three hours time.[61]

This narrative makes it clear that her edifying extempore prayer was sanctioned and even encouraged. It is worth noting that apart from Ridge, who was another of her friends,[62] only women were in the room when she began speaking: some Calvinists took the view that, while St Paul prohibited women from teaching men, nothing prevented from women writing to, advising, and even preaching to, each other.[63]

The only person to write negatively about Melville's long poem was, somewhat ironically, her youngest son. Samuel Colville evidently rebelled against his mother and her circle, since he was getting into trouble for writing satires from the 1640s.[64] Satires and pasquils were written by the godly as well as the unregenerate (all too pointed epigrams were part of the reason why Andrew Melville was consigned to the Tower); neither party held a monopoly on contemptuous dismissal of alternative points of view.[65] But Colville made a specific target of his mother and her associates. His *Mock-Poem or Whig's Supplication* is an imitation of Samuel Butler's *Hudibras*, first published in 1663. It was in two parts: the earliest dated manuscript of the first half is from 1667[66]; and the second part may have been completed a little later, since it ends with an ode to London which focuses on the great rebuilding after the fire of 1666. Like his mother; Colville commanded an extensive audience. In his 1681 preface, he states that the poem was passing from hand to hand in manuscript.[67] The first London edition was 1681, the first Edinburgh edition 1687, and there were two more before 1700.

The *Mock-Poem* opens with a panorama of defeated and outlawed Whigs, which is to say Calvinists like his mother and her friends, lying

[61] Livingstone, 'Memorable Characteristics', vol. I, 347.
[62] Ibid., 342.
[63] Thompson, *John Calvin*, 43–5.
[64] In a letter of 1631 to John Livingstone, Elizabeth indicates that her youngest child's behaviour had long troubled her. Three of Samuel's pasquils survive: see James Maidment (ed.), *A Book of Scotish Pasquils, 1568–1715* (Edinburgh: William Paterson, 1868), 144 and 394–5.
[65] McGinnis and Williamson, 'Politics, Prophecy, Poetry', 16–17; and Maidment (ed.), *Scotish Pasquils*, 11–12.
[66] Aberdeen, University Library MS 103.
[67] The Brotherton Library in Leeds has no less than seven manuscripts, five of which were owned by contemporary Scots; the Bodleian has two, Aberdeen, two. There must have been a considerable number in circulation.

about in disarray. He pokes fun at his mother specifically and not just generically. In the preface, he (or a friend) sums up his life:

> Samuel was sent to France
> To learn to sing and dance
> And play upon a Fiddle
> Now he's a man of great esteem,
> His Mother got him in a dream
> At Culross on a griddle.[68]

This insouciant verse depends on the reader recognising an association between Lady Culross and dreaming. Later in the poem, a long exposé of the uncouthness of Scottish Calvinists, he testifies to the continuing wide circulation of his mother's poem when he writes:

> We'll read on the *True Converts Mark*,
> Or we will read on *Bessie Clark*
> Or else on *Bakers Heavenly Beam*
> Or on the *Lady Culross Dream*,
> Which sundry drunken Asses flout,
> Not seeing the Jewel within the Clout.[69]

Colville's target was the impoverished poetics of his mother's circle rather than its religion as such; he was sincerely Protestant.[70] But the key point for present purposes is that Melville was received, whether by admirers or detractors, as a Calvinist poet, not a woman poet. There is nothing in her reception, positive or negative, which makes a point of her gender.

Melville and her son stand for two opposing strains in Scottish culture. It would be easy to come away with the conclusion that in the seventeenth century a Presbyterian monoculture was succeeded after the Restoration by a more Anglophile, literary and outward-looking Scotland, but this impression has a great deal to do with what was and was not published. In the first half of the seventeenth century, the General Assembly of the Kirk was highly aware of the power of the press

---

[68] He may have spent time in France, as this rhyme suggests, since his brother Alexander taught at the Protestant academy in Sedan in France till the late 1640s.

[69] The first may be John Andrewes, *The conuerted mans new birth ... with an excellent marke, to know the childe of God* (London: N. O[kes] and I. N[orton], 1629), or Jean Taffin, *Of the marks of the children of God*, which went through eight London editions. The second is W. Livingstone, *Conflict in Conscience of ... Bessie Clarksone* (Edinburgh: Wreittoun, 1630). The third could be Joshua Miller (not Baker), *A became of Light Darted Thorough the Clouds* (London: for H.C. and L.L., 1650).

[70] He also published Samuel Colville, *The Grand Impostor Discovered; or, an Historical Dispute of the Papacy and Popish Religion* (Edinburgh, for the author, 1673).

and exerted effective control over Scottish printers.[71] However, English poetry, such as Campion's *Book of Airs*, was scribally circulated, as were pasquils and other counter-cultural material.[72] In the second half of the century, Charles II restored episcopacy, and a more secular, flippant, cynical and libertarian approach to the business of living began to find printed expression, but it did not emerge out of nowhere. *Ane Godlie Dreame* was reprinted for one set of Scottish readers, the *Mock-Poem* for another, through the second half of the seventeenth century and beyond. Colville's poem, dismissive as it is, suggests the continued widespread popularity of his mother's writing, while, at the same time, bearing witness to deep national political and religious divisions. But the same was true in England, where readers of Rochester and Aphra Behn coexisted with the far larger readership of *Pilgrim's Progress* and Francis Quarles's *Emblemes*.

[71] Raymond, *Pamphlets and Pamphleteering*, 161–201, points to the General Assembly's capacity to control printers. See also David Stevenson, 'A Revolutionary Regime and the Press: The Scottish Covenanters and Their Printers, 1638–51', *The Library*, 6th ser., 7 (1985), 315–37 at 321–2.

[72] Sebastiaan Verweij, *The Literary Culture of Early Modern Scotland: Manuscript Production and Transmission, c. 1560–1625* (Oxford: Oxford University Press, 2016).

20

Political Writing across Borders

Mihoko Suzuki

Charlotte Stanley, Countess of Derby, is a familiar figure in the history of the English Civil Wars for having heroically (and successfully) defended her husband's seat, Latham House, from a Parliamentarian siege.[1] Contemporary newsbooks notably refer to her as one who "stole the Earles breeches" and "prov[ed] her selfe of the two, the better Souldier."[2] Yet what is not as well known – or emphasized – is that she was born in France as Charlotte de la Trémoille and grew up during the French religious wars in which her father, Claude, participated on both sides: first as a royalist, and later, after his conversion, as a leader of the Huguenots. Although she herself never returned to France after her marriage at the Hague to James Stanley, then Lord Strange, in 1626, in her forty-year correspondence with her sister-in-law Marie de la Tour d'Auvergne (1601–65), Duchess of Trémoille – some written in cypher – she discusses extensively the politics of the civil wars in both England and France.[3]

Stanley's letters exemplify women's political writing across the borders of England and France during the mid-seventeenth century, when civil wars in both countries produced a heightened interest in the contemporary political situation across the Channel, and when Henrietta Maria, daughter of the French king Henri IV (and sister of Louis

---

[1] A contemporary account, BL Add. MS 22655, *A Brief Journal of the Siege against Latham House*, refers to Stanley's status as a foreigner in passing: as "a woman, a *Stranger* divorced from her Friends" (fol. 8ʳ, emphasis added) without specifying that she was French. Antonia Fraser, *The Weaker Vessel: Woman's Lot in Seventeenth-Century England* (New York: Knopf, 1984), 165–9, does refer to her extraction as a French Huguenot and her French accent even in her old age, though the majority of the account concerns the siege.

[2] See *The Scottish Dove* 112 (December 3–10, 1645), 887; and *A Perfect Diurnall* 123 (December 1–8, 1645), 990.

[3] These letters were discovered in the nineteenth century in the "bottom of a barrel," and portions have been included in Madame [Henriette de] Guizot de Witt, *The Lady of Latham; Being the Life and Original Letters of Charlotte de la Trémoille, Countess of Derby* (London: Smith, Elder & Co, 1869). Subsequent citations to this edition are included parenthetically. The Duchess of Trémoille added the key to the cypher as well as dated the letters (vi). For a recent account, see Kmec, "'A Stranger Born.'"

XIII), took refuge in Paris, eventually establishing an exile court in St Germain-en-Laye.

None of Stanley's surviving letters concern the siege at Latham House or the execution of her husband by the Parliamentarians. Yet letters do survive, in which she discusses and analyzes the politics of civil war, engaging in debate with her sister-in-law concerning, for example, the significance of religion for the Parliamentarian cause:

> If the Parliament had for their end religion and the glory of God, as you think they have, they would not act with the cruelty and injustice which characterize all they do. As for religion, they have so deceived the people that now, when they perceive their errors, and groan under the burden of their tyranny, even those who have been the most attached to their cause deplore our misery and their own. They would find it hard to tell you their creed, where there are as many religions as families.[4]

Here we see the slippage between the political and religious positions of participants in the French and English civil wars: the Huguenot Duchess of Trémoille apparently has expressed sympathy for the Parliamentarians (though her husband has converted to Catholicism), while the Countess of Derby, daughter of a Huguenot leader, takes a royalist position and attacks the Puritans as hypocrites.

Yet, even so, her letters include critiques of Charles I and Henrietta Maria, characterizing the court and public affairs as riddled with "confusion" and "disorder," the king promoting unworthy courtiers, and the queen's activities in France being "very hurtful to us" – even though her daughter was named Henrietta Maria after the queen who was most likely her godmother: "but she cares neither for what she says nor does, provided she can recover her position" (116). She goes so far as to state, "every one is ashamed of her" (121). Stanley's political observations go beyond her own interests to that of the "nation" and "the people," so that she avers: "I greatly fear the nation is not at the end of its misery ... In times like these one cannot think much of one's own individual troubles" (123). The importance to Stanley of national politics over familial bonds is exemplified in her will that bequeathed her son Charles, who had become a parliamentarian, "the sum of five pounds" (158) – effectively disinheriting him for his political apostasy.[5]

---

[4] Guizot de Witt, *Lady of Latham*, 132.
[5] In his *ODNB* article on Stanley, John Callow attributes this disinheritance to her displeasure over her son's marriage.

Even before the outbreak of the English Civil Wars, during the conflict between England and France centered on Buckingham's attempt to support the Huguenots during the siege of La Rochelle, Stanley is anxious to bring peace between her native and adopted country. In a letter addressed to her mother, she states, "All of this makes me despair of peace. If it were in my power to make any overtures in this direction, which it is not, my distance from Court would prevent me from doing so" (31). This imperative to mediate between the two countries in order to achieve peace underlies her critique of Henrietta Maria – like Stanley a Frenchwoman who became English upon her marriage, and whose position as queen gives her more political standing than Stanley – when she states, "I believe also that peace will only come through those who have begun the war. As for the queen, she interferes with nothing, and thinks only of how to kill time. The King and she live very happily together" (31).[6]

Just as we can surmise from Stanley's letters that her French sister-in-law expressed a strong interest in politics across the Channel, so we have explicit evidence from women who wrote memoirs during the Fronde of their knowledge and interest in the English Civil War during this period as a possible precursor or exemplum to their own civil war.[7] For example, Madame de Motteville, the confidante of Anne of Austria, the queen regent, recounts Henrietta Maria's counsel to Anne to heed the example of her husband Charles, who "had undone himself only for want of knowing the real Truth of Things."[8] Motteville's dramatic account notably parallels fictional letters in contemporary pamphlet literature (collectively called the *Mazarinades*) that has Henrietta Maria counsel Anne "to heed my example ... it's the People who make Kings, and Kings must maintain the People, rather than allow them to groan under the

---

[6] Noting that Stanley was "scarcely older than Henrietta Maria," Guizot de Witt, *Lady of Latham*, 31, explains her "anxiety for public welfare and the desire to see peace re-established between France and England" as arising from "her natural human interests in the character of wife and mother" rather than from a properly political interest.

[7] "The Fronde" designated a series of civil wars between 1648 and 1653, during the minority of Louis XIV, in which the nobility rose up against the regime of Cardinal Mazarin and Louis's mother and regent Anne of Austria. It was dubbed the "woman's war" for the political and military prominence of women, the *frondeuses*, such as the Duchess of Montpensier (the Grande Mademoiselle), the cousin of Louis XIV, and Madame de Longueville, the sister of Louis, the Grand Condé.

[8] Françoise de Motteville, *Memoirs for the History of Anne of Austria, Wife of Lewis XIII of France; and Regent of that Kingdom from his Death to the Accession of her Son Lewis XIV*, 5 vols. (London: John Darey, 1726), vol. II, 384. For a fuller discussion of Motteville and the "English connection," see Suzuki, "Women's Political Writing."

slavery and tyranny of a celebrated Tyrant."[9] Although Motteville is not as explicitly critical of Mazarin and Anne as the political pamphlets supporting the *frondeurs*, her account indicates the cost to monarchical sovereignty of underestimating public discontent and anger; in this respect, Motteville's complex political analysis parallels Stanley's, who, though a royalist, nevertheless expressed strong criticism of Henrietta Maria and Charles.

Stanley and Motteville's "ambiguous royalism" parallels that of Margaret Cavendish, who accompanied Henrietta Maria into exile in France and then married Charles's general William Cavendish – also exiled in France after the military defeat he suffered at the Battle of Marston Moor. Cavendish's political writing reflects her immersion in French culture – despite her assertion that she did not know French. Although scholars of early modern women's writing have expanded the scholarship on the political aspects of women's writing, they have still largely confined their investigations within the English national context. During the political turbulence of the mid-seventeenth century civil wars in both England and France, when the English court found itself in exile in France, it is not surprising that women in both countries wrote about politics that went beyond their national borders.

Margaret Cavendish and the French Connection

While Stanley carries on a debate with her sister-in-law in France concerning the English Civil Wars and Motteville discusses the political situation across the Channel as a monitory example in her memoirs, Margaret Cavendish's "French connection" is more oblique, though she actually lived in France for four years attending Henrietta Maria's court in exile as well as during the first years of her marriage to William. Indeed, her connections to French literary culture have been addressed only by a few, most likely because of her oft-noted assertion that she did not know French.[10] In one of the prefaces to *Natures Pictures* Cavendish claims that she does not "understand any Language but English, which is my native Language," though this statement appears in the context

---

[9] Françoise de Motteville (?), *Lettre de la Reyne d'Angleterre, a la Reyne Regente, en faveur de la France, & pour la Paix du Royaume* (Letter from the Queen of England to the Queen Regent in favor of France and for the Peace of the Kingdom) (Paris: Pierre Variquet, 1649), 5.

[10] See Scott-Douglass, "Enlarging Margaret," 149 and 164–9, on Cavendish, the *femme forte*, and the *frondeuses*; and Chalmers, *Royalist Women Writers*, 40–6 and 52–3, on Cavendish's use of the *femme forte* – as inflected by Henrietta Maria – in her plays and in one of her frontispiece portraits.

of defending her use of "the English that is spoken in this age," which includes "such words as belong to other Nations, being mixed therein."[11] This statement and the consequent assumption that she did not speak or read French has discouraged Cavendish scholars from investigating connections between her works and the literature and culture of France.[12] Yet I suggest that she seeks to reaffirm her Englishness and her self-representation as an English writer after her sojourn in France; her strategic protestation thereby calls attention to the fact that her English is hybrid, just as the cultural foundation and context of her writings may also be mixed. Moreover, a few pages following her statement concerning her disability, Cavendish reveals in "The Judgement" that she herself was considering the relationship between England and France. This short piece, in which two gentlemen who have traveled in both England and France are asked by a third to discuss the merits of the two countries, invites us to consider the significance of the French connection in her works. Here Cavendish follows the tradition of Sir John Fortescue's *De Laudibus Legum Angliae* (*In Praise of the Laws of England*, c. 1470) and Sir Thomas Smith's *De Republica Anglorum* (*On the Republic of England*, 1583) – political treatises comparing England to France – as well as the *Mazarinades* that compare France and England.

Cristina Malcolmson has argued that William Cavendish brought back to England Harley MS 4431 of Christine de Pizan's works, now in the British Library.[13] If so, Cavendish would have been aware not only of the *City of Ladies*, which includes illustrations of the text as well as a miniature of Christine presenting her works to Isabeau of Bavaria, but also of other texts of political import included in this manuscript. Christine's *Boke of the Faytes of Armes and of Chyvalrye* had been translated into English and published in 1489 by William Caxton, who had been commissioned by Henry VII to translate and publish the work for the benefit

---

[11] Margaret Cavendish, *Natures Pictures* (London: A. Maxwell, 1671), n.p. Cavendish may also have been keen to separate herself from the association of eroticism/sensuality with French. See Juliet Fleming, "*The French Garden*: An Introduction to Women's French," *English Literary History*, 56 (1989), 19–51.

[12] In Cavendish, *Sociable Letters*, 70, she satirically portrays "Mrs. H. O." who behaves after "the French Mode" and "speaks French like a Native," indicating that such women were considered to be self-dramatizing and frivolous. In another letter, however, she discusses reading a translation of a French book (*Sociable Letters*, 79 and 134). See also Whitaker, *Mad Madge*, 89–90, on Cavendish's exposure to paintings of *femmes fortes*, including Rubens's series on Marie de' Medici, who had visited her family at Colchester in 1638, and on Cavendish's "alternative model of feminine behavior … based on the fashion for heroic women" (153).

[13] Malcolmson, "Christine de Pizan's *City of Ladies*."

of "euery gentylman born to armes & all manere men ... captaynes/
souldiours." Although the title page does not carry Christine's name as
author, the texts prominently include references by Christine to herself
as author, references that call attention to her gender. Given William's
purchase of the Harley MS, his position as Charles I's general during the
civil war, his advice to the future Charles II concerning government in
the role as his governor, as well as Margaret's authorship of his life, which
focuses on his military career, it is probable that the Cavendishes would
have been familiar with Christine's work "of armes and of chyvalrye," as
well as "of polycye."[14] Cavendish's notion of the body politic is very similar to Christine's. In addition, her striking self-awareness as an author and
her production of a substantial *oeuvre* in various genres is unprecedented
for a woman writer in England, but clearly has an illustrious precedent in
Christine de Pizan.[15]

William's purchase of the Harley manuscript is an example of his support of his wife's avocation as a woman writer; their frequent authorial
collaboration would also suggest that William's knowledge of French
would have given Margaret access to relevant French texts. In fact, in the
Preface to *The Worlds Olio* (1655), Cavendish features a husband who
imparts what he has learned to his wife, suggesting the likelihood that
Margaret gained knowledge of French texts that she might have had difficulty reading on her own.[16] David Norbrook, in arguing for a republic
of letters among early modern women, discusses the importance for
Cavendish of Marie de Gornay as well as Anna Maria van Schurman, as
the most prominent women intellectuals in Europe, despite the absence
of reference to either of these writers in Cavendish's writings.[17]

Material in the memoirs of Anne Marie Louise Orléans, Duchess
of Montpensier – the cousin of Louis XIV and niece of Henrietta
Maria – suggests some possible connections with the Cavendishes.
Montpensier repeatedly discusses her meetings with Henrietta Maria,
who sought to arrange a match between her niece and her son, the future

---

[14] See: Christine de Pisan, *Here begynneth the table of the rubryshys of the boke of the fayt of armes and of chyvalrye* (London: William Caxton, 1489); Christine de Pisan, *Here begynneth the booke whiche is called the body of polycye* (London: Joh[a] Scot, 1521).
[15] Scott-Douglass, "Self-Crowned Laureates."
[16] For a discussion of Cavendish's relationship to Montaigne, see Mihoko Suzuki, "The Essay Form as Critique: Reading *The World's Olio* through Montaigne and Bacon (and Adorno)," *Prose Studies: History, Theory, Criticism* 22.3 (1999), 1–16.
[17] Norbrook, "Women, the Republic of Letters, and the Public Sphere."

Charles II.[18] The memoirs also mention Christina of Sweden who was visiting the French court, and whom Cavendish represents as Queen Masc in the *Apocryphal Ladies* (1662).[19] In her memoirs, Montpensier discusses her love of horses, which led her to order them from England.[20] Given William Cavendish's expertise in horses, as exemplified in his book, *La méthode nouvelle de dresser les chevaux* (1657), this common equestrian interest suggests an additional link between Montpensier and the Cavendishes. Montpensier's letters to Motteville, which voice her skepticism on the subject of marriage, accords with the satirical treatment of marriage that characterizes Cavendish's plays.[21]

Although the Penguin edition of Cavendish's *The Blazing World* presents it as "the only known Utopia fiction by a seventeenth-century woman writer," Montpensier also wrote a utopia in the 1650s, *Relation de l'isle imaginaire*. It is significant that at least in England, utopias had been written from a position of political prerogative, by males who held high office such as Thomas More and Francis Bacon; only in the mid-seventeenth century when women were beginning to assert such prerogative were these two examples, which exhibit some notable similarities, produced. Montpensier includes an extended description of dogs of different colors, which corresponds to Cavendish's oft-noted different-colored hybrid creatures in *The Blazing World*. After describing different kinds of dogs, such as the greyhound, the spaniel, and the bulldog, Montpensier's narrator goes on to say, "the queen is black, with white and red; the king is white, and the princes of blood are usually grey and black or black and grey."[22] Montpensier's interest in animals and the political – she asserts that dogs form a kind of republic, as others have claimed that ants and bees do, but with more awareness and reason – closely corresponds to Cavendish's throughout her *oeuvre*.[23]

---

[18] Anne-Marie-Louise-Henriette-d'Orléans, Duchess of Montpensier, *Memoirs of Mademoiselle de Montpensier, Grand-daughter of Henri Quatre, and Niece of Queen Henrietta-Maria. Written by Herself*, 3 vols. (London: Henry Coberun, 1848), vol. I, 125, 173–4.

[19] Montpensier, *Memoirs*, vol. II, 44–53.

[20] Montpensier, *Memoirs*, vol. I, 375–8.

[21] DeJean (ed. and trans.), *Against Marriage*. On Cavendish's satire of marriage and its relation to dramatic form, see Mihoko Suzuki, "Margaret Cavendish and the Female Satirist," *Studies in English Literature 1500–1900*, 37, 3 (Summer 1997), 483–500.

[22] Anne-Marie-Louise-Henriette-d'Orléans, Duchess of Montpensier, *La Relation de l'isle imaginaire, et L'histoire de la Princesse de Paphlagonie* (s. n.,1659), 46. Translation mine.

[23] On this, see Mihoko Suzuki, "Animals and the Political in Lucy Hutchinson and Margaret Cavendish," *The Seventeenth Century*, 30 (2015), 229–47.

Cavendish's *The Blazing World* also bears comparison to another utopia, Cyrano de Bergerac's *L'Autre monde* (*Other World*) – privately circulated before it was published in 1657 – which features materialism and atomism in keeping with Cavendish's thought.[24] Cyrano's indictment of man's arrogation of "sovereignty" and "natural mastery" over animals, through setting traps and killing them, a perspective not common during this period, closely approximates Cavendish's hunting poems – on the hare and the stag. Moreover, Cyrano's "Histoire des oiseaux" and Cavendish's "A Dialogue of Birds" both include statements that birds do not understand the meaning of human speech that they mimic. Finally, the contradictory political statements in the eight *Mazarinades* he wrote – for and against Mazarin – recall Cavendish's similarly dialogical statements on both sides of the civil war.

An even more salient connection between Cavendish and the most prolific woman writer in France during this period, Madeleine de Scudéry, can be found in the orations by women that Scudéry included in *Femmes illustres* (1642), especially since Cavendish indicates that she sought precedents in writing her orations (though she characteristically does not explicitly name Scudéry, or any other writer who preceded her in this genre). Scudéry includes "harangues," as she calls them, by Cleopatra to Mark Antony, Lucretia to Collatine, Mariam to Herod, and Agrippina to the Roman people. These constitute striking departures from Ovid's *Heroides*, comprised of letters to an absent and most often faithless beloved, for Scudéry's speakers seek to persuade their addressees through oratory (appended to each oration is an account of its effect on the listeners). Significant for Cavendish's *Orations*, Scudéry's preface, "Aux dames [To the Ladies]," asserts that she seeks to correct the mistake that oratorical art was unknown to women and that the ancients maintained that women possess eloquence without artifice and without effort.[25]

---

[24] Line Cottegnies suggests that the "potentially damning impact of being associated with Cyrano and his notorious reputation as a libertine and an atheist" led Cavendish to omit a reference to him in the preface to some of the 1688 copies of *The Blazing World*. See "Margaret Cavendish and Cyrano de Bergerac: A Libertine Subtext for Cavendish's *Blazing World* (1666)?" *XVII–XVIII: Bulletin de la société d'études anglo-américaines des XVIIe et XVIIIe siècles*, 54 (2002), 165–85 at 167–9. She also points out that the Cavendishes and Cyrano "frequented the same circles" in Paris (172), and that the two works share many similarities.

[25] [Madeleine de Scudéry], *Les Femmes Illustres, ou Les Harangues Heroïques, de Monsieur de Scudery* (Paris: Augustin Courbé, 1655), sig. aiiᵛ–aiiiʳ. This preface is not included in the English translation of 1656, *A Triumphant Arch Erected and Consecrated to the Feminine Sexe: By M. de Scudery: Englished by I. B. Gent* (London: William Hope and Henry Herringman, 1656), whose translator's preface emphasizes women's "beauties" that have subdued "the *Arms*, *Scepters*, and *Crowns* of so many monarchs" (sig. A3ᵛ) rather than women's capacity for oratory.

Yet Cavendish goes beyond Scudéry by not only publishing the orations under her own name – Scudéry's works were published under the name of her brother Georges, though she herself acknowledged her identity as author, which was widely known – but also by having her speakers address political subjects to public audiences. By contrast, Scudéry's heroines address their beloveds, husbands, or other family members – except in the oration by Agrippina, where, Scudéry explains, her overwhelming grief as a widow of Germanicus led her to address the Roman people.[26]

Another work by Scudéry that merits consideration in this context is *Artamenes or the Grand Cyrus* (1649–53), whose ten volumes were published during the Fronde years; its English translation was published in 1653 and dedicated to Cavendish's sister-in-law, Anne Lucas.[27] Scudéry herself dedicated the work to Madame de Longueville, a prominent *frondeuse* and the sister of Condé, the leader of the aristocrats against Mazarin; in the dedication, she compared Longueville to her hero Cyrus. The 1656 edition carries a portrait of Longueville as the frontispiece. In the novel itself, Longueville is represented by Mandana, the daughter of the King of Cappadocia; her brother Condé is represented by Mandana's beloved, Cyrus.[28] Not only does Mandana seek to establish peace between Cyrus and Philadaspes, rivals for her love, "to the end they might become more serviceable unto her Father" the king, but she also outlines qualities required to win her love, qualities which are notably political ones: "that his valour be not too cruell: that he love victory better then bloud, that his fury last no longer then fight: That he be ever civil ... That sweetness and clemency be his predominant qualities" (1:92).

---

[26] [Madeliene de Scudéry], "Agripine au people Romain" in *Les Femmes Illustres*, 368. (This oration is not included in the 1656 English translation.) However, Scudéry undercuts her own "argument" through Agrippina's oration, where she asserts that Germanicus communicated his valor to her (so that she contributed to the defeat of Arminius, enemy of Rome), reminds her audience that she is "of the blood of Augustus" (her grandfather), and successfully incites the people to demand justice from the Senate and Tiberius against Piso, responsible for Germanicus's death (379, 386–9). Indeed, nearing the conclusion of her oration, she exhorts her audience to punish Germanicus's enemies, for he deserved consideration as "a grandson of Antony, a nephew of Augustus, and a *husband of Agrippina*" (385; emphasis added). Thus Jane Donawerth and Julie Strongson's assertion that Scudéry "demonstrate[d] her humanist oratorical credentials without violating the gender norms of her society" does not adequately reflect the complexity of Scudéry's negotiation of those gender norms: Donawerth and Strongson (eds.), "Volume Editors' Introduction," in Scudéry, *Selected Letters*, 21.

[27] Madeleine de Scudéry, *Artamenes, or, The Grand Cyrus*, 10 parts in 5 vols. (London: Printed for Humphrey Moseley and Thomas Dring, 1653–5).

[28] See Erica Harth, *Ideology and Culture in Seventeenth-Century France* (Ithaca: Cornell University Press, 1983), 97–102, on the topicality of the *Grand Cyrus* that "fulfills the ambiguity of the word *histoire*" (101).

Mandana is thus represented as a level-headed and "reasonable" princess who is first and foremost impressed by Cyrus's political qualities:

> A Prince who hath saved the life of the King my Father, who hath a thousand and a thousand times exposed his own for him, who hath received so many wounds; Conquered so many Provinces; won so many Battles; took a King a Prisoner; prevented a dangerous Conspiracy; and who has long loved me, without telling me of it, or displeasing me. (2:39)

Her actions toward him are also governed by reason, for example when she decides to separate from him in light of the prophecy that Cyrus will conquer Asia, which would include her father's kingdom; indeed, Mandana is of stronger resolve than Cyrus, who is overcome by love for her. Later, when she does fall in love with him, she considers her love of a man "worthy to command all others" (2:65) to be honorable; because she believes her passion to be just, she allows herself to love him. Neither Mandana nor Thomris (another prominent queen in the narrative who sends out spies against surprise attacks) are engulfed by love like Racine's heroines; they are governed by reason and act according to political exigencies. By contrast, when Philadaspes falls in love with Mandana, he declares: "I did not so much as consult with my own reason; it was love only which was my adviser in the entreprise" (2:105). When Mandana refuses him, he becomes subject to volatile and uncontrollable passions: "sometimes all violence, sometimes all submission ... deep silent melancholy ... sometimes extream anger" (2:118). Scudéry exemplifies this lack of control on the part of males in the repeated abduction of Mandana by Philadaspes and later Philadaspes's confidant Mazares who himself falls in love with her; both carry Mandana away in a boat – a device Cavendish also uses at the beginning of *The Blazing World* (1666).

As in Cavendish's works, Scudéry's *Grand Cyrus* examines the question of male vs. female sovereignty. She states that Cappadocians did not much care for having a king; and that they loved Princess Mandana so well that they desired to have her for their queen. In "Assaulted and Pursued Chastity" (1656), Travellia becomes vice-gerent as a result of strong popular acclaim; Cavendish explores the question of elective monarchies, as does Scudéry, whose Mandana discusses with Artamenes whether people will change a monarch displeasing to them. The conversations between Mandana and Artamenes on topics suitable for rulers, such as different ways of making war and different ways of governing, are very much in keeping with Cavendish's interest in these topics in works such as "The She-Anchoret" and the *Orations*.

Philadaspes's mother, Queen Nitocris, "one of the greatest and wisest Princess of the world" (2:78), was queen from an early age because of her father's death; renowned for her wisdom and prudence, she voluntarily submits herself to, in her own words, "the necessity of State affaires, and the good of my people," and resolves "to receive a husband by the universal allowance of my subjects" (2:101). Her people, acting according to "the powerfull reason of state which would have all causes and pretences of civill wars removed," propose a husband other than the man she loves, and she abides by their decision "without the least shew of repugnancy ... and lived very well with her husband" (2:102). In "Assaulted and Pursued Chastity," the Queen of Amity similarly demonstrates a concern for her people's wishes in choosing a husband; both Scudéry and Cavendish in these instances approvingly represent monarchs who do not insist on absolutist prerogative but seek counsel from their people in order to act in accordance with the interest of the state. Accordingly, Scudéry states, "in other Kingdoms ... they say, the Prince is above the Lawes; but in Assyria, the Lawes are used to be above the Prince, whose Glory it is to be subject unto them" (2:104).

Victor Cousin claims, based on Scudéry's correspondence, that Scudéry "was not in the least a *frondeuse*," and that she detested the disorders of 1648 and 1649 and strongly supported the monarchy. At the same time, he states that she was not a "Mazarine" either, for she never praised the cardinal in her letters. Cousin concludes that her concern for her country led her to believe that Condé was the only one who, having saved the monarchy before, could save it again.[29] Though acknowledging Scudéry's simultaneous loyalty to Condé and the monarchy (if not to the actual monarch), Joan DeJean sees the composition and publication of the volumes of the *Grand Cyrus* that followed the trajectory of the civil war as a "novelistic production that nearly marked the downfall of the absolute monarchy," considering its political subversion to be the founding gesture of the French novel.[30] This difficulty in reconciling Scudéry's political statements, exemplified in the commentary by both Cousin and DeJean, recalls the similar problem with Cavendish, who also made contradictory statements for and against the monarchy. Scudéry does excoriate those who would seek to bring the English Revolution to France

---

[29] Victor Cousin, *La Société française au XIIe siècle, d'après "Le Grand Cyrus" de Mlle de Scudéry*, 2 vols. (Paris: Didier, 1858), vol. I, 37–8.
[30] Joan DeJean, *Tender Geographies: Women and the Origins of the Novel in France* (New York: Columbia University Press, 1991), 45.

and play the roles of Cromwell and Fairfax; yet the evidence of *Cyrus* indicates that Scudéry admired and sought to praise the most prominent *frondeuse*, Longueville.[31] Finally, Scudéry's collaborative authorship with her brother Georges – the works were published under his name – closely parallels the collaboration between Cavendish and her husband William.

Cavendish's years in France brought her in contact not only with the texts that I have discussed, but with many personages of the French aristocracy and the Fronde. In fact Carol Barash has suggested that Cavendish modeled her career on the *précieuses* and that she imitated the *frondeuses* in her appearance and self-representation, such as her wearing masculine dress, titling herself "princess," and considering herself, by virtue of her class, welcome to participate in such events as meetings of the Royal Society. Although Barash does not elaborate upon the specific use Cavendish made of these cultural paradigms in her works, she does go on to suggest that Cavendish's deprecation of women as a group while demanding political rights for high-ranked women is derived from the *précieuse* literary ideal of the *femme forte*.[32] Amy Scott-Douglass examines more extensively the connection between Cavendish and those she calls the three Margarets: Margaret of Anjou, Margaret de Bethune, and Margaret de Rohan, focusing on the double example of military action and writing that these women represented for Cavendish.[33] And Hero Chalmers argues that Cavendish's use of the *femme forte* in her works exemplifies the vital role played by royalism in fostering Cavendish's startling emergence"; she claims that "[t]he 'heroick' image is fundamental to the way in which Margaret Cavendish situates herself (and is situated by others) in relation to royalist literary production, royalist readers, and royalist iconography."[34]

Yet the picture of these *frondeuses* that emerges from my reading of numerous *Mazarinades* is not exactly royalist; I would agree with historian Nina Gelbart's claim that the Fronde can be considered as the forerunner of the French Revolution.[35] Addressing the flowering of women's writing during the absolutist reign of Louis XIV, Germaine de Staël and Joan DeJean, more recently, have argued that women's writing stands

---

[31] See Cousin, *La Société*, vol. I, chap. 1, on Madame de Longueville.

[32] Barash, *English Women's Poetry*, 35–6.

[33] Scott-Douglass, "Enlarging Margaret," 149.

[34] Chalmers, *Royalist Women Writers*, 1, 55.

[35] Gelbart, *Feminine and Opposition Journalism in Old Regime France: Le Journal des Dames* (London: University of California Press, 1987), xv. Accordingly, throughout her work Gelbart designates the opposition press of the eighteenth-century "*frondeur* journalism."

in contradiction to the absolutism that by its nature denies all forms of difference.[36] We might extend de Staël and DeJean's observation, which concerns women's writing per se, to suggest that despite an overt or stated allegiance to royalism, the very act by women of voicing political opinions stands in contradiction to the fundamental ideology of patriarchal absolutism that would deny women such prerogatives.

Taking Barash's and modifying Chalmers's assumption of an unequivocally royalist use by Cavendish of the *femme forte*, I suggest that her writings reflect her exposure to the Fronde and the influence of the *frondeuses* in a more complex way. The female community she establishes in the *Convent of Pleasure* can be read in the framework of the salon culture with which Cavendish came into contact during her exile, or the female community Montpensier established after being exiled by Louis XIV. There is pathos in the fact that these female communities Cavendish constructed in her writings were unavailable to her in her lived experience; in fact, her intellectual companions were predominantly male, starting with her husband and brother-in-law Charles, but also Jasper Mayne and others whose letters to her about her work were collected by her husband after her death. The most prominent English women writers of her day, Lucy Hutchinson and Katherine Philips, both reveal interest in or awareness of Cavendish but there was no actual contact among these writers.[37]

The Amazonian warriors of *Bell in Campo*, the cross-dressed Affectionata in *Loves Adventures*, and Travellia in "Assaulted and Pursued Chastity," who engage in military action as well as exercise political power, have contemporary referents in the *frondeuses* such as Montpensier and Madame de Longueville.[38] Given her and her husband's interest in the theater and playwriting, Cavendish was most likely acquainted with the plays of Corneille, which were performed at the royal palace as well as attended in the theaters by members of the French court. As John Lough has shown, aristocratic women constituted a significant part of the French theater audience and could influence the fate of plays, the fame

---

[36] Germaine de Staël, "Des Femmes qui cultivent les lettres," vol. II, chapter 4, in *De la littérature*, 2 vols. (Paris: Maradan, 1800), vol. II, 333; DeJean, *Tender Geographies*, 11.

[37] Norbrook, "Margaret Cavendish and Lucy Hutchinson; and Salzman," *Reading Early Modern Women's Writing*, 190.

[38] Both *Bell in Campo* and *Loves Adventures* were written during the 1650s and included in Cavendish's *Playes* (1662). On the implications for women's political participation in *Bell in Campo*, see Suzuki, *Subordinate Subjects*, 189–95; and in *Loves Adventures*, see Mihoko Suzuki, "Gender, the Dramatic Subject, and Female Authorship: *Loves Adventures* and the Shakespearean Example," in Romack and Fitzmaurice, *Cavendish and Shakespeare*, 103–20.

of authors, and even dramatic trends.[39] A number of scholars have suggested that Corneille fashioned his impressively self-reliant and politically engaged heroines after the *frondeuses* and that the *frondeuses* in turn took his heroines as their models. Indeed, the heroic aspiration after *gloire* in Corneillian drama certainly would have resonated with Cavendish, who repeatedly announced that she wrote in pursuit of Fame.

The idea of glory, and what Ian Maclean calls "the literature of prestige" especially prevalent during the regency of Anne of Austria, most likely encouraged and justified Cavendish's explicit pursuit of public recognition, "Fame," unusual for a woman writer in seventeenth-century England, although the 1656 edition of Scudéry's *Artamène* prominently features as frontispiece to Part I an allegorical representation of "La Renommée [Fame]."[40] In the preface to *Poems and Fancies*, Cavendish states that hers is "an Age when effeminate spirits rule, as most visible they doe in every Kingdome" and that therefore women should "take the advantage, and make the best of our time, for fear their reigne should not last long; whether it be in the Amazonian Government, or the Politick Common-wealth, or in flourishing Monarchy."[41] Significantly, at the time of her writing, the "effeminate Ruler" in England would have been Charles, and a "flourishing Monarchy" was non-existent, replaced by the "Politick Common-wealth." In France, given the minority of Louis, Anne of Austria was regent; in place of the ineffectual Gaston d'Orléans, the uncle of Louis XIV, Montpensier, as his daughter, fulfilled the role as sovereign lord of Orléans and one of the leaders of the Fronde, even pointing cannons at Louis' forces during the battle of St Antoine. In a number of ways, then, this passage indicates that Cavendish's pursuit of Fame, following the example of the *frondeuses*, cannot be characterized as unequivocally royalist.

Because the *frondeuses* were aristocrats and antimonarchical – though they professed allegiance to Louis while criticizing Mazarin and Anne of Austria – they display affinities with what I have called the "ambiguous royalism" of Cavendish.[42] They provide a model for Cavendish, who valued her aristocratic status but who also expressed what can only be characterized as antimonarchical sentiments. To take just one example,

[39] John Lough, *Seventeenth-Century French Drama: The Background* (Oxford: Clarendon, 1979), chapter 4, "Audiences."
[40] Ian Maclean, *Woman Triumphant: Feminism in French Literature, 1610–1652* (Oxford: Clarendon Press, 1977), 74. See Jane Stevenson (Chapter 19) in this volume, on early modern women's fame.
[41] Cavendish, *Poems and Fancies* (1653), fol. Aa1ᵛ.
[42] See Suzuki, *Subordinate Subjects*, 182–202.

Cavendish provides a surprisingly critical analysis in the *Orations* of the causes of the civil war and Charles's responsibility for his own downfall, an analysis that substantially agrees with that of the Parliamentarians.[43]

A salient – and empowering, from the point of view of women – contradiction existed within Salic Law, which forbade women from ascending to the throne but in fact gave them executive powers as regents, as Christine de Pizan pointed out in the many examples she cites in *The Book of the City of Ladies* and also as witnessed in recent French history with the examples of Catherine de' Medici and Anne of Austria. The contradiction between theory and practice underlies Cavendish's negotiation of her subordinate position as wife, admittedly to a prominent aristocrat, into a position that enabled her to participate in the literary, and arguably the political public sphere through her publications that her husband sponsored–by writing approving dedications and financing their printing in handsome folio formats and disseminating them to university libraries and prominent thinkers of the day.

Thus Cavendish, like her French counterparts, adroitly exploited her position in patriarchy during the civil wars. Madame de Longueville parlayed her position as sister of Condé and led the *frondeurs* during her brother's imprisonment, just as Montpensier displaced her ineffectual father in playing active political and military roles during the Fronde; both played the role of political double or surrogate to male members of their families. Similarly, Cavendish refashioned her position as a subordinate wife of a man of superior rank into that of a woman writer whose career was at once made possible and enthusiastically endorsed by her husband. Moreover, combining a reference to the *frondeuses*, who acted on behalf of their male kin, and her own relationship with her husband, Cavendish has her warrior heroines in *Bell in Campo* and *Loves Adventures* join battle along with their husbands or on their behalf. Above all, Cavendish writes in order to achieve the extraordinary celebrity that the *frondeuses* achieved; indeed, the political effects of her published writing proved to be just as important as the political activity that gave renown to the *frondeuses*. In this respect, it is significant that she appends to *The Life of ... William Cavendish* (1663) reflections on politics, especially in reference to the civil war, not only by her husband, but by herself. For according to Gelbart, the press during the Fronde disseminated the assumption that women had the right to know, judge,

---

[43] Ibid., 184–5.

and be involved in events, to support and participate in factions, and in general to challenge the established order.[44] This was an assumption that was shared by women petitioners in England across the Channel, but the aristocratic French women would have provided a more congenial model for Cavendish than the women of lower rank who were at times excoriated as "fishwives" and "oyster women" by the popular press.[45]

In the preface to *Natures Pictures*, Cavendish indicates that because direct political action is closed to her (and here she must have been thinking of women involved in government like the *frondeuses*), she considers her writing to be compensatory, or by implication an alternative way in which to achieve Fame: "And since all heroick Actions, publick Imployments, powerfull Governments, and eloquent Pleadings are denied our Sex in this age, or at least would be condemned for want of custome, is the cause I write so much" (fol. C1^r). The enumeration of the activities denied English women indicates that her writing seeks to enact imaginatively these activities closed to her sex: "the heroic actions, publick imployments, and powerfull Governments" are dramatized in her plays such as *Loves Adventures* and *Bell in Campo*, and the eloquent pleadings in the *Orations*. In the *Natures Pictures* itself, she commends to her readers in particular "The She-Anchoret," in which she describes the exchanges between the title character and various questioners on the nature of justice, the best form of government and other political subjects. "The She-Anchoret" recommends Monarchy, preferring a "Tyrant King" to a "factious Councell" (327) indicating a disillusioned and demystifying pragmatism that seeks the lesser of two evils rather than an unequivocal endorsement of one over the other.

These examples indicate that although Cavendish stated that women should not involve themselves in politics, she herself did so through her extensive publications. Her *Orations* debate political subjects and her plays construct imaginary scenes of political participation, thereby constituting important political interventions in themselves. And the *Life* of her husband, which became a source of the later history of the English Civil Wars, provides a political and military assessment of the royalist defeat by indicting the negative roles played by Charles I and Henrietta Maria. Cavendish slyly accomplishes this critique by inking out passages

---

[44] Gelbart, *Feminine and Opposition Journalism*, 19.
[45] Cavendish herself also petitioned Parliament in pursuit of her husband's estate, as she recounts in her autobiography, Margaret Cavendish, *A True Relation*, in *Natures Pictures* (London: J. Martin and J. Allestrye, 1656).

that describe Charles's parsimony and failure to support his generals, which in fact called attention to them in some copies where the inking out is incomplete; in yet other copies, the crossed-out content is written in. For example, in discussing Charles I's command to William to lead his troops, Cavendish strikes the passage: "without receiving any pay or allowance from His Majesty," thereby indicting Charles for providing inadequate support to the military operations on his behalf by his most loyal general.[46] The importance of this betrayal can be gleaned in the corrective (and normative) statement by the King's ambassadors in "Assaulted and Pursued Chastity": "he will repay your charges and expenses in this war, although his own is great, and his loss is more."[47] In this respect, the conflict between the monarch and aristocrats that was the focus of the French Fronde had much resonance for Cavendish's reflection on Newcastle's and her own political position vis-à-vis Charles II. In the *Sociable Letters*, moreover, Cavendish calls Charles "Lord C. R.," criticizing him in comparison to William: "he is an Effeminate Man, fitter to Dance with a Lady, than to Fight with an Enemy; nor do I wonder that the Lord N.W. [William Newcastle] practices Riding, Fencying, Vaulting, Shooting, Hunting, Fortifying, Navigating, and the like, because he is a Heroick man, fitter to Conquer a Nation, than to Dance a Galliard or a Courant."[48] This devastating critique of Charles, though it may thinly disguise its object of criticism by calling him C. R., parallels Cavendish's criticisms of him in the *Life* that were at times visible "under erasure."

Cavendish's French contemporaries were considered to have turned away from politics to writing after the failure of the Fronde. A salient example is Montpensier, who began writing her memoirs as well as her stories and utopia after Louis sent her into exile in 1653. Similarly, the last volume of Scudéry's *Artamène*, published after the failure of the Fronde, turns to the story of Sappho, away from heroic action to writing. In the cases of Montpensier and Scudéry, as in the case of Cavendish, participation in the literary after exclusion from the political can be considered as a turn to a compensatory alternative, but the literary constitutes not simply a retreat, but a continuation of political activity in discursive form – for it is not simply action that is political.

Cavendish's statement that she knew only English should not preclude her involvement in and response to a dense and compelling French

[46] Cavendish, *Life of the Duke*, 9.
[47] Cavendish, "Assaulted and Pursued Chastity," in Cavendish, *Natures Pictures*, 105.
[48] Cavendish, *Sociable Letters*, 33.

political and cultural context. During her four years in Paris she witnessed the beginning of the Fronde; she later spent a decade in Antwerp, from where many *frondeurs* launched attacks. Attending to these cross-Channel connections enables us to see more clearly the transcultural nature of Cavendish's political writings. Indeed Cavendish's ambivalence about monarchy, despite her position as the wife of a prominent aristocrat with close ties to Charles I, has significant parallels with the *frondeuses*'s aristocratic anti-monarchism.

Just as Stanley and her sister-in-law in France energetically discussed the English Civil Wars and Motteville explicitly applied the "English example" to the political situation in France, so Cavendish implicitly but no less productively thought with the "French example" to arrive at her own political position. An acknowledgment of writing "across borders" revises the prevailing assumption that women on both sides of the Channel confined themselves to their own national culture as the context of their thinking about politics, with notable implications. Such a shift in perspective gives proper due to the active and informed interest these writers took in historical events and ideas from beyond their national context that in turn shaped – and complicated – their political writings.

English Women's Writing and Indigenous Medical Knowledge in the Early Modern Atlantic World

Edith Snook

Women's writing in early modern England was in small but significant ways engaged with the Columbian Exchange, which saw new biological materials circulate around the Atlantic region after 1492.[1] European diseases killed many Indigenous people in their territories, stretching from what is now Newfoundland to Argentina. At the same time, Europeans (probably incorrectly) blamed those of the Caribbean and Florida for syphilis.[2] European plants and animals were introduced to the Americas, while plants from that region, such as sassafras, sarsaparilla, guaiacum, and tobacco, began to be used in European remedies, and foods, such as chocolate, tomatoes, and squash, became part of European cuisine and naturalized to European gardens.[3] This biological exchange was deeply informed by an imperialist ideology that justified colonial expansion, to the long-lasting detriment of the Indigenous peoples of the Americas. As Londa Schiebinger argues, '[t]he botanical sciences served the colonial enterprise and were, in turn, structured by it'.[4] Describing English relationships with Indigenous people in the West Indies, Schiebinger

---

[1] See Alfred W. Crosby, *The Columbian Exchange: Biological and Cultural Consequences of 1492* (Westport, CN: Greenwood, 1972).

[2] Scholars are still debating the veracity of the early modern claim that what came to be called syphilis originated in the Americas. Mary Lucas Powell and Della Collins Cook (eds.), *The Myth of Syphillis* (Gainesville: University Press of Florida, 2005), argue that venereal syphilis was not present in North America before the arrival of Columbus. However, also using bone evidence, Bruce M. Rothschild, 'History of Syphillis', *Clinical Infectious Diseases* 40 (2005), 1454–63, argues that it was. Andrew Lawlor, 'Searching for Syphilis's Origins', *Science*, 332 (22 April 2011), 417, contends it was transmitted to the Americas from Asia in the pre-Columbian period. Ivana Anteric et al., 'Which Theory for the Origin of Syphilis is True', *Journal of Sexual Medicine*, 11.12 (2014), 3112–8, argue that syphilis was present in Croatia prior to 1492.

[3] On the harm to Indigenous people of the introduction of new plants to their culture, see for example Beverly Soloway, '"mus co shee": Indigenous Plant Foods and Horticultural Imperialism in the Canadian Sub-Arctic', *Canadian Bulletin of Medical History*, 32 (2015), 253–73.

[4] Schiebinger, *Plants and Empire*, 11.

contends that such bioprospecting was not 'an unencumbered search for truth characterized by open communication of the best results', as scientists then preferred to see it; rather, 'conditions were hard in biocontact zones. Mortality was high; informants were unwilling. The search for potential life-saving new drugs was mired in relations of conquest, commerce, and slavery'.[5] African slaves being brought to the Americas and Indigenous peoples already there were themselves agents of biological change, with Africans instigating rice cultivation in the region and developing hybrid medical knowledge, and Indigenous people being regarded by the English as sources of knowledge about nature, albeit sources Settlers and medical writers treated with some suspicion.[6] Nevertheless, English importation of drugs from the region expanded significantly in the seventeenth century alongside settlement.[7]

This chapter is interested in the representation of knowledge of the *materia medica* of the Americas in early modern English women's writing. Women have not so far occupied an especially prominent role in the history of early modern European bioprospecting, perhaps because men wrote the travel narratives and learned medical texts that are key sources in understanding medicine in an Atlantic context. A key scholar to explore gender, Schiebinger investigates in *Plants and Empire* how the knowledge of abortifacients did not move to England, writing a history of early eighteenth-century agnotology. Yet even before this, English women writers were constructing knowledge of medical plants from the Americas, a few in literature and many more in their domestic recipe collections – a socially significant form of writing at an historical moment in which domestic medical practice was integral to the provision of care in England. This study of recipes is particularly informed by Pamela H.

---

[5] Londa Schiebinger, 'Prospecting for Drugs: European Naturalists in the West Indies,', in Londa Scheibinger and Claudia Swan (eds.), *Colonial Botany: Science, Commerce, and Politics in the Early Modern World* (Philadelphia: University of Pennsylvania Press, 2005), 119–33. For a wider survey of early European observations of Indigenous people's herbal knowledge, see Vogel, *American Indian Medicine*, 36–110. Vogel explores European observations of Indigenous medicine, European conceptions of their own superiority, and the reluctance of some – Settler and Indigenous – to exchange knowledge about medicines.

[6] Judith Ann Carney, *Black Rice: The African Origins of Rice Cultivation in the Americas* (Cambridge, MA: Harvard University Press, 2001); Parrish, 'American Curiosity', 215–306. On resistance to foreign medicines in England, see Andrew Wear, *Knowledge and Practice in Early Modern English Medicine, 1550–1680* (Cambridge University Press, 2000), 48, 72–3; and on Settler resistance, see Parsons, 'Medical Encounters', and Jennifer Mylander, '"How-To" Books: Impractical Manuals and the Construction of Englishness in the Atlantic World', *Journal for Early Modern Cultural Studies*, 9 (2009), 123–46.

[7] On drug importation, see Patrick Wallis, 'Exotic Drugs and English Medicine: England's Drug Trade, c. 1550–c. 1800', *Social History of Medicine*, 25 (2012), 20–46.

Smith's exploration of how craft knowledge overlapped with and contributed to the development of early modern science. Smith argues for the historical impact of 'vernacular science', efficacious knowledge developed through the practice of artisans that had recipes as its primary literary form.[8] To look at how English women engaged with Indigenous knowledge, this chapter tracks the stories told about the *materia medica* of the Americas and its Indigenous sources in Aphra Behn's fiction and drama and in women's recipe collections, where I focus on sarsaparilla and sassafras, two popular plants from across the Atlantic. I want to argue first that Indigenous knowledge functioned for the English in the early modern period as a kind of vernacular science, as knowledge developed through labour and experience, and then that women, as users of this knowledge, are part of a culture that in recipes both forgets this history of sources and remembers Indigenous practices and technologies.

Women's Literature

There are not a large number of literary works by early modern Englishwomen concerned with the Americas: Hester Pulter writes two poems about New England moose, and arguably the fantastical new worlds discovered by Margaret Cavendish's heroines in *Assaulted and Pursued Chastity* and *The Blazing World* reflect her thinking on the Americas. The writer most invested in medicinal plants, however, is Aphra Behn, who likely travelled to Surinam and is well known for her writing about the Americas. The narrative of *Oroonoko* (1688) is based on the historical circumstance that the slave trade was bringing Africans to Surinam to work on sugar plantations, and it ends with Oronooko, her enslaved African hero, smoking a pipe of tobacco.[9] What I am interested in is how Behn's narrator suggests that Surinam's Indigenous inhabitants (historically, the Carib and Arawak people) understand its natural resources: they know 'all the places where to seek the best Food of the country, and the Means of getting it; and for very small and unvaluable Trifles, supply us with that 'tis impossible for us to get'.[10] This sense of the richness of resources accords to a degree with Neil L. Whitehead's description of the region as then one of great natural diversity, 'actively

---

[8] Smith, 'Making as Knowing'.

[9] Iwanisziw, 'Behn's Novel Investment in "Oroonoko"', discusses tobacco in *Oroonoko* and *The Widow Ranter*, drawing connections to Oronooko's name (Oronoko tobacco was grown in the Chesapeake area).

[10] *Oroonoko*, in *Works of Aphra Behn*, Summers (ed.), vol. III, 60.

sustained by native ecological practices', where the 'diversity of flora, fauna, and environment was matched by a florescence of human social and cultural forms'.[11] If Behn allows, however, that the people know where to find food, she does not see them cultivating or valuing it. That food stuffs could be traded for 'trifles' follows what Jeffrey Knapp argues is a 'common colonial logic' in the European estimation of those they deem 'savage': 'they always hold the wrong thing in "precious estimation" – not gold, for instance, but trifles'.[12] Behn's perspective on Indigenous people accounts neither for their work with the natural world, nor their alternative system of cultural values.[13]

Similarly, when Behn describes a medicine man and his remedies, she constructs the Indigenous people as 'very Superstitious' and the 'Great *Peeie*, that is Prophet' as

> bred to all the little Arts and cunning they are capable of; to all the Legerdemain Tricks, and Slight of Hand, whereby he imposes upon the Rabble; and is both a Doctor in Physick and Divinity. And by these Tricks makes the Sick believe he sometimes eases their Pains; by drawing from the afflicted part little Serpents, or odd Flies, or Worms, or any Strange thing; and though they have besides undoubted good Remedies, for almost all their Diseases, they cure the Patient more by Fancy than by Medicines; and make themselves Fear'd, Lov'd, and Reverenc'd.[14]

When the narrator asserts that they could have 'good Remedies' but instead turn to 'fancies', 'cunning', and 'tricks', she gives the proper use of nature – remedies – to Europeans. Even as her narrative acknowledges the value of Indigenous knowledge in Settler survival, it dismisses that knowledge as superstitious, fanciful, political theatre.

Tobacco underpins the narrative of *The Widow Ranter*. Staged in 1689 and printed in 1690, the play attracts colonists to Virginia to grow tobacco, which appears as a subversive, dramatic prop for the Widow Ranter, who contravenes gender norms by smoking.[15] The Indigenous characters in the play, a king and queen, have no relationship with tobacco, although seventeenth-century English observers noted that both the Powhatan and Virginia Algonquin people who lived in the region

[11] Neil L. Whitehead, 'Native Peoples Confront Colonial Regimes in Northeastern South America (c. 1500–1900)', in Frank Salomon and Stuart B. Schwarts (eds.), *The Cambridge History of the Native Peoples of the Americas*, 3 vols. (Cambridge University Press, 1999), vol. III, 390–1.

[12] Jeffrey Knapp, 'Elizabethan Tobacco', *Representations* 21 (1988), 26–66 at 35.

[13] On how Indigenous people valued gold for its smell, brilliance, and 'cosmological significance', see Whitehead, 'Native Peoples', 395.

[14] Behn, *Oroonoko*, in *Works*, vol. III, 102.

[15] Aphra Behn, *The Widow Ranter*, in *Works*, vol. VII, 306.

cultivated and used tobacco.[16] Tobacco, moreover, is central to many Native American stories and sacred rituals, and for the people of the Eastern Woodlands (which includes Virginia) it was a medicine, a status indicator, and gift of friendship and hospitality.[17] Yet, in the play, tobacco belongs only to the Settlers. Friendly and Dullman have plantations, and as the play explores questions of class and colonial governance, tobacco planting emerges as a proper realm for the lower-class colonists' activity. Timerous, a poor councilor, previously 'set and stript Tobacco', and in the end, he promises to return 'to my old trade again, bask under the shade of my own Tobacco, and Drink my Punch in Peace'. With his turn from governance to farming, the plot suggests a move from chaos to peace.[18] The epilogue, 'Spoken by a Woman', commends the medicinal qualities of tobacco in defending the play: 'Farce is a Food proper for your lips,/ As for *Green-Sickness*, crumpt Tobacco-pipes'.[19] Tobacco is a valuable English commodity, a pleasure, a proper focus of lower-class labour, and a medicine (if curing green sickness is not a common virtue according to English herbals). It is not, however, a plant that the Indigenous people of the Powhatan Confederacy are shown knowing anything about. The play forgets where tobacco came from, who taught the colonists to smoke, and, with *Oroonoko*, queries not only who can own the plants of the Americas but who can claim to know them properly.

Women's Recipes

Recipes were perhaps the most culturally pervasive form of women's writing engaged in Atlantic knowledge exchange, with recipes including multiple ingredients from the Americas appearing well before Behn's late seventeenth-century work. Recipes, too, raise questions of English

[16] Alexander von Gernet, 'North American Indigenous *Nicotiana* Use and Tobacco Shamanism: The Early Documentary Record, 1520–1660', in Joseph C. Winter (ed.), *Tobacco Use by Native North Americans* (Norman: University of Oklahoma Press, 2000), 66–70.

[17] Penelope B. Drooker, 'Pipes, Leadership, and Interregional Interaction in Protohistoric Midwestern and Northeastern North America', in Sean Rafferty and Rob Mann (eds.), *Smoking and Culture: The Archaeology of Tobacco Pipes in Eastern North America* (Knoxville: University of Tennessee Press, 2004), 73–124; Joseph C. Winter, 'Traditional Uses of Tobacco by Native Americans', in Winter (ed.), *Tobacco Use*, 14–20.

[18] Behn, *Widow Ranter*, in *Works*, vol. VII, 302 and 351. On tobacco and American identity, see Peter C. Herman, '"We all smoke here": Behn's *The Widow Ranter* and the Invention of American Identity', in Robert Appelbaum and John Wood Sweet (eds.), *Envisioning an English Empire: Jamestown and the Making of the North Atlantic World* (Philadelphia: University Press of Pennsylvania, 2005), 254–74.

[19] Behn, *Widow Ranter*, in *Works*, vol. VII, 354.

indebtedness, remembering, and forgetting. In the past decade, recipes have inspired a lively scholarly discussion. Sara Pennell and Amy Tigner explore ingredients from the Americas in cookery recipes and how they, as Pennell contends, erase their 'outlandish connections'.[20] Elsewhere, Pennell, as well as Alisha Rankin and Lynette Hunter, argue for the import of women's work and practical knowledge for seventeenth-century science.[21] Wendy Wall discusses the recipe as a literary form that constructed knowledge on the grounds of '*techne* (labour)' and '*praxis* (experience)' and used 'systems of naming' that 'marked the recipe's travels within a community of potential knowledge conferrers'.[22] Writing about the creation of traditional Indigenous knowledge across the Atlantic, Peter Newhouse argues that it 'arises out of careful observation and careful thought carried out within a particular cognitive framework, reflective of an underlying mode of thought or cognitive orientation towards the world. It is also transmitted in a particular fashion under particular circumstances'; it is a system, he adds, with which Western knowledge has been in 'continuous contact' since the fifteenth century.[23] Even more than Aphra Behn's work, recipes provide very specific evidence of this cross-cultural circulation of knowledge, a story that is also about early modern women's lives as expert, authoritative participants in communities, families, and modes of thought of the Scientific Revolution.[24] To illustrate this point, I want to focus on sarsaparilla and sassafras, two ingredients commonly found in women's recipes. A deciduous tree native to what is now the eastern United States, sassafras was a valuable seventeenth-century commodity that inspired expeditions to and temporary settlements in Massachusetts and Virginia.[25] Sarsaparilla is a vine, which was between 1566 and 1610 the second most valuable drug import and between 1617 and 1638 the sixth most valuable, outstripping sassafras until the end of the century.[26]

---

[20] Pennell, 'Recipes and Reception'; Tigner, 'Preserving Nature'.
[21] Alisha Rankin, 'How to Cure the Golden Vein: Medical Remedies as *Wissenschaft* in Early Modern Germany', in Meyers and Cook (eds.), *Ways of Making*, 113–37; Pennell, 'Perfecting Practice?'; Hunter and Hutton, *Women, Science and Medicine*.
[22] Wall, *Recipes for Thought*, 228, 231.
[23] David Newhouse, 'Indigenous Knowledge in a Multicultural World', *Native Studies Review* 15.2 (2004), 150–4.
[24] On recipes as life-writing, see Field, '"Many hands hands"'.
[25] Russell M. Magnaghi, 'Sassafras and Its Role in Early American History', *Terrae Incognitae*, 29 (1997), 10–21.
[26] Wallis, 'Exotic Drugs', 31. For a survey of early European representations of sassafras and sarsaparilla, see J. Worth Estes, 'The European Reception of the First Drugs from the New World', *Pharmacy in History*, 37 (1995), 7–8.

Before I turn to women's recipes, I want to consider how sassafras and sarsaparilla entered English pharmacology, where they would remain until the nineteenth century. They are represented at first in herbals and travel narratives as ingredients that Europeans learned about from Indigenous people in the Caribbean and North America. An early, influential herbal to catalogue ingredients from the Americas was the Spaniard, Nicolás Monardes's sixteenth-century *Historia medicinal de las cosas que se traen de nuestras Indias Occidentales que sirven en medicina* (1565).[27] This work was translated into Latin, Italian, French, German, and English (by John Frampton, a merchant) and printed in 1577, 1580, and 1596 in England as *Joyfull newes out of the newe founde worlde*. Monardes's work was cited in travel narratives and used and cited in later English herbals.[28]

Recounting stories from contact zones told to him by travelers, Monardes indicates that sarsaparilla came from New Spain where 'the Indians did use it for great medicine, with the which they did heale many and divers diseases'. He credits the Spanish with the name – they believe that the plant is the same as one found in Spain – but its medical uses are 'Indian' knowledge. They beat sarsaparilla in a mortar and water to create a jelly that, when strained, was a thick drink that would be taken throughout the day as the patient fasted.[29] This method he says is better than any other, but they also prepare it by washing it, cutting it small, putting it in an earthenware pot with water, and letting it infuse for twenty-four hours before setting it over a fire so three pots boil down to one.[30] It cures 'Reumes or Runnings, or windinesse, the evill of women, of the Mother, or any other cause or occasion what soever'.[31] A second section on the sarsaparilla of Guayaquil (then a village, now the largest city in Ecuador) indicates that the Indigenous women there taught the Spaniards to use a water made from the rind of the plant, using the method above, but boiling it until half, rather than two thirds,

---

[27] On Monardes, see Daniela Bleichmar, 'Books, Bodies, and Fields: Sixteenth-Century Transatlantic Encounters with the New World *Materia Medica*', in Schiebinger and Swan (eds.), *Colonial Botany*, 83–99.

[28] Estes, 'European Reception', 14–15, traces the gradual appearance of American ingredients in European herbals. Gerard was the first to offer an extended discussion of multiple plants from the region. Thomas Hariot, *A Briefe and True report of the Newfoundland of Virginia* (Frankfurt: John Wechel, 1590), 9, refers the reader to Monardes as he reports on sassafras.

[29] Nicolás Monardes, *Joyfull Newes Out of the New-found Worlde*, trans. John Frampton (London: E. Allde, 1596), fols. 15ᵛ–16ʳ.

[30] Monardes, *Joyfull Newes*, fols. 16ʳ–16ᵛ refers to his earlier description of the method for measurement (fol. 12ʳ).

[31] Monardes, *Joyfull Newes*, fols. 18ʳ⁻ᵛ.

evaporates.[32] In these stories, Indigenous people, including women, have judgement, technologies of measurement and pulverizing, and proven knowledge of medical remedies.

In later English herbals, the story of sarsaparilla's origins is more briefly told, and it is placed within the Galenic system. Placed under the entry for bindweed – Parkinson as 'Pricklye Bindweede', and Gerard as 'rough' bindweed – sarsaparilla is, for Gerard, 'Zarza Parilla, or the prickly Binde-weed of America' from Peru and Virginia. Gerard complains about the lack of information beyond Monardes, but affirms it is hot and dry and 'good for all manner of infirmities wherein there is hope of cure by sweating'.[33] Parkinson disputes Monardes's view that 'Sarsaparilla of America', brought to England from America via Spain, is the same as that already known, and argues that it is a distinct plant. Some use it is as a powder, he says, some by boiling it in water so long that it makes a cream, and others as a decoction in water, boiled to half or a third.[34] Although these uses are in line with Monardes's, Parkinson does not follow him in saying that the 'some' who used sarsaparilla as a decoction and cream include Indigenous people.

As to sassafras, Monardes traces it to Florida, reporting that he learned about the tree from a Frenchman who reported on how the French in Florida had grown ill, but 'the Indians did shewe them this tree, and the manner how they should use it, and so they did and were healed of many evilles, which surely bringeth admiration'.[35] The Spanish too were cured by the tree, 'shewed to them by the Indians'.[36] Monardes explains the method they use for preparation in a way that again accords the practitioners experience and judgement:

> They digged up the roote of this tree, and tooke a piece thereof, such as it seemed to them best, they cutte it small into very thin and little peeces, and cast them into water, at discretion, as much as they sawe was needefull, lyttle more or lesse, and they sodde it the tyme that seemed sufficient for to remaine a good colour, and so they dranke in the morning fasting, and in the daytime, and at dynner, and supper, without keeping any more weight, or measure ... by this they were healed of so many griefes, and evill diseases, that to heare of them what they suffred.[37]

---

[32] Ibid., fol. 81ᵛ.
[33] John Gerard, *The Herball or Generall Historie of Plantes* (London: Thomas Johnson, 1636), 859–61; John Parkinson, *Theatrum Botanicum* (London: Thomas Cotes, 1640), 173–6.
[34] Parkinson, *Theatrum*, 176.
[35] Monardes, *Joyfull Newes*, fol. 46ʳ.
[36] Ibid., fol. 46ᵛ.
[37] Ibid.

He adds that 'the Indians' also put the leaves, after stamping them, on bruises, and that they call it 'Pauamé'.[38] Monardes's list of its virtues includes comforting the liver and treating swellings, griefs of the head and stomach, lameness, and gout.[39] John Gerard also records the names for sassafras in French as 'Pauame', but gives it an English one, too: 'Ague tree', since its virtue is healing ague. He contends that the plant is hot, dry, and cleansing, and that it helps dropsy, removes stoppage of the liver, cures agues and fevers, and provokes urine.[40] John Parkinson, like Monardes, credits the French with bringing knowledge of sassafras to 'the Christian world' from Florida, where it had been learned by them 'of the Natives' who called it 'Pauame' or 'Winanke'. The decoction, he says, 'is familiarly given in all cold diseases', a perspective that treats Indigenous practice of creating a decoction as common English knowledge. Yet he adds to his list of how the decoction will treat obstructions of the liver and spleen, rheumes, 'defluxions of the head', and strengthen the parts, noting that 'the Indians use of the leaves being bruised to heale their wounds, and sores' – as if that remedy remains unfamiliar and theirs alone.[41]

Nicholas Culpeper's very popular *A Physical Directory* (1649), an English translation of the *Pharmacopoeia Londinensis* (1618), published by the College of Physicians to guide apothecaries in approved remedies, erases Indigenous origins altogether.[42] Sarsaparilla is 'somewhat hot and dry, helpful against pains in the head, and joynts, they provoke sweat, and are used familiarly in drying Diet-drinks'.[43] Sassafras is 'hot and dry in the Second degree, it opens obstructions or stoppings, it strengthens the breast … it breaks the stone staies vomiting, provokes urine, and is very profitable in the French pocks'.[44] No mention is made of the Americas or its peoples. These herbals are telling a story. In Monardes's version, it is the experience and knowledge of Indigenous peoples that could inform European practice. In Gerard's and Parkinson's herbals, it does too, but they cite only Monardes, and the traces of the Indigenous knowledge of the plants fade to names and practices that have not been

---

[38] Ibid., fols. 47ᵛ–48ʳ.
[39] Ibid., fols. 48ʳ–50ᵛ.
[40] Gerard, *Herball*, 1524–5.
[41] Parkinson, *Theatrum*, 1606–7.
[42] The first edition, in Latin, *Pharmacopoea Londinensis* (London: Edward Griffin, 1618), includes 'Smilax aspera' (rough bindweed) and 'sassafras' in its catalogue of simples (sig. Dd1ᵛ–Dd2ʳ).
[43] Nicholas Culpeper, *A Physicall Directory* (London: Peter Cole, 1649), 17.
[44] Culpeper, *Physicall Directory*, 24.

adopted; Indigenous knowledge that is used becomes simply English, approved even by the College. In becoming 'familiar' and English, the ingredients also shift from an Indigenous cultural framework to a European, Galenic one. For Martha Robinson, this move to the Galenic system 'meant that the English assumed from the beginning that they were capable of knowing more about Indian medicine than the Indians did. The Indians might have remedies that "worked," but they required superior English understanding to explain how or why they worked'.[45] Knowledge of sassafras and sarsaparilla is constructed on the grounds of such forgetting and transformation as well.

So what then of women's recipes? How did they approach these ingredients? They say nothing about the ingredients' Atlantic origins, but their methodologies, crucially, are very much like those Monardes's reporters encountered in the Americas: infusions and decoctions that make a drink, or occasionally, a broth. Other types of medicines, such as ointments, troches, electuaries, pills, or plasters, do not appear. The recipes of Lady Frances Catchmay (d. 1629) contain one long recipe using sarsaparilla and sassafras: 'An approved medicen for the french disease: Called the frenche pox' appears near the end of the recipes in the original hand, dated to about 1625. In the recipe, sarsaparilla cut into one-inch pieces and sassafras 'very thinne shaved' are boiled in water, then licorice, hermodactyl, and white wine are added, and the concoction is boiled again. More water is added, the conction is left to seeth before more ingredients are added, and the drink is finally cooled and strained. The recipe ends with detailed instructions on its use, the time of day it should be taken and with what, and it finally concludes with a specific and personal commendation: 'I wish you could understand how assuredly I doe beleeve that this god willinge, will helpe any one of how longe continuance soever, if a man may be credulous in any experience then he may trust to this that I have proved above thre hundred tymes all wth very good successe'.[46] In this recipe book, sassafras and sarsaparilla are part of Lady Catchmay's experience as a medical practitioner, one that she is concerned that her children will continue to understand. A preface to the

[45] Martha K. Robinson, 'New Worlds, New Medicines: Indian Remedies and English Medicine in Early America', *Early American Studies*, 3.1 (2005), 97.
[46] Wellcome Library, MS 184a, Lady Frances Catchmay, *A Booke of Medicens*, c. 1625, fols. 25^v–26^r. Katrina Rutz, 'The Catchmay Project', *Early Modern Recipes Online Collective*, July 2014, http://emroc.hypotheses.org/ongoing-projects/frances-catchmay, provides evidence that Catchmay was buried in Gloucestershire, the only thing known about her life.

collection states that it was left to her son Sir William Catchmay, who should let all of his sisters and brothers have a copy of it.[47]

Grace (Sharington) Mildmay, Lady Mildmay (c. 1552–1620), the wife of Anthony Mildmay, mistress of Apethorpe Hall in Northamptonshire, and author of meditations and advice, left an extensive recipe archive.[48] Mildmay's recipes are collected in a scribally prepared, quarto-sized volume to which she added further marginal notes and recipes, and in another scribally prepared folio compiled by her daughter, Mary Fane, Countess of Westmorland, entitled 'Certaine breife Collections and observations disgested into Fowre bookes' as 'The treasure of this my worthy Mothers minde'.[49] The recipes in the quarto volume use many exotic and expensive ingredients, including multiple remedies using sarsaparilla and sassafras, many of which are for infusions and decoctions. 'A compounded Ale, to open obstructions' uses large quantities, mixing half a pound of sarsaparilla and other ingredients with twelve gallons of ale, boiling this down, adding yeast, stewing it and distilling it, then hanging in the liquid a bag of the residue of the ingredients for ten or twelve days, and finally adding hermodactyl (a root imported from the East) and nutmeg.[50] 'The cure of the pockes, ye surest shortest and easiest that ever was found' is a multi-stage cure that begins with bleeding the patient and fasting, and then giving the patient a decoction of sarsaparilla, hermodactyl, licorice, and anise seeds, infused for twenty-four hours in water and boiled down, to which senna has been added. In one section of the manuscript, Mildmay adds in her own hand multiple recipes for diets – drinks for health – that involve sassafras. Two diets list sassafras as their first ingredient but boil different ingredients with china root and water to create the drink.[51] Multiple recipes involving sarsaparilla begin two pages later. All boil sarsaparilla with other ingredients in water. 'A diet broth, to take as a breakefast, every morning' mixes sarsaparilla, china root, agrimony, betony, violet flower, mace, and a crust of bread to make a broth 'of the strength of a good chicken'.[52] Another diet, 'A good diet & course of phisick for spring & fall, to preserve health & to rectifie putrified humors in the body: by Mr Poe',

[47] Wellcome MS 184a, Catchmay, *Booke*, fol. 2ᵛ.
[48] On Mildmay and medicine, see Hellwarth, '"Be unto me as a precious ointment"', and Linda Pollock, *With Faith and Physic: The Life of a Tudor Gentlewoman, Lady Grace Mildmay, 1552–1620* (London: Collins and Brown, 1993), 92–109.
[49] NRO W(A) Misc. Vol. 33, *Lady Grace Mildmay's Medical Papers*; NRO W(A) Misc. Vol. 32, *Lady Grace Mildmay's Medical Papers*.
[50] NRO W(A) Misc. Vol. 33, Mildmay, 119.
[51] Ibid., 132.
[52] Ibid., 134–6.

recommends a sequence of daily purges and diet drinks, the drink being a decoction of six ounces of sarsaparilla and one ounce of sassafras, aloes, and fennel seeds added to water and boiled down.[53]

The other recipe collection prepared by the Countess of Westmorland includes sarsaparilla and sassafras in the treatment of specific diseases. A diet for the decay of memory is created by placing sarsaparilla and sassafras and other ingredients in a linen bag and infusing it in ale.[54] A recipe treating an inflamed face with swelling recommends taking a mastic pill, the application of an oil, and drinking a china broth 'made with opening rootes and cooleing hearbes', and then taking every morning with the broth 'searsed powder of Sarsaparilla' which will produce sweat, the only recipe recommending taking sarsaparilla in powder form.[55] A course of physic for the falling sickness, 'Experienced upon a maide of twentie five yeares who had that disease from her childhood, and was parfectly cured by the same', recommends after a purge a 'dyet made of sassaphras' created by infusing sassafras alone in water and boiling it down. This cure, the recipe reports, was undertaken over the course of three years and works 'to mollifie all hardnes; to moysten all drynes; and to sett the head; harte; and spirituall parts free from all convulsions'.[56] In Mildmay's recipe collection, the use of sassafras and sarsaparilla are part of a medical practice that is experimental, grounded in experience, and engaged with her male contemporaries.

The manuscript recipe collection of Anne (Harrison) Fanshawe, Lady Fanshawe (1625–80), best known for her biography of her diplomat husband Richard Fanshawe, includes remedies using sarsaparilla. While the collection also records recipes from Spain, these are from her mother Margaret Harrison. Near the beginning of the manuscript, which was begun in 1651, is a recipe from her mother 'For Melancholy and heaveness of spiretts', which boils sarsaparilla in white wine with raisins of the sun and hermodactyl, and adding licorice, anise seeds, and chamomile flowers to make a drink that can be used three or four times a day; a second drink, to be given when the patient is thirsty, is made by adding this decoction to ale.[57] Another recipe from 'My Mother' – 'To make an

---

[53] Ibid., 140.
[54] NRO W(A) Misc. Vol. 32, Mildmay, fol. 19^v.
[55] Ibid., fol. 44^r.
[56] Ibid., fols. 9^v–10^r.
[57] Wellcome Library, MS 7113, Lady Anne Fanshawe, *Recipe book of Lady Ann Fanshawe*, 1651–1707, fols. 4^{r-v}. On hermodactylus, see Steven Blankaart, *The Physical Dictionary* (London: Samuel Crouch, 1702), 106.

Excellent opening and purging Drinke for the Liver' – puts sarsaparilla, 'sliced and bruised', polipody of the oak (a fern grown at the root of oak trees), 'Sena of Alexandria' (grown in Syria, Persia, and Arabia), yellow dock root, rhubarb, and other herbs and seeds into a bag with a piece of lead and places the bag in a barrel of ale; on the first day, the recipe recommends, 'squeeze the juice out of the Bagge in the drinke 3 or 4 times, letting the bagge hang in the drinke continually, then let them work together'.[58] After steeping, the drink should be given two hours before dinner and supper, at the beginning of May 'or at the fall of the Leafe' and is good for the liver, 'any Dropsicall humour, or the scurvy, or Foulenes of Blood'.[59] In this collection, the remedies are part of Fanshawe's maternal inheritance.

The first recipe collection to be published under female authorship was that of Elizabeth (Talbot) Gray, Countess of Kent (1582–1651), whose *Choice Manual of Rare Secrets in Physick* (1653) was printed multiple times through the second half of the seventeenth century and into the eighteenth century. With her sister, Althea Talbot, and Queen Henrietta Maria, the Countess of Kent was, according to Lynette Hunter, 'part of a group of people investigating the new experimental science and interested in new approaches to knowledge'.[60] And indeed, *The Queen's Closet Opened*, printed first in 1655 and several times thereafter, contains recipes using sassafras and sarsaparilla, including recipes from Dr Butler, Dr Lukener, and Francis Bacon.[61] Like these, the remedies in the Countess of Kent's collection deploy sarsaparilla as part of an infusion or in a decoction. 'A Medicine very good for the Dropsie, or the Scurvy, and to clear the blood' has two parts to be mixed together, one part an ale infused with brooklime, watercress, water mint, and scurvy grass, and the other a water infused with guaiacum (a West-Indian wood) and sarsaparilla.[62] 'The Diet against Melancholy' also infuses ingredients – sena, rhubarb, polipody of oak, sarsaparilla, and other seeds and spices – in ale.[63]

[58] On senna, see Blankaart, *Physical Dictionary*, 279–80. On polypodium of oak, see J[ohn] B[ullokar], *An English Expositor* (London: John Legatt, 1641), sig. M3[v].

[59] Wellcome MS 7113, Fanshawe, *Recipe*, fol. 5[r].

[60] Lynette Hunter, 'Women and Domestic Medicine: Lady Experimenters, 1570–1620' in Hunter and Hutton (eds.), *Women, Science and Medicine*, 93–4.

[61] [W.M.], *The Queens Closet Opened* (London: Nathaniel Brook, 1655), 2–3, 68–9, 70–1, 93, 134, and 281.

[62] Elizabeth Grey, *A Choice Manual of Rare and Select Secrets in Physick and Chyrurgery* (London: [G. D.], 1653), 30–1.

[63] Grey, *Choice*, 108–9. Robert Burton, *The Anatomy of Melancholy*, Nicolas K. Kiessling, Thomas C. Faulkner, and Rhonda L. Blair (eds.), 6 vols. (Oxford University Press, 1990), vol. II, 250, also

Water-based, 'An excellent Syrupe to purge' boils down sarsaparilla, 'Sena Alexandrina', 'Polipodium of the Oak', prunes, ginger, anise, cumin and caraway seeds, and other ingredients with added sugar to create a syrup.[64]

In all of these recipes, sarsaparilla and sassafras have become part of an English culture of intellectual exchange, among women, scholars, physicians, families, and acquaintances. It is a culture rooted in a creative, experiential epistemology. Lady Catchmay offers assurances that she has tried her remedy 300 times, and Mildmay assesses why her recipe worked on a twenty-five-year-old woman. No two recipes are exactly alike, although the ingredients are prepared in many similar ways, and sassafras and sarsaparilla are repeatedly used with some of the same ingredients (china root, polipody of oak, and senna, for instance). It is a culture that depends on knowledgeable labour, with some recipes demanding a great deal of attention with their sometimes long lists of ingredients and multi-day (even multi-year) courses, and every one presuming a knowledge of the technique.

The knowledge exchanges explicitly recorded, however, do not include Indigenous people. Arguing for the importance of memory to early modern women's writing in the British Atlantic world, Kate Chedgzoy contends that recipes manifested cultural memory by their practical knowledge, as the embodied memory of repeated practices.[65] The recipes discussed here also remember, explicitly in their named contributors, but also implicitly in their reliance on Indigenous methodologies for using sassafras and sarsaparilla. They recall Monardes's reports that Indigenous people used infusion and decoction and that they made a powder of sarsaparilla. They recall reports that Indigenous people cut the sassafras and sarsaparilla into small pieces and that in decoction the liquid should be reduced by a certain fraction (as in Mildmay's assertion, 'Boyle all in iii gallons, to a gallon & an halfe'.[66] They recall European observations that the ingestion of these drinks should be accompanied by fasting.[67] And even though most of Monardes's reports suggest the use of simples (composed of a single ingredient), and many of these recipes are for

recommends 'the decoction of China roots, Sassafras, Sarsaparilla, Guaiacum. China, saith Manardus, makes a good colour in the face, takes away melancholy, and all infirmities proceeding from cold'.

[64] Grey, *Choice*, 57–8.
[65] Chedgzoy, *Women's Writing in the British Atlantic World*, 22.
[66] On small pieces, see Wellcome MS 184a, Catchmay, *Booke*, fol. 25ᵛ and NRO W(A) Misc. Vol. 33, Mildmay, 135; on reduction, see NRO W(A) Misc. Vol. 33, Mildmay, 134.
[67] On fasting, see NRO W(A) Misc. Vol. 33, Mildmay, 134 and Vol. 32, fol. 19ᵛ.

compound waters, the addition of other ingredients was found in the Americas, too. Arthur Barlow reports in 'The Voyage made to the Coasts of America', printed in Hakluyt's *Principal Navigations*, of the people that he encounters on Roanoke Island: 'all the yere after they drink water, but it is sodden with Ginger in it and blacke Sinamon, and sometimes Sassaphras, and divers other wholesome, and medicinable hearbes and trees'.[68] All of these techniques – decoction, diet drinks, and fasting – are existing components of European medical practice, but the legitimacy of their use with sassafras and sarsaparilla was learned from people across the Atlantic.

I am not saying here that Indigenous medicine is the same as English Galenic medicine, even though in the early modern period, there are obviously notable similarities.[69] Indigenous knowledge about nature is forged on a different relationship with nature, one rooted in the spiritual, in the observation of the local, and in the knower's relationship with plants and animals, where there are obligations and responsibilities, where one is transformed by that knowledge.[70] Jason Hall discusses, for instance, how the medical knowledge of the Maliseet people (on whose unceded territory I reside) included a sense of kinship with plants, a kinship alien to European systems of thought.[71] What I am interested in making visible is the unacknowledged intellectual debt established in recipes. Writing about chocolate and tobacco, Mary Norton argues that 'European uses of goods had their origins in Native American technologies, material forms, therapeutic knowledge, and symbolic investments', an intellectual syncretism nevertheless accompanied by a repudiation of knowledge deemed 'savage'.[72] Perhaps because they were not associated with religious practices, knowledge of sassafras and sarsaparilla is not characterized in this way. Yet English writing about them still soon forgets Indigenous sources, even as it remembers their practices and builds

---

[68] Arthur Barlow, 'The first voyage made to the coasts of America' in Richard Hakluyt (ed.), *The Third and Last Volume of the Voyages, Navigations, Traffiques, and Discoveries of the English Nation* (London: George Bishop, 1600), 249.

[69] Clara Sue Kidwell, 'Native American Systems of Knowledge' in Philip J. Deloria and Neal Salisbury (eds.), *A Companion to American Indian History* (Malden, MA: Blackwell Publishing, 2004), 87–102.

[70] Kidwell, 'Native American'; and Newhouse, 'Indigenous', 139–54. See also Parsons, 'Medical Encounters', 65–6, who discusses how a relationship with nature informed practices of observation and the creation of remedies.

[71] Jason Hall, 'Maliseet Cultivation and Climatic Resilience on the Wəlastəkw/St. John River During the Little Ice Age', *Acadiensis*, 44.2 (2015), 3–25.

[72] Marcy Norton, *Sacred Gifts, Profane Pleasures: A History of Tobacco and Chocolate in the Atlantic World* (Ithaca: Cornell University Press, 2008), 10.

them into English social relationships, women's labour, and their creation of medical knowledge through that caring work.

Conclusion

The Cherokee American/Canadian writer Thomas King says in *The Truth about Stories*, 'The truth about stories is that that's all we are'; 'stories were medicine', he adds, and 'a story told one way could cure, that the same story told another way could injure'.[73] The stories in the texts considered here are injurious in not recounting how Europeans were indebted to Indigenous knowledge, even as soldiers, settlers, and travellers in the Americas and physicians, apothecaries, and domestic practitioners back in England depended on that knowledge. Aphra Behn's *Oroonoko* does not represent the Indigenous people of Surinam as the author of remedies, nor those from Virginia in *The Widow Ranter* as knowledgeable about tobacco. Recipes, too, forget, even as they use practical knowledge from across the Atlantic. This is not unique to women's recipes, although more explicit recognition was sometimes forthcoming, as in John Josselyn's *New England Rarities Discovered* (1672), where a recipe 'For Colds', after the description of sumach, states: 'The English use to boyl it in Beer, and drink it for Colds; and so do the Indians, from whom the English had the Medicine'.[74] Like this recipe, early modern women's writing, in literature and recipes, has a story to tell about medical knowledge in an Atlantic context. The story that we tell about it should include all participants.[75]

---

[73] Thomas King, *The Truth about Stories: A Native Narrative* (Toronto: House of Anansi Press, 2003), 92.
[74] John Josselyn, *New-Englands Rarities Discovered* (London: G. Widdowes, 1672), 60.
[75] Thank you to Emily Skov-Nielsen for her research assistance and to Dr Rachel Bryant for her feedback.

Lady Anne Clifford's Great Books of Record: *Remembrances of a Dynasty*

Jessica L. Malay

From many noble progenitors I hold

Transmitted lands, castles, and honors which they sway'd of old

Anne Clifford, *Life of Mee*[1]

The Lady Anne Clifford, Countess of Dorset, Montgomery and Pembroke, and Baroness Clifford of Skipton in her own right (1590–1676) was the daughter of George, third Earl of Cumberland (1558–1605), an important courtier and maritime adventurer in Elizabeth I and later James I's courts. Her mother, Margaret Russell (1560–1616), came from the powerful Russell family, Earls of Bedford. Her aunt, Anne Russell, Countess of Warwick (1549–1604), was one of Elizabeth I's extraordinary gentlewomen of the privy chamber, serving the queen from 1559 until Elizabeth's death, waiting upon the queen in the final hours of her life. Anne Russell's position at the centre of female political power for over forty years influenced both her sister Margaret and her niece Anne, and contributed to their determination to pursue Anne Clifford's rights to the Clifford hereditary lands[2] after George Clifford's death (1605). All Anne Clifford's works, from her autobiographies (in various forms)[3] to her historical and antiquarian work, which is given best expression in her *Great Books of Record,* are in some way related to Anne Clifford's

---

[1] Clifford, *Great Books,* 1.

[2] The lands in Westmorland and in Craven, Yorkshire, that descended to the Clifford's through royal grants, including Brougham and Appleby castles in Westmorland and Skipton Castle in Yorkshire.

[3] The 1603 memoir. The 1616, 1617, 1619 diary exists in four manuscript copies: Belfast, Northern Ireland, D3044/G/5, PRONI; Longleat Archives, Wiltshire, Portland Papers, Portland MS 23; Kent History and Library Centre, Maidstone, Kent, MS U269/3/3/5; Bod MS. Eng. misc. d. 133. The 1589–1649 memoir and 1650–76 yearly summaries make up the bulk of the third volume of the *Great Books of Records,* all three sets are now held by the Cumbria Archive Service, Kendal. The 1676 daybook is in the private collection at Dalmain House, Cumbria. See also Clifford, *Great Books*; and Clifford, *Anne Clifford's Autobiographical Writing.*

inheritance battle, which was the defining experience in her life.[4] This is made clear by entries in her daybook of 1676, where she recalls just two days before her death: 'I rememberd how this day was 60 years did I and my blessed Mother in Brougham Castle in Westmorland, where wee then lay, give in our answer in writing that wee would not stand to the Award the then four chief Judges meant to make concerning the lands of mine Inheritance'.[5] And while the battles over Anne Clifford's inheritance, fought on a number of fronts, were the initial catalyst for Anne Clifford's early historical and antiquarian interests, the *Great Books of Record* (along with her other textual and visual projects) became much more than an assertion and protection of her rights.[6] They informed her understanding of her own life within the complex and ever creative dynamics of time.

Margaret Russell in the Archives

Anne Clifford's first husband, Richard Sackville, third Earl of Dorset, once wrote to her, 'I love and hold [you] a sober woman, your lands onlie excepted which transportes you beyond your self and make you devoid of all reason'.[7] Margaret Russell disagreed. Russell believed that the fight for the Clifford hereditary lands was fundamentally reasonable, and imperative for the benefit and security of Richard and Anne's future progeny and in defence of the direct hereditary descent of the houses first of Veteriponts and then Cliffords for nearly 500 years. This dynastic impetus can be seen in Margaret Russell's letters in the early days of the lawsuits. She complains to Edward Bruce, Lord Kinloss: 'My enemys cannot accuse mee for anie faults soe much as for trusting in the laws of this land, for the right of my Daughter's Inheritance, or soe to overthrowe a noble house which right of hers I have now lay'd down at his Majesty's feete, (her Right coming from Women heretofore & nowe going to Women againe)'. She continues that Anne Clifford was 'the first Daughter & sole heire to an Earl since the time of the Conquest left without any land at all, & the first of all times as I think, that was so deceitfully wrested out of

---

[4] See Peter Sherlock (Chapter 16) in this volume, for a discussion of Clifford's motives in her commissioning of dynastic funeral monuments.

[5] Dalemain Archives, Dalemain House, Penrith, Cumbria, Anne Clifford's Daybook, 20 March 1676 entry.

[6] These include her *Great Picture* (Abbot Hall Gallery, Kendal, Cumbria), her *Claim and Title of the Lady Anne Clifford to the Baronies of Clifford, Westmorland and Vescy* (see WDHOTH 1/13, Cumbria Archive Service, Kendal; MS 104, Lincoln's Inn Library, London; MS 105, Queen's College, Oxford) and other manuscript publications she commissioned.

[7] Cumbria Archive Service, Kendal (CAS Kendal), HOTH Box 44, Anne Clifford, Letter, 1617.

the Lands of her Inheritance'.[8] Margaret Russell based her legal and moral strategy on primary evidence. And while Anne Clifford was only fifteen at the time of her father's death, it is apparent that Margaret Russell included her in the activities and discussions surrounding the inheritance battle. Anne Clifford's early education in historiography under the tutelage of Samuel Daniel also informed her understanding of how the historical moment could have relevance in contemporary concerns.

The inheritance battle began in earnest with George Clifford's death in 1605, though it is likely that George Clifford intended to secure the inheritance of the Clifford hereditary lands for his brother, Francis, by the mid-1590s (George's only surviving son Robert died in 1591, leaving Anne as the sole heir 'of his body').[9] It is also clear that Margaret Russell had already begun to develop a strategy to thwart his wishes. By the time of his death George was clearly aware that Margaret would challenge any attempt to disinherit their daughter, drawing upon her diminished but still potent political capital. Still, George Clifford sought to avoid a legal confrontation through his will by settling £15,000 on Anne upon her marriage and making generous arrangements for Margaret's support after his death.[10] In the 1590s he agreed a jointure for his wife which gave Margaret life control of the vast Clifford estates in Westmorland including Appleby and Brougham castles and the forest of Whinfell. This jointure agreement was assured by Parliament and gave Margaret substantial economic and political power in the north during her widowhood.[11] However, Margaret Russell dismissed his supposed generosity to Anne Clifford, describing it as 'a portion that many Merchant's daughters have had', telling her daughter that 'your ancient inheritance from your forefathers from a long descent of Ancestors is richly worth a hundred thousand pounds'.[12] Margaret Russell used her jointure resources to fund the legal battles she undertook to secure Anne Clifford's inheritance.

Samuel Daniel relates how Margaret Russell uncovered compelling evidence of Anne Clifford's legal rights to the Clifford hereditary lands, describing how these rights were 'brought to light unto the knowledge of the world by your [Russell's] wisdom and industry, out of the records of this Kingdom miraculously after the death of my Lord her father'.[13]

---

[8] Portland Papers, PO/VOL. XXIII, Anne Clifford, Letter, 1608, 51–2.
[9] Clifford, *Great Books*, 660–8.
[10] TNA PROB 11/108, Will of George Clifford; and Clifford, *Great Books*, 656.
[11] Clifford, *Great Books*, 656–7; Parliamentary Archives, London, HL/PO/PB/1/1592/35Eliz1n17.
[12] Portland Papers, Clifford, Letters, 77 and 69.
[13] Portland Papers, Clifford, Letter, 63.

Daniel refers to Russell's discovery of key documents that proved the ancient Clifford estates were entailed on the Crown. This entail stipulated that the Clifford hereditary lands could only be passed from parent to child, the 'heir of the body' – male or female – in direct line of succession. Should there be no direct heir of the previous holder of the lands, the lands returned to the Crown. Henry VIII was so concerned about the attempts of some of his subjects to circumvent the Crown entail that he reiterated its inviolability by statute in 1542.[14] Margaret Russell's discovery of key charters that proved the ancient Clifford lands were entailed on the Crown could not be ignored, and led to eleven years of legal wrangling in which Margaret very nearly succeeded in securing the Clifford hereditary lands for Anne. Unfortunately, James I's unwavering support for Francis Clifford, George's brother, and the death of key allies – Robert Cecil, first Earl of Salisbury (who favoured Francis) and Prince Henry (who favoured Richard Sackville) in 1612, and Margaret Russell herself in 1616 – led to the King's Award, an agreement brokered by the King in which Richard Sackville was given £20,000 if he agreed that the Clifford hereditary lands should descend first to Francis Clifford and promised to pursue no further legal action related to these lands. Anne Clifford was to remain as heir, in accordance to her father's will, after the male heirs of Francis Clifford. Anne Clifford never signed this agreement, which meant that Sackville had to put up sureties for her behaviour, increasing their marital discord. This also meant that later, when Anne inherited the Clifford hereditary lands in 1643, she was not bound by the agreement and thus had greater freedom in her use and disposition of the lands.[15] Despite Anne's loss in legal terms with the King's Award in 1617, the documents that Margaret Russell uncovered helped Anne to justify her disobedience to her husband, leading gentlemen in the land (including the Archbishop of Canterbury) and the King in regard to the Clifford lands. The documents sustained her belief in the rights of women to inherit and provided role models for female governance.

The narratives she found in the ancient Clifford documents, and which she later includes in her *Great Books*, told her, for example, of her ancestor Isabella de Veteripont, who brought one part of the Veteripont

---

[14] 32 Henry VIII 36, *Statutes of the Realm, Volume III (1509–1545)*, 11 vols. (London: Dawsons, 1817), 788–9.

[15] In 1608 James I granted by letters patent to Francis Clifford the Clifford hereditary lands, effectively removing the Crown entail and releasing the lands from Crown interest (Clifford, *Great Books*, 734–8). These letters, coming after the fact, did not undermine Anne Clifford's legal case, but later benefited her as she was able to leave the lands as she chose.

inheritance to the Cliffords and served as sole authority in her area of Westmorland during her widowhood, including exercising her office of sheriff of Westmorland in her own person. Anne Clifford could also identify with Isabella's legal defeat at the hands of Edmund, brother to Edward I, where she lost the custody of her son and the control of his inheritance during his minority. Anne suggests in her biographical sketch of Isabella, that it was thought 'the greife thereof shorten[ed] her daies, for she dyed within a while after'.[16]

This struggle with the most powerful men of the realm resonated with Anne Clifford, who never forgot her humiliation and defeat at the hands of James I. Another of her ancestors who appears in her *Great Books* was Alice de Lacy[17] a landowner and third Countess of Salisbury and fourth Countess of Lincoln *suo jure* (in her own right). Edward II imprisoned her in 1322 and forced her to hand over many of the lands she had inherited from her father to the Crown. The examples of these two women, along with what Anne Clifford always maintained was her own mistreatment at the hands of King James, may be reflected in her underlining of the passage: 'Many of us are sicke of Kings diseases in our private fortune: Wee are Kings to our Suppliants', and her emphatic annotation in her own hand, 'Most True'.[18]

Despite the unfortunate experiences of these female ancestors at the hands of kings, the ancient documents discovered in the course of the Clifford inheritance battle attested to the primacy of female inheritance in the original and subsequent acquisitions of land and political power by the Cliffords and reveal that the women of the Clifford dynasty founded, maintained and protected the political dominance of the Cliffords in Westmorland and parts of Yorkshire. This was a potent narrative for Anne Clifford that sustained her in her determination to uphold her rights for herself and, after 1614, for her daughter Margaret.

Anne Clifford: Editor, Compiler, Author

There is evidence that even after the King's Award in 1617 Anne Clifford continued to amass documents related to the Cliffords and the Clifford hereditary lands. And while hindered from pursuing any legal actions

---

[16] Clifford, *Great Books*, 238.
[17] Ibid., 188–94.
[18] John Barclay, *Barclay His Argenis* (London: G. P[urslowe] for Henry Seile, 1625), 197. Anne Clifford's copy is Hunt CSmH RB 97024.

that violated the King's Award, she was able to push forward her claim to the title and rights of the barony of Clifford, which was not covered by the award.[19] She was also free to pursue actions related to her interest as heir to the Clifford hereditary lands,[20] including policing her rights under the award by undertaking the claims and entries which she authorized in 1628, 1632 and 1637.[21] During this period she continued a variety of legal and personal manoeuvres to secure her place as heir as it became clear that her cousin Henry Clifford would have no male heir. Anne understood that these ancient deeds, patents, wills and other documents would help ensure that she or her daughter Margaret, should Anne predecease her cousin, would inherit the Clifford hereditary lands without challenge. She married the powerful Philip Herbert, Earl of Montgomery and Pembroke, in 1630 for the same purpose. As the inevitability of her inheritance became assured in the late 1630s, the documents provided exempla and precedents for the reorganization and governance of her estates, including records of her hereditary rights and examples of female authority. In 1641, Francis Clifford, fourth Earl of Cumberland, died, and on 11 December 1643 his son Henry, last male heir of the Cliffords of the North, also died. Anne Clifford inherited the Clifford hereditary lands with no opposition. This became the catalyst for her production of the *Great Books of Record*, where she brought order and narrative form to the documents that had sustained her in her insistence on her rights for nearly forty years.

The difficulty in forming an adequate description of the *Great Books* lies in the diversity and scope of this textual production. The *Great Books* are an imposing work of just over 635,300 words, written on double or elephant folio sheets (approximately 26 × 17 inches) on fine paper watermarked with either an anchor and star or a fleur-de-lis (both in circles) bound in three large volumes. They contain four large genealogical illustrations (see Figure 22.1) and several other drawn 'descents' illustrating the maternal ancestry. Many of the copies of documents included in the *Great Books* are accompanied by a sketch of the seal attached to the original document. The purpose of these sketches was to verify the authenticity of the document, but the effect is to produce an engaging visual experience for the reader. Traces of use are also retained in the *Great*

---

[19] Clifford, *Great Books*, 775–6.
[20] By 1622 Henry Clifford had yet to produce a male heir. His son Francis (b. 1619) and Henry (b. 1622) both died in infancy. His last child, a daughter Frances, was born in 1626.
[21] Clifford, *Great Books*, 776–89.

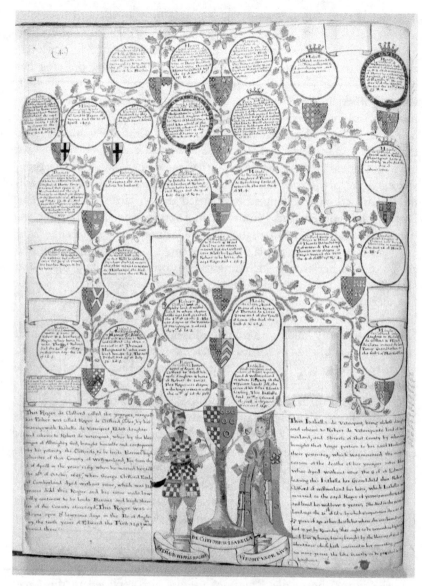

Figure 22.1 Clifford's *Great Books of Record*: Descent of Roger de Clifford III and
Isabella de Veteripont
WDCAT/16, Vol. 1, 4. Printed with permission of Cumbria Archive Centre, Kendal

Books, revealing a rich reading history after the period of production. Many pages include marginal notes in the hands of Anne Clifford, her secretaries and later readers. There is also a great deal of underscoring and marginal brackets, most often by Anne Clifford, but again also by later readers (see Figure 22.2). Evidence of use is also made clear by the additional documentary and narrative material entered into two sets of the *Great Books* by Anne Clifford's grandson Thomas Tufton and his daughter Margaret (Countess of Leicester and Baroness Clifford). It appears that initially four sets were produced, while a planned set to be produced on vellum sheets was never completed.[22] Three of these sets survive today in the Cumbria Archive Service, Kendal.[23] On the title page of the first volume of the *Great Books* Anne Clifford proudly proclaims:

> The cheife of which records in this booke was, by the care and paynefull industrie of that excellent Ladey Margarett Russell Countess Dowager of Cumberland, gotten out of the severall offices and courts of this kingdome, to prove the right and tytle, which her onely childe, the Lady Anne Clifford, now Countess Dowager of Pembrooke, Dorsett and Montgomery, had to the inheritance of her father and his auncestors.

This statement has misled scholars into attributing the bulk of the material present in the *Great Books* to the activities of Margaret Russell (and her deputies).[24] Certainly these sets include the original documents discovered by Margaret Russell that were used as key pieces of evidence in the inheritance lawsuits. However, the key word in the title page is 'chiefe', indicating the most important documents in relation to the Crown entail, rather than the bulk of material later included in the *Great*

---

[22] This intention to produce a copy in vellum may have been suggested by Kenelm Digby's "Digbiorum Pedigree" (Sherborne Castle, Dorset). This illustrated history of the Digby family from Henry I to Charles I, completed in 1634, is a sumptuous production on vellum that contains copies of charters and other documents, along with illustrations of monuments and heraldic insignia.

[23] WDCAT/16 and WDHOTH 1/10 (2 sets, one initially kept at Hothfield, but brought to Appleby in the twentieth century, and one that remained at Skipton from Anne Clifford's time until the sale of Skipton Castle in the 1950s when it was integrated into the Hothfield collection, now housed at CAS, Kendal). WDCAT/16 descended from Anne Clifford's great granddaughter, Mary Tufton, daughter of Thomas Tufton, into the Levenson-Gower family and was sold to the Cumbria Archive service in 2004 by a member of this family. The set kept at Appleby during Anne Clifford's life and after her death, and consulted by eighteenth- and nineteenth-century historians, is missing. For a detailed discussion of these sets, see Malay, "Introduction", in Clifford, *Great Books*, 19–25.

[24] Some twentieth-century scholars have suggested that Margaret Russell simply commissioned her lawyers, especially St Loe Kniveton, to search out these documents; they may indeed have done the actual legwork, but Daniel and Anne Clifford make clear that Margaret was directly responsible for the activities which unearthed these documents.

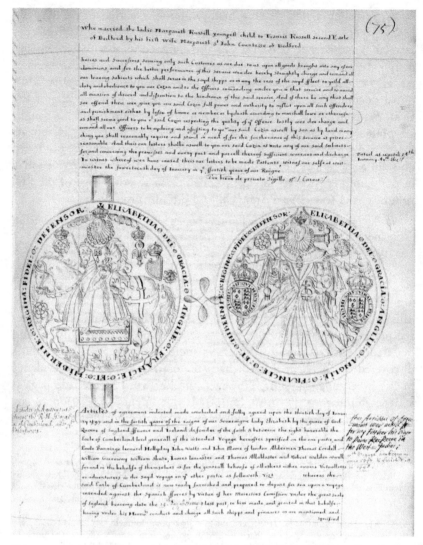

Figure 22.2   Page from Clifford's *Great Books of Record*
WDCAT/16, Vol. 3, 75. Printed with permission of Cumbria Archive Centre, Kendal

Books. Anne Clifford always identifies the documents secured by her mother; for example, she writes in the margin of Isabella de Veteripont's suit to King Edward I:

> In the receipt of the Exchequor is this long prosidendo … which is a speciall record, to prove the title of Ann Countes of Pembrook etc. to her inheritance in Westmerland and Craven, and was first taken out of that office by Margarett Countess Dowager of Cumberland her religious and excellent mother with great industry and dificulty the 28 of November the 6 yeare of King James (1608).[25]

This is typical of the way in which Anne Clifford identified the 'chiefe' documents discovered by her mother. However the *Great Books* contain much material collected after the lawsuits. These include material provided by a number of antiquarians, individuals and even her husbands. That Anne Clifford examined and sought out and sorted through manuscript material herself is shown by her annotations on a number of manuscripts. She notes in her own hand in the margin of one document included in the *Great Books*: 'This other Great Inquisition was founde by mee in Skipton Castell in the yeare 1650'.[26] Her work with a number of historians and antiquarians of the period will be discussed below.

However, the *Great Books* are not simply books of legal precedents, but are instead a powerful narrative of the Veteripont and Clifford dynasties for over 600 years. That she intended to create a narrative is clear by the way in which she organized the material and her inclusion of biographical narratives following the documents connected to each Veteripont and Clifford Lord.[27] These she composed using documentary material along with chronicle and other narrative sources where possible. As one reads Anne Clifford's narrative, it becomes clear she is not simply telling the story of a powerful dynasty. Instead, this is a narrative that foregrounds and celebrates the role of women in establishing, maintaining and empowering the family.

Anne Clifford credits Margaret de Toeni (c. 1118–85) with founding all the Clifford dynasties of England. Margaret was the daughter and sole heir of Ralph de Toeni of Clifford Castle in Herefordshire. She married Walter (d. 1190), a younger son of Richard Fitzponz, a Norman knight.

---

[25] Clifford, *Great Books*, 230.
[26] Ibid., 596.
[27] The term 'Lord' is here used to indicate the person who exercised the rights and authority of lordship over the Clifford (and earlier Veteripont) lands, and was at times female as in the case of Isabella de Veteripont.

Anne Clifford announces the records of Walter de Clifford with: 'Walter de Clifford who first tooke that sirname after he was possessed of the castle, honor, and manor of Clifford in Herefordshire in right of his wife Margaret de Tony who first tooke that sirname after he was possessed'. She reiterates this claim in his genealogical descent, thus emphasizing that his rights to Clifford Castle and his name came from Margaret de Toeni and were held by the right and title of the female.[28]

Anne Clifford also gives much room to the evidences of the Veteripont family through whom the Westmorland lands came to the Cliffords (see Figure 22.1). Again, she begins with a woman, her foremother Idonea de Bulli (d. 1235),[29] who married Robert, first Lord Veteripont. Anne Clifford states:

> Hee marryed as apeares by records Idonea daughter and heire of John de Busley ... and shee brought the said landes and honnors with other great possessions (as apeares by these records) to her said husband Robert de Veteripont. Shee was so great a womman in those times as thatt King John when hee gave the landes in Westmorland and the sherifwick in that countie to her said husband in the pattent of the graunt of them, did make mention of her.[30]

Anne Clifford praises Idonea not only for the lands she brought to her husband but also for her active governance of these and the Westmorland lands given to the couple by King John[31] which would later form the Clifford hereditary lands in Westmorland: 'Shee out lived her husband seven yeares and dyed his widdow in [1235]. And shee held the landes in Westmorland, till her death as apeares by the Pipe Rowles'. Anne Clifford also praises Idonea for her piety, describing how in her widowhood she endowed religious institutions.[32] This was Anne Clifford's narrative strategy throughout her *Great Books* – to illustrate how women built and sustained the Clifford dynasty through material and spiritual means, often despite the destructive actions of males, whose involvement in the political battles of their respective periods often put the dynasty in grave jeopardy.

---

[28] Clifford, *Great Books*, 160, 161.

[29] The earliest document in the *Great Books* is connected with Idonea de Builli – the charter of Rupe Abbey in 1088 by her uncle.

[30] Clifford, *Great Books*, 81.

[31] King John granted Robert de Veteripont, first Lord Veteripont, the Westmorland lands including the castles of Brough, Brougham, Pendragon and Appleby, as well as the sheriffwick of Westmorland in 1203. These would remain the Clifford hereditary lands in Westmorland and descend to Anne Clifford in 1643 – see Clifford, *Great Books*, 38–9.

[32] Clifford, *Great Books*, 81.

This is apparent early in the *Great Books*. In 1203, Robert de Veteripont, third Lord Veteripont, nearly lost the lands in Westmorland granted to his grandfather because of his support of Simon de Montfort. However, as Anne Clifford explains, 'after the said Robert de Veteripont's death, the said King Henery the third seazed all the landes into his owne handes, butt after the fiftieth yere of his raigne hee restored the said landes to his two daughters and heires Isabella and Idonia'.[33] And while clearly this act by Henry was motivated by a desire to reward his supporters, Roger de Leyburne and Roger de Clifford, the fact remains that the property was retained through the female body.

These two sisters were inspirational for Anne Clifford, evidenced not only by the way in which she narrates their lives in the *Great Books*, but also her use of them as role models in her life. In 1660 she rebuilt Idonea's castle of Pendragon, which had lain in ruins since 1342. This was hardly necessary given she had four other newly repaired castles, but it is clear she wished to inhabit Idonea's castle once again. Idonea died in 1333 at the age of 73. Her portion of the Veteripont inheritance in Westmorland, which included Pendragon and Brough castles, descended to Robert, first Lord Clifford of Skipton Castle, thus reuniting the Veteripont lands in Westmorland granted by King John. Her sister, Isabella de Veteripont, inherited the other portion of the Westmorland grant – Appleby and Brougham castles and the sheriffwick of Westmorland. Isabella married Roger de Clifford (1248–82), and her influence on Anne Clifford is most powerfully proved by the fact that Anne named her second daughter Isabella (her first daughter was named Margaret after her mother). Anne Clifford writes that Isabella 'ought to bee remembred of her posterity with honnour and reverence in that shee brought soe faire and noble an inheritance unto them which by God's blessing hath continewed to her successors for so many generations as the paralell thereof is hardly to bee founde in the kingdome'. She makes the point here that Isabella was the foremother of the Clifford dynasty in Westmorland and Yorkshire, with a direct line of male descent for fourteen generations, beginning with Isabella and ending with George Clifford,[34] though Anne would assert that it continued through her and her daughter Margaret and Margaret's numerous progeny. Isabella was

---

[33] Ibid., 112.

[34] From 1273 to 1605, beginning with the birth of Robert, first Lord Clifford, and ending by Anne Clifford's reckoning with the death of her father in 1605, but continuing through her female body including her eleven grandchildren from her daughter Margaret.

also remarkable because, as Anne Clifford explains, 'this Isabella ... in her owne person and sate herselfe upon the benche as hereditary Sherriffess of Westmorland, upon tryalls of life and deathe, an honnour which no womman in this kingedome hath hetherto attayned but herselfe [Anne Clifford]'.[35] Anne used her position as Sheriff of Westmorland to establish and maintain her authority in the region, much as she imagined Isabella had once done.

Anne Clifford was also keen to emphasize the role of women in the survival of the Clifford dynasty. She creates a dramatic narrative in both documents and her biographical sketch of the dramatic role Margaret Bromflete (Baroness Vescy *suo jure*) played in the survival of the Clifford dynasty. Margaret's husband John, ninth Lord Clifford, sided with the Lancastrians during the fifteenth-century War of the Roses. His murder of the Earl of Rutland, immortalized in Shakespeare's *Henry VI*, part 3, at the Battle of Wakefield, earned him the title of 'Butcher Lord' – he died shortly after at the Battle of Towton. With Edward IV on the throne (elder brother of the Earl of Rutland) and the Clifford hereditary lands forfeit, the Clifford dynasty was threatened with extinction. During this period Margaret Bromflete took refuge at her property in Londesborough. Her two sons, six-year-old Henry and five-year-old Richard, were at considerable risk of being murdered according to Anne Clifford, and so Margaret hid them. Anne recalls the romantic tale that Margaret placed Henry with a shepherd family during his youth. This Henry was called 'Shepherd Lord', though in all likelihood he spent only a few years in rural retreat at the Cumberland houses of his step-father Sir Lancelot Threlkeld and at Londesborough. And while some question whether the boys were ever at risk of assassination in the early years of Edward IV,[36] Anne Clifford believed they were and credited Margaret Bromflete with ensuring their physical and political survival. Anne Clifford believed that Henry's future was secured through Margaret's actions and her lands and title which descended to him. It was this inheritance that made him (at least according to Anne Clifford) an attractive enough marital prospect to conclude a marriage with Anne St John in 1486. This Anne was first cousin to the new King Henry VII, and Anne Clifford attributes to this marriage the return of all the Clifford hereditary lands intact to Henry Clifford:

---

[35] Clifford, *Great Books*, 153.
[36] Henry was given a pardon in 1472 by Edward IV.

Which King (as is thought) did restore the said Lord to his landes honors and estate the rather because hee did then marry that cozen german of his. For though the said Kinge favoured him because his father and grandfather were slayne in the service of the House of Lancaster, yet by tradition it is receyved that the cause cheifely why hee restored his landes and honnors was because hee marryed the said King's cozen germain Anne St John.[37]

This connection to the Crown was to lead to even greater honours for the Clifford family through women. Anne St John's son Henry, eleventh Lord Clifford, was brought up with the young prince Henry, later Henry VIII, and was made first Earl of Cumberland. He married Margaret Percy (d. 1543), who brought with her the Percy fee in Yorkshire.[38] These aristocratic honours and connections to the Tudors reached their climax with the marriage of Henry, twelfth Lord Clifford and second Earl of Cumberland, to the Lady Eleanor Brandon, daughter of Mary Tudor, one-time Queen Consort of France and younger sister to Henry VIII. Anne Clifford describes her as 'this high borne princess Elianor Countess of Cumbreland' who was 'grandchilde to King Henery the seventh, neice to King Henery the eight, and cozen german to King Edward the sixth, Queene Mary, and Queene Elizabeth, and to James the fifth King of Scotland' (see Figure 22.2)[39] From this marriage came one surviving child, Margaret Clifford, later Countess of Derby who at one point was, according to the will of Henry VIII, next heir to the throne of England after Elizabeth I. Anne Clifford's father was half-brother to this Margaret, and his mother Anne Dacre was the second wife of Henry, second Earl of Cumberland, after the death of Eleanor Brandon.

Primary Sources: A New Antiquarianism

That Anne Clifford intended to foreground the essential contributions of women to the Clifford dynasty in the *Great Books* is clear. The books provide evidence that Anne Clifford believed that women were as capable of, and indeed in many ways better suited to, governance than men. And this is perhaps most audaciously illustrated in her suggestion that Henry VII held the throne of England through the right of his wife Elizabeth of York, daughter to Henry IV, and not through conquest. In the *Great*

---

[37] Clifford, *Great Books*, 554.
[38] The Percy fee seigniory was made up of the western part of Craven, Yorkshire, and gave the Cliffords nearly complete control of the region of Craven, Yorkshire.
[39] Clifford, *Great Books*, 619.

Books she writes, 'Elizabeth Queen of England eldest daughter and [who was] at length heire to King Edward the 4th'.[40]

The documents that Anne Clifford amassed and organized into the Clifford dynastic narrative in the *Great Books* puts into context Margaret Russell's comment about Anne Clifford's 'right coming from Women heretofore & nowe going to Women againe'. The Clifford name came from Margaret de Toeni, and the Westmorland estates (always the chief object of Margaret and Anne, so much so they were willing to relinquish claim to the Skipton and Craven holdings) descended directly from Idonea and Isabella de Veteripont. This evidence also bolstered first Margaret Russell and then Anne Clifford's resolve; as Margaret puts it in a letter to James I, Anne 'is sole Heyre now to her deceaced father & her noble Anecestors & is thereby rightfully, by the laws of this Land Baroness Clifford Westmorland and Vesey & high Sheriffess of that County by Inheritance & Ladie of the Honour of Skipton in Craven'.[41] It was this assurance, proved by documentary evidence, that sustained Anne Clifford in her determination not to relinquish her claim to the Clifford hereditary lands, no matter the political jeopardy and personal distress this caused. The *Great Books of Record* are a textual celebration of Anne Clifford's ultimate success against all the odds. Certainly one could end one's discussion of the *Great Books* on this note; however, Anne's close work and management of the *Great Books* project suggest that her interest in historical texts and material was deeply rooted. Her work was focused on her family, but the *Great Books* provide evidence that Anne Clifford was also a participant in the intellectual climate of seventeenth-century antiquarianism.

Graham Parry describes the early modern antiquarian movement as a 'convergence of Renaissance scholarship and Reformation concerns of national identity and religious ancestry',[42] and this is a perfectly reasonable way to assess the interest of the large number of individuals who engaged in historical research in the period. But perhaps Simonds D'Ewes best captures the attraction ancient documents held for individuals, describing his first visit to the Tower of London, then the equivalent of a national archive (and the source of many of the key documents discovered by Margaret Russell). On 4 September 1623, D'Ewes wrote

[40] Ibid., 615.
[41] Portland Papers, Clifford, Letter, 50–1.
[42] Graham Parry, *The Trophies of Time: English Antiquarians of the Seventeenth Century* (Oxford: Oxford University Press, 1995), 2.

in his diary that 'after dinner I went to the Tower there to see some records, and how I liked them, and through Gods mercye, happening upon a Charter of Edward the Confessors. I liked it well, and resolved to … [come] hither twice a week'. In his autobiography he expands upon this entry, noting that 'from this day forward I neuer whollie gaue ouer the studie of Records, but spent manie dayes & moneths about it to my great content and satisfaction'. D'Ewes, like Anne Clifford, was fascinated by the 'excellencies' of both 'historicall & nationall' matters, and came to value, as many others including Margaret Russell did, ancient documents as primary sources.[43] While less detailed, a marginal note by Anne Clifford in the *Great Books* also communicates her great pleasure in archival research; she comments in her own hand: 'This other Great Inquisition [concerning Skipton castle] was founde by mee in Skipton Castell in the yeare 1650'.[44]

This excitement in ancient documents and their use as primary sources likely developed early in Anne Clifford because of their importance in proving her rights to the Clifford hereditary lands, while the *Great Books* project shows her lifelong antiquarian interests. However, it was not only the material – the manuscripts and physical remains – that interested Anne Clifford. Her productions also reveal an involvement in emerging historiographical methodology which favoured the use of primary evidence over chronicle or narrative sources. It was this use of primary sources that challenged the narrative of George and later Francis Clifford concerning the right descent of the Clifford hereditary lands in the inheritance dispute. Margaret Russell looked to ancient charters to prove Anne Clifford's right as the 'heir of the body' of her father and the Crown entail. This was a strategy that was becoming increasingly popular in legal practices of St Loe Kniveton, Thomas Athowe, John Greenwood (who were employed by Russell) and other Gray's Inn lawyers who challenged the dominance of legal precedence in court proceedings, insisting instead on the importance of primary documents in the establishment of property rights. This interest in primary documents was also informing historical research with the lawyer and historian William Fleetwood, an early proponent of the use of primary resources in law and in historical discourse.[45]

---

[43] J. Sears McGee, *An Industrious Mind: The Words of Sir Simonds D'Ewes* (Stanford: Stanford University Press, 2015), 55.

[44] Clifford, *Great Books*, 596

[45] J. D. Alsop, 'William Fleetwood and Elizabethan Historical Scholarship', *Sixteenth Century Journal*, 25 (1994), 155.

John Hall, a Gray's Inn lawyer and political writer, explained the attraction of primary sources: 'for hee that writes a generall History, must be necessitated to borrow from others & they perhaps from mis-reports'.[46] He believed that chronicle sources could be fallible, and that primary documents were better suited to historical discourse as they allowed one to 'discover the inner side of Negotiations, and events' and thus 'draw a better estimate of things, and deduce more certaine, and unquestioned axiomes'.[47] Here Hall drew upon the Oxford lectures of Degory Whear, which were published in Latin in 1623.[48] Anne Clifford's close association with a number of leading antiquarians of the period makes it clear that she was heavily invested in these methodical discussions. The *Great Books*, her letters and accounts provide evidence of Anne Clifford's relationships with these antiquarians, including William Dugdale, Augustine Vincent, Simonds D'Ewes, John Selden, Robert Cotton, Matthew Hale, Charles Fairfax and especially her close associate Roger Dodsworth. These relationships show that she was well placed to participate in the development of historiography of the period as she employed and extended contemporary historical practice in her *Great Books*.

She designed for the *Great Books* a strict and formal structure, organizing material in chronological order in sections devoted to each Lord and his (or her) immediate family. In each section she included complete transcriptions of primary documents, first in the original language (Latin or Anglo-French) followed by an English translation. These documents include headings that alert the reader to the important element or theme of each document. At the end of each Lord's section she composed a biographical summary drawing upon the documents, chronicle sources (which she used carefully and often challenged) and at times evidence from material sources such as tombs, castles, ruins and even trees. She ended each section with an annotated index. These methodological practices were to a certain extent employed in other manuscript and published historical/genealogical works in a more modest way.[49] Other antiquarians she worked with amassed large collections

---

[46] See Raymond Joad, 'John Hall's *A Method of History*: A Book Lost and Found', *English Literary Renaissance*, 28 (1998), 295.

[47] John Hall, *Advancement of Learning* (London: John Walker, 1649), 36.

[48] Degory Whear, *De ratione et methodo legendi historias* (Oxford: Iohnnes Lichfield and Guilielmus Turner, 1623); Joad, 'John Hall's *A Method of History*', 272.

[49] Two examples of these are John Smyth's *Lives of the Berkeleys* and Thomas Herbert's histories of the Herbert family, the *Herbertorum Prosapia* (Cardiff Central Library, Phillips 5.7, Cardiff) and the *Origo Praeclara Herbertorum* (at Wilton House archives until 1989, now lost).

of transcribed and primary documents but never completed the work of a single print or manuscript compilation.[50] Anne Clifford's *Great Books* are methodologically sophisticated. They are well organized, of wide scope and communicate a consistent narrative. The work was produced in manuscript but it is a carefully designed manuscript production in multiple copies.

A Living Text

In this way Anne Clifford developed her history of the Cliffords (which was always in the end a history of herself) far beyond existing historical models, extending her work from a genealogical impulse to place it within a larger narrative of European history. The *Great Books* illustrate how familial networks knit England together, collapsing physical distance through social relationships. For centuries the Cliffords owned property and exercised influence not only in Yorkshire and Westmorland but throughout England, Wales, Scotland and Ireland. Anne's work provides valuable insight into the way in which aristocratic power was established and maintained for centuries. Parry asserts that the antiquarian impulse of the seventeenth century was fuelled by concerns of national identity. The *Great Books*, composed in the midst of the civil wars of the 1640s and 1650s, have much to say about national identity, promoting a view of an ideally ordered society disrupted repeatedly by war, or as Anne Clifford once suggested, by 'King's diseases'. It was this ideal society that Anne Clifford, troubled by recalcitrant tenants, marching armies, billeted soldiers and a disordered Church, sought to re-form in the 'lands of her inheritance'.

And thus finally, while certainly an innovative historical project, the *Great Books* find their most powerful expression as autobiography. At the end of the third volume Anne Clifford maintained a yearly summary of the key events of her own life that often referred back to earlier periods recorded in the *Great Books*, embedding autobiography within a larger historical narrative. Anne Clifford places herself at the nexus of Clifford dynastic history and by association the broader national history. Her extensive use of biblical references in her autobiographical section and elsewhere in the *Great Books*, drawn mainly from the Old Testament prophets, shows that she saw herself as operating beyond dynastic and

---

[50] A good example of this was Roger Dodsworth, whose work was only partially ordered and published by William Dugdale.

national history, embodying a metaphorical Israel in a covenant relationship with God.

The *Great Books* also functioned as a living text that was continually shaped and in use during Anne Clifford's life and beyond her death. Her accounts note the careful addition of her yearly autobiographical summaries, rebinding, and the copying out of portions for particular uses. Anne Clifford inhabited the *Great Books* in ways that make them unique as a historical work. These later annotations and readerly marks reveal her understanding of her identity as derived from her heritage, her relationship with her immediate and extended family, her relationship with the land and her understanding of God's purpose for her. The books embed her within both a particular time and place, while also unmooring time and space, allowing her to inhabit the past, present and future simultaneously. Perhaps her grandson Thomas Tufton recognized this at least obliquely. After Anne Clifford's death he wrote this tribute to her in the *Great Books*: 'This noble and pious Lady ... with such great care and resolucion preserved and defended her undoubted right to this northern estate ... to whose vertuous and excellent memory, her succeeding posteriety owe many great obligations'.[51]

The last document recorded in the *Great Books* is dated 1734. It is a patent granting the 1299 Barony of Clifford to Margaret Tufton, Countess of Leicester.[52] She used both the evidence in the *Great Books* and the example of her great-grandmother Anne Clifford to claim her rights. She then recorded the document within the *Great Books*, adding her own presence amongst those of her ancestors and at the same time reaching ahead through the *Great Books* to future generations. Anne Clifford designed her *Great Books* to function beyond her own life. They were certainly designed to advertise her mother's great efforts on her behalf, serving as a memorial to Margaret Russell. They communicate what Anne Clifford believed was her godly duty and response to the pursuit, receiving and management of the 'lands of her inheritance'. She believed they would be useful in continuing to secure the rights of her progeny, though she may have been surprise that they continue to operate as a site for historical research. The *Great Books* give unprecedented insight into both the individual Anne Clifford and changes in culture over the span of 600 years.

---

[51] Clifford, *Great Books*, 905.
[52] Ibid., 926–7.

Select Bibliography

Primary Sources and Editions

Ascham, Roger. *The Scholemaster*. London: John Day, 1570.

Askew, Anne. *The Examinations of Anne Askew*. Edited by Elaine V. Beilin. Oxford: Oxford University Press, 1996.

Bacon, Anne. *The Letters of Lady Anne Bacon*. Edited by Gemma Allen. Camden Society, 5th Series, Vol. 44. Cambridge: Cambridge University Press, 2014.

An Apology or Answer in Defence of the Church of England: Lady Anne Bacon's Translation of Bishop John Jewel's Apologia Ecclesiae Anglicanae. Edited by Patricia Demers. Cambridge: Modern Humanities Research Association, 2016.

Ballard, George. *Memoirs of Several Ladies of Great Britain Who Have Been Celebrated for Their Writings or Skill in the Learned Languages, Arts and Sciences*. Edited by Ruth Perry. Detroit: Wayne State University Press, 1985.

Barker, William. *The Nobility of Women by William Bercher (1559)*. Edited by Warwick Bond. Roxburghe Collection, 142 London: Chiswick Press, 1904.

Behn, Aphra. *The Novels of Mrs. Aphra Behn*. Edited by Ernest A. Baker. London: Routledge & Sons, 1905.

The Works of Aphra Behn. Edited by Montague Summers. 6 vols. London: William Heinemann, 1915.

The Works of Aphra Behn. Edited by Janet Todd. 7 vols. London: William Pickering, 1992.

Bentley, Thomas. *The Monument of Matrons*. 5 vols. London: Henry Denham, 1582.

Bess of Hardwick's Letters: A Complete Correspondence, c. 1550–1608, www.bessof-hardwick.org; 2013.

Bradstreet, Anne. *Several Poems*. Boston: John Foster, 1678.

The Tenth Muse Lately Sprung Up in America. London: Stephen Bowtell, 1650.

The Works of Anne Bradstreet. Edited by Jeannine Hensley. Cambridge, MA: Harvard University Press, 1967.

The Complete Works of Anne Bradstreet. Edited by Joseph R. McElrath, Jr. and Allan P. Robb. Boston, MA: Twayne Publishers, 1981.

Anne Bradstreet. Edited by Patricia Pender. Early Modern Women's Research Network Digital Archive, 2017, http://hri.newcastle.edu.au/emwrn/da/index.php?content=digitalarchive.

Cary, Mary. *The Resurrection of the Witnesses and Englands Fall*. London: D. M. for Giles Calvert, 1648.

Cary, Elizabeth. *Elizabeth Cary, Lady Falkland: "The Tragedy of Mariam, the Fair Queen of Jewry' with 'The Lady Falkland: Her Life'"* Edited by Barry Weller and Margaret W. Ferguson. Berkeley and London: University of California Press, 1994.

    Elizabeth Cary/Lady Falkland: Life and Letters. Edited by Heather Wolfe. Cambridge: RTM Publications, 2001.

    The Tragedy of Mariam, the Fair Queen of Jewry. Edited by Ramona Wray. London and New York: Bloomsbury, 2012.

Cavendish, Margaret. *Poems and Fancies*. London: T. R. for J. Martin, and J. Allestrye, 1653.

    Playes. London: A. Warren, for John Martyn, James Allestry, and Tho. Dicas. 1662.

    Poems and Phancies. London: William Wilson, 1664.

    Sociable Letters. London: William Wilson, 1664.

Cavendish, William. *Dramatic Works by William Cavendish*. Edited by Lynn Hulse. Oxford: The Malone Society, 1996.

Clifford, Anne. *Anne Clifford's Autobiographical Writing, 1590-1676*. Edited by Jessica L. Malay. Manchester: Manchester University Press, 2018.

    The Diary of Anne Clifford. Edited by Katherine O. Acheson. New York: Garland, 1995.

    Great Books of Record. Edited by Jessica L. Malay. Manchester: Manchester University Press, 2015.

Collins, An. *An Collins: Divine Songs and Meditacions (1653)*. Edited by Sidney Gottleib. Tempe, AZ: Medieval and Renaissance Texts and Studies, 1996.

Cummings, Brian, ed. *The Book of Common Prayer: The Texts of 1549, 1559, and 1662*. Oxford: Oxford University Press, 2011.

Davies, Eleanor (Lady Douglas). *The Benediction from the A: lmighty O:mnipotent*. S.I. [s. n.], 1651.

DeJean, Joan, ed. and trans. *Against Marriage: The Correspondence of La Grande Mademoiselle*. Chicago: University of Chicago Press, 2002.

Douglas, Margaret, and Others. *The Devonshire Manuscript: A Woman's Book of Courtly Poetry*. Edited by Elizabeth Heale. Toronto: CRRS/ITER, 2012.

Eardley, Alice, ed. *Lady Hester Pulter: Poems, Emblems, and "The Unfortunate Florinda."* Toronto: CRRS/ITER, 2014.

Elizabeth, I., Queen of England. *A Godly Medytacyon of the Christen Sowle*. Edited by John Bale. Wesel: van der Straten, 1548.

    Queen of England. *Elizabeth I: Collected Works*. Edited by Leah S. Marcus, Janel Mueller, and Mary Beth Rose. Chicago: University of Chicago Press, 2002.

    Queen of England. *Elizabeth I: Translations, 1544–1589*. Edited by Joshua Scodel and Janel Mueller. Chicago: University of Chicago Press, 2009.

Erasmus, Desiderius. *Precatio dominica in septem portiones distribute*. Basel: Johann Bebel, 1523.

A Deuoute Treatise vpon the Pater Noster. Translated by Margaret More Roper. London: Thomas Berthelet, 1526.

Fox, Margaret Askew Fell. *Womens Speaking Justified, Proved and Allowed of by the Scriptures, All Such as Speak by the Spirit and Power of the Lord Jesus.* London: [s. n.], 1666.

Grey, Jane. *An Epistle of the Ladye Jane.* London: John Day, 1554.

Grymeston, Elizabeth. *Micelanea. Meditations. Memoratives.* London: Melch. Bradwood for Felix Norton, 1604.

Hallett, Nicky, ed. *Lives of Spirit: English Carmelite Self-Writing of the Early Modern Period.* Aldershot: Ashgate, 2007.

Hawley, Susan. *A Briefe Relation of the Order and Institute, of the English Religious Women at Liège.* n.p., 1652.

Herbert, Mary Sidney. *Collected Works of Mary Sidney Herbert, Countess of Pembroke.* Edited by Margaret P. Hannay and Noel J. Kinnamon. 2 vols. Oxford: Clarendon, 1998.

Heywood, Thomas. *Gynaikeion: or, Nine Books of Various History. Concerning Women.* London: Printed by Adam Islip, 1624.

Hodgson-Wright, Stephanie, ed. *Women's Writing of the Early Modern Period, 1588–1688: An Anthology.* Edinburgh: Edinburgh University Press, 2002.

Hutchinson, Lucy. *On the Principles of the Christian Religion.* London: Longman, Hurst, Rees, Orme, and Brown, 1817.

Order and Disorder. Edited by David Norbrook. Oxford: Blackwell, 2001.

The Works of Lucy Hutchinson, Volume I. Edited by Reid Barbour and David Norbrook. Oxford: Clarendon Press, 2012.

Jewel, John. *An Apologie or Answere in Defence of the Churche of Englande.* Translated by Anne Bacon. London: Reginald Wolfe, 1564.

Joscelin, Elizabeth. *The Mother's Legacie to Her Unborne Child.* 2nd ed. London: John Haviland for William Barrett, 1624.

Lanyer, Aemilia. *The Poems of Aemilia Lanyer: Salve Deus Rex Judaeorum.* Edited by Susanne Woods. Oxford: Oxford University Press, 1995.

Latz, Dorothy, ed. *"Glow-worm Light": Writings of Seventeeenth-Century English Recusant Women from Original Manuscripts.* Salzburg: University of Salzburg Press, 1989.

Leigh, Dorothy. *The Mother's Blessing.* London: John Budge, 1616; reprint 1636.

Lock, Anne. *The Collected Works of Anne Vaughan Lock.* Edited by Susan M. Felch. Tempe, AZ: Arizona Center for Medieval and Renaissance Studies, 1999.

Luther, Martin. *Exposition of the Lord's Prayer.* Translated by Henry Cole. London: James Nisbet, 1844.

Makin, Bathsua. *An Essay to Revive the Antient Education of Gentlewomen.* London: Thomas Parkhurst, 1673.

Matchinske, Megan, ed. *Mary Carleton and Others, the Carleton Bigamy Trial.* Tempe, AZ: ACMRS/ITER, 2018.

Melville, Elizabeth. *Poems of Elizabeth Melville, Lady Culross.* Edited by Jamie Reid Baxter. Edinburgh: Solsequium, 2010.

Milton, John. *Eikonoklastes in Answer to a Book Intitl'd Eikon Basilike, the Portrature of His Sacred Majesty in His Solitudes and Sufferings.* London: Matthew Simmons, 1649.

More, Thomas. *The Supplycacyon of Soulys.* London: W. Rastell, not after 25 October 1529.

Nichols, John, ed. *The Progresses, Processions and Magnificent Festivities of King James the First.* 4 vols. London: J. B. Nichols, 1828.

Nims, John Frederick. ed. *Ovid's Metamorphoses: The Arthur Golding Translation 1567.* Philadelphia: Paul Dry Books, 2000.

Ochino, Bernardino. *Sermons of Barnardine Ochine of Sena.* Translated by Anne Cooke Bacon. London: R. Carr for W. Redell, 1548.

  Certayne Sermons of the Ryghte Famous and Excellente Clerke. London: John Day, ca. 1551.

  Fourtene Sermons of Barnardine Ochyne, Concernyng the Redestinacion and Eleccion of God. Tranlated by Anne Cooke. London: John Day and William Seres, 1551.

Orlando: Writing by Women in the British Isles from the Beginnings to the Present. Edited by Susan Brown, Patricia Clements, and Isobel Grundy. http://orlando.cambridge.org.

Ostovich, Helen, and Elizabeth Sauer, eds. *Reading Early Modern Women: An Anthology of Texts in Manuscript and Print, 1550–1700.* New York: Routledge, 2004.

Parr, Susanna. *Susanna's Apologie against the Elders.* London: Henry Hall for T. Robinson, 1659.

Parr, Katherine. *Katherine Parr: Complete Works & Correspondence.* Edited by Janel Mueller. Chicago: University of Chicago Press, 2011.

Perdita Manuscripts. www.amdigital.co.uk/m-products/product/perdita-manuscripts-1500-1700/.

Plat, Hugh. *The Floures of Philosophie (1572) by Hugh Plat and A Sweet Nosgay (1573) and The Copy of a Letter (1567) by Isabella Whitney.* Edited by Richard Panofsky. Delmar, NY: Scholars' Facsimiles and Reprints, 1982.

Richardson, Elizabeth. *A Ladies Legacie to Her Daughters.* London: Thomas Harper, 1645.

Russell, Elizabeth Cooke Hoby. *The Writings of an English Sappho.* Edited by Patricia Phillippy. Translations from Greek and Latin by Jaime Goodrich. Toronto: CRRS/ITER, 2011.

Scudéry, Madeleine de. *Selected Letters, Orations, and Rhetorical Dialogues.* Edited by Jane Donawerth and Julia Strongson. Chicago: University of Chicago Press, 2004.

Seymour, Anne, Margaret Seymour, and Jane Seymour. *Le Tombeau de Marguerite de Valois.* In *Printed Writings, 1500–1640. Part 2: Anne Margaret and Jane Seymour.* Aldershot: Ashgate, 2000.

Shell, Marc. *Elizabeth's Glass. With "The Glass of the Sinful Soul" (1544) by Elizabeth I and Epistle Dedicatory" and "Conclusion" (1548) by John Bale.* Lincoln and London: University of Nebraska Press, 1993.

Speght, Rachel. *The Polemics and Poems of Rachel Speght.* Edited by Barbara Lewalski. Oxford University Press, 1996.

Starr, Nathan, ed. "The Concealed Fansyes: A Play by Lady Jane Cavendish and Lady Elizabeth Brackley." *PMLA* 46 (1931): 802–38.

Swetnam, Joseph. *The Arraignment of Lewd, Idle, Froward, and Unconstant Women.* London: George Purslowe for Thomas Archer, 1615.

Teague, Frances, Margaret Ezell, eds. and Jessica Walker, assoc. ed. *Educating English Daughters: Late Seventeenth-Century Debates by Bathsua Makin and Mary More.* Tempe, AZ: ACMRS/ITER, 2016.

Trapnel, Anna. *Anna Trapnel's Report and Plea, or, a Narrative of Her Journey into Cornwal.* London: Thomas Brewster, 1654.

Turberville, George. *The Heroycall Epistles of the Learned Poet Publius Ouidius Naso, in English verse.* London: Henry Denham, 1567.

Tyrwhit, Elizabeth. *Elizabeth Tyrwhit's Morning and Evening Prayers.* Edited by Susan M. Felch. Aldershot: Ashgate, 2008.

Ward, Mary. *Mary Ward 1585–1645: "A Briefe Relation . . ." with Autobiographical Fragments and a Selection of Letters.* Edited by Christina Kenworthy-Browne. Woodbridge: Boydell for Catholic Record Society, 2008.

Whitney, Isabella. *A Sweet Nosgay.* London: Richard Jones, 1573.

The Copy of a Letter, Lately Written in Meeter, by a Yonge Gentilwoman: To Her Vnconstant Louer. London: Richard Jhones, 1567.

Who Were the Nuns? Edited by Caroline Bowden and James E. Kelly. http://wwtn.history.qmul.ac.uk.

Women Writers in England, 1350–1850. Edited by Susanne Woods. https://global.oup.com/academic/content/series/w/women-writers-in-english-1350-1850-wwe/?cc=gb&lang=en&.

Women Writers Online. www.wwp.northeastern.edu/wwo.

Woolf, Virginia. *A Room of One's Own and Three Guineas.* Edited by Anna Snaith. Oxford University Press, 2015.

Wroth, Mary. *The Poems of Lady Mary Wroth.* Edited by Josephine A. Roberts. Baton Rouge: Louisiana State University Press, 1992.

The First Part of the Countess of Montgomery's Urania. Edited by Josephine A. Roberts. MRTS 140. Binghamton, NY: Medieval and Renaissance Texts and Studies, 1995.

The Second Part of the Countess of Montgomery's Urania. Edited by Suzanne Gossett, Janel M. Mueller, and Josephine A. Roberts. Tempe, AZ: Medieval and Renaissance Texts and Studies, 1999.

Mary Wroth's Poetry: An Electronic Edition. Edited by Paul Salzman. http://wroth.latrobe.edu.au/all-poems.html.

Secondary Sources

Albano, Caterina. "Visible Bodies: Cartography and Anatomy." In *Literature, Mapping, and the Politics of Space in Early Modern Britain,* ed. Andrew Gordon and Bernhard Klein, 89–106. Cambridge: Cambridge University Press, 2001.

Allen, Gemma. "'a briefe and plaine declaration': Lady Anne Bacon's 1564 Translation of the Apologia Ecclesiae Anglicanae." In *Women and Writing, c. 1340–1650: The Domestication of Print Culture*, ed. Anne Lawrence-Mathers and Phillipa Hardman, 62–76. Rochester, NY: Boydell & Brewer, 2010.

The Cooke Sisters: Education, Piety, and Politics in Early Modern England. Manchester: Manchester University Press, 2013.

Anderson, Penelope. *Friendship's Shadows: Women's Friendship and the Politics of Betrayal in England, 1640–1705*. Edinburgh: Edinburgh University Press, 2012.

Austern, Linda Phyllis. "The Conjuncture of Word, Music, and Performance Practice in Philips's Era." In *The Noble Flame of Katherine Philips: A Poetics of Culture, Politics, and Friendship*, ed. David L. Orvis and Ryan Singh Paul, 213–41. Pittsburgh, PA: Duquesne University Press, 2015.

Barash, Carol. *English Women's Poetry, 1649–1714: Politics, Community, and Linguistic Authority*. Oxford: Oxford University Press, 2000.

Bath, Michael. *Emblems for a Queen, the Needlework of Mary Queen of Scots*. London: Archetype Publications, 2008.

Baxter, James Reid. "Presbytery, Politics and Poetry: Maister Robert Bruce, John Burel and Elizabeth Melville." *Records of the Scottish Church History Society*, 34 (2004): 6–27.

"Elizabeth Melville, Calvinism and the Lyric Voice." In *James VI and I, Literature and Scotland: Tides of Change, 1567–1625*, ed. David J. Parkinson, 151–72. Leuven: Peeters, 2012.

Beal, Peter. *In Praise of Scribes: Manuscripts and Their Makers in Seventeenth-Century England*. Oxford: Clarendon Press, 1998.

Beilin, Elaine V. *Redeeming Eve: Women Writers of the English Renaissance*. Princeton University Press, 1987.

"Writing Public Poetry: Humanism and the Woman Writer." *Modern Language Quarterly*, 51 (1990): 249–71.

"A Woman for All Seasons: The Reinvention of Anne Askew." In *Strong Voices, Weak History*, ed. Pamela Benson and Victoria Kirkham, 341–64. Ann Arbor: University of Michigan Press, 2005.

Bicks, Caroline, and Jennifer Summit, eds. *The History of British Women's Writing, Volume II: 1500–1610*. Basingstoke: Palgrave Macmillan, 2010.

Blain, Virginia, Isobel, Grundy, and Patricia, Clements, eds. *Feminist Companion to Literature in English*. New Haven and London: Yale University Press, 1990.

Bowden, Caroline, and James E. Kelly, eds. *The English Convents in Exile, 1600–1800*. 6 vols. London: Pickering and Chatto, 2012–2013.

Boyd, Brogan. "The Masque and the Matrix: Alice Egerton, Richard Napier, and Suffocation of the Mother." *Milton Studies*, 55 (2014): 3–52.

Braidotti, Rosi. *The Posthuman*. Cambridge: Polity Press, 2013.

Brant, Clare, and Diane Purkiss, eds. *Women, Texts and Histories, 1575–1760*. New York and London: Routledge, 1992.

Burke, Victoria. "Elizabeth Ashburnham Richardson's 'motherlie endeavors' in Manuscript." In *English Manuscript Studies, 1100–1700*, Volume IX, ed. Peter Beal and Margaret Ezell, 98–112. Oxford: Blackwell, 2000.

"Manuscript Miscellanies." In *Cambridge Companion to Early Modern Women's Writing*, ed. Laura Knoppers, 54–67. Cambridge: Cambridge University Press, 2009.

Burke, Victoria, and Marie-Louise Coolahan. "The Literary Contexts of William Cavendish and His Family." In *Religion, Culture and Society in Early Modern Nottinghamshire*, ed. Martyn Bennett, 115–41. Lewiston: Edwin Mellen Press, 2005.

Burke, Victoria, and Jonathan Gibson, eds. *Early Modern Women's Manuscript Writing: Selected Papers from the Trinity/Trent Colloquium*. Aldershot: Ashgate, 2004.

Burton, Ben, and Elizabeth Scott-Baumann, eds. *The Work of Form: Poetics and Materiality in Early Modern Culture*. Oxford: Oxford University Press, 2014.

Campbell, Julie D., and Maria Galli Stampino, eds. *In Dialogue with the Other Voice in Sixteenth-Century Italy*. Toronto: CRRS/ITER, 2011.

Chalmers, Hero. "Dismantling the Myth of 'Mad Madge': The Cultural Context of Margaret Cavendish's Authorial Self-Presentation." *Women's Writing*, 4 (1997): 323–40.

Royalist Women Writers, 1650–1689. Oxford: Oxford University Press, 2004.

Chedgzoy, Kate. *Women's Writing in the British Atlantic World: Memory, Place and History, 1550–1700*. Cambridge: Cambridge University Press, 2007.

Chew, Elizabeth V. "Si(gh)ting the Mistress of the House: Anne Clifford and Architectural Space." In *Women as Sites of Culture*, ed. Susan Shifrin, 167–82. Burlington, VT: Ashgate, 2002.

Cho, Sumi, Kimberlé Williams Crenshaw, and Leslie McCall. "Toward a Field of Intersectionality Studies: Theory, Applications, and Praxis." *Signs: Journal of Women in Culture and Society*, 38, 4 (2013): 785–810.

Clark, Elizabeth A. "Sex, Shame, and Rhetoric: En-gendering Early Christian Ethics." *Journal of the American Academy of Religion*, 59 (1991): 221–45.

Clarke, Elizabeth. "The Garrisoned Muse: Women's Use of the Religious Lyric in the Civil War Period." In *The English Civil Wars in the Literary Imagination*, ed. Claude Summers and Ted-Larry Pebworth, 130–43. Columbia, MO: University of Missouri Press, 1999.

Clarke, Danielle. "Nostalgia, Anachronism, and the Editing of Early Modern Women's Texts." *Text: an Interdisciplinary Annual*, 15 (2000): 187–209.

The Politics of Early Modern Women's Writing. New York: Longman, 2001.

"'Formed into Words by Your Divided Lips': Women, Rhetoric and the Ovidian Tradition." In *"This Double Voice": Gendered Writing in Early Modern England*, ed. Danielle Clarke and Elizabeth Clarke, 61–85. Basingstoke: Palgrave Macmillan, 2000.

"Producing Gender: Mary Sidney Herbert and her Early Editors." In *Editing Early Modern Women*, ed. Sarah C. E. Ross and Paul Salzman, 40–59. Cambridge: Cambridge University Press, 2016.

Clarke, Danielle, and Elizabeth, Clarke, eds. *"This Double Voice": Gendered Writing in Early Modern England*. Basingstoke: Palgrave Macmillan, 2000.

Clarke, Danielle, and Marie-Louise, Coolahan. "Gender, Reception, and Form: Early Modern Women and the Making of Verse." In *The Work of Form: Poetics and Materiality in Early Modern Culture*, ed. Ben Burton and Elizabeth Scott-Baumann, 144–61. Oxford: Oxford University Press, 2014.

Clarke, Elizabeth, and Lynn Robson. "Why Are We 'Still Kissing the Rod'? The Future for the Study of Early Modern Women's Writing." *Women's Writing*, 14, 2 (2007): 177–93.

Coles, Kimberley Anne. *Religion, Reform, and Women's Writing in Early Modern England*. Cambridge: Cambridge University Press, 2008.

Coolahan, Marie-Louise. *Women, Writing, and Language in Early Modern Ireland*. Oxford: Oxford University Press, 2010.

Cooke, Anne. "Widowhood and Linguistic Capital: The Rhetoric and Reception of Anne Bacon's Epistolary Advice." *English Literary Renaissance*, 31 (2001): 3–33.

Coolahan, Marie-Louise. "Single-Author Manuscripts, Poems (1664), and the Editing of Katherine Philips." In *Editing Early Modern Women*, ed. Sarah C. E. Ross and Paul Salzman, 176–95. Cambridge: Cambridge University Press, 2016.

Crawford, Julie. "The Case of Lady Anne Clifford; Or, Did Women Have a Mixed Monarchy?" *PMLA*, 121, 5 (2006): 1682–9.

    Mediatrix: Women, Politics, and Literary Production in Early Modern England. Oxford: Oxford University Press, 2014.

Crenshaw, Kimberlé. "Demarginalizing the Intersection of Race and Sex: A Black Feminist Critique of Antidiscrimination Doctrine, Feminist Theory and Antiracist Politics." *University of Chicago Legal Forum*, 139 (1989): 139–67.

Daybell, James, and Andrew Gordon, eds. *Cultures of Correspondence in Early Modern Britain*. Philadelphia: University of Pennsylvania Press, 2016.

de Groot, Jerome. "Coteries, Complications and the Question of Female Agency." In *The 1630s: Interdisciplinary Essays on Culture and Politics in the Caroline Era*, ed. Ian Atherton and Julie Sanders, 189–209. Manchester: Manchester University Press, 2006.

Demers, Patricia. "Margaret Roper and Erasmus: The Relationship of Translator and Source," *Women Writing Et Reading Magazine*, 1 (2006): 3–8.

    "'Nether bitterly nor brablingly': Lady Anne Cooke Bacon's Translation of Bishop Jewel's Apologia Ecclesiae Anglicanae." In *English Women, Religion, and Textual Production, 1500–1625*, ed. Micheline White, 205–17. Burlington, VT: Ashgate, 2011.

Dolan, Frances. *Dangerous Familiars: Representations of Domestic Crimes in England, 1550–1700*. Ithaca, NY: Cornell University Press, 1994.

Duffy, Eamon. *The Stripping of the Altars: Traditional Religion in England, 1400–1580*. New Haven, CT: Yale University Press, 1992.

    Marking the Hours: English People and Their Prayers 1240–1570. New Haven, CT: Yale University Press, 2006.

Eardley, Alice. "Recreating the Canon: Women Writers and Anthologies of Early Modern Verse." *Women's Writing*, 14, 2 (August 2007): 270–89.

Evett, David. "Some Elizabethan Allegorical Paintings: A Preliminary Enquiry." *Journal of the Warburg and Courtauld Institutes*, 52 (1989): 149–65.

Ezell, Margaret J. M. *The Patriarch's Wife: Literary Evidence and the History of the Family*. Chapel Hill, NC: University of North Carolina Press, 1987.

   "The Myth of Judith Shakespeare: Creating the Canon of Women's Literature in the Twentieth Century." *New Literary History*, 21 (1990): 579–92.

   Writing Women's Literary History. Baltimore and London: The Johns Hopkins University Press, 1993.

   Social Authorship and the Advent of Print. Baltimore, MD: John Hopkins University Press, 1999.

   "The Laughing Tortoise: Speculations on Manuscript Sources and Women's Book History." *English Literary Renaissance*, 38 (2008): 331–55.

   "Editing Early Modern Women's Manuscripts: Theory, Electronic Editions, and the Accidental Copy-Text." *Literature Compass*, 7 (2010): 102–9.

Felch, Susan M. "'Halff a Scrypture Woman': Heteroglossia and Female Authorial Agency in Prayers by Lady Elizabeth Tyrwhit, Anne Lock, and Anne Wheathill." In *English Women, Religion, and Textual Production, 1500–1625*, ed. Micheline White, 147–66. Burlington, VT: Ashgate, 2011.

   "The Backward Gaze: Editing Elizabeth Tyrwhit's Prayerbook." In *Editing Early Modern Women*, ed. Sarah C. E. Ross and Paul Salzman, 21–39. Cambridge: Cambridge University Press, 2016.

Ferguson, Margaret W. *Dido's Daughters: Literacy, Gender and Empire in Early Modern England and France*. Chicago: University of Chicago Press, 2003.

Ferguson, Margaret W., Maureen, Quilligan, and Nancy, J. Vickers, eds., *Rewriting the Renaissance: The Discourses of Sexual Difference in Early Modern Europe*. Chicago: University of Chicago Press, 1986.

Felski, Rita. "Context Stinks." *New Literary History*, 42 (2011): 573–91.

Field, Catherine. "'Many Hands Hands': Writing the Self in Early Modern Women's Recipe Books." In *Genre and Women's Life Writing in Early Modern England*, ed. Michelle Dowd and Julie Eckerle, 49–63. Aldershot: Ashgate, 2007.

Flanders, Julia. "The Body Encoded: Questions of Gender and the Electronic Text." In *Electronic Text: Investigations in Method and Theory*, ed. Kathryn Sutherland, 127–44. Oxford: Clarendon Press, 1997.

Foster, Donald W. "Resurrecting the Author: Elizabeth Tanfield Cary." In *Privileging Gender in Early Modern England*, ed. Jean R. Brink, 141–74. Kirkville, MO: Sixteenth-Century Journal Publishers, 1993.

Frye, Susan. *Pens and Needles: Women's Textualities in Early Modern England*. Philadelphia: University of Pennsylvania Press, 2010.

Genette, Gérard. *Palimpsests: Literature in the Second Degree*. Lincoln, NE: University of Nebraska Press, 1997.

Gilbert, Sandra M., and Susan Gubar. *The Madwoman in the Attic: The Woman Writer and the Nineteenth-Century Literary Imagination*. New Haven, CT: Yale University Press, 1979.

eds. *The Norton Anthology of Literature by Women: The Traditions in English.*
    2nd ed. New York: W. W. Norton, 1996.
Gillespie, Katharine. "'This Briny Ocean Will O'erflow Your Shore': Anne
    Bradstreet's 'Second World' Atlanticism and National Narratives of Literary
    History." *Symbiosis*, 3 (1999): 99–118.
Goldberg, Jonathan. *Desiring Women Writing: English Renaissance Examples.*
    Stanford: Stanford: University Press, 1997.
    "Lucy Hutchinson Writing Matter." *English Literary History*, 73.1 (Spring
    2006): 275–301.
Goodrich, Jaime. "Thomas More and Margaret More Roper: A Case for
    Rethinking Women's Participation in the Early Modern Public Sphere."
    Sixteenth Century Journal, 39 (2008): 1021–40.
    "The Dedicatory Preface to Mary Roper Clarke Basset's Translation of
    Eusebius' Ecclesiastical History [with text]." *English Literary Renaissance*, 40
    (2010): 301–20.
    Faithful Translators: Authorship, Gender, and Religion in EarlyModern England.
    Evanston, IL: Northwestern University Press, 2014.
    "A Poor Clare's Legacy: Catherine Magdalen Evelyn and New Directions in
    Early Modern Women's Literary History." *English Literary Renaissance*, 46
    (2016): 3–28.
Gowing, Laura. *Domestic Dangers: Women, Words, and Sex in Early Modern
    London.* Oxford: Clarendon, 1996.
Graham, Elspeth et al., eds. *Her Own Life: Autobiographical Writings by
    Seventeenth-Century Englishwomen.* London: Routledge, 1989.
Gray, Catherine. *Women Writers and Public Debate in 17th-Century Britain.*
    New York: Palgrave Macmillan, 2007.
Green, Ian. *Print and Protestantism in Early Modern England.* Oxford: Oxford
    University Press, 2000.
Greer, Germaine et al., eds. *Kissing the Rod: An Anthology of Seventeenth-Century
    Women's Verse.* London: Virago Press, 1988.
Grundy, Isobel, and Susan Wisemen, eds. *Women, Writing, History, 1640–1740.*
    London: B. T. Batsford, 1992.
Hackel, Heidi Brayman. "The Countess of Bridgewater's London Library."
    In *Books and Readers in Early Modern England: Material Studies*, ed.
    Jennifer Anderson and Elizabeth Sauer, 138–59. Philadelphia: University of
    Pennsylvania Press, 2002.
    Reading Material in Early Modern England: Print, Gender, and Literacy.
    Cambridge: Cambridge University Press, 2005.
Hackel, Heidi Brayman, and Catherine E. Kelly, eds. *Reading Women: Literacy,
    Authorship, and Culture in the Atlantic World, 1500–1800.* Philadelphia:
    University of Pennsylvania Press, 2009.
Hageman, Elizabeth H. "Afterword: The Most Deservedly Admired
    Mrs. Katherine Philips—Her Books." In *The Noble Flame of Katherine
    Philips: A Poetics of Culture, Politics, and Friendship*, ed. David L. Orvis and
    Ryan Singh Paul, 311–24. Pittsburgh, PA: Duquesne University Press, 2015.

Hannay, Margaret P., ed. *Silent but for the Word: Tudor Women as Patrons, Translators, and Writers of Religious Works*. Kent, OH: Kent State University Press, 1985.

Harris, Johanna, and Elizabeth Scott-Baumann, eds. *The Intellectual Culture of Puritan Women, 1558–1680*. Basingstoke: Palgrave, 2015.

Harvey, Elizabeth D. *Ventriloquized Voices: Feminist Theory and English Renaissance Texts*. London and New York: Routledge, 1992.

Heller, Jennifer Louise. *The Mother's Legacy in Early Modern England*. Aldershot: Ashgate, 2011.

Hellwarth, Jennifer Wynne. "'Be unto me as a precious ointment': Lady Grace Mildmay, Sixteenth-Century Female Practitioner." *Dynamis* 19 (1999): 95–117.

Hickerson, Megan L. "'Ways of Lying': Anne Askew and the Examinations." *Gender & History*, 18 (2006): 50–65.

Hinds, Hilary. *God's Englishwomen: Seventeenth-Century Radical Sectarian Writing and Feminist Criticism*. Manchester: Manchester University Press, 1996.

Hobby, Elaine. *Virtue of Necessity: English Women's Writing 1648–88*. London: Virago Press, 1988.

Hosington, Brenda M. "England's First Female-Authored Encomium." *Studies in Philology*, 93 (1996): 117–63.

"Tudor Englishwomen's Translations of Continental Protestant Texts: The Interplay of Ideology and Historical Context." In *Tudor Translation*, ed. Fred Schurink, 121–42. New York: Palgrave Macmillan, 2011.

"Lady Margaret Beaufort's Translations as Mirrors of Practical Piety." In *English Women, Religion, and Textual Production, 1500–1625*, ed. Micheline White, 184–204. Burlington, VT: Ashgate, 2011.

Howard, W. Scott. "An Collins and the Politics of Mourning." In *Speaking Grief in English Literary Culture: Shakespeare to Milton*, ed. Margo Swiss and David A. Kent, 177–96. Pittsburgh, PA: Duquesne University Press, 2002.

ed. *An Collins and the Historical Imagination*. Aldershot: Ashgate, 2014.

Hunter, Lynette, and Sarah, Hutton, eds. *Women, Science and Medicine 1500–1700: Mothers and Sisters of the Royal Society*. Thrupp: Sutton, 1997.

Hurley, Anne Hollinshed, and Chanita Goodblatt, eds. *Women Editing/Editing Women: Early Modern Women Writers and the New Textualism*. Newcastle: Cambridge Scholars, 2009.

Hutcheon, Linda. *A Theory of Adaptation*. New York: Routledge, 2006.

Hutson, Lorna. *The Usurer's Daughter: Male Friendship and Fictions of Women in Sixteenth-Century England*. London and New York: Routledge, 1994.

"The 'Double Voice' of Renaissance Equity and the Literary Voices of Women." In *"This Double Voice": Gendered Writing in Early Modern England*, ed. Danielle Clarke and Elizaeth Clarke, 142–63. Basingstoke: Palgrave Macmillan, 2000.

Iwanisziw, Susan B. "Behn's Novel Investment in Oroonoko: Kingship, Slavery and Tobacco in English Colonialism." *South Atlantic Review* 63 (1998): 75–98.

James, Susan. *The Feminine Dynamic in English Art, 1485–1603: Women as Consumers, Patrons and Painters*. Farnham: Ashgate, 2009.

Jed, Stephanie. "The Tenth Muse: Gender, Rationality, and the Marketing of Knowledge." In *Women, Race, and Writing in Early Modern England*, ed. Margo Hendricks and Patricia Parker, 195–208. New York: Routledge, 1993.

Jones, Ann Rosalind. "Apostrophes to Cities: Urban Rhetorics in Isabella Whitney and Moderata Fonte." In *Attending to Early Modern Women*, ed. Susan D. Amussen and Adele Seef, 155–75. Newark: University of Delaware Press, 1998.

"Maidservants of London: Sisterhoods of Kinship and Labor." In *Maids and Mistresses, Cousins and Queens: Women's Alliances in Early Modern England*, ed. Susan Frye and Karen Robertson, 21–32. Oxford: Oxford University Press, 1999.

Kaufman, Peter Iver. "Absolute Margaret: Margaret More Roper and 'Well Learned' Men." *Sixteenth Century Journal*, 20 (1989): 443–56.

Kelso, Ruth. *Doctrine for the Lady of the Renaissance*. Urbana: University of Illinois Press, 1956.

Kinney, Clare R. "The Masks of Love: Desire and Metamorphosis in Sidney's New Arcadia." *Criticism*, 33 (1991): 461–90.

ed. *Mary Wroth. Ashgate Critical Essays on Women Writers in England, 1550–1700*. Vol. IV. Farnham: Ashgate, 2009.

Kmec, Sonja. "'A Stranger Born': Female Usage of International Networks in Times of War." In *The Contending Kingdoms": France and England 1420–1700*, ed. Glenn Richardson, 147–60. Aldershot: Ashgate, 2008.

Knight, Leah. "Reading Across Borders: The Case of Anne Clifford's 'Popish' Books." *Journal of the Canadian Historical Association*, 25 (2014): 27–56.

Knoppers, Laura Lunger, ed. *Cambridge Companion to Early Modern Women's Writing*. Cambridge: Cambridge University Press, 2009.

Kroll, Richard W. F. *The Material Word*. Baltimore, MD: The Johns Hopkins University Press, 1991.

Kunin, Aaron. "From the Desk of Anne Clifford." *English Literary History*, 71 (2004): 587–608.

Lamb, Mary Ellen. *Gender and Authorship in the Sidney Circle*. Madison, WI: University of Wisconsin Press, 1990.

"Out of the Archives: Mary Wroth's Countess of Montgomery's Urania." In *Editing Early Modern Women*, ed. Sarah C. E. Ross and Paul Salzman, 197–214. Cambridge: Cambridge University Press, 2016.

"The Cooke Sisters: Attitudes toward Learned Women in the Renaissance." In *Silent but for the Word: Tudor Women as Patrons, Translators, and Writers of Religious Works*, ed. Margaret P. Hannay, 107–25. Kent, OH: Kent State University Press, 1985.

Lay, Jenna. *Beyond the Cloister: Catholic Englishwomen and Early Modern Literary Culture*. Philadelphia: University of Pennsylvania Press, 2016.

Levin, Carole. "Lady Jane Grey: Protestant Queen and Martyr." In *Silent but for the Word: Tudor Women as Patrons, Translators, and Writers of Religious*

Works, ed. Margaret P. Hannay, 92–106. Kent, OH: Kent State University Press, 1985.

Llewellyn, Nigel. *Funeral Monuments in Post-Reformation England*. Cambridge: Cambridge University Press, 2000.

Loewenstein, David. *Treacherous Faith: The Specter of Heresy in Early Modern English Literature and Culture*. Oxford: Oxford University Press, 2013.

Loewenstein, David, and Janel Mueller, eds. *The Cambridge History of Early Modern Literature*. Cambridge: Cambridge University Press, 2002.

Longfellow, Erica. *Women and Religious Writing in Early Modern England*. Cambridge: Cambridge University Press, 2004.

Looser, Devoney. *British Women Writers and the Writing of History, 1670–1820*. Baltimore and London: The Johns Hopkins University Press. 2001.

Lux-Steritt, Laurence, and Carmen Mangion, eds. *Catholicism and Spirituality: Women and the Roman Catholic Church in Britain and Europe, 1200–1900*. Basingstoke: Palgrave, 2010.

Lyne, Raphael. "Intertextuality and the Female Voice after the Heroides." *Renaissance Studies*, 22 (2008): 307–23.

Mack, Phyllis. *Visionary Women: Ecstatic Prophecy in Seventeenth-Century England*. Berkeley, CA: University of California Press, 1992.

Magnusson, Lynne. "Imagining a National Church: Election and Education in the Works of Anne Cooke Bacon." In *The Intellectual Culture of Puritan Women, 1558–1580*, ed. Johanna Harris and Elizabeth Scott-Baumann, 42–56. Basingstoke: Palgrave, 2015.

Malay, Jessica L. "The Marrying of Anne Clifford: Marriage Strategy in the Clifford Inheritance Dispute." *Northern History* 159, 2 (2012): 251–64.

"Constructing Narrative of Time and Place: Anne Clifford's Great Books of Record." *Review of English Studies*, 66, 277 (2015): 859–75.

"Beyond the Palace: The Transmission of Political Power in the Clifford Circle." In *Family Politics in Early Modern Literature*, ed. Hannah Crawforth and Sarah Lewis. London: Palgrave Macmillan, 2017.

Malcolmson, Cristina, and Mihoko Suzuki, eds. *Debating Gender in Early Modern England, 1500–1700*. New York: Palgrave, 2002.

Malcolmson, Cristina. "Christine de Pizan's City of Ladies in Early Modern England." In *Debating Gender in Early Modern England, 1500–1700*, ed. Cristina Malcolmson and Mihoko Suzuki, 15–35. New York: Palgrave, 2002.

Mandell, Laura. "Gendering Digital Literary History: What Counts for Digital Humanities." In *A New Companion to Digital Humanities*, ed. Susan Schreibman, Ray Siemons, and John Unsworth, 511–23. Oxford: Wiley Blackwell, 2015.

Marcus, Leah S. "Editing Queen Elizabeth I." In *Editing Early Modern Women*, ed. Sarah C. E. Ross and Paul Salzman, 139–55. Cambridge: Cambridge University Press, 2016.

Marotti, Arthur F. *Manuscript, Print and the English Renaissance*. Ithaca, NY: Cornell University Press, 1995.

Marshall, Peter. *Religious Identities in Henry VIII's England.* Aldershot: Ashgate, 2006.

Matchinske, Megan. *Writing, Gender and State in Early Modern England: Identity Formation and the Female Subject.* Cambridge Studies in Renaissance Literature and Culture 26. Cambridge: Cambridge University Press, 2002.

    Women Writing History in Early Modern England. Cambridge: Cambridge University Press, 2009.

McGrath, Lynette. *Subjectivity and Women's Poetry in Early Modern England: Why on the Ridge Should She Desire to Go?* Aldershot: Ashgate, 2002.

McQuade, Paula. "'Except that they had offended the Lawe': Gender and Jurisprudence in The Examinations of Anne Askew." *Literature and History,* 3rd ser. 3 (1994): 1–14.

    ed. *Catechisms Written for Mothers, Schoolmistrisses, and Children, 1575–1750.* Aldershot: Ashgate, 2008.

    "A Knowing People: Early Modern Motherhood, Female Authorship, and Working-Class Community in Dorothy Burch's A Catechism of the Several Heads of the Christian Religion." *Prose Studies* 32, 3 (December 2010): 167–86.

    Catechisms and Women's Writing in Seventeenth-Century England. Cambridge: Cambridge University Press, 2017.

Meakin, H. L. *The Painted Closet of Anne Bacon Drury.* Farnham: Ashgate, 2013.

Miller, Shannon. *Engendering the Fall: John Milton and Seventeenth-Century Women Writers.* Philadelphia: University of Pennsylvania Press, 2008.

Milling, Jane. "Siege and Cipher: The Closet Drama of the Cavendish Sisters." *Women's History Review,* 6 (1997): 411–26.

Millman, Jill Seal, and Gillian Wright, eds. *Early Modern Women's Manuscript Poetry.* Manchester: Manchester University Press, 2005.

Molekamp, Femke. *Women and the Bible in Early Modern England: Religious Reading and Writing.* Oxford: Oxford University Press, 2013.

Mueller, Janel. "Prospecting for Common Ground in Devotion: Queen Katherine Parr's Personal Prayer Book." In *English Women, Religion, and Textual Production, 1500–1625,* ed. Micheline White, 127–46. Burlington, VT: Ashgate, 2011.

Mullan, David George, ed. *Women's Life Writing in Early Modern Scotland: Writing the Evangelical Self.* Aldershot: Ashgate, 2003.

Munro, Ian. "The City and Its Double: Plague Time in Early Modern London." *English Literary Renaissance,* 30 (2000): 241–61.

Myers, Anne M. "Construction Sites: The Architecture of Anne Clifford's Diaries." *English Literary History,* 73 (2006): 581–600.

Narveson, Katherine. *Bible Readers and Lay Writers in Early Modern England.* Aldershot: Ashgate Press, 2012.

Ng, Su Fang. *Literature and the Politics of Family in Seventeenth-Century England.* Cambridge: Cambridge University Press, 2007.

Norbrook, David. "Margaret Cavendish and Lucy Hutchinson: Identity, Ideology and Politics." *In-Between,* 9 (2000): 179–203.

"Women, the Republic of Letters, and the Public Sphere in the Mid-Seventeenth Century." *Criticism*, 46, 2 (Spring 2004): 223–40.

Orgel, Stephen. "The Case for Comus." *Representations*, 81 (2003): 31–45.

Parrish, Susan Scott. *American Curiosity: Cultures of Natural History in the Colonial British Atlantic World*. Chapel Hill: The University of North Carolina Press, 2006.

Parsons, Chris. "Medical Encounters and Exchange in Early Canadian Missions." *Scientia Canadensis*, 31 (2008): 49–66.

Pender, Patricia. "Reading Bale Reading Anne Askew: Contested Collaboration in the Examinations." *Huntington Library Quarterly*, 73 (2010): 507–22.

Early Modern Women's Writing and the Rhetoric of Modesty. London: Palgrave, 2012.

"Editing Early Modern Women in the Digital Age." In *Editing Early Modern Women*, ed. Sarah C. E. Ross and Paul Salzman, 255–69. Cambridge University Press, 2016.

Pender, Patricia, and Rosalind Smith, eds. *Material Cultures of Early Modern Women's Writing*. Basingstoke: Palgrave, 2014.

"Afterword: Reading Early Modern Women and the Poem." In *Early Modern Women and the Poem*, ed. Susan Wiseman, 244–52. Manchester: Manchester University Press, 2013.

"Editing Early Modern Women in the Digital Age." In *Editing Early Modern Women*, ed. Sarah C. E. Ross Paul and Salzman, 255–69. Cambridge: Cambridge University Press, 2016.

Pennell, Sara. "Recipes and Reception: Tracking 'New World' Foodstuffs in Early Modern British Culinary Texts, c. 1650–1750." *Food and History*, 7 (2009): 11–34.

"Perfecting Practice? Women, Manuscript Recipes and Knowledge in Early Modern England." In *Early Modern Womens' Manuscript Poetry Selected Papers from the Trinity/Trent Colloquium*, ed. Victoria Burke and Jonathan Gibson, 237–58. Aldershot: Ashgate, 2004.

Phillippy, Patricia. "The Maid's Lawful Liberty: Service, the Household and 'Mother B' in Isabella Whitney's A Sweet Nosegay." *Modern Philology*, 95 (1998): 439–62.

"'Herself Living, to Be Pictured': 'Monumental Circles' and Women's Self-Portraiture." In *The History of British Women's Writing, Volume III: 1610–1690*, ed. Mihoko Suzuki, 129–51. Basingstoke: Palgrave, 2011.

"Living Stones: Lady Elizabeth Russell and the Art of Sacred Conversation." In *English Women, Religion, and Textual Production, 1500–1625*, ed. Micheline White, 17–36. Burlington, VT: Ashgate, 2011.

Women, Death and Literature in Post-Reformation England. Cambridge Cambridge University Press, 2002.

Quilligan, Maureen. *Incest and Agency in Elizabeth's England*. Philadelphia University of Pennsylvania Press, 2005.

Raber, Karen, ed. *Ashgate Critical Essays on Women Writers in England 1550–1700: Elizabeth Cary*. Farnham: Ashgate, 2009.

Rankin, Deana. "'A More Worthy Patronesse': Elizabeth Cary and Ireland." In *The Literary Career and Legacy of Elizabeth Cary, 1613–1680*, ed. Heather Wolfe, 203–22. New York: Palgrave, 2007.

Raylor, Timothy. "Newcastle's Ghosts: Robert Payne, Ben Jonson, and the 'Cavendish Circle'." In *Literary Circles and Cultural Communities in Renaissance England*, ed. Claude J. Summers and Ted-Larry Pebworth, 92–114. Columbia and London: University of Missouri Press, 2000.

Raymond, Joad. *Pamphlets and Pamphleteering in Early Modern Britain*. Cambridge: Cambridge University Press, 2003.

RECIRC: The Reception and Circulation of Early Modern Women's Writing, 1550–1700. www.nuigalway.ie/English/marie_louise_coolahan.html.

Rich, Adrienne. Foreword: "Anne Bradstreet and Her Poetry." In Anne Bradstreet, *The Works of Anne Bradstreet*, ed. Jeannine Hensley, ix–xxii. Cambridge, MA: Harvard University Press, 1967.

Roberts, Josephine. "Editing the Women Writers of Early Modern England." *Shakespeare Studies*, 24 (1996): 63–70.

Roberts, Sasha. "Feminist Criticism and the New Formalism: Early Modern Women and Literary Engagement." In *The Impact of Feminism in English Renaissance Studies*, ed. Dympna Callagan, 67–92. New York and London: Palgrave, 2007.

Robin, Diana. *Publishing Women*. University of Chicago Press, 2007.

Robinson, Lillian S. "Treason Our Text: Feminist Challenges to the Literary Canon." *Tulsa Studies in Women's Literature*, 2 (1983): 83–98.

Romack, Katherine, and James Fitzmaurice. *Cavendish and Shakespeare: Interconnections*, Aldershot: Ashgate: 2006.

Ross, Sarah Gwyneth. *The Birth of Feminism*. Cambridge, MA: Harvard, 2009.

Ross, Sarah C. E. *Women, Poetry, and Politics in Seventeenth-Century Britain*. Oxford: Oxford University Press, 2015.

Ross, Sarah C. E., and Elizabeth Scott-Baumann. "Anthologizing Early Modern Women's Poetry: Women Poets of the English Civil War." In *Editing Early Modern Women*, ed. Sarah C. E. Ross and Paul Salzman, 215–31. Cambridge: Cambridge University Press, 2016.

   eds. *Women Poets of the English Civil War*. Manchester: Manchester University Press, 2017.

Ross, Sarah C. E., and Paul Salzman, eds. *Editing Early Modern Women*. Cambridge: Cambridge University Press, 2016.

Salzman, Paul. *Reading Early Modern Women's Writing*. Oxford: Oxford University Press, 2006.

   "Identifying as (Women) Writers." In *The History of British Women's Writing, Volume III: 1610–1690*, ed. Mihoko Suzuki, 33–47. Basingstoke: Palgrave, 2011.

Sanders, Julie. "Caroline Salon Culture and Female Agency: The Countess of Carlisle, Henrietta Maria, and Public Theatre." *Theatre Journal*, 52 (2000): 449–64.

Schiebinger, Londa L. *Plants and Empire: Colonial Bioprospecting in the Atlantic World*. Cambridge, MA: Harvard University Press, 2004.

Schiebinger, Londa, and Claudia Swan, eds. *Colonial Botany: Science, Commerce, and Politics in the Early Modern World*. Philadelphia: University of Pennsylvania Press, 2007.

Schleiner, Louise. *Tudor and Stuart Women Writers*. Bloomington, IN: Indiana University Press, 1994.

Scodel, Joshua. *The English Poetic Epitaph: Commemoration and Conflict from Jonson to Wordsworth*. Ithaca and London: Cornell University Press, 1991.

Scott-Baumann, Elizabeth. *Forms of Engagement: Women, Poetry, and Culture, 1640–1680*. Oxford: Oxford University Press, 2013.

Scott-Douglass, Amy. "Self-Crowned Laureates: Towards a Critical Revaluation of Margaret Cavendish's Prefaces." *Pretexts: Literary and Cultural Studies*, 9 (2000): 27–49.

"Enlarging Margaret: Cavendish, Shakespeare, and French Women Warriors and Writers." In *Cavendish and Shakespeare: Interconnections*, ed. Katherine Romack, and James Fitzmaurice, 147–78. Aldershot: Ashgate: 2006.

Shell, Alison. *Catholicism, Controversy and the English Literary Imagination, 1558–1660*. Cambridge: Cambridge University Press, 1999.

Sherlock, Peter. "Monuments, Reputation and Clerical Marriage in Reformation England: Bishop Barlow's Daughters." *Gender and History*, 16 (2004): 57–82.

Monuments and Memory in Early Modern England. Aldershot: Ashgate, 2008.

Showalter, Elaine. *A Literature of Their Own: British Women Novelists from Brontë to Lessing*. London: Virago, 1982.

A Jury of Her Peers: American Women Writers from Anne Bradstreet to Annie Proulx. New York: Vintage, 2009.

Skura, Meredith. "The Reproduction of Mothering in Mariam, Queen of Jewry: A Defense of 'Biographical' Criticism." *Tulsa Studies in Women's Literature*, 16 (1997): 27–56.

Smith, Nigel. *Perfection Proclaimed: Language and Literature in English Radical Religion 1640–1660*. Oxford: Clarendon Press, 1989.

"The Rod and the Canon," *Women's Writing* 14 (2007): 232–45.

Smith, Helen. *"Grossly Material Things": Women and Book Production in Early Modern England*. Oxford: Oxford University Press, 2012.

Smith, Pamela H. "Making as Knowing: Craft as Natural Philosophy." In *Ways of Making and Knowing: The Material Culture of Empirical Knowledge*, ed. Pamela H. Smith, Amy R. W. Meyers, and Harold J. Cook, 17–47. Ann Arbor, MI: University of Michigan Press, 2014.

Snook, Edith. *Women, Reading, and the Cultural Politics of Early Modern England*. Aldershot: Ashgate, 2005.

"Jane Grey, 'Manful' Combat, and the Female Reader in Early Modern England." *Renaissance and Reformation / Renaissance et Réforme*, 32 (2009): 47–81.

Stevenson, Jane B. *Women Latin Poets*. Oxford: Oxford University Press, 2005.

"Women and the Cultural Politics of Printing." *The Seventeenth Century*, 24 (2009): 205–37.

"Reading, Writing and Gender in Early Modern Scotland." *The Seventeenth Century*, 27, 3 (Autumn 2012): 335–74.

Stevenson, Jane B., and Peter Davidson, eds. *Early Modern Women Poets (1529–1700): An Anthology.* Oxford: Oxford University Press, 2001.

Stewart, Alan. "The Voices of Anne Cooke, Lady Anne and Lady Bacon." In *"This Double Voice": Gendered Writing in Early Modern England*, ed. Danielle Clarke and Elizabeth Clarke, 88–102. Basingstoke: Palgrave Macmillan, 2000.

Summers, Claude J., and Ted-Larry Pebworth, eds. *Literary Circles and Cultural Communities in Renaissance England.* Columbia and London: University of Missouri Press, 2000.

Summit, Jennifer. *Lost Property: The Woman Writer and English Literary History, 1380–1589.* Chicago: University of Chicago Press, 2000.

Suzuki, Mihoko. "Anne Clifford and the Gendering of History." *Clio* 30 (2001): 195–229.

Subordinate Subjects: Gender, the Political Nation, and Literary Form in England 1588–1688. Aldershot: Ashgate, 2003.

ed., *Anne Clifford and Lucy Hutchinson.* Burlington, VT: Ashgate, 2009.

ed., *The History of British Women's Writing, Volume III: 1610–1690.* Basingstoke: Palgrave, 2011.

"Women's Political Writing: Civil War Memoirs." In *Routledge History of Women in Early Modern Europe*, ed. Amanda Capern, 2018.

Targoff, Ramie. *Common Prayer: The Language of Public Devotion in Early Modern England.* Chicago: University of Chicago Press, 2001.

Tigner, Amy L. "Preserving Nature in Hannah Woolley's The Queen-Like Closet; or Rich Cabinet." In *Ecofeminist Approaches to Early Modernity*, ed. Jennifer Munroe and Rebecca Laroche, 129–49. New York: Palgrave Macmillan, 2011.

Travitsky, Betty S., ed. *The Paradise of Women: Writings by Englishwomen of the Renaissance.* New York: Columbia University Press, 1989.

Subordination and Authorship in Early Modern England: The Case of Elizabeth Cavendish Egerton and her "Loose Papers." Tempe, AZ: ACMRS, 1999.

Travitsky, Betty S., and Patrick Cullen, eds. *The Early Modern Englishwoman: A Facsimile Library of Essential Works.* London: Routledge, 1996.

Trentien, Whitney. "Isabella Whitney's Slips: Textile Labor, Gendered Authorship, and Early Modern Miscellany." *Journal of Medieval and Early Modern Studies*, 45 (September 2015): 505–21.

Trill, Suzanne. "Early Modern Women's Writing in the Edinburgh Archives: A Preliminary Checklist." In *Writing Women in Medieval and Early Modern Scotland*, ed. Sarah Dunnigan et al., 201–25. Basingstoke: Palgrave, 2004.

van den Berg, Sara J., and W. Scott Howard. "Milton's Divorce Tracts and the Temper of the Times." In *The Divorce Tracts of John Milton: Texts and Contexts*, ed. Sara J. van den Berg and W. Scott Howard, 1–35. Pittsburgh, PA: Duquesne University Press, 2010.

Van Wyhe, Cornelia, ed. *Female Monasticism in Early Modern Europe: An Interdisciplinary View.* Aldershot: Ashgate, 2008.

Vogel, Virgil J. *American Indian Medicine.* Norman, OK: University of Oklahoma Press, 1970.

Walker, Claire. *Gender and Politics in Early Modern Europe: English Convents in France and the Low Countries.* Basingstoke: Palgrave, 2003.

Wall, Wendy. *The Imprint of Gender: Authorship and Publication in the English Renaissance.* Ithaca, NY: Cornell University Press, 1993.

Recipes for Thought: Knowledge and Taste in the Early Modern English Kitchen. Philadelphia: University of Pennsylvania Press, 2016.

Wallace, David. *Strong Women: Life, Text, and Territory 1347–1645.* Oxford: Oxford University Press, 2011.

Whitaker, Katie. *Mad Madge: The Extraordinary Life of Margaret, Duchess of Newcastle.* New York: Basic Books, 2002.

White, Helen C. *The Tudor Books of Private Devotion.* Madison, WI: University of Wisconsin Press, 1951.

White, Micheline. "Women Writers and Literary-Religious Circles in the Elizabethan West Country: Anne Dowriche, Anne Lock Prowse, Anne Lock Moyle, Ursula Fulford, and Elizabeth Rous." *Modern Philology*, 103, 2 (2005): 187–214.

ed. *English Women, Religion, and Textual Production, 1500–1625.* Burlington, VT: Ashgate, 2011.

"Women's Hymns in Mid-Sixteenth-Century England: Elisabeth Cruciger, Miles Coverdale, and Lady Elizabeth Tyrwhit." *ANQ*, 24, 1 (2011): 21–32.

"The Perils and Possibilities of the Book Dedication: Anne Lock, John Knox, John Calvin, Queen Elizabeth, and the Duchess of Suffolk." *Parergon*, 29, 2 (2012): 9–27.

Wiesner, Merry E. *Women and Gender in Early Modern Europe.* Cambridge: Cambridge University Press, 2000.

Wilcox, Helen. "Anne Clifford and Samuel Pepys: Diaries and Homes." *Home Cultures: The Journal of Architecture, Design and Domestic Space*, 6 (2009): 149–6.

"'ah famous citie': Women, Writing, and Early Modern London." *Feminist Review*, 96 (2010): 20–40.

"The 'finenesse' of Devotional Poetry: An Collins and the School of Herbert." In *An Collins and the Historical Imagination*, ed. W. Scott Howard, 71–85. Aldershot: Ashgate, 2014.

Williams, Deanne. *Shakespeare and the Performance of Girlhood.* Basingstoke: Palgrave Macmillan, 2014.

Williamson, George. *Lady Anne Clifford.* Kendal, Cumbria: Titus Wilson, 1922.

Wilson, Jean. "Ethics Girls: the Personification of Moral Systems on Early Modern English Monuments." *Church Monuments*, 13 (1998): 87–105.

Wiseman, Susan. *Conspiracy and Virtue: Women, Writing, and Politics in Seventeenth Century England.* Oxford University Press, 2006.

"'Romes wanton Ovid': Reading and Writing Ovid's Heroides 1590–1712." *Renaissance Studies*, 22 (2008): 295–306.

ed. *Early Modern Women and the Poem*. Manchester: Manchester University Press, 2013.

"No 'Publick Funerall'? Lucy Hutchinson's Elegy, Epitaph, Monument." *The Seventeenth Century*, 30 (2015): 207–28.

Wolfe, Heather. "Reading Bells and Loose Papers: Reading and Writing Practices of the English Benedictine Nuns of Cambrai and Paris." In *Early Modern Women's Manuscript Writing: Selected Papers from the Trinity/Trent Colloquium*, ed. Victoria Burke and Jonathan Gibson, 135–56. Aldershot: Ashgate, 2004.

Wray, Ramona. "Anthologizing the Early Modern Female Voice." In *The Renaissance Text: Theory, Editing Textuality*, ed. Andrew Murphy, 55–72. Manchester: Manchester University Press, 2000.

"Editing the Feminist Agenda: The Power of the Textual Critic and Elizabeth Cary's The Tragedy of Mariam." In *Editing Early Modern Women*, ed. Sarah C. E. Ross and Paul Salzman, 60–76. Cambridge: Cambridge University Press, 2016.

Wright, Gillian. *Producing Women's Poetry: Text and Paratext, Manuscript and Print*. Cambridge: Cambridge University Press, 2013.

Wynne-Davies, Marion. *Women Writers and Familial Discourse in the English Renaissance: Relative Values*. Basingstoke: Palgrave Macmillan, 2007.

Ziegler, Georgianna. "Hand-Ma[i]de Books: The Manuscripts of Esther Inglis." In *English Manuscript Studies, 1100–1700*, vol. IX, ed. Peter Beal and Margaret Ezell, 73–87. Oxford: Blackwell, 2000.

"Women Writers On-line: An Annotated Bibliography of Web Resources." *Early Modern Literary Studies*, 6, 3 (2001). http://extra.shu.ac.uk/emls/06-3/ziegbib.htm.

Index

CPSIA information can be obtained
at www.ICGtesting.com
Printed in the USA
LVHW03*1226300718
585364LV00002B/5/P

9 781107 137066